A STUDY OF HISTORY

A STUDY

ARNOLD TOYNBEE

OF HISTORY

a new edition revised and abridged
by the author and Jane Caplan
507 illustrations 90 in colour
23 maps and charts

THAMES AND HUDSON

CONTENTS

FOREWORD

THIS BOOK is an attempt to do what its title suggests: I have tried to look at Mankind's history as a whole. This means looking at it from the start down to the present year 1972, and it also means looking at it globally.

In the time-dimension our view is bound to be out of scale. During the first half million, or perhaps one million, years after our pre-human ancestors had become human, we were primitives who have left no record except a few bones and a quantity of palaeolithic tools. Agriculture and the domestication of animals and pottery-making and weaving are only about ten thousand years old; civilization is only about five thousand years old, and most of what we know about human history is limited to these comparatively recent times. To see history globally in the geographical sense is less difficult than to see it in time-depth; but, in order to take a balanced global view, we have to rid ourselves of the illusion that the particular country, civilization, and religion that happens to be ours is, on that account, central and superior. For the historian, his ancestral standing-ground is an accidental impediment to seeing the global panorama in its true proportions.

But why study history at all? Why concern ourselves with anything beyond the range of our own time and place? At the present day there is a practical reason for taking a wider view. Within the last five hundred years, the whole face of the globe, together with its air-envelope, has been knit together physically by the amazing advance of technology, but Mankind has not yet been united politically, and we are still strangers to each other in our local ways of life, which we have inherited from the times before the recent 'annihilation of distance'. This is a terribly dangerous situation. The two World Wars and the present worldwide anxiety, frustration, tension, and violence tell the tale. Mankind is surely going to destroy itself unless it succeeds in growing together into something like a single family. For this, we must become familiar with each other; and this means becoming familiar with each other's history, since Man does not live just in the immediate present. We live in a mental time-stream, remembering the past and looking forward – with hope or with fear – to an oncoming future.

This present-day practical reason for studying history comprehensively is obvious and cogent. But, even if we were not moved to study history by a concern for self-preservation, we should be moved by curiosity; for curiosity is one of the distinctive faculties of human nature. We should still feel curiosity about the Universe in which we find ourselves, even if we were completely prosperous and secure – and no human society, at any time or anywhere, has yet come within sight of attaining these two ideal goals.

I know this from my own experience. I have been prompted to study history by a lifelong curiosity. I was historical-minded from as early an age as I can remember. My mother was an historian, and her interest in history was infectious and stimulating. I was also brought up with a great-uncle who had been a sailor. He had been the captain of an East-

Indiaman (a three-masted square-rigged sailing-ship), and his stories of his voyages to India and China excited me. So, out of curiosity, I had been studying history from the start, though I had grown up in the illusion that I was going to live out my life in a rational, orderly, and peaceful world. It was not until August 1914, when I was in my twenty-sixth year, that I became aware of a practical reason for studying history comprehensively. It was the outbreak of the First World War that woke me up to an awareness of the realities. The same event also revealed to me a possible method of handling the enormous mass of historical information with which a comprehensive study of history has to cope.

The year 1914 caught me at the University of Oxford, teaching the history of classical Greece. In August 1914 it flashed on my mind that the fifth-century BC historian Thucydides had had already the experience that was now overtaking me. He, like me, had been overtaken by a fratricidal great war between the states into which his world had been divided politically. Thucydides had foreseen that his generation's great war would be epoch-making for his world, and the sequel had proved him right. I now saw that classical Greek history and modern Western history were, in terms of experience, contemporary with each other. Their courses ran parallel. They could be studied comparatively. I soon also came to see that Greek history and Western history were two specimens of a species which had a number of other representatives. I counted up to twenty-one civilizations; I now count up to at least thirty-one, besides a few more that were abortive. For a comparative study, twenty or thirty specimens are enough.

I had been educated for studying history comprehensively by my mother, by my uncle, by Thucydides, and by two other Greek historians, Herodotus and Polybius, who had each written panoramic histories of as much of the world as came within their horizon. As a child, I had chafed at being made to learn the names of the counties of England and the dates of English kings. The kings of Israel and Judah, who allegedly so often did evil and so seldom did good, had aroused my curiosity about their Assyrian and Egyptian neighbours, some of whose impressive monuments I could gaze at in the British Museum. An intensive study of Greek and Latin literature, embracing poetry and philosophy as well as history, had widened my mental horizon. Thucydides in August 1914 had given me a shock that I am feeling still. In 1915 and 1916, about half the number of my school fellows were killed, together with proportionate numbers of my contemporaries in other belligerent countries. The longer I live, the greater grows my grief and indignation at the wicked cutting-short of all those lives. I do not want my grandchildren and great-grandchildren to have the same fate. The writing of this book has been one of my responses to the challenge that has been presented to me by the senseless criminality of human affairs.

I have been working on *A Study of History* from 1920 to 1972. In the summer of 1920 I made a first shot which missed fire. In the summer of 1921, in the train between Istanbul and Calais, I jotted down the headings of 'Parts', most of which will be found in the present revised and illustrated version. The unabridged work runs to twelve volumes. From 1927 to 1939 I was racing against the coming Second World War, and I got the sixth of the first six volumes published forty days before the Second World War broke out. I published volumes vii–x in 1954, volume xi ('Historical Atlas and Gazetteer') in 1959, volume xii ('Reconsiderations') in 1961.

From 1924 to 1956 I was sandwiching my work on *A Study of History* with producing, for the Royal Institute of International Affairs in

London, an annual survey of current international affairs, and then a political history of the Second World War, in partnership with my wife. These two large and long-continuing undertakings were complementary to each other. I could not have done either job if I had not also been doing the other simultaneously. I have always had one foot in the present and the other in the past. I have kept the same footing in this revised and illustrated version of my Study, and here I have also peered into the future. When one is studying the present and the past, to turn a blind eye to the future would be impossible, and, if it were possible, it would be perverse.

The present revised and illustrated version of *A Study of History* is a co-operative enterprise. It has been produced by agreement between the Oxford University Press and Thames and Hudson, and the work has been carried out by Miss Jane Caplan and me in collaboration.

In its present form the book differs in several ways both from the original twelve volumes and from the abridgment of the first ten volumes by D. C. Somervell.

This is the first illustrated version, and the illustrations, with the accompanying captions, give the book a new dimension. Pictures not only reinforce a text; they are able to convey a great deal that words cannot express adequately. The illustrations have been found by Mrs Bruckner of Thames and Hudson. They have been chosen, out of a number that Mrs Bruckner provided, in consultation with Miss Caplan and me, and the captions have been drafted by Miss Caplan and approved by me.

Both Miss Caplan and Mrs Bruckner had to master the plan and contents of the book in its original form before Miss Caplan could find and fill the gaps revealed by the passage of time and before Mrs Bruckner could illustrate the book in Miss Caplan's and my joint new version of it. This was a formidable task, and I am deeply grateful to these two colleagues who have performed it. This hard work of theirs has made possible the collaboration that has resulted in the present version of the book. I could not have produced this version single-handed. It is, as I have said, a co-operative piece of work; but, in pointing this out, I have one reservation to make. Criticisms of the book should be aimed at me alone. My ideas are more vulnerable than my colleagues' researches.

The present version is, like Somervell's, an abridgment, but here the book has been shortened on different lines, and room has been found for topics that were not included either in Somervell's version or in the original first ten volumes. Somervell succeeded in reproducing, in epitome, the whole structure of volumes i–x, and inevitably he had to leave out most of the historical examples with which I had supported my theses. In those parts of the original that are included in the present version, it has been possible to retain much more of the detail. Portions of the supplementary volume xii ('Reconsiderations') have now been incorporated, for the first time, in the main body of the book.

It has also been possible to take account of events and discoveries of later dates than 1961, the year in which the volume of 'Reconsiderations' was published. For instance, the ironic history of the defeats of sucessive 'improvements' in the art of war has been carried several steps further, (unhappily this is still an unfinished story), and the formerly unknown history of the indigenous civilizations of Africa to the south of the Sahara has been given its due place side by side with the other regional civilizations. In 1927, the year in which I started making my notes for the first ten volumes of the book, it was supposed that Tropical and

Southern Africa had been a region that had had no history before the arrival of the Arabs and the West Europeans. Since then, the history of this major part of Africa has been largely retrieved, partly by archaeological exploration and partly by a closer study of the earliest surviving documentary evidence. We know now that, in Tropical Africa, the arts of agriculture and metallurgy have a history that can compare with their history in Western Europe. The early history of civilization in Eastern Asia, and East Asian economic and social history of all periods, have also been brought into much clearer focus. While we have been at work, China has been regaining her normal role of playing one of the major parts in the world's affairs. In the present edition of this Study, we have tried to take account of these and other recent additions to the knowledge and understanding of human affairs.

In the *Odyssey*, the second of the two great epic poems of classical Greece, there is a tale about the kidnapping of the sea-god Proteus by a Greek rover, Menelaus, who had lost his way on his journey home from the siege of Troy. Proteus could be made to tell his captor's fortune if the captor could hold him fast, but this was difficult; for Proteus's retort to being kidnapped was to keep on changing his shape – hence the word 'protean' in English. History is protean. You have no sooner caught history in one shape than it changes shape like Proteus – sometimes almost out of all recognition.

To change shape is in the very nature of history, because it is in the nature of history to go on adding to itself. History has added more than fifty-eight years to its length between August 1914, when I had my first impulse to write this book, and the publication date of the present volume. Each addition changes the whole; for the whole of the past looks different in the light of our additional experience of life. For instance, Thucydides's Greece looked different to me in August 1914 from what it had looked like to me in July 1914, because, in between, the First World War had broken out, and this was indeed a portentous addition to the previous sum of world history.

The First World War was portentous, but its portentousness was not unique. There had been other sudden events that had likewise changed the appearance of the whole historical landscape: for instance, the political unification of China in 221 BC; Alexander's crossing of the Hellespont in 334 BC, the Arabs' eruption out of Arabia in AD 633, and the Mongols' eruption out of the north-east Asian steppes in the thirteenth century. There have been still more portentous events that have been gradual: for instance, the development of Greek and Chinese philosophy and of Jewish monotheism, and the spread of the missionary religions and of agriculture and of the harnessing of water-power. The age in which we are now living is not peculiar in generating new events that make all the past look different. At the same time, our age is perhaps peculiar in two respects.

One peculiar feature of our age is the acceleration of the pace of change to an unprecedented degree as a result of 'the annihilation of distance' through the extraordinary recent advance of technology. History is now being made so fast that it is constantly taking us by surprise. The second peculiar feature of our age is that the past has become doubly protean. Its appearance has been changing not only in the light of our current new experience, but also in the light of the archaeologists' new discoveries. They have been making revolutionary new discoveries, and they have also been making revolutionary new interpretations of some of their previous discoveries. Archaeologists compensate for being methodical by being temperamental, and drastic changes of fashion in archaeological theory have accentuated the drastic changes in the archaeologists' picture of the past that would have been called for in any case by the increase in their knowledge of the facts.

The archaeologists' discoveries, in the Americas as well as in the Old World, since Napoleon's invasion of Egypt in 1798 have been indispensable, though volatile, contributions to the comparative study of civilizations. Since then, the archaeologists have disinterred the relics of some civilizations – e.g. the Sumero-Akkadian, the Indus culture, the Minoan, the Mycenaean, the Mayan, and the Shang period of the civilization of China – which had fallen into complete oblivion. They have also brought to life the Pharaonic Egyptiac Civilization, whose massive monuments had never ceased to be conspicuous, by deciphering its records, and they have subsequently deciphered the records of the Sumero-Akkadian and Mycenaean Civilizations and those of the Chinese Shang dynasty. The civilizations that have thus been made accessible for historians by the archaeologists have increased the number of known civilizations to a figure at which a comparative study of them has become possible. At the same time, the archaeologists have been changing the shape of history at the dawn of civilization as rapidly as the scientists, technicians, dictators, and conquerors have been changing history's shape in the twentieth century.

For these reasons the present version of this book differs widely from the original version in the ten volumes published between 1934 and 1954, and, for the same reasons, the present version in its turn is bound to be put out of date by the continuing flow of events and increase of knowledge. Neither history nor any other human activity can be definitive so long as the human race continues to exist. This book will have served its purpose if it helps its readers to take a comprehensive view of the formidable but fascinating flux of human affairs.

ARNOLD TOYNBEE

PART I

THE SHAPE OF HISTORY

I begin my Study by searching for a unit of historical study that is relatively self-contained and is therefore more or less intelligible in isolation from the rest of history. I reject the present-day habit of studying history in terms of national states; these seem to be fragments of something larger: a civilization. In so far as Man needs to classify information before interpreting it, this large-scale unit seems to me to be less distorting than a smaller scale. After defining my unit, and looking at pre-civilizational societies, I try to establish a 'model' for histories of civilizations, taking my cue from the course of Hellenic, Chinese, and Jewish history. By combining their principal features, I propose a composite model which seems to fit the histories of most of the civilizations we know. I conclude by assembling a list of civilizations past and present.

SUBJECTIVITY:
A PARTIAL VISION

Men see largely what they expect to see, and they record what seems to them important. Judged from the standpoint of a modern geographer, this thirteenth-century *Mappa Mundi* is absurd, but on its own terms it is a logical picture of a Christian world. At the top of a flat disk is the east – the source of the Christian religion – marked by Eden and Adam and Eve, with Jerusalem below. Europe, Africa, and Asia are conveniently grouped together in a scheme that embodies some but by no means all of the geographical knowledge of the time. The result is a philosophical model, not a guide for travellers.

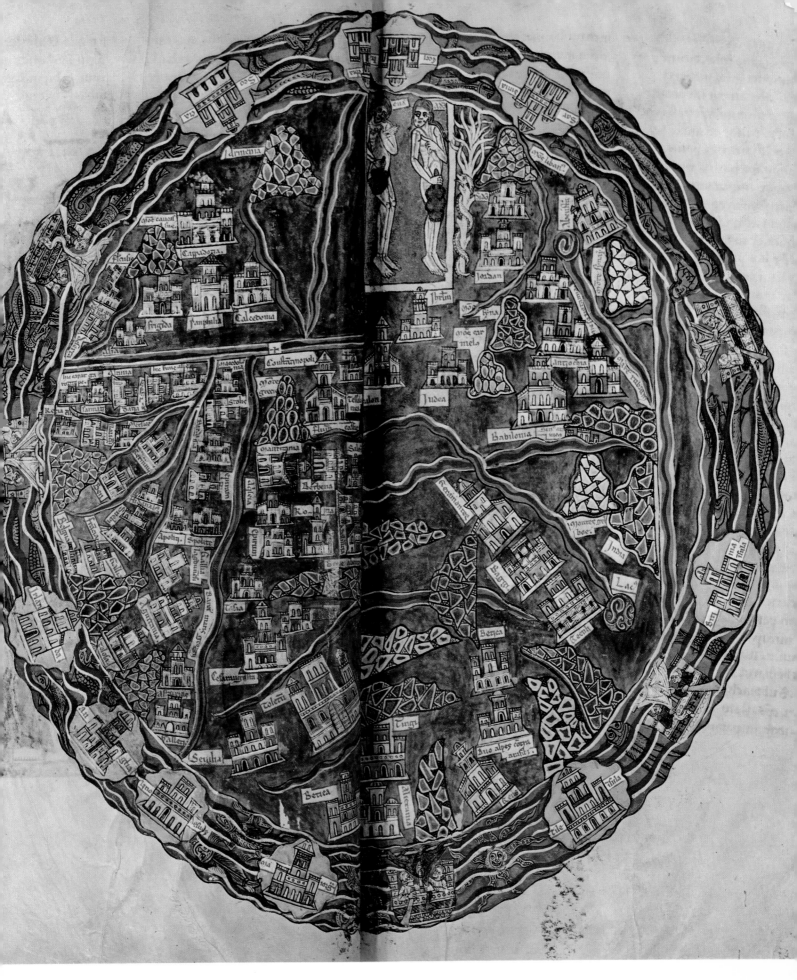

plates 2, 3

SUBJECTIVITY:
DIVERSITY IN UNITY

An identical religious belief can be given totally different cultural interpretations. The seventeenth-century Ethiopian painting of the Deposition, above, sees the scene in terms of contemporary local conventions. A Mughal artist in sixteenth-century India, opposite, attempts faithfully to copy his European model, but the physical types of the Virgin and those around her are unmistakably Indian.

'FIXING' THE UNIVERSE:
MODELS OF THE WORLD

The need to see a pattern in a mysterious universe is as old as the human race. The Aztec 'map' of the Five World Regions, above, identifies four past worlds at the cardinal points, and the present Earth in the centre; each is represented by the god who directs its history. The Buddhist mandala, opposite, is a chart of a more abstract metaphysical world: a geometric diagram that assists meditation on a mysterious ultimate reality.

plates 6, 7

HELLENIC AND CHINESE MODELS

The Hellenic Civilization provides the evidence for a model of continuous development: thus the Christian stylite, seeming to grow from his Greek column, suggests a symbol of this movement which culminated in the birth of a new but related Christian civilization.

Chinese history, by contrast, is marked by a pattern of alternating cycles of unity and disunity, order and disorder, progress and decline. The Chinese philosophers, right, are studying the Yin-Yang symbol which represents this spiral movement, Yang being equated with dynamism and action, while Yin symbolizes inertia and passivity. The historian's task is to combine the significant features of these Hellenic and Chinese patterns, creating a realistic model that can be applied to the histories of other civilizations.

plates 8, 9

THE JEWS:
A DIASPORAN MODEL

The 'diasporan' model takes account of societies which have been geographically dispersed and partly merged in the life of alien societies, but which maintain their own spiritual unity and distinctiveness through adherence to a common cultural tradition. The clearest example is the Jews.

These two scenes seem to be perfectly typical of their time and place – Renaissance Italy, left, and eighteenth-century Germany, right. Yet they are both from Hebrew liturgical manuscripts and both show the celebration of the Passover, part of that ritual which, beneath all the differing conventions and fashion, kept the Jewish community alive.

plates 10, 11

THE COST OF POWER

The organization of labour was a major step on the road to civilization, but it also divided society into a ruling minority and a productive majority. The wealth produced by Egyptian peasants supported the ceremonious luxury of the pharaoh and his wife, above, and the Assyrian emperor's slaves, opposite, laboured to build his palace as a monument to imperial prestige. In the pre-industrial age, these costly enterprises drained the resources of an inadequate peasant economy and were significant causes of the instability of successive empires.

26

plate 12

AN OBJECTIVE VISION

The world from space, as twentieth-century Man has for the first time been able to see it. Historical horizons have in a comparable way rolled back during this century, opening the way for Man to achieve an 'ecumenical' vision of all the civilizations he has created.

1 The relativity of historical thought

The Aethiopians say that their gods are snub-nosed and black-skinned and the Thracians that theirs are blue-eyed and red-haired. If only oxen and horses had hands and wanted to draw with their hands or to make the works of art that men make, then horses would draw the figures of their gods like horses, and oxen like oxen, and would make their bodies on the model of their own.[1] XENOPHANES.

IN ANY AGE of any society the study of history, like other social activities, is governed by the dominant tendencies of the time and the place. The Western World in our age has been living under the dominion of two institutions: the industrial system of economy and a hardly less complicated system of politics which we call 'Democracy' as a short title for responsible parliamentary representative government in a sovereign independent national state. These two institutions, the one economic and the other political, attained a general supremacy in the Western World at the close of the age preceding our own[2] because they offered provisional solutions for the chief problems with which that age had been confronted. Their enthronement signified the completion of the age which had sought and found salvation in them; their survival bears witness to the creative power of our predecessors; and we, who did not create them, have grown up under their shadow. In the industrial system and the parliamentary national state we still live and move and have our being; and the power of these two inherited institutions over our lives is reflected in the hold which they possess over our imaginations. Their prestige is apparent at almost every point in the work of our historians.

The industrial system has a human aspect in the division of labour and a non-human aspect in the application of modern Western scientific thought to the physical environment of human life. Its method of operation is to maintain, up to the maximum of its productive capacity, an incessant output of such articles as can be manufactured from raw materials by the mechanically co-ordinated work of a number of human beings. These features of the industrial system have been reproduced in the theory and even in the practice of Western thought in the twentieth century.

When I was a child I used to stay from time to time in the house of a distinguished professor of one of the physical sciences. There was a study lined with bookshelves, and I remember how, between one visit and another, the books used to change. When first I knew the room, many shelves were filled with general literature, with general scientific works, and with general works on that branch of science in which my host was an expert. As the years passed, these shelves were invaded, one after another, by the relentless advance of half a dozen specialized periodicals – gaunt volumes in grim bindings, each containing many monographs by different hands. These volumes were not books in the literary sense of the word, for there was no unity in their contents and indeed no relation whatever between one monograph and another beyond the very feeble link of their all having something to do with the branch of science

in question. The books retreated as the periodicals advanced. I afterwards rediscovered them in the attics, where the *Poems* of Shelley and *The Origin of Species*, thrown together in a common exile, shared shelves of a rougher workmanship with microbes kept in glass bottles. Each time I found the study a less agreeable room to look at and to live in than before.

These periodicals were the industrial system 'in book form', with its division of labour and its sustained maximum output of articles manufactured from raw materials mechanically. In my dislike of those rows of volumes I used to regard them as the abomination of desolation standing in the place where it ought not, but I am now ready to believe that they may not have been out of place in a physical scientist's work-room in the early years of the twentieth century of our era. Since the industrial system, in its non-human aspect, is based on physical science, there may well be some kind of 'pre-established harmony' between the two; and so it is possible that no violence is done to the nature of scientific thought through its being conducted on industrial lines. At any rate, this may well be the right way of handling any branch of physical science in its early stages – and all our modern Western science is still very young, even compared with the age of the Western Society – since discursive thought of any kind needs an initial supply of 'data' on which to work. The same method, however, has latterly been applied in many realms of thought beyond the bounds of physical science – to thought which is concerned with life and not with inanimate Nature, and even to thought which is concerned with human activities.[3] Historical thought is among these foreign realms in which the prestige of the industrial system has asserted itself; and here – in a mental domain which has had a far longer history than our Western Society and which is concerned not with things but with people – there is no assurance that the modern Western industrial system is the best régime under which to live and to labour.[4]

The subjugation of this ancient kingdom of historical thought by the modern industrialism of Western life is illustrated in the career of Theodor Mommsen. In his younger days Mommsen wrote a great book, which certainly will always be reckoned among the masterpieces of Western historical literature. This book was *The History of the Roman Republic*, published in 1854–56; but Mommsen had hardly written it before he became almost ashamed of it and turned his magnificent energy and ability into other channels. Mommsen made it his life work to organize the exhaustive publication of Latin inscriptions and the encyclopaedic presentation of Roman Constitutional Law. *Das Römische Staatsrecht* and the *Corpus Inscriptionum Latinarum* were the monuments by which, in later life, he would have preferred to be remembered; and the volumes of his collected works – a congeries of unrelated monographs and articles – are like so many volumes of a learned periodical which happens to have had only one contributor. In all this, Mommsen was representative of the

GOD IN MEN'S IMAGE

1, 2, 3 Christian iconography seen through Islamic, Congolese, and Chinese eyes.
Despite the common theme, the objects each mirror the artist's own particular
cultural and racial environment.

Western historians of his generation – a generation in which the prestige of the industrial system imposed itself upon the 'intellectual workers' of the Western World. Since the days of Mommsen and Ranke, historians have given their best energies to the 'assemblage' of raw materials – inscriptions, documents, and the like – in 'corpus'es and periodicals; and, when they have attempted to 'work' these materials 'up' into 'manufactured' or 'semi-manufactured' articles, they have had recourse, once again, to the division of labour and have produced synthetic histories like the several series of volumes published in successive versions by the Cambridge University Press. Such series are monuments of the laboriousness, the 'factual' knowledge, the mechanical skill, and the organizing power of our society. They will take their rank with our stupendous tunnels and bridges and dams and high-rise buildings and giant jet-planes and spacecraft, and their editors will be remembered among the famous Western engineers. In invading the realm of historical thought, the industrial system has given scope to great strategists and has set up marvellous trophies of victory. Yet, in a detached onlooker's mind, the doubt arises whether this conquest may not, after all, be a *tour de force* and the confidence of victory the delusion of a false analogy.

Some historical teachers of our day deliberately describe their 'seminars' as 'laboratories' and, perhaps less consciously but no less decidedly, restrict the term 'original work' to denote the discovery or verification of some fact or facts not previously established.[5] At the furthest, the term is extended to cover the interim reports upon such work which are contributed to learned journals or to synthetic histories. There is a strong tendency to depreciate works of historical literature which are created by single minds, and the depreciation becomes the more emphatic the nearer such works approximate to being 'Universal Histories'. For example, H. G. Wells's *The Outline of History* was received with unmistakable hostility by a number of historical specialists. They criticized severely the errors which they discovered at the points where the writer, in his long journey through time and space, happened to traverse their tiny allotments. They seemed not to realize that, in reliving the entire life of Mankind as a single imaginative experience, Wells was achieving something which they themselves would hardly have dared to attempt – something, perhaps, of which they had never conceived the possibility. In fact, the purpose and value of Wells's book seem to have been better appreciated by the general public than by the professional historians of the day.

The industrialization of historical thought has proceeded so far that it has even reproduced the pathological exaggerations of the industrial spirit. It is well known that individuals or communities whose energies are concentrated upon turning raw materials into light, heat, locomotion, or manufactured articles are inclined to feel that the discovery and exploitation of natural resources is a valuable activity in itself, apart from the value for Mankind of any results produced by the process. They are even tempted to feel it reprehensible in other people when they neglect to develop all the natural resources at their disposal; and they themselves readily become slaves to their fetish if they happen to live in a region where natural resources, and

opportunities for developing them, abound. This state of mind appears to European observers to be characteristic of a certain type of American businessman; but this type is simply an extreme product of a tendency which is characteristic of our Western World as a whole; and our contemporary European historians sometimes ignore the fact that in our time the same morbidity, resulting in the same loss of proportion, is also discernible in their own frame of mind.

The point may be brought home by an illustration. After Alexander the Great had broken up the Achaemenian Empire, the dynasty of the Ptolemies built some of the fragments into a Great Power based on Egypt, while the Seleucids built up another Great Power out of the former provinces of the Empire in Asia. No one who studies these two Great Powers in their historical perspective can doubt which of them is the more interesting and important. The Seleucid Monarchy was the bridal chamber in which the Hellenic and Syriac Civilizations were married, and their union there produced titanic offspring: to begin with, a divine kingship as a principle of association between city-states which was the prototype of the Roman Empire, and then a whole series of syncretistic religions: Mithraism, Christianity, Manichaeism, and Islam. For nearly two centuries the Seleucid Monarchy was the greatest field of creative human activity that existed in the world; and long after it had fallen the movements generated during its comparatively brief span of existence continued to mould the destinies of Mankind. Compared with this, the marriage of Hellenism with the Egyptiac Civilization in the Ptolemaic Empire was unfruitful. The introduction into the Roman Empire of the worship of Isis and of certain forms of economic and social organization is really all that can be placed to its account. Owing, however, to a climatic accident, the amount of raw information regarding these two monarchies which happens to be accessible to us is in inverse ratio to their intrinsic importance in history. The dry-as-dust soil of Upper Egypt yields the scientific Western excavator a wealth of papyri, beyond the dreams of the scholars of the Renaissance, and these papyri afford minute information regarding local methods of agriculture, manufacture, trade, and public administration, whereas the history of the Seleucid Monarchy has to be pieced together mainly from scattered coins and inscriptions and from fragments of literary records. The only new source of information here that is comparable to the Ptolemaic-Age papyri from Upper Egypt is the Seleucid-Age clay tablets from Babylonia. The significant point is that the Ptolemaic papyri have attracted almost all the spare energies of Western scholarship in the field of ancient history, and that the comparatively large number of scholars who have been devoting themselves to elucidating the minutiae of papyrus texts have tended to measure the historical importance of the Ptolemaic Monarchy by the amount of raw material accessible for the reconstruction of its history and by the intensity of the labour which they themselves have devoted to this reconstructive work.

An outside observer is tempted to regret that part of this energy was not reserved for equally intensive work upon the relatively meagre quantity of materials that is at our disposal for the reconstruction of Seleucid history. One additional gleam of light thrown upon the darkness of this page might add more to our understanding of the history of Mankind than floods of light thrown upon the social and economic organization of Ptolemaic Egypt. And, beyond this, the observer is moved to a psychological reflexion. He suspects that the scholar who has become a Ptolemaic papyrologist has seldom asked himself the prior question: 'Is Ptolemaic Egypt the most interesting and important phenomenon to study in the particular age of the particular society to which it belonged?' More probably he has asked himself instead: 'What is the richest mine of unworked raw material in this field?' And, finding that the answer is 'Ptolemaic papyri', he has become a papyrologist for the rest of his working life without thinking twice about it. Thus in modern Western historical research, as in modern Western industry, the quantity and location of raw materials threaten to govern the activities and the lives of human beings. Yet there is little doubt that our imaginary papyrologist has made a wrong choice by all humane standards. Intrinsically, the Seleucid Monarchy and not the Ptolemaic Monarchy is the field in which the pearl of great price awaits the historical explorer. For this judgment it is sufficient to quote the authority of Eduard Meyer [6] – a scholar who was not without honour in his own generation, though he used his mastery of modern scientific equipment and technique in order to write 'Universal History' in the great tradition of the *Essai sur les Mœurs* or *The History of the Decline and Fall of the Roman Empire*, like some son of Anak born out of due time.

This tendency for the potter to become the slave of his clay is so evident an aberration that a corrective may be found for it without abandoning the fashionable analogy between the processes of historical thought and the processes of industry. In industry, after all, to be hypnotized by the raw material does not pay. The successful industrialist is the man who first perceives that there is a strong economic demand for some particular commodity or service, and then lays hands upon just those raw materials and that manpower with which, at a profit to himself, he can manufacture that object or perform that service efficiently. Raw materials and manpower which do not happen to serve the purpose have no interest for him. In other words, he is a master of natural resources, and not their slave, and so he becomes a captain of industry and makes his fortune.

But historical thought is not, in truth, analogous to industrial production. In the world of action, we know that it is disastrous to treat animals or human beings as if they were stocks and stones. Why should we suppose this treatment to be any less mistaken in the world of ideas? Why should we suppose that the scientific method of thought – a method which has been devised for thinking about inanimate Nature – should be applicable to historical thought, which is a study of living creatures and indeed of human beings? When a professor of history calls his 'seminar' a 'laboratory', is he not wilfully expatriating himself from his natural environment? Both names are metaphors, and either metaphor is apt in its own sphere. The historian's *seminarium* is a nursery-garden in which living ideas about living creatures are taught to shoot. The physical scientist's *laboratorium* is – or was till the other day [7] – a workshop in which manufactured or semi-manufactured articles are

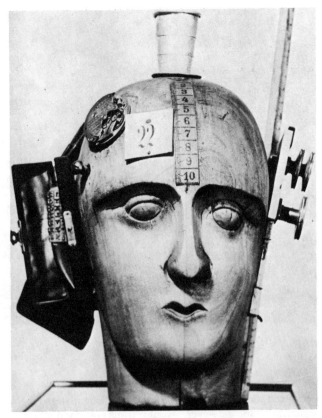

4, 5 INDUSTRIALISM AND NATIONALISM, the twin obsessions of modern Western Man. *The Spirit of our Time*, above, depicts the mechanization of the human intellect. Below, images of militant nationalism superimposed on a jubilee post-card portrait of Kaiser William II.

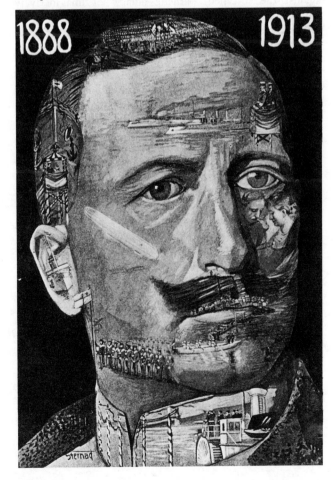

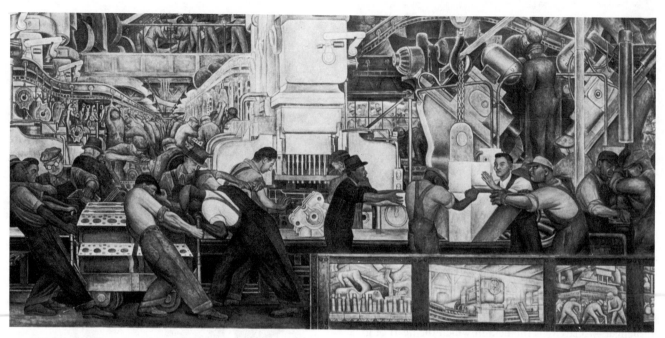

MAN AND HIS MASTER   6 A mural commissioned by the Ford Motor Works, Detroit, solemnly celebrates Man's subordinate place in the industrial process.

produced mechanically out of inanimate raw materials. No practical man, however, would think of conducting a nursery-garden on the principles of a factory or a factory on the principles of a nursery-garden; and, in the world of ideas, the corresponding misapplications of method ought to be avoided by scholars. We are sufficiently on our guard against the so-called 'pathetic fallacy' of imaginatively endowing inanimate objects with life. We now fall victims to the inverse 'apathetic fallacy' of treating living creatures as if they were inanimate.

If the industrial system had been the sole dominant institution in contemporary Western life, the influence of its prestige over Western historical thought might have broken down under its own weight; for the industrial system can be applied to historical thought only by a very drastic division of labour. In industry, the division of labour is readily (perhaps too readily) accepted by Mankind as a price which has to be paid for material well-being; and there appears – or appeared till recently – to be little repugnance to it in that realm of thought which is concerned with the physical Universe. It is conceivable that, as Bergson suggests, the mechanism of our intellect is specifically constructed so as to isolate our apprehension of physical Nature in a form which enables us to take action upon it.[8] Yet, even if this is the original structure of the human mind, and if other methods of thinking are in some sense unnatural, there also exists a human faculty, as Bergson goes on to point out, which insists, not upon looking at inanimate Nature, but upon feeling life and feeling it as a whole.[9] This deep impulse to envisage and comprehend the whole of life is certainly immanent in the mind of the historian; and such violence is done to it by the division of labour which the analogy of the industrial system imposes on historical thought, that our historians would almost certainly have revolted against this tyranny if there had not been a second dominant institution in contemporary Western life which has appeared to make unity of vision still compatible with

the industrialization of historical thought. This second institution, which has peacefully divided with the industrial system the allegiance of modern Western historians, is the sovereign state, which is inspired in our 'democratic' age by the spirit of nationality.

Here, again, an institution dominating a particular age of a particular society has influenced the outlook and activity of historians who happen to have been brought up under its shadow. The spirit of nationality is a sour ferment of the new wine of democracy in the old bottles of tribalism. The ideal of our modern Western democracy has been to apply in practical politics the Christian intuition of the fraternity of all Mankind; but the practical politics which this new democratic ideal found in operation in the Western World were not ecumenical and humanitarian but were tribal and militant. The modern Western democratic ideal is thus an attempt to reconcile two spirits and to resolve two forces which are in almost diametrical opposition; the spirit of nationality is the psychic product of this political *tour de force*; and the spirit of nationality may be defined (negatively but not inaccurately) as a spirit which makes people feel and act and think about a part of any given society as if it were the whole of that society. This strange compromise between democracy and tribalism has been far more potent in the practical politics of our modern Western World than democracy itself. Industrialism and nationalism, rather than industrialism and democracy, are the two forces which have exercised dominion *de facto* over our Western Society in our age; and, during the century that ended about AD 1875, the Industrial Revolution and the contemporary emergence of nationalism in the Western World were working together to build up 'Great Powers', each of which claimed to be a universe in itself.

Of course this claim was false. The simple fact that there were more Great Powers than one proved that no single one of them was coextensive with the sum total of that society which embraced them all. Every Great Power,

34

however, did succeed in exerting a continual effect upon the general life of society, so that in some sense it could regard itself as a pivot round which the whole of society revolved; and every Great Power also aspired to be a substitute for society in the sense of being self-contained and self-sufficient, not only in politics and economics but even in spiritual culture. The state of mind thus engendered among the people of communities which constituted Great Powers spread to communities of lesser calibre. In that age in the history of our Western Society, all national states, from the greatest down to the least, put forward the same claim to be enduring entities, each sufficient unto itself and independent of the rest of the world. The claim was so insistently advanced and so widely accepted that the true duration and true unity of the Western Society itself were temporarily obscured; and the deep human impulse to feel life as a whole, which is perpetually seeking to find satisfaction in the changing circumstances of life as it passes, attached itself to particular nations rather than to the larger society of which those nations were members. Such fixations of social emotion upon national groups became almost universal, and historians have been no more immune from them than other people. Indeed, the spirit of nationality has appealed to historians with special force, because it has offered them some prospect of reconciling the common human desire for unity of vision with the division of labour imposed upon them by the application of the industrial system to their work. To grapple with 'Universal History' on industrial principles is so evidently beyond the compass even of the most gifted and the most vigorous individual that, for a scientific historian, the admission that unity could not be found in anything short of 'Universal History' would be tantamount to renouncing unity of vision altogether – a renunciation which would take the light out of any historian's landscape. If, however, he could seize upon a unit of historical thought which was of more manageable proportions yet was still in some sense a universe too, the psychological problem of reconciling his intellect with his emotions might be solved; and such a solution appeared to be offered by the principle of nationality.

On this account the national standpoint has proved specially attractive to modern Western historians, and it has been commended to their minds through more than one channel. They have been led to it not only because it has been prevalent in the communities in which they have grown up, but also because their raw material has presented itself to a large extent in the form of separate national deposits. The richest mines which they have worked have been the public archives of Western governments. Indeed, the abundance of this particular natural resource is what chiefly accounts for their astonishing success in increasing their volume of production. Thus our historians have been drawn partly by professional experience, partly by a psychological conflict, and partly by the general spirit of their age, in one and the same direction.

The lengths to which this tendency may go can be observed in the work of a distinguished historian belonging to one of the greatest nations of the modern Western World. Camille Jullian was one of the most eminent authorities on the 'prehistory' of that portion of continental Europe which at the present time constitutes the territory

7 By contrast, a scene from the Chaplin film *Modern Times* lampoons the dwarfing of Man by the machines he has created.

8　Arc de Triomphe, Paris, 1806–36

9　Brandenburg Gate, Berlin, 1789

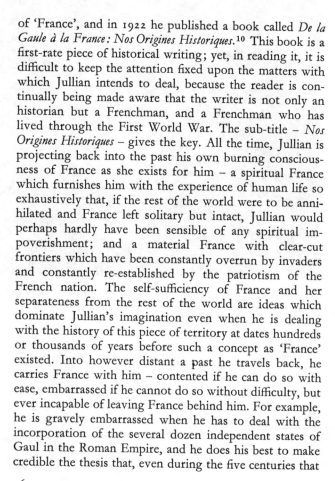

of 'France', and in 1922 he published a book called *De la Gaule à la France: Nos Origines Historiques*.[10] This book is a first-rate piece of historical writing; yet, in reading it, it is difficult to keep the attention fixed upon the matters with which Jullian intends to deal, because the reader is continually being made aware that the writer is not only an historian but a Frenchman, and a Frenchman who has lived through the First World War. The sub-title – *Nos Origines Historiques* – gives the key. All the time, Jullian is projecting back into the past his own burning consciousness of France as she exists for him – a spiritual France which furnishes him with the experience of human life so exhaustively that, if the rest of the world were to be annihilated and France left solitary but intact, Jullian would perhaps hardly have been sensible of any spiritual impoverishment; and a material France with clear-cut frontiers which have been constantly overrun by invaders and constantly re-established by the patriotism of the French nation. The self-sufficiency of France and her separateness from the rest of the world are ideas which dominate Jullian's imagination even when he is dealing with the history of this piece of territory at dates hundreds or thousands of years before such a concept as 'France' existed. Into however distant a past he travels back, he carries France with him – contented if he can do so with ease, embarrassed if he cannot do so without difficulty, but ever incapable of leaving France behind him. For example, he is gravely embarrassed when he has to deal with the incorporation of the several dozen independent states of Gaul in the Roman Empire, and he does his best to make credible the thesis that, even during the five centuries that

intervened between the generation of Julius Caesar and the generation of Sidonius Apollinaris, the local individuality of Gaul was a more important fact in the life of its inhabitants than their membership in an Empire which embraced the whole *orbis terrarum* of the Mediterranean basin. On the other hand, Jullian cannot contain his delight when he discerns the lineaments of France upon the face of Europe in the Neolithic Age. Here is a passage[11] which occurs at the end of a brilliant reconstruction of certain aspects of Neolithic life through an examination of the trails along which the Neolithic people did their travelling:

We can now speak of these essential routes by means of which, to a large extent, France was created. Equally, this traffic did not go beyond the boundaries which will later become those of Gaul, as if the value of these boundaries were already recognized in the human consensus.

Here, in the twinkling of an eye, the scientific Western historian of the Neolithic Age has been transfigured into the French patriot in AD 1918, crying: 'Ils ne passeront pas!'

This is perhaps an extreme case of the emotional and intellectual substitution of a nation for Mankind. At the same time, when the nation thus magnified happens to be France, the degree in which history is thrown out of perspective is the least possible in the circumstances. After all, some entity corresponding to the name 'France' actually has maintained its individuality within the universe of our Western Society for a millennium and, though a thousand years is not a long time in the history of Mankind, it covers almost the whole lifetime of our own Western Society,

10 Dewey Victory Arch, New York, 1899

11 '1000 Years of Russia' monument, Novgorod, 1862

which began to emerge from the ruins of the Roman Empire only about 250 years before France herself began to emerge as a distinct element in this new Western World. Moreover, France, since her emergence, has continuously played a central and a leading part in Western history; and thus, while Jullian's attempt to present the Roman Empire or the Neolithic Age in terms of France is a palpable *tour de force*, the distortion is not so apparent to the eye when modern Western history is focused from the French standpoint, with France in the centre and everything else on the periphery. France perhaps approaches nearer than any other national state to being co-central and coextensive with the whole of our Western Society. If, however, instead of France, we were to take Norway or Portugal, or even Holland or Switzerland, and attempt to write the history of Western Society round any one of these countries, we can see at once that the attempt would break down. As a *reductio ad absurdum*, let us try to imagine ourselves writing the history of the Western Society round one of those national states which did not attain their statehood till after the termination of the First World War. That would involve writing the history of a society which has been in existence for more than twelve centuries round a nation whose existence is not yet securely established. Whether a Czechoslovak or a Jugoslav national consciousness yet exists has hardly ceased to be a debatable question. Certainly such consciousnesses were non-existent as recently as three quarters of a century ago; and even if we attempted to present the history of the West in terms of the constituent parts of these nascent nationalities – in terms, that is, of Czechs or Slovaks or Croats or Serbs, whose

history as distinct groups goes back further – the absurdity, while less great in terms of relative age, would be greater in terms of relative population and territorial extension. Western history cannot be comprehended in terms of nationalities of this calibre. Indeed, far from being able to write a Slovako- or Croato-centric history of the West, we should find it impossible to write even a Slovako-centric history of Slovakia or a Croato-centric history of Croatia. In contrast to France, Slovakia and Croatia fall so far short of constituting historical universes in themselves that, when isolated, they cease to be intelligible. It would be impossible to write intelligible histories of Slovakia or Croatia in which those territories, or their peoples, were given the role of protagonists, even in their own small corners of the broad Western stage. It would be impossible, in their case, to distinguish from their external relations an internal history which was something specifically their own. It would be found that every experience which they underwent and every activity into which they entered had been shared by them with other communities whose share had been greater than theirs, and in attempting to make their history intelligible we should find ourselves extending our field of vision to include one after another of these other peoples. Possibly we should have to extend it until we had included the whole of our Western Society. In any case, the intelligible field, when we found it, would certainly prove to be some field of which Slovakia or Croatia itself was a small and comparatively unimportant fraction.[12]

The emergence of national states which have no history that is intelligible in isolation signifies the arrival of a new age and indicates what its character is to be. The general conditions of our Western Society have already become profoundly different from those which were in the ascendant during the century ending about AD 1875 and which have stamped the minds of Western historians with an impress which they still retain. Down to about 1875, the two dominant institutions of industrialism and nationalism were working together to build up Great Powers. After 1875 they began to work in opposite directions – industrialism increasing the scale of its operations beyond the compass of the greatest of the Great Powers and feeling its way towards a worldwide range, while nationalism, percolating downwards, began to implant a separate consciousness in peoples of so small a calibre that they were incapable not only of forming Great Powers but even of forming minor states possessed of full political, economic, and cultural independence in the established sense of those terms.

The cumulative effect of the two world wars has brought to the surface a tendency which had been at work for nearly half a century before 1914. In 1918 Austria-Hungary, one of the eight Great Powers which had been on the map in 1914, broke up. At the same date the break-up of the Ottoman Empire was completed. The Second World War was followed by the break-up of the British, French, and Dutch colonial Empires, and the number of Great Powers was reduced to two, while the total number of juridically sovereign independent states was increased, in the course of the next quarter of a century, to about 140. The greater the number of nominally sovereign states, the smaller their average area, population, wealth, and economic and military capacity are bound to be. Today the two surviving Great Powers still overshadow the rest of the world, but the characteristic states of the new age are not units that can be thought of as being universes in themselves; they are states whose nominal independence is manifestly limited on the military or economic or cultural plane or on all these planes alike. Even the two surviving Great Powers are being dwarfed in the economic sphere by the worldwide scale on which industrialism has now come to conduct its operations. Some states are still kicking violently against the pricks. They are attempting to salvage their dwindling independence by pursuing militant monetary and tariff and quota and migration policies. Some states, however, are also confessing, by deeds that are more eloquent than words, that they cannot stand alone. The 'developing' countries are seeking financial and technological aid from the 'developed' countries, and the states of Western Europe – which, for four and a half centuries, ending in 1945, fought round after round of wars with each other to prevent any one of them from dominating the rest – are now trying to unite voluntarily, on a footing of equality with each other, in a European economic community.

These multiple tendencies can be summed up in a single formula: in the new age, the dominant note in the corporate consciousness of communities is a sense of being parts of some larger universe, whereas, in the age which is now over, the dominant note in their consciousness was an aspiration to be universes in themselves. This change of note indicates an unmistakable turn in a tide which, when it reached high-water mark about the year 1875, had been flowing steadily in one direction for four centuries. It may portend a return, in this respect, to the conditions of the preceding phase (the so-called 'medieval' phase) of Western history, when the consciousness of the Western Society was dominated by institutions like the Papacy and the Holy Roman Empire which incorporated some aspects of its life as a whole, while kingdoms and city-states and fiefs and other local institutions were felt to be something parochial and subordinate. At any rate, that is the direction in which the tide seems to be flowing now – as far as it is possible to discern its direction so short a time after it has turned.

If this observation is correct, and if it is also true that historians cannot abstract their thoughts and feelings from the influence of the environment in which they live, then we may expect to witness in the near future a change in the outlook and activities of Western historians corresponding to the recent change in the general conditions of the Western Society. Just as, at the close of the age which we have left behind, the historians' work was brought into conformity with the industrial system and their vision was caught and bounded by the idea of nationality, so, in the new age upon which we have entered, they will probably find their intelligible field of study in some landscape where the horizon is not restricted to the boundaries of a single nationality, and will adapt their present method of work to mental operations on a larger scale.

This raises two questions, one of immediate interest: 'What is the intelligible field of study which Western historians will discover for themselves in this new age?', and another of permanent importance: 'Is there some intelligible field of historical study which is absolute and not merely relative to the particular social environment of particular historians?' So far, our inquiry seems to have brought out the fact that historical thought takes a deep impress from the dominant institutions of the transient social environment in which the thinker happens to live. If this impress proved to be so profound and so pervasive as actually to constitute the *a priori* categories in the historian's mind, that conclusion would bring our inquiry to an end. It would mean that the relativity of historical thought to the social environment was absolute; and in that case it would be useless to gaze any longer at the moving film of historical literature in the hope of discerning in it the lineaments of some abiding form. The historian would have to admit that, while it might be possible for him to work out a morphology of his own mind by analysing the influences exerted upon it by the particular society in which he lived, it was not possible for him to discover the structure of that society itself, or of the other societies in which other historians and other human beings had lived in different times and places. That conclusion, however, does not yet confront us. So far, we have simply found that in the foreground of historical thought there is a shimmer of relativity, and it is not impossible that the ascertainment of this fact may prove to be the first step towards ascertaining the presence of some constant and absolute object of historical thought in the background. Our next step, therefore, is to take up the search for an intelligible field of historical study independent of the local and temporary standpoints and activities of historians upon which we have focused our attention hitherto.

2 The field of historical study

IN SETTING OUT to look for some objective 'intelligible field of historical study', it seems best to start with what is the usual field of vision of contemporary Western historians, that is, with some national state. Let us pick out, from among the national states of the West, whichever one seems most likely, at first sight, to correspond to our contemporary historians' ideal of what their field should be, and then let us test their outlook in this instance in the light of the 'historical facts' (taking 'historical facts' in the popularly accepted sense and begging provisionally the prior philosophical question as to the meaning of the word 'fact' in this term).[1]

Great Britain seems as good a choice as any. She is a national state that has been a Great Power. Her principal constituent, England, who merged herself in Great Britain about 250 years ago without any breach of continuity or change of identity, is as old a figure in Western history as France, and on the whole as important a figure, though she has performed quite a different historical function. Her peculiar merit for our purpose is that, to an exceptional degree, she has been kept in isolation – first by certain permanent features of physical geography, and secondly by a certain policy on the part of her statesmen in the age during which she has been most creative and most powerful. As regards her geographical isolation, the shores of an island provide frontiers which are incomparably more clear-cut than the land-frontiers of France, however precise and eternal Jullian may have felt those land-frontiers to be. For instance, we should not smile at Jullian if he had made the discovery that the Neolithic trails in Britain broke off along the same line at which the roads and railways of Britain break off today, or if he quoted *et penitus toto divisos orbe Britannos*[2] in describing the position of Britain in the Roman Empire. As regards her political isolation, Britain has been something of an *alter orbis*.[3]

We shall not easily discover a Western nation which has been more isolated than she has been and which yet has played so prominent a part over so long a span of Western history. In fact, if Great Britain (as the heir and assign of England) is not found to constitute in herself an 'intelligible field of historical study', we may confidently infer that no other modern Western national state will pass muster.

Is English history, then, intelligible when taken by itself? Can we abstract an internal history of England from her external relations? If we can, shall we find that these residual external relations are of secondary importance? And in analysing these, again, shall we find that the foreign influences upon England are slight in comparison with the English influences upon other parts of the world? If all these questions receive affirmative answers, we may be justified in concluding that, while it may not be possible to understand other histories without reference to England, it is possible, more or less, to understand English history without reference to other parts of the world. The best way to approach these questions is to direct our thought backwards over the course of English history and recall the principal chapters.

In this inverse order, we may take those chapters to be:
(a) the establishment of the industrial system of economy (since the last quarter of the eighteenth century of our era);
(b) the establishment of responsible parliamentary government (since the last quarter of the seventeenth century);
(c) the expansion overseas (beginning in the third quarter of the sixteenth century with piracy and developing gradually into a worldwide foreign trade, the acquisition of tropical dependencies and the foundation of new English-speaking communities in overseas countries with temperate climates);
(d) the Reformation (since the second quarter of the sixteenth century);
(e) the Renaissance, including the political and economic as well as the artistic and intellectual aspects of this movement (since the last quarter of the fifteenth century);
(f) the completion of the feudal system (since the eleventh century);
(g) the conversion of the English from the religion of the so-called 'Heroic Age' to Western Christianity (since the last years of the sixth century).

This summary glance backwards from the present date over the general course of English history would appear to show that the further back we look the less evidence do we find of self-sufficiency or isolation. The conversion, which was really the beginning of all things in English history, was the direct antithesis of that: it was an act which merged half a dozen isolated communities of barbarians in the common weal of a nascent Western Society. As for the feudal system, Marc Bloch[4] has shown that a system of protective relationships had been developing in England since the seventh century, and that the furtherance of this development in the ninth century was largely the result of an external stimulus, the Danish invasions. After the Conquest, the imported Norman institutions and administrative practices penetrated virtually the whole of society. Thus it may fairly be said that any account of the establishment of the feudal system in England would not be intelligible unless France and Scandinavia, at least, were also brought into the picture. As for the Renaissance, in both its cultural and its political aspects it is universally admitted to have been a breath of life from Northern Italy. If, in Northern Italy, humanism, absolutism, and the balance of power had not been cultivated in miniature, like seedlings in a sheltered nursery-garden, during two centuries that fall approximately between AD 1275 and AD 1475, they could never have been bedded out north of the Alps from about 1475 onwards. The Reformation, again, was not a specifically English phenomenon, but a general movement in the Promethean North of Western Europe (where the Baltic, the North Sea, and the Atlantic all beckoned towards new

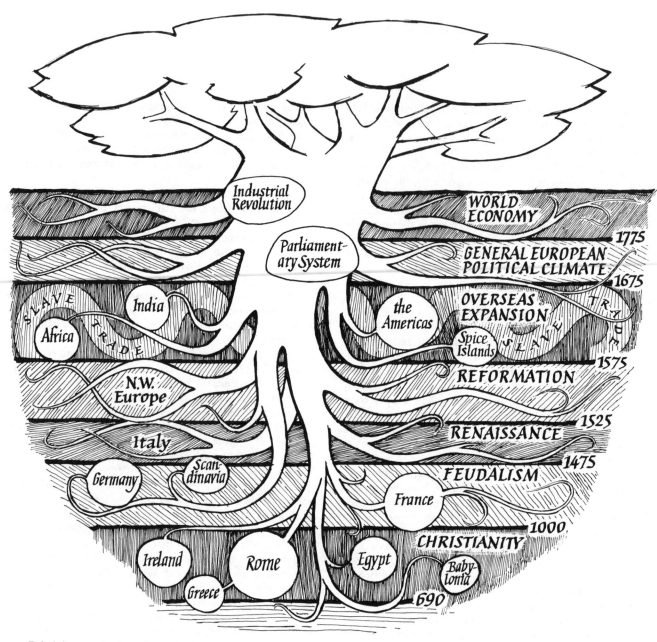

12 Britain's roots in the cultures of the world.

worlds) for emancipation from the Epimethean South (where the western Mediterranean held the eye fixed upon worlds that were dead and gone). In the Reformation, England did not take the initiative, nor did she take it even in the competition between the European nations of the Atlantic sea-board for the prize of the new worlds overseas. She won that prize as a comparatively late comer, in a series of struggles, which lasted for several centuries, with Powers which were before her in the field. In order to understand the history of English expansion overseas, it is necessary to appreciate the consequences of all the general European wars, and indeed to take into account all the vicissitudes of the European balance of power, from about

the last quarter of the fifteenth century onwards – in fact, to extend the field of vision across the whole horizon of modern Western history.

It remains to consider the two latest chapters: the geneses of the parliamentary system and of the industrial system – institutions which are commonly regarded as having been first evolved locally on English soil and afterwards propagated from England into other parts of the world. For our purpose, these are the crucial chapters in English history. Are these two chapters intelligible in insular terms? No, they are not, in the judgment of recognized authorities. 'General History', Lord Acton holds,[5] 'naturally depends on the action of forces which are not national, but proceed from wider causes. . . . Bourbons and Stuarts obeyed the same law, though with a different result.' In other words, the parliamentary system, which was the local result in England, was the product of a force which was not peculiar to England, but was operative in England and in France simultaneously. As for the Industrial Revolution, it 'cannot be explained in purely British terms, for this country formed part of a wider economy, which we may call the "European economy" or the "world economy of European maritime states".'[6]

Thus British national history is not, never has been, and almost certainly never will be an 'intelligible field of study' in isolation; and if that is true of Great Britain, it must surely be true *a fortiori* of any other national state. Therefore, if we are to pursue our quest, it is clear that we must take some larger entity than the nation as our field.

A society is confronted in the course of its life by a succession of problems, which every member has to solve for himself as best he may. The presentation of each problem is a challenge to undergo an ordeal, and through this series of ordeals the members of the society progressively differentiate themselves from each other. On each occasion some fail, while others succeed in finding a solution; and, again, some of the solutions found are imperfect or commonplace or inimical to success in solving subsequent problems, while others are exact or original or fertile in possibilities of further progress. As ordeal follows ordeal, some members of the society at some moment fail to adjust themselves, and fall by the way; others struggle on, strained or warped or stunted; others grow in wisdom and stature, and in making their own way discover new avenues for a general advance of the society to which they belong. Throughout, it is impossible to grasp the significance of a particular member's behaviour under a particular ordeal without noting the similar or dissimilar behaviour of his fellows and without viewing the successive ordeals as a series of events in the life of the whole society.

Thus English history does not become intelligible until we view it as the history of a wider society of which Great Britain is a member in company with other national states, each of which reacts, though each in its own way, to the common experiences of the society as a whole. Similarly, Venetian history has to be viewed as the history of a temporary sub-society including Milan, Genoa, Florence, and the other 'medieval' city-states in Northern Italy; Athenian history as the history of a society including Thebes, Corinth, Sparta, and the other city-states of Greece in the Hellenic Age. In each case we have to think in terms of the whole and not of the parts; to see the chapters of the story as events in the life of the society and not of some particular member; and to follow the fortunes of the members, not separately but concurrently, as variations on a single theme or as contributions to an orchestra which are significant as a harmony but have no meaning as so many separate series of notes. In so far as we succeed in studying history from this point of view, we find that order arises out of chaos in our minds and that we begin to understand what was not intelligible before.

This method of interpreting 'historical facts' will perhaps be made clearer by a concrete example, which may be taken from the history of the city-states of the Hellenic World during the four centuries falling approximately between 725 and 325 BC.

Soon after the beginning of that age, the society of which these numerous states were all members was confronted with the problem of the pressure of population upon the means of subsistence – means which the Hellenic people at that time were apparently obtaining almost entirely by raising a varied agricultural produce in their home territories for home consumption. When the crisis came, different states contended with it in different ways. Some, like Corinth and Chalcis, disposed of their surplus population by seizing and colonizing agricultural territories overseas – in Sicily, Southern Italy, Thrace, and elsewhere – where the native population was either too sparse or too incompetent to resist invasion. The Greek colonies thus founded simply extended the geographical area of the Hellenic Society without altering its character. The agriculture which they practised and the institutions under which they lived were substantially reproductions of the conditions which they had left behind them in their home countries.

On the other hand, certain states sought solutions which entailed a variation in their way of life. Sparta, for instance, satisfied the land-hunger of her citizens not by colonizing overseas territories outside the previous geographical limits of the Hellenic World[7] but by attacking and conquering her nearest Greek neighbours in Messene. The consequences were that Sparta obtained her necessary additional lands only at the cost of obstinate and repeated wars with neighbouring peoples of her own calibre; that, even when the conquest was completed, the retention of the conquered territories required a permanent military effort; and that this permanent strain bore upon Sparta herself and not upon some independent daughter-state overseas who would have been responsible for her own security. In order to meet this situation, Spartan statesmen were compelled to militarize Spartan life from top to bottom – which they did by reinvigorating and adapting certain primitive social institutions, common to a number of Greek communities, at a moment when, in Sparta as elsewhere, these institutions were on the point of disappearing.[8]

Athens reacted to the population problem in a different way again. At first she neglected it – neither planting colonies overseas nor conquering the territory of her Greek neighbours – until the pressure threatened to find vent in a social revolution. At that point, when the solutions sought by other states were no longer open to her, she discovered an original solution of her own by specializing her agricultural production for export, starting manufactures also for export, and then developing her political institutions so as to give a fair share of political power to the new classes which had been called into being by these economic innovations. In other words, Athenian statesmen averted a social revolution; and, discovering this solution for the common problem as far as it affected themselves, they incidentally opened up a new avenue of advance for the whole of the Hellenic Society. This was what Pericles meant when, in the crisis of his country's material fortunes, he claimed that she was 'the education of Hellas'.[9] In so far as she lived unto herself, as a city-state, Athens came to grief before that age of Hellenic history had reached its close. In so far as she lived for Hellas, Pericles' claim was justified by the event; for in the next age of Hellenic history, which began about 325 BC, the new ideas and institutions which had been worked out by Athens in order to discover a particular solution for the general problem of the preceding age were adopted by the rest of the Hellenic Society (which by then had expanded far beyond the narrow domain of the Greek-speaking peoples) as their common social heritage. This phase of Hellenic history is commonly called 'the Hellenistic Age', but 'the Atticistic Age' is the proper name for it.[10]

From this angle of vision, which takes not Athens or Sparta or Corinth or Chalcis but the whole of the Hellenic Society as its field, we are able to understand both the significance of the histories of these several communities during the period 725–325 BC and the significance of the transition from this period to that which followed. Questions are answered to which no answer could be found so long as we looked for an intelligible field of study in Chalcidian history or Corinthian history or Spartan history or Athenian history examined in isolation. From this point of view it was merely possible to observe that Chalcidian or Corinthian history was in some sense normal, whereas Spartan and Athenian history departed from the norm in different directions. It was not possible to explain the way in which this departure took place; and historians were reduced to suggesting that the Spartans and Athenians were already differentiated from other Greeks by the possession of special innate qualities at the dawn of Hellenic history. This was equivalent to explaining Spartan and Athenian development by postulating that there had been no development at all, and that these two particular Greek peoples were as peculiar at the beginning of the story as at the end of it. That hypothesis, however, is in contradiction with established historical facts. In regard to Sparta, for example, the excavations conducted by the British Archaeological School at Athens have produced striking evidence that, down to about the middle of the sixth century BC, Spartan life was not abnormal in the ways which thereafter were to differentiate it so sharply from life in other Hellenic communities. After the middle of that century there was a revolutionary change which has to be explained, and an explanation can be found only through looking at Spartan history in this period as a special local response to an ordeal which confronted the whole of the Hellenic Society. The special characteristics of Athens, which she communicated to the whole Hellenic World in the so-called 'Hellenistic' Age (in contrast to Sparta, whose peculiar turning proved to be a blind alley), were likewise acquired characteristics, the genesis of which can only be apprehended from a general standpoint. It is the same with the differentiation between Venice, Milan, Genoa, Florence, and the other city-states in Northern Italy in the so-called 'Middle Ages' of our Western history, and with the differentiation between France, Spain, the Netherlands, Great Britain, and the other national states of the West in more recent times. In order to understand the parts, we must first focus our attention upon the whole, because this whole is the field of study which is intelligible in itself.

In this progressive differentiation of the components of a society, Hellenic history, during the four centuries 725–325 BC, displays the same configuration as 'medieval' North Italian history and as modern Western history as a whole; but, though this episode of Hellenic history is comparable to these two other episodes, it is not contemporary with them. Chronologically, it is anterior. The origins of the Western Society can be traced back to the last phase of Hellenic history – to its Graeco-Roman phase – but not further back than that; and this chronological relation of Western history to Hellenic history reveals the limits of the backward extension of our Western Society in time. The spatial extension of this 'intelligible field', while wider than that of any single nation belonging to it, is narrower, even in its most extensive spatial cross-section, than the entire surface of the Earth and than the whole living generation of Mankind; and we now find that its backward extension in time, while somewhat longer than that of any single nation belonging to it, is not so long, even when we take into account the length of its roots underground, as the span of time during which the species of society of which it is a representative has been in existence.

Our provisional conclusions can be stated as follows:

(a) The 'intelligible fields of historical study', whose limits we have roughly established by working outwards and backwards from the standpoint of our own country in our own day, are societies which have a greater extension, in both space and time, than national states or city-states, or any other political communities.

(b) Such political communities (national states, city-states, and the like) are not only narrower in their spatial extension and shorter-lived in their time-extension than the respective societies to which they belong, but their relation to these societies is that of inseparable parts to indivisible wholes. They are simply articulations of the true social entities and are not independent entities in themselves. Societies, not states, are 'the social atoms' with which students of history have to deal.

(c) The societies of which national states like Great Britain or city-states like Athens are parts, while they are (unlike their parts) independent entities in the sense that each of them constitutes, by itself, an 'intelligible field of historical study', are at the same time related to one another in the sense that they are all representatives of a single species of society.

(d) No one of the particular societies which we have been studying embraces the whole of Mankind or extends spatially over the whole habitable and traversable surface of the planet or is coeval with the species of which it is one representative. Our Western Society, for example, which is still alive, was not conceived until the Hellenic Society had passed its maturity, while the Hellenic Society – even if (as is not the case) it proved, on being traced back, to be one of the original representatives of the species – has been extinct for thirteen and a half centuries, so that in any case its complete life-span would fall short of the still uncompleted life-span of the species by that much already.

(e) While the continuity between the histories of one society and another is very much slighter in degree than the continuity between different chapters in the history of any single society (indeed, so much slighter as virtually to differ in kind), yet in the time-relation between two particular societies of different age – namely, the Western and the Hellenic – we have observed features indicating a nexus which we may describe metaphorically as 'affiliation'.

13 SOCIETY AS AN ORGANISM Leviathan, 'King of the Proud', from Hobbes's treatise. The image here reproduces the fallacious belief that societies consist of crowds, not relationships.

3 Some definitions of terms

1 SOCIETY

SOCIETY is the total network of relations between human beings. The components of society are thus not human beings but relations between them. In a social structure 'individuals are merely the *foci* in the network of relationships'.[1] The famous frontispiece of Hobbes's *Leviathan*, displaying society as a gigantic human figure composed of a multitude of life-sized human figures, is an anthropomorphic misrepresentation of reality; and so is the practice[2] of speaking of human beings as 'members' of society or of one or other of its component institutions (e.g. a club, a church, a class, a family, a 'corporation'). A visible and palpable collection of people is not a society; it is a crowd. A crowd, unlike a society, can be assembled, dispersed, photographed, or massacred.

2 CULTURE

I agree with, and adopt, P. Bagby's definition of culture as being 'regularities in the behaviour, internal and external, of the members of a society, excluding those regularities which are clearly hereditary in origin'.[3] Bagby adds[4] that, in virtue of being 'the patterned or repetitive element in

history', 'culture is history's intelligible aspect'. A. L. Kroeber proposes[5] a definition in four points, of which the first three agree with Bagby's definition. Kroeber's fourth point is that culture embodies values. I agree with, and adopt, this point too.

3 CIVILIZATION

This pseudo-Latin word is a modern French coinage, and Dr Johnson refused to include the English counterpart of it in his dictionary of the English language. Since then, it has become current in all modern languages in the meaning of a particular kind or phase of culture that has been in existence during a particular age. In the present state of knowledge the Age of Civilization appears to have begun approximately five thousand years ago.

Bagby proposes[6] that we should take our cue from the etymology of the word 'civilization' and should define civilization as 'the kind of culture found in cities'. And he proposes to define 'cities' as being 'agglomerations of dwellings many (or, to be more precise, a majority) of whose inhabitants are not engaged in producing food'.

In a society which produces an economic surplus, a division of labour is possible. Specialist minorities, freed from the work of food production, can monopolize social tasks which were formerly the responsibility of all participants in the society.

14   Warriors from Benin, sixteenth or seventeenth century AD

Bagby's definition comes near to hitting the mark. Yet it will not quite serve. Nor will V. G. Childe's coinage of the phrase 'the Urban Revolution' (on the analogy of 'the Industrial Revolution') as a synonym for the emergence of the species of culture known as 'civilization'.[7] There have been city-less societies that have nevertheless been in process of civilization. But we have, I believe, to go further, and to equate civilization with a state of society in which there is a minority of the population, however small, that is free from the task, not merely of producing food, but of engaging in any other of the economic activities – e.g. industry and trade – that have to be carried on to keep the life of the society going on the material plane at the civilizational level. These non-economic specialists – professional soldiers, administrators, and perhaps, above all, priests – have certainly been city-dwellers in the cases of most of the civilizations known to us.[8]

I agree with H. Frankfort[9] in rejecting the view that 'such changes as an increase in food-production or technological advances (both, truly enough, coincidental with the rise of civilization) . . . explain how civilization became possible'. A. N. Whitehead surely hits the truth in a passage, quoted by Frankfort in this context, in which he declares that 'in each age of the world distinguished by high activity, there will be found at its culmination, and among the agencies leading to that culmination, some profound cosmological outlook, implicitly accepted, impressing its own type on the current springs of action'.[10]

Christopher Dawson is making the same point when he says that 'behind every civilization there is a vision'.[11] On this view, to which I adhere, the presence in a society of a minority liberated from economic activities is an identification-mark of civilization rather than a definition of it. Following Whitehead's lead, I should define civilization in spiritual terms. Perhaps it might be defined as an endeavour to create a state of society in which the whole of Mankind will be able to live together in harmony, as members of a single all-inclusive family. This is, I believe, the goal at which all civilizations so far known have been aiming unconsciously, if not consciously.

4 SOCIETIES

I use the words 'societies' in the plural and 'a society' in the singular to mean particular historical exemplifications of the abstract idea 'society' which has been examined above. The relation of 'societies' or 'a society' to 'society' is the relation of one or more representatives of a class of phenomena to the class that it represents.

Since I use the word society to mean the total network of relations between human beings, I use the words 'societies' and 'a society' to denote particular networks that can be analysed as being combinations of a number of institutions that are their components, but which cannot be identified as being, themselves, components of any more comprehensive network. If one defines societies in these terms, one finds that there are several kinds of them. In other words, one finds that the genus 'society' consists of several species. There are, for instance, pre-civilizational societies, societies in process of civilization, and societies that are embodiments of higher religions. The pre-civilizational societies again fall into a number of different sub-classes: Lower

Palaeolithic, Upper Palaeolithic, Mesolithic, Neolithic, Chalcolithic. The last three of these sub-classes, or at any rate the last two, have more in common with civilizations than they have with their Palaeolithic predecessors.

Though, according to my definition, societies are systems of relations that are not components of other societies, they are not, in my view, Leibnizian monads. All societies exert a constant reciprocal influence on each other. The extant representatives of the species are being influenced, in different degrees, not only by all their surviving contemporaries but also by the legacies of all societies that have come and gone up to date.

Every social network is the carrier of a culture, and it is impossible in practice to study a society and its culture apart from each other.

5 CIVILIZATIONS

I use the word 'civilizations' in the plural and 'civilization' in the singular to mean particular historical exemplifications of the abstract idea 'civilization' which has been examined above. The relation of 'civilizations' or 'a civilization' to 'civilization' is the relation of one or more representatives of a class of phenomena to the class that it represents. The class represented by civilizations is one species of the genus 'culture'. Every civilization is carried on the network of a society, and it is impossible in practice to study a civilization and its society apart from each other.

A civilization can be defined as being 'an intelligible field of study'; as being the common ground between the respective individual fields of action of a number of different people; and as being a representative of a particular species of society. These definitions are compatible with each other, and something essential would be missing if any one of them were left out. The first of these definitions is, of course, put in subjective terms. Its approach to the definition of a civilization is epistemological. The other two definitions are objective. They are attempts to describe the reality that the inquirer's mind believes (and believes correctly, in my view) that it has apprehended in the phenomena. Ideally, any definition that we make of anything whatsoever ought to be made in this dual form, considering that the duality of subject and object, and the problem of what the true relation between them is, are inherent in all thinking.

A civilization is an intelligible field by comparison with its component communities – nations, city-states, millets, castes, or whatever else these components may happen to be. In general, a larger unit of study is likely to be more intelligible than a smaller one, considering that nothing can be completely intelligible short of the sum total of reality. This, however, cannot be intelligible either, because things are intelligible only to minds, and, *ex hypothesi*, there would be no mind, outside the sum total of reality, to be the subject of this object. Accordingly, the intelligibility of phenomena, on whatever scale, can never be more than partial and imperfect. This indicates that a civilization is 'an intelligible field of study' in a relative sense only.

The common ground between a number of different people's individual fields of action is an alternative phrase for describing what, in this chapter, I have called a network of relations between a number of human beings. A network

15 Egyptian scribe, Fifth Dynasty

16 Buddhist priest, Japan, ninth century AD

of relations, being a phenomenon in the time-dimension as well as in the space-dimension, will have phases. The civilizations whose histories are on record so far are objective realities that have all had geneses; most of them have also grown, over various periods of time, to various extents; some of them have had breakdowns; and some of them have then gone through a process of disintegration ending in dissolution. In crediting civilizations with histories in a pattern of phases, I am not personifying them or conceiving of them in anthropomorphic terms. A non-human intelligible field of study – for instance, a crystal – can also be an objective reality that changes in a regular pattern of phases.

Civilizations are invisible, just as constitutions, states, and churches are, and this for just the same reasons. But civilizations, too, have manifestations that are visible, like the Prussian state's gold-crowned eagles and spiked helmets, and like the Christian Church's crosses and surplices. Set side by side an Egyptiac, an Hellenic, and a pre-Renaissance[12] Western statue. It will be impossible to mistake which of these is the product of which school of sculptors. The distinctiveness of each of the three artistic styles is not only visible; it is definite – more definite than any of the visible products or emblems of any church or state. By exploring the range, in space and time, of a civilization's distinctive artistic style, one can ascertain the spatial and temporal bounds of the civilization that this style expresses. As Kroeber points out,[13] an artistic style is a sensitive indicator of historical connexions. Within the ambit of any one civilization the various styles 'tend towards a certain consistency among themselves',[14] and 'styles are the very incarnation of the dynamic forms taken by the history of civilization'.[15] Our ability, Kroeber adds, to locate an unassigned work of art to its place in a style sequence implies that the development of a style follows a one-way course. 'A style is a strand in a culture. . . . It is also a selective way. . . . Where compulsion or physical or physiological necessity reign, there is no room for style.' In being selective, a style, as well as a state, is an expression of will.[16] Bagby, too, observes[17] that 'the art-historians have shown that the styles of works of art are not absolutely indefinable', and that 'something of the same kind is done by the anthropologist and the culture historian. He too feels a common flavour in the diverse features of a culture or a period; he too tries to point out the observable qualities which give rise to this feeling.'[18] Frankfort points out[19] that 'we recognize it [the character of a civilization] in a certain coherence among its various manifestations, a certain consistency in its orientation, a certain cultural "style" which shapes its political and its judicial institutions, its art as well as its literature, its religion as well as its morals'.

The visible works of art that reveal so much about their civilization are merely expressions of it. They are not the civilization itself. That remains invisible, like a church or a state. When the anthropologist or the cultural historian tries to analyse the observable qualities that have been his clues to the diagnosis of a culture, he analyses them, as Bagby notices,[20] in terms of ideas and values.

4 The need for a comprehensive study of human affairs

THE DEMAND for a comprehensive study of human affairs is inspired by several motives. Some of these are permanent and some temporary; some are disinterested, some self-regarding. The strongest and most estimable of these is curiosity. This is one of the distinctive traits of human nature. No human being seems to be altogether without it, though the degree of its strength varies enormously as between different individuals. In the field of human affairs, curiosity prompts us to seek a panoramic view in order to gain a vision of reality that will make it as intelligible as is possible for a human mind. 'History certainly justifies a dictum of Einstein, that no great discovery was ever made in science except by one who lifted his nose above the grindstone of details and ventured on a more comprehensive vision.'[1] A panoramic view will at any rate be a less misleading reflexion of reality than a partial view. And, while it is true that in the search for knowledge and understanding, as in all human activities, human achievements are never complete, it is one of Man's virtues that he has the intelligence to be aware of this and has the spirit to go on striving, with undiminished zest, to come as near to his goal as his endowment of ability will carry him.

Another motive for the quest for a panoramic view of human affairs, and indeed of the whole of the phenomenal Universe, is more self-regarding. The phenomena appear to be innumerable, and the Universe infinite, to the diffracting human mind; and this experience of being adrift in a boundless sea, without chart or compass, is terrifying for a being whose powers are finite. In this disconcerting human situation our first recourse is to make believe that the ocean is not as big as it looks; we try to play on it the tricks of partition and omission; but, in playing them we see through them, and then the only recourse left is the formidable one of trying to fling our mental net over the Universe as a whole. Needham points out[2] that 'one of the greatest stimulatory factors of primitive science' was 'the need for at least *classing* phenomena, and placing them in some sort of relation with one another, in order to conquer the ever-recurring fear and dread which must have weighed so terribly on early men'.

This anxiety in the face of the phenomena spurs human minds, always and everywhere, into 'fixing' the phenomena by finding a pattern in them; but it has been accentuated in the present-day world as a result of the world's sudden unification by means of modern science and technology. The same unprecedented scientific and technological advances that have unified the world by 'annihilating distance' have put it into Mankind's power to annihilate itself by making war with atomic weapons. We are now waking up to the truth that we have unintentionally put ourselves in a new position in which Mankind may have to choose between the two extreme alternatives of committing genocide and learning to live henceforward as a single family.[3] The human race's survival is now once again in doubt for the first time since Man established his ascendancy over non-human Nature – a feat that he achieved part way through the Palaeolithic Age. This time it is human nature that threatens Mankind with extinction. The recurrence of the ancient threat from this new quarter is a challenge to all human beings to subordinate their traditional parochial loyalties to a new paramount loyalty to Mankind itself. The recurrent threat's source in human nature is a challenge to us to study human affairs in order to bring them under control.

In a world that has been unified in both space and time, a study of human affairs must be comprehensive if it is to be effective.[4] It must include, not only the whole of the living generation, but also the whole of the living generation's past. In order to save Mankind we have to learn to live together in concord in spite of traditional differences of religion, civilization, nationality, class, and race. In order to live together in concord successfully, we have to know each other, and knowing each other includes knowing each other's past, since human life, like the rest of the phenomenal Universe, can be observed by human minds only as it presents itself to them on the move through time. Historical forces can be more explosive than atom bombs. For our now urgent common purpose of self-preservation it will not be enough to explore our common underlying human nature. The psychologist's work needs to be supplemented by the archaeologist's, the historian's, the anthropologist's, and the sociologist's. We must learn to recognize and, as far as possible, to understand, the different cultural configurations in which our common human nature has expressed itself in the different religions, civilizations, and nationalities into which human culture has come to be articulated in the course of its history. 'All of human history is relevant to present and future human needs.'[5] 'The knowledge of the history of Mankind should be one of Mankind's common possessions.'[6]

We shall, however, have to do more than just understand each other's cultural heritages, and more even than appreciate them. We shall have to value them and love them as being parts of Mankind's common treasure and therefore being ours too, as truly as the heirlooms that we ourselves shall be contributing to the common stock. Without the fire of love, the dangerous fissures in Mankind's social solidarity cannot be annealed. Danger, even when it is as extreme as ours is today, is never a sufficient stimulus in itself to make men do what is necessary for their salvation. It is a poor stimulus because it is a negative one. A cold-blooded calculation of expediency will not inspire us with the spiritual power to save ourselves. This power can come only from the disinterested pursuit of a positive aim that will outrange the negative one of trying to avoid self-destruction;[7] and this positive aim can be given to men by nothing but love.

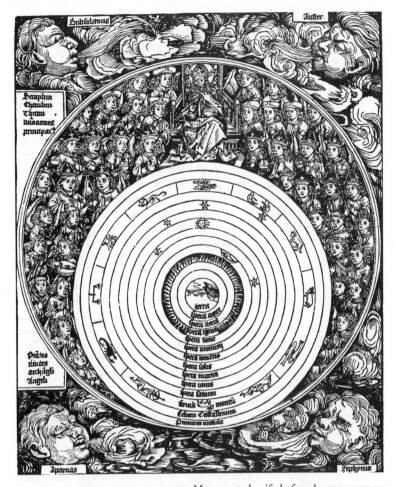

17, 18 CHARTING THE COSMOS Man must classify before he can comprehend. The pre-Copernican panorama of the Universe, above, defines it as a series of spheres, protected by the Heavenly Host. An Aztec calendar stone projects the world's history, showing the sun (centre) surrounded by symbols of the destruction of worlds past and present.

5 The transitional societies

THE SPECIES of society with which this book is mainly concerned are the civilizations and the higher religions. These loom large in our retrospective view, because they are the major living institutions and because we know far more about them than about their antecedents. The reason, however, why they are topical and familiar is that they are things of yesterday. The oldest of the higher religions are barely 2500 years old; the oldest of the civilizations are only 5000 years old. By far the longest epoch of Mankind's history so far has been the Lower Palaeolithic Age. This may have lasted for half a million years, reckoning from the date at which our ancestors became recognizably human.[1] By comparison, the Upper Palaeolithic Age, which dawned perhaps 30,000 years ago, was brief, yet its duration was long in terms of the time-scale of the civilizations, and longer still on the time-scale of the higher religions. Moreover, in both the Old World and the Americas, the dawn of civilization was separated culturally, as well as chronologically, from the end of the Upper Palaeolithic Age by a transitional series of cultures. We must not ignore these earlier and longer chapters of human history if we have recognized the need for making a comprehensive study of human affairs.

Upper Palaeolithic Man had been a hunter, but, in the north-west quarter of the Old World, he lost this means of livelihood when the recession of the latest in a succession of glacial ages brought in its train disconcerting changes in the regional flora and fauna. In Northern Europe, that once mighty hunter, Magdalenian Man, failed to respond to this challenge from his environment. Some of his humbler contemporaries to the south and south-east also partly died out. Some of them decamped still further southwards, in step with the southward drift of the savannahs at the expense of the tropical forest. But some of them held their ground and made history.

The type or phase of culture that was transitional between the Upper Palaeolithic and the civilizations of the first generation which arose in the Lower Tigris-Euphrates valley and the Lower Nile valley c. 3000 BC is commonly known as Neolithic, in allusion to its characteristic tool, the ground-stone axe, which was much more potent than even the finest of Upper Palaeolithic Man's chipped or flaked flints. However, agriculture and, to an almost equal degree, the keeping of domestic animals, which was the normal concomitant of agriculture in the region where the agriculture of the Old World originated, are the essence of the Neolithic culture and are its greatest enduring legacy to cultures of subsequent phases that are 'higher' in the sense of having been built up on Neolithic foundations, whether or not they are higher in terms of spiritual achievement and value.

By achieving the agricultural-pastoral revolution, human beings made themselves into active partners of Nature instead of continuing to be parasites on her like their human predecessors and like all other kinds of living creatures except some of the social insects. Both vegetable and animal husbandry are fruits of foresight, forethought, perseverance, and self-control, and require an unfailing practice of these virtues to keep them going. Husbandmen have to take thought, not only for the morrow, but for the next year; and, however hungry they may be, they must not eat the seed-corn or slaughter the cows, ewes, and she-goats that yield them milk, besides replenishing their herds and flocks. The reward of husbandry is the production of a food supply that can maintain a denser population in greater security than hunting and food-gathering can. But to describe this revolution solely in technological and economic terms would be to give an inadequate account of it. Before the epiphany of higher religion led to the extrication of the religious activities from the secular side of life, all social and cultural activities were religious activities as well. Husbandry, both vegetable and animal, certainly had a religious, as well as an economic, aspect to begin with; and the agricultural-pastoral revolution might never have been achieved if it had not been a religious revolution in one of its aspects.

Primitive agriculture had produced no surplus food and therefore no reserves for maintaining specialists; the only division of labour had been between men and women, and each local community had been self-sufficient.[2] The new arts that arose in the Afrasian oases during the fourth millennium BC required male specialists, and this indicates that a certain surplus must by then have been accruing.[3] Metallurgy is a full-time occupation;[4] 'metallurgical lore is the first approximation to international science',[5] and metallurgy destroys Neolithic self-sufficiency – requiring, as it does, not only smiths, but miners, smelters, and carriers.[6] The fourth-millennium inventions – metallurgy, the wheel, the ox-cart, the pack-ass, the sailing ship – provided the technological foundations for a new economic organization which could undertake a task that Afrasian Man had not yet attempted: the reclamation, for agriculture, of the jungle-swamps in the great Afrasian basins and valleys. This work presupposed a mastery of the arts of irrigation, and irrigation in its turn demanded an elaborate economic and social framework, since without them there could be no public works;[7] and without these the fourth-millennium technological inventions would not have enabled Afrasian Man to achieve his great new enterprise.

No doubt every technological revolution is also a social one in the sense that technological changes are both consequences and causes of social changes. R. J. Braidwood points out[8] that the nature of the surviving evidence for pre-civilizational culture yields a picture in which technology looms too large. But, in contrast to the Neolithic revolution, which had been a technological one first and foremost, the civilizational revolution was a social and cultural one in its essence. The technological stages of history – food-gathering, food-production, industrialism – do not correspond to its cultural stages.[9] The Neolithic technological

19 Ass driver, Egyptian, Fifth Dynasty

THE NEOLITHIC
TECHNOLOGICAL REVOLUTION

Pack-ass, ox-cart, and sailing-ship all represented
major advances in inventive technique and the
harnessing of non-human power. Technically, such
inventions immensely increased Man's command
over his environment; but in social and psychological terms they marked the beginning of Man's
sense of imprisonment in his culture.

20 Model of a cart, Syrian, third millennium BC

21 Sailing-ship, Minoan, c. 2000 BC

49

WATER POWER AND HUMAN POWER

The earliest irrigation schemes required an unprecedented degree of social co-operation and coercion; they permanently altered men's relations with each other as well as with the physical environment.

22 The 'Scorpion' King cuts the first sod of an irrigation canal in Egypt. The scene symbolizes the restoration of peace and order after the conquest of Lower Egypt by the South.

23 Raising water by means of the *shaduf*. The pole, hinged on an upright, has a bucket at one end and a balance on the other; the counterpoised weight allows the bucket to be filled, lifted, and swung round with little effort.

revolution, in which food-production supplanted food-gathering, was a technological change of the same order of magnitude and momentousness as the modern Western Industrial Revolution in which muscle-power was replaced by harnessed inanimate power as Man's material means of manufacture and locomotion.[10] There was no comparable technological change during the intervening age. 'The technological and economic differences between civilization and the pre-civilizational phases of food-production were differences of degree.'[11] On the other hand, this intervening age saw, in the emergence first of civilization and then of higher religion, the two greatest single cultural changes in human history so far. The civilizational stage of culture could not have been achieved if it had not been preceded by the invention of food-production and the other concomitant and subsequent technological advances that have been noticed just above. But the emergence of civilization was, in itself, an event on a non-technological plane. It was brought about by developments on the spiritual plane.[12] So far from being caused, or accompanied, by any fresh technological advance, it was soon followed by an arrest of the movement of technological advance that had been set going in the Neolithic technological revolution.[13] Conversely, the Neolithic technological revolution had cost a spiritual price. 'The hunter's wide-ranging life had freed Man's spirit; agriculture made it a prisoner of the clod.'[14]

'All through the Near East the best sites were reclaimed with toil.'[15] The undertaking required the production, collection, and storing of a large food-surplus to feed a great labour-force diverted from food-production to large-scale public works bringing in no immediate return in the form of foodstuffs. This labour-force had to be raised, controlled, and directed. Neither task would have been possible without a governing minority possessed of both immense ability and immense authority;[16] for the task was heart-breaking as well as back-breaking, and the scale of it was so vast that the ordinary labourer can hardly have foreseen in imagination the fruits of his efforts.[17] He must have been induced to work in faith or have worked under coercion. More probably, he was driven by both these forces simultaneously. It is significant that, in both Sumer and Egypt at the dawn of history, the reclaimed land is the property of a god,[18] and that this god is represented by effective economic and political institutions managed by a ruling minority.

It was this disciplined corporate effort, with a religious faith as its inspiration and with the necessary political authority and technological equipment at its command, that reclaimed the Afrasian river basins and valleys for agriculture. 'Unless a markedly different rainfall and weather pattern could be postulated for four or five thousand BC, which we doubt, extensive life in alluvial Mesopotamia would have been literally impossible without irrigation.'[19] 'The alluvial valleys of the great rivers offered a more exacting environment, but also greater material rewards for its exploitation. In them, Copper-Age villages turned into Bronze-Age cities.'[20] 'The food-producing revolution was perhaps the turning-point in the human career, but it was through the urban revolution that the consequences of the turn were realized.'[21] The biggest and

24 The union of the Upper and Lower Nile, consummated by two deities who tie their emblems of papyrus and lotus round a motif symbolizing unity.

25 Map, *c.* 1300 BC, of irrigation canals on a royal estate near Nippur, Mesopotamia. The water-ways run through the fields; the circles represent villages.

most difficult of the primary feats of civilization – the creation of the land of Sumer out of the marshes of the Lower Tigris-Euphrates basin – was also the earliest. Sumer was about the size of Denmark, and by about 2500 BC the yield from the crops grown on these ex-marshes was eighty-six-fold.[22] The limited enterprise of creating Upper Egypt out of the Lower Nile valley seems to have been achieved later – possibly to some extent under the stimulus of what the Sumerians had already accomplished. The reclamation of the Nile delta – a task on the scale of the creation of Sumer – may have been completed only in the Early Dynastic Age of Egypt. If so, it will have been earlier than the reclamation of the Indus valley. The reclamation of the marshlands in the basins of the East Asian rivers seems to have come decidedly later.

Thus the reclamation of the river valleys of Afrasia for agriculture was in truth a response to the challenge of the progressive desiccation of Afrasia in the present Post-glacial or Inter-glacial Age. The cultivation of the minor oases, which had been the first response to this challenge, had turned out not to be enough in itself to make Afrasia permanently habitable by Man under post-pluvial conditions. In the end he was confronted with a choice between emigrating, as was done by the pioneers who carried agriculture from Afrasia to the ends of the Old World, and reclaiming the Afrasian swamps, as was done eventually by the makers of the earliest Old-World civilizations. The reclamation of the swamps was a permanent solution, because the new fields thus brought under cultivation were irrigated perennially by rivers whose sources rose outside the arid zone, and whose waters continually refertilized the soil with silt drawn by erosion from a virtually inexhaustible supply. In the reclaimed river valleys Man could be sure of making a livelihood so long as he continued to do organized and disciplined hard labour. Desiccation was the challenge; the lands of Sumer and Egypt were the response. But this bare statement would be a misleading simplification of the story. It does not become intelligible until we have also taken account of the primitive agricultural societies that made the transition to the earliest of the civilizations from the latest of the Upper Palaeolithic food-gathering and hunting societies. Even Upper Palaeolithic Man lacked the technology, as well as the organization, for coping with the jungle-swamps. Man had to put himself through a transitional apprenticeship before he could venture on the enterprise of civilization.

The intervention of this transitional stage between the primitive level of culture and the higher level that we call 'civilization' is not peculiar to the Old World; we find the same phenomenon in the history of the Americas.

6 The comparative study of civilizations

IN SETTING OUT to make a comprehensive survey of human affairs, I have started by questioning the recent Western practice of making all human history culminate in the Western inquirer's own country in his own time. Since I happen to be an Englishman, I have asked myself whether it is credible that the England of my time is the culmination of history, and I have concluded that this view would be a nationalistic hallucination. (This hallucination is considerably less credible for an Englishman in 1972 than it was in 1927, the year in which I started to make my notes for this book.) I have recognized that England, taken by itself, is not, in fact, an 'intelligible field of study', either in my time or at any earlier date since the time when such a thing as England first became discernible on the political map. I have therefore looked for a minimum unit, of which England is a part, which might be found intelligible if treated as being self-contained, and I have found this in the Western Civilization. In the act of thus identifying my native specimen of a species of society that is not only larger than a nation-state but is also more intelligible, in virtue of approaching nearer to being self-contained, I have found myself confronted by two pertinent facts. First, the West is not all the world; the world is divided between the West and a number of other living civilizations. In the second place, the fact that the West and its contemporaries are still going concerns signifies that their histories are not yet finished; and at least one complete specimen of the history of a civilization is a necessary first piece of material evidence for a study of the species.

I have therefore probed backwards in time, towards the origins of my own native Western Civilization, till I struck the latter end of an earlier one, the Graeco-Roman (alias the Hellenic), to which the Western Civilization is affiliated through the Christian Church. The history of this Hellenic Civilization is a complete specimen of its kind. It has certainly come to an end, for in my day there is no longer any Hellenic Civilization in existence. It has long ago been superseded by two successors: the Western Civilization and the West's sister and contemporary, the Byzantine Civilization. The history of the Hellenic Civilization also certainly does not extend backwards in time beyond our ken, for it is known to have had, not only successors, but also a predecessor, the Minoan-Helladic-Mycenaean (alias Aegean) Civilization. Here, then, in the history of the Hellenic Civilization, is the specimen history of a civilization for which I have been looking. It has one general merit and two special merits for a Western inquirer. Its general merit is its completeness. It has an identifiable beginning and end, and the whole story, in between, is on record, at least in outline. Its special merits are its link with Western history and its familiarity to a Westerner. Even if he has not been educated in the Greek and Latin classics, he will be likely to know more about Hellenic history than about the history of any other civilization outside his own.

Now that I have found my complete specimen of the history of a civilization, how am I to use it for my purpose? This purpose is to explore ways and means of organizing a comprehensive study of human affairs; and, from the start of my inquiry, I have rejected the customary presentation of history that leads the whole of it up to the inquirer's own time and place. This means rejecting a single-track chart of history; for it is only by making it all lead up to oneself that one can persuade oneself that history runs along a single line, and single-track charts of history will not work. Multiple-track charts are the only kind that will fit the phenomena as we find them.

A multiple-track chart, however, presents an intellectual problem that a single-track chart does not raise: the problem of organizing the data. So long as one is following a single track, no such problem arises. The observer has merely to take events as he finds them; he finds them in a sequence, and a sequence can be reproduced in a narrative. But as soon as he refuses to keep to a single track any longer, the observer finds himself with a number of simultaneous phenomena on his hands. These cannot be dealt with in a single narrative, because they do not constitute a single sequence. A number of different narratives have now to be brought into some kind of relation with each other, and *ex hypothesi* this relation cannot be the narrational one, since it is not possible to be telling more than one story at a time. When we have to establish a relation between two or more series of concurrent events, this requires us to take a synoptic view of them, and that in turn requires us to study them comparatively.

A comparative study of a number of specimens means noting their likenesses and differences with a view to discovering whether or not there is a standard type to which they conform, notwithstanding their individual peculiarities. But in order to make our comparison with any assurance we have also to satisfy ourselves that the specimens we are proposing to compare are properly comparable.[1] Here are two intellectual operations that are required as soon as we adopt a multiple-track chart of the phenomena in place of the self-regarding and misleading single-track one; and this is where the construction of a model can, I believe, serve us in good stead.

A 'model', in the sense in which this word has come to be used apropos of scientific investigation, is a symbol that is being used as an instrument.

A symbol is not identical or coextensive with the object that it symbolizes. If it were this, it would be, not a symbol of the thing, but the thing itself. It would be an error to suppose that a symbol is intended to be a reproduction of the thing that it is really intended, not to reproduce, but to illuminate. The test by which a symbol stands or falls is not whether it does or does not faithfully reproduce the object to which it points; the test is whether it throws light on that object, or obscures our understanding of it. The effective symbol is the illuminating one, and effective symbols are an indispensable part of our intellectual apparatus. If a symbol is to work effectively as an instrument for intellectual action – that is to say, as a 'model' – it has to be simplified and sharpened to a degree that reduces it to something like a sketch-map of the piece of reality to which it is intended to serve as a guide – a sketch-map, not a photograph taken from a U-2 aeroplane.

Whether a model resembles anything in the outside world can be discovered only by verification. When we verify a model by testing how far it does or does not correspond to the phenomena, this is, of course, not an end in itself but only a means to an end. Our ulterior purpose is not to learn whether the model is or is not valid; it is to get new insight into the structure and nature of reality by applying a model that is valid and is therefore an effective tool. How far the model is or is not valid is not a matter of any intrinsic interest in itself.

The operation of constructing a model is different from the operation of testing whether it fits the phenomena.[2] But, so far from its being proper to dissociate the two operations from each other, it would seem to be impossible to obtain sure results from either of them if they are not carried out in conjunction. The model has to be constructed out of only a fraction of the total body of data, or we should never be able to mount it for use in investigating the remainder. But, just on this account, the structure will remain tentative and provisional until it has been tested by application to all the rest of the data within our knowledge.[3] Conversely, our picture of the data as a whole will remain chaotic until we have found a model that brings out in them a pattern of specimens of a species.

Unless we bring these two operations into conjunction with each other by conducting them simultaneously and interdependently, we cannot tell whether or not our provisional model provides a genuine clue to some principle of order in the apparent chaos, or whether this particular model must be modified or supplemented or discarded in favour of another. Nor can we tell whether the items in a particular conglomeration of data that we have picked out of the chaos, like a child picking spillikins out of a heap, have any significant common features, or whether they merely happen to have hung together accidentally. In performing each of the two operations, we have provisionally to anticipate the results of the other operation. The untested results of each provide a test – and this the only test at our disposal – of the other operation's validity.

The test of the 'model' that I have found in the history of the Hellenic Civilization is whether or not this 'model' proves to fit the history of other societies of the same species. In order to apply this test I have to take for granted, provisionally, the list of civilizations that I present, and seek to justify, in chapter nine. The testing of my 'model' by applying it to this still untested list is going to lead me to modify the 'model' itself by combining it with a second 'model' offered by the history of the Sinic Civilization. It is also going to lead me to the conclusion that a single 'model', even a composite one, will not suffice for organizing all the data in the form of a comparative study.

CULTURAL UNITY AND POLITICAL
DISUNITY IN THE HELLENIC WORLD
AT ITS ZENITH

A single style stamps these coins, which
come from nine independent city-states:
fruitful competition contained within a
common culture.

27 Peparethos, *c.* 500–480 BC   28 Abdera, *c.* 520–515 BC

29 Macedonia, *c.* 500–480 BC   30 Itanus, *c.* 450 BC   31 Boeotia, *c.* 446–426 BC

32 Naxos, *c.* 460 BC   33 Aenus, *c.* 455–432 BC   34 Maronea, *c.* 400–336 BC

7 Hellenic and Chinese models

I NOW have to apply my Hellenic model to the rest of the field of the histories of civilizations. Before applying it, I will dissect it, and will then apply the component parts one by one. This procedure seems likely to be illuminating, because we shall find that different parts fit the phenomena in different degrees and in different numbers of instances. I shall keep in mind M.R.Cohen's counsel to 'give special note to those facts that fail to fit into preconceived patterns'.[1]

My Hellenic model comprises more than the internal history of the Hellenic Civilization. It also includes this Civilization's relations with contemporary civilizations whose participants it annexed to its internal proletariat; its relations with Christianity; and finally its relations, through Christianity, with the subsequent Orthodox Christian and Western Civilizations. This configuration of historical events can be analysed into the following elements.

One element is the configuration of the Hellenic Civilization's own political history. At the earliest stage of Hellenic history of which we have any record, there is a sharp contrast between the cultural unity of the Hellenic World and its political disunity. We find it divided up politically into a number of sovereign independent states whose citizens recognize that they are all partakers in a common culture yet are not inhibited by this from going to war with each other. In the course of time these fratricidal wars become so devastating that they bring the civilization to grief. When it is on the point of dissolution it wins a reprieve through the belated political unification of the Hellenic World in the Roman Empire. This brings temporary peace and order, but at the prohibitive price of a series of 'knock-out blows' ending in the overthrow of all political Powers except for the one surviving victor. By the time when the Hellenic 'universal state' is established by Rome, the Hellenic World is already so seriously exhausted and demoralized that it proves unable to maintain its universal state in perpetuity; and the break-up of the Roman Empire spells the Hellenic Civilization's dissolution.

COMPETITION DEGENERATES INTO WAR

35 The outbreak of the Peloponnesian War (431/430 BC) precipitated the Hellenic World into four centuries of devastating fratricidal conflict. A relief shows the siege of a Greek city in Asia Minor, with Greek fighting Greek. (Lycian, *c.* 400 BC.)

36 CHRISTIAN INHERITORS A fourth-century mosaic *Victory of the Eucharist* uses the traditional imagery of a Roman military triumph to symbolize the victory of Christianity over paganism.

37 BARBARIAN USURPERS Here, a classic Roman style is 'borrowed' to commemorate the victory of the Lombard King Agilulf. (Seventh century A D.)

A second element is the configuration of the Hellenic Civilization's social history after its 'breakdown'. The leading minority in the society comes to depend more and more on force, and less and less on attraction, for maintaining its ascendancy. This change in the character of its relation with the majority alienates both the dominant minority's subjects within the Hellenic Civilization's domain and the primitive peoples beyond its borders who have previously been attracted towards it. These two classes turn respectively into an internal and an external 'proletariat' (in the sense of a class that is 'in' society but not 'of' it). The internal proletariat is swollen in numbers by the addition of barbarians from the external proletariat and of representatives of foreign civilizations who are forcibly incorporated in the Hellenic Civilization's internal proletariat through military conquest.

A third element is the configuration of the Hellenic Civilization's religious history in the same phase. The internal proletariat creates a higher religion, Christianity,

that draws its inspiration from one of the non-Hellenic civilizations whose representatives have been incorporated in the Hellenic internal proletariat. Christianity converts the Hellenic World and also its barbarian invaders. An attempt to organize a counter-religion, Neoplatonism, professedly drawing its inspiration from native Hellenic sources, is a failure. The Christian Church, in which the Christian religion has taken social form, serves as a chrysalis out of which two new civilizations, the Eastern Orthodox Christian (alias Byzantine) and the Western Christian, eventually emerge after a cultural interregnum.

A fourth element is the part played by 'the external proletariat' (the barbarians). Their creativity expresses itself in epic poetry, and their nationalism in the adoption of Christianity in heretical forms (e.g. Arianism) or of religions related by origin to Christianity (e.g. Islam). The barbarians conquer the Hellenic universal state militarily and establish successor-states on its domain. But their contribution to the creation of the new civilizations is slight compared to 'the internal proletariat's' contribution. The matrix of the new civilizations is the Christian Church, not the Roman Empire's barbarian successor-states.

A fifth element is a series of 'renaissances' of the Hellenic culture in the course of the histories of the two 'Hellenistic' civilizations: the Byzantine and the Western. These renaissances are attempts to draw inspiration from Hellenism direct, and not merely indirectly through the medium of the Hellenic element in Christianity.

Let us now see how far these several elements in my Hellenic model fit the histories of civilizations other than the Hellenic.

The combination of cultural unity with political disunity, which we find in the Hellenic World at the dawn of its history, appears to be widespread. It is the situation in all known living pre-civilizational societies, according to Bagby. Its frequency is not surprising, for, after all, there are only two possible alternatives: if a society is not united politically, it is necessarily divided. So political disunity, taken by itself, is too general a feature to have much significance. The significant political configuration in my Hellenic model is the revolutionary change from disunity to unity as a result of a series of ever more devastating wars which have brought the civilization to grief before political unity is achieved. And, in the histories of the civilizations, this configuration is a frequent one. For instance, it occurs – in unmistakable counterparts of the Hellenic pattern – in the histories of the Andean and Middle American Civilizations (if we now regard civilization in Middle America as being continuous and unitary, and see the Aztec Empire as its universal state in the making). The same pattern is also unmistakable in the histories of the Syriac, Sinic, Indic, and Sumero-Akkadian Civilizations, the Eastern Orthodox Christian Civilization in Russia, and the Far Eastern Civilization in Japan. Syria was unified politically in the Assyrian Empire and its successors the Neobabylonian Empire and the Achaemenian Empire, China in the Ch'in (Ts'in) and Han Empire after the period of 'the Contending States', India in the Maurya Empire after a similar period of fratricidal inter-state warfare, the Sumero-Akkadian World in the Empire of Agade and in the subsequent Empire established by the Third Dynasty of Ur and re-established momentarily by Hammurabi, Russia in the Muscovite Empire, Japan in the unitary régime established by the Tokugawa Shogunate.

In the history of the Egyptiac Civilization the political configuration of our Hellenic model can be identified if it is accepted that there was a period in which the nomes (cantons) of Egypt were so many sovereign independent states, perpetually going to war with each other, and that this was followed by a period in which first Upper Egypt and then the whole of the Nile valley below the First Cataract was united politically in the so-called 'Old Kingdom'.[2] This configuration conforms to the Hellenic model, but the chronology does not. In the history of the Hellenic Civilization the revolutionary change from disunity to unity on the political plane came in the last chapter of the story, after the warfare between the contending states had not only brought the Hellenic Civilization to grief but had carried it to the verge of dissolution. In the history of civilization in Egypt there was the same revolutionary change, but it came at the very beginning. The age, if there

38, 39, 40 RECURRING RENAISSANCES Three times between 500 and 1500 Western culture returned to its Hellenic source – in the Carolingian Renaissance (top, St Matthew in the guise of a classical philosopher), the twelfth-century Renaissance (centre, Madonna and Child at Autun) and 'the' Renaissance in fifteenth-century Italy (below, Madonna and Child).

was one, of the contending Egyptian cantons was 'prehistoric' in the sense of being 'pre-civilizational'. In Egypt political unification was simultaneous with the dawn of civilization, and it was followed by the most creative period of Egyptiac history, instead of being followed by dissolution and preceded by breakdown and disintegration, as it was in Hellenic history. When we find an identical configuration in the histories of two civilizations appearing at two quite different stages and performing two quite different functions, this suggests that the common feature may mask a radical difference between the fundamental structures of the two histories.

The structure of the West's sister-civilization, the Eastern Orthodox Christian or Byzantine, conforms to the Egyptiac model. In Eastern Orthodox Christendom the interregnum following the break-up of the Roman Empire was immediately succeeded by the establishment of political unity through a successful revival, here, of the Roman Empire – an achievement that presents a sharp contrast to the series of abortive revivals of the Roman Empire in the West from Charlemagne's attempt onwards.

The second element in my Hellenic model – the disintegration of a broken-down society into an internal and an external proletariat – does occur in a considerable number of non-Hellenic instances. In Hellenic history this second element is closely associated with the third: the creation, by the internal proletariat, of a higher religion in which the inspiration comes from a foreign source. This third element is a key-part of the model, since the church in which the higher religion embodied itself in the Hellenic case served as the chrysalis out of which two new civilizations emerged. It is therefore important to discover whether the pattern of the history of the Christian Church is a standard one which can be detected in a number of other instances, or whether it is something exceptional.

In order to test this we must first analyse this pattern into its elements. The Christian Church arose among the proletariat of one disintegrating civilization; its inspiration came from a different civilization; it easily overcame a counter-church professedly inspired by the native traditions of the civilization in whose domain the victorious church had made its appearance; the victorious church converted the world in which it had triumphed, and also this world's barbarian invaders. It brought to birth two new civilizations which can hardly be regarded as being mere continuations of the preceding Hellenic Civilization within whose bosom Christianity had made its first appearance. It is true that the Western and Byzantine Civilizations are Hellenistic, but they are distinguished from the Hellenic Civilization itself by being also Christian, and Christian from the start.

Perhaps the closest parallel to the history of Christianity at the western end of the Old World is the history of the Mahayanian version of Buddhism at the eastern end of it. The source of the Mahayana's inspiration, like the source of Christianity's, was foreign to the world in which the rising religion made its fortune. Christianity made its fortune in the Hellenic World but drew its inspiration from a Syriac source; the Mahayana made its fortune in the Sinic World but drew its inspiration from an Indian source. Again, the Mahayana made its way among the proletariat of the

Sinic Society, in the sense that it attracted native Chinese who were in revolt against the Confucian tradition and barbarian invaders who were suspicious of it. Furthermore, the progress of the Mahayana evoked a counter-church, the Taoist Church, which was remarkably similar to the Neoplatonist Church in being constructed out of a native philosophy to combat a foreign religion and in trying to steal this foreign religion's thunder by imitating those features of it that made it attractive. These resemblances between the Mahayana and Christianity are impressive; but beyond this point the histories of the two religions do not any longer run parallel.

In the Western and Byzantine Worlds Christianity won a monopoly which it retained for centuries, even if it is losing it now. The Neoplatonist counter-church, as well as the four established Hellenic philosophies – Platonism, Aristotelianism, Stoicism, Epicureanism – have all been stone-dead by now for at least fourteen hundred years. Hellenism has survived only in so far as Christianity chose to take it over. Byzantine and Western attempts at renaissances of Hellenism drawn direct from the fountain-head have been superficial and ephemeral. In so far as the Western and Byzantine Societies are now ceasing to be Christian, they are still inescapably ex-Christian. Their cultural heritage is so thoroughly saturated with Christianity that it is impossible for them to disengage themselves from their Christian past (as is demonstrated, for example, by the transparentness of the Communist ideology's Judaeo-Christian origins). In Eastern Asia, history has run a less revolutionary course. Here the Mahayana never succeeded, even at the height of its vigour and power, in driving off the field either the Taoist counter-church or Confucianism, which was the established Sinic philosophy. In China at the opening of the twentieth century, Confucianism and Taoism, as well as the Mahayana, were still alive, and this was more than eighteen hundred years after the Mahayana had made its first lodgment in China, and more than a thousand years since the end of the Mahayana's partial ascendancy, which had lasted from the break-up of the United (Western) Ch'in (Ts'in) régime early in the fourth century of the Christian era down to the official persecution of Buddhism in AD 842–45. Until AD 1911 the Sinic universal state was still a going concern, and was still being administered by Confucian-educated civil servants. This universal state, the traditional system of administering it, the civil service which knew how to make the system work, and the Confucian-educated gentry that was the civil service's perennial source of recruitment constituted, together, one single great integrated institution. The continuity of this institution may be held to have counted for more than even the most violent of the breaches in the continuity of other elements of civilization in China.

This issue of continuity versus discontinuity is raised by the contrast between Christianity's triumph in the former domain of the Hellenic Civilization and Buddhism's failure to achieve the same apparently manifest destiny in Eastern Asia. The same issue is raised in regard to the history of civilization in India by a metamorphosis of indigenous Indian religion which was so revolutionary as to be comparable to the introduction of foreign religions – the Mahayana and Christianity – into China and the Hellenic

World. In Indian society the master activity was not the civil administration, as it was in Chinese society; it was the religious ministry. The Brahman caste was therefore the Indian counterpart of the Chinese Confucian-educated gentry; and the Brahmans managed to maintain their monopoly of the religious ministry in India in spite of the radical transformation of the spirit, as well as the practice, of Indian religion in the course of a millennium running from the beginning of the second century BC.

It will now be evident that the different elements in my Hellenic model are not all of equal service as keys for elucidating uniformities in the configuration of the histories of civilizations. The political configuration of the Hellenic model recurs, as we have already reckoned, in the histories of at least nine other civilizations. On the other hand, this element in the Hellenic model entirely fails, as we have seen, to fit the political history of the Egyptiac World. The configuration of Egyptiac political history is not only different; it is antithetical. In Hellenic history the universal state is the last phase; in Egyptiac history it is the first. And, when we come to the procreation of affiliated civilizations through the agency of a higher religion serving as a chrysalis, we find the Hellenic model failing to provide a key more often than it succeeds.[3] This element in the model does recur, as we have seen, in Chinese and Indian history, and perhaps in Egyptiac history too; but, in each of these other instances, the break in continuity does not seem decisive enough to entitle me to confirm my provisional interpretation of what comes after the break as being the history of a new civilization.

Since Hellenic history has turned out, on trial, not to provide a model that fits the histories of all the other civilizations, let us see how far Chinese history, when put to the same test, will serve as an alternative model to Hellenic history or as a supplement to it. If we take a retrospective view of Chinese history, surveying its course backwards into the past from AD 1911, the date of the fall of the Ch'ing (Manchu) régime, we find that it displays a strongly pronounced configuration. This span of Chinese history – and it is a long span – presents itself as a series of successive realizations of the ideal of a universal state, punctuated by intermediate lapses into disunion and disorder. The phases of both kinds have varied considerably in length, so that the rhythm is cyclical without having any regular periodicity. The succession of unitary phases runs back from the Ch'ing (Manchu) régime to the Ming and the Yüan (Mongol), with intervening bouts of disunion that have been relatively brief. The pre-Yüan bout of disunion lasted for about 150 years; the preceding unitary Sung régime for 167 years; the bout of disunion before that for about half a century; the unitary T'ang régime, with its Sui overture, for more than three centuries before that; the preceding bout of disunion for about four centuries (reckoning back, beyond the collapse of the United Ch'in (Ts'in), to the collapse of the Posterior Han); the previous unitary Han régime, with its Ch'in (Ts'in) overture, for about four centuries, punctuated by two sharp but short bouts of anarchy in AD 9–25 and 207 BC–202 BC.

This is manifestly the configuration of Chinese history from the fall of the Ch'ing unitary régime in AD 1911 back to the establishment of the Ch'in (Ts'in) unitary régime in

221 BC. After 1911 China experienced another bout of disunion, and this ended in 1949 with the establishment of a new unitary régime under communist auspices. However, we cannot be sure that the introduction of this alien Western ideology has not brought with it a decisive break in Chinese history and a change in its political configuration; and thus we cannot predict whether the old familiar pattern of alternating rounds of unity and disunity will continue to operate in the traditional style. It is true that China was captured by a non-Chinese philosophy or religion once before in the shape of Buddhism, and that, after seeming to have prevailed, this Indian religion was eventually overpowered by the indigenous Chinese *Weltanschauung*; but we do not know now whether this indigenous *Weltanschauung* is going to prove potent enough to reassert itself victoriously once again.

China's future is enigmatic. On the other hand there is no uncertainty about the past facts in the span of Chinese history that ended in the political unification of China in 221 BC. We have noticed that, from the Han Age inclusive back to the dawn of the Sinic Civilization, the configuration of Chinese history conforms to the Hellenic model. At the earliest date at which the record of Chinese history comes into clear focus – and this is no earlier than the ninth or eighth century BC – China makes her appearance on the scene as a politically disunited world of local states, and the political unity that she eventually attained under the Ch'in (Ts'in) and Han dynasties was the consequence of a long-drawn-out series of ever more devastating interstate wars. Throughout the age preceding the political unification of 221 BC, China was, however, already a unity on the cultural plane; and on this plane her greatest intellectual creative work was done during the politically catastrophic period of the Contending States, before her political unity was achieved. This was the age of the founders of almost all the schools of Chinese philosophy, including Confucius himself, whose school was eventually canonized as the classical one. Confucius was a conservative. He never dreamed of an effective political unification of the Chinese World. Ch'in Shih Hwang-ti's work would have shocked him; and Han Liu P'ang's modification of it would have pleased him hardly any better. Confucius, like Plato and Aristotle, took political disunity for granted. This authentic configuration of early Chinese history – including the contemporaneity of political disunity and intellectual achievement – bears an unmistakable resemblance to the configuration of early Hellenic history, and differs entirely from the pattern of subsequent Chinese history with its configuration of intellectual torpidity and political unity punctuated by bouts of disunion that are abnormal and temporary.

However, it is this later configuration, which did not establish itself before 221 BC, that has been taken by Chinese scholars since the Han Age as their model for Chinese history as a whole. Consequently, this model could not be applied to early Chinese history without doing violence to the facts: and the scholars did this violence rather than renounce their quest of self-consistency and symmetry.

Having correctly observed that the later unitary régimes were conscious and deliberate restorations of the Ch'in (Ts'in)-Han unitary régime, Chinese scholars assumed that this too must have been a restoration of some earlier régime, and accordingly they extrapolated their series of phases of unity, backwards in time, through a Chou and a Shang and a Hsia restoration of an ideal polity supposedly founded by primordial sages. These sages are perhaps gods reduced to human stature; the Hsia régime is legendary, so far as we know; the Shang and Chou régimes were realities; their historicity is attested by surviving material remains of their cultures, including such instructive contemporary documents as the Shang inscriptions on 'oracle bones'. But there is no evidence to suggest that either the Shang or the Chou régime was a polity of the same order as the Ch'in (Ts'in) and Han régimes and their subsequent avatars. *Pace* the traditional presentation of Chinese history, the effective unification that Shih Hwang-ti achieved and that Liu P'ang salvaged must in truth have been an unprecedented achievement, as the work of Caesar and Augustus was in the Hellenic World.

The Chinese scholars' traditional model for Chinese history actually fits Egyptiac history better. It fits the facts of Egyptiac history from beginning to end. In the Egyptiac 'Old Kingdom' we have, at the dawn of history, a unitary régime which is neither legendary like the Hsia nor shadowy like the Chou, but is authentic and substantial. And, from the first beat of the alternating rhythm of unity and disunity in the Old Kingdom, this rhythm marches on through the First Intermediate Period of Egyptiac history, the Middle Kingdom, the Second Intermediate Period, the New Kingdom, and a series of revivals of the New Kingdom in which, as in the corresponding stage of Chinese history, the empire-builders' role comes to be filled more and more frequently by foreigners – in the Egyptiac case, Libyans, Ethiopians, Assyrians, Persians, Macedonians, Romans – with indigenous dynasties putting in an appearance more and more rarely.

The application of the traditional Chinese model would make the same nonsense of early Hellenic history as it makes of early Chinese history. On the other hand, the model fits well enough if, starting from the Roman Empire, the surveyor moves, not backward, but forward, in time from the year 31 BC and keeps his eye fixed on the Empire's central and eastern sections, which were the heart-land of this Hellenic universal state and came to be the seat of the imperial government after its location at Nicomedia by Diocletian in AD 284 and at Constantinople by Constantine I in AD 324–30. In this heart-land the alternating rhythm declares itself unmistakably. The punctuations of disunity and disorder in AD 69 and AD 193–97 were repeated and intensified in an agonizing half century of anarchy running from 235 to 284. The subsequent Diocletianic-Constantinian restoration was followed by a collapse after the imperial army's disastrous defeat by the Goths at Adrianople in 378. But this dangerous reverse, too, was quickly retrieved by a steady recovery in the course of the fifth century. A fresh collapse was brought upon the Hellenic universal state by Justinian I (*imperabat* AD 527–65). He overstrained it through his misguided attempt at re-expansion; and this over-exertion was followed by a fresh bout of anarchy, lasting from 602 to 717, which was at least as agonizing, and was twice as long, as the bout in the years 235–84. But in 717 the universal state was restored once more by Leo Syrus; and, after that, unity and order

were maintained till 1071; were re-established in 1081; and were maintained again till 1186. The revolt of the Bulgars in that year, and the Western Christians' sack of Constantinople and partition of the East Roman Empire in 1204, precipitated a chaos that lasted for nearly two hundred years. But, in the later decades of the fourteenth century, unity was restored, yet again, by the 'Osmanlis. The new 'Caesar of Rome' (*Qaysar-i-Rum*) re-expanded the restored universal state up to the limits in South-Eastern Europe and in the Tigris-Euphrates basin that had been attained by the Emperor Trajan (*imperabat* AD 98–117); and this Turkish Roman Empire maintained itself for some four hundred years (AD 1372–1774), with punctuations of disaster and disorder at the turn of the sixteenth and seventeenth centuries and again after the failure, in 1683, of the second Ottoman siege of Vienna. The defeat of the Ottoman Empire in the Russo-Ottoman war of 1768–74 was the beginning of the end. Yet, even after that, there was a rally in the first half of the nineteenth century. In South-Eastern Europe the Ottoman Empire did not finally break up till 1878, and in South-West Asia not till 1918. The last Ottoman *Qaysar-i-Rum* was deposed – and the office abolished – by the Emperor's own subjects in AD 1922, 116 years after the renunciation of the title of Roman Emperor by the last holder of it in the West.

Here, in an epilogue to Hellenic history which has its starting-point in 31 BC, we have a counterpart of the pattern of Chinese history since 221 BC which is almost as exact a replica of it as the course of Egyptiac history is from beginning to end. And in the Levant, as in China, this persistent rhythm does not peter out till a date that, today, is still within living memory. The Hellenic universal state, however, had some backward outlying provinces round the shores of the western basin of the Mediterranean, including Italy and Rome itself, the semi-barbarian city that had been the universal state's political nucleus. To complete our test of the applicability of the Chinese model to the history of the western end of the Old World, we must apply it in the extreme west too; and the experiment will show that here, from AD 378 onwards, the Chinese model fails to fit the historical facts as signally as it fails in the Hellenic World as a whole down to 31 BC and in China itself down to 221 BC. The traditional Chinese model is equally inapplicable to the histories of the Middle American and Andean Civilizations, which the Hellenic model fits so well.

Our survey of the histories of civilizations in terms of the traditional Chinese model has shown that this, like the Hellenic, fails to fit all cases. Indeed, its only perfect fit is its application to Egyptiac history, and this only on condition that we leave the 'prehistoric' age out of account. The traditional Chinese model does not fit the early history of any other civilization, not even that of civilization in China itself. Paradoxically, it can give only a negative account of the age in which its own revered patron-philosopher Confucius lived, though Confucius was a child of his age, besides being an innovator under the guise of an archaist. The traditional Chinese model has to write the Confucian Age off as part of an intermediate period between the Western Chou and the Imperial Ch'in (Ts'in). From the date of the establishment of a universal state onwards, the Chinese model does fit Hellenic and subsequent Byzantine history well, the history of the Tigris-Euphrates basin and Iran passably, the history of India barely. But it does not fit Western, Middle American, or Andean history at all. And, in a pattern that presents history as an alternation of universal states and lapses from them, and ignores both local states and diasporás, there is no place for the Jews. The Jews lost their local state, never managed (as most other peoples have never managed) to become empire-builders, but have managed (unlike most other peoples) to preserve their national identity without having a state or even a national home. In world history seen through Chinese spectacles, the Jews would pass unnoticed both in the age of the Prophets and in the age of the Pharisees.

It will be seen that the shortcomings of the traditional Chinese model are at least as great as those of the Hellenic one. Yet the Chinese model, like the Hellenic, is illuminating as far as it goes, and the two models, looked at in relation to each other, are more than twice as illuminating as each of them is by itself. The Hellenic model is as widely applicable to the earlier phase in the histories of civilizations as the Chinese model is to the later phase; and an improved model can be constructed by combining the later phase according to the Sinic model with the earlier phase according to the Hellenic.[4] This composite model for the histories of civilizations shows these societies starting as unities on the cultural plane without being united on the political plane. This régime is favourable to social and cultural progress; but its price is chronic warfare between the local states; this warfare becomes more intense and more devastating as the society grows in strength; and sooner or later it produces a social breakdown which, after a long-drawn-out 'time of troubles', is belatedly retrieved by the establishment of a universal state. This universal state is subject to recurrent lapses into anarchy; but, whether these intermediate periods are short or long, they are apt to be surmounted by the restoration of political unity. There must be some strong force making for the maintenance and, after lapses, for the restoration of unity, when once the original achievement of unity has come to pass; for the phenomenon of restoration occurs again and again, and this even after 'intermediate periods' that have been so long and so anarchic that they might have been expected to have made an irreparable break in the tradition.

This new model fits a great majority of the indisputable specimens of the species of society that we have called 'civilizations'. The Egyptiac Civilization is unique in having achieved political unity at the opening of its history; but, as we have observed, there was an antecedent age of political disunity here too, if we take into account the pre-civilizational stage of history in Egypt. The Middle American, Andean, and Hellenic Civilizations are exceptional in having experienced only a single spell of the universal state stage instead of the normal experience of an initial spell followed by a series of restorations. But, in the Hellenic Civilization's case, this is true of the sequel only in the westernmost section of its domain. Western historians are apt to be preoccupied by what happened in these backward outlying territories, because this is the history of their own civilization. But the sequel to the fall of the Roman Empire in its central and eastern provinces is at least as significant;

and in this area the sequel conformed to the Chinese pattern: there was a series of revivals of the universal state, beginning in AD 717 and not coming to a final close till 1922.

The composite Helleno-Sinic model, which is evidently the standard pattern, is explicable in human terms in all its stages. For example, when we examine a civilization's age of growth, we shall not be surprised to find that a period in which a society is articulated into a number of politically separate local communities, all sharing one common culture, should be a time of creativity and progress. The stimulus that comes from direct personal intercourse works more powerfully in a small community than in a large one; life in a small community that is in active and competitive intercourse with neighbours of its own size and kind is more stimulating still, since this is a social structure that combines the stimulus of intimacy with the stimulus of a wider horizon. A classic exposition of the cultural advantages of a régime of political disunity within a unitary economic and cultural field has been given by Hume in his essay *Of the Rise and Progress of the Arts and Sciences*. But these blessings have their price in the currency of inter-state warfare; and a point may come when the toll taken by this is greater than any benefit that the stimuli of variety and competition can confer. If the balance becomes decidedly adverse, the society breaks down. It might be asked why a society does not forestall its breakdown, or at any rate retrieve it, by promptly applying the remedy of political unification to which it does eventually have recourse. Why do people put up with a long-drawn-out 'time of troubles' before bringing themselves to get rid of warfare by submitting to a universal state? The answer is that human beings are creatures of habit, and that the régime of local sovereignties has won such a hold on people's hearts in the age when it was producing a balance of advantage that it takes a long experience of its subsequent disastrous effects to induce its former beneficiaries to abandon their allegiance to it when they have become its victims.

When once, however, a universal state has been established, it is not surprising that this régime should win a hold on people's hearts in its turn. The peace and order that the achievement of political unity brings with it are appreciated by contrast with a foregoing 'time of troubles' that had become intolerable before it was transcended; and the loss of stimulus now seems a cheap price to pay for the inestimably precious boon of being rescued from the jaws of destruction and guaranteed against a recurrence of this fearful threat so long as the universal state lasts.[5] With the passage of time, a universal state's hold over its subjects' hearts is apt to increase, unless the empire-builders have been aliens who have persistently made themselves odious.[6] It is easy to understand why a universal state, once established, should be restored again and again when it has broken down. But we still have to ask ourselves why, when once it has been established, there should be any 'intermediate periods' at all, considering that normally the maintenance of the universal state is desired by at least a majority of its subjects.

The declines and falls of universal states can be interpreted as being the after-effects of mortal wounds that have been inflicted by society on itself during the foregoing

61

41 The upper register of this stone engraving represents anarchy, showing an attempt to assassinate the Ch'in founder of the Sinic universal state; the lower register symbolizes order: two legendary sovereigns wield geometrical instruments, and the symmetrical patterns below represent 'Good Government'. (Second century AD.)

'times of troubles'; and this lassitude, if not exhaustion, would explain the lapse in the maintenance of a universal state; but it would not explain how a society that has lacked the vitality to maintain its universal state can subsequently summon up enough vitality to re-establish it. In seeking to account for the alternating rhythm that seems normally to prevail in the history of a civilization from the date of the first establishment of its universal state, we need not rest content with the Chinese account of this rhythm as being a manifestation, in human affairs, of a fundamental cosmic rhythm of Yin and Yang that is itself inexplicable and axiomatic. The rhythm does run through the histories of universal states, but there is a human explanation of it. It is an explanation in economic terms.

A universal state is a heavy charge on the economy of a civilization. It requires, for its maintenance, a well-paid professional civil service and professional defence force; and the cost of these services will rise if it is one of the laws of the history of a universal state that, with the passage of time, the administrative and military personnel is apt to become more numerous as the institutions of local self-government decay and as the pressure of the trans-frontier barbarians increases. If the universal state – and, with it, the society incapsulated in it – is to be able to meet these rising costs without being crushed by them, it must be able to draw upon a commensurately rising productivity; but, in the Age of the Civilizations to date, the economy has been more or less static most of the time in the greater part of the *Oikoumene*.

The deliberate application of science to technology in the West is something recent and unprecedented. Even today, when the Industrial Revolution has been in progress for some two hundred years and has spread from Britain, where it originated, to the ends of the Earth, the greater part of the human race is still in the pre-industrial stage. The last economic revolution before this was the enhancement of the productivity of agriculture through water-control, some time before the close of the fourth millennium BC, which transformed inhospitable swamps and jungles into the cradles of the Sumero-Akkadian and Egyptiac Civilizations.[7] But only a fraction of the cultivable part of the Earth's surface is capable of being made to give a comparable yield. Moreover, even in the most favourable environments, the technique of agriculture remained virtually static until the beginning of the present application of science to the improvement of crops and livestock; and this, like the present Industrial Revolution, dates back only to eighteenth-century Britain. Thus the normal economic basis of civilization, till a very recent date, has been a static agriculture at a level of productivity that in most places has been not much higher than that attained in Neolithic societies in the Pre-civilizational Age. But a civilization is a much more costly social structure than a Neolithic society is, and its costs are perhaps at their maximum when the civilization is organized politically in a universal state, and when this universal state has been in existence for some time. The inability of a pre-scientific agricultural economy to bear this economic load is evidently one of the causes of the unwished-for collapses by which so many universal states have been overtaken so many times in succession.

The importance of the part played by the economic factor in determining whether a universal state is to collapse or is to survive can be gauged by comparing the respective fortunes of the Roman Empire in its different sections. The western provinces, in which the Empire collapsed in the fifth century of the Christian Era, were relatively backward economically; the central and eastern provinces, in which, in the same century, the Empire survived, were the principal seats of the Hellenic World's industry and trade; and their relative economic strength more than counterbalanced the relative unfavourableness of their strategic position. Though the centre and the east were more directly exposed than the west was to assaults from the Eurasian Nomads of the Great Western Bay of the steppe, and from the Sasanian power in Iran and 'Iraq, the Empire managed here to hold its own; and, though it did collapse, here too, in the seventh century, it might have continued to survive in these economically stronger sections if, in the sixth century, the Emperor Justinian had not taxed their strength too severely in attempting to reconquer the derelict west. Thereafter, when, in the eighth century, the Hellenic universal state was re-established in the two rival shapes of the East Roman Empire in Anatolia and the Carolingian Roman Empire in Gaul, history repeated itself through the operation of the same economic causes. The Carolingian Empire swiftly collapsed; the East Roman Empire survived, without any further collapse, for three and a half centuries (AD 717–1071). The reason for this diversity of fortunes, this time once again, was that Anatolia in this age was economically capable of carrying the load of a universal state, whereas contemporary Transalpine Western Europe was not. It is significant that in the East Roman Empire, during the century immediately preceding the disaster of AD 1071,

there had been increasing symptoms of social and economic ill-health in the Empire's heart-land, Anatolia.

These are dramatic illustrations of the survival value of economic productivity for a universal state. Yet, hitherto, the rulers of universal states have seldom been alive to this. More often they have been either indifferent to possibilities of technological advance or positively hostile to these, on the reckoning that any technological change is a menace to economic equilibrium and hence also to the social and political stability that the founders of the universal state have established with such difficulty. Certainly the Roman imperial government did not ever realize, at any stage of its history, that technology, as exemplified in Hero of Alexandria's invention of a turbine engine, could have solved the Hellenic universal state's intertwined problems of finance and defence. And in the western provinces in the fourth century of the Christian Era, when the Empire was fighting for survival there, no attention was paid to possibilities of dealing with manpower shortage and with defence logistics by mechanization, though a set of projects for this was published in an anonymous memorandum *De Rebus Bellicis*.[8] In universal states at both ends of the Old World the public authorities seem normally to have confined their action to collecting the land-tax and turning the screw harder on the taxable cultivators or their landlords when agricultural production has declined or public expenses have mounted.

It is significant that, in China, the local state of Ch'in (Ts'in), which eventually established a universal state for the first time by overthrowing the last of its competitors in 221 BC, was also the state which, in the fourth century BC, had distinguished itself among its competitors by systematically revolutionizing its social and economic structure with a view to increasing the population's productivity and putting the increased product at the government's disposal. But it is also significant that, when this régime was extended to the whole of China by the founder of the universal state, Ch'in Shih Hwang-ti, it provoked vehement opposition. After Shih Hwang-ti's death his régime was quickly overthrown; and both he and the 'Legist' school of philosophers, whose theories had been the inspiration of the Ch'in government's practice, were execrated in the subsequently established Chinese tradition. The school of philosophy that was officially established by the Han Emperor Wu-ti (*imperabat* 140–87 BC), and that maintained its monopoly, off and on, from that time till AD 1911, was not the 'Legist' school, but the Confucian. And Confucianism has not been sympathetic towards non-agricultural economic enterprise, though it has understood the value of water-control for agriculture and for communications.

The inadequacy of the economic substructure goes far towards explaining the successive collapses of universal states, not only in China, but in other regions where they have been erected on the same economic and social basis. It explains, for instance, the collapse of the Old Kingdom of Egypt, the fifth-century collapse of the Roman Empire in its western provinces, the ninth-century collapse of the Carolingian avatar of the Roman Empire in the same region, and also the eleventh-century collapse of the Byzantine avatar of the Roman Empire in Anatolia. In all these four cases occurring at the opposite end of the Old World to

PEASANT PRODUCTION · 42 The estate owner, Menna, watches the activities of his peasants. A fellah is being punished and other officials make their reports, while underneath, cattle are driven across the harvested grain to thresh it before it is winnowed. (Egyptian, Eighteenth Dynasty.)

China, the economic basis of the universal state was almost exclusively agricultural, and the burden on the peasantry of maintaining a universal state – a burden that is heavy even under the best régime – became intolerable when landlords armed with official authority shook off governmental control and added their private exactions to the government's demands.

If the cause of the recurrent collapse of those universal states that have come and gone so far is, in truth, economic, the recent change in Mankind's economic situation, thanks to the modern Western Industrial Revolution, promises better prospects for a future universal state on a literally worldwide scale. Modern technology accompanied by a deliberate reduction in the birth-rate as well as in the death-rate would give an unheard-of buoyancy to a future world-state's finances. Instead of being constrained to take an intolerable toll from a poor and static peasant economy, a future world-state could afford to subsidize a revolution in the peasantry's traditional Neolithic way of life through a worldwide application of science and technology to peasant agriculture.

If this is indeed the outlook for a future world-state, that is fortunate for the human race. For the same unprecedented scientific and technological progress that has opened up these prospects of higher production has already produced weapons that would turn war into genocide if they were ever to be used. And the possibility that they may be used will remain open so long as our present-day world remains divided on the political plane, as it now is, among a number of sovereign independent states. In our present situation we can no more afford than our predecessors could, in their 'times of troubles', to let this perilous political disunity continue. But we also cannot afford, in the age of atomic weapons, to let the now imperative political unification of all Mankind come about, in the traditional way, through war *à outrance* ending in the destruction of all the competing Powers but one. Mankind will have to reach political unity through agreement; and, if and when this unity has once been attained, we shall not be able to afford to see the old alternating rhythm of lapses and recoveries reassert itself. For, in the Atomic Age, any lapse into disunity and disorder would be a threat to the existence of the human race. This is an unprecedently difficult problem for statesmanship. But we may take heart if it is true that the technological revolution which has presented this problem to the future architects of a world-state is also going to ease for them the economic problem that has repeatedly worsted their predecessors.

64

8 A Jewish model

NORMALLY the establishment of a universal state, even for no longer than a single spell, has resulted in a permanent obliteration of the identities of the local states and peoples that have been incorporated in it. A classic case is that of 'the Lost Ten Tribes'. Today the population of the Kingdom of Israel, a state which was wiped off the map by the Assyrian Empire in 722 BC, is represented *in situ* only by a few hundred Samaritans in the neighbourhood of Nablus. The Israelites who were deported were completely absorbed into the population of the countries in which they were settled. Their loss of identity was not an exception; it was the rule. It has become famous only because the rule was exceptionally broken by the history of the Israelites' kinsmen, the people of Judah, after their local kingdom, in its turn, had been wiped off the map by the Neobabylonian Empire in 586 BC. The Jews were twice uprooted from their original homeland by Nebuchadnezzar and twice by the Romans. And, before their second uprooting by the Romans in AD 135, they had been subjects of five Empires in turn: the Neobabylonian, the Achaemenian, the Ptolemaic, the Seleucid, and the Roman. From AD 135 to AD 1948 there was no such thing as a Jewish state[1] and not even such a thing as a Jewish 'national home' in the sense of a territory that was substantially Jewish in population without being under Jewish rule. Yet, without the political framework of a state or the territorial basis of a home, the Jews have managed to preserve their separate identity, as a people, from 586 BC – the year that saw the obliteration of the Kingdom of Judah – down to the present day. They have preserved it as a scattered minority (diasporá) living among non-Jewish majorities in countries outside the former frontiers of the extinct Kingdom of Judah and hundreds or thousands of miles away from its historic capital, Jerusalem.

This feat is remarkable and exceptional, but it is not unique. The Jews are not the only uprooted people who have achieved it. For example, it has also been achieved by the Parsees since the destruction of the Sasanian Persian Empire by the Primitive Muslim Arab conquerors; by the Monophysite Christians since the Muslim Arabs' conquest of Syria, Egypt, and Armenia; and by the Nestorian Christians since the fifth century, when they found asylum in the Sasanian Empire from their Orthodox Christian persecutors in the Roman Empire. From the completion of the Ottoman conquest of the former territories of the East Roman Empire down to the revolt of the 'Osmanlis' Greek subjects in the Morea in 1821, the Greek Orthodox Christians were partially uprooted and scattered, yet managed, in diasporá, to preserve their identity as a community, Jewish-fashion. In Russian Orthodox Christendom, members of some of the dissenting Christian sects have escaped from their Orthodox persecutors by migrating to the outer fringe of the Russian Empire or to regions beyond the Russian frontiers. The Molokane have found asylum in Transcaucasia and Eastern Siberia, the Skoptsy in Rumania, the Dukhobors in Canada. In Western Christendom the members of the Society of Friends (the Quakers), whose earliest recruits came from rural districts in the north of England, have tended, in England at any rate, to move from their native countryside into the cities, because in an urban environment it has been easier for them to avoid a conflict with the authorities over their conscientious objection to paying tithes to the Episcopalian Established Church. The migration of the Quakers into the cities has also been the story of the Huguenot refugees from France in Holland, Britain, and Germany.

However, the Jewish diasporá provides the best material for the construction of a model of the diasporá type of community. Of all the diasporás in our list it is the most famous, the most influential, and also perhaps the most unhappy, at least so far, in its relations with the gentile majorities among whom it has been living. It has also been in existence longer than any of the others, and has been more completely divorced from the cultivation of the land in its original home.

If, on these considerations, we take the Jewish diasporá as our model for this species of community, we shall find in it the following elements. First, there is the diasporá's determination to retain its historic identity in circumstances in which most communities have resigned themselves to losing theirs. Having been deprived of its state and its home and been reduced to living as a minority – and a scattered one – abroad, the uprooted community has found new means of maintaining its cohesion and continuity under these adverse conditions. It maintains them now through the voluntary observance of an exacting religious ritual and law. The second element is the diasporá's motive for being unwilling to merge itself in the majority among whom it has come to live. It cherishes its separate identity because it believes itself to be the depository of a religious revelation of unique significance and value. A third element in the configuration of the Jewish diasporá is its recognition of the truth that it will fail to survive if it does not provide itself with an adequate economic basis. Since it has no state of its own and no national home, economic power is the only form of power within its reach; and a community must command power of some kind in order to hold its own in the world. Even economic power is difficult for a diasporá to obtain. It has lost its hold on agriculture, which has been Man's primary and staple source of livelihood since the Neolithic Age, and, in the alien countries in which it has been scattered, it has been excluded, more often than not, from public life, and even from the liberal professions, as a penalty for its refusal to adopt the religion of the local majority. A diasporá must make its fortune out of whatever economic occupations the majority leaves open to it. The least obstructed opening has usually been retail trade. But, whatever the economic opportunity has been, the diasporá has always managed to win from it the economic resources required for its survival. On the economic as well as on the spiritual plane, penalization has proved to be an unusually powerful stimulus.[2]

'CIVILIZATION IS
DERACINATION':
THE JEWS IN DIASPORÁ

A tenacious observance of traditional religious ritual preserved Jewish community life in alien societies.

43 Above, Sephardic Jewish family gathers with its household for the Passover in eighteenth-century Amsterdam.

44 The Ulmann family of Basel (1831) celebrates *Succot*, the Jewish harvest festival, under the traditional tabernacle or awning.

This model derived from the Jewish diasporá fits all the other specimens on our list more or less closely. In all these cases religion has supplied the motive for the will to preserve the scattered community's identity, while economic prowess in some non-agricultural occupation has provided the means of putting this will to survive into effect. If we now simplify the model, we shall find that the religious species of diasporá is one representative of a more comprehensive genus. Two of the most conspicuous diasporás in the present-day world are the Scottish and the Lebanese. Like the Jews, Parsees, Huguenots, and Quakers, the Lebanese and the Scots abroad are conspicuously successful in business; but the pressure that has moved them to seek their fortunes abroad has been economic, not religious or political. Neither the Lebanese nor the Scots have lost their country; both have been masters in their own house,[3] and neither have been persecuted, either at home or abroad, for clinging to their ancestral religion.[4] They have been victims, not of their fellow men, but of Nature. Their native countries are poor countries, and they have been driven abroad by the difficulty of making a livelihood at home.[5]

What is common to diasporás of the religious species represented by the Jews and the secular species represented by the Scots abroad is the transformation of a social structure. In both cases we are watching a community changing the basis of the cohesion that maintains its distinctive identity. It is changing over from an originally territorial basis, on which it has been held together by having a national home and a national government of its own, to a cultural and occupational basis, on which it is held together by having common memories, beliefs, manners and customs, and skills. Both the Jews and the Scots are on this road, though the Scots have not yet travelled far from the starting-point, while the Jews have long since reached the terminus. Looked at in a wider setting that includes the alien majority among whom the diasporá has been scattered, this change through which both Jews and Scots have been passing is a change from a vertical organization of society to a horizontal one. The communities into which society is articulated are undergoing a metamorphosis from having been so many local cells to becoming so many ubiquitous strata coexisting with each other over an identical area, which, in principle, may be coextensive with the whole habitable surface of the globe.

We can follow the history of this metamorphosis. 'Civilization is deracination.'[6] The Jewish diasporá was a product, in the Fertile Crescent, of two interrelated social developments: an intensification of social intercourse and an increase in urbanization. The growing social intercourse took the peaceful forms of commercial and cultural exchanges, as well as the violent forms of war and deportation; the growing cities served as melting-pots in which the intercourse could lead to fusion. As far as we know, this process started in the Fertile Crescent earlier than anywhere else. Indeed the relative facility of physical communications between the centres of settled life in this region in the Postglacial Age is one of the factors that account for the Fertile Crescent's having been the cradle of civilization. Since the fifth and fourth millennia BC, when civilization was incubating there, the Fertile Crescent has always been precocious. Time and again something that has made its first appearance in this nursery-garden of higher culture has eventually become worldwide. And the history of the diasporá type of social organization is an instance of the Fertile Crescent's habit of giving a lead to the rest of the world.

The 'annihilation of distance' by the progress of technology applied to physical means of communication opens up the vista of a future society that will embrace the whole habitable and traversable surface of the planet, together with its air-envelope, and will unite the human race in a single comprehensive society. In such an ecumenical society, diasporás, not territorially compact local units, seem likely to be the most important of the global society's component communities, and we may guess that the majority of these future diasporás will not be the products of the dispersal of communities that were originally local, and that they will not be held together by ethnic or even by religious bonds. Their spiritual bond will be some common concern or common profession. The world's physicists already constitute one global diasporán community; the world's musicians are another; the world's physicians and surgeons are in process of becoming a third. Take note of the announcements in the press of the meetings of international conventions, and you will realize that the network of global diasporán communities is growing rapidly in a society in which long-distance telephone calls and air-mail and round-the-world services of passenger-planes are enabling people who have a spiritual affinity with each other, in virtue of sharing some common concern, to communicate and co-operate effectively, wherever their local domiciles may happen to be.

The Jewish diasporá maintained its cohesion for twenty-four centuries, running from the sixth century BC, during which Mankind's physical means of communication were still confined to the wind-power that drove sailing-ships and the muscle-power of donkeys and horses and camels. This astonishing achievement gives the measure of what can be expected in an age in which the physical power of inanimate Nature is being harnessed for human purposes by human technology in an always increasing number of forms.

The accelerating improvement in means of communication of all kinds may do more to promote the creation of diasporás by facilitating it than Assyrian war-lords were ever able to do by force. In a society that is 'annihilating distance', world-wide diasporás, rather than local national states, look like 'the wave of the future'. The transformation of the world into a cosmopolis favours social organization on a non-local basis. It is a well-known feature of urban life that city-dwellers associate, not with their next-door neighbours, but with kindred spirits scattered all over the metropolitan area. In a village one must consort with one's next-door neighbour, willy-nilly. In a great city with a highly developed transportation system, one has a far wider choice of friends and companions. Now that the world is becoming one city, we may expect to see associations based on neighbourhood come to be overshadowed by others based on spiritual affinity; that is to say, by diasporás in the broadest sense of the term in which this includes ubiquitous scattered minorities that are held together by religious and other ties of all kinds that are independent of locality.

45 France, fourteenth century

46 Italy, sixteenth century

47 Holland, seventeenth century

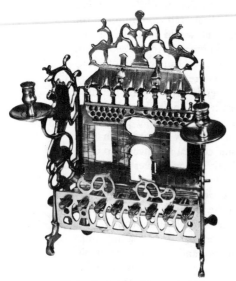

48 Poland, eighteenth century

49 'Iraq, eighteenth century

50 Holland, eighteenth century

THE CULTURE OF THE JEWISH DIASPORÁ

A traditional ritual object, the *hanukkah* candle-stick, in different artistic styles each reflecting the local culture.

51 Austria, eighteenth century

52 Jerusalem, nineteenth century

53 *Tashlekh*, a purification ceremony. The celebrants cast objects from their pockets into running water; the figures scattered across the landscape suggest a poignant metaphor of the Jewish dispersion. (Polish, nineteenth century.)

If this forecast is justified, we need our Jewish model for a diasporá, as well as our Hellenic model for the transition from local states to a universal state and our Chinese model for the alternating rhythm of a universal state's successive lapses and rallies. Each of these models is an indispensable mental tool for the comparative study of civilizations, because each of them gives us the key to one of the major configurations of human society and culture during the Age of Civilizations so far. Each configuration is the product of a resolution of forces. In each case Man's attempt to achieve an aim that is of major importance to him can be seen contending with the problems and the penalties that his pursuit of this particular aim brings with it. In the Hellenic model we see Man in process of civilization pursuing the possibilities of creativity that are offered by a régime of extreme local diversity and independence, until the strife which is the price of this régime reaches a pitch of intensity at which society finds itself constrained to purchase peace through unity at the cost of resigning itself to an uninspiring uniformity. In the Jewish model we see Man in the same chapter of his history clinging to some revelation, discovery, achievement, or way of life that he feels to be of

supreme significance and value, and therefore exerting himself to preserve the separate identity of the 'Chosen People' that is the custodian of this pearl of great price. The 'Chosen People's' belief in its national mission gives it the spirit to maintain itself in diasporá after losing its national state and even its national home – and this in a situation in which the rest of society has resigned itself to the merger of national individualities in the ecumenical unity that is the price of peace. In the Chinese model we see *soi-disant* civilized Man exerting himself to preserve this ecumenical unity, once established, and to restore it each time that it breaks up. He restores it because he cannot bear the strife and disorder that the return of disunity brings with it. Each of these endeavours is an attempt to satisfy one of Man's fundamental requirements. But the histories of civilizations down to the present date do not give us any assurance that these fundamental requirements can all be fulfilled simultaneously. The extent to which Man in process of civilization succeeds in reconciling these requirements with each other gives one measure of Man's capacity for living as the social animal that he has to be if he is to survive.

9 A survey of civilizations

IN CHAPTER SEVEN I have tried to construct an Helleno-Sinic 'model' for the normal configuration of the societies of the species 'civilizations', and, in order to do this, I have had to make two postulates. I have not only had to recognize the existence of other societies of the species of which the Hellenic and the Sinic are two representatives; I have also had provisionally to give names to some of those other civilizations and to assign limits to them in both space and time. The present chapter is an attempt to draw up a definitive list of civilizations with the aid of the Helleno-Sinic model that I have proposed in chapter seven. The criterion for the inclusion of a society in this list is its conformity to the Helleno-Sinic model.

In the drawing up of any list of civilizations that is intended to be 'canonical', the application of a model as a test of eligibility cannot be completely objective, and therefore cannot be indisputable. There is bound to be an element of subjectivity, and therefore of arbitrariness, which it will be impossible to eliminate.

For instance, the Western, Hellenic, and Sinic Civilizations have each had contemporaries of the same species. Each of these has, of course, claimed to be coextensive with Civilization itself; but palpable facts prove that this claim is illusory, like the Jews' claim that the Jews themselves are the unique 'Chosen People' and that the rest of Mankind are 'Gentiles'. The coexistence of a number of contemporary civilizations, each of which is an authentic representative of the species, is demonstrable, but this matter of incontrovertible fact raises the question whether, in a set of contemporary civilizations, the components of this set are completely independent of each other. If we conclude that some of them have an affinity with others, we then have to examine the character of this affinity, and also its degree.

In the set of civilizations that are still 'going concerns', the Western Civilization and the Sinic can be pronounced to be independent of each other. The Western Civilization is 'affiliated' to the Hellenic, and is also affiliated to the Syriac in virtue of its religion, since Christianity has its roots in what we may call an Helleno-Syriac 'culture-compost'. By contrast, the Sinic Civilization is not 'affiliated' to any antecedent society of its own species, and, though in the course of its history it did adopt Buddhism, which was a religion of alien origin, the source of Buddhism was different from the source of Christianity.

Thus the relation between the Western and the Sinic Civilization is one of complete independence of each other. By contrast, the Western Civilization has an affinity with the Eastern Orthodox Christian Civilization and with the Islamic, since Islam, as well as Eastern Christianity, has its roots in an identical Helleno-Syriac 'culture-compost'. There is a still closer affinity between the Sinic Civilization on the one hand and the Korean, Japanese, and Vietnamian Civilizations on the other hand. These three civilizations have been inspired by the Sinic, but they have developed their loans from the Sinic Civilization on lines of their own

that are distinctive enough to entitle them to rank as separate civilizations of a sub-class that we may label 'satellites', in contrast to 'independent' civilizations such as the Sinic, the Western, and the Hellenic and Syriac, to both of which the Western Civilization is 'affiliated'.

We have, however, to distinguish between 'satellite' civilizations, which are separate representatives of the species, though their link with one of the 'independent' civilizations (or with two or more of these in succession) is very close, and the provinces of a 'full-blown' civilization. Some of these provinces may have so distinctive a provincial style that they might almost equally well be classified as being separate civilizations of the 'satellite' class. How, for instance, are we to classify the culture of Italy in the last millennium BC and the first five centuries of the Christian Era? Is this Italic culture merely a strongly pronounced provincial version of the Hellenic Civilization, or is it a separate civilization, though one that is a 'satellite' of the Hellenic? In such cases as this, the classification will inevitably be subjective and arbitrary, and therefore opinions will differ and there will be no objective criterion to validate one of the conflicting opinions and to invalidate the others.

We are confronted with a similar residuum of uncertainty when we pass from relations in the space-dimension to relations in the time-dimension. The history of the Western Civilization cannot be regarded as being a mere epilogue to the history of the Hellenic Civilization. The Western 'Roman Empire of the German People' ('The Holy Roman Empire') has been too feeble an avatar of the Roman Empire, and its role in Western history has been too slight, to allow us, on the strength of this ghost of the Roman Empire, to regard Western history as being a mere prolongation of Hellenic history. Moreover, through Christianity, the Western Civilization is related to the Syriac Civilization as well as to the Hellenic. Therefore we have to classify the Western culture not only as an independent one, in the sub-class of 'affiliated' civilizations, but, having once conceded this status to the Western Civilization, we have to concede the same status to the Eastern Orthodox Christian Civilization and to the Islamic, since these two cultures are rooted in the same Helleno-Syriac 'culture-compost' as the Western Civilization.

The concession to Eastern Orthodox Christian history of an identity of its own, instead of regarding it as an epilogue to Hellenic history, is, however, questionable. In contrast to the Roman Empire's shadowy avatars in the West, its avatars in Eastern Orthodox Christendom have been, as has already been noted, as substantial as the avatars of the Ch'in-Han Empire in China. On the strength of this phenomenon in China, I have interpreted the whole of Chinese history, from the Shang Age down to the fall of the Ch'ing dynasty in AD 1911, as being the continuous history of one and the same civilization, which I have labelled the 'Sinic'. Having conceded this, am I justified in not also conceding that the Hellenic Civilization survived in the

Levant until the liquidation of the Ottoman Roman Empire in A D 1922? Conversely, I have conceded that the adoption of Christianity and Islam brought with it a break of cultural continuity that requires us to classify the Western, Eastern Orthodox Christian, and Islamic cultures as separate civilizations. Am I then justified in having refused to classify as a separate civilization, merely 'affiliated' to the Sinic, the phase of Chinese culture that is subsequent to the adoption, in China, of Buddhism?

Thus the assignment of a particular culture to one class or another would still be debatable in some borderline cases, even if there were agreement about the classification itself. It might be agreed that there is a breach of continuity between Hellenic history and Western history. It might also be agreed that the history of Pharaonic Egypt is continuous from the date of the union of the two crowns, soon after the beginning of the third millennium B C, to the second century of the Christian Era; but these two cases are at opposite extremities of the gamut, and, in between, there is a series of gradations, within which it is impossible to affix labels with the same precision. Again, it might be agreed that, among the civilizations that are still 'going concerns', the Western and the Sinic Civilizations are completely independent of each other; but the Russian Civilization's relation with the Eastern Orthodox and the Western would be subject to dispute.

The inclusion of the African Civilizations should be clarified.[1] The term is here taken to include the politically organized pre-Islamic and pre-Christian societies of the Western Sudan and of Central and Eastern Africa, but not those fragmentary African communities whose economic and political institutions were rudimentary. It can hardly be denied that Africa south of the Sahara was 'on the move' long before the arrival of the modern Westerners who put Africa 'on the map' in contemporary Western eyes. The rise of indigenous civilizations in sub-Saharan Africa was stimulated by the spread of metallurgy from Egypt in the last millennium B C[2] and by still obscure influences from Kush and Meroe[3] – countries in the Nile valley, south of Egypt, whose culture had been partly derived from Egypt but was also partly an original creation of their own.

The kingdoms in the Nile valley to the south of the First Cataract and to the north of the White Nile swamps were Monophysite Christian for about eight centuries before they were conquered and converted by Muslim Arabs in the fourteenth century of the Christian Era. Moreover, the major exotic influence on the indigenous African Civilizations to the south of the Sahara in the Western as well as in the Eastern Sudan came from the Islamic Society, which has been in contact with sub-Saharan Africa since the Muslim Arab conquest of Egypt and North-West Africa in the seventh century of the Christian Era.[4] Indeed, the outstanding achievements of indigenous civilizations in Africa are to be found in those areas in which the penetration of Islamic influences has been the most thorough – e.g. the belt of open country to the south of the Sahara and to the north of the Nilotic swamps.[5] But the indigenous African cultures were already long since established before the arrival of Islam, and in the Congo basin and at the southern end of the Rift Valley there were African cultures that were not affected by either Islam or the modern West before the nineteenth century.[6]

Although the non-Islamic communities were for the most part non-literate, and hence subject to crucial limitations on their economic and political expansion,[7] the existence of cities, which is Bagby's and Childe's criterion for civilization,[8] is attested in Islamic and non-Islamic Africa alike. The needs and rewards of trade called into existence both cities and the organized and centralized administration that an urbanized society requires.[9] The development of intensive agriculture and the profits of commercial enterprise permitted the rise of non-productive élites – kings, administrators, scholars, priests – who were supported out of the economic surplus.[10] My own definition of civilization in ethical terms[11] is also applicable to Africa, now that the richness of Africa's religious and philosophical heritage is at last being revealed to Western eyes.[12]

A Western observer must be struck, however, by a crucial deficiency in the world-explaining cosmologies which have been evolved, in fascinating diversity, among the indigenous African communities. These highly integrated systems for establishing Man's relationship with the human and non-human world do certainly permit a highly practical classification of the complex data of his material and spiritual experience, as these would appear to a pre-scientific society. Yet this very self-sufficiency, which is an advantage in so far as it is a solution for the problem of coming to terms with a hostile but more or less predictable environment, becomes a positive bane when once the stable equilibrium which it establishes so successfully is disturbed by factors for which no explanation is forthcoming from traditional experience.[13] In this situation, the equilibrium ossifies into conservatism, or else is so utterly disrupted and devalued that a community dissolves into uncertainty. In the former case, unprecedented problems or stimuli will have been neutralized by being absorbed somehow into the existing patterns of social and mental organization; in other words, the system shows little capacity for positive and fruitful responses to challenges.[14] These fates of being 'arrested'[15] on the threshold of growth, or being doomed to a premature death, await any society which lacks an internal capacity for innovation and initiative; and we may infer both from the evidence of Africa's history and from what we know today of African philosophies that at crucial points in the development of Africa the crippling limitations of mental rigidity took their toll.[16]

All the same, the temporary Western domination of Africa during the 'colonial' period has led Westerners to underestimate the African achievement. The values of the aggressive Western Society of the nineteenth century were largely determined by the recently adopted Western objective of technological innovation, and alien societies that did not come up to this arbitrarily imposed technological standard were classified in Western minds as barbaric, primitive, savage. Today, however, the perpetuation of these views convicts those who hold them of obstinate prejudice. An unbiased observer will credit Africa with achievements comparable to those in other societies – and such societies have been the normal type, so far – in which an obsessive concern with technology has not been allowed to overshadow everything else. It will be recognized that Africa has made a special – perhaps not yet adequately recognized – contribution to Mankind's cultural achievements in the spheres of social relations and of Man's relations with non-human Nature.

The list of civilizations cannot be conclusive and is subject to the various reservations discussed above. The chart shows the time-spans of all the civilizations except for those possible satellite civilizations whose claim to rank as separate seems dubious.[17]

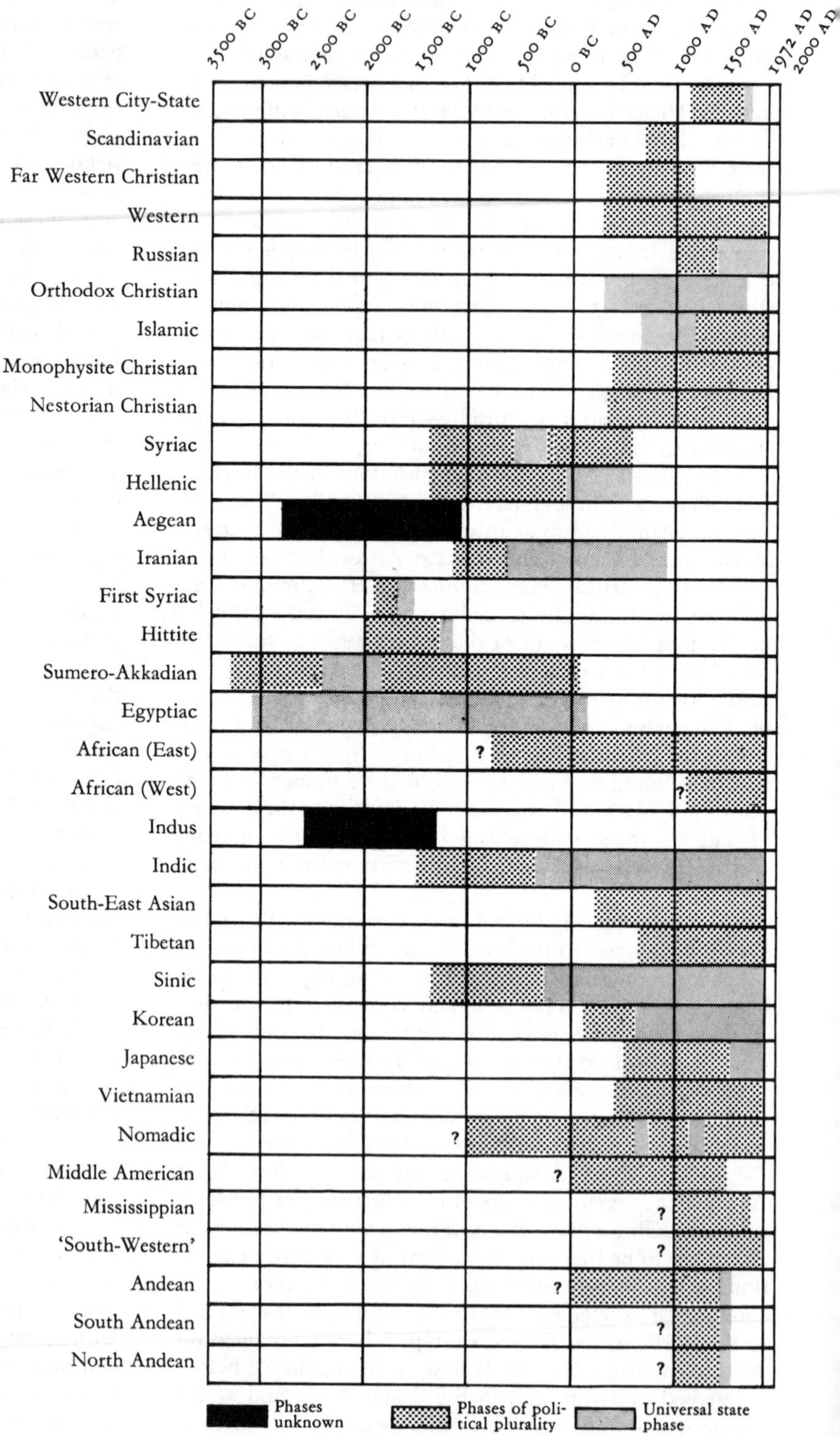

I FULL-BLOWN CIVILIZATIONS

A INDEPENDENT CIVILIZATIONS

Unrelated to others

Middle American
Andean[18]

Unaffiliated to others

Sumero-Akkadian[19]
Egyptiac
Aegean[20]
Indus
Sinic

Affiliated to others

Syriac *to* Sumero-Akkadian, Egyptiac, Aegean, and Hittite
Hellenic *to* Aegean
Indic *to* Indus
African *first to* Egyptiac, *then to* Islamic, *then to* Western[21]
Orthodox Christian ⎫
Western ⎬ *to both Syriac and Hellenic*
Islamic ⎭

B SATELLITE CIVILIZATIONS

Mississippian ⎫
'South-Western'[22] ⎬ *of Middle American*
North Andean[23] ⎫
South Andean[24] ⎬ *of Andean*
?Elamite[25] *of Sumero-Akkadian*
Hittite[26] *of Sumero-Akkadian*
?Urartian[27] *of Sumero-Akkadian*
Iranian *first of* Sumero-Akkadian, *then of* Syriac
?Meroitic[28] *of Egyptiac*
Korean ⎫
Japanese ⎬ *of Sinic*
Vietnamian ⎭
?Italic[29]
South-East Asian *first of* Indic, *then*, in Indonesia and Malaya only, *of* Islamic
Tibetan[30]
Russian *first of* Orthodox Christian, *then of* Western
Nomadic *of* sedentary civilizations adjacent to Eurasian and Afrasian steppes

II ABORTIVE CIVILIZATIONS[31]

First Syriac, eclipsed by Egyptiac
Nestorian Christian, eclipsed by Islamic
Monophysite Christian, eclipsed by Islamic
Far Western Christian, eclipsed by Western
Scandinavian, eclipsed by Western
Medieval Western City-State Cosmos, eclipsed by modern Western

54 The civilizations of the world, 3500 BC to AD 2000 illustrating the successive phases of their growth.

PART II

THE GENESES
OF CIVILIZATIONS

Having rounded up my horses, I now set myself to put them through their paces. What is it that brings a civilization to birth? I first try race and then environment, and I find both these explanations unsatisfying, because they assume that living beings are subject to inexorable laws of Nature, like dead matter. So I look for an explanation in terms of life, which in human affairs means free will. I find this in the insights of mythology and religion, which show creation as the outcome of an encounter – a process that I shall describe as challenge-and-response. I then try to discover the limits within which the interplay of challenge-and-response is effectively creative in practice. I do this by examining a number of test cases, and I find that, although a strong stimulus is needed to bring a civilization into existence, the challenge must not be so severe as to stifle creativity.

plate 13

THE BIRTH OF CIVILIZATION

What is the force that injects dynamic movement into an inert cosmos? This Indian picture of the fertilized 'world-egg' illustrates the Tantric Buddhist conception of life's constitution: the undifferentiated unity of pure Being must be broken up into separate categories before conscious life is possible, starting with the distinction between the passive female life-principle and the male element of activating energy. The idea that the dialectical interaction of opposites culminates in progressive motion has served in many other ages and societies as a key for understanding the nature of creation and the process of growth: in Greece the forces were identified as love and hate, in China as Yin and Yang, in the modern West as thesis and antithesis.

plates 14, 15

RACE AND
CREATIVITY

Does one part of humanity have more of the creative spark than another? Modern Western racists regard the white races as congenitally superior, but the medieval West divided Mankind according to religion, not race. Moorish Muslim Spain was, in medieval Christian eyes, a 'dark' civilization, but baptism, above, gave its members a passport into the 'white' Western Society. Opposite, race is no barrier to entry into the medieval artist's paradise.

plates 16, 17

CHALLENGE-AND-RESPONSE
IN CHRISTIAN SYMBOLISM

'Challenge-and-response' is a formula describing the free play of forces that provokes new departures in individual or social life. An effective challenge stimulates men to creative action, but it necessarily disturbs a pre-existent harmony and may therefore have at first the appearance of evil. In terms of Christian theology, Christ's sacrifice leads to a higher harmony with God, yet this could not have been attained without the Fall. Thus the medieval *Tree of Death and Life*, above, bears both skull and crucifix: it is at the same time the Old Testament tree of knowledge and sin, and the New Testament tree of the cross and redemption. The same idea inspires Blake's watercolour, opposite: Christ himself leads Adam and Eve out of paradise, for their sin makes possible his revelation of God's redeeming love.

plate 18

THE STIMULUS
OF HARD COUNTRIES

Easy environments present no challenge to Man: it is the hard country that stimulates him to creative action. From the barren wilderness of the Judaean desert, the Israelites wrested a spiritual intuition of the unity and omnipotence of God – a feat of understanding that far outmatched the achievements of their contemporaries in less demanding climes.

80

plate 19

THE STIMULUS
OF PENALIZATIONS

Religious discrimination offers the same potential challenge as a harsh physical environment. In Japan the Western traders and native Christian converts shown here were persecuted with a severity that has scarcely been equalled in the entire history of religious penalization, yet both endured their painful treatment for more than two centuries until toleration was granted in the nineteenth century.

plate 20

ABORTIVE CIVILIZATIONS:
THE CHALLENGE THAT OVERWHELMS

A strong challenge often provokes a highly creative response, but there comes a point where its severity is no longer stimulating but overwhelming. A ninth-century wall painting from the 'Christian temple' in Qarakhocho is a monument to the long-dead Nestorian Christian community in Central Asia, a burgeoning civilization extinguished in the act of coming to birth when it was faced with the insuperable challenge of a massive Arab invasion. Though individual members rose to the occasion, the society as a whole could not resist the tide, and its identity was submerged in an alien culture and an alien religion.

STATIC PAST

The mimesis, or social imitation, of ancestors in precivilizational societies is stultifying; the dead weight of meticulously observed customary practice obstructs innovation and social progress.

55 Ancestor altar in the shrine of the Oba (king) of Benin, the Oba supported by his attendants.

DYNAMIC FUTURE

By contrast, when the same mimesis is directed towards living personalities, social movement is possible. Creative leaders are not patriarchs but pioneers; they attract a following through merit, not tradition.

56 An apotheosis of Peter the Great shows the Russian Emperor standing on a pyramid composed of his military victories, flanked by portraits of previous Tsars.

10 The nature of the geneses of civilizations

IN MAKING my list of civilizations, I have grouped these in sets, and my labels for these sets show that there are more ways than one in which a civilization can come into existence. A civilization may emerge through the spontaneous mutation of some pre-civilizational society. This is the mode of genesis of the civilizations that I have labelled 'unrelated to others' and 'unaffiliated to others'. Alternatively, a pre-civilizational society may be stimulated into changing into a civilization by the influence of some civilization that is already in existence. This is the class of civilizations that I have called 'satellites'. This label is simply a mark of this particular kind of origin; it does not imply that the 'satellite' civilization is necessarily inferior either in cultural quality or in historical importance to the pre-existing civilization that has given it its initial stimulus. For instance, the Russian Civilization is, in origin, a 'satellite' of the Eastern Orthodox Christian Civilization of the East Roman Empire and Bulgaria; it has latterly become a 'satellite' of the Western Civilization; but it has produced distinctive achievements of its own, and, in some of these, it has surpassed the Eastern Orthodox Christian Civilization, under whose influence the Russian Society raised its culture above its previous pre-civilizational level. A civilization can also come into existence, not through the mutation of a pre-civilizational society, but through the disintegration of one or more civilizations of an older generation and the transformation of some of their elements into a new configuration. This is the social and cultural process that I have labelled 'affiliation'. The Eastern Orthodox and Western Christian Civilizations and the Islamic Civilization are 'affiliated', in this usage of the word, to the Hellenic and Syriac Civilizations.

In this third form of genesis, older civilizations are followed and replaced by younger representatives of the same species of society. In the two other forms of genesis, there is a change of species. A civilization comes into existence through a mutation of a society that has previously been a pre-civilizational one. When we find one species of society changing into another, we have to look for the features in which the differences between the two species reside.

The difference between civilizations and pre-civilizational societies does not consist in the presence or absence of institutions; for we find that institutions, being the vehicles of the impersonal relations in which all societies have their existence, are attributes of the whole genus and therefore common properties of the two species. Pre-civilizational societies have their own characteristic institutions – the spirit of the year, with his dramatic cycle of seasonal experiences; totemism and exogamy; tabus, initiations, and age-classes; segregations of the sexes, at certain stages of life, in separate communal establishments – and some of these institutions are certainly as elaborate and perhaps as subtle as those which are characteristic of civilizations.

Nor are civilizations distinguished from pre-civilizational societies by the division of labour; for though in general this plays a more important part in their lives, and its importance tends to increase as they grow, we can discern at least the rudiments of the division of labour in the lives of pre-civilizational societies also. For instance, primitive kings, who seem like undifferentiated 'all-round men' by contrast with the executive heads of political communities in societies which are in process of civilization, can be seen to be specialists when we observe them in their own social environment and compare them with the rank-and-file of their tribesmen. Primitive magicians and smiths and minstrels are specialists in the same degree.

Indeed, the division of labour may be a necessary condition of the existence of institutions and therefore a generic feature in the lives of societies, since it is difficult to imagine how institutions could exist without in some way being embodied in the persons of particular human beings who are thus invested with special social functions.

The complement and antidote to the division of labour is social imitation or mimesis,[1] which may be defined as the acquisition, through imitation, of social 'assets' – aptitudes or emotions or ideas – which the acquisitors have not originated for themselves, and which they might never have come to possess if they had not encountered and imitated other people in whose possession these assets were already to be found. Mimesis, too, is a generic feature of social life.[2] Its operation can be observed both in pre-civilizational societies and in civilizations. It operates, however, in different directions in the two species. In pre-civilizational societies, as we know them, mimesis is directed towards the older generation of the living members and towards the dead ancestors who stand, unseen but not unfelt, at the back of the living elders, reinforcing their power and enhancing their prestige. In a society where mimesis is thus directed backward towards the past, custom rules and the society remains static. On the other hand, in societies in process of civilization, mimesis is directed towards creative personalities which command a following because they are pioneers on the road towards the common goal of human endeavours. In a society where mimesis is thus directed forward towards the future, 'the cake of custom'[3] is broken and the society is in dynamic motion along a course of change and growth.

In this contrast between a dynamic movement and a static condition, we have come at last upon a point of difference between civilizations and primitive societies; but when we ask ourselves whether the difference thus empirically observed is permanent and fundamental, we find that the answer is in the negative.

If we only know of pre-civilizational societies in a static condition, this is merely an accidental consequence of the fragmentariness of our knowledge. All our 'data' for the study of societies of this kind happens to come from representatives of the species which are in the last phases of their histories; but, where direct observation fails us, a train of reasoning informs us that there must have been earlier phases in the histories of the pre-civilizational societies in which these were moving more dynamically than any civilizations have ever moved yet, as far as our knowledge goes. Pre-civilizational societies must be prior to humanity, since Mankind could not have become human except in a social environment; and this mutation of our pre-human ancestors into human beings, which was accomplished, in circumstances of which we have no record, under the aegis of pre-civilizational societies, was a more profound change, a greater step in growth, than any progress which Man has yet achieved under the aegis of civilizations.

Pre-civilizational societies, as we know them by direct observation, may be likened to people lying torpid upon a ledge on a mountain-side, with a precipice below and a precipice above; civilizations may be likened to companions of these 'Sleepers of Ephesus' who have just risen to their feet and have started to climb on up the face of the cliff; while we, for our part, may liken ourselves to observers whose field of vision is limited to the ledge and to the foot of the upper precipice and who have come upon the scene at the moment when the different members of the party happen to be in these respective postures and positions. At first sight we may be inclined to draw an absolute distinction between the two groups, acclaiming the climbers as athletes and dismissing the recumbent figures as paralytics: but on second thoughts we shall find it more prudent to suspend judgment.

After all, the recumbent figures cannot be paralytics in reality; for they cannot have been born on the ledge, and no human muscles but their own can have hoisted them to this halting-place up the face of the precipice below. So far from being paralytics, they must be seasoned athletes who have successfully scaled the 'pitch' below and are still taking a well-earned rest from their recent labours.[4] On the other hand, their companions who are climbing at this moment have only just left this same ledge and started to climb the face of the precipice above; and, since the next ledge is out of sight, we do not know how high or how arduous this next 'pitch' may be. We only know that it is impossible to halt and rest before the next ledge, wherever that may lie, is reached. Thus, even if we could estimate each present climber's strength and skill and nerve and courage, we could not judge whether any of them have any prospect of gaining the unseen ledge above, which is the goal of their present endeavours. We can, however, be sure that some of them will never attain it.

We can see many of our climbers already falling – some to their death and others to an ignominious life-in-death on the ledge below. These others lie side by side with the decomposing corpses of their companions who – *felices opportunitate mortis*[5] – have escaped the pains of failure through annihilation, and also side by side with the recumbent forms of those apparent paralytics who have not yet essayed the 'pitch' by which these unfortunates have already been defeated. Disqualified from essaying the 'pitch' again and denied the *coup de grâce* of annihilation, they would lie 'fast bound in misery and iron',[6] enduring the torments of Prometheus with the vulture devouring his liver, if the gods did not take pity on them and grant them insensibility by turning them into stone, to weather away, with the lapse of centuries, like Niobe on the flank of Mount Sipylus. By the time when we have come on the scene, a majority of the climbers on the precipice above our ledge have fallen to meet one or other of the penalties of defeat – petrifaction or annihilation – and there are only a few to be seen still working their way upward. If we could look down the face of the precipice below our ledge to the next ledge beneath, and translate ourselves back into the age when this lower 'pitch' was the scene of action, we should almost certainly discover that the mountaineers who have attained our ledge, to rest from their labours before essaying the 'pitch' next above, are in a still smaller minority by comparison with the unnumbered and unremembered casualties which the scaling of that 'pitch' likewise cost in its time.

We have now followed out our simile far enough to have ascertained that the contrast between the static condition of pre-civilizational societies, as we know them, and the dynamic motion of societies in process of civilization is not a permanent and fundamental point of difference, but an accident of the time and place of observation. All the pre-civilizational societies which we now observe at rest must once have been in motion; and all societies which have entered upon the process of civilization may come to rest sooner or later in one way or another. Some have come to rest already by relapsing, long before the goal has been attained, to the level of primitive humanity from which they have started. The condition of these *ci-devant* civilizations which have failed in their endeavours is static like the condition of those pre-civilizational societies which are extant today because they have succeeded in theirs. In every other respect, there is all the difference between them; and this difference – the difference between failure and success – is wholly in the pre-civilizational societies' favour. These societies, as we see them today, are static because they are recuperating from the strain of a successful effort to attain the state in which they now persist. Their stillness is the stillness not of death but of sleep; and, even if they may be destined never to awake, they are at least still alive. The *ci-devant* civilizations are static because they have lost their lives in an unsuccessful attempt to transcend the state into which they have now relapsed. Their stillness is the stillness of dead things in decay; and they are dead equally beyond doubt and beyond recall, whether they happen to be disintegrating as rapidly as a putrefying corpse or as slowly as a rotting tree-trunk or a weathering rock.

We have failed to find the immediate object of our search, a permanent and fundamental point of difference between pre-civilizational societies and civilizations; but incidentally we have obtained some light on the ultimate objective of our present inquiry: the nature of the geneses of civilizations. Starting with the mutation of pre-civilizational societies into civilizations, we have found that this consists in a transition from a static condition to a dynamic activity; and we shall find that the same formula holds good for the alternative mode of emergence of civilizations through the secession of proletariats from the dominant minorities of pre-existent civilizations which have lost their creative power. Such dominant minorities are static by definition; for to say that the creative minority of a civilization in growth has degenerated or atrophied into the dominant minority of a civilization in disintegration is only another way of saying that the society in question has relapsed from a dynamic activity into a static condition. Against this static condition, the secession of a proletariat is a dynamic reaction; and in this light we can see that, in the secession of a proletariat from a dominant minority, a new civilization is generated through the transition of a society from a static condition to a dynamic activity, just as it is in the mutation which produces a civilization out of a primitive society. The geneses of all civilizations – the unrelated and the related class alike – could be described in a sentence written by a Western philosopher-statesman of our age one month after the close of the First World War:

> There is no doubt that mankind is once more on the move. The very foundations have been shaken and loosened, and things are again fluid. The tents have been struck, and the great caravan of Humanity is once more on the march.[7]

Can we yet say anything more about the transition from a static condition to a dynamic activity in which the genesis of every civilization consists? We know this much more already: this instance of the transition is not unique. When we were studying it in our simile of the mountain-side, we realized that the ledge on which we saw the pre-civilizational societies lying dormant and the *ci-devant* civilizations lying dead, while the societies in process of civilization were scaling the face of the precipice above, was only one ledge in a series, the other terms of which were outside our field of vision. All extant pre-civilizational societies must have reached our ledge from an unseen ledge below, and all societies in process of civilization are endeavouring to reach an unseen ledge above; and, for all we know, the number of other ledges above this and below that may be infinite in both directions.

The height of the cliff-face that towers above us is beyond our powers of estimation, but we do know what is the goal that we are seeking in the perilous climb in which some human societies are now engaged. Within less than 2500 years after the emergence of the earliest of the civilizations, the earliest of the higher religions and philosophies appeared, and each of these post-civilizational societies has pointed out Mankind's goal and has given us prescriptions for attaining it. Thus, though the goal of Mankind's continuous and increasing endeavours is still out of sight, we know, nevertheless, what it is. We can discern it, without having to divine the future, by looking inwards; for Mankind's goal is written large in the constitution of human nature. What changed our pre-human ancestors into human beings like ourselves was the acquisition of consciousness and will. These two spiritual faculties are human nature's distinguishing marks; and their character is ambivalent. They are both a treasure that gives us hope and a burden that puts us in peril. Their emergence in Man has split the unity of the Universe, and broken its harmony, for every conscious, wilful, human soul. The price of human knowledge and freedom is an intellectual and a moral relativity. Each of us sees the Universe divided between himself and all the rest of it; and each of us seeks to make

57 The goal of human endeavours. The soul arduously climbs towards God by a ladder, its rungs marked with the virtues that lead to transcendent understanding. Engraving from *Il Monte Sancto di Dio*, 1477.

THE DARK AND THE LIGHT

58 According to Chinese art theory, the central peak in a landscape must be surrounded by lower hills 'which cluster around it, their Yin and Yang sides (dark and light) clearly distinguished' – from a treatise by the court painter T'ang-Tai.

himself the centre round which all the rest shall revolve. This constitution of human nature sets human nature's goal. Its goal is to transcend the intellectual and moral limitations that its relativity imposes on it. In terms of Judaic theism, human nature's intellectual goal is to see the Universe as it is in the sight of God, instead of seeing it with the distorted vision of one of God's self-centred creatures. Human nature's moral goal is to make the self's will coincide with God's will, instead of pursuing self-regarding purposes of its own. The Indian philosophies and religions set the same goal for us in terms of their supra-personal vision of ultimate reality.

Few, if any, human souls have been entirely unaware of this goal or entirely indifferent to it. The saints have dedicated themselves to the pursuit of it, and some saints have come within a hair's breadth of attaining it – as it has seemed to spectators of ordinary spiritual stature, though never to the spiritual athletes themselves. A human soul's – even a saint's soul's – fight with self-centredness is unceasing. The saints testify to the truth of this from their own spiritual experience; and this means that the next ledge, if some of the present climbers do succeed in reaching it, will not be a permanent abode for human souls. Like the ledge below it, that is within our field of vision, it will be only a temporary camping-ground. Even if some future generation of Mankind were to make, unanimously, a spiritual effort that would transfigure human society into a communion of saints, rest would not be one of the rewards of this spiritual achievement. Even in a saintly society the victory over self-centredness, collective and individual, would never be complete, and the effort would therefore have to be unremitting. This means that the next ledge will be the scene of a spiritual struggle that will not be less intense than the struggle to climb, from ledge to ledge, up the face of the cliff.

Nor will the next ledge be the last. For all we know, the heights above us, that are still waiting to be scaled, may be far higher than those that we have scaled already, and the depths of these, which are now below us, are unfathomable. The pre-civilizational societies that are extant today are far above the level of Primitive Man. Most of them are representatives of Neolithic Man – the inventor of agriculture and the tamer of most of our domesticated animals. A very few of them are representatives of Upper Palaeolithic Man, and this able and enterprising hunter and food-gatherer was already on the move. He had left behind him the more rudimentary technology and economy of his Lower Palaeolithic predecessor. Lower Palaeolithic Man may have lain dormant on his ledge for half a million years; and this is all but a fraction of the time-span of Mankind's human existence so far. Lower Palaeolithic Man had to recuperate from his pre-human ancestors' *tour de force* of becoming human; for this was not only the earliest of Mankind's achievements; it was also a greater and a harder feat than any that Mankind has performed since then. We should have to descend below the ledge from which sub-man rose to Man in order to find the level of the common ancestor of Mankind and the anthropoids. And how many hundreds and thousands of lower ledges should we have to leave behind us in our descent if we sought to trace the rise of mammals from the lowest vertebrates and of vertebrates from the rudimentary forms in which life itself first emerged out of the abyss?

Without venturing down that dark descent or even allowing ourselves to speculate whether the alternating series of ledge and precipice, precipice and ledge, is infinite or finite, we can observe that the alternation between horizontal and perpendicular surfaces on the mountain-side repeats itself in a kind of pattern, and that the corresponding alternation between a static condition and a dynamic activity in the energies of the living creatures that are seeking to scale the mountain similarly recurs in a kind of rhythm. This rhythm has been pointed out by a number of observers, living in different ages of different societies, who all agree in regarding it as something fundamental in the nature of the Universe.

Herbert Spencer sees the Universe moving from 'an indefinite, incoherent homogeneity to a definite, coherent heterogeneity' through a series of 'integrations' and 'differentiations'.[8] Hegel sees the history of Mankind as a spiral development, a series of movements from one form of unity through a phase of disunity and on to reintegration on a higher plane.[9] Saint-Simon sees the histories of civilizations as a series of alternating 'organic' and 'critical' periods.[10] Twenty-three centuries before the appearance of these eighteenth-century and nineteenth-century Western philosophers, an Hellenic man of science, Empedocles, attributed the changes in the face of the Universe, of which we are empirically aware, to the alternate ebb and flow of two forces which are complementary to one another and at the same time antithetical: an integrating force which he calls 'love' and a disintegrating force which he calls 'hate'. 'Without contraries there is no progression.'[11]

The two alternating forces or phases in the rhythm of the Universe which Empedocles calls 'love' and 'hate' have also been detected – quite independently of the movement of Hellenic thought – by observers in the Sinic World, who have named them 'Yin' and 'Yang'.[12] The nucleus of the Sinic character which stands for Yin seems to represent dark coiling clouds overshadowing the Sun, while the nucleus of the character which stands for Yang seems to represent the unclouded Sun-disk emitting its rays. In the original everyday usage, Yin appears to have signified the side of a mountain or a valley which is in the shadow, and Yang the side which is in the sunshine. Sinic philosophers pictured Yin and Yang as two different kinds of matter. As substances, Yin symbolized water and Yang fire. As phases of the Universe, they symbolized the seasons; and the regular annual alternation of the seasons suggested the Sinic conception of how Yin and Yang are related to one another. Each in turn comes into the ascendant at the other's expense; yet even at the high tide of its expansion it never quite submerges the other, so that, when its tide ebbs, as it always does after reaching high-water mark, there is still a nucleus of the other element left free to expand, as its perpetual rival and partner contracts, until it arrives in due course at the opposite turning-point where the whole movement begins all over again.

Of the various symbols in which different observers in different societies have expressed the alternation between a static condition and a dynamic activity in the rhythm of the Universe, Yin and Yang are the most apt, because they convey the measure of the rhythm direct and not through some metaphor derived from psychology or mechanics or mathematics. We will therefore use these Sinic symbols in this Study henceforward; and we shall find that this notation lends itself readily to the music of other civilizations. In the *Magnificat* we shall hear Yin's song of joy at passing over into Yang:

My soul doth magnify the Lord, and my spirit hath rejoiced in God my Saviour;
For he hath regarded the lowliness of his handmaiden.

In the Chorus Mysticus which is the culmination of the Second Part of *Faust* we shall hear Yang's song of joy at passing back again, when his race is run, into Yin:

Alles vergängliche
Ist nur ein Gleichnis;
Das Unzulängliche,
Hier wird's Ereignis;
Das Unbeschreibliche,
Hier ist's getan;
Das ewig-Weibliche
Zieht uns hinan.[13]

In the self-revelation of the Spirit of the Earth to the scholar who evokes this mighty power by the vehemence of his mental strife, we shall hear the very beat of the alternating rhythm itself:

In Lebensfluten, im Tatensturm
Wall' ich auf und ab,
Webe hin und her!
Geburt und Grab
Ein ewiges Meer,
Ein wechselnd Weben,
Ein glühend Leben,
So schaff' ich am sausenden Webstuhl der Zeit
Und wirke der Gottheit lebendiges Kleid.[14]

59 Yin-Yang symbol.

RACE AND THE HUMAN RACE
60, 61   The medieval Christ offers
salvation to all Mankind, but modern
Man presumes to divide and grade
the human race.

11 The cause of genesis: race?

Vis inertiae, entrenched in custom, may account for Man's pause, at the pre-civilizational level of culture, for perhaps half a million years; but why is it that, within the last five thousand years, certain members of the human race, in certain societies, have so far overcome their inertia as to pass out of this Yin-state into a new fit of Yang-activity? The more weight we attach to *vis inertiae* as a negative retarding factor, the greater the momentum which we must ascribe to the positive factor, whatever it may be, which has set human life in motion again by its impetus.

There are several alternative directions in which this positive factor may be looked for. It may be sought in some special quality in the human beings who have made this particular transition from Yin to Yang on the occasions of which we have knowledge; or it may be sought in some special feature in the environments in which the transition has taken place; or again it may be sought in some inter-action between the microcosm and the macrocosm, in some prowess of the race when confronted with some challenge from the environment. Let us explore these alternatives one by one. Let us consider first the factor of race, and second the factor of environment, each in and by itself. If neither factor appears capable, in isolation, of generating the momentum for which, *ex hypothesi*, we have to account, then we must find our unknown quantity in some product of the two factors, if we are to find it at all. It may be that, when they interact under certain conditions, they produce effects which do not follow from their action under other conditions either separately or together – as air and petrol vapour, when mixed in a carburettor and introduced into a combustion-chamber, produce explosions powerful enough to drive the engine of a motor-car, though the air in the atmosphere and the petrol in the petrol-tank remain inert.

'Race' is the term used to denote some distinctive innate quality in any genus or species or other class or group of living creatures. The racial elements which concern us here are distinctive psychic or spiritual qualities, possibly innate in certain societies of human beings, which may prove to be the positive factor impelling these societies towards civilization. All discussions of race, so far, in which race is considered from our point of view, depend on the postulate that there is a permanent and precise correlation between hypothetical racial characteristics of a psychic order in human beings and the racial characteristics which are manifest in our human bodily physique. The distinctive marks of physical race leap to the eye – even when the eye is untrained and the distinctions are subtle and minute.

In the Western World of our day, 'racial' explanations of social phenomena are much in vogue. Racial differences of human physique, regarded as immutable in themselves and as bearing witness to likewise immutable racial differences in the human psyche, are supposed to account for the differences which we observe empirically between the fortunes and achievements of different human societies. The present vogue of racialism in the West, however, has really little to do with current scientific hypotheses. A prejudice so strong as this cannot be accounted for by a cause so rational. Modern Western racial prejudice is not so much a distortion of Western scientific thought as a pseudo-intellectual reflexion of Western race-feeling; and this feeling, as we see it in our time, is a consequence of the expansion of our Western Civilization over the face of the Earth since the last quarter of the fifteenth century of our era. The feeling has been aroused by contact, often under untoward conditions, between societies whose representatives happen to stand at opposite extremes of the range of variety in physical race which is to be found in *Homo sapiens*.[1]

Our modern Western race-feeling was unknown in the Western Society in earlier times and has failed to assert itself in certain sections of this Western Society down to this day. During the so-called 'Dark Ages' and 'Middle Ages' – that is to say, during the ten centuries ending in about the last quarter of the fifteenth century of our era – the members of the Western Society, when they thought of Mankind as a whole, were accustomed to divide the human family into two categories, as we divide it nowadays. The principle of division, however, was utterly different. Instead of dividing Mankind, as we do, into white people and coloured people, our forefathers divided it into Christians and heathen; and we are bound to confess that their dichotomy was better than ours both intellectually and morally. It was better intellectually because a human being's religion is a vastly more important and significant factor in his life than the colour of his skin, and is therefore a vastly better criterion for purposes of classification. Again, the dichotomy into Christians and heathen is better morally than the dichotomy into white and coloured, because the gulf between religions, unlike the gulf between races, is not impassable. It is a division between sheep in the fold and sheep astray on the mountains, not between sheep and goats.

In the eyes of the medieval Western Christian, when he looked abroad upon the world, the heathen, wandering unkempt in the wilderness, were neither incurably unclean nor irretrievably lost. Potentially, they were Christians like himself; and he looked forward to a time when all the lost sheep would be gathered into the fold. Indeed, he looked forward to this with assurance as the foreordained con-summation of terrestrial history, the fulfilment of God's purpose in the world. In this spirit, Western artists used to portray one of the three Magi as a black. How different from the spirit in which the white-skinned Western Protestant of modern times regards his black-skinned con-vert. The convert may have found spiritual salvation in the white man's faith; he may have acquired the white man's culture and learnt to speak his language with the tongue of an angel; he may have become an adept in the white man's economic technique, and yet it profits him nothing so long as he has not changed his skin. Surely he can retort that it profits the white man nothing to understand all mysteries and all knowledge and have skill so that he can move mountains, so long as he has not charity.

62 BLACK MAGUS *The Adoration*, by Hans Baldung, follows the common medieval practice of depicting one of the three Magi as a black.

This medieval Western freedom from the prejudice of race-feeling has survived among Western peoples who have remained more or less in the medieval phase of our Western Civilization: for instance, the Spaniards and Portuguese and the descendants of Spanish and Portuguese settlers who founded new Western communities in America.[2]

The Arabs and all other white Muslims, whether brunets or blonds, have always been free from colour-prejudice *vis-à-vis* the non-white races; and, at the present day, Muslims still make that dichotomy of the human family which Western Christians used to make in the Middle Ages. They divide Mankind into believers and unbelievers who are all potentially believers; and this division cuts across every difference of physical race. This liberality is more remarkable in white Muslims today than it was in white Western Christians in our Middle Ages; for our medieval forefathers had little or no contact with peoples of a different colour, whereas the white Muslims were in contact with the blacks of Africa and with the dark-skinned peoples of India from the beginning and have increased that contact steadily, until nowadays whites and blacks are intermingled, under the aegis of Islam, through the length and breadth of Pakistan and Africa. Under this searching test, the white Muslims have demonstrated their freedom from race-feeling by the most convincing of all proofs: they have given their daughters to black Muslims in marriage.

The races which have made the most numerous and the most brilliant contributions to those civilizations which have emerged within the last five thousand years are all of them still represented, besides, in pre-civilizational societies which have not risen above the level of barbarism or even above the level of savagery. If we classify by hairiness, we can confront the Nordic specimens of *Homo hirsutus* who have helped to create the Indic and Hittite and Hellenic and Western and Russian Civilizations, and the Orthodox Christian Civilization in South-Eastern Europe, with their poor relations the Hairy Ainu and the Australian aborigines and the Veddahs and the Todas, who have remained on the pre-civilizational level down to this day. If we classify by colour, we can confront the white men who have helped to create perhaps half the civilizations of which we know with our latter-day white barbarians: the fair-haired, blue-eyed highlanders of North-West Africa who have defied both the assaults and the blandishments of one civilization after another in the fastnesses of the Rif and the Atlas and Kabylia; their Nomadic kinsmen in the Sahara, whose deficiency of pigment is betrayed in their hair and eyes even when their skins are tanned by a scorching sun; the fair-haired, blue-eyed highlanders of Albania, who long contrived to evade civilization in fastnesses which overlook the high road between Greece and Rome; the highlanders of the Caucasus, who are such magnificent specimens of the white race that our Western ethnologists have taken their name in vain as a scientific term for the whole breed of *Homo pallidus*; the highlanders of Kurdistan; the highlanders of the borderland between Afghanistan and India; and – once again – the Ainu who, despite the whiteness of the skin that peeps through their shaggy fur, have fought the losing battle of barbarism against 'the yellow peril' of the East Asian Civilization in Japan. Again, we can confront the yellow men who have created the Sinic Civilization with the yellow barbarians who still survive, in a few scattered enclaves, among the mountains that divide the southern watershed of the Yangtse from the southern coastline of China, and with the yellow savages in some pockets of the interior of the Indo-Chinese peninsula. We can confront the brown creators of the Indic Civilization with the wild tribes of continental India – Bhils and Ghonds and the like – and with the head-hunters of Sumatra and Borneo. We can confront the Incas with the Araucanian barbarians of Chile and with the savages of Amazonia and of the Tierra del Fuego. We can confront the Mayas and the Toltecs with 'the noble savage' of North America who has established his fame as the redskin *par excellence*.

Our records show that the barbarians who still survive as such are a remnant of barbarian populations which the neighbouring civilizations have assimilated, and that this process of assimilation is still going on. If we had taken our survey of white barbarians two centuries ago instead of today, our list would have included the Scottish highlanders, who have been completely assimilated by the Western Society during the half-dozen generations that have come and gone since 1745. If the survey is taken again two centuries hence, it may seem as strange then to our descendants that the Albanians and the Rifis should have still been barbarians in our time as it seems to us now that the Scottish highlanders should have still been barbarians

in the reign of King George II. Similarly, a survey of yellow barbarians taken about the year 1000 BC would have returned as barbarians almost the whole of the Chinese people of today except those living in two relatively small areas, in the lower and the middle basin of the Yellow River, to which the Sinic Civilization was confined in that early age. The enlargement of the borders of civilizations and the recruitment of their manpower by the assimilation of their barbarian neighbours has been one of the constant features in the lives and activities of civilizations since this species of society first came into existence.

If we assume that all human beings of all races are capable of civilization, this process of assimilation, which is an empirically established fact, is also a fact which presents no difficulties to the understanding.

Retardations of the advance from barbarism to civilization can be accounted for by the interplay between a human nature which is common to all Mankind and certain exceptionally unfavourable circumstances in the local environments of some sections of the human family during certain periods of time.

The foregoing considerations will perhaps be sufficient to guard us against the error of supposing that some special quality of race in some fraction of Mankind is the positive factor which, within the last five thousand years, has shaken part of Mankind out of the Yin-state which we call 'the integration of custom' into the Yang-activity which we will decide to call 'the differentiation of civilization'.

63 BLACK SAINT
The Meeting of Saint Erasmus and Saint Mauritius, by Mathias Grünewald.

SAME ENVIRONMENT, DIFFERENT CULTURES   64, 65   While the Eurasian steppes supported a fully-fledged Nomadic Civilization, top, the similar prairie lands of North America have never given rise to an indigenous Nomadic Civilization.

12 Environment?

THE EXPANSION of a society sometimes brings its carriers into contact with peoples that differ from them in physique and in culture. These differences present a problem; and modern Westerners have solved this problem to their own satisfaction by improvising the concept of race. Hellenic minds were confronted with the same problem in consequence of a similar expansion of the Hellenic Society, which began towards the close of the eighth century BC, and they solved the problem – also to their own satisfaction – by working out a theoretical explanation on quite different lines. The Hellenic solution was superior to the Western solution in all points. It was more imaginative, more rational, and more humane; and, above all, it was unprejudiced. The self-regarding element which is so general, so prominent, and so ugly a feature in our Western race-theories is conspicuous by its absence here. For, so far from being roused to race-consciousness by contact with human beings who were not as they were, the Hellenes drew an inference which made them more sceptical about race than they had been before. They explained the manifest differences between themselves and their newly discovered neighbours as being the effects of diverse environments upon a uniform human nature, instead of seeing in them the outward manifestations of a diversity that was somehow intrinsic in human nature itself.

The *locus classicus* in which the Hellenic 'environment theory' may be studied is a treatise entitled *Influences of Atmosphere, Water, and Situation* which dates from the fifth century BC and is preserved among the collected works of the Hippocratean School of Medicine. As the best exposition of the theory in any literature within our range, this monograph deserves quotation:

The countries which have the greatest and the most frequent seasonal variations of climate also have the wildest and most highly diversified landscape and present the greatest array of mountains, forests, plains, and meadow-lands, while in countries where the seasonal variations are slight the uniformity of landscape is at its maximum. Consideration will show that the same equations hold good for human nature. Human physiognomies may be classified into the well-wooded and well-watered mountain type, the thin-soiled waterless type, the meadowy marshy type, the well-cleared and well-drained lowland type. Here, too, there is the same effect of environmental variation upon physique; and, if the variation is great, the differentiation of bodily type is increased proportionately. . . .[1]

The environment-theory of the geneses of civilizations has none of the moral repulsiveness of the race-theory, yet intellectually it is no less vulnerable. Both theories attempt to account for the empirically observed diversity in the psychical behaviour and performance of different fractions of Mankind by supposing that this psychical diversity is fixedly and permanently correlated, in the relation of effect to cause, with certain elements of diversity, likewise given by empirical observation, in the non-psychical domain of Nature. The race-theory finds its differentiating natural cause in the diversity of human physique, the environment-theory finds it in the diversity of the climatic, topographical, and hydrographical conditions in which different human societies live; but this discrepancy between the two theories is not fundamental. They are merely two different attempts to find a solution for the same equation by assigning different values to the same unknown quantity. The structure of the equation which is postulated in the two theories is identical; and neither can stand if the common underlying formula will not bear examination. The essence of the formula is a correlation between two sets of variations; and this correlation must be demonstrated to be fixed and permanent – it must maintain itself in every instance under all conditions – before any theories founded on it can claim the status of scientific laws. Under this test, we have already seen the race-theory break down; and we shall now see the environment-theory fare no better.

For instance, the steppes of Eurasia and Arabia and North Africa have been occupied, till within living memory, for perhaps nearly four thousand years past, by pastoral Nomadic peoples whose way of life is both highly distinctive and remarkably uniform throughout their physiographically and climatically distinctive and uniform habitat. Then does the physiography and climate of these pastoral Nomads' environment account for the character of their culture? If we confine our survey to the steppes on the mainland of the Old World, it does reveal the correlation between type of environment and type of society which is demanded by the theory that similar environments always and everywhere produce similar societies, not by mimesis, but on the principle of the uniformity of Nature. Under further tests, however, the correlation breaks down. For we find that the other areas in the world which offer environments for Nomad societies – the prairies of North America, the llanos of Venezuela, the pampas of Argentina, the Australian grasslands in western Queensland and western New South Wales – have not fulfilled the requirements of the environment-theory by producing independent Nomadic societies of their own. Their potentialities are not open to question. They have been realized by the enterprise of the Western Society in modern times; and the pioneering Western stockmen – North American cowboys and South American gauchos and Australian cattlemen – who have won and held these untenanted ranges for a few generations, in the van of the advancing plough and mill, have captivated the imagination of Mankind as triumphantly as the Scythian and the Tatar and the Arab. The potentialities of the American and Australian steppes must have been powerful indeed if they could transform into Nomads, if only for a generation, the pioneers of a society which had no Nomadic traditions, having lived by agriculture and manufacture ever since it first emerged. It is all the more remarkable that the peoples whom the first Western explorers found in occupation had never been stimulated by the potentialities of the environment into Nomadism, but had found no better use for these Nomads' paradises than to use them as hunting-grounds – remaining on the pre-pastoral hunting and food-gathering level of economy to the end.

If we next test the environment-theory by a survey of areas resembling the Lower Nile valley, our experience will be the same. All Greeks who came into contact with Pharaonic Egypt in the Hellenic Age of the Greek people's history were struck by features of the Egyptiac Civilization that, in Greek eyes, were peculiar. Herodotus attributes these peculiarities of the Egyptiac culture to peculiarities of the physical environment in which this culture took shape. 'The climate in which the Egyptians live is alien [to the climate of the Hellenic World], and, besides that, the nature of their river is unique. This explains why the Egyptians have established for themselves manners and customs that, for the most part, are entirely opposite to those of the rest of Mankind.'[2] Herodotus's Hippocratean explanation of the idiosyncrasies of the Egyptiac Civilization would be convincing if we found the same manners and customs in force in all other countries, anywhere on the face of this planet, in which the climate and physiography are comparable to those of the lower valley and the delta of the river Nile. We cannot, of course, expect to find any country in which the physical setting of the Egyptiac Civilization is duplicated exactly, but it is duplicated approximately in the Lower Tigris-Euphrates basin and in the Indus basin. In each of these two other regions, the physical conditions are, in several key features, the same as in Egypt. There is the same encompassing steppe, dry climate, and ample supply of water and alluvium provided by great rivers which rise in distant rain-swept and snow-capped highlands; and, in both of these comparable settings, civilizations resembling the Egyptiac Civilization did arise. But when we extend our survey, the correlation breaks down. The environment offered by the lower valleys of the Nile and of the Indus and of the Tigris and Euphrates is also offered by the valleys of the Rio Grande and the Colorado river in the south-western United States. Under the hands of the modern European settler, equipped with the resources of a civilization which he has brought with him from the other side of the world, these rivers of America have performed the miracles which the Nile and Euphrates once performed for Egyptiac and Sumeric irrigation-engineers; but this magic has never been taught by the Colorado or the Rio Grande to people who were not adepts in it already through having learnt it elsewhere, and who, besides possessing the skill, also had the spirit to apply this skill where opportunities offered themselves.

Many more cases could be cited in which an environment of some particular type has been turned to account by one human society when another human society has failed to make anything of the same potential assets. But the two cases of potentially irrigable river-basins and potential pastures on the steppe suffice to show that environment, like race, is not the cause of the geneses of civilization.

'Environment' is a relative term. It implies the existence, the presence, and the action of some other party. This other party is some living creature; and the environment of every living creature is the sum total of the rest of the Universe. For instance, a human being's environment consists of the whole of non-human Nature, both inanimate and animate, together with all his fellow human beings (includ-ing the dead as well as the living). Above all, a person's environment includes the human nature of the person himself. This last-mentioned constituent of a human being's environment – the internal spiritual constituent – is the key to the person's relations with all the rest of his environment's constituents; for, if a human being fails to master Nature within himself, he will fail to master it in the rest of the Universe that lies outside him. He may 'understand all mysteries and all knowledge',[3] but the most highly accomplished technical expertise will profit him nothing if he is not also in command of himself.

As for that element in Man's environment that consists of non-human Nature, this has been in existence for countless aeons before the unknown date at which our ancestors became human in the act of awaking to consciousness. We can also forecast that non-human Nature will still be there for further countless aeons after the unknown future date at which the human race will have become extinct. In the history of non-human Nature (if we could imagine the pre-human and post-human chapters of this history being recorded by some non-human observer) the period during which one of the constituents of the Universe has been Mankind will have been as brief as the twinkling of an eye. But for Man, so long as he exists, non-human Nature has significance only by virtue of being a part – though it is not the most important part – of Man's environment. When the Universe is regarded from Man's standpoint,

the facts of geography are the facts as they are approached. . . . This world, without man, is not environment, is not our world. . . . Without man, environment does not exist.[4]

No product of nature can be considered a natural resource until man wants it for his use and has techniques for exploiting it. Thus, rich, swampy land is not a natural resource unless man can drain it and cultivate it; nor were coal, gold, or uranium ore of any importance until man wanted them and had means of using them.[5]

Thus Greek thinkers were mistaken in supposing that the variety of the non-human constituent of Nature which is Mankind's habitat is the cause of the variety of human culture, and that there is an invariable correlation between types of culture and types of physiography and climate. 'The facts of geography are the facts as they are approached' by Man. This is true, but, if it is true, so too must be the converse proposition. The man who approaches the facts of geography either possesses or lacks the equipment for coping with these facts; and the key part of Man's equipment is not his technology; it is his spirit. If Man does not have the vision, initiative, persistence, and, above all, self-command that are required for engaging in the enterprise of taking advantage of the potentialities of some geographical fact, the best tools will not, by themselves, enable Man to do this job. In Man, the decisive factor – the factor that tips the balance either towards success or towards failure – is not race, and it is not skill either; it is the spirit in which Man responds to the challenge of the sum total of Nature that has become Man's environment as a result of Man's own appearance in the Universe. This sum total includes the nature of Man himself, as exemplified in *Homo sapiens* and in the individual representatives of this species – that is to say, in particular persons.

13 Challenge-and-response

I HAVE been searching for the positive factor which, within the last five thousand years, has shaken part of Mankind out of the 'integration of custom' into the 'differentiation of civilization'. The dawn of civilization was not the first occasion on which the rhythm of human history underwent this change. This had happened already when some human societies on the fringes of the Fertile Crescent had invented agriculture. It had happened, before that, when some earlier societies had broken away from the routine – perhaps, by then, half a million years old – of making Lower Palaeolithic tools, and had invented the much more competent Upper Palaeolithic technique. The most radical of all new departures in human history had been the original one in which Man's pre-human ancestors had turned into human beings. Thus the search for the explanation of such new departures is a search for the origin, not only of civilization, but of humanity itself.

In my search up to the present point, I have been experimenting with the play of soulless forces – *vis inertiae* and race and environment – and I have been thinking in the deterministic terms of cause-and-effect. Now that these manoeuvres have ended, one after another, in my drawing blank, I am led to consider whether my successive failures may not point to some mistake in method. Perhaps I have fallen a victim to 'the apathetic fallacy' against which I sought to put myself on guard at the outset of my inquiry.[1] Have I not erred in applying to historical thought, which is a study of living creatures, a scientific method of thought which has been devised for thinking about inanimate Nature? And have I not also erred further in treating the outcomes of encounters between persons as cases of the operation of cause-and-effect? The effect of a cause is inevitable, invariable, and predictable. But the initiative that is taken by one or other of the live parties to an encounter is not a cause; it is a challenge. Its consequence is not an effect; it is a response. Challenge-and-response[2] resembles cause-and-effect only in standing for a sequence of events. The character of the sequence is not the same. Unlike the effect of a cause, the response to a challenge is not predetermined, is not necessarily uniform in all cases, and is therefore intrinsically unpredictable. I will now look at my problem with new eyes. I will see 'persons' where, so far, I have been seeing 'forces'. I will picture the relations between persons as being challenges that evoke responses, instead of causes that produce effects. I will follow Plato's lead: I will turn away from the formulae of science in order to hearken to the language of mythology.

So far, by the process of exhaustion, we have made one discovery: the cause of the geneses of civilizations is not simple but multiple; it is not an entity but a relation. We have the choice of conceiving this relation either as an interaction between two inhuman forces – like the petrol and the air which interact in the engine of a motor-car – or as an encounter between two personalities. Let us yield our minds to the second of these two conceptions. Perhaps it will lead us towards the light.

An encounter between two superhuman personalities is the plot of some of the greatest stories and dramas that the human imagination has conceived. An encounter between Yahweh and the Serpent is the plot of the story of the Fall of Man in the Book of Genesis; a second encounter between the same antagonists (transfigured by a progressive enlightenment of Syriac souls) is the plot of the New Testament which tells the story of the Redemption; an encounter between the Lord and Satan is the plot of the Book of Job; an encounter between the Lord and Mephistopheles is the plot of Goethe's *Faust*; an encounter between Gods and Demons is the plot of the Scandinavian *Voluspà*; an encounter between Artemis and Aphrodite is the plot of Euripides' *Hippolytus*.

We find another version of the same plot in that ubiquitous and ever-recurring myth – a 'primordial image', if ever there was one – of the encounter between the Virgin and the Father of her Child. The characters of this myth have played their allotted parts on a thousand different stages under an infinite variety of names: Danae and the Shower of Gold; Europa and the Bull; Semele the stricken Earth and Zeus the Sky that launches the thunderbolt; Creusa and Apollo in Euripides' *Ion*; Psyche and Cupid; Gretchen and Faust. The theme recurs, transfigured, in the Annunciation. This protean myth even found favour for a time with those Western cosmogonists of our own day who propounded the theory that the planetary system was the issue of a close conjunction between the Sun and another passing star.

Their hypothesis was that in the remote past our sun was an ordinary star without planets. Then, about twenty million years [*sic*] ago, another star on its journey through space passed very close to the sun. The gravitational attraction between the two bodies swung them about one another and eventually the other star passed on. But in this close encounter great tides of gaseous matter would have been torn from the sun; some of this would fall back, some might have followed the passing star into space, but a certain amount would remain under the gravitational field of the sun, circling around it. These gases eventually condensed into smaller fragments, which finally accreted into larger and larger bodies to form the planets.[3]

This is no more than a restatement, in the incongruous accents of modern astronomy, of the mythological encounter between the Sun goddess and her ravisher that is so familiar a tale in the mouths of the untutored children of Nature.

Let us try to analyse the plot of this story or drama which repeats itself in such different contexts and in such various forms. We may begin with two general features: the encounter is thought of as being a rare or even a unique event; and it has consequences which are vast in proportion to the vastness of the breach which it makes in the customary course of Nature.

Even in the easy-going world of the Hellenic mythology, where the gods saw the daughters of men that they were fair, and had their way with so many of them that their victims

66 SATAN'S CHALLENGE, GOD'S RESPONSE The Devil's intrusion into
God's Universe provokes a renewal of divine creativity. Blake's watercolour
dramatically emphasizes Satan's vigorous movement, in contrast to God's
majestic immobility. Beneath them, Job, 'perfect and upright'.

67 'Am I a God? I feel the light' (*Faust*). Faust's restless search for more than human knowledge is a challenge to God, yet is accepted by Him as the alternative to a sterile inertia.

could be marshalled and paraded in poetic catalogues,[4] such incidents never ceased to be sensational affairs and invariably resulted in the births of heroes. In the versions of the plot in which both the parties to the encounter are superhuman, the rarity and the momentousness of the event are apt to be thrown into stronger relief. In the Book of Job, 'the day when the sons of God came to present themselves before the Lord, and Satan came also among them' is evidently thought of as being an unusual occasion; and so is the encounter between the Lord and Mephistopheles in the 'Prologue in Heaven' (suggested, of course, by the passage in the Book of Job) which starts the action

of Goethe's *Faust*.[5] In both these dramas, the consequences on Earth of this unusual encounter in Heaven are tremendous. The single ordeals of Job and Faust represent, in the intuitive language of fiction, the infinitely multiple ordeal of Man; and, in the language of theology, the same vast consequence is represented as following from the superhuman encounters that are portrayed in the Book of Genesis and in the New Testament. The expulsion of Adam and Eve from the Garden of Eden, which follows from the encounter between Yahweh and the Serpent, is nothing less than the Fall of Man; the passion of Christ in the New Testament is nothing less than Man's Redemption.

68 FALL AND REDEMPTION Without Man's Fall, God would be unable to reveal his self-sacrificing love: the temptation of Eve and Christ's Crucifixion are linked in the common medieval symbol of a Tree of Death and Life.

In the New Testament, the uniqueness of the divine event is of the essence of the story; and this has been a stumbling-block to the Western intellect ever since the geocentric conception of the material universe was first impugned by the discoveries of modern Western astronomy.

Yet this modern astronomical conception of immensity, which appeared, only yesterday, to confute the ageless myth of the unique divine event, may appear to rehabilitate it tomorrow: for the immensity of the reputed extent of empty space is out of all proportion to the immensity of the reputed number of the stars; and it follows from this that any encounter between two stars would be an almost inconceivably rare event. Thus, in the portrayal of a conjunction of our Sun and another star, which was supposed

to have led on to the appearance of life on Earth, the rarity and momentousness of the event turn out to be almost as much of the essence of the story as they are in the Book of Genesis and in the New Testament, where the encounters are between God and the Devil and the consequences are the Fall and the Redemption of Man. The traditional plot of the play has a way of reasserting itself in exotic settings.

The play opens with a perfect state of Yin. In the Universe, Balder keeps all things bright and beautiful through keeping himself alive. In Heaven,

> Die unbegreiflich hohen Werke
> Sind herrlich, wie am ersten Tag.[6]

On Earth, Faust is perfect in knowledge; Job is perfect in

goodness and prosperity;[7] Adam and Eve, in the Garden of Eden, are perfect in innocence and ease; the virgins – Gretchen, Danae, Hippolytus – are perfect in purity and beauty. In the astronomer's universe, the Sun, a perfect orb of incandescent matter, is travelling on an unimpeded course through Space. In the biologist's universe, the species is in perfect adaptation to its environment.

When Yin is thus complete, it is ready to pass over into Yang. But what is to make it pass? A change in a state which, by definition, is perfect after its kind can be started only by an impulse or motive which comes from outside. If we think of the state as being one of physical equilibrium, we must bring another star to raise a tide on the spherical surface of the Sun, or another gas to evoke an explosion from the inert air in the combustion-chamber of the motor-engine. If we think of the state as being one of psychic beatitude or *nirvana*, we must bring another actor on to the stage: a critic to set the mind thinking again by suggesting doubts; an adversary to set the heart feeling again by instilling distress or discontent or fear or antipathy; in fact, an enemy to sow tares in the field;[8] an access of desire to generate *karma*. This is the role of the Serpent in the Book of Genesis, of Satan in the Book of Job, of Mephistopheles in Goethe's *Faust*, of Loki in the Scandinavian mythology, of Aphrodite in Euripides' *Hippolytus* and Apollo in his *Ion*, of the passing star in modern Western cosmogony, of the environment in the Darwinian theory of evolution. In the language of a modern Western philosopher, 'To jolt the individual . . . and also . . . to break up the collective frameworks in which he is imprisoned, it is indispensable that he should be shaken and prodded from outside. What would we do without our enemies?'[9]

The role is interpreted most clearly when it is played by Mephistopheles. First, the Lord propounds it in the Prologue in Heaven:

> Des Menschen Tätigkeit kann allzuleicht erschlaffen,
> Er liebt sich bald die unbedingte Ruh';
> Drum geb' ich gern ihm den Gesellen zu,
> Der reizt und wirkt und muss als Teufel schaffen.[10]

Afterwards, Mephistopheles gives the same account of his role in introducing himself, on Earth, to Faust:

> Ich bin der Geist, der stets verneint!
> Und das mit Recht; denn alles, was entsteht,
> Ist wert, dass es zugrunde geht;
> Drum besser wär's, dass nichts entstünde.
> So ist denn alles, was ihr Sünde,
> Zerstörung, kurz das Böse nennt,
> Mein eigentliches Element.[11]

Finally, Faust explains the adversary's role, by implication, from his own experience, in his dying speech:

> Nur der verdient sich Freiheit wie das Leben
> Der täglich sie erobern muss.[12]

The impulse or motive which makes a perfect Yin-state pass over into a new Yang-activity comes from an intrusion of the Devil into the universe of God. The event can best be described in these mythological images because they are not embarrassed by the contradiction that arises when the statement is translated into logical terms. In logic, if God's universe is perfect, there cannot be a Devil outside

it, while, if the Devil exists, the perfection which he comes to spoil must have been incomplete already through the very fact of his existence. This logical contradiction, which cannot be resolved logically, is transcended intuitively in the imagery of the poet and the prophet, who give glory to an omnipotent God yet take it for granted that He is subject to two crucial limitations.

The first limitation is that, in the perfection of what He has created already, He cannot find an opportunity for further creative activity. If God is pictured as transcendent, then

> Die unbegreflich hohen Werke
> Sind herrlich, wie am ersten Tag;[13]

the works of creation are as glorious as ever they were but they are not 'changed from glory to glory'.[14] At this point, the principle that 'where the spirit of the Lord is, there is liberty'[15] fails; and, if God is pictured as immanent, the same limitation still holds:

> Der Gott, der mir im Busen wohnt
> Kann tief mein Innerstes erregen,
> Der über allen meinen Kräften thront
> Er kann nach aussen nichts bewegen.[16]

The second limitation upon God's power is that when the opportunity for fresh creation is offered to Him from outside, He is bound to take it. When the Devil challenges Him, He cannot refuse to take the challenge up. 'Live dangerously', which is the Nietzschian Zarathustra's ideal, is God's necessity. This limitation is illustrated in the Parable of the Tares:

So the servants of the householder came and said unto him: 'Sir, didst not thou sow good seed in thy field? From whence, then, hath it tares?' He said unto them: 'An enemy hath done this.' The servants said unto him: 'Wilt thou then that we go and gather them up?' But he said: 'Nay; lest, while ye gather up the tares, ye root up also the wheat with them. Let both grow together until the harvest.'[17]

God is bound to accept the embarrassment that is thrust upon Him by the Devil because He can refuse only at the price of renouncing His own purposes and undoing His own work – in fact, at the price of denying His own nature and ceasing to be God, which is either an impossibility or another story.

If God is thus not omnipotent in logical terms, is He still mythologically invincible? If He is bound to take up the Devil's challenge, is He equally bound to win the ensuing battle? In Euripides' *Hippolytus*, where God's part is played by Artemis and the Devil's by Aphrodite, Artemis is not only unable to decline combat but is doomed to defeat. The relation between the Olympians – all peers of one another in a barbarian war-lord's war-band – is anarchic:

> 'Twas the will
> Of Cypris that these evil things should be,
> Sating her wrath. And this immutably
> Hath Zeus ordained in heaven: no God may thwart
> A God's fixed will; we grieve but stand apart.[18]

And Artemis can only console herself by making up her mind that one day she will play the Devil's role herself to Aphrodite's hurt:

> My hand shall win its vengeance, through and through
> Piercing with flawless shaft what heart soe'er
> Of all men living is most dear to Her.[19]

Thus, in Euripides' version of the plot, the victory in the battle falls to the Power which assumes the Devil's role, and the outcome is not creation but destruction. In the Scandinavian version, destruction is likewise the outcome of Ragnarök – when 'gods and demons slay and are slain'[20] – though the unique genius of the author of *Voluspà* makes his Sibyl's vision pierce the gloom to behold the light of a new dawn beyond it. On the other hand, in another version of the plot, the combat which follows the unavoidable acceptance of the challenge takes the form, not of an exchange of fire in which the Devil has the first shot and cannot fail to kill his man, but of a wager which the Devil is apparently bound to lose. The classic works of art in which this wager-motif is worked out are, of course, the Book of Job and Goethe's *Faust*; and it is in *Faust*, again, that the points are made most clear.

After the Lord has accepted the wager with Mephistopheles[21] in the Prologue in Heaven, the terms are agreed on Earth, between Mephistopheles and Faust, as follows:

Faust. Werd ich beruhigt je mich auf ein Faulbett legen,
    So sei es gleich um mich getan!
    Kannst du mich schmeichelnd je belügen
    Dass ich mir selbst gefallen mag,
    Kannst du mich mit Genuss betrügen,
    Das sei für mich der letzte Tag!
    Die Wette biet' ich!
Mephistopheles.   Topp!
Faust.   Und Schlag auf Schlag!
    Werd' ich zum Augenblicke sagen:
    'Verweile doch! Du bist so schön!'
    Dann magst du mich in Fesseln schlagen,
    Dann will ich gern zugrunde gehn!
    Dann mag die Totenglocke schallen,
    Dann bist du deines Dienstes frei,
    Die Uhr mag stehn, der Zeiger fallen,
    Es sei die Zeit für mich vorbei![22]

The bearing of this mythical compact upon our problem of accounting for new departures can be brought out by identifying Faust, at the moment when he makes his bet, with one of those 'awakened sleepers' who have risen from the ledge on which they had been lying torpid, and have started to climb on up the face of the cliff, in our simile of the climbers' 'pitch'.[23] In the language of our simile, Faust is saying: 'I have made up my mind to leave this ledge and climb this precipice in search of the next ledge above. In attempting this, I am aware that I am courting danger and deliberately leaving safety behind me. I am aware that if once I pause I shall fall, and that if once I fall I shall fall to destruction. Yet, for the sake of the possible achievement, I am ready to take the inevitable risk.'

In the story as told in this version of the plot, the intrepid climber, after an ordeal of mortal dangers and desperate reverses, succeeds in the end in scaling the cliff triumphantly. In both Job and *Faust*, the wager is won by God; and again, in the New Testament, the same ending is given, through the revelation of a second encounter between the same pair of antagonists, to the combat between Yahweh and the Serpent which, in the original version in the Book of Genesis, had ended rather in the manner of the combat between Artemis and Aphrodite in the *Hippolytus*.[24]

Moreover, in Job and *Faust* and the New Testament alike, it is suggested, or even declared outright, that the wager cannot be won by the Devil; that the Devil, in meddling with God's work, cannot frustrate but can only serve the purpose of God, who remains master of the situation all the time and gives the Devil rope for the Devil to hang himself. This seems to be implied in Jesus's words to the chief priests and captains of the Temple and the elders: 'This is your hour and the power of darkness',[25] and in his words to Pilate: 'Thou couldest have no power at all against me, except it were given thee from above.'[26] And the implication is worked out in the following passage from the pen of a modern Christian theologian:

Not *through* pain and defeat and death does Christ come to victory – and after Him all we who are Christ's because of Him – but . . . these things *are* the victory. . . . It is . . . in the Risen Christ that we can see how evil, against which we yet must strive, runs its course and is found at the end to be the good which it seemed to be resisting and destroying: how God must abandon us in order that He may be the more sure of us.[27]

So, in Goethe's *Faust*, in the Prologue in Heaven, after the wager has been offered and taken, the Lord declares to Mephistopheles,

    Du darfst auch da nur frei *erscheinen*,[28]

and announces that He gladly gives Mephistopheles to Man as a companion, because he

    reizt und wirkt und *muss*, als Teufel, *schaffen*.[29]

Stranger still, Mephistopheles, when he opens his attack upon Faust, introduces himself to his intended victim as

    Ein Teil von jener Kraft
    Die stets das Böse will und stets das Gute schafft.[30]

In fact, Mephistopheles, notwithstanding the fearful wickedness and suffering which he manages to produce, is treated throughout the play as a buffoon who is destined to be a dupe. This note is struck by the Lord Himself in the passage just quoted from the Prologue in Heaven, where He proceeds:

    Ich habe deinesgleichen nie gehasst.
    Von allen Geistern die verneinen
    Ist mir der Schalk am wenigsten zur Last.[31]

The same note persists throughout the first part of the play and is intensified in the second, until, in the scene of his final discomfiture,[32] which is written in a deliberately comic vein, Mephistopheles is turned into a positive figure of fun. Faust repeats, in his dying speech, the very words

    Verweile doch, du bist so schön

on which his wager with Mephistopheles turns; and Mephistopheles gloats over the corpse in the belief that he is the winner; but he has congratulated himself too soon; for Faust has recited the crucial formula not affirmatively apropos the present, but only conditionally apropos the future:

    Zum Augenblicke *dürft'* ich sagen
    'Verweile doch, du bist so schön!' . . .
    Im Vorgefühl von solchem hohen Glück
    Geniess' ich *jetzt* den höchsten Augenblick.[33]

Mephistopheles has not won the wager after all; and he is ignominiously pelted off the stage with volleys of roses strewn by a chorus of *putti*, who distract him with their sensuous charms while they spirit away the dead Faust's immortal part from under his nose. In his mingled self-pity and self-contempt for so much labour lost, Mephistopheles cuts a poorer figure than the discomfited Shylock in the dénouement of *The Merchant of Venice*.

These ludicrously discomfited villains who have been created by our two great modern Western dramatists have their prototype in the Scandinavian Loki: a figure who played his part in a traditional and anonymous drama which was performed as a religious rite before it crystallized into a myth. In this ritual drama, Loki

was the sacral actor whose business was to draw out the demon, to bring the antagonism to a head and thus to prepare for victory, – hence the duplicity of his nature. . . . Such a figure has to bear the blame of the tricks and feints necessary to provoke the conquest of life, he becomes a comic figure, the trickster who is predestined to be overreached.[34]

Has the Devil really been cheated? Did God accept a wager which He knew all the time that He could not lose? That would be a hard saying; for, if that were true, the whole transaction would have been a sham. God would have been risking nothing. He would not have been 'living dangerously', after all; and, surely, 'Nothing venture, nothing win.' An encounter that was no encounter could not produce the consequence of an encounter – the vast cosmic consequence of causing Yin to pass over into Yang.

The truth is that, when one of God's creatures is tempted by the Devil, God Himself is thereby given the opportunity to recreate the world. By the stroke of the adversary's trident, all the fountains of the great deep are broken up. The Devil's intervention has accomplished that transition from Yin to Yang, from static to dynamic, for which God had been yearning ever since the moment when His Yin-state became complete, but which it was impossible for God to accomplish by Himself, out of His own perfection. And the Devil has done more for God than this; for, when once Yin has passed over into Yang, not the Devil himself can prevent God from completing His fresh act of creation by passing over again from Yang to Yin on a higher level. When once the divine equilibrium has been upset by the Satanic instability, the Devil has shot his bolt; and the restoration of equilibrium on a new plan, in which God's purpose is fulfilled, lies wholly within God's power.

Thus the Devil is bound to lose the wager, not because he has been cheated by God, but because he has overreached himself.[35] He has played into God's hands because he would not or could not deny himself the malicious satisfaction of forcing God's hand. Knowing that God would not or could not refuse the wager if it were offered, the Devil did not observe that God was hoping, silently but eagerly, that the offer would be made. In his jubilation at obtaining an opportunity to ruin one of God's choicest creatures, the Devil did not foresee that he would be giving God Himself an opportunity to renew the whole work of creation. And so God's purpose is fulfilled through the Devil's instrumentality and in the Devil's despite.[36]

It will be seen that this dénouement of the plot turns upon the role of God's creature who is the object of the wager;

Two engravings from nineteenth-century editions of Goethe, illustrating the beginning and the end of the drama, have something of the directness of the earlier popular Faust legend.

69   Satan challenges God.

70   The Devil and Heaven fight for Faust's soul.

71, 72 KNOWLEDGE THROUGH SUFFERING The anguish suffered by Job and by Christ on the Cross culminates in an otherwise unattainable power of understanding.

and here again we find ourselves beset by logical contradictions on all sides. A Job or a Faust is at once a chosen vessel and a vessel of destruction; and, in the fact of being subjected to his ordeal, he has already fulfilled his function, so that it makes no difference to the drama in Heaven whether he, on Earth, is blasted by the fire or whether he emerges more finely tempered. Even if the Devil has his way with him – even if his destruction is complete – God's purpose is nevertheless fulfilled and the Devil's purpose frustrated; for, in spite of the sacrifice of the creature, the Creator lives, while, through the sacrifice of the creature, the work of creation proceeds:

Of old hast Thou laid the foundation of the Earth, and the Heavens are the work of Thy hands.
They shall perish, but Thou shalt endure. Yea, all of them shall wax old like a garment; as a vesture shalt Thou change them, and they shall be changed.
But Thou art the same, and Thy years shall have no end.[37]

Again, this chosen vessel of destruction which is the object of the wager between God and the Devil is their common field of action, the arena in which they do battle, the stage on which they play; but he is also the combatants as well as the arena and the dramatis personae as well as the stage. Created by God and abandoned to the Devil, he is seen, in the prophet's vision, to be an incarnation of both his Maker and his Tempter, while, in the psychologist's analysis, God and the Devil alike are reduced to conflicting psychic forces in his soul – forces which have no independent existence apart from the symbolic language of mythology.

The conception that the object of the wager between God and the Devil is an incarnation of God is familiar. It is the central theme of the New Testament. The conception that the object of the wager is at the same time an incarnation of the Devil is less familiar but perhaps not less profound. It is expressed in the encounter between Faust and the Earth Spirit, who prostrates Faust by proclaiming Faust's likeness to the spirit whom he understands – the still unmanifested Mephistopheles:

Faust. Der du die weite Welt umschweifst,
　　　Geschäftiger Geist, wie nah fühl' ich mich dir!
Geist. Du gleichst dem Geist den du begreifst,
　　　Nicht mir! (*Verschwindet*).
Faust (*zusammenstürzend*). Nicht dir?
　　　Wem denn?
　　　Ich Ebenbild der Gottheit!
　　　Und nicht einmal dir![38]

It remains to consider the role of this 'Devil-God', this part and whole, this creature and incarnation, this arena and combatant, this stage and player; for, in the wager version of the plot, the encounter between the Powers of Hell and Heaven is only the prologue, while the passion of a human figure on Earth is the substance of the play.

In every presentation of this drama, suffering is the keynote of the human protagonist's part, whether the part is played by Jesus of Nazareth, or by Job, or by Faust and Gretchen, or by Adam and Eve, or by Hippolytus and Phaedra, or by Hoder and Balder. 'He is despised and rejected of men; a man of sorrows, and acquainted with grief.'[39] 'He will be scourged, racked, shackled, blinded with hot irons and be put to every other torment, ending with being impaled.'[40] Faust makes his entry in a state of utter disillusionment with his mastery of human knowledge;[41] turns to magic only to receive a shattering rebuff from the Earth Spirit;[42] and then accepts from Mephistopheles an initiation into the life of sense and sex which leads him to the tragic moment in Margaret's prison, at the dawn of her dying day, when he cries, like Job,[43] in his agony: 'O, would that I had never been born.'[44] Gretchen, entering carefree,[45] is made to pass through the Valley of the Shadow of Death:

> Mein Ruh' ist hin,
> Mein Herz ist schwer;
> Ich finde sie nimmer
> Und nimmermehr.[46]

The subjective experience of the human being who is cast for this part is conveyed with unusual vividness and poignancy in the following dream of a woman undergoing an operation under insufficient ether, which is cited by William James:

A great Being or Power was traveling through the sky, his foot was on a kind of lightning as a wheel is on a rail, it was his pathway. The lightning was made entirely of the spirits of innumerable people close to one another, and I was one of them. He moved in a straight line, and each part of the streak or flash came into its short conscious existence only that he might travel. I seemed to be directly under the foot of God, and I thought he was grinding his own life up out of my pain. Then I saw that what he had been trying with all his might to do was to *change his course*, to *bend* the lightning to which he was tied, in the direction in which he wanted to go. I felt my flexibility and helplessness and knew that he would succeed. He bended me, turning his corner by means of my hurt, hurting me more than I had ever been hurt in my life, and at the acutest point of this, as he passed, I *saw*. I understood for a moment things that I have now forgotten, things that no one could remember while retaining sanity. The angle was an obtuse angle, and I remember thinking as I woke that had he made it a right or acute angle, I should have both suffered and 'seen' still more, and should probably have died....

If I had to formulate a few of the things I then caught a glimpse of, they would run somewhat as follows:—
The eternal necessity of suffering and its eternal vicariousness. The veiled and incommunicable nature of the worst sufferings; – the passivity of genius, how it is essentially instrumental and defenceless, moved, not moving, it must do what it does; – the impossibility of discovery without its price; – finally, the excess of what the suffering 'seer' or genius pays over what his generation gains. (He seems like one who sweats his life out to earn enough to save a district from famine, and just as he staggers back, dying and satisfied, bringing a lac of rupees to buy grain with, God lifts the lac away, dropping *one* rupee, and says,'That you may give them. That you have earned for them. The rest is for ME.') I perceived also, in a way never to be forgotten, the excess of what we see over what we can demonstrate.[47]

Objectively, the ordeal consists of a series of stages which the sufferer has to pass through in order to serve God's purpose.

In the first stage, the human protagonist in the drama takes action – in reaction to an assault from the tempter – which sets up a change from passivity to activity, from rest to motion, from calm to storm, from harmony to discord, in fact from Yin to Yang. The action may be either dyna-

mically base, as when the Ancient Mariner shoots the Albatross or Loki shoots Balder with the blind God Hoder's hand and the mistletoe shaft; or dynamically sublime, as when Jesus, in the temptation in the wilderness which immediately follows his baptism in Jordan, rejects the traditional Jewish role of the militant Messiah who was to raise the Chosen People to dominion in this world by the sword.[48] The essence of the act is not its moral character but its dynamic effect. The Ancient Mariner's act changes the fortunes of the ship and her crew; Jesus's act gives the conception of the Messiah a new turn and therewith a power which had not resided in it before.[49] The corresponding act in the ordeal of Job is his cursing of the day of his birth[50] – a protest which raises the whole issue of Job's deserts and God's justice. In the ordeal of Faust, the point is elaborated and brought out more clearly.

Before Mephistopheles intervenes, Faust is already making efforts on his own account to break out of his Yin-state – his unsatisfyingly perfect mastery of human knowledge. He seeks escape from his spiritual prison through the arts of magic and is repelled by the Earth Spirit;[51] he seeks escape through suicide and is checked by the song of the choir of angels;[52] he is driven back from action to meditation; yet his mind still runs upon action and transposes 'Im Anfang war das Wort' into 'Im Anfang war die Tat.'[53] At that moment, already, Mephistopheles is present in a theriomorphic disguise; but it is not till the tempter stands before him in human form that Faust performs his dynamic act by cursing the whole moral and material universe.[54] Therewith, the foundations of the great deep are loosed; and an invisible choir of spirits laments and exults that the old creation is shattered and a new creation begun.

> Weh! Weh!
> Du hast sie zerstört,
> Die schöne Welt
> Mit mächtiger Faust;
> Sie stürzt, sie zerfällt!
> Ein Halbgott hat sie zerschlagen!
> Wir tragen
> Die Trümmern ins Nichts hinüber,
> Und klagen
> Über die verlorne Schöne.
> Mächtiger
> Der Erdensöhne,
> Prächtiger
> Baue sie wieder,
> In deinem Busen baue sie auf!
> Neuen Lebenslauf
> Beginne
> Mit hellem Sinne,
> Und neue Lieder
> Tönen darauf.[55]

In the song of these spirits, whom Mephistopheles claims as his own,[56] the first note of Yang resounds. The hymn of the Archangels –

> Die unbegreiflich hohen Werke
> Sind herrlich, wie am ersten Tag –

is now transcended.

So, too, in the Scandinavian universe, when, at Loki's prompting, blind Hoder performs his unwittingly dynamic act and Balder is slain,

Life is blighted and the curse spreads from the gods to the dwelling-place of human beings. The thoughts of men are darkened and confused by the upheaval in nature and the tumult of their own minds, and in their distraction men violate the very principles of life. The bonds of kinship give way to blind passion: brothers fight with one another, kinsmen shed their own blood, no one trusts his fellow; a new age dawns: the age of swords, the age of axes; the ears of men are filled with the din of shields being splintered and of wolves howling over the bodies of the slain.[57]

In the story of the Fall of Man in the Book of Genesis, the dynamic act is Eve's eating of the fruit of the tree of knowledge at the Serpent's prompting; and here the application of the myth to new departures in history is direct. The picture of Adam and Eve in the Garden of Eden is a reminiscence of the Yin-state to which pre-civilizational Man attained in 'the food-gathering phase' of economy, after he had established his ascendancy over all the rest of the flora and fauna of the Earth – the state which is remembered in the Hellenic mythology as 'the times of Cronos'.[58] The Fall, in response to the temptation to taste the fruit of the tree of the knowledge of Good and Evil, symbolizes the acceptance of a challenge to abandon the achieved integration and to venture upon a fresh differentiation out of which another integration may – or may not – arise. The expulsion from the Garden into an unfriendly outer world in which the Woman must bring forth children in sorrow and the Man must eat bread in the sweat of his face, is the ordeal which the acceptance of the Serpent's challenge has entailed. The sexual intercourse between Adam and Eve, which follows, is an act of social creation. It bears fruit in the birth of two sons who impersonate two nascent civilizations: Abel the keeper of sheep and Cain the tiller of the ground.[59]

The equation of civilization with agriculture, and progress with toil, is also to be found in Hellenic literature in the famous line of Hesiod

The price of achievement is toil; and the gods have ruled that you must pay in advance,[60]

which is echoed in Virgil's

It was father Jupiter's will that the farmer's path should not be easy. He gave the lead in the laborious task of turning the sod. He sharpened our human wits with anxiety. He did not tolerate the sloth that would have let his realm decay.[61]

In more general terms and with less poetic imagery, the same story is retold by Origen – a thinker who, in the second century of our era, became one of the fathers of the Christian Church without ceasing to be an Hellenic philosopher:

God, wishing Man's intelligence to be exercised everywhere, in order that it might not remain idle and without a conception of the arts, created Man with needs, in order that sheer need might force him to invent arts for providing himself with food and providing himself with shelter. It was better for those who would not have used their intelligence in seeking after a philosophic knowledge of God that they should be badly enough off to use it in the invention of arts, rather than that they should be well enough off to leave their intelligence altogether uncultivated.[62]

The first stage, then, in the human protagonist's ordeal is a transition from Yin to Yang through a dynamic act – performed by God's creature under temptation from the adversary – which enables God Himself to resume His creative activity. But this progress has to be paid for; and it is not God – a hard master, reaping where He has not sown, and gathering where He has not strawed[63] – but God's servant, the human sower, who pays the price.

The second stage in the human protagonist's ordeal is the crisis. He realizes that his dynamic act, which has reliberated the creative power of his Master and Maker, has set his own feet on a course which is leading him to suffering and death. In an agony of disillusionment and horror, he rebels against the fate which, by his own act, he has brought upon himself for God's gain. The crisis is resolved when he resigns himself consciously to be the instrument of God's will, the tool in God's hands; and this activity through passivity, this victory through defeat, brings on another cosmic change. Just as the dynamic act in the first phase of the ordeal shook the Universe out of Yin into Yang, so the act of resignation in the second phase reverses the rhythm of the Universe – guiding it now from motion towards rest, from storm towards calm, from discord towards harmony, from Yang towards Yin again.

In the cry of an Hellenic poet, we hear the note of agony without a note of resignation to follow:

Would that my lot had not been cast
Among the race that's fifth and last!
Would that I'd died before their day
Or lived when they had passed away![64]

The tragedy rises to a higher level in the Scandinavian vision of Odin, on the eve of Ragnarök, mentally striving to wrest the secret of Fate from the powers that hold it – not in order to save himself alive but for the sake of the Universe of gods and men who look to him, the All Father, to preserve them. In the passion of Jesus, we are initiated into the whole psychological experience.

When Jesus first realizes his destiny, in the course of his last journey from Galilee to Jerusalem, he is master of the situation; and it is his disciples, to whom he communicates his intuition immediately before,[65] and again immediately after,[66] his transfiguration, who are perplexed and dismayed. The agony comes upon him, on the eve of his passion, in the Garden of Gethsemane,[67] and is resolved in the prayer: 'O my Father, if this cup may not pass away from me except I drink it, Thy will be done.'[68] Yet the agony recurs when the sufferer is hanging on the Cross, where the final cry of despair – 'My God, My God, Why hast Thou forsaken me?'[69] – precedes the final words of resignation: 'Father, into Thy hands I commend my spirit',[70] and 'It is finished'.[71]

The same experience of agony and resignation is presented – here in purely psychological terms – in the Epistle to the Romans, where the cry – 'O wretched man that I am! Who shall deliver me from the body of this death?' – is followed by the antiphony: 'I thank God through Jesus Christ our Lord. So then with the mind I myself serve the law of God, but with the flesh the law of sin.'[72]

The same experience, again, is narrated to the Wedding-Guest by the Ancient Mariner, who has brought upon himself the ordeal of 'life-in-death' by his criminal yet none the less dynamic act of shooting the Albatross:

> Alone, alone, all, all alone,
> Alone, on a wide wide sea!
> And never a saint took pity on
> My soul in agony.
> The many men, so beautiful!
> And they all dead did lie:
> And a thousand thousand slimy things
> Lived on; and so did I.

In this ordeal, the curse is lifted when the sufferer resigns himself to the consequences of his act and has a vision of beauty where he had only perceived hideousness so long as his heart had remained hard:

> O happy living things! No tongue
> Their beauty might declare:
> A spring of love gushed from my heart,
> And I blessed them unaware:
> Sure my kind saint took pity on me,
> And I blessed them unaware.
>
> The self-same moment I could pray;
> And from my neck so free
> The Albatross fell off, and sank
> Like lead into the sea.

This is the turning-point in the romantic odyssey. The divine powers which had becalmed the ship now magically waft her to port and bring the villain – or the hero – of the ballad home to his own country.

So, too, Job humbles himself to God at the end of his colloquy with his friends, when Elihu has shown how God is just in His ways and is to be feared because of His great words in which His wisdom is unsearchable, and when the Lord Himself, addressing Job out of the whirlwind, has challenged the sufferer to continue the debate with Him.

Then Job answered the Lord and said:
'Behold, I am vile. What shall I answer thee! I will lay mine hand upon my mouth.
'Once have I spoken, but I will not answer; yea, twice, but I will proceed no further. . . .
'I know that Thou canst do everything, and that no thought can be withholden from Thee. . . .
'Therefore have I uttered that I understood not – things too wonderful for me, which I knew not. . . .
'I have heard of Thee by the hearing of the ear, but now mine eye seeth thee.
'Wherefore I abhor myself, and repent in dust and ashes.'[73]

In this Syriac poem, the psychology is crude. The resignation comes, not through a spiritual intuition in the soul, but through a physical manifestation to the eye of God's irresistible force. In Goethe's version of the drama, the sequence of agony and resignation holds its place as the crisis and the culmination of the plot – Gretchen passes through it in the last scene of Part I[74] and Faust, in his turn, at the climax of Part II[75] – but the ethos is transformed beyond recognition.

In the scene in Gretchen's prison, in the grey dawn of her last day, Mephistopheles seeks to take advantage of Gretchen's agony in order to induce her to forgo her salvation by escaping her doom. It seems the easiest enterprise that

REBELLION TO RESIGNATION

73 'Let the day perish wherein I was born.' Job's inability to understand God's purpose in his ordeal moves him to deny his faith in God's goodness.

74 'He that reproveth God, let him answer it.' God answers Job out of the whirlwind. Watercolours by William Blake.

he has yet essayed. His victim is distraught with horror at the imagination of what lies before her; it is the hour at which human vitality is at its lowest ebb; the pains of death are imminent; the prospect of escape is offered suddenly and unexpectedly; and it is Gretchen's lover Faust himself who implores her to flee with him through the magically opened prison doors. Yet Gretchen, raving in her agony, seems insensible to Faust's appeal, until at last Mephistopheles, in his impatience, intervenes himself. That is the moment of the tempter's defeat; for Gretchen, recognizing him for what he is, awakes from her frenzied trance and takes refuge in the judgment of God – no longer rooted to the spot in a nightmare like the Aeschylean Cassandra, but deliberately rejecting, like the Platonic Socrates, a possibility of escape of which she is fully aware:

Margarete. Was steigt aus dem Boden herauf?
           Der! Der! Schick' ihn fort!
           Was will er an dem heiligen Ort?
           Er will mich!
Faust.   Du sollst leben!
Margarete. Gericht Gottes! Dir hab' ich mich übergeben!
Mephistopheles (zu Faust). Komm! Komm! Ich lasse dich mit ihr
           im Stich.
Margarete. Dein bin ich, Vater! Rette mich!
           Ihr Engel! Ihr heiligen Scharen,
           Lagert euch umher, mich zu bewahren!
           Heinrich! Mir graut's vor dir.
Mephistopheles. Sie ist gerichtet!
Stimme (von oben).   Ist gerettet!
Mephistopheles (zu Faust).   Her zu mir!
        (Verschwindet mit Faust).
Stimme (von innen, verhallend). Heinrich! Heinrich![76]

In the third stage, the reversal of the cosmic rhythm from Yang towards Yin, which was initiated in the second stage, is carried to completion. At the climax of Ragnarök, when Thor has met the Dragon and Odin the Wolf,

'The sun is darkened, the earth sinks back into the waves, stars rain down, and the flames leap up and lick the heavens.' But then 'the barking' of the Wolf 'is heard for the last time as the world-fire flickers down.' And 'when the roar and the voices are stilled, the earth once more rises out of the sea in evergreen freshness; brooks leap down the hills; . . . The Gods meet among self-sown fields, they call to mind the tale of deeds and former wisdom, and in the grass before their feet the golden tables are found lying. A new hall rises golden-roofed and fairer than the Sun. Here a race of true-hearted men will dwell and rejoice in their hearts' desire. Then from above descends the mighty one, all powerful. The dusky dragon flies past, brushing the ground with his wings weighted down by dead bodies; he sinks into the abyss and disappears.'[77]

In this new creation, which the ordeal of one of God's creatures has enabled God to achieve, the sufferer himself returns to a state of peace and harmony and bliss on a higher level than the state which he left behind when he responded to the tempter's challenge. In the Book of Job, the achievement is startlingly crude – the Lord convinces Job that He is answerable for His acts to no man – and the restoration is naïvely material: 'the Lord blessed the latter end of Job more than his beginning' by giving him fairer daughters than those that he had lost and twice as many

sheep and camels and oxen and asses.[78] In the New Testament, the agony and resignation and passion of Jesus achieve the Redemption of Man and are followed by the Redeemer's resurrection and ascension. In the Scandinavian mythology, Odin returns to life after hanging upon a tree, and has keener vision in his one eye than he had before he plucked out his other eye and cast it from him as the purchase-price of wisdom.[79] In Goethe's *Faust*, the last scene of the second part, in which the Virgin Goddess, with her train of penitents, grants an epiphany to the pilgrims who have scaled the rugged mountain to its summit, is the counterpart of the Prologue in Heaven with which the first part of the play opens. The two scenes correspond, as, in the Christian version of the myth, Man's state of blessedness after the Redemption corresponds to his state of innocence before the Fall. The cosmic rhythm has come round, full circle, from Yin through Yang to Yin; but the latter Yin-state differs from the former with the difference of spring from autumn. The works of creation, which the Arch-angels hymned[80] and which Faust's curse shattered,[81] arise in splendour again, to be hymned by the Pater Profundus;[82] but this time they are in the tender shoot instead of being ripe for the sickle. Through Faust's dynamic act and Gretchen's act of resignation, the Lord has been enabled to make all things new; and, in this new creation, the human protagonists in the divine drama have their part. Gretchen, whose salvation had been proclaimed by the voice from Heaven at the dawn of her last day on Earth, appears,

75 CONSUMMATION Angels raise Faust's soul to Heaven. A twentieth-century interpretation by Max Beckmann.

transfigured as Una Poenitentium, in Mary's train, and the *visio beatifica* is vouchsafed to Faust, who rises to join her, transfigured as Doctor Marianus.

> Das Unzulängliche,
> Hier wird's Ereignis;
> Das Unbeschreibliche,
> Hier ist's getan.[83]

Thus the manifestation of God as a hard master proves not to have been the ultimate truth. The ordeal of God's creature appears in retrospect as a revelation, not of God's callousness or cruelty, but of His love.

> So ist es die allmächtige Liebe
> Die alles bildet, alles hegt.[84]

'For whom the Lord loveth He chasteneth, and scourgeth every son whom He receiveth.' – '*Pathei mathos*'.[85]

Finally, the sufferer triumphant serves as a pioneer. 'Strait is the gate and narrow is the way which leadeth unto life, and few there be that find it.'[86] The human protagonist in the divine drama not only serves God by enabling Him to renew His creation, but also serves his fellow-men by pointing a way for others to follow.[87] Job's intercession averts the Lord's wrath from Job's friends.[88] Gretchen's intercession wins for Faust the *visio beatifica*.[89] When Jesus first foreshadows his ordeal to his disciples, he proclaims, 'If any man will come after me, let him deny himself and take up his cross and follow me',[90] and on the eve of his passion he adds, 'And I, if I be lifted up from the Earth, will draw all men unto me.'[91]

By the light of mythology, we have gained some insight into the nature of challenges and responses. We have come to see that creation is the outcome of an encounter, or – to retranslate the imagery of myths into the terminology of science – that genesis is a function of interaction. We shall now regard race and environment in a new light and shall place a different interpretation upon the phenomena. We shall no longer be on the look-out for some simple cause of the geneses of civilizations which can be demonstrated always and everywhere to produce an identical effect. We shall no longer be surprised if, in the production of civilizations, the same race, or the same environment, appears to be fruitful in one instance and sterile in another. Indeed, we shall not be surprised to find this phenomenon of inconstancy and variability in the responses produced, on different occasions, by one and the same challenge, even when that challenge is an interaction between the same race and the same environment under the same conditions. However scientifically exact the identity between two or more situations may be, we shall not expect the respective outcomes of these situations to conform with one another in the same degree of exactitude, or even in any degree at all. In fact, we shall no longer make the scientific postulate of the uniformity of Nature, which we rightly made so long as we were thinking of our problem in scientific terms as a function of the play of inanimate forces. We shall be prepared now to recognize, *a priori*, that, even if we were exactly acquainted with all the racial, environmental, or other data that are capable of being formulated scientifically, we should not be able to predict the outcome of the interaction between the forces which these data represent. We

should be unable because, on this plane of action, the 'forces' are persons.

The unpredictability of the outcomes of encounters between persons is a familiar datum of experience. A military expert cannot predict the outcome of a battle or a campaign from an 'inside knowledge' of the dispositions and resources of both the opposing general staffs, or a bridge expert the outcome of a game or a rubber from a similar knowledge of all the cards in every hand. In both these analogies, 'inside knowledge' is not sufficient to enable its possessor to predict results with any exactness or assurance, because it is not the same thing as complete knowledge. There is one thing which must remain an unknown quantity to the best-informed onlooker, because it is beyond the knowledge of the combatants, or the players, themselves; and their ignorance of this quantity makes calculation impossible, because it is the most important term in the equation which the would-be calculator has to solve. This unknown quantity is the reaction of the actors to the ordeal when it actually comes. 'Physical causes only operate through the hidden principles which play a part in forming our spirit and our character.'[92] A general may have an accurate knowledge of his own manpower and munition-power and almost as good a knowledge of his opponent's; he may also have a shrewd idea of his opponent's plans; and, in the light of all this knowledge, he may have laid his own plans to his own best advantage. He cannot, however, foreknow how his opponent, or any of the other men who compose the force under his opponent's command, will behave, in action, when the campaign is opened and the battle joined; he cannot foreknow how his own men will behave; he cannot foreknow how he will behave himself. Yet these psychological momenta, which are inherently impossible to weigh and measure and therefore to estimate scientifically in advance, are the very forces which actually decide the issue when the encounter takes place. The military genius is the general who repeatedly succeeds in divining the unpredictable by guesswork or intuition; and most of the historic military geniuses – commanders of such diverse temperament and outlook as Cromwell and Napoleon – have recognized clearly that manpower and munition-power and intelligence and strategy are not the talismans that have brought them their victories. After estimating all the measurable and manageable factors at their full value – insisting that 'God is on the side of the big battalions', that 'God helps those who help themselves', that you should 'trust in God and keep your powder dry' – they have admitted frankly that, when all is said and done, victory cannot be predicted by thought or commanded by will because it comes in the end from a source to which neither thought nor will have access. If they have been religious-minded, they have cried 'Thanks be to God which giveth us the victory';[93] if they have been sceptical-minded, they have ascribed their victories – in superstitious terms – to the operations of Fortune or to the ascendancy of their personal star; but, whatever language they have used, they have testified to the reality of the same experience: the experience that the outcome of an encounter cannot be predicted and has no appearance of being predetermined, but arises, in the likeness of a new creation, out of the encounter itself.

MAN'S VICTORY

76 The abrupt transition from irrigated fields to arid desert, in the Northern Sudan,
indicates the supreme effort required to wrest cultivation from wasteland.

14 The arduousness of excellence

IN THE preceding chapter we decided that the cause of the geneses of civilizations must be sought in a pattern of interaction which we have called 'challenge-and-response'. In contrast to the effect of a cause, the response to a challenge is not invariable and is therefore not predictable. An identical challenge may evoke a creative response in some cases but not in others.

What are the situations in which creative responses have actually been evoked by challenges on the evidence of past human experience? If we turn to examine the range of stimuli to which human communities have been exposed, we shall not be surprised to find ourselves rejecting the popular view that civilizations tend to be generated in environments which offer unusually easy conditions of life to Man. The fallacy of this view springs from a failure to see in the genesis of a civilization an act of creation involving a process of change in time. The final appearance, as it looks when the drama of genesis has been played to the finish, is thoughtlessly equated with the primitive appearance of the same scene before it was taken in hand by Man to serve as the stage for a great human action. For example,

we are accustomed to regard Egypt as a paradise, as the most fertile country in the World, where, if we but scratch the soil and scatter seed, we have only to await and gather the harvest. The Greeks spoke of Egypt as the most fit place for the first generations of men, for there, they said, food was always ready at hand, and it took no labour to secure an abundant supply.[1]

But, as the author goes on to say,

there can be no doubt that the Egypt of today is a very different place from the Egypt of pre-agricultural times. There has been a great, but gradual, change in the physical condition of the whole country. . . . The agricultural Egypt of modern times is as much a gift of Man as it is of the Nile.[2]

In fact, of course, the fallacious popular view entirely overlooks the stupendous human effort involved, not only in once transforming the prehistoric jungle-swamp of the Lower Nile valley into the fertile Land of Egypt, but also in perpetually preventing this magnificent but precarious work of men's hands from reverting to its primeval state of Nature, and in maintaining it to the present day as 'a going concern'. The virgin wildernesses of the Bahr-al-Jabal in the Upper Nile valley still testify today to the feat performed further north by the pioneers who, some five thousand years ago, succeeded in transforming similar tracts of inhospitable jungle-swamp into an ordered network of dikes and fields, where soil and water are subject to human control for the service of human purposes. A geographer may object that this particular comparison is invalidated by the difference in scale between the two areas here in question;[3] but he will surely be persuaded by the spectacle of places where a recalcitrant Nature, once tamed by human heroism, has broken loose again and actually reasserted her old ascendancy over some site that was once

77 Sustaining the effort: a chain of water-holes forms a lifeline for Man in the desert.

the homeland of a civilization or the scene of some other signal human achievement. We will try to clinch our argument by reviewing some instances of such reversions, where the primeval state of Nature and the subsequent works of Man and the eventual reversion of Nature to her primeval state are all displayed on one spot like geological strata.

One remarkable example is the present state of the homeland of the Mayan Civilization in Mexico. Far from the works of the Mayas being 'going concerns' today, their sole surviving monuments are the ruins of the immense and magnificently decorated public buildings which now stand in the depths of the tropical forest, remote from any present human habitations. The forest has literally swallowed them up, like some sylvan boa-constrictor, and is now dismembering them at its leisure: prising their fine-hewn, close-laid stones apart with its writhing roots and tendrils. But these masterpieces of Mayan architecture which are now being strangled by the forest must have been built as works of supererogation with the surplus of an energy which, for leagues around, had already transformed the forest into fruitful fields. They were the trophies of Man's victory over Nature; and, at the moment when they were raised, the retreating fringe of the vanquished and routed sylvan enemy was perhaps barely visible on the horizon. To the human beings who looked out over the world from those vantage-points then, the victory of Man over Nature must have seemed utterly secure; and the transitoriness of human achievements and the vanity of human wishes are poignantly exposed by the ultimate return of the forest. Yet that is not the most significant lesson to be learnt from the present state of Copan or Tikal or Palenque. The ruins

NATURE'S REVENGE

78 A temple at Angkor submerged in the ever-encroaching jungle.

speak still more eloquently of the intensity of the struggle with the physical environment which the creators of the Mayan Civilization must have waged victoriously in their day. In her very revenge, tropical Nature testifies unwillingly to the courage and the vigour of the men who once, if only for a season, succeeded in putting her to flight and keeping her at bay.

The creeper-covered ruins of Angkor teach us the same lesson; and the no less arduous feat of conquering the parched plains of Ceylon for agriculture is commemorated in the breached bunds and overgrown floors of the tanks which were once constructed on the wet side of the hill-country, on a colossal scale, by the Sinhalese converts to the Indic religion of the Hinayana. These missionaries of the Indic Civilization in Ceylon once achieved the *tour de force* of compelling the monsoon-smitten central highlands to give water and life to the wide plains below, which Nature had condemned to lie parched and desolate.

It is a remarkable fact of Ceylon's history that it was in the flat northern part of the island, the dry zone, that [her] early civilisation flourished. . . . A remarkable system of irrigation was developed by the Sinhalese over many generations – a very astounding and admirable achievement in early civil engineering.

The irrigation system in a flat country must, of course, be based on the conservation of water in reservoirs and the construction of channels to supply water to the maximum possible acreage around them. The ancient Sinhalese constructed reservoirs with remarkable skill. Some of them were of considerable size, great artificial lakes, and many of these 'tanks' . . . were skilfully connected with each other to form a vast irrigation system. Modern irrigation engineers have evinced much admiration for the way in which the ancient Sinhalese succeeded in their irrigation schemes, which are far from easy, even to their modern counterparts. . . . The construction of these early irrigation systems was a remarkable practical feat. They required constant attention, and their construction and maintenance must be regarded as the leading feature of early Sinhalese economic life. . . .

When it is remembered that, for example, the tank known as Minneriya had (and has) a bund several miles long and about 50 feet high, it becomes clear that a very large labour force must have been employed, and very carefully organized. This particular tank is 4,560 acres in extent when full of water. . . . It was fed by a canal 25 miles in length, dug in the fourth century [A.D.]. Another canal, which brought water to Anuradhapura, was 54 miles long, and irrigated 180 square miles; for the first 17 miles of this canal the gradient is only 6 inches to the mile, which aptly illustrates the ability of the irrigation engineers of those times.[4]

But this fertile countryside survived in its man-made state only so long as Man did not relax his grip upon his hostile physical environment. When the internecine wars of the eleventh century of the Christian Era destroyed the tank-building dynasty and checked the continuous human exertions which had been required to produce and maintain this miraculous transformation in the face of Nature, those irrigated and cultivated and populated plains relapsed into their primeval barrenness – a state which no man has since aspired or dared to alter. Can we watch Nature flaunting her ultimate triumph over these works of Man, and still doubt that the conditions in which they were performed were not unusually easy but unusually difficult?

79 Monument of men's former victory over the forest: stele at Yaxchilan.

80 'A country of skin and bones' – denuded landscape at Cape Sounion, in Attica.

15 The stimulus of hard countries

Now THAT we have found that a harsh environment is not inimical to civilization but rather the contrary, are we warranted in formulating the further proposition that the stimulus towards civilization grows stronger in proportion as the environment grows more difficult? Let us put this to the test by reviewing the evidence empirically, first making a distinction between the stimuli presented by the physical and by the human environment. We shall begin by comparing physical environments which present different degrees of difficulty.

The Aegean area, the birthplace of two successive civilizations, presents unusual difficulties which become fully apparent only when the area is viewed in its geographical setting, against the foil provided by the regions round about. I can testify to this from personal experience. On my first visit to the Aegean, I came and went by sea, and the abrupt transition from the terrain of England to that of Greece had the effect of dulling my imaginative appreciation of the contrast. On my second visit, I again arrived by sea, but I broke my stay in Athens by making several reconnaissances into regions just outside the Aegean area. First I went to Izmir (Smyrna) and into the interior of Anatolia; next I went to Istanbul (Constantinople) and again into Anatolia from that quarter; and then I went to Thessalonike (Salonica) and into Macedonia. Finally, I returned to England overland, travelling by rail from Istanbul to Calais. In the course of these expeditions, I found myself on each occasion travelling out of country that was bare, barren, rocky, mountainous, and broken into fragments by the estranging sea, into country that was greener and richer and softer, in which the mountain-ranges were replaced by rolling hills, and the sea-filled gulfs and straits by broad cultivable river valleys. The cumulative effect of these successive contrasts was very powerful, for they showed the Aegean area in its true colours as a region of unusual difficulty by comparison not only with England but with every region adjoining it. In this light I realized the deep meaning of the words which Herodotus puts into the mouth of the Spartan Damaratus: 'Hellas has a foster-sister Poverty who never leaves her; but she has brought in a guest in the shape of Virtue, the child of Wisdom and Law; and by Virtue's aid Hellas keeps Poverty at bay and Servitude likewise.'[1]

Similar contrasts in the physical environment, capped by corresponding contrasts in the local variety of civilization, may be observed in the interior of the Aegean area itself. For instance, if one travels from Athens along either the railway or the speedway for cars which eventually lead through Thessalonike into the heart of Europe, one passes on the first stage of the journey through a stretch of country which gives to Central or Western European eyes an anticipatory glimpse of their own familiar scenery. After climbing slowly round the eastern flanks of Mount Parnes through a typical Aegean landscape of stunted pines and jagged limestone crags, the traveller is astonished to find himself running into a lowland country of gently undulating deep-soiled ploughlands. This unexpected landscape is a 'sport'; in the lifetime of the Hellenic Civilization it was called Boeotia, and in Hellenic minds the word 'Boeotian' had a quite distinctive connotation. It stood for an ethos that was rustic, stolid, unimaginative, brutal – an ethos out of harmony with the prevailing genius of the Hellenic culture. The discord between the Boeotian ethos and Hellenism was accentuated by the fact that just round the corner of Parnes lay Attica, 'the Hellas of Hellas': the country whose ethos was the quintessence of Hellenism lying cheek by jowl with the country whose ethos affected normal Hellenic sensibilities like a jarring note.

The point of interest for our present purpose is that this profound cultural contrast was geographically coincident with an equally striking contrast in the physical environment. For Attica is 'the Hellas of Hellas' not only in her soul but in her physique. She stands to the other countries of the Aegean as those Aegean countries stand to the regions around. If you approach Greece by sea from the west, you may flatter yourself that your eye has grown accustomed to the Greek landscape – beautiful and forbidding at once – before the view is shut out as you pass through the deep cutting of the Corinth Canal. Yet when your ship emerges from the Isthmus at last, you will still be shocked by an austerity of landscape in the Saronic Gulf for which the scenery on the other side of the Isthmus has not fully prepared you; and this austerity attains its climax when you round the corner of Salamis and see the land of Attica spread before your eyes up to the summits of Pentelicus and Hymettus.

In Attica, with her abnormally light and stony soil, the process of denudation by erosion, which Boeotia has escaped down to this day, was already complete in Plato's time, as witness his own account of it.

Contemporary Attica may accurately be described as a mere relic of the original country. . . . In consequence of the successive violent deluges which have occurred within the past nine thousand years . . . there has been a constant movement of soil away from the high altitudes. . . . What remains of her substance is like the skeleton of a body emaciated by disease, as compared with her original relief. All the rich soft soil has moulted away, leaving a country of skin and bones.[2]

What did the Athenians do with their poor country when she had lost the buxomness of her Boeotian youth? We know that they did the things which made Athens 'the education of Hellas'. When the pastures of Attica dried up and her ploughlands wasted away, her people turned to devices of their own: olive-cultivation and the exploitation of the subsoil. To make a living from the produce of his olive-groves, the Athenian had to pack his Attic oil into jars and ship it overseas and exchange it on the Scythian market for grain – necessities which called into existence the Attic potteries and the Attic merchant marine, and also, since international trade requires a money economy, the Attic silver-mines. All these things together – exports, industries, merchant ships, and money – required the protection and defrayed the upkeep of a navy. Thus the

81 Harvesting olives, the principal export crop; from a fifth-century vase.

82 Merchant ship, vehicle of Athenian trade, as depicted on a kylix of the sixth century BC.

83 Enterprise: Arkesilas, King of Cyrene, supervises the weighing and packing of wool for the overseas trade. Cyrene was one of many Greek colonies founded in Asia Minor in the seventh century BC.

84 Passivity: a stolid Boeotian figurine of a mourning woman.

erosion of their soil in Attica stimulated the Athenians to acquire the command of the sea from one end of the Aegean to the other, and beyond; and therewith the riches that they had lost were recovered a hundredfold. But these riches grasped through the sea – riches beyond the dream of the Boeotian ploughman whose deep-soiled fields had never failed him – were merely the economic foundation for a political and artistic and intellectual culture which made Athens 'the education of Hellas', and 'Attic salt' the antithesis of Boeotian animality. On the political plane, the Athenian industrial and seafaring population constituted the electorate of the Athenian democracy, while Attic trade and sea-power provided the framework for that international association of Aegean city-states which took shape in the Delian League under Athenian auspices. On the artistic plane, the prosperity of the Attic potteries gave the vase-painter the opportunity for creating a new form of beauty; and the extinction of the Attic forests compelled Athenian architects to wrestle with the medium of stone and so create the Parthenon instead of resting content with common log-built structures. And finally the Athenians were exposed to all the foreign intellectual and cultural currents that washed ashore with their merchants and mariners; the city gathered the whole of contemporary Hellenic culture to itself in order to transmit it to posterity seasoned with 'Attic salt' and ennobled by the Attic impress.

The contrast between Boeotia and Attica is not the only illustration offered by the Aegean area in the age of the Hellenic Civilization. Boeotia had another neighbour in Chalcis, a city facing the mainland on the island of Euboea. In the hinterland behind Chalcis lay the Lelantine Plain, a ploughland no less rich than Boeotia itself; but unfortunately – or fortunately – for the Chalcidians the plain was narrow, and hence their farmers, brought up short in their search for new land against the precipitous flanks of the towering peak of Dirphys, were stimulated to seek their fresh ploughlands abroad. Sailing out into the Aegean, they founded a new Chalcidice on the coasts of Thrace to the north and east, and another in Sicily to the south and west. Of course, the Chalcidians' response to the challenge of land-shortage in their native Euboea is not to be compared with the feats to which the erosion of Attica stimulated the Athenians; for, where the latter achieved a qualitative transformation of their economy, the Chalcidians performed the merely quantitative act of adding field to field. Yet Chalcis too made a mark – albeit a fainter mark than the Athenian – upon Hellenic history, for it was through her farmer-settlers overseas that the barbarians of Macedonia and Latium were drawn into the orbit of the Hellenic culture. In their degree the Chalcidians reacted to the prick of necessity's spur, while comfortable Boeotia cared for none of these things.

The enlargement of the area of the Hellenic World *c.* 725–525 BC, in which the Chalcidians played this prominent part, offers us another celebrated illustration of our theme through the contrast between the two Greek colonies of Calchedon and Byzantium, which were planted respectively in 685 and 668 BC on the Asiatic and on the European side of the southern entrance to the Bosphorus. Herodotus tells us that, about a century and a half after the foundation of these two cities, the Persian statesman Megabazus passed that way and, hearing that Calchedon had been planted seventeen years before Byzantium, he nicknamed Calchedon 'the city of the blind'; by this he meant that it was inconceivable that men of vision should have deliberately chosen to found their settlement on the patently worse of two available sites.[3] But his observation was epigrammatic rather than acute; for it is easy to be wise after the event, and by Megabazus's day the respective destinies of the two cities were already manifest. Calchedon had remained an ordinary Greek transmarine agricultural settlement, no different from scores of others planted round the Mediterranean coasts. Meanwhile, Byzantium was already growing into one of the busiest ports of the Hellenic World, and was fairly launched on the career which was to culminate in her becoming the ultimate capital of an Orthodox Christian universal state. Thus, by Megabazus's time any comparison between the respective advantages of Byzantium and Calchedon would naturally turn upon their respective facilities as ports; and on this test the eligibility of Byzantium was incomparably the greater. Byzantium not only possessed the natural harbour of the Golden Horn, which had no counterpart on the opposite coastline where Calchedon stood. More than that, the set of the current which comes down the Bosphorus from the Black Sea favours any vessel trying to make the Golden Horn from either direction, while it impedes any vessel heading for the open beach of Calchedon. The founders of Calchedon would have been blind men indeed if, in the face of these twin facts, they had deliberately chosen their location in preference to Byzantium as the site for a port.

In reality, of course, the founders of Calchedon made their historic choice on a quite different consideration; as they approached the coasts of the Bosphorus they looked at the landscape and chose their site with eyes that were not blind at all, but were simply farmers' eyes and not mariners'. They planted their city on a sheltered strip of fertile coast, and settled down to raise the crops that they had always raised at home. For their purpose they could not have chosen better, and we may picture the founders of Byzantium – arriving from Greece seventeen years later in search of new land for their own ploughs – cursing the Calchedonians for their perspicacity and themselves for their tardiness as they turned away from this smiling Bithynian riviera, now crowned by Calchedon's walls, towards the much less inviting opposite coast of Thrace. Moreover, these unfortunate late comers settled down to till the soil of their little peninsula only to see the fruits of their labours carried off systematically year after year by the marauding Thracian tribes of the hinterland.[4] The Byzantine settlers found that they were caught in an interminable and insoluble war with a barbarian adversary who was both too numerous and powerful to be beaten off by force of arms, and too voracious and determined to be bought off with tribute.

After all, then, the Calchedonians' vision and perspicacity would seem to be vindicated by the calamitous fate which met the Byzantines. Yet this is not the true moral of the story: the true moral is that, when the Byzantines found themselves perpetually subject to this prohibitive handicap on land, they were stimulated to turn to the sea, and to indemnify themselves for their ruinous losses as farmers by making handsome profits as merchants and mariners. Under this powerful stimulus, to which the prudent Calchedonian farmers were never exposed, the Byzantines made the most of their straits and discovered that the 'Golden Horn' was a cornucopia. Byzantium, occupying a site midway between the economic foci of the Aegean and the Black Sea, and dominating the narrow passage through which all trade must pass, held the key to the prosperity of the Hellenic World – a guardianship from which she learnt to derive the greatest possible wealth and influence. Thus the vast divergence between the destinies of Byzantium and Calchedon is not explained by Megabazus's epigram. It was not the blindness of the Calchedonians but the ferocity of the barbarian hordes that made Byzantium's fortune, for she had been taught a lesson by necessity which the sheltered Calchedonians were never even set to learn.

If we turn now to the Syriac World, we shall find a similar correlation between the relative distinction achieved by its inhabitants, and the relative physical difficulty of the environments in which they found themselves at the end of the post-Mycenaean *Völkerwanderung*. The Syriac Civilization has above all three great feats to its credit. It discovered the Atlantic Ocean; it invented an alphabetic system of writing which is the ancestor of all systems in use today except the Chinese, Japanese, and Korean; and it arrived at a particular conception of God which is common alike to Judaism, Zoroastrianism, Christianity, and Islam, and alien alike from the Egyptiac, Sumero-Akkadian, Indic, and Hellenic veins of religious thought and feeling. But in the progress of the Syriac Civilization towards these achievements it was not the favoured Arameans of Damascus or of the fertile Orontes valley who took the lead, nor yet those tribes of Israel who halted east of Jordan on the rich pastures of Gilead.[5] More remarkable, the primacy in the Syriac World was not retained by the Philistine Sea Peoples, who came not as barbarians but as the heirs of an Aegean Civilization, and took as their prize the broad maritime plain from Ekron to Gaza. The discovery of the Atlantic was not made by these Lords of the Plain of Shephelah, whose ancestral seafaring tradition became buried, with their seed-corn, in the deep ploughlands of their new home. When they came to feel the need to expand, they turned their backs on the sea to conquer the arid lowlands of Beersheba and the well-watered valleys of Esdraelon and Jezreel, meeting their fate at last when they challenged the hill-tribesmen of Israel and Judah for the mastery of Palestine. The discovery of the Atlantic, and the invention of the consonantal alphabet, was left to the Phoenicians, a remnant of the native Canaanite people of Syria who had retreated during the invasions into the rugged middle quarter of the coast. Phoenicia presents a remarkable physical contrast to the Shephelah chosen by the Philistine settlers in their passage to the south. On this part of the coast, there is no broad plain and no gradation between littoral and hill-country; the mountain-range of Lebanon rises almost sheer out of the sea, grudging the coast-dwellers any foothold of their own and cutting them off from the plains of the interior. Thanks to the unattractiveness of their homeland, the Phoenicians survived the Philistine incursion into Syria; and thanks to its

85, 86 The Phoenician genius expressed itself in the revolutionary invention of the alphabet; and in ships like this Phoenician sailors explored and colonized the Western Mediterranean and the Atlantic coast of North Africa.

ungenerous crags they actually took over from their new neighbours that tradition of long-distance navigation which the Philistines now discarded. While the Philistines were browsing on Shephelah like sheep in clover and were moving inland in search of fresh pastures, the Phoenicians launched outwards from their inhospitable coast into the open sea, and won a second home for the Syriac Civilization in the western basin of the Mediterranean and on the coasts of the Ocean beyond.

The physical discovery of the Atlantic, however, is surpassed as a feat of human prowess by the spiritual discovery of monotheism; and this achievement was contributed by a Syriac community that had been stranded by the *Völkerwanderung* in a physical environment which was still less inviting than the Phoenician coast. Washed up on the empty hills of Ephraim and Judah, the Israelite pioneers of the Nomadic Hebrew tribes transformed themselves from wandering stock-breeders into sedentary husbandmen, scratching a sparse living from the weak and stony soil of the deforested heights. Such was the obscurity of this shabby clan of peasants that, even as late as the fifth century B C, when all the great Prophets of Israel had said their say, the name of Israel was unknown to Herodotus and the Land of Israel still masked by *Palaistine*[6] in the Herodotean panorama. Yet, in the power of their spiritual understanding, the Israelites surpassed the military prowess of the Philistines and the maritime prowess of the Phoenicians. In the barren and land-locked highlands of Israel there was immanent a divine inspiration which made this wild and unnoticed country a means of grace to those who settled there, and a crucible for the forging of one of Mankind's greatest spiritual treasures.

87 'This is God's hill, in which it pleaseth him to dwell.' The home of the Israelites: desert between Jerusalem and Jericho, with the mountains of Moab in the distance.

16 The stimulus of penalizations

WHEN WE PASS from the physical to the human environment, we find that, *mutatis mutandis*, the phenomena are the same. A social group which is penalized, for example, by exclusion from certain fields of activity, is apt to respond to the challenge of discrimination by concentrating its energies on other fields and developing an exceptional proficiency in these. Penalization can thus have an effect as stimulating as that produced by a physical challenge; we can illustrate this by examining the reactions of different groups to the challenge of religious discrimination.

The disabilities suffered by Nonconformist Protestants in the Western World offer an example of the penalization of a group which belonged to the same society as its oppressors. In England, after the Restoration of AD 1660, the Dissenting Protestant denominations were subjected to a galling though not wholly intolerable discrimination, and this had the effect of stimulating them to distinguish themselves in the professions which they were permitted to practise: the members of the Society of Friends in industry and banking, for example, and other Dissenters and Nonconformists in retail trade. These Protestants were able to exist and prosper within their own society; but the more rigorous persecution of the English Puritans earlier in the same century, or of the American Mormons two hundred years later, stimulated each of these sects into reacting with proportionately greater vigour. Finding no room for themselves in the same country as their persecutors, they each in their own day went out into the wilderness, with no more support than their own courage and vision, to establish their ideal commonwealths on virgin soil; and thus they acted as pioneers of their civilization as well as guardians of their faith.

Another situation arises when the respective adherents of the penalized and the privileged denominations belong to two different civilizations which are both 'going concerns'. This can be illustrated from the *ancien régime* of the Ottoman Empire, where we find an Orthodox Christian Society incorporated in the alien body of a Muslim universal state. Here the subject Christians were excluded from the practice of government, from the military and 'liberal' professions, and, to some extent, from the ownership and even from the cultivation of land. The effect of this severe discrimination was to stimulate the penalized Christians into learning to excel in the humbler trades, which remained open for Christian practitioners. Among these Greek Christian inhabitants of Constantinople, one coterie – the so-called 'Phanariots' who lived in the northwest corner of the city within the Theodosian Wall – were stimulated by the challenge of penalization to such a degree that they actually rose to be the virtual partners and potential supplanters of the 'Osmanlis themselves in the political administration and control of the Ottoman Empire. Under the aegis of the re-established Orthodox Patriarchate, the Phanar ghetto became a rallying-point for Greek-speaking Orthodox Christians; and the Phanariot minority developed two special accomplishments. As merchants on the grand scale, their commercial relations with the Western World gave them a first-hand familiarity with Western customs and Western languages. As managers of the Ecumenical Patriarchate's affairs, they acquired a wide practice and close understanding of Ottoman administration, since the Patriarch was the official intermediary between the Padishah and all his Orthodox Christian subjects, not merely those who were under the Ecumenical Patriarch's ecclesiastical jurisdiction. These two accomplishments made the fortune of the Phanariots when, in the long-drawn-out conflict between the Ottoman Empire and the Western World, the tide definitely turned against the 'Osmanlis after their second unsuccessful siege of Vienna in AD 1682–83.

The military decline of the 'Osmanlis confronted them with two formidable problems. They now had to negotiate at the conference-table with the Western Powers whom they could no longer defeat in the field; and for the first time they had to consider the feelings of their Orthodox Christian subjects, whom they could no longer be sure of holding down by force. In other words, the Ottoman Empire could no longer dispense with skilled diplomatists and skilled administrators; and the necessary fund of experience, of which the 'Osmanlis found themselves destitute in the hour of their need, was opportunely placed at their disposal by the Phanariots. In consequence, the 'Osmanlis were constrained to disregard the precedents and tamper with the principles of their own régime by waiving, for the Phanariots, the condition that non-Muslim aspirants to a career in the Ottoman public service must become converts to Islam. The Ottoman government had taken the first steps in this direction even before the disaster of 1683 had forced their hand. Between 1669 and 1716, the Phanariots were given the monopoly of four high offices of state which had become key positions in the new political situation. In the course of the next hundred years the political power of the Phanariots was steadily enhanced by the influence and patronage which these offices carried with them, and by the increasing need, in the face of intensified Western pressure, for the services of the one element in the Ottoman Empire which could cope with 'the Western Question'. By the end of the eighteenth century it had begun to look as if the Phanariots were firmly set on a path which would eventually lead them to a senior partnership in the Ottoman firm.

In the event, however, the Phanariots failed to achieve their 'manifest destiny';[1] they forfeited their prize because they allowed their energies to be diverted from the peaceful penetration of the Ottoman state to the violent road of nationalist revolt. The Greeks were the first to succumb to the virus of a Western nationalism that began to permeate the Ottoman Empire towards the end of the eighteenth century, and between the outbreak of the French Revolution and the outbreak of the Greek War of Independence (*gerebatur* AD 1821–29) they fell under the spell of two incompatible aspirations. They had not given up the old

88 Christians in a Muslim state: Eastern Orthodox Christian prelate; a sixteenth-century Turkish drawing made for a member of the Phanariot community in Constantinople.

Phanariot ambition of entering into the whole heritage of the 'Osmanlis and keeping the Ottoman Empire intact under Greek instead of Turkish management; and at the same time they had conceived the new ambition of establishing a sovereign independent national state of their own – a state that could be no more than a gobbet of the Empire's dismembered carcass. The incompatibility of the two aims was conclusively demonstrated in 1821, when simultaneous attempts were made by the Phanariot Prince Ypselandes to make himself master of the Ottoman Empire, and by the Maniot chieftain Mavromikhalis to carve out an independent Greece. The resort to arms spelled the ruin of the Phanariot aspirations in any case, for it produced an electric effect upon the 'Osmanlis. The reed on which they had been leaning for more than a century had pierced their hand;[2] and their fury at this betrayal nerved them to break the treacherous staff in pieces and to stand again at all costs on their own feet. In 1821, the 'Osmanlis retorted to Ypselandes's act of war by destroying at one blow the fabric of power which the Phanariots had been peacefully building up for themselves since 1669; and this was the first step in a century-long process of eradicating all non-Turkish elements from the remnant of the 'Osmanlis' heritage. Moreover, this first explosion of Greek nationalism not only kindled the first spark of Turkish nationalism; it had precisely the same effect upon the non-Greek subject nationalities of the Ottoman Empire; and thus the 'manifest destiny' of the Phanariots and the future of the Ottoman Empire were together brought to naught.

Without extending our field of vision beyond the bounds of the Ottoman Empire, we can find another example of our theme in the Roman Catholic 'Levantines'. These immigrants from Western Europe were permitted to reside within the Ottoman Empire on sufferance, and the only escape from the religious discrimination to which they were subject was to become 'renegades' – a step which not only raised them from the degradation of being treated as pariahs, but threw open to them the highest positions in the Ottoman state. But, in the Levantine community as in the Phanariot, apostasy was the exception, not the rule, despite the strength of the inducements to it. In Galata on the north shore of the Golden Horn, and in the other 'Échelles du Levant', the Catholic *ra'iyeh*[3] lived a ghetto-life which was not far different from the life of the Orthodox Christian *ra'iyeh* in the Phanar or the life of the Jews in the West down to the time of the French Revolution. The Levantines duly developed the specific vices and virtues which the ghetto demands: in its stifling atmosphere they must either respond to the challenge of religious penalization in the same manner as other men, or succumb.

Our final set of examples is drawn from a third situation, in which the adherents of the penalized denomination belong to a civilization which survives only as a fossil or diasporá[4] within another living civilization. Let us glance at some of the diasporás of the Syriac Society and of its Christian successors which have been scattered, from time to time, during the much-interrupted and long-drawn-out courses of these societies' histories. The medium in which all of them have been preserved is a religious medium; their religious idiosyncrasies, which have safeguarded their identities and perpetuated their existence, have also exposed them to religious discrimination at the hands of the alien societies in which they live; this penalization has taken the usual form of exclusion from certain walks of life; and it has evoked the usual reaction in its victims.

The Jews, for example, overcame the handicap which their religious idiosyncrasy entailed by holding their own successfully as traders and financiers in a great variety of human environments. The Parsees, for their part, played the same role in the Indic World as the Jews played elsewhere, and showed the same elasticity and initiative as the Jews in using their special skills and experience to good effect in a variety of circumstances. The Armenian Gregorian Monophysites too, who started their career by holding out against their Orthodox Christian persecutors in the Roman Empire, revealed a similar ability and adaptability, until at the present day the Armenian merchant has become as ubiquitous as his Parsee counterpart. The Jacobite Monophysites in Syria and the Coptic Monophysites in Egypt have reacted locally in the same way to the same challenges.

By contrast with the Monophysites, the Nestorian Christians found life in the Roman Empire impossible, and they transferred their headquarters to 'Iraq and Iran, where they held their own not only as men of business but as physicians, under the relatively tolerant Sasanid and Umayyad and 'Abbasid régimes; and they did not perish in the social cataclysm which overwhelmed these regions at the break-up of the 'Abbasid Caliphate, when Baghdad was sacked by the Mongols in AD 1258. Before this catastrophe overtook their base of operations in the Islamic Empire, the Nestorians had already learnt to make themselves at home in other human environments at the ends of the earth. In one direction, they made their way by sea along the west coast of India, and established a sphere of their own at the extremity of the Indian peninsula, where their descendants or converts (captured from Nestorianism for Monophysitism) survive to this day as 'Saint Thomas's Christians' in Kerala. In another direction they ventured out overland, beyond the furthest outposts of the Syriac and Iranian Worlds in Transoxania, into the heart of the great Asian steppe, and made their way across the whole breadth of the wilderness until they emerged on the other side in China. These continental Nestorian pioneers who once won a footing in Central and Eastern Asia have left no survivors. Yet, although in this sense they have been less successful than their co-religionists who followed the maritime route to India, they succeeded in making a greater mark upon the history of Mankind in their briefer day.

In Eastern Asia the Nestorians were an active element in society in the Age of the T'ang (*imperabant* AD 618–907); and in the oases of the Eurasian steppe they succeeded in converting the sedentary Turkish Uighurs and came near to establishing a distinctive Far Eastern Christian Civilization.[5] It is true that this *tour de force* was abortive. The prospect was compromised in AD 737, when the oases of Transoxania were incorporated in the Arab Empire, and the *coup de grâce* was delivered when the semi-Nestorianized Nomads of the high steppe were successively defeated by the pagan chief of the Mongols, Chingis Khan. Even so, the Nestorian pioneers were able, thanks to their local

89, 90 Armenian and Jewish merchants, uprooted from their native soil, penalized for their religion, yet successful in trade.

91 Shrine of Saint Thomas at Meliapore. Though the Saint's mission and death in India are probably legendary, his reputed burial-place was a centre of pilgrimage for Indian Christians.

monopoly of the elements of a higher culture, to hold their own after the overthrow of their Nomad patrons; the Mongol conqueror took them into his service as scribes and accountants and recorders. For the best part of a century, while the centre of gravity of the Mongol Empire still remained on the steppe and its seat of government in 'Prester John's' country at Qaraqorum, the archives of the Great Khan's court were kept by Nestorian Christian secretaries. The Nestorians even made some distinguished Mongol converts. Hulagu Khan, who sacked Baghdad and devastated 'Iraq in AD 1258, had a Nestorian wife; and Hulagu's advance-guard, which captured Damascus in AD 1260, was commanded by a Nestorian general. It will be seen that the history of these Nestorian Christian Turkish Uighurs bears a certain resemblance to the history of the Orthodox Christian Greek Phanariots. They too just missed their 'manifest destiny'; yet, in response to the challenge of penalization, they had developed certain special accomplishments which so enhanced their social value in the human environment in which they lived that they were virtually taken into partnership by the rulers of a great empire.

92 Stone stele, erected near Ch'ang Ngan in AD 781, records the mission of Nestorian Christianity to China.

93 Nestorian jewelled crosses, found in Central Asia. (Eighth to tenth century AD.)

17 Abortive civilizations

WE HAVE NOW reached a point at which we can bring our present argument to a head. We have found out that civilizations come to birth in environments that are unusually difficult and not unusually easy; and this has led us to establish, by an examination of the effects of penalization, a general rule which may be expressed in the formula: 'the greater the challenge, the greater the stimulus'. However, we still have to find out whether the validity of this rule is absolute or limited. In other words, if we increase the severity of the challenge *ad infinitum*, do we thereby ensure an infinite intensification of the stimulus, and, by the same token, an infinite increase of energy in the response evoked by it? Or do we reach a point beyond which an increase in severity brings in diminishing returns? And if we go beyond this point, do we reach a further point at which the challenge becomes so severe that the possibility of responding to it successfully is eliminated altogether?

In order to offer a convincing answer to these questions, we must be able to present unequivocal evidence of instances in which a challenge has proved to be excessive. The excessiveness of a challenge will not be conclusively demonstrated by the mere fact that a particular party has failed to respond to the challenge in question on a particular occasion. This would prove nothing in itself, because almost every challenge that has eventually evoked a victorious response turns out, on further inquiry, to have baffled or broken one respondent after another before the moment when, at the hundredth or perhaps the thousandth summons, the victor has entered the lists at last. For instance, the physical challenge of the Northern European forests effectually baffled Palaeolithic Man. Unequipped with the implements for felling the trees, and ignorant in any case of how to turn the rich underlying soil to account by cultivation, Palaeolithic Man simply avoided the forests there and settled on sand-dunes and chalk-downs. Yet his experience does not prove that the challenge of the forests was in itself prohibitively excessive; for, where he remained baffled, his Neolithic and Bronze-Age and Iron-Age successors were able to make some impression with the aid of their superior tools and technique, until, eventually, the pioneers of the Western Christian Civilization and of the Russian Civilization took in hand and mastered the forest from the Atlantic to the Urals.

The political intrusion of Hellenism upon the Syriac and Iranian Worlds in the train of Alexander the Great presented a standing challenge to these two societies.[1] Were they or were they not to rise up against the intrusive civilization and cast it out? Confronted with this challenge, they made a number of attempts to respond, all of which took a religious movement as their vehicle. The Zoroastrian and Jewish reactions were failures; the Nestorian and Monophysite reactions were failures; the Islamic reaction was a success.

Zoroastrianism and Judaism were expressions, in religious terms, of the Iranic and the Syriac Civilizations respectively. These two civilizations, which had been thrown on the defensive by Hellenism, had each successfully flowered long before they had been hit by the Hellenic impact. Nestorian and Monophysite Christianity were abortive attempts to bring new civilizations to birth.

An abortive civilization may be defined as one whose adherents have, at the start, tried and failed to perform some particular role which has afterwards been performed successfully by the adherents of some other civilization. When this happens, the first of the two competing incipient civilizations is eclipsed. It either disappears completely or survives as a remnant in holes and corners. We have just noted that Nestorianism and Monophysitism were two successive attempts to shake off an Hellenic ascendancy over the Christian Church and the Roman Empire. This ascendancy had become an anachronism in the fifth century of the Christian Era, in a world in which, by then, the former Syriac and Hellenic cultures had blended into a 'compost'[2] that had become the common culture of all the former Syriac and Hellenic peoples except the Jews and the Samaritans. Neither the Nestorians nor the Monophysites proved strong enough to get the better of the Hellenic 'Imperialists' (Melchites). The Nestorians were driven out of the Roman Empire; the Monophysites were driven underground. However, the enterprise which these anti-Roman Christians had tried and failed to carry out was eventually achieved by the Muslims. In consequence the Syro-Hellenic 'culture-compost' produced an Islamic Civilization, while the Nestorians and Monophysites have survived only in diasporá or in fastnesses. Wherever we find that one civilization has been supplanted by another, this gives us a clue. Any supplanted civilization is a potential candidate for a place on the list of civilizations that have been abortive.

In the cases that we have noticed so far, we have found that a challenge which has defeated some competitors has eventually been met successfully by another competitor, but such sequences of historical events do not provide us with the unequivocal evidence which we need in order to discover whether a challenge may be so severe as to be inherently insuperable. We may find a more fruitful approach to this problem if we adopt a method of comparison in three terms. If we start from an instance in which a challenge has evoked a successful response, and then compare this with examples of the response of a similar party both to less severe and to more severe challenges, we may find that our starting-point will fall into a middle place between two extremes. In other words, if we establish that the two extremes represent challenges that are respectively too weak and too severe to stimulate a creative response, we shall have discovered where the optimum degree of severity lies, and we shall have found out that the interaction of challenge-and-response is subject to the well-known law of diminishing returns.

Let us look at this through the example of a series of encounters between Islam and Christendom. On various occasions, the expanding waves of these two religious movements collided with each other, and, if we take a comparative view of these collisions, we shall observe that they presented a sequence of challenges of varying violence which evoked responses of varying success. When the Muslims made their incursion into France in AD 732, a Western Society, which was only just beginning the struggle to establish itself, was confronted by a band of conquerors who had leapt from victory to victory in pushing out the bounds of their dominions from the southern shore of the Mediterranean. Yet the sequel to this striking challenge showed that it was not excessive, for, far from killing off its respondent, it stimulated the nascent Western Christian Society to repulse the invaders and begin a successful career of political and cultural self-articulation.

The West, however, was only one of several points at which the Islamic-Christian collision occurred. In the South, Islam was challenging Monophysite Christendom in Abyssinia (the present-day Ethiopia), and this encounter will offer us an example of a response that failed because the local presentation of the challenge was too weak. The reason for the peculiar survival to this day of the Abyssinian fossil of Monophysitism is the virtual impregnability of the highland fastness in which it is enclosed. The waves of successive cultural invasions have washed ineffectually round the rock on which this primitive fossil is stranded, without either engulfing it or stimulating it to higher effort. Abyssinian Monophysitism remained a stagnant and isolated fragment of Christianity; the challenge of Islam

INEFFECTIVE CHALLENGE 94 Physical geography shielded the Ethiopian Christians from external stimuli: the community vegetated in isolation. Roof of a thirteenth-century church carved from the living rock at Lalibela.

was ineffective here because, like all other challenges up to the time when modern technology brutally breached Abyssinia's natural barriers, the impact of Islam on Abyssinia was weakened to a point far below the optimum degree of severity by the impregnability of the local physical environment.

On the other hand, the response of Transoxanian Nestorianism in the East to the Islamic challenge was a failure for the opposite reason. Such was the severity of the challenge that it actually prevented a 'Far Eastern Nestorian Christian Civilization' from being born. This embryonic Far Eastern Christian Civilization in a Nestorian chrysalis was germinating in the Oxus–Jaxartes basin before it was rendered abortive; and the blow which robbed it of its

chance of coming to life was the definitive annexation of the region to the Arab Empire in AD 737–41. Before this conquest, all the local conditions in the area appeared to be in favour of the genesis of a new civilization there. There had been a long and thorough intermingling of cultures: Iranian and Syriac and Hellenic and Indic. There had been an equally long and thorough intermingling of races: an indigenous Iranian peasantry had been overlaid by a deposit of Iranian-speaking Nomads in the second century BC, and by two further layers of Turkish-speaking Nomads in the fifth and sixth centuries of the Christian Era. This fruitful diversity of the human element was preserved and accentuated by the character of the physical environment. The concentration of the sedentary inhabitants into a

INSURMOUNTABLE CHALLENGE   95   The incipient Nestorian Christian civilization in Central Asia was overwhelmed by the Muslim Arabs before it could take root. Wall-painting from the 'Christian temple' in Qarakhocho.

number of separate fortified oases had resulted in the social articulation of the country into a number of politically independent but economically and culturally interconnected city-states. These maintained good relations with their Ephthalite and subsequent Turkish overlords, who had the sense to realize that the prosperity of master and subject alike derived from the transit-trade along the East–West caravan route, and hence depended upon the guarantee of safe and unobstructed passage through their dominions. To these beneficial human and physical conditions was added the religious stimulus of a vigorous Nestorianism, carried into Central Asia and as far as China by the adherents of the faith who had fled from persecution in the Roman Empire.

Thus in the middle of the seventh century of the Christian Era the new embryonic civilization in Transoxania had every prospect of coming to birth. The cause of its premature extinction is to be found in its failure to respond to the menacing challenges presented by the Muslim Arabs' intrusion. A prolonged resistance to the Arab invaders and the devastating intervention of the Türgesh (Western Turkish) Nomads threatened to produce conditions of such intense anarchy that the trade-routes could not have been kept open; and, once these were cut, the life-blood of Transoxania would flow out unstaunched. The Arabs offered a choice between an unmitigated economic catastrophe and a moderated form of political servitude in which the loss of local independence was made more tolerable by the prospect of access to the markets of the Arab Empire, spanning a hinterland from Khurasan to the Atlantic. By accepting, as they did, a peace that was not an unconditional surrender, the Transoxanians escaped the alternative of economic annihilation; but at the same time their acquiescence in being incorporated in an alien universal state had the inevitable effect of stifling the embryo of their own civilization. In this case, the price of response to the challenge had been prohibitively high.

We can now arrange our series of collisions between Islam and the various Christendoms in a sequence. The impact of the Islamic wave upon Abyssinian Monophysitism was so feeble that it hardly administered any perceptible stimulus. Its stronger impact upon Western Christendom was highly stimulating, as is demonstrated by the vigour of the response. The impact upon Nestorian Christendom caught and stifled this society in embryo, while it was still too weak to make a successful response to the challenge. It is evident that the severity of the Islamic challenge to Western Christendom was of the optimum degree, and that the challenges to Abyssinian Monophysite Christendom and to Central Asian Nestorian Christendom were both equally remote in degree from the favourable mean. Here we have a criterion for distinguishing between civilizations that come to flower and civilizations that are abortive. We can see why Western Christianity and Islam each gave birth to a civilization, whereas Nestorian and Monophysite Christianity each failed to achieve this. Islam had proved strong enough to defeat the ascendancy of the Hellenic 'Imperialists'; the West, in its turn, had proved strong enough to defeat Islam. On the other hand, Nestorian and Monophysite Christianity had each been worsted by the 'Orthodox' Christianity of the Hellenic 'Imperialists', and they did not benefit when the ascendancy of Orthodox Christianity was eventually overthrown by Islam. In Abyssinia, as we have seen, the impact of Islam on Monophysite Christianity was too slight to be stimulating, whereas, in Transoxania, the impact of Islam on Nestorian Christianity was so strong that its effect was crushing. Consequently, Islam eclipsed these two varieties of Christianity and entered into their heritage. Monophysite Christianity survived only as a diasporá, except in the highland fastnesses of Abyssinia and Armenia; Nestorian Christianity survived only in the highlands of Kurdistan and in the swamps and jungles of Kerala, at the southwestern extremity of India.

PART III

THE GROWTHS
OF CIVILIZATIONS

A civilization that has successfully come to birth has surmounted the first and highest hurdle, but will it then automatically go on from strength to strength? The evidence of some societies whose growth has been arrested after birth suggests that this does not always happen, and so I am led on to investigate the nature of growth itself. A society continues in growth, it seems, when a successful response to a challenge provokes a fresh challenge in its turn, converting a single movement into a series. I am then driven to ask whether the successive steps in this sequence of challenge-and-response lead in some direction. The notion of inevitable progress towards a predictable goal seems to me to be inappropriate in the human sphere, but I find that in a general way the growth of a society can be measured in terms of the increasing power of self-determination won by the society's leaders; and I believe that the future fate of a civilization lies in the hands of this minority of creative persons.

plate 21

THE ARREST OF GROWTH

Mongol Nomads in conversation. A civilization that attempts some extraordinary *tour de force* may find itself, not defeated outright, but arrested in a state of immobility, its energies wholly absorbed in meeting this single great challenge. The Central Asian Nomads were condemned to this fate: they successfully mastered the problem of adaptation to the harsh exigencies of life on the steppes, but in doing so they became the slaves of their environment, unable to make any fresh creative advance.

plate 22

THE ELAN OF GROWTH

Birth is a single act: growth is a continuous process. The movement of challenge-and-response becomes a self-sustaining series if each successful response provokes a disequilibrium requiring new creative adjustments. The Promethean myth embodies this progressive *élan*, for Prometheus, after defying a tyrannical Zeus by bringing the forbidden power of fire to Man, persuades him of the need to allow Mankind's perpetual development. Medieval accounts of the myth added a Christian slant to the pagan original, seeing in Prometheus not a rebel against God but His partner in the Creation. In this fifteenth-century miniature, Prometheus is shown first travelling with his torch through the spheres of the Universe, and, in the centre, animating the inert figure of Man in paradise. Here the Promethean fire is shown as a literally life-giving force, but it had an additional symbolic significance as the fire of knowledge or intellectual curiosity, Prometheus's punishment then being seen as a metaphor of the dangerous fruits of inquiry.

18 Examples of the arrest of growth

DO THE GROWTHS of civilizations present a genuine problem? Our inquiries up to this point have shown us beyond doubt that the problem of the geneses of civilizations is a real one, and we have done our best to offer some solutions to it. But do we now need to seek any further? When birth is once achieved, does not growth follow of itself? The answer to this question seems to be that birth may not automatically be followed by growth. In addition to those specimens of developed and abortive civilizations that we have already identified, we can find examples of a third type of society, or of communities within a society: namely, those which have not been abortive yet have not continued to develop either, but which have been arrested after birth.

The common feature of the arrested societies and communities is that they have all alike been immobilized as the result of having attempted, and achieved, a *tour de force*. They are responses to challenges which lie on the very borderline between the stimulating and the excessive. While the abortive civilizations have attempted a feat of birth which is overwhelmingly hard, and have been defeated, the arrested societies have won this first round, but have thereby ensured their own defeat in the next. In the imagery of our fable of the climbers' 'pitch',[1] the representatives of the arrested societies are like climbers who happen to have started to scale the precipice in places where they are soon brought up short against beetling projections of the cliff-face. Neither defeated nor daunted, as other more timid or more prudent souls might be, these over-audacious climbers accept the challenge and grapple with the jutting crag, only to find themselves, at the next moment, clinging to its projecting face in a rigid posture from which they dare not budge. All their skill and vigour and boldness is now absorbed in a supreme effort to save themselves from falling, and they have no margin of energy for climbing on until they have reached a normal surface again. They are performing an astonishing acrobatic feat, but a feat in the realm of statics and not in the realm of dynamics. Their motto – and eventual epitaph – is 'J'y suis, j'y reste.'

A society may in practice be arrested at any stage in its life after it has once come to birth, and we shall see[2] that the phenomenon of arrest can be observed in several societies after their breakdown, in the last phase of their lives. Equally, a single community within a civilization may become arrested while its neighbours continue to develop. This happened to the Ottoman Turks when they leaped from being a pastoral Nomadic community to becoming an imperial Power. They faced the unprecedented challenge of having to govern vast subject populations, and, trying to cope with this novel political problem, they created intractable and inflexible institutions which precluded any further social development. The Spartans brought a similar fate upon themselves when, in answer to the Hellenic Society's common problem of population pressure in the eighth century BC, they expanded their territory by conquest within Hellas, and found all their creative energies absorbed in the effort to maintain their control over a hostile population of their own kind.

In addition to these examples, there are other societies which seem to have embarked on or performed the initial *tour de force* of birth, only to find themselves incapable of sustaining a movement of growth. Such are the Esquimaux, who have developed a highly distinctive and superbly well adapted Arctic culture, which has, however, made them the prisoners of the harsh environment that they set out to conquer, since the primary task of surviving uses up all their power. Such too are the many segmentary communities of the African World, who live in a physical and ideological environment which seems to inhibit the growth of large and flexible communities. Whenever such a community threatens to become too large to be sustained by the traditional institutions and practices of the tribe, a section breaks off from the parent community, and goes off to found a new tribal society. Thus the exigencies which led to the creation of such a rigid framework of social and practical life condemn the community to isolation and impotence.

The outstanding example of an arrested society is, however, the Eurasian Nomadic Society. The Nomads have taken up the challenge of the steppe, an element of physical Nature which is no less demanding than the Arctic snows or the tropical jungles. Indeed, the steppe bears more resemblance to another highly uncongenial element, the ocean, than it does to any area of dry land. Steppe-surface and water-surface have this in common, that they are both accessible to Man only as a pilgrim and a sojourner. Neither offers him anywhere on its broad expanse (apart from the islands and oases) a place where he can rest and stay and settle down to a sedentary existence. Both provide strikingly greater facilities for travel and transport than those parts of the Earth's surface upon which human communities are accustomed to live in permanence; but both exact (as the penalty for trespassing upon them) the necessity of constantly 'moving on', or else 'moving off' their surface altogether and finding some standing-ground upon *terra firma* somewhere beyond the coasts which respectively surround them. Thus there is a real similarity between the Nomadic herds which range the steppe in search of pasturage, and the fishing-fleet which plies the ocean in quest of shoals; between the convoy of merchantmen which exchanges the products of the opposite shores of the sea, and the camel-caravan by which the opposite shores of the steppe are linked with one another; between the water pirate and the desert raider; and between those explosive movements of population which impelled Achaeans, Norsemen, or Crusaders to take to their ships and break like tidal waves upon the coasts of Europe and the Levant, and those other movements which impelled Arabs or Scythians or Turks or Mongols to swing out of their orbit on the steppe and to break, with equal violence and equal suddenness, upon the settled lands of Egypt or 'Iraq or Russia or India or China.

It will be seen that the Nomads' response to the challenge of Nature is a *tour de force*; but, in the absence of a satisfactory body of archaeological evidence, the historical incentive which provoked this achievement must remain a matter of conjecture. The problem is one of dating, for we have no information which would allow us to assign the historical origin of Central Asian pastoral Nomadism to any exact time in any particular place.[3]

In exploring Man's earliest attempts to tame and harness his physical environment, it is possible to apply a model of development according to which the modes of economic production are assumed to have become progressively more sophisticated, succeeding each other in stages from hunting and gathering through the domestication of plants and animals to a settled form of mixed agricultural and pastoral farming; and, on this pattern, Nomadism might be supposed to be an alternative system that diverged from the standard development at the stage of animal domestication, for Nomadism is essentially a highly specialized form of stockbreeding. Attempts have been made, for example, to link the stages in this process to climatic change, the inference being that, as the degree of desiccation increased, so, first, the herds of wild animals hunted by Man disappeared, obliging communities which had formerly lived entirely by hunting to eke out their livelihoods under less favourable conditions by taking to a rudimentary form of agriculture and by domesticating wild animals by providing them with the food that they could no longer find for themselves. Later, as the process of desiccation intensified, so, in turn, these sedentary farmers and pastoralists were evicted, according to this theory, from the shrinking areas of cultivable land and were forced to adopt a more mobile form of pastoral production on the surrounding steppe, moving with their herds seasonally from place to place in quest of patches of temporary pastureland.[4] More recently the hypothesis of demographic pressure has been advanced to explain the successive changes in production, on the supposition that, in response to the growth of population and in default of any ability to improve existing production techniques, early Man was forced to diversify his means of support, by learning, for example, the art of domesticating plants and animals.[5] Either of these two theories might account satisfactorily for the institution of pastoral Nomadism, but they can be no more than unverified conjectures where no supporting archaeological evidence exists; and we are not entitled to assume that the limited evidence supplied by the excavation of any one site may be applied by analogy to the vast areas that have been utilized for pastoral Nomadism at one time or another.

In the first place, then, we cannot date even approximately the supposed successive changes in the modes of agricultural production; and if this process is shrouded in mystery, then the mystery is at its most impenetrable in the case of the origins of pastoral Nomadism, for, by definition, mobile human clans and their herds are the least likely of any prehistoric communities to have left sufficiently durable signs of their habitation or passage for the spades of modern archaeologists to dig up and bring to light again. Moreover, we even have no warrant for assuming that Nomadism began as an alternative response to environmental challenges, whether of climate or population or

96 Life in a Nomad camp, from a fourteenth-century Mongol drawing.

97 Ainu fishermen on a frozen river in Japan. The Ainu long remained a static, sub-Arctic hunting and fishing community outside the pale of the growing Japanese Civilization.

anything else – that is, as a response which diverted the peoples that adopted it from the main current of agricultural development and into what eventually proved to be a backwater. It is also conceivable that, so far from being imported on to the arid steppe by an exodus from farming communities, Nomadic stockbreeding was an original and unprecedented method devised by the ancient inhabitants of the steppe for meeting the challenges imposed by their parsimonious environment at a stage of their prehistory that may have been remote, though it must, of course, have been later than the stage at which they had acquired the domesticated animals that became their mainstay.

Precise evidence on the origins of Nomadism has not come to light so far. On the other hand, there is no uncertainty about the inherent severity of the challenge to which the Nomadic way of life was a response, and none, again, about the vigour of that response or about the tenacity with which it was sustained. The Nomad grapples with an outstandingly hostile environment in the strength of a highly developed pastoral art; but, in order to practise this art successfully under exceedingly exacting conditions, he has to develop a special skill, and, in order to exercise this skill, he has also to develop special moral and intellectual powers. Pastoral Nomadism is one of the most specialized forms of economic activity, for – lacking a settled place of residence and the opportunity for cultivation – the Nomad is almost exclusively dependent upon the single resource of his herds, from which he must obtain his food, clothing, housing, fuel, and transport, and at the same time a surplus which he can exchange with peoples on the periphery of the steppe for necessities of life like metals and cereals. The Nomads' mobility is tremendous, by contrast with the relative stationariness of agricultural peoples, but it is nevertheless limited by the immense logistical problems of organizing the movement of relatively large groups of men and animals in a barren and inhospitable environment. The Nomad must manœuvre himself and his family and his flocks and his herds over the vast spaces of the steppe from pasture to pasture, in conformity with the climatic year-cycle which determines the capacity of successive pasture-grounds for feeding his animals; he must calculate distance and direction with fair accuracy if he is not to lose himself on the open wastes or miss those widely dispersed watering-points and pasturages without which he and his migrant flocks will perish; and the Nomad patriarch cannot wrest victory out of this perpetual economic campaign without exercising – and exacting from the human beings and animals under his authority – those virtues of forethought and self-reliance and physical and moral endurance which a military commander exercises, and exacts from his troops, when Man is at war with Man and not with physical Nature. The *tour de force* of Nomadism demands a rigorously high standard of behaviour and physique, and a highly developed instinct of loyalty and clan solidarity; without these characteristics the disciplined train that winds across the steppe will disintegrate into atomized fragments, each incapable of keeping alive in isolation. It is hardly surprising that the very achievement of such a masterly degree of discipline should have exacted from the society that has accomplished it a penalty of equivalent magnitude.

The Nomads' penalty is in essence the same as the Esquimaux's. The formidable physical environment which they have succeeded in conquering has insidiously enslaved them, in ostensibly accepting them as its masters. The Nomads, like the Esquimaux, have become the perpetual prisoners of a cycle of movement; they have to be permanently in motion as their herds exhaust one pasture after another. Thus, in acquiring the initiative on the steppe, the Nomads have forfeited the initiative in the world at large. It is true that they have not passed across the stage of the histories of civilizations without leaving their mark, and the internal articulation of their own civilization has some outstanding achievements to its credit. The vigorous artistic creations of the Scythians, one of the earliest Nomadic peoples with whom the Western World came into contact, are as impressive as any produced by their sedentary contemporaries; and, a thousand years later, the great Nomadic Empires of the Turks and the Mongols gave rise to astonishingly robust and vivid cultures, based on thriving capitals such as Ögödei Khan's Qaraqorum. Yet here surely is the clue to the frailty of the true Nomadic Civilization: except in those periods in history when it has broken out of its own domain and burst upon its sedentary neighbours and established a temporary authority over realms outside the steppe, the Nomadic Society has been condemned to languish in the wastes of its own barren environment, perpetually on the move in small clans and bands. The social instrument which has permitted a wonderfully effective economic utilization of a hostile terrain has also proved an insurmountable impediment to higher cultural development.

98 Nomad art: detail from a Scythian scabbard, showing two gods, each of whom faces a sacred tree, an image taken from Mesopotamian mythology.

19 The criterion of growth

HAVING SATISFIED OURSELVES that the growths of civilizations do present a problem, we must now try to solve this problem by inquiring what the nature of growth may be; or, in other words, we must try to identify the criterion of growth. Let us start our inquiry by invoking the aid of mythology, a power which has already helped us in an earlier chapter, and see whether the insights of Aeschylus's Promethean Trilogy can throw some light on our present subject.

The myth of the Book of Job and of Goethe's *Faust* gave us an insight into the nature of the geneses of civilizations,[1] and the Promethean myth may now offer us a clue to the nature of their growths. In the Aeschylean version, Zeus loses his battle against the challenger. Unlike the God of Job or of Faust, Zeus is here not yearning for the stimulus which will permit him to perform a fresh creative act, but rather he is anxious to stay as he is and to keep the Universe around him at a standstill; the challenge presented to Zeus by Prometheus, which calls the temper and policy of Zeus in question, moves Zeus to inflict a vindictive persecution upon his challenger; and in this act, which overthrows his cherished equilibrium, Zeus brings about his own defeat, while Prometheus, through suffering, wins his way to victory.

The Aeschylean Zeus is seen for what he is in an audacious pre-classical era before people had become 'afraid of the solvent and destructive effects of free speculation [but were] still looking to the powers of the human intellect, to reason and free inquiry, as the great emancipators'.[2] Zeus's feat was the overthrow of his divine predecessor Cronos; and, having accomplished this *tour de force* and mounted the throne of Olympus, he has no other idea except to keep himself enthroned there, in solitary, motionless, tyrannical state with his foot on the neck of a prostrate Universe. Zeus, however, has not conquered Cronos by his own unaided powers, but with the help of Prometheus; and he has to be saved in spite of himself, as Aeschylus divined, by the challenge of his erstwhile ally. Whereas Zeus has no other wish than to preserve his position in a static eternity, Prometheus is an insatiable creator, a kindler of fire, a probing progressive mind – a mythical personification of the growth process, the Bergsonian *élan vital*. He knows that, unless Zeus keeps on the move, the new ruler of Olympus will inevitably be overthrown in his turn, like Cronos before him; and therefore he gives Zeus no peace.

> When first he mounted on his father's throne
> Straightway he called the gods, and gave each one
> His place and honours. So he wrought his plan
> Of empire. But of man, unhappy man,
> He had no care: he counselled the whole race
> To uproot, and plant a strange brood in its place.
> And none took stand against that evil mind
> Save me. I rose. I would not see mankind
> By him stamped out and cast to nothingness. . . .[3]

Failing to convince Zeus by power of reason that his static Universe is not a world at peace but a desert, Prometheus sets the will of Zeus at defiance, and leads Mankind onward and upward, inspiring his protégé and pupil with his own spirit.

> A thing of no avail
> He was, until a living mind I wrought
> Within him, and new mastery of thought.[4]

For this thwarting of his will, Zeus takes his revenge upon Prometheus by turning against him the whole battery of his superhuman force.

> Mercy I had for man; and therefore I
> Must meet no mercy, but hang crucified
> In witness of God's cruelty and pride.[5]

In this contest, Prometheus is physically at Zeus's mercy. Yet the victory is in Prometheus's hands; for no torture that Zeus can inflict is able to overcome Prometheus's willpower; and this will-power guards a secret that Zeus fain would know. The secret is that, if Zeus persists in his static and tyrannical posture, he is dooming himself to be overthrown, like his predecessor, by the brute force which he has deliberately enthroned in place of thought. This secret is the key of Zeus's own destiny, and in *Prometheus Bound* we are shown Zeus trying, and failing, to wrest Prometheus's secret from him. Although the other two plays of the trilogy are no longer extant, we have enough evidence to suggest that, in the end, Prometheus and Zeus are reconciled: Zeus learns the lesson of forgiveness, and agrees to spare his enemy and to allow the human race to develop. So Zeus had, after all, a glimmer of the 'Promethean light' within himself which he could not wholly extinguish; and his conflict with Prometheus kindled into flame a spark that was latent all the time in Zeus's soul.

On the plane of mythology Zeus and Prometheus are presented as two separate human personalities, but in a psychological analysis they can be seen as being two impulses in a single human soul which interpenetrate each other, however vehement their conflict, because it is the same soul that feels them both. We can apply this psychological interpretation to the action of human souls in social situations. For example, supposing that, in the infancy of the Hellenic Society towards the close of the second millennium BC, the lethargy of the North-West Greek-speaking barbarian invaders, who had squatted among the débris of the derelict Aegean Civilization, had nowhere been stirred by a current of Promethean mental energy, then all Hellas would have vegetated in perpetuity like 'Dorian' Crete. But in some of these barbarian souls, as in the mythical Zeus, the dying spark of a civilizing ethos was rekindled, and through this Promethean *élan* the infant Hellenic Society was released from its static bondage to a dead social fabric and was carried forward from genesis into growth. The Promethean *élan* of the human intellect which Aeschylus portrayed in mythical imagery has been described in philosophical terms by Bergson.

99, 100 PROMETHEUS THE CREATOR In Greek mythology, Prometheus – rebel against Zeus, disturber of Olympian harmony – was also the creator of the human race; above, Prometheus forms the skeleton of Man from clay and water in the likeness of gods. Below, his own protector, the helmeted goddess Athene, completes the work by breathing life into the inanimate effigy.

Man, as he issued from the hands of Nature, was a being who was both intelligent and social, with a sociality which was calculated to reach its term in diminutive societies and with an intellect which was destined to serve both the individual life and the group life. But the intellect, dilating by its own efforts, has entered upon an unexpected development. It has liberated human beings from servitudes to which they had been condemned by the limitations of their nature. Under these conditions it has proved not impossible for certain human beings, with particularly rich [psychic] endowments, to reopen that which had been closed, and to perform, at least for themselves, that which it would have been impossible for Nature to perform for humanity at large. Their example has eventually carried away the rest of Mankind, at least in imagination.[6]

Can we translate these insights into our own language of challenge-and-response? So far, in our investigations, we have been content to note certain rather obvious truths about the nature of challenges: we have observed that neither an excessive nor a deficient challenge can evoke a creative response, and that a challenge which lies just on the border of excessiveness – which at first sight seems to be the most stimulating challenge of all – will tend to exact a fatal penalty from its respondents in the shape of an arrest in their development.[7] And here, of course, lies the secret of growth for which we are searching; for, on the long view, the optimum challenge must be the one which not only stimulates the challenged party to achieve a single successful response, but also stimulates him to acquire a momentum that carries him on a step further: from achievement to fresh struggles, from the solution of one problem to the presentation of another, from momentary rest to reiterated movement, from Yin to Yang again. The single, finite movement from a disturbance to a restoration of equilibrium is not enough, if genesis is to be followed by growth. To convert the movement into a repetitive, recurrent rhythm, there must be an *élan* which carries the challenged party through equilibrium into an overbalance which exposes him to a fresh challenge and thereby inspires him to make a fresh response in the form of a further equilibrium ending in a further overbalance – and so on in a progression which is potentially infinite. In earthly language:

> So tauml' ich von Begierde zu Genuss
> Und im Genuss verschmacht' ich nach Begierde.[8]

In heavenly language:

> Komm! Hebe dich zu höheren Sphären!
> Wenn er dich ahnet, folgt er nach.[9]

Is there any direction or purpose in this continually repeated rhythm of growth? In encountering this question we shall be wise to remind ourselves that the idea of 'direction' can have no literal application except in the physical world, and that we must be on our guard against going astray when we apply the same idea in the psychic field.

It goes without saying that the direction [of successive steps in human progress] is the same as soon as we have agreed upon calling these movements steps in progress. Each movement will in fact then have to be defined as a step forward. But this is merely a metaphor; and if there were really a pre-existing direction along which Mankind had been content to advance, moral revivals would be predictable: the need of a creative effort for each of them would not be there. The truth is that one can always take the latest of them, define it by a concept, and say that the others contained a greater or lesser quantity of what the concept includes, and that consequently all of them were stations on the road to this. But things take this form only in retrospect. In reality, the changes were qualitative and not quantitative, and they therefore defied prediction. There was, however, one side on which they presented in themselves, and not merely in their conceptual transcripts, a factor common to them all. They were all of them attempts to open what was closed. . . . To push our analysis further, we must add that these successive efforts were not exactly the progressive realization of an ideal, because no idea that had been forged in anticipation would be able to represent the sum of acquisitions each of which, in creating itself, would be creating a special idea of its own. Yet all the same, this diversity of efforts might well sum itself up in something unique: an *élan*.[10]

A teleological formula might be adequate to express any single term in the progression, but it would become misleading when applied to the total of the whole series. The continuity of growth is not spatial but summative. As far as direction goes, the line of movement plotted out by the succession of responses to challenges may be exceedingly erratic; but this has little or no symbolic significance, because the continuous progress that is achieved by the Promethean *élan*, as its response to one challenge exposes it to another challenge *und so weiter*, cannot be registered at all in the form of a curve. This progress has rather to be conceived of in terms of control or organization, as a progressive and cumulative increase both in outward mastery of the environment and in inward self-determination or self-articulation on the part of the individual or society that is in the process of growth.

The conquest of the external environment, be it human or physical, does not by itself constitute the criterion of growth, attractive though this simple formula may appear at first sight. We can easily find examples which contradict this view. The Sinic Civilization, for instance, was pushing out the bounds of its political dominion, and thus experiencing a period of growth in terms of geographical expansion, precisely at a time when it was undergoing a process of violent social disintegration in the period of the Contending States (771–221 BC). In the field of technology too there is no invariable correlation between the mastery of new techniques and the progress of civilization; we have already seen, for instance, in our survey of arrested societies, that societies may remain static even though technique improves.[11] Again, the sheer technical expertise which has enabled Man to conquer and control his outer environment may frequently be the seal of his doom, if he proves incapable of surmounting the challenges that impinge on his soul from within.[12] True growth consists in a progressive change of emphasis and transfer of energy and shifting of the scene of action out of the field of the macrocosm and into that of the microcosm; and in this new arena victorious responses to challenges do not take the form of overcoming an external obstacle, but manifest themselves instead in a progressive self-articulation. When we watch an individual human being or a human society making successive responses to a succession of challenges, and when we ask ourselves whether this particular series of

101, 102 PROMETHEUS THE BRINGER OF FIRE Prometheus's dual mythological roles as the creator of Man and as the defiant bringer of fire from God to Man have often been compounded into a single image, to show Prometheus animating the figure of Man by means of fire.
Below, Prometheus travels through the spheres between Heaven and Earth to bring fire to Man; illustration from a fifteenth-century Flemish manuscript. Beneath, while Jehovah gives shape to Chaos, Prometheus animates Man with his torch in paradise: a medieval Christian illustration to Ovid's *Metamorphoses* sanctifies the pagan tradition by putting the Hellenic creation myth into the iconographical language of Genesis.

103 Prometheus's revolt against Zeus has led to a new kind of creation: he raises his torch to the Sun's fire which flows through his body to give life to the figure of Man.

104 The three episodes of the Prometheus myth. In the sky, Prometheus kindles his torch at the Sun's chariot; on the left, he fires the frozen statue of Man, and, opposite, he is bound to a tree by Hermes to await his punishment.

responses to challenges is to be interpreted as a manifestation of growth, we shall arrive at the answer to our question through observing whether, as the series proceeds, the action does or does not tend to shift from the first to the second of the two fields aforesaid. The presence or absence of this movement of transference gives us our criterion for the presence or absence of growth in a series of responses to challenges. In practice, of course, the action is not confined to the one or the other of these fields exclusively, but the process of growth implies that, in each successive bout, the action on the external field is counting for less, and the action on the internal field for more, in deciding the issue between victory and defeat. In order to illuminate these rather abstract reflexions on the nature of growth, let us turn to an example drawn from history, and attach our speculations to evidence.

In Hellenic history the earlier challenges all emanated from the external environment. After the break-up of the Aegean Civilization, the remaining inhabitants of lowland Greece were faced with the challenge of achieving some security against the aggressive brigands of the adjacent highlands. The lowlanders successfully solved their problem of self-defence by attaining a military mastery over their neighbours. Yet the very success of their response to this first challenge exposed them to a second. A victory which had ensured the peaceful pursuit of agriculture in the lowlands gave a momentum to the growth of population, until it reached a density which the

Hellenic homeland could no longer support. This problem of over-population was met by the expedient of an overseas expansion which again, in its turn, exposed the respondents to a new human challenge from the rival Phoenician and Etruscan colonists of the colonized countries. This challenge was actually presented when the expansion of the Greeks was checked for some two centuries (*c.* 525–325 BC) by the counter-pressure of their non-Greek neighbours: in the critical year of 480 BC Greece was compelled to fight for her existence on two fronts simultaneously – against the Carthaginians in Sicily and against Xerxes' Persians in Greece itself. Thereafter, this formidable challenge was triumphantly surmounted in the course of the four centuries beginning with Alexander's passage of the Hellespont in 334 BC. Alexander overthrew the Achaemenian Empire, thereby opening the way for Hellenism to dominate the main body of the Syriac World, and the Egyptiac and Sumero-Akkadian and Iranian and Indic Worlds into the bargain. The Romans overthrew the Carthaginians and gained the upper hand over the European barbarians, thus opening the way for a fresh expansion of Hellenism westwards. Thanks to these triumphs, the Hellenic Society now enjoyed a respite of some five or six centuries – from the latter part of the fourth century BC to the early decades of the third century of the Christian Era – during which no serious challenge from the external environment was presented to it. But this did not mean that the Hellenic Society was exempt from challenges altogether

during this period. On the contrary, this was a period of decline: that is to say, a period in which Hellenism was confronted with challenges to which it failed to respond with success. If we now look at these challenges, we shall observe that they were all of them new versions of old challenges which had already been met victoriously on the external field, but which had been translated, in that very act, from the environment of the Hellenic Society into that Society's own life.

For example, the Hellenic Society had resisted the external military challenge of the Persians and the Carthaginians in 480 BC with two potent weapons – the Athenian navy and the Syracusan dictatorship; but these two instruments which were so successful in performing their immediate functions also produced severe internal strains and stresses within the Hellenic body social – a competition for hegemony between Athens and Sparta, a degeneration of the Athenians' hegemony over their maritime allies into a tyranny, and a Sicilian reaction against Syracusan domination – and these in their turn presented the Hellenic Society with a challenge which it proved unable to meet and which eventually resulted in a social breakdown. Thus a challenge which in 480 BC had been presented as an impact of external political forces reappeared in 431 BC (in the great Atheno-Peloponnesian War) as an internal conflict within the society itself.

In the next chapter of Hellenic history, corresponding effects followed from the expansion of Hellenism, east and west, in the tracks of the Macedonian and Roman armies. The military victories of Hellenic arms, which exempted Hellenism from any further external challenge for some five or six hundred years, could achieve this result only by transferring the field of challenge-and-response from outside to inside the ambit of the Hellenic World. The long military struggle against external enemies was translated into the civil wars of the rival Macedonian *diadochi* and rival Roman dictators. The economic competition between the Hellenic and the Syriac Societies for the mastery of the Mediterranean was reflected within the bosom of the Hellenic Society in the devastating domestic warfare between the Oriental plantation-slaves and their Hellenic masters. Likewise the cultural conflict between Hellenism and the Oriental civilizations reappeared, after the Hellenic culture had successfully asserted its supremacy over the others, as an internal crisis within Hellenic souls: a crisis that declared itself in the emergence of Isis-worship and astrology and the Mahayana and Mithraism and Christianity and a host of other syncretistic religions.

We can detect a similar transference of the field of action in the encounters between the Western Civilization and the Asian and African Worlds today. The reaction against an aggressive Western imperialism has resulted in the successful political emancipation of these societies from an alien dominion or domination; but the external impact of Westernism, in the shape of the imposed apparatus of political and economic colonialism, has dissolved only to become transformed into an internal conflict within these societies between the alien civilization and the indigenous ethos. Not only are the resulting cultural stresses clearly apparent within these societies, but the Western Society – which until recently had enjoyed an extended period of exemption from external challenges – is also now exposed to the rebounding effects of these attempts on the part of its former subjects and satellites to respond to a challenge which had originally been presented by the West itself.

The phenomenon of transference can be observed in the response to physical as well as human challenges; for the triumph of the Western Civilization over its material environment has been followed by a similar transmutation of external into internal challenges. The problems of mastering physical Nature on the economic plane – of transforming the raw materials provided by Nature into products useful to Man – have been triumphantly met by Western *Homo faber*; but these achievements in the technical sphere have created immense problems in the realm of human relations. Economic competition has accentuated international stresses and strains; in the domestic life of some communities the tension between capital and labour has produced cataclysmic upheavals; and these two disruptive movements have combined on a worldwide scale to create the glaring contemporary problem of the differences between the standards of living of different fractions of Mankind who have now been brought into economic relations with one another by the world-encompassing nexus of commerce and finance.

On the military plane, too, the crucial challenge is no longer technological but psychological. Our mastery of the techniques of destruction may still be capable of refinement, but can hardly be enhanced, since we already have the capacity to annihilate the physical and human world utterly; so the challenge presented to scientific minds by the material secrets of atomic physics has been transformed into a moral challenge for all Mankind.

On this showing, we may perhaps persist in the view that a given series of successful responses to successive challenges is to be interpreted as a manifestation of growth if, as the series proceeds, the action tends to shift from the external environment – whether human or physical – to the *for intérieur* of the growing personality or growing civilization. In so far as this grows and continues to grow, it has to reckon less and less with challenges delivered by alien adversaries that demand responses on an outer battlefield, and more and more with the challenges that are presented by itself to itself on an inner arena. Growth means that the growing personality or civilization tends to become its own environment and its own challenge and its own field of action. In other words, the criterion of growth is a progress towards self-determination; and progress towards self-determination is a prosaic formula for describing the miracle by which life enters into its kingdom.

If self-determination is the criterion of growth, and if self-determination means self-articulation, we can analyse the process by which civilizations actually grow if we investigate the way in which they progressively articulate themselves. In a general way, it is evident that a society in the process of civilization articulates itself through the individual human beings who 'belong' to the society, or to whom the society 'belongs'. Society itself, as we have said in an earlier chapter,[13] is not a collection of persons but is a network of relations; it is the field of interaction of two or more agents. It is not itself the source of social action, for a source is *ex hypothesi* other than a field. A society is the medium of communication through which human beings interact with each other, and it is human individuals and not human societies that 'make' history.

This truth is stated forcibly and insistently by Bergson in the work which we have already quoted in this chapter.

We do not believe in the 'unconscious' [factor] in history: the 'great subterranean currents of thought', of which there has been so much talk, only flow in consequence of the fact that masses of men have been carried away by one or more of their own number. . . . It is useless to maintain that [social progress] takes place by itself, bit by bit, in virtue of the spiritual condition of the society at a certain period of its history. It is really a leap forward which is only taken when the society has made up its mind to try an experiment; this means that the society must have allowed itself to be convinced, or at any rate allowed itself to be shaken; and the shake is always given by *somebody*.[14]

The individuals who perform this service to society, and who thereby bring about the growth of the societies in which they arise, are superhuman in a very literal sense, for they have attained a supreme self-mastery which manifests itself in a rare power of self-determination. These are the souls who, to use Bergson's language, have felt the direction of the *élan vital*; they are 'privileged human beings whose desire it is . . . to set the imprint [of the *élan*] upon the whole of Mankind and – by a contradiction of which they are aware – to convert a species, which is essentially a created thing, into creative effort; to make a movement out of something which, by definition, is a halt.'[15]

The creative personality feels the impulse of internal necessity to transfigure his fellow men by converting them to his own insight; and the emergence of a genius of this kind – whether a religious mystic like Christ and the Buddha, or a political leader like Lenin and Gandhi – inevitably precipitates a social conflict, as society struggles to cope with the disequilibrium produced by his creative energy. Equilibrium will be restored if the individual's vision can be translated into society's practice – if the creative mutation in the microcosm is answered by an adaptative modification of the macrocosm; and growth will be assured if this movement proceeds in a dynamic series of continual alternations, from integration through differentiation to reintegration and thence to a redifferentiation that is still not the end of the story. But what if the creative personality fails to carry society with him, or allows his spiritual leadership to degenerate into an oppressive and sterile tyranny? If we have argued that growth is a concomitant of the creative energy of self-determination, then we must see too whether we can interpret breakdown in terms of the loss of this power.

PART IV

THE BREAKDOWNS
OF CIVILIZATIONS

Why have some civilizations broken down in the past? I do not believe that civilizations are fated to break down, so I begin by exposing the fallacious arguments of the determinists. Having rejected determinist explanations, I look for an alternative. I find, first, that the very process by which growth is sustained is inherently risky: the creative leadership of a society has to resort to social 'drill' in order to carry along the uncreative mass, and this mechanical device turns against its masters when their creative inspiration fails. I then have to account for the failure of creativity, and I ascribe it to the spiritual demoralization to which we human beings seem to be prone on the morrow of great achievements – a demoralization to which we are not bound to succumb, and for which we ourselves therefore bear the responsibility. Success seems to make us lazy or self-satisfied or conceited. I muster a series of notable historical examples to show how this actually happens and how human beings have erred in each case.

plates 23, 24

DETERMINISM OR FREE WILL?

Men have often been tempted to deny free will and retreat into deterministic explanations of the flux of life, especially during periods of social crisis. A seventeenth-century English trencher, above, borrows its theme from the wheel-imagery of cyclical philosophies: Plenty, Pride, Plea (i.e. litigation), and Poverty are linked in an inevitable sequence, though Peace, in the centre, may offer escape. Poussin's *Dance of Human Life*, below, also looks back to the medieval wheel of fortune, but introduces a positive element of free choice. Beneath the Sun's chariot, moving on its unchangeable course, figures of Transience and Time watch the rhythmic dance of Poverty, Labour, Plenty, and Luxury. The dancers are locked in a single movement and governed by the laws of the cosmos; but the inclusion of Labour – substituted here for the more common medieval figure of resigned Humility – contradicts the determinist imagery by suggesting that men's conscious efforts may break the fateful cycle.

Speke your coiecture; how kend this figure. Plentie. That peace maketh plentie; plentie; pryde; plee; & poutie. Amongh the con tarily all in this place; Hath peetie where entereth pride to prate; the med place equally.

plates 25, 26

CREATIVE RESPONSE, MECHANICAL RESPONSE

The growth of a civilization lies in the hands of a creative minority. This élite must have the power not only to cope successfully with the challenges to which their society is exposed, but also to carry along with them the majority of uncreative people. Saint Francis of Assisi epitomizes the creative personality who can impart inspiration to other souls 'like light caught from a leaping flame'. Giotto's fresco, right, illustrates the vision of the Saint that moved Pope Innocent III to sanction the Franciscan Order's foundation: according to one account, the Pope 'saw the Lateran Basilica about to fall, when a little poor man, of mean stature and humble aspect, propped it with his own back and saved it from falling.' This dream convinced Innocent that Francis was the Church's spiritual saviour.

Such power of inspiration is, however, rare. More often, a society's leaders must rely on the dull obedience instilled by social drill to induce the rank-and-file to follow their leader; but this common device carries a built-in risk of failure. The soldiers, opposite, are men welded into a machine: they are no longer individuals with personal responses and the power of self-determination, but a mechanical corps, at the mercy of others, and liable to demoralization if leadership fails, or to rebellion if it degenerates into tyranny.

plates 27, 28

IDOLIZATION OF
THE PAST: VENICE

Infatuated with her medieval glory, Venice failed to respond creatively to the challenges of the modern world. In the sixteenth century, Tintoretto could show Venice truthfully as the 'Queen of the Adriatic', above; but two centuries later the giant statues of Mars and Neptune, presiding over the Doge's coronation, opposite, are no more than empty symbols of an idolized past.

plates 29, 30

IDOLIZATION OF
AN INSTITUTION:
ORTHODOX CHRISTENDOM

The Orthodox Christian Society compromised its future by reviving and idolizing a ghost of Roman imperial absolutism: the authoritarian rule of a church-dominated state crushed and distorted social growth. The eleventh-century Empress and Emperor, above, flank the figure of Christ in authentic symbolism of the spiritual patronage that the secular power appropriated. The creative potential that was thus condemned to sterility can be glimpsed in the works of genius created in the fourteenth century, when – too late – the decline of imperial power liberated energies that had been repressed for centuries: the vigour and movement that the artist has breathed into his mosaic of the first steps of the Virgin, opposite, make a telling contrast to the stiff formalism of earlier official art.

plates 31, 32

IDOLIZATION OF A TECHNIQUE:
WARFARE

Military history provides a continuing illustration of the disastrous effects of relying on an old-fashioned technique instead of pressing on to meet the future with creative innovations. The classic example is the legendary duel between Goliath and David, above, in which the armour-plated giant, confident of yet another victory, is unexpectedly defeated by an insignificant and harmless-looking shepherd boy. Altdorfer's celebrated painting, *Alexander's Victory*, opposite, commemorates the historic victories of the co-ordinated cavalry and phalanx of Macedon over the militarily conservative armies of contemporary Greece and Asia.

plate 33

THE INTOXICATION OF VICTORY:
AMBITION OVERLEAPS ITSELF

A sad Ecclesia – the Catholic Church in Rome – watches her
desertion by her papal spouse Clement V, who carries a falcon
symbolic both of calamity and holy love. The picture, from a
fifteenth-century manuscript, commemorates the 'Babylonish
Captivity' of the Papacy under the French kings at Avignon,
which began during Clement's pontificate in 1309. The Captivity
and the ensuing Great Schism were the sequel to a disastrous
series of misjudgments by successive Popes, whose obsession
with worldly success tempted them to overreach themselves.
The Papacy's decline as a spiritual force, culminating in the
Reformation, is a classic example of the catastrophic effects of
blinding ambition.

20 Is determinism convincing?

ONE OF THE perennial infirmities of human beings is to ascribe their own failures to the operation of forces which are entirely beyond their control and immeasurably wider in range than the compass of human action. This mental manœuvre, which promises to convert an importunate sense of humiliation into a new assurance of self-importance – by setting the great engine of the Universe in motion in order to break one human career – is among the most insidious of 'the Consolations of Philosophy'. It is particularly attractive to sensitive minds in periods of decline and fall; and in the decline and fall of the Hellenic Civilization it was a commonplace of different schools of philosophers to explain the social decay which they deplored but could not arrest as the incidental and inevitable effect of an all-pervasive 'cosmic senescence'. This was the philosophy of the Epicurean Lucretius in the last generation of the Hellenic time of troubles before the Hellenic Society obtained the temporary relief of the *Pax Augusta*.

> The Universe itself is not exempt.
> Its ramparts will be stormed; and this dread breach
> Will make of it a foul putrescent ruin.
> The mischief has begun. Why, our own age
> Is broken-backed already. Mother Earth
> Has lost her strength. Today she finds it hard
> To bring forth pygmies – she who once brought forth
> The life of all the ages; hers the feat
> Of bearing the huge frames of monstrous beasts. . . .
> Our bright crops and our smiling vineyards too
> Are Earth's gift, her spontaneous gift, to men.
> Hers the sweet younglings, hers the smiling pastures.
> Alas! Today, these hardly reach full growth,
> Though human work now comes to Nature's aid.
> We work our teams, and teamsters too, to death,
> Wear out our tools, yet hardly match Earth's needs.
> Our fields demand more work, yet grudge work's fruits.
> Shaking his head, the aging ploughman sighs.
> His work has gone for nothing, he laments.
> The present? A sad contrast to the past.
> He envies the good fortune of his sire.
> The ancients, he laments, were godly men.
> They made a living, made it with great ease,
> From holdings that are dwarfed by ours today.
> The wizened grape-vine's woeful husbandman
> Arraigns time's ruthless rush and pesters Heaven,
> Blind to the Universe's slow decay,
> Worn down by aeons, destined for the grave.[1]

The theme recurs in a work of controversy which was written by one of the Fathers of the Western Christian Church some three hundred years later, under the impression of the stricken Hellenic Society's next relapse into a time of tribulation which had found Cyprian a pagan scholar and which saw him a Christian martyr before the crisis passed:

You ought to be aware that the age is now senile. It has not now the stamina that used to make it upstanding, nor the vigour and robustness that used to make it strong. This truth is proclaimed, even if we keep silence . . . by the world itself, which testifies to

its own decline by giving manifold concrete evidence of the process of decay. There is a diminution in the winter rains that give nourishment to the seeds in the earth, and in the summer heats that ripen the harvests. The springs have less freshness and the autumns less fecundity. The mountains, disembowelled and worn out, yield a lower output of marble; the mines, exhausted, furnish a smaller stock of the precious metals; the veins are impoverished, and they shrink daily. There is a decrease and deficiency of farmers in the fields, of sailors on the sea, of soldiers in the barracks, of honesty in the market-place, of justice in court, of concord in friendship, of skill in technique, of strictness in morals. When a thing is growing old, do you suppose that it can still retain, unimpaired, the exuberance of its fresh and lusty youth? Anything that is near its end and is verging towards its decline and fall is bound to dwindle. The Sun, for instance, radiates his beams with a less brilliant and fiery splendour when he is setting, and the Moon grows thin, with her horns all eaten away, when she is on the wane. The tree which was once so green and so luxuriant turns sterile later on, as its branches wither up, and grows ugly with old age; and old age likewise stops the flow of the spring, until the bounteous outpouring of its welling source dwindles into a bare trickle. This is the sentence that has been passed upon the world; this is the law of God: that what has been born must die, and what has grown up must grow old, and what has been strong must lose its strength, and what has been great must be diminished; and that this loss of strength and loss of stature must end, at last, in annihilation.[2]

We can perhaps hear an echo of Cyprian's pessimism in the concern voiced in our own generation at the allegedly imminent exhaustion of our Earth's store of natural resources; and we are even familiar with the idea of a cosmic sentence of death, since it has been repeated by those Western physical scientists who have postulated the ultimate disintegration of all matter in accordance with the Second Law of Thermodynamics.[3] But even if we were to accept this now disputed proposition, this sentence upon the material cosmos would bear with it none of that promise of spiritual liberation – through the extinction of our consciousness or else through its etherealization[4] – which it bore for Lucretius and for Cyprian; for our Western cosmologists present a time-chart on which human history and cosmic history are plotted on such utterly different scales that, from the practical standpoint, they can be regarded as quite out of relation with each other.

Mankind is young. . . . Our civilization is still in its infancy, and the Earth itself is not half-way through its career; it is more than 4,000 million years old, but in 4,000 million years from now it will probably still exist.[5]

Accordingly, the latter-day Western advocates of a predestinarian or deterministic explanation of the breakdowns of civilizations appeal instead to a law of senescence and death with a shorter wave-length, for which they claim jurisdiction over the whole kingdom of life on this planet. One of the most celebrated members of this school, Oswald Spengler, argued that a civilization is comparable with an organism, and that it is subject to the same process of childhood, youth, maturity, and old age as a human being or any other living organism.[6] But we have already noted in an earlier chapter[7] that societies are not in fact living organisms in any sense. In subjective terms they are the intelligible fields of study; and in objective terms they are the common ground between the respective fields of activity of a number of individual human beings, whose individual energies are the vital forces which operate to work out the history of a society, including its time-span.

Who can decree or forecast what the characters and the interactions of all these actors are to be, or how many of them are to appear upon a particular stage from first to last? To declare dogmatically, with Spengler, that every society has a predestined time-span is as foolish as it would be to declare that every play that is written is bound to consist of an equal number of acts.

Spengler does not strengthen the determinist case when he abandons the simile of an individual organism for the simile of a species of organisms or a genus:

The *habitus* of any group of organisms includes, among other things, a definite life-span and a definite *tempo* of development; and no morphology of history can dispense with these concepts. ... The span of a generation – whatever creature may be in question – is a numerical value of almost mystical significance. And these relations are also valid for all civilizations – and this in a way that has never before been dreamt of. Every civilization, every archaic age, every rise and every downfall, and every inevitable phase of each of these movements, has a definite time-span which is always the same and which always recurs with symbolic emphasis. What is the significance of the fifty-year period in the rhythm of political, intellectual, and artistic life which is prevalent in all civilizations? ... What is the significance of the millennium which is the ideal life-span of all civilizations, considered in proportion to the individual human being's 'three-score years and ten'?[8]

The conclusive answer to these questionings is that a society is not a species or genus, any more than it is an organism. It is itself an individual representative of some species of the genus 'societies', and the individual human beings who are the 'members' of a society are representatives of a species or genus likewise. But the genus of which we human beings are the individuals is neither the Western Society (or the Hellenic Society or any other society) in particular nor the genus of societies in general, but the genus *Homo*; and this simple truth absolves us from any obligation to examine here the Spenglerian dogma that genera and species have preordained life-spans on the analogy of the individual organisms in which the biological genera and species are represented. Even if we suppose for a moment that the genus *Homo* has a limited mandate for existence on the face of this planet, a brief consideration of the actual historical duration of biological genera and species to date shows at once that it is as impossible to link up the breakdown of any civilization with this hypothetical expiry of the mandate of the genus *Homo* as it is to link it up with the dissolution of the material Universe into radiation. The genus *Homo* is believed to have been in existence, in a recognizably human form, for between 300,000 and 500,000 years already,[9] as against the 5000 or so years that have elapsed since the first emergence of the societies called 'civilizations'. What warrant is there for assuming that the mandate of this genus (if it really is subject to any mandate) is not good for another 500,000 years at least? And, to come to grips again with our immediate problem of the breakdowns of civilizations, what ground is there for suggesting that these breakdowns are accompanied by any symptoms of physical or psychic degeneration in the individual human beings who happen to be alive in a society at the time of its dissolution? Were the Athenians of the generation of Socrates and Euripides and Thucydides and Pheidias and Pericles, who were overtaken by the catastrophe of 431 BC, intrinsically poorer creatures in soul or body than the generation of Marathon, who shone in retrospect in the illusively intensified light of an age which appeared more glorious than it actually had been in contrast with the age that followed?

An explanation of the breakdowns of civilizations in terms of the supposed science of eugenics perhaps appears to be suggested by Plato in a famous passage of *The Republic*:

A society with the ideal constitution is not easily thrown out of equilibrium; but, after all, everything that has a genesis is foredoomed to eventual disintegration, and even the ideal constitution will not endure in perpetuity, but will break down in the end. The breakdown is connected with the periodic rhythm (with a short wave-length for short-lived creatures and a long wave-length for those at the other end of the scale) which is the rhythm of life in the animal as well as in the vegetable kingdom, and which is the determinant of both physical and psychic fecundity. The specific laws of human eugenics will baffle both the reason and the intuition of our trained ruling minority, in spite of all their intellectual power. These laws will elude them; and one day they will beget children inopportunely. ...[10]

Plato contrived a fantastically intricate numerical formula to express the wave-length of human life, and postulated that social disintegration would follow upon the neglect of this mathematical law of eugenics by a society's leaders. Even so, it is plain that Plato does not represent the racial degeneration, to which he attributes the social breakdown, as being an automatic or predetermined event, but rather as being an intellectual mistake, a failure of technique: a lapse in the sphere of human action.

There is, in any case, no warrant for following Plato in accepting racial degeneration as even a secondary link in the chain of causation through which a social breakdown leads on to a decline. For although, in times of social decline, the members of the declining society may seem to dwindle into pygmies or to stiffen into cripples, by contrast with the kingly stature and magnificent activity of their forbears in the age of social growth, to ascribe this malady to degeneration is a false diagnosis. The biological heritage of the epigoni is the same as that of the pioneers, and all the pioneers' endeavours and achievements are potentially within their descendants' reach. The malady which holds the children of decadence fast bound in misery and iron[11] is no paralysis of their natural faculties as human beings but a breakdown and disintegration of their social heritage, which debars them from finding scope for their unimpaired faculties in effective and creative social action. The dwarfing of the epigoni is the effect of social breakdown and not its cause.

We have now discarded three predestinarian explanations of the breakdowns of civilizations: the theory that

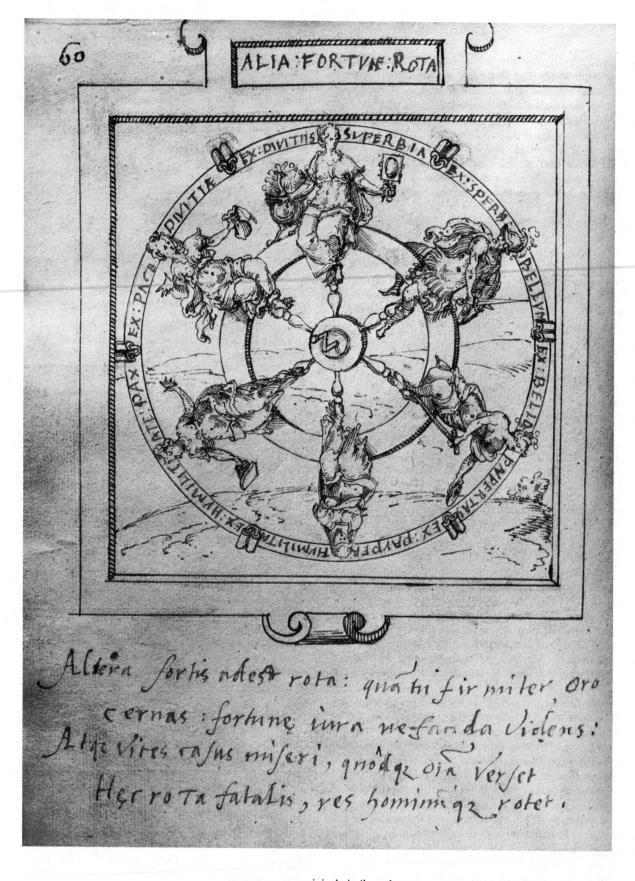

THE WHEEL, original simile and permanent symbol of the cyclic philosophy.

105 *Rota fortunae*: this version of the wheel of fortune interprets the idea in terms of a sequence of moral responses: from peace wealth, from wealth pride, from pride war, from war poverty, from poverty humility, from humility peace.

106 *Rota fatalis*: Western wheel of fate, using the same imagery of predetermined cycles.

107 *Rota vitalis*: Indic wheel of life, symbolic of the eternal round of procreation.

they are the incidental consequence of a running-down of the clockwork of the physical Universe; the theory that a civilization, like a living organism, has its own inherent life-span and life-curve; and the theory that the breakdown of any civilization at any given date is due to the racial degeneration of its human components. We still have to consider one further predestinarian hypothesis, which assumes that civilizations succeed one another by a law of their nature which is the common law of the cosmos, in a perpetually recurrent cycle of alternating birth and death.[12]

The application of this theory of cycles to the history of Mankind was a natural corollary to the sensational astronomical discovery, which appears to have been made in the Babylonic World by the end of the third millennium BC[13] and which was popularized by Greek astronomers after the fourth century BC, that the three conspicuous and familiar astronomical cycles – the terrestrial cycle of day-and-night and the lunar cycle of the month and the solar cycle of the year – were not the only instances of periodic recurrence in the movements of the heavenly bodies; that there was also a larger co-ordination of stellar movements which embraced all the planets as well as the Earth and Moon and Sun; and that 'the music of the spheres', which was made by the harmony of this heavenly chorus, came round full circle, chord for chord, in a cycle of great cosmic months and years which dwarfed the solar year into insignificance. The inference was that the annual birth and death of the terrestrial vegetation, which was manifestly governed by the solar year-cycle, had its counterpart in a recurrent birth and death of all things on the time-scale of the cosmic year-cycle; and minds which came under the spell of this idea were apt to project this pattern of periodicity into every object of their thought.[14]

Hellenic literature abounds in references to this cyclic philosophy. Plato was evidently fascinated by it, for the theme recurs throughout his writings.

Athenian Stranger. Do you feel that the ancient legends have any truth in them?

Cleinias of Crete. Which legends?

Stranger. The legends of repeated destructions of the human race by floods and plagues and many other catastrophes, in which only a tiny remnant of Mankind survived.

Cleinias. Why, certainly, the whole of that body of legend carries conviction with everybody.[15]

Elsewhere Plato develops this brief exposition of the cyclic hypothesis, applying it to the history of the Hellenes[16] and to the pattern of the cosmos as a whole, which he represents as a perpetual alternation of catastrophe and rehabilitation.[17] The same doctrine reappears in Virgil's poetry:

The last age of the Sibyl's song is here.
The sequence of the ages starts again.
The past returns – the Virgin, Saturn's Realm –
A new race from High Heaven descends to Earth. . . .
Another Tiphys steers another Argo,
Laden with heroes; yes, and other wars
Bring great Achilles once again to Troy.[18]

But where Virgil sees a triumphant renewal of an heroic age, Marcus Aurelius, writing some two hundred years later under the shadow of a melancholy age, feels only the desolation of endless repetition:

There is a deadly monotony about the cyclic motion of the cosmos – up and down, world without end. . . . Soon we shall be buried under the Earth, and next the Earth herself will be transformed, and then whatever has arisen out of her transmutation will undergo the same process again and again to infinity.[19]

This philosophy of sheer recurrence, which intrigued, without ever quite captivating, the Hellenic genius, came to dominate contemporary Indic minds.

Hindu thinkers had evolved a cyclic theory of time. The cycle was called a *kalpa* and was equivalent to 4,320 million earthly years. The *kalpa* is divided into 14 periods and at the end of each of these the universe is recreated and once again Manu (primeval man) gives birth to the human race. At the moment we are in the seventh of the 14 periods of the present *kalpa*. Each of these is divided into 71 Great Intervals and each of these is divided respectively in 4 *yugas* or periods of time. The *yugas* contain respectively 4,800, 3,600, 2,400, 1,200 god-years (one god-year being 360 human years), and there is a progressive decline in the quality of civilization. We are now in the fourth of these *yugas*, the *kaliyuga* when the world is full of evil and wickedness, and thus the end of the world is by comparison imminent, though there are several millennia yet before the end![20]

Are these 'vain repetitions'[21] of the Gentiles really the law of the Universe and, therefore, incidentally the law of the histories of civilizations? If we find that the answer is in the affirmative, we can hardly escape the conclusion that we are the perpetual victims of an everlasting cosmic practical joke, which condemns us to endure our sufferings and to overcome our difficulties and to purify ourselves of our sins – only to know in advance that the automatic and inevitable lapse of a certain meaningless measure of time cannot fail to stultify all our human exertions by reproducing the same situation again and again *ad infinitum*, just as if we had never exerted ourselves at all.

This conclusion may be tolerable to an unusually robust intellect in an unusually sanguine mood. A modern Western philosopher has even succeeded in making the 'law of eternal recurrence' a matter for rejoicing:

Sing and bubble over, O Zarathustra, heal your soul with new songs, so that you may bear your great destiny, that was never yet the destiny of any man! For your animals well know, O Zarathustra, who you are and must become: behold, *you are the teacher of eternal recurrence*, that is now *your* destiny! . . . Behold, we know what you teach: that all things recur eternally, and we ourselves with them, and that we have already existed an infinite number of times before, and all things with us. . . .[22]

Aristotle, too, shows no signs of distress when he pricks the bubble of his own philosophy by making the casual observation, in the middle of a treatise on meteorology, that

in human history the recurrence of identical scientific views does not happen just once or twice or a small number of times; it happens *ad infinitum*.[23]

In another passage, Aristotle deals with the problem of periodicity in human affairs, through the concrete example of the implications of a recurrence of the Trojan War, as if these implications were nothing more than an intellectual conundrum.[24] He contemplates with a dispassionate calm the proposition that 'human life is a vicious circle' of repetitive genesis and decay, and feels no pang. Virgil, too, in the passage that we have already quoted, dismisses the recurrent Trojan War as a slight and momentary recrudescence of the Old Adam, which simply serves as a foil to the swiftly and securely redawning golden age. Yet, when the poet returns from his day-dream of an earthly paradise regained to resume the spiritual burden of his own tormented generation, he confesses that the heroic warfare of the Achaeans in the pre-Hellenic interregnum has led on, through a continuous chain of *karma*, to the internecine warfare of the Roman war-lords.

In full, long since, with Roman blood,
We have atoned for Trojan breach of faith. . . .
A world where right spells wrong, and wrong spells right!
So many wars! So many shapes of crime!
The plough despised! The ploughman reft away!
The widowed fields unkempt! The sickle's curve
Melted to mould a sword-blade's stiff straight edge. . . .
Neighbours break bonds of friendship, take up arms;
The wicked war-god rages everywhere.
The pace is quickening like the chariots' pace
When they burst out to speed along the course.
No use, poor charioteer, to draw thy reins.
Thy chariot's masters are thy racing steeds.[25]

Is the Trojan War to recur innumerable times over, when it is fated each time to precipitate an age-long avalanche of wickedness and woe? This question, which Virgil dares not face, is answered by Shelley in a chorus which begins as a Virgilian reminiscence and ends on a note which is altogether Shelley's own:

The World's great age begins anew,
  The golden years return,
The Earth doth like a snake renew
  Her winter weeds outworn:
Heaven smiles, and faiths and empires gleam
Like wrecks of a dissolving dream. . . .

A loftier Argo cleaves the main,
  Fraught with a later prize;
Another Orpheus sings again,
  And loves, and weeps, and dies;
A new Ulysses leaves once more
Calypso for his native shore.

Oh! write no more the Tale of Troy,
  If Earth Death's scroll must be!
Nor mix with Laian rage the joy
  Which dawns upon the free,
Although a subtler Sphinx renew
Riddles of death Thebes never knew. . . .

Oh cease! Must Hate and Death return?
  Cease! Must men kill and die?
Cease! Drain not to its dregs the urn
  Of bitter prophecy.
The World is weary of the Past:
Oh might it die or rest at last!

If the law of the Universe is really the sardonic law *plus ça change plus c'est la même chose*,[26] no wonder that the poet cries for the Buddhist release from a wheel of existence which may be a thing of beauty so long as it is merely guiding the stars in their courses, but which is an intolerable tread-mill for our human feet.

Does reason constrain us to believe that the cyclic movement of the stars is also the movement of human history? What, 'in the last analysis', are those movements of Yin-and-Yang and challenge-and-response which we have taken some intellectual pleasure in discerning and bringing to light? Certainly, in these movements of the forces that weave the web of human history, an element of sheer recurrence can be detected; indeed, it stares us in the face. Yet the shuttle which shoots backwards and forwards across the loom of time in a perpetual to-and-fro is all this time bringing into existence a tapestry in which there is manifestly a progress towards an end and not just an 'endless repetition' in the likeness of the shuttle's own action. The transition from Yin to Yang, in any given case, is no doubt one repetition of a repetitive action; yet this repetition is neither vain nor stale, since it is the necessary condition for an act of creation which is new and spontaneous and unique.[27] Similarly, the response to a challenge which provokes a further challenge and thereby evokes a further response which is likewise provocative in its turn no doubt sets up a cyclic movement. Yet we have seen that it is precisely this kind of response – the response which inaugurates a cyclic movement by providing for its own successor – that releases the Promethean *élan* of social growth.[28]

The simple truth is that, in any analysis of rhythm, we have to distinguish between the movements of the part and those of the whole, and between the natures of the means and of the ends. There is no law of pre-established harmony which decrees that the end must have the same nature as the means, or the whole the same movement as the part; and this is immediately obvious in the case of the wheel, which is the original simile and permanent symbol of the whole cyclic philosophy. The movement of the wheel is admittedly repetitive in relation to the wheel's own axle; but the wheel has been manufactured and fitted to its axle only in order to become a part of a vehicle; and the fact that the vehicle can move only in virtue of the wheel's circular movement round the axle does not compel the vehicle itself to travel like a merry-go-round in a circular track. The wheel is indispensable to the vehicle as a means of locomotion, but it is incapable of dictating the course on which the vehicle is to move. The course depends upon the manipulation of the reins or the steering-gear by the driver. Indeed, if the relations between the wheel and the vehicle – or part and whole, or means and end – are governed by any law at all, it is not a law of identity but a law of diversity, under which a repetitive movement of the wheel (or the part or the means) brings about a non-repetitive movement of the vehicle (or the whole or the end); conversely, the end attains its unique realization, and the whole its unique individuality, and the vehicle its unique goal, through the repetitive employment of similar means and the repetitive juxtaposition of standard parts and the repetitive revolutions of the wheel round its axle.

This harmony of two movements – a major irreversible movement which is borne on the wings of a minor repetitive movement – is perhaps the essence of what we mean by rhythm; and we can discern this play of forces not only in the mechanized rhythm of our man-made machinery but likewise in the organic rhythm of life. The annual procession of the seasons, which brings with it the annual blossom and decay of vegetation, has made possible the secular evolution of the vegetable kingdom. The sombre cycle of birth and reproduction and death has made possible the evolution of all higher animals up to Man himself. The pumping-action of the lungs and heart enables the human being to live out his life; the bars of music, and the feet, lines, stanzas, and cantos of poetry enable the composer and the poet to expound their themes; the cyclic rotation of the praying-wheel carries the Buddhist towards the goal of *nirvana*; and even the wheel of existence, from which the Buddhist discipline promises release, produces the abiding burden of *karma* which is handed on, to be aggravated or mitigated, from one incarnation-cycle to the next and thereby transforms a trivial round into a tragic history. The repetitive 'music of the spheres' dies down to an undertone in an expanding Universe of nebulae and star-clusters which are apparently receding from one another with incredible velocity, while the relativity of the space-time framework gives to each successive position of the vast astral arrays the irrevocable historic uniqueness of a dramatic 'situation' in some play in which the actors are human personalities.

Thus the detection of periodic repetitive movements in our analysis of the process of civilization does not by any means imply that the process itself, to which these contributory movements minister, is of the same cyclic order as they are. On the contrary, if any inference can be drawn legitimately from the periodicity of these minor movements, we may rather infer that the major movement which they bear along on their monotonously rising and falling wings is of the diverse order, or, in other words, that it is not recurrent but progressive. This interpretation of the movement of life in terms of two modes of rhythm has been precisely expressed in the philosophies of the African Civilizations, and perhaps at its most sophisticated in the cosmogony of the Dogon people of the Western Sudan.

Their conception of the universe is based, on the one hand, on a principle of the vibrations of matter, and on the other, on a general movement of the universe as a whole. The original germ of life is symbolized by the smallest cultivated seed. . . . This seed, quickened by an internal vibration, bursts the enveloping sheath, and emerges to reach the uttermost confines of the universe. At the same time this unfolding matter moves along a path which forms a spiral or helix. . . . Two fundamental notions are thus expressed: on the one hand the perpetual helical movement signifies the conservation of matter; further, this movement . . . is held to represent the perpetual alternation of opposites – right and left, high and low, odd and even, male and female – reflecting a principle of twin-ness, which ideally should direct the proliferation of life. These pairs of opposites support each other in an equilibrium which the individual being conserves within itself. On the other hand, the infinite extension of the universe is expressed by the continual progression of matter along this spiral path.[29]

This tentative conclusion is sufficient for our purpose at the moment. We are not condemned to believe in the cyclic version of predestinarianism as the supreme law of our human history; and this was the last form of the necessitarian doctrine with which we had to contend. The goddess with whom we have to do battle is not *Saeva Necessitas*[30] with her lethal armoury, but, on the evidence of the fates of civilizations in past history, only probability, whom mortal valour wielding mortal weapons may one day drive ignominiously off the field. The civilizations which have already died are not 'dead by fate'; and therefore a living civilization such as the Western Civilization is not doomed inexorably in advance *migrare ad plures*: to join the majority of its kind that have already suffered shipwreck. The divine spark of creative power is instinct in ourselves; and, if we have the grace to kindle it into flame, then 'the stars in their courses'[31] cannot defeat our efforts to attain the goal of human endeavours.

108 Creative leadership: Moses, inspired by God to set a society in motion towards a territorial and divine inheritance.

21 The mechanicalness of mimesis

IF WE HAVE PROVED to our satisfaction that the breakdowns of civilizations are not brought about by the operation, either recurrent or progressive, of forces which are outside human control, we still have to find the true causes of these catastrophes; and the conclusions that we reached in our earlier chapter on the nature of growth[1] will provide us with a sure pointer in our present search. We found there that growth is the concomitant of self-determination; can we now reverse this, and argue that breakdowns come about as a result of the loss of this power of self-determination? In other words, shall we find that civilizations have met their deaths not from the assault of an external and uncontrollable assassin, but by their own hands?

This was the conclusion which was divined with a sure intuition by a modern Western poet.

> In tragic life, God wot,
> No villain need be! Passions spin the plot:
> We are betray'd by what is false within.[2]

And Meredith's flash of insight is not a new discovery of nineteenth-century Western wisdom, like the Origin of Species or the Law of the Conservation of Energy. A century earlier the genius of Volney had casually exploded the eighteenth-century doctrine of the natural goodness and automatic improvement of human nature by testifying that 'the source of his calamities . . . resides within Man himself; he carries it in his heart'.[3] The same truth is declared in a fragment of Menander, which almost anticipates Meredith's own words:

> Things rot through evils native to their selves,
> And all that injures issues from within.[4]

And a Western Christian bishop reached the same conclusion in the fourth century of the Christian Era: 'The enemy is right inside you, the cause of your erring is there inside, I say, shut up in ourselves alone.'[5]

The concept of self-determination as a religious issue is also found in the philosophies of the African Civilizations, which see the misfortunes that befall a man or his community as the fruits not of fate but of sin; in other words, as the results of irresponsible behaviour. 'Onipa ne asem, say the Akan [a West African people]: it is mankind that matters – meaning, in this context, that any man can always be responsible for himself.'[6]

This truth about the lives of human beings is equally true of the lives of societies. A Hellenic philosopher, Dicaearchus, is reported to have maintained – in a lost work called How Men go to Destruction – that the greatest danger to Man is Man. Volney applied his intuition that 'the source of his calamities . . . resides within Man himself' to the destruction of bodies politic, in lieu of the untenable hypothesis that communities, like individuals, have a limited life-span and a formulated life-curve;[7] and this is anticipated in a passage of Saint Cyprian, in which the African Father applies the same truth to the entire field of social life.[8]

You complain of the aggression of foreign enemies; yet, if the foreign enemy were to cease from troubling, would Roman really be able to live at peace with Roman? If the external danger of invasion by armed barbarians were to be stamped out, should we not be exposed to a fiercer and a heavier civil bombardment, on the home front, in the shape of calumnies and injuries inflicted by the powerful on their weaker fellow citizens? You complain of crop-failures and famines: yet the greatest famines are made not by drought but by rapacity, and the most flagrant distress springs from profiteering and price-raising in the corn-trade. You complain that the clouds do not disgorge their rain in the sky, and you ignore the barns that fail to disgorge their grain on terra firma. You complain of the fall in production, and ignore the failure to distribute what is actually produced to those who are in need of it. You denounce plague and pestilence, while really the effect of these scourges is to bring to light, or bring to a head, the crimes of human beings: the callousness that shows no pity for the sick, and the covetousness and rapine that are in full cry after the property of the dead.[9]

In this passage a man of penetrating insight and deep feeling has given the true explanation of the breakdown which had cut the growth of the Hellenic Civilization short some 600 or 700 years earlier, and which had brought the broken-down society to all but the last stage of its decline and fall in Cyprian's own day. The Hellenic Civilization had broken down because, in its growth-stage, at some point something had gone wrong on the home front with that interaction between individuals through which the growth of a growing civilization is achieved.

What is the weakness that exposes a growing civilization to this risk of stumbling and falling in mid-career and losing its Promethean élan? If we recall our analysis of growth in a previous chapter,[10] we shall realize that, on our own showing, the risk of such a collapse is constant and acute, because it lies in the very nature of the course which a growing civilization is obliged to take.

This course is not the narrow way 'which leadeth unto life – and few there be that find it'.[11] Although the few that find this way are precisely those creative personalities who set a civilization in motion and carry it forward, they cannot simply lay aside every weight and run the race that is set before them,[12] because, being 'social animals', they cannot go on moving forward themselves unless they can contrive to carry their fellows with them in their advance; and the uncreative rank-and-file of Mankind, which in every known society has always been in an overwhelming majority, cannot be transfigured en masse in the twinkling of an eye.

Perfection . . . is not possible while the individual remains isolated: the individual is obliged, under pain of being stunted and enfeebled in his own development if he disobeys, to carry others along with him in his march towards perfection, to be continually doing all he can to enlarge and increase the volume of the human stream sweeping thitherward.[13]

In these conditions, which are inherent in the very nature of social life, the creative personalities are challenged to attempt a *tour de force*: 'to convert a species, which is essentially a created thing, into creative effort; to make a movement out of something which . . . is a halt'.[14]

This *tour de force* is not impossible to achieve; and indeed there is a perfect way: the 'strenuous intellectual communion and intimate personal intercourse' that impart the divine fire from one soul to another 'like light caught from a leaping flame'.[15] Yet it is an unpractical counsel of perfection to prescribe this way, as Plato prescribes it, to the exclusion of others; for the inward spiritual grace through which an unillumined soul is fired by communion with a saint is almost as rare as the miracle that has brought the saint himself into the world. The world in which the creative personality finds himself, and in which he has to work, is a society in which his fellows are ordinary human beings. His task is to make his fellows into his followers; and Mankind in the mass can only be set in motion towards a goal beyond itself by enlisting the faculty of mimesis, or imitation.[16] For this mimesis is a kind of social drill;[17] and the dull ears that are deaf to the unearthly music of Orpheus's lyre are well attuned to the drill-sergeant's raucous word of command. The rank-and-file can only catch their leader up by taking a short cut, and they can only find room to march by deploying into the broad way that leadeth to destruction.[18] When the road to destruction has perforce to be trodden on the quest of life, it is perhaps no wonder that the quest should sometimes end in disaster.

Moreover, there is a weakness in the actual exercise of mimesis, quite apart from the way in which the faculty may be exploited. For, if it is true that mimesis is a kind of drill, it is also true that drill is a kind of mechanization of human movement and life; and our concept of the 'machine' has an ambiguous connotation. When we talk of 'a delicate mechanism' or 'mechanical ingenuity' or 'a skilled mechanic', the words call up the general idea of a triumph of life over matter and the particular idea of the triumph of human will and thought over the physical environment of a human society. The invention of machinery immensely extends Man's power over Man's environment by so manipulating inanimate objects that they are made to carry out human purposes, as the drill-sergeant's commands are executed by his platoon of mechanized human beings.

Nature herself has implicitly complimented Man upon his mechanical ingenuity by anticipating him in the use of mechanical devices. She has made an audaciously extensive use of them in the piece of natural mechanism with which we are most familiar: her *chef d'œuvre*, the human body. In the heart and lungs she has constructed two self-regulating machines which are models of their kind; and, by adjusting these organs to the performance of their appointed tasks with such perfection that they 'work automatically', Nature has released a margin of our muscular and nervous and psychic energies from the monotonously repetitive task of making breath follow breath and heart-beat follow heart-beat, and has set these marginal energies free to do the 'original work' of locomotion and sensation and thought. This is the trick by which, in the evolution of organic life, she has succeeded in building up ever more and more elaborate organisms. At every stage in this advance she has acted as Orpheus acts when he resorts to

MACHINE SUBSERVIENT
109 Ingenious rotary machine for comparative study of several books.

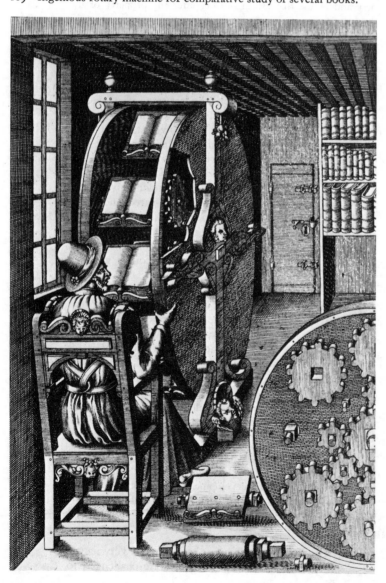

MACHINE DOMINANT   110   Streamlined working men, faceless and docile.

the methods of the drill-sergeant. In each successive organism in her ascending series she has introduced the maximum possible amount of drill, or, in other words, of automation. In fact, a natural organism is made up, like a human society, of a creative minority and an uncreative majority of 'members'; and in a growing organism, as in a growing society, the majority is drilled into following the minority's lead mechanically.

When we have lost ourselves in admiration of these natural and human mechanical triumphs, it is disconcerting to be reminded that there are other phrases – 'machine-made goods', 'machine-like movements', 'mechanical behaviour', 'the party machine' – in which the connotation of the word 'machine' is exactly the reverse. Yet there is no doubt about it: in each of the phrases in this second group the idea that is suggested is not the triumph of life over matter but the mastery of matter over life; and, instead of experiencing a thrill of self-confidence and pride, we feel a shock of humiliation and misgiving as we realize that the master-tool of life and mind, which promises to give them a boundless dominion over the material Universe, may actually turn in their hands into an instrument for their own subjugation to the Kingdom of Ancient Night.

A bondage lurking under shape of good –
Arts in themselves beneficent and kind,
But all too fondly followed and too far.[19]

The powers which, one moment ago, seemed to have discovered the secret of setting the Universe on fire, now suddenly turn out to have quenched their own flame and put out their own light by rashly smothering the spark under its potential fuel.

This Janus-like quality in the nature of machinery is disconcerting because at first sight it seems like a betrayal; but on second thoughts it becomes apparent that it is 'all in the game'. For the mechanic to denounce his machine because it has 'caught him out' is as irrational as it would be for the losing team in a tug-of-war to blame their rope for their defeat when they have gone out of their way to challenge the other team to a trial of strength and have woven the rope with their own hands in order to make the match playable. The discomfited team's error has lain in taking it for granted that, when once battle was joined, it could not fail to win. Yet the team's rope does not, of course, in itself guarantee a victory to either side. It is merely a neutral way and means for a trial of strength in which the issue is not a foregone conclusion. And, in the cosmic tug-of-war between life and matter, this neutral function is fulfilled by everything that comes under the category of machinery. Machines are ambiguous in their essence, and to call this ambiguity a betrayal is to convict oneself of being the bad workman who complains of his tools. *Homo faber* has apprenticed himself to a dangerous trade; and anyone who sets out to act on the principle of 'nothing venture, nothing win' is manifestly exposing himself to the risk of losses as the price of putting himself in the running for the victor's crown.

If this risk is involved in Man's use of machinery for dealing with his physical environment, it must be incurred, *a fortiori*, when he resorts to the device of mechanization in his relations with himself and his fellow men.[20] An expedient which is dangerous to life when it is employed in the struggle between life and matter becomes a sheer *tour de force* when life attempts to exploit it against life itself.

Thus a risk of catastrophe proves to be inherent in the use of the faculty of mimesis, which is the vehicle of mechanization in the medium of human nature; and it is evident that this inherent risk will be greater in degree when the faculty of mimesis is called into play in a society which is in dynamic movement than when the same faculty is given rein in a society which is in a state of rest. The weakness of mimesis lies in its being a mechanical response to a suggestion from some alien source, so that the action that is performed through mimesis is, *ex hypothesi*, an action that would never have been performed by its performer upon his own initiative. Thus all action that proceeds from mimesis is essentially precarious because it is not self-determined; and the best practical safeguard against the danger of its breaking down is for the exercise of the faculty of mimesis to become crystallized in the form of habit or custom. In 'the cake of custom'[21] the double-edged blade of mimesis is comfortably padded. But the breaking of 'the cake of custom' is of the essence of the change through which the passive Yin-state of a pre-civilizational society gives way to the dynamic Yang-drive.[22] In this movement the edged tool of mimesis is not discarded, but is employed with enhanced effect now that the breaking of 'the cake of custom' has laid its cutting edges bare. This baring of the blade means the removal of a safeguard; and the necessity of using the tool of mimesis without the protection of a customary régime – a necessity which is the price of growth – condemns a growing civilization to live dangerously. Indeed, the danger is perpetually imminent, since the condition which is required for the maintenance of the Promethean *élan* of growth is a condition of unstable equilibrium in which 'the cake of custom' is never allowed to set hard before it is broken up again.[23] In this hazardous pursuit of the goal of human endeavours there can never be such a thing as a provisional insurance against the perils which mimesis entails. There can only be an ultimate and radical solution of the problem through the complete elimination of mimesis in a society which has transformed itself into a

MACHINE MAN   111   Victims of corrupted power, drilled into passivity.

112   Destructive leadership: the totalitarian state – an impersonal Moloch, devouring
the lives and land of his people.

communion of saints; and this consummation, which is nothing less than the attainment of the goal, has never been even distantly approached by any known civilization hitherto.

In the meantime – and, on the scale of human lives, the time is long-drawn-out – the mechanized column of route is perpetually in danger of coming to a halt or of falling out of formation on the march if ever the rank-and-file are left to act without a lead in some situation without a precedent. The abyss which always yawns open before the feet of human beings who are taking the broad road towards civilization is continually revealed in abnormal accidents like shipwrecks or fires, which usually evoke exhibitions of astonishing demoralization as well as astonishing heroism; and the depth of this moral abyss is still deeper where the abnormal ordeal is not a natural accident but a social malady like a war or a revolution. In the history of Man's attempt at civilization hitherto there has never been any society whose progress in civilization has gone so far that, in times of revolution or war, its members could be relied upon not to commit atrocities. To confine ourselves to the history of our own society in our own generation, we can cite the behaviour of the Nazis in the Second World War and of the Western forces in Korea in 1950–51 and of the Americans in Vietnam in the 1960s and of the French settlers and professional soldiers in Algeria in 1954–62 and of the French police at home in Paris in 1968 as proof positive that, in certain conditions of abnormality and under a certain degree of strain, atrocities will be committed by members of the least uncivilized societies that have yet existed. In times of stress the mask of civilization is torn away from the primitive countenance of raw humanity in the rank-and-file; but the moral responsibility for the breakdowns of civilizations lies upon the heads of the leaders.

The creative personalities in the vanguard of a civilization who have had recourse to the mechanism of mimesis are exposing themselves to the risk of failure in two degrees, one negative and the other positive.

The possible negative failure is that, undesignedly and perhaps unconsciously, the leaders may infect themselves with the hypnotism which they have deliberately induced in their followers; and in that event the docility of the rank-and-file will have been purchased at the disastrous price of a loss of initiative in the officers. 'If the blind lead the blind, both shall fall into the ditch.'[24] If the mechanical rhythm by which ninety per cent of an organism is made subservient to the rest, in order that the remaining ten per cent of energy may be concentrated on creative evolution, is extended to the whole, then 'a marvel of mechanical ingenuity' is degraded into the monstrosity of 'a machine-like automaton'. The difference between ninety per cent and one hundred per cent of mechanization is all the difference in the world; and there is just this kind of difference between a society that is in growth and a society that has become arrested.

The arrested societies which we surveyed in an earlier chapter[25] have achieved so close an adaptation to their environment that they have taken its shape and colour and rhythm instead of impressing the environment with a stamp which is their own. The equilibrium of forces in their life is so exact that all their energies are absorbed in the effort of maintaining the position which they have attained already, and there is no margin of energy left over for reconnoitring the course of the road ahead. In the cases of arrest we have a classic illustration of the negative failure in which the leaders themselves become hypnotized by the drill which they have inculcated into the rank-and-file. In this predicament the column comes to a dead halt, at whatever point on its route it may happen to find itself at the moment, simply because there is nobody left at the head of the column to give fresh orders.

This negative failure, however, is seldom the end of the story. In abandoning Orpheus's music for the drill-sergeant's word of command, the leaders have played upon the faculty of mimesis in the rank-and-file by an exertion of power – as a substitute for the uncoercive play of the charm of genius that is attractive only to kindred spirits. In the interaction between leaders and led, mimesis and power are correlatives; and power is a force which is perhaps rarely brought into play without being abused. In any event, the tenure of power is an abuse in itself if those who hold the power have lost the faculty of leadership. Accordingly, the halt of the column of route, which we have pictured in our military simile, is apt to be followed by mutiny on the part of the rank-and-file, and by 'frightfulness' on the part of the officers – who make a desperate attempt to retain by brute force an authority which they have ceased to merit by any signal contribution to the common weal. The result is a hideous pandemonium, in which the military formation breaks up into an Ishmaelitish anarchy. This is the positive failure which is the nemesis of the resort to mimesis in the life of a growing civilization; and in the language of another simile this failure is familiar to us already. It is that 'disintegration' of a broken-down civilization which declares itself in the 'secession of the proletariat' from a *ci-devant* band of leaders which has degenerated into a 'dominant minority'.[26] The successive transformations of the prophet into the drill-sergeant and of this martinet into a terrorist explain the declines and falls of civilizations in terms of leadership.

In terms of relation or interaction, the failure of the Promethean *élan* declares itself in a loss of harmony. In the movement of life a change in any one part of a whole ought to be accompanied by sympathetic adjustments of the other parts if all is to go well; but when life is mechanized one part may be altered while others are left as they have been, and a loss of harmony is the result. In any whole a loss of harmony between its component parts is paid for by the whole in a corresponding loss of self-determination; and the fate of a declining civilization is described in Jesus's prophecy to Peter:

When thou wast young, thou girdedst thyself, and walkedst whither thou wouldest; but when thou shalt be old . . . another shall gird thee and carry thee whither thou wouldest not.[27]

A loss of self-determination is the ultimate criterion of breakdown, for – as we suggested by anticipation at the beginning of this chapter – it is the inverse of the criterion of growth. In the succeeding chapters we shall examine some of the forms in which this loss of self-determination through loss of harmony is manifested.

22 The reversal of roles

ANOTHER ASPECT of that failure of self-determination which we have been considering is the apparent nemesis of creativity. It looks as if it were uncommon for the creative responses to two or more successive challenges in the history of a given society to be achieved by one and the same minority or individual. So far from this being the rule, the party that has distinguished itself in dealing with one challenge is apt to fail conspicuously in attempting to deal with the next. This ironical and disconcerting yet apparently normal inconstancy of human fortunes is one of the dominant motifs of the Attic drama, and it is discussed by Aristotle, in his *Poetics*, under the name of *peripeteia*, or 'the reversal of roles'.[1] It is also one of the principal themes of the New Testament.

In the drama of the New Testament a Christ whose epiphany on Earth in the person of Jesus is, in Christian belief, the true fulfilment of Jewry's long-cherished Messianic hope is nevertheless rejected by a school of Scribes and Pharisees which, only a few generations back, has come to the fore at a critical juncture by leading an heroic Jewish revolt against the triumph of Hellenization. Yet now, in this far more momentous crisis, the Jews that comprehend and accept the – in Christian eyes – authentic Jewish Messiah's message are the least within the community, the publicans and the harlots.[2] The Messiah himself comes from 'Galilee of the Gentiles';[3] and his greatest executor, Paul, is a Hellenized Jew from Tarsus, a city beyond the traditional horizon of the Promised Land. In the numerous presentations of the drama of *peripeteia* in the parables and incidents of the Christian Testament, the roles that are reversed are sometimes played by the Pharisaic élite and the outcasts from the Jewish fold,[4] and at other times by Jewry as a whole and the Gentiles;[5] but whether it is the Pharisees who are challenged, as in the parable of the Pharisee and the Publican,[6] or the Jewish community itself, as in the parable of the Good Samaritan,[7] the moral is the same:

The stone which the builders rejected, the same is become the head of the corner.[8]

In its own historical setting, the Christian rendering of the theme of *peripeteia* is a variation on an ancient rendering in the Jewish Scriptures. The New Testament and the Old Testament are, both alike, regarded as instruments through which God has bequeathed a supernatural heritage to human beneficiaries; and the common plot of a twice played tragedy is a reversal of roles through a transfer of God's priceless gift from an apparently assured recipient to one with far less apparently promising prospects. In the original performance of the play it is Esau, the first-born, who sells his birthright to his younger brother Jacob; and in the second performance it is the heirs of Jacob who, by their rejection of Christ, now forfeit their prize to Esau. The Christian version of the plot thus presents a double *peripeteia*, a reversal of a reversal; but the literal historical sequence depicted in the New Testament has at the same time a deeper significance as an allegory of a mystery which is illustrated in the course of history because it lies at the heart of life. On this plane the operation of the principle of *peripeteia* is proclaimed in the New Testament in terms that transcend the historical limits of a particular time and place:

If any man desire to be first, the same shall be last of all and servant of all.[9] He that is least among you, the same shall be great.[10]

And the actors in the reversal of roles are, in this context, neither Pharisees-and-Publicans nor Jews-and-Gentiles, but are adults-and-children:

Except ye be converted and become as little children, ye shall not enter into the kingdom of heaven. Whosoever, therefore, shall humble himself as this little child, the same is greatest in the kingdom of heaven. And whoso shall receive one such little child in my name, receiveth me.[11]

This paradoxical *peripeteia* between sophistication and simplicity was affirmed by Jesus in a quotation from Jewish Scripture:

Out of the mouth of babes and sucklings thou hast perfected praise.[12]

The mystery symbolized here in the reversal of roles between children and adults flashes out of its sheath of allegory in the exultant phrases of Saint Paul:

God hath chosen the foolish things of the world to confound the wise; and God hath chosen the weak things of the world to confound the things which are mighty; and base things of the world, and things which are despised, hath God chosen, yea, and things which are not, to bring to nought things that are: that no flesh should glory in his presence.[13]

But what is the explanation of a principle which plays so prominent a part both in the New Testament and in the Attic drama? In the absence of the deeper insight which posterity has gained through sharper suffering, primitive minds were inclined to give a cynical answer to this question. They sought to explain the downfalls of pre-eminent human beings as acts of external powers that were human in their ethos but were superhuman in potency. They supposed the overthrowers of great men to be gods and their motive to be envy. 'The envy of the gods' is one of the *Leitmotivs* of primitive mythology, and it was a subject of special fascination for Hellenic thought.

God loves to cut short everything that overtops its kind. In this way a great army is destroyed by a small army in certain circumstances – as, for instance, when God in His envy sends down panic upon them, or thunder. Then they perish, and their last state is unworthy of their first. God suffers no one to be proud except Himself.[14]

This passage from Herodotus occurs in a fictitious speech from the mouth of Xerxes' uncle Artabanus, after Xerxes has announced his project of conquering Hellas; and Herodotus makes Xerxes, in the course of his address, incur the envy of no fewer than three great gods: Poseidon,

113 SURFEIT – OUTRAGEOUS BEHAVIOUR – DISASTER According to Herodotus, Croesus flaunted his vast prosperity and happiness before Solon, but was warned by the sage that no man could be judged happy until his end were known. His pride wounded, Croesus dismissed Solon in fury; but he went on to suffer a series of disastrous misfortunes, culminating in his capture by Cyrus who condemned him to death by burning. On the pyre, Croesus remembered Solon's words and called out his name, moving Cyrus to mercy; but the raging flames were only extinguished when Apollo intervened.

through his announcement of his intention to bridge the Hellespont; Zeus, through his boast that he will divide with him the lordship of the Universe; and Helios, through his declared intention of extending the range of his own dominion from sunrise to sunset.[15] In this tragedy of Xerxes' greatness and fall the protagonist irrevocably seals his own doom when, on the eve of his passage of the Hellespont, on the road to defeat, the spectacle of his grand army and armada tempts him to declare himself divinely happy. The moment after uttering this blasphemy, Xerxes recollects himself; but it is too late now for repentance.

In a more serious vein the same thesis is pronounced by Herodotus in the parables of Croesus and of Polycrates.[16] The Herodotean godhead shows a touch of human kindness in the parable of Croesus, who is as wantonly presumptuous as Xerxes, yet manages to save his soul alive by a repentance at the eleventh hour; but the divine attributes of malignity and implacability reveal themselves, naked and unashamed, in the parable of Polycrates. He seeks to anticipate the wrecking of his fortunes through 'the envy of the gods' by marring his own prosperity through his own act, but is frustrated when his favourite signet-ring, which he has to this end cast ceremoniously into the sea, is miraculously and untowardly restored to him by the implacable Divinities. This Herodotean note is recaptured by Horace, an accomplished Latinizer of Greek verse and Hellenic ethos, in a meditation on the fatal consequences of human audacity:

> Nothing is too difficult for us mortals to dare;
> In our folly we aspire to scale Heaven itself.
> By our crimes we foil Jove,
> Who would fain forget his wrath and cease to hurl his bolts.[17]

Or we may quote the words of a Roman philosopher-poet whose testimony is even more impressive, considering that he had made it his life-work to preach the illusoriness of the belief that there is any supernatural intervention in human affairs.

> Do not the nations tremble, and proud kings
> Shudder, convulsed by fear of wrath divine?
> They count their guilty deeds and reckless words.
> The dreadful day of reckoning – has it come?[18]

The cynical explanation of the working of the Universe that was postulated by Lucretius in a disintegrating Hellenic Society was given in the Sinic World too in a comparable time of troubles:

> Stretch a bow to the very full,
> And you will wish you had stopped in time;
> Temper a sword-edge to its very sharpest,
> And you will find it soon grows dull....[19]

And, if we turn to a world more remote from the Hellenic in ethos in spite of its geographical proximity, we shall find in the book of an Israelitish prophet of the eighth century BC a curiously close anticipation of the words which Herodotus put into the mouth of Artabanus some three hundred years later:

The day of the Lord of hosts shall be upon every one that is proud and lofty, and upon every one that is lifted up; and he shall be brought low.... And the loftiness of man shall be bowed down; and the Lord alone shall be exalted in that day.[20]

This philosophy is found too in Ecclesiastes, which was written in the second century BC under the influence, perhaps, not only of the Jewish tradition but also of post-Herodotean Hellenic thought;[21] and even some two centuries after this we can find, in the Gospel according to Saint Luke, the suggestion that God's intervention in human affairs is due in the first place to a desire to exercise power, and only secondly to a concern for justice and mercy:

He hath shewed strength with his arm; he hath scattered the proud in the imagination of their hearts.
He hath put down the mighty from their seats, and exalted them of low degree.[22]

It was a Greek and not a Jew who, with an insight reaped from his own spiritual travail, first proclaimed the truth that the cause of *peripeteia* is not to be found in the intervention of any external power but is an aberration in the soul of the sufferer himself, and that the name of this fatal moral evil is not envy but sin.

A grey word liveth, from the morn
  Of old time among mortals spoken,
That man's Wealth waxen full shall fall
Not childless, but get sons withal;
And ever of great bliss is born
  A tear unstaunched and a heart broken.

But I hold my thought alone and by others unbeguiled;
'Tis the deed that is unholy shall have issue, child on
    child,
Sin on sin, like his begetters; and they shall be as they were.
But the man, who walketh straight, and the house thereof,
    tho' Fate
Exalt him, the children shall be fair.[23]

The sinner is brought to destruction not by God's act but by his own. His offence lies, not in rivalling his Creator, but in deliberately making himself utterly unlike him; and God's part in this human tragedy is not active but passive. The sinner's bane is not a divine envy, but a divine inability to continue to use as an instrument of creation a creature that has insisted upon alienating itself from the life of its Creator.[24] The sinful soul comes to grief because, so long as it wills to sin, God's grace is unable to inspire and inform it. According to this view, *peripeteia* – the reversal of roles – is produced by the inward spiritual working of a moral law, and not by the impact of some external agency; and, if we examine the plot of this psychological tragedy, we shall discern two variations on it. In one version the subject errs through an untimely passivity, while in the other he rushes actively to seek his doom.

The passive aberration to which a creative human being is prone in the sequel to an achievement is to 'rest on his oars' in a fool's paradise where he dreams that, by having exerted himself once upon a time, he has won a title to 'live happily ever after'. Short of this degree of folly, the victor in yesterday's battle is apt to dream that, if time does refuse to stand still, then he has merely to repeat mechanically the motions that served him so well last time in order to be sure of overcoming any new challenge. It is plain that the creative individual who yields to this passive mood is falling into the posture of the arrested society[25] which has achieved so exact an equilibrium with its environment that

it becomes its slave instead of remaining its master. In the case of an arrested society this posture is only tenable so long as the environment happens to remain constant, and it spells disaster as soon as the environment begins to change. The same fate awaits a creative individual or minority which has become infatuated with his own works. In the Syriac legend of the Creation, the completion of the physical Universe resulted in a static paradise, and it needed the Serpent's undesignedly beneficent intervention to liberate God's energies for performing a fresh act of creation in spite of Himself.[26] In terms of modern Western physical science the nemesis of creativity, in this passive form, is seen in the over-specialization of a species which condemns it to extinction if it becomes incapable of adapting itself to a change in the environment.

If the moral of this passive aberration that overtakes some creative spirits is 'let him that thinketh he standeth take heed lest he fall',[27] we shall find that 'pride goeth before destruction, and an haughty spirit before a fall'[28] is the epitaph of those others who rush to seek their doom.

This second version of the plot is familiar in Greek literature as a tragedy in three acts: *koros* (surfeit), *hybris* (outrageous behaviour), and *ate* (disaster) – an active psychological catastrophe in which the subject, spoilt by success, loses his mental and moral balance and courts disaster by attempting the impossible. It was the commonest theme in what we now know of the fifth-century Athenian drama: the story of Agamemnon in Aeschylus's play of that name, and of Xerxes in his *Persae*; of Ajax in Sophocles' play of that name, of Oedipus in his *Oedipus Tyrannus*, and of Creon in his *Antigone*; and the story of Pentheus in Euripides' *Bacchae*. In Plato's words:

If one sins against the laws of proportion and gives something too big to something too small to carry it – too big sails to too small a ship, too big meals to too small a body, too big powers to too small a soul – the result is bound to be a complete upset. In an outburst of *hybris* the overfed body will rush into sickness, while the jack-in-office will rush into the unrighteousness that *hybris* always breeds.[29]

In these two variant versions of a single plot, we can discern and comprehend the nemesis of creativity; and, if it is true in 'real life' that the successful creator of one chapter is severely handicapped, by his very success, in endeavouring to resume the creative role in the next, then it is plain that we have here run to earth a very potent cause of the breakdowns of civilizations. We can see that in the drama of social life this nemesis of creativity would bring on social breakdowns directly in two distinct ways. First, it would seriously diminish the number of candidates for the creator's role in the face of any given challenge, since it would tend to rule out those who had responded successfully to the last challenge; and these, *ex hypothesi*, were potential creators before their very success threatened to sterilize their creativity in the act of demonstrating it. In the second place, this frequent sterilization of the *ci-devant* creators would handicap the society in its next ordeal out of all proportion to the mere numerical ratio between a handful of lost leaders and a host of creative spirits; for, *ex hypothesi* again, the very past achievement which has fatally disqualified them from achieving anything further has also brought them to the front and lodged them in key

114 'The first shall be last; and the last shall be first': a Christian allegory, showing the proud man cast to destruction, while the meek man is raised to Heaven. (Florentine engraving, 1470–80.)

positions where their senile impotence to create is aggravated by their lasting potency *ex officio* to thwart and hinder.

Can this nemesis of creativity be averted? Clearly it can; for otherwise every civilization that ever came to birth would be arrested inexorably at the threshold of life, whereas we know that the great majority of civilizations[30] have avoided this fate and have gone on from strength to strength. Yet the way of salvation is narrow and difficult to find. The question is, 'How can a man be born when he is old? Can he enter a second time into his mother's womb and be born?'[31] And the answer is that, 'except ye be con-

verted and become as little children, ye shall not enter into the kingdom of heaven.'[32]

How often do creative minorities which have discovered a successful response to one challenge then qualify themselves, through a spiritual rebirth, to take up the next challenge and the next? And how often do they disqualify themselves by fatuously 'resting on their oars' or by wilfully rushing down the steep place that leads from *koros* through *hybris* into *ate*? Our best hope of finding an answer to this question lies in resorting to our usual method of making an empirical survey.

23 Athens and Venice: the idolization of an ephemeral self

WHILE the attitude of 'resting on one's oars' may be described as the passive way of succumbing to the nemesis of creativity, the negativeness of the mental posture does not certify an absence of moral fault. A fatuous passivity towards the present springs from an infatuation with the past; and this infatuation is the sin of idolatry which, in the primitive Hebrew scheme of religion, is the sin most apt to evoke the vengeance of 'a jealous god'. Idolatry may be defined as an intellectually and morally purblind worship of the part instead of the whole, of the creature instead of the Creator, of time instead of eternity.[1] It is an abuse of the highest faculties of the human spirit, and its effect is to transform one of 'the ineffably sublime works'[2] of God into an 'abomination of desolation'.[3] In practical life this moral aberration may take the comprehensive form of an idolization of the idolater's own personality, or own society, in some ephemeral phase of the ceaseless movement which is growth; or, again, it may take the limited form of an idolization of some particular institution or technique which has once stood its devotee in good stead. Let us look at each of these forms of idolatry in turn.

A notorious example of the idolization of an ephemeral self is presented by Athens, who succumbed to the nemesis of creativity by becoming infatuated with her transitory role as 'the education of Hellas'.

We have seen[4] how Athens earned a temporary claim to this magnificent title through her triumphant conquest of the physical and human challenges that faced her in her early career, and through the supremely brilliant domestic culture that she went on to create. Her gifts to Hellas were indeed immense; yet the very occasion on which the title 'the education of Hellas' was conferred upon her might have reminded her sons that their achievement was far from perfect. The phrase was coined by Pericles in the funeral oration[5] which he delivered in praise of the Athenian dead in 431–430 BC – the first year of an Atheno-Peloponnesian War which was the outward visible sign of an inward spiritual breakdown in the life of the Hellenic Society. This fatal war had broken out because Athens had proved unable to conquer the next challenge set by her own outstanding domestic successes: the challenge of being called upon to create an Hellenic political world order. In the circumstances of the year 431–430 BC the orator's proclamation of Athens as 'the education of Hellas' should therefore not have moved his audience to a thrill of self-adulation, but rather have moved them to 'abhor' themselves and 'repent in dust and ashes'.[6] The military overthrow of Athens in 404 BC, and the greater moral defeat which the restored Athenian democracy inflicted upon itself in 399 BC by the judicial murder of Socrates, did indeed provoke one contemporary Athenian man of genius to repudiate Athens and almost all her works.[7] Yet this gesture neither profited Plato himself nor impressed his fellow-citizens; and the epigoni of those Athenian pioneers who had made their city 'the education of Hellas' sought to vindicate their claim to a forfeited title by the perverse method of proving

themselves unteachable. They idolized the dead self of Athens as she had been, for a fleeting moment, in the Periclean Age; and they thereby debarred a post-Periclean Athens from having any part or lot in later Hellenic acts of creation.

On the political plane, Attic egoism brought successive disasters upon Athens as she repeated the errors which, in 404 BC, had resulted in the loss of her own political primacy in Hellas and in the breakdown of the Hellenic Civilization as a whole. Her inveterate egoism ruined the Hellenic World's chance of countering the threat of Macedonian domination in the fourth century BC; and it was not until she found herself hopelessly outclassed by the new Great Powers of titanic calibre which were rising on the periphery of the Hellenic World that Athens reluctantly renounced her pretence to the status of an Hellenic Great Power. Even then, her reading of the lesson was fatally negative, for she withdrew into a selfish isolation from which she looked on passively while Rome delivered knock-out blows to rival titans, and overwhelmed Athens' own neighbours, who had been attempting – without Athenian help – to avert this catastrophe by the expedient of federation. With a supreme inconsequence Athens waited until Rome's world power had been placed on an impregnable basis by the overthrow of all serious competitors, and then she abandoned her latter-day policy of isolation and plunged into the mêlée on the anti-Roman side. She paid for her folly in 86 BC, when the Roman conqueror Sulla took the city of Athens by storm; and, though Athens was spared annihilation – for the sake, as Sulla explained, of the living Athenians' dead ancestors[8] – and though she survived as a *chef d'œuvre* of architecture and a seat of intellectual life, this last absurd excursion into the arena of international politics was the inglorious end of Athenian political history.

The Athenians stand convicted of having brought their political misfortunes upon themselves through the moral fault of infatuation with their own past; and it is here that we must look for the psychological cause of their inveterate self-stultifying egoism. This explanation will be confirmed if we take a comparative view of the contemporary creative achievements of certain other Hellenic communities which conspicuously lacked the Athenians' intellectual endowment, but were also, by the same token, exempt from the incubus of a Periclean halo.

Take, for example, the Athenian Xenophon's contemptuous description of his Achaean and Arcadian comrades in the motley band of Greek mercenaries which, in 401 BC, was seeing service with the Achaemenian pretender Cyrus.[9] In this miniature Hellas-under-arms Xenophon observed, half irritably and half condescendingly, that the Achaeans and Arcadians were more wayward, impulsive, improvident, refractory to discipline, and in fact in every way more crude and barbaric, than the representatives of the more sophisticated and progressive Hellenic communities of the day, like his own Athenian self or his Spartan and Boeotian friends. Xenophon's observation was apt at

CIVIC APOTHEOSES
115 The goddess Athene, a monumental example of civic pride; Late Hellenistic statue.

the time; yet so rapidly were the roles reversed that the Arcadian historian Polybius (*vivebat c.* 202–120 BC) could not only severely condemn the fourth-century Athenian politician Demosthenes for his narrow parochialism, but could compare his poor statesmanship unfavourably with the political wisdom of Polybius's own Arcadian forebears in the same generation.[10]

This accurate comparative judgment was even more conspicuously valid for the ensuing period of Hellenic politics. In the third century BC it was Achaea and Arcadia that led the movement to liberate Hellas from her Macedonian shackles, and that devised the political system of voluntary federation which was the sole means by which the small city-states could maintain their national independence without sacrificing their local autonomy. Even the rigidly traditionalist Spartan state found a new power of flexibility and experimentation which temporarily lifted it out of its centuries-old lethargy. Only Athens, in this critical moment when Hellas was desperately trying to stave off her fate, remained coldly aloof and lethally negative.

This torpor of Athens in her latter days comes out still more strikingly when we turn our attention from politics to culture; for culture, even more than politics, was the sphere of activity in which Athens excelled in the spring-time of her history, and in this field her *floruit* came later and lasted longer. In the souls of Euripides and Thucydides and Socrates and Plato the very onset of the political adversity that was heralded by the outbreak of the Atheno-Peloponnesian War had the effect of a challenge which evoked the highest moral and intellectual flights of the Attic spirit; and the fourth century BC, which saw the beginnings of the political autumn of Athenian history, marked the height of its cultural summer. The decline was slow, but by Polybius's time Athens could no longer claim to possess a monopoly of the higher Hellenic culture; and even in the field of philosophy, which she appeared to have made peculiarly and inalienably her own, the conceit of being 'the education of Hellas' led her into a suicidal self-betrayal.

The rejection of Paul by the Athenians is the analogue of his Master's rejection by the Jews. Though Paul preached by public colloquy, according to Athenian custom, his message of the Resurrection proved an insuperable stumbling-block to an Athenian generation which was infatuated with a Stoic and Epicurean past.[11] Paul's first impression of Athens as a 'city wholly given to idolatry' was indeed a true intuition of Athens as she had come to be in the Apostle's day. Athens refused to be charged with a spiritual mission which she might have taken as the crown of her long philosophic preparation; and the function of serving as a seed-bed in which the germs of Hellenic philosophy and Syriac religion would mingle and blend was fulfilled, not by Attica, but by Asia Minor.

Three centuries after Paul's departure, when the Cappadocian Fathers of the Church were laying the ecclesiastical foundations of a new social order, Athens was inspiring the Emperor Julian with his tragically academic dream of a paganism reminted in a Christian image and resuscitated by artificial respiration. A hundred years further on, Athens was the scene of a strange cultural alliance between a scholastic intellectualism and an archaistic revival of primitive superstitions which the live genius of Hellenic philosophy had apparently strangled with ease, a thousand years before, in its Ionian infancy. In this age, when Hellenism was at bay in an Attic fastness, the first and last things in the Hellenic tradition – its lowest and highest elements – thus entered, at Athens, into a desperate defensive *union sacrée*. The activities of these latter-day professors of a senile Attic pedantry were eventually snuffed out by the long-delayed enforcement of the imperial government's decree against paganism, when the University of Athens was closed in AD 529. The ejected Athenian professors sought refuge in Asia with Rome's Sasanian enemies; yet in migrating eastwards to the Zoroastrian Chosroes' Ctesiphon they were actually moving nearer to the very source of the aggressive Syriac culture whose far-projected radiation had just completed the disintegration of Hellenism in its homeland. If the Syriac spirit was strong enough, even in an Helleno-Syriac syncretism such as Christianity, to make it impossible any longer to lead the life of an Hellenic philosopher in Athens, how could that life conceivably be lived in Ctesiphon, where the people's religion was Christianity in its Nestorian form, while the government's religion was a Zoroastrianism which was an undilutedly and militantly anti-Hellenic expression of the Iranian genius? It is not surprising that the Athenian refugees soon found themselves incurably homesick for the inhospitable world whose dust they had shaken off their feet with so antique a gesture. Fortunately this tragi-comedy had a happy ending. When Chosroes negotiated peace terms with Rome in AD 533, he had a special clause inserted in the treaty which secured the readmission of his protégés into Roman territory with a guarantee of liberty for them to live out their lives as pagans unmolested by the imperial police. This Attic addiction to idolatry did not die finally with its last professional adepts: the first successful re-establishment of the cult of images in Orthodox Christendom was the work of the Athenian-born Empress Irene (*imperabat* AD 780–802).

We have now glanced at the political and cultural role played by Athens during the long-drawn-out process of the disintegration of the Hellenic Society; and our cursory survey has brought to light a paradoxical fact. Here is a period of Hellenic history which might aptly be labelled 'the Atticistic Age', in acknowledgment of the truth that the creative work of Athens in the age immediately preceding had left the strongest impress upon the Hellenic Society of the time; and yet, in an age which bears this conspicuous stamp of Attic achievements in the past, Athens makes herself conspicuous – once again, but this time in exactly the opposite way – through the absence of any contemporary Attic contributions to the solution of current Hellenic problems.

The Attic paradox, for which we have found an explanation in Athens' fatal aberration of idolizing her dead self, has a parallel in the Western World in the similar contrast between the respective roles that Italy has played in successive chapters of Western history.

If we scrutinize the countenance of the Western Society in that 'modern' chapter of its history which runs from the latter part of the fifteenth century of our era to the latter part of the nineteenth, we shall find that its modern

116 A voluptuous Venice, enthroned in the clouds among the Olympians, is crowned by Victory. Detail from a ceiling painting by Veronese in the Council Hall of the Doge's Palace, sixteenth century.

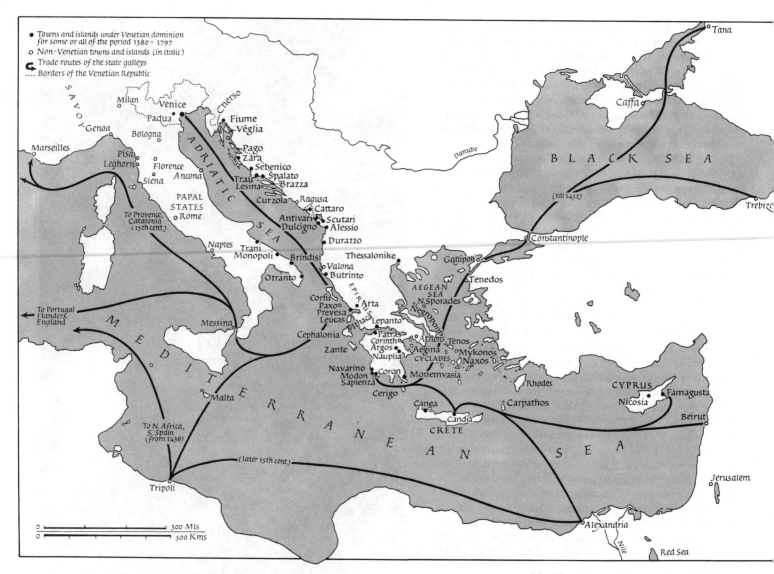

117   The Venetian maritime empire, 1380–1797.

economic and political efficiency, as well as its modern
aesthetic and intellectual culture, is of a distinctively
Italian origin. The unrivalled creativity of Italy in the
fourteenth and fifteenth centuries was the original driving-
force behind the movement of Western Civilization during
the ensuing span of four centuries, which might aptly be
called our 'Italistic Age';[12] and here we find ourselves confronted, once more, by the Attic paradox; for, throughout
a period of our common Western history which bore the
image and superscription of Italian acts of creation in the
past, the contemporary Italian contributions to the general
life of the age were conspicuously inferior to those of
medieval Italy's modern Transalpine converts. The comparative cultural sterility of Italy during the four-hundred-years'
span of history which began in about A D 1475 was manifest
in all the former homes of Italian culture, but out of a
cluster of examples we may be content with citing Venice
as a particularly poignant illustration of a malady which
afflicted every one of Italy's historic city-states.

At the dawn of the sixteenth century, Venice seemed
superficially to have been more successful than most of her

neighbours in holding her own during a critical period of
changing political circumstances. She had not lost her
independence to a Transalpine conqueror, as Milan had,
nor had she fallen victim to an Italian empire-builder, as
Siena had to Florence and Bologna to the Papacy. Instead,
she had managed to acquire an empire of her own, and
furthermore to retain it without being driven to renounce
the luxury of continuing to live under her ancestral republican constitution. Her success was by no means accidental,
but was the reward of a clear-headed and unslumbering
statesmanship; and the quality of this statesmanship can be
tested by comparing it with Athenian behaviour in corresponding situations. If Venice succeeded in gaining and
holding an empire without having to submit to a despotism
at home, this was because she avoided the strain which
imperialism tends to impose upon communities that indulge
in it; and she achieved this negative but by no means negli-
gible success by making her dominion so tolerable that her
subject-cities were not tempted to rebel against it. In
corresponding circumstances Athens had made her tyranny
so odious that her subject-allies yearned only for release

118, 119   Doge's Palace and Campanile of Saint Mark's, Venice, and a replica at Piran in Istria.

SIGNPOSTS OF
VENETIAN IMPERIAL POWER

120   Venetian fort at Herakleion, Crete.

121, 122   Venetian lions on gateways at Nauplion and at Corfu.

THE DECEPTIONS OF PRIDE

123 The infamous sack of Constantinople by Crusaders in 1204 was seen by Venice merely as a glorious episode in her long commercial career.

124 Venice's naval victory in 1668 over the Turks at Candia gratified her pride but brought no solid advantage: the town was lost again in 1669.

from it, even at the price of accepting another servitude. The inferiority of Athenian to Venetian statesmanship comes out as clearly in its handling of the problem of how a small state at the geographical centre of an international system should keep its footing after it has been dwarfed by the rise of new titans on an expanding periphery. The persistent ineptitude of the Athenians in coping with this problem affords a remarkable contrast to the masterliness of Venetian diplomacy, which managed to stave off for nearly three hundred years that partition of the Republic's Italian dominions among the Transalpine Powers which was the grand design of the League of Cambrai (1508).

The secret of Venice's success was an ability to rise above the vice of self-worship to which Athens owed her failures. But the success of modern Venice has been only relative and negative; on the whole and in the end, Venice failed to make any fresh creative contribution to the life of the society in which she managed to survive; and this Venetian failure can be explained by the fact that Venice, too, did succumb, in her own way, to the nemesis of creativity.

In the field of domestic politics the infatuation with a dead self which had nerved Venice to maintain her own medieval republican constitution at the same time inhibited her from anticipating or emulating the modern constitutional achievements of Switzerland or the Northern Netherlands by transforming her latter-day Italian empire into a federal state on a republican basis. While Venice was never so wrong-headed as to oppress her subject-cities, she was also never so broad-minded as to take them into partnership; and so, in AD 1797, when the Venetian Republic was overthrown by Napoleon, the political régime in the Venetian dominions was still just what it had been in AD 1339: that is, a mild hegemony under which a number of subject-communities had to take their orders from a single privileged sovereign state.

Again, in the field of foreign policy, the extraordinary skill with which modern Venetian statesmanship succeeded in maintaining the integrity of the latter-day Venetian dominions in Italy, without involving Venice herself in efforts beyond her strength, did not find its counterpart in the contemporary policy of Venice in the Levant. In her dealings with the Western Powers, Venice took care not to exhaust her limited energies, yet in the east she defied the overwhelming strength of the 'Osmanlis in the forlorn hope of defending her ancient Levantine empire. Through her unseasonable intransigence in the War of Candia (gerebatur AD 1645–69), Venice permanently weakened her stamina without any result beyond the unprofitable satisfaction of knowing that she had compelled the Ottoman Power to pay an exorbitant price for its victory.

The modern Venetian idolization of the medieval Venetian Empire in the Levant, which inspired the Venetians to this vain act of self-immolation, drove them on to renew the unequal struggle at the first opportunity. When the tide turned against the 'Osmanlis after their second unsuccessful siege of Vienna in AD 1682–83, the Venetians hastened to intervene on the anti-Ottoman side, and their efforts were momentarily rewarded by their acquisition of large tracts of Ottoman territory on the mainland. But the victory was ephemeral, for in 1715 the Venetians duly lost all their new conquests, and more into the bargain, and the

125   The frivolity of eighteenth-century Venice can be seen as a psychological compensation for the years of intolerable strain. Carnival Scene by Canaletto.

only permanent effect of their ill-judged intervention was to create a diversion which allowed the Habsburgs and the Romanovs to extend their own empires at the 'Osmanlis' expense. Indeed, this Venetian policy was unprofitable economically as well as politically, for the territorial possessions that Venice had been seeking to retain or acquire were by this time commercially valueless, owing to the diversion of the mainstream of trade from the Mediterranean to the Atlantic. Thus the Levantine stake for which Venice played her ruinous game against Turkey was nothing more substantial than a passion to 'save her face' by retaining the cumbersome territorial tokens of a past political greatness. The fact that this passion should have mastered the habitually cool and calculating Venetian mind is a striking testimony to the deadliness of the malady of self-idolization.

The nemesis of Venetian medieval creativity took a stern material shape in the massive military fortifications which modern Venice has left as her cenotaph in her old Levantine *places d'armes*; and the same writing on the wall is no less plainly manifest in the melancholy works of art which were being created at home. At first sight it may seem incredible that the seventeenth- and eighteenth-century Venetians who were living that elegantly frivolous carnival life which the music and pictures commemorate were the same flesh and blood that fought and died in the Levantine wars; but second thoughts tell us that the very sharpness of the contrast in ethos proves the two moods complementary. The intolerable strain which modern Venice was incurring in the Levant demanded, and received, in psychological compensation, an Epicurean relaxation of Venetian life at home. In Canaletto's meticulous portraits of a Venice from whose atmosphere the sunlight has faded we seem to see the ashes of a holocaust in which the Venetians had burned their energies out since the days when they had savoured the full-blooded colours of Titian and Tintoretto; and the same note of 'dust and ashes' struck the poet Browning's ear in 'A Toccata of Galuppi's'.

Here you come with your old music, and here's all the good it
 brings.
What, they lived once thus at Venice, where the merchants were
 the kings,
Where Saint Mark's is, where the Doges used to wed the sea with
 rings?

What? Those lesser thirds so plaintive, sixths diminished, sigh
 on sigh,
Told them something? Those suspensions, those solutions –
 'Must we die?'
Those commiserating sevenths – 'Life might last! we can but
 try!'

177

THE LAST SPARK DIES   126 In 1797 Venice was overthrown by Napoleon. Celebrations round the
Tree of Liberty were staged in Saint Mark's Square.

Yes, you, like a ghostly cricket, creaking where a house was
    burned:
'Dust and ashes, dead and done with, Venice spent what Venice
    earned!
'The soul, doubtless, is immortal – where a soul can be
    discerned.'

Nor was this Epimethean chapter of Venetian history,
for which Galuppi has written the dirge and Canaletto
painted the hatchment, the last phase of Venice's participation in the life of the Western World. Venice, together with
the rest of Italy, has been reprieved from an eighteenth-
century life-in-death by undergoing a nineteenth-century
Risorgimento. Superficially this recent Italian social miracle
might seem to testify that Venice has eventually triumphed
over the nemesis of her previous creativity by facing it out
and living it down; but, when we look for the creative
forces by which the *Risorgimento* was actually achieved, we
shall observe that they almost all arose outside the bounds
of those historic city-states which were the seed-beds of
Italian creativity in the Middle Ages. If modern Italy
eventually rose again, this was because the stage was so set
that the outcome did not depend upon the actors' own
merits, but was decided by the play of irresistible external
forces. The first strong political stimulus was the temporary
incorporation of Italy in the Napoleonic Empire, which
brought her into association with modern France. The
first strong economic stimulus was the reopening of the
trade route through the Mediterranean between Western
Europe and India – an eighteenth-century English fancy

which was transformed into a reality by the after-effects of
Napoleon's invasion of Egypt. The troubling of Mediterranean waters by the wash of French and English hulls
broke in vivifying waves upon Italian shores, when the
building of a railway from Cairo to Suez was followed up,
in 1869, by the opening of the Suez Canal. These Transalpine stimuli did not, of course, produce their full effects
in Italy until they had communicated themselves to Italian
agents; but the Italian creative forces by which the *Risorgimento* was brought to fruition did not arise on any Italian
ground that had already borne the harvest of a medieval
Italian culture.

In the economic field, the first Italian port to win a share
for itself in modern Western maritime trade was neither
Venice nor Genoa, but Leghorn – the modern creation of a
Tuscan Grand Duke who planted it with a settlement of
Iberian crypto-Jewish refugees; and it was these immigrants, and not the descendants of the native pioneers of
commerce, who made Leghorn's fortune in the seventeenth
and eighteenth centuries. In the political field, the unification of Italy was the achievement of an originally Transalpine principality which scarcely had a foothold on the
Italian side of the Alps before the eleventh century, and
which did not lose the last of its Transalpine possessions
until 1860. Piedmont, the Cisalpine base of the dominions
of the House of Savoy, was Transalpine in spirit and
tradition, with little share in the city-state culture of Cisalpine Italy; and this sense of being alien from the rest of
Italy persisted even after the Savoyard state's centre of

127 The 1848 rising against Austria was inspired by past glories, but no amount of heroism could revive them.

gravity had shifted to the Italian side of the mountains in the fourteenth century. Not until 1848 did the House of Savoy throw in its lot with the Italian people, by laying aside its own parochial ambitions and putting itself at the head of a national movement of unification.

In 1848 the Austrian régime in Lombardy and Venetia was threatened simultaneously by a Piedmontese invasion and by risings in Venice and Milan and the other cities within the Habsburgs' Italian provinces; and it is interesting to reflect upon the difference in the historical significance of these two anti-Austrian movements which took place at the same time and which both figure officially as blows struck in a common cause. The risings in Venice and Milan were strokes struck for liberty, no doubt, and were no less heroic for being unsuccessful; but the vision of liberty which inspired them was the recollection of a medieval past. Compared with the heroism of the Venetian insurgents, the Piedmontese military performance in 1848–49 was not very creditable; yet Piedmont survived the disgrace of its shameful defeat at Novara to take its revenge ten years later at Magenta; and the British-like constitution which Charles Albert granted to his subjects in 1848 survived his abdication to become the basis of the constitution of a united Italy. By contrast, the incontestably valorous feats of Milan and Venice were not repeated and both cities thereafter sank back passively into the arms of their Austrian rulers and waited for the work of liberation to be performed by Piedmont and her Transalpine ally France.

The explanation for this contrast is that the Venetians and the Milanese were virtually foredoomed to failure because the spiritual driving-force behind them was still that idolization of their own dead selves, as medieval city-states, which had been defeating the finest efforts of Italian statesmanship since the time of Machiavelli. The nineteenth-century Venetians who responded to Manin's call in 1848 were fighting for Venice alone, and not for Piedmont or Milan or even for Padua. They were striving to restore an obsolete Venetian Republic and not to create a new Italian national state; for this reason their enterprise was a forlorn hope, whereas Piedmont could survive a more shameful defeat because the Piedmontese were not the slaves of an unforgettable historic past: they were psychologically free to identify themselves with the dominant political forces of the day and to throw themselves into the novel enterprise of creating a unified Italian state.

On this showing the revolts of 1848 played an essentially negative role in the Italian *Risorgimento*; indeed, their immediate failure was an indispensable preliminary to the success which crowned the struggles of 1859–70. In 1848 the idols of a medieval Milan and a medieval Venice were so cruelly battered and defaced that at last they lost their fatal hold upon the idolaters' souls; and it was this belated effacement of a medieval Italian past in the seats of its former greatness that cleared the ground for a successful Italian *Risorgimento* under the leadership of the one modern Italian state that was free from the spiritual incubus of overpoweringly poignant medieval memories.

128 Caesaro-Papism: the concentration of secular and religious authority in the single person of the East Roman Emperor is signalized in a tenth-century ivory of Christ crowning the Emperor Constantine VII.

129 Caesar and Pope: opposite, Saint Peter gives spiritual power to Pope Leo III and temporal power to the Emperor Charlemagne, reflecting the actual division of authority in the nascent Western Christian World of the ninth century A D.

THE NEMESIS of creativity, which we have just been studying in the form of an idolization of an ephemeral self, may also take the form of an idolatrous worship of some ephemeral institution: and, although an institution is manifestly a lesser idol than the human self which was its author, both alike are created things and, as such, unfit to be made recipients of a worship that is due to none but their Creator. A moral and intellectual aberration which thus remains in essence the same is not made any the less deadly by being indulged in on a narrower human range. A classic case in which the idolization of an institution brought an entire civilization to grief is the infatuation of Orthodox Christendom with a ghost of the Roman Empire, an ancient institution which had fulfilled its historical function and completed its natural term of life before the Orthodox Christian Society made its fatal attempt to resuscitate it.

Signs of the breakdown of the Orthodox Christian Civilization were visible by the end of the tenth century of the Christian Era, the most prominent of these being the outbreak of the disastrous Bulgaro-Roman War of AD 976–1018. This disaster overtook Orthodox Christendom, and blighted its growth, barely three hundred years after its first emergence out of the chaos of the post-Hellenic interregnum; and this growth-span is miserably short by comparison with the life-history of Western Christendom – a sister-civilization which was coeval with Orthodox Christendom in its birth, and which has not demonstrably broken down even now, nearly a thousand years after the date at which its twin civilization entered on its time of troubles.

How are we to account for this striking difference between the fortunes of two societies which started life at the same moment and in the same circumstances? The actual outcome, as the passage of a thousand years has unfolded it before our eyes today, is the more remarkable considering that it is the exact inverse of what would have been prophesied by any impartial observer who might have happened to make a comparative study of Orthodox and Western Christendom in the middle of the tenth century of our era. An observer at such a date would certainly have declared that the Orthodox Christian Civilization's prospects were brighter than those of this Society's Western sister. He would have recalled that, two and three hundred years before, Arab invaders had overrun all of North-West Africa and the Iberian peninsula and had passed the line of the Pyrenees before they had met with any effective resistance from Western Christendom, whereas Orthodox Christendom had brought the Arabs' eastern offensive to a halt at the line of the Taurus and had thus saved all of its Anatolian patrimony from the Umayyad Power. Our hypothetical observer could have gone on to point out that the means by which Orthodox Christendom had achieved this success was by rallying and concentrating its hardpressed forces through an evocation of a ghost of the Roman Empire; and this great political work of the Emperor Leo Syrus (*imperabat* A D 717–41) would have

appeared to him all the more brilliant by contrast with the miserable failure of the corresponding attempt in the West, when this was made by Charlemagne two generations later.

Why was it, then, that the Orthodox Christian Civilization so soon belied its early promise, while the Western Civilization has so very much more than made up for an unpromising start? The explanation lies precisely in the contrast between Charlemagne's failure and Leo's success. If Charlemagne's attempted resuscitation of the ghost of the Roman Empire had not been a fiasco, then the infant Western Civilization on whose shoulders he had imposed

this crushing incubus might well have succumbed. If the West was saved in this way by Charlemagne's failure, we may find that, inversely, the Orthodox Christian Society was ruined by Leo's very success. Leo's achievement, in effectively reviving the institution of the Roman Empire on Orthodox Christian soil, was a response that was over-successful to a challenge that was excessive; and the over-strain of this *tour de force* exacted its penalty in the shape of a malformation. The outward symptom was a premature and excessive aggrandizement of the state in Orthodox Christian social life at the expense of all other institutions.

EMPEROR

130 Mosaic portrait of Justinian, dominating his church at Ravenna as he dominated the whole Eastern ecclesia.

The inward aberration was the idolization of a particular historic polity which had been conjured back from the grave and been decked out in the prestige of an emotionally glorified past in order to save a nascent society from imminent destruction. If we look at the Constantinopolitan Empire in this light, and not in the rarefied glow of its superficial military achievement, we shall find that we must turn back to an earlier page of its history in order to understand the long process by which successive emperors squandered their true heritage and sacrificed it on the altar of an impious presumption.

In the last chapter of the history of the Roman Empire, which may be taken, for our present purpose, as having begun with the death of the Emperor Theodosius the Great in AD 395, there had been, at first, a notable differentiation in the fortunes of the Hellenic universal state in its Latin provinces on the one hand and in its Greek and Oriental provinces on the other. In the Latin provinces there had been an immediate financial, political, and social collapse; the framework of the Empire had broken up, and the political vacuum had been occupied by the automatically emancipated proprietors of the great agricultural estates and leaders of powerful barbarian war-bands, while the Church had stepped into the social breach. Meanwhile, in an age which thus saw the dissolution of the Empire in the West, the imperial régime in the Greek and Oriental provinces succeeded in riding out one after another of the waves by which its counterpart in the Latin provinces was being broken up. By strong-minded statesmanship and determined military reform Leo the Great (*imperabat* AD 457–74) had released the Empire in the East from its perilous dependence upon barbarian mercenaries from the no-man's-land beyond the imperial frontiers; and his successors Zeno and Anastasius wrestled successfully with the problems of administrative and financial reform and parried the doctrinal dispute that threatened to split the Greek from the Oriental provinces of the Empire.[1] In fine, the imperial régime in the Constantinopolitan Empire distinguished itself, throughout the fifth century, by determined efforts to maintain the Empire as 'a going concern' which stand out in sharp contrast to the contemporary 'defeatism' of the imperial régime in the West; and for the moment these efforts seemed to have been rewarded with a triumphant success. Yet by the sixth century the contrast was shown to be, after all, superficial and impermanent. Everything that Leo and Zeno and Anastasius had sedulously and cumulatively gathered in was scattered to the winds in the single reign of Justinian (*imperabat* AD 527–65), who was betrayed, by an idolization of the vanished Empire of Constantine and Augustus, into indulging the same prodigious ambition, with the same disastrous results, as his latter-day Austrasian mimic Charlemagne. The slender store of energy which had been so carefully hoarded up and so conscientiously bequeathed to him by his predecessors was burnt up by Justinian in his abortive effort to restore the territorial integrity of the Empire by reincorporating in it the lost Latin provinces in Africa and Europe. His death in AD 565 was the signal for a collapse of the Empire in the Greek and Oriental provinces which resembled the collapse in the West after the death of Theodosius the Great – except that it came with redoubled swiftness and force in revenge for having been staved off for 170 years longer. In the almost un-intermittent warfare that supervened in the 152 years between Justinian's death and Leo Syrus's accession, the Constantinopolitan Empire lost its Oriental provinces and Justinian's African conquests to the Arabs, while its European provinces in South-Eastern Europe and in Italy were overrun by the Slavs and Lombards. Thus, *de facto*, the Roman Empire perished in its central and eastern provinces after the death of Justinian as, after the death of Theodosius, it had perished *de facto* in the West.

There were, indeed, certain indications that a nascent Orthodox Christian Society was, in the seventh century, about to enter – tardily but decidedly – on the same course that had already been chosen for the sister society of Western Christendom by Pope Gregory the Great (*pontificali munere fungebatur* AD 590–604). After the break-up of the Empire in the West, it may be said that, broadly speaking, the vacuum left by the dissipation of political authority into plural and parochial units was eventually filled by the ecclesiastical authority of an ecumenical Church, symbolized in the Roman Patriarchate or Papacy. Gregory's achievement in the West was nearly paralleled in the East by the Orthodox Patriarch Sergius (*patriarchico munere fungebatur* AD 610–38), who could have had a similar chance of creating an ecumenical ecclesiastical alternative to the vanished Empire when the Emperor Heraclius, hard pressed by the Sasanian advance against Constantinople in AD 618, planned to shift the seat of imperial authority to Carthage. In the event, it was Sergius himself who forced Heraclius to renounce this plan, and thereby ensured the survival of an imperial régime centred on Constantinople. If Heraclius had succeeded in withdrawing, the Orthodox Christian Patriarchate of Constantinople might, we may guess, have played the same part as its Western counterpart; it might have transfigured the face of its society. But, by his very *tour de force* of transforming Heraclius into a hero *malgré lui*, Sergius ruled out for himself the opportunity of playing Gregory's heroic role; and, more than that, he kept open for Leo Syrus the opportunity for giving Orthodox Christian history a quite un-Western turn a hundred years later. For, by his threefold achievement of salvaging the prestige of the Empire and establishing the prestige of Constantinople and retrieving the Asiatic patrimony of Orthodox Christendom from the clutches of Oriental invaders, Sergius bequeathed to Leo Syrus the indispensable material for that solid reconstruction of a Roman Empire, based on Orthodox Christian soil in Asia Minor, which was Leo's formidable handiwork. And the restoration of the Empire precluded a development of the Ecumenical Patriarchate in the style of the Papacy.

The ghost of the Roman Empire which was successfully evoked on Orthodox Christian ground in the eighth century of the Christian Era materialized in a substantial and efficient centralized state which maintained itself for nearly five hundred years. In its main features this Eastern *Imperium Redivivum* succeeded in being what it set out to be. It was a recognizable reproduction of the original Roman Empire, and it anticipated the political development of Western Christendom by some seven or eight hundred

EMPRESS
131 Theodora, wife of Justinian, given equal prominence as befitted her position in the East Roman state.

IMPERIAL GOVERNMENT
132 Soldiers and ministers from Justinian's retinue, members of an administrative and military system unknown in the West.

years; for no state comparable to the eighth-century East Roman Empire ever made its appearance in the Western World until after the radiation of Italian efficiency into the Transalpine kingdoms at the turn of the fifteenth and sixteenth centuries. The new Orthodox Christian Power was founded, to begin with, on a solid territorial basis: for Leo and his successor Constantine V succeeded in reuniting a block of territory from Adrianople in the Balkan peninsula to Caesarea in eastern Asia Minor, together with the scattered islands of the Aegean archipelago and beach-heads of continental territory round the coasts of Italy and the Balkan peninsula. The extent of this territory gave the Orthodox Christian Power great material resources; the compactness of its torso offered it the possibility of maintaining these resources intact; and the conservation of the Empire's energy was the cardinal principle of imperial statesmanship from Leo's reign onwards for two centuries. The efficiency with which Leo and his successors were able to avoid over-ambitious military adventures and un-profitable entanglements was itself the fruit of two East Roman institutions – a standing army and a permanent civil service – which were both virtually unknown in the West at any time between the fifth century and the fifteenth. These two institutions were conceivable only in a state which could command the economic and cultural resources to provide for the education of a professional military and administrative establishment; and it was the educated corps of officers and the educated hierarchy of civil servants which alone made it possible for the resuscitated ghost of the Roman Empire in Orthodox Christendom to achieve its most remarkable and most unfortunate triumph, the effective subordination of Church to state. It is in the relations between Church and state that the histories of Orthodox Christendom and Western Christendom show the widest and most momentous divergence; and here we can locate the parting of the ways that respectively led the Western Society forward along the path of growth and the Orthodox Christian Society along a path that was to end in destruction.

Leo Syrus and his successors on the East Roman imperial throne succeeded in attaining a goal which in the West was never approached by Charlemagne or Otto I or Henry III. The East Roman emperors, in their own dominions, turned the Church into a department of state and the Ecumenical Patriarch into a kind of imperial Under-Secretary of State for Ecclesiastical Affairs, with a status that was professional but a tenure that was by no means secure. In relegating the Church to this position, the East Roman emperors were simply putting into effect one important part of their programme of making the restoration of the Roman Empire a solid reality; for this relation between Church and state was precisely that which had been contemplated by Constantine the Great when he decided to take the Christian Church under his patronage; and this Constantinian conception had actually been realized *de facto* in the history of the later Roman Empire from the reign of Constantine himself to the reign of Justinian inclusive.

Constantine's policy of incorporating the Christian Church in the body politic of the Roman Empire was highly successful. The Church fell into the place which he had designed for it, and it did not make any motion to assert its independence until action was forced upon it by the catastrophe of its protector's demise. Thereafter, the Popes, as well as the Patriarchs, persisted in lamenting the loss of their comfortable imperial carapace and in attempting to find their way back into it. In Western Christendom this dilemma was solved by the reintegration, in the Papal *Respublica Christiana*, of Church and state through the subordination of a multiplicity of local states to a single ecumenical Church which was the principle of unity and the source of authority in the Western Christian body social; and this 'hierocratic' constitution of society was a wholly new creation.[2] In the corresponding chapter of Orthodox Christian history, there was no comparable creative act, because in an earlier chapter the Orthodox Christian Society, by achieving its successful restoration of the Roman Empire, had renounced the possibility of creation in favour of the easier course of idolizing an institution which was a legacy from the past; and this natural yet disastrous aberration accounts for Orthodox Christendom's premature downfall.

In this Orthodox Christian idolization of the ghost of the Roman Empire which Leo Syrus had evoked, the subordination of the Orthodox Church to the East Roman state was the crucial act; and this act was conscious and whole-hearted. In Leo's own assertion – 'Imperator sum et sacerdos'[3] – we hear the founder of the East Roman Empire making the 'Caesaro-papistical' claim of a Constantine in the imperious accents of a Justinian. We shall not be surprised to find that Leo's success in imposing the imperial government's overriding authority upon the Church in the greater part of his dominions is the first link in a fatal chain of causation which ends in the breakdown of the Orthodox Christian Civilization some two and a half centuries later.

If we study the tragedy of Orthodox Christian history, we shall observe that the destructive effect of Leo Syrus's deed of reincorporating the Church in the state declares itself in two distinct ways – one of them general and the other particular.

The general effect was to check and sterilize the tendencies towards variety and elasticity and experimentation and creativeness in Orthodox Christian life; and we can roughly measure the extent of the damage done to the development of the Orthodox Christian Civilization in this way by noting some of the conspicuous achievements of the sister-civilization of the West, in the corresponding stage of its growth, that have no Orthodox Christian counterparts. In the Orthodox Christian body social in its growth-phase, we not only find nothing that corresponds to the Hildebrandine Papacy; we also miss the rise and spread of self-governing universities, corresponding to the new Western centres of intellectual activity at Bologna and Paris, and of self-governing city-states, corresponding to the new Western centres of life in Central and Northern Italy and in Flanders.[4] Moreover, the Western institution of feudalism, which was independent of and in conflict with the medieval Western Church and the medieval city-states, was, if not entirely absent in the East, at least effectively repressed, like the Orthodox Church – with the unfortunate consequence that, like the Church, this feudalism asserted

itself belatedly and violently in Orthodox Christendom when the weakening of the imperial Power gave it its opportunity at last.

This eventual self-assertion of both feudalism and the Church in the Orthodox Christian World shows that, in these two spheres at any rate, the relative sterility and monotony of Orthodox Christian life in the preceding chapter of history were not due to any lack of vitality or creative power in the Orthodox Christian body social, but to the artificial and temporary repression of these faculties by *force majeure*; for, of all the seeds that had been planted in the Orthodox Christian social landscape, one – the 'Caesaro-papal' East Roman *Imperium Redivivum* – shot up with such abnormal speed and vigour that it completely outstripped its fellows and blighted their growth. In contrast to the diverse and well-proportioned institutions flourishing in the West, the landscape in Orthodox Christendom now presented a painful picture of that disharmony which is the penalty of misgrowth.

The view that it was repression, and not sterility, that prevented the healthy growth of the Orthodox Christian Society will be reinforced if we look at some of those rare flashes of creative genius which the Orthodox Christian Society emitted at certain points in space and time at which it happened to be free from its almost ubiquitous imperial incubus.

To the west of Thrace, for example, in an area which was spared the full weight of the imperial régime, the Orthodox Christian Church found in Macedonian Mount Athos a base of operations for its counter-offensive against the imperial Power; and in still more distant Calabria a handful of Basilian monks, who had been expelled from their Sicilian monasteries by the island's African Muslim conquerors, succeeded in reconverting a derelict and supine province into a settled and orderly community – an achievement equal to that of the Irish monks who had set out to recapture a paganized England in the sixth and seventh centuries. This same Calabrian monastic settlement was later the home of a vein of vigorous religious speculation and philosophy which stood in strong contrast to what is popularly supposed to be the narrow 'Byzantine' ethos.

Even more significant are those flashes of Orthodox Christian creative genius that blaze out beyond the range of the East Roman imperial régime by eluding it in its time-dimension. Perhaps the most astonishing example of this creativity is the fourteenth-century mosaic decoration in the *ci-devant* monastery church of Chora, which is now the Kahriye Camii Museum. Here, within the boundaries of the imperial capital, we can still gaze today at this exhibition of an Orthodox Christian art which was able to achieve in the intractable material of the Byzantine artist's choice, at a date by which the imperial government had become enfeebled, an effect of movement and life that is scarcely surpassed by any contemporary Italian work in oil or tempera.

Two hundred years later, after the Orthodox Christian Society had been disburdened of the leaden cope of the East Roman Empire in order to be draped in an Ottoman funeral-pall, we can detect an afterglow of the deceased civilization. In Domenico Theotokopoulos 'El Greco' (*vivebat* AD 1541–1614) the Orthodox Christian island of

133 The fourteenth-century flowering of Byzantine art: mosaic from the Kahriye Camii.

Crete gave the Western World an artist whose art would appear to be the antithesis of the rigid canon of the Athoan iconists. And yet, in spite of appearances, El Greco's inspiration must have derived from a native idiom, since it was so manifestly remote from the contemporary style of painting in the West that it was long regarded as an unintelligible *lusus naturae*.

This case may also remind us of another tragic feature in Orthodox Christendom's fate. Both the good and the evil that this luckless society has done have largely accrued to some other society's benefit.

Like El Greco at Rome and Toledo, the Basilian monks in Calabria did their pioneer work for the future advantage of the alien Christendom in the West; and there is a more notorious example of the same involuntary altruism to the profit of the same neighbour in the fructification of the culture of the West, at the beginning of the modern chapter of Western history, through the Western discovery of the literature of the Hellenic Civilization among the ruins of the sister Christendom's collapsing edifice. This fruitful Western discovery could never have been made if Orthodox

Christian piety had not sedulously preserved these precious monuments of a common parent-culture through the tempests and earthquakes of the post-Hellenic interregnum, in order to bring them out of its treasure-house in a Byzantine renaissance which began in the same generation as the Carolingian renaissance and continued until the fifteenth century. This preservation and resurrection of the mighty works of the Hellenic genius in the bosom of the Orthodox Christian Society ought to have brought its due reward in the fullness of time by inspiring Orthodox Christendom – as it did afterwards most effectively inspire Western Christendom – to achieve original works of its own; but in Orthodox Christian cultural history there was never any struggle for emancipation from Hellenic leading-strings corresponding to that 'Battle of the Books' between the Ancients and Moderns which was waged in the West through decade after decade of the seventeenth century until there could be no mistake about the Moderns' victory.

Accordingly in Orthodox Christendom the reborn Hellenic culture, like the East Roman *Imperium Redivivum*, became an incubus instead of a stimulus. It was not until

134   The *Agony in the Garden* (*c.* 1585) by the Cretan artist El Greco, last heir of the Byzantine tradition.

its transmission to the lively mental environment of fifteenth-century Italy that this potent mental tonic was able to produce its proper stimulating effect; and thus, as it turned out, Orthodox Christendom actually performed her pious cultural labour for her Western sister's benefit.

The notorious evil deed of the Orthodox Christian Society which redounded to the advantage of the West was the extermination of the Paulicians, a sect which seems to have been a local survival in Armenia and Asia Minor of the archaic 'Adoptionist' school of Christianity.[5] Asia Minor had been the seed-bed of Christianity, and in fulfilling this historical function the Asiatic peninsula had produced a rich experimental variety of the crop with which it had been so successfully sown. One of the first-fruits of this Asiatic inheritance had been the iconoclastic movement, which was suppressed after more than a century of conflict (AD 726–843). But the unconventional Asiatic religious spirit which had thus been repressed in the metropolitan provinces of the East Roman Empire still remained incarnate in the Paulicians, and when, at some date in the ninth century, the Paulicians set up a militant

republic of latter-day saints in a remote and barely accessible no-man's-land between the Empire and the 'Abbasid Caliphate, they offered to the dissident elements in Asia Minor a rallying-point which was independent of the waning fortunes of iconoclasm. If this interesting Paulician community had been allowed to survive, it might conceivably have saved the life of Orthodox Christendom by preserving for it, and eventually restoring to it, those vital elements in the Orthodox Christian social heritage which were incompatible with an East Roman régime in which the Church was subjected to the state *de facto*. In the imperial capital at Constantinople and in the Paulician headquarters at Tephrike the component elements of the Orthodox Christian religious genius were polarized. As soon as the conflict over the status of icons had been terminated by the definitive rejection of iconoclasm, the imperial government set out to extirpate the Paulician heresy; and the military as well as the theological strength of the East Roman Empire was thrown into the conflict. In a war *à outrance* between powers so unequally matched the outcome could not be in doubt, though it might be long delayed; and, after a

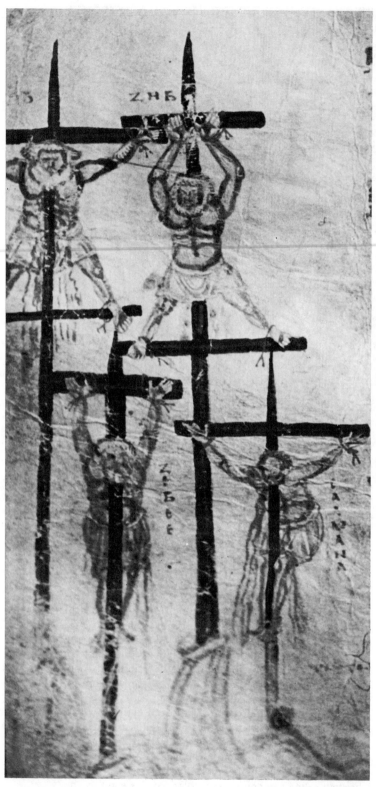

ORTHODOX INTOLERANCE

135 The brutality that could be unleashed by religious controversy is apparent in this ninth-century Biblical illustration. The artist was surely aware of such events as the extermination of the Paulicians, the Orthodox Church's unimaginative response to ideological challenge.

struggle which lasted from 843 to 875, the hornet's nest at Tephrike was smoked out by the master of the imperial beehive at Constantinople.

From the East Roman government's standpoint this was a famous victory; for the vehemence of the Empire's assault upon the Paulicians betrayed a conviction that the existence of the Paulician Republic was a menace to the Empire's security. Considering the incompatibility of principle between the two régimes, we may well believe that the official view was right; but we may also pass the private judgment that in this matter the East Roman Empire's victory was the Orthodox Christian Society's defeat. In eliminating the Paulicians the East Roman government did the same disservice to Asia Minor that the Christian 'successor-states' of the Umayyad Caliphate did to the Iberian peninsula when they expelled the Jews and the Muslims, or Louis XIV to France when he expelled the Huguenots, or the National Socialist régime to Germany when it expelled the Jews and liberals. Nor did the crushing of the Paulicians by the East Roman government make Orthodox Christendom immune against the dualistic form of religion which the East Roman Paulicians had adopted.

Thanks to the imperial Power's policy of deportation, batches of Paulicians were planted on the Bulgarian frontier of the Empire, in Thrace, in AD 755 or 757; and further deportations followed the destruction of the Paulician centre of military operations at Tephrike in AD 872, thus giving them a fertile new mission-ground. Within a century the laborious weeding operations of the East Roman Emperor Basil I had been more than offset by the assiduous sowing of the Bulgarian 'dualist' heresiarch Bogomil. This man of destiny was a Slavophone priest of the Orthodox Church in Bulgaria. We do not know whether he derived his dualism from his country's new Paulician neighbours or thought it out independently for himself. In Bulgaria in the tenth century, social conditions were bad enough to suggest, without any prompting from abroad, that goodness was not omnipotent in the Universe. In any case, Bogomil's dualism spread far and wide over the continent of Europe, finding a second base of operations in Bosnia, and eventually appearing in the Latin World under the name of 'Catharism'. In Western, as in Orthodox, Christendom the appearance of these goats among the sheep evoked active counter-measures, and the East Roman Emperor Basil's militant policy against the ninth-century Paulicians was echoed 350 years later in Pope Innocent III's anti-Albigensian Crusade.[6] Was this war of extermination that was levied in Christ's name by the Papacy at the height of its power the sin that doomed the master-institution of Western Christendom to meet with its tremendous downfall? Whatever the answer to this question may be, it is certain that the tragedy of Albi reproduced the tragedy of Tephrike on a larger material scale; yet a challenge to which Orthodox Christendom had responded only with a bloody crime evoked in the West an act of creation as well as an act of destruction. The Franciscan and Dominican responses to the challenge which Catharism presented to Western Christianity at the turn of the twelfth and thirteenth centuries put fresh life in the West into the Christian institution of monachism, for Francis and Dominic brought the monks out of their rural cloisters and thrust them into the world to minister to the spiritual needs of Western Europe's growing urban population. We look in vain for any Orthodox Christian parallel to this movement. In Orthodox Christendom, Paulicianism was not only denied the opportunity of performing any creative act of its own; it was not permitted there even to create by proxy through calling into play the creative powers of its Orthodox opponents and destroyers.

Having now surveyed the general effect of East Roman 'Casearo-papism' in stunting the growth and pruning out the variety of Orthodox Christian life, we can next examine the particular way in which this overwhelming institution was directly responsible for the breakdown of the Orthodox Christian Civilization.

We have already observed in passing[7] that the outward visible sign of this breakdown was the great Bulgaro-Roman War of AD 976–1018. We may now go on to observe that, while one of the belligerents in this war was that simulacrum of the Roman Empire which had been established in the nucleus of a nascent Orthodox Christian World, the other belligerent was the most important among the neighbouring barbarian communities that had been incorporated in a growing Orthodox Christian body social in the process of its expansion. In other words, the expansion and the breakdown of the Orthodox Christian Society were intimately connected with each other. In an earlier chapter[8] of this Study we noted that mere expansion is not in itself the criterion of growth. At the same time, when a society which does bear the genuine marks of growth is found simultaneously to be expanding in the geographical sense, we might expect *a priori* that the expansion would recruit the growing society's strength. This was, in fact, the effect of the expansion of Western Christendom in the four centuries beginning with the reign of Pope Gregory the Great (*fungebatur* AD 590–604), when the outlying regions of Northern and Central Europe were successively incorporated in the body social of Western Christendom. In contrast to the fruitful effects of this Western expansion, the corresponding expansion of Orthodox Christendom did nothing to enhance that society's strength and vitality, but, on the contrary, precipitated its breakdown by setting the lists for an internecine struggle between the Bulgarian converts and their East Roman instructors. We can compare the conversion of the Bulgars in the ninth century with the corresponding conversion of the Saxons by the Franks in the preceding hundred years. In the West, the conversion of these pagan neighbours was followed by their firm incorporation in the political and social fabric of Western Christendom; but the contemporary Orthodox Christian Bulgars were divided from their new East Roman co-religionists by a deeper moral gulf than had existed between them a hundred years earlier, when the gulf had been religious as well as political.

Before we attempt to explain this striking difference in the respective effects of the Western and the Orthodox Christian Society's expansion, we should note another difference that was antecedent. By comparison with the performance of Western Christendom, Orthodox Christendom was astonishingly slow in addressing itself to the task of enlarging its own borders through the conversion of the barbarians at its European gates. After an early and apparently abortive spurt of missionary activity in the Western Illyricum in the seventh century, the pagan inhabitants of the Balkan peninsula were ignored for the best part of two hundred years. The conversion of Bulgaria to Orthodox Christianity did not take place until 864, by which time Western Christendom had, for its part, not only recaptured all of the ground that had formerly been held in this quarter of Europe by the Roman Empire, but had pushed beyond this old frontier and penetrated as far as the Elbe. This extreme inequality of achievement in the European mission-field is even more striking when we remember that the Orthodox Church had kept its hands free from one formidable handicap to missionary work which the Western Church had imposed upon itself. In Western Christendom it was taken for granted from the outset that Latin must be the exclusive and universal liturgical language, irrespective of the native vernacular of the Church's converts. On this linguistic question the Western ecclesiastical authorities were intransigent, even at the risk of losing the allegiance of their new converts. In sharp contrast to this tyranny of Latin in the West, the Orthodox Christian Church cultivated a remarkably liberal policy. It made no attempt to confer upon the Greek language the liturgical monopoly which the Western Church conferred upon Latin as a matter of course; and there can be no doubt that this policy of translating the Liturgy into the local vernacular gave Orthodox Christendom a signal advantage over Western Christendom in the field of missionary enterprise. On this showing, the *de facto* success of Western Christendom in outstripping Orthodox Christendom in the mission-field will appear more paradoxical than ever. To resolve this paradox we must suppose that the advantage accruing to Orthodox Christendom from its linguistic liberalism was heavily outweighed by some formidable handicap; and as soon as we look for this handicap it leaps to the eye.

The missionary work of the Orthodox Church was crippled by the subjection of the Ecumenical Patriarchate to the secular authority of the East Roman imperial government; for this servitude of the Orthodox Church to the East Roman state presented a painful dilemma to all prospective converts to the Orthodox faith. If they accepted Christianity at the Ecumenical Patriarch's hands, and so came under his ecclesiastical jurisdiction, the change that they were making in their own status would not be only a change of religious belief and practice. In accepting the Patriarch's ecclesiastical jurisdiction they would be accepting implicitly, in the same act, the political sovereignty of the Patriarch's secular master. In other words, they really had to choose between a persistence in their ancestral paganism and a conversion to Christianity which involved a forfeiture of their political independence; and, in the circumstances, it is not surprising that they should flinch from making this latter choice – notwithstanding the inducement of being permitted to employ their mother tongue for the celebration of the Christian Liturgy. This was a dilemma which did not confront those barbarians who were invited into the Christian fold by the missionaries of the Western Church; for the acceptance of the ecclesiastical jurisdiction of the Roman See, though it involved a submission to the linguistic tyranny of the Latin language, did not carry with it the more formidable servitude of acknowledging the political sovereignty of a foreign government. Although the Papacy eventually succeeded in its second attempt to resuscitate a ghost of the Roman Empire in the West, neither the Carolingian nor the Saxon incarnation of this Western *Imperium Redivivum* was either universal or permanent; for instance, the English remained loyal sons of the Roman Church without following Pope Leo III's example of paying allegiance to the imperial authority of Charlemagne; and their relations with the Holy See thus were not affected by the evocation of the Western Holy Roman Empire.

The expansion of Orthodox Christendom could not proceed on these happy lines because the subjection of the patriarchal to the imperial Power was there not an empty form but a stern reality; and the unfortunate consequences which this difference entailed were not slow to work themselves out when in 864 the East Roman government felt itself compelled at last to secure the conversion of Bulgaria.

The inherent disastrousness of the Orthodox Church's subjection to the East Roman state, which disclosed itself in this emergency, is thrown into relief by the fact that, in this affair as in others, the East Roman government displayed its customary moderation. A disastrous institutional structure inexorably produced its inevitable effect in spite of a statesmanlike policy.

To begin with, the conversion of Bulgaria to Orthodox Christianity in 864 was brought about by an East Roman naval and military demonstration. This misuse of political power for religious purposes was indeed tactful by comparison with the bitter religious wars waged by Charlemagne in a corresponding situation. Nevertheless, the Bulgarian Khan Boris reacted strongly to even this light touch of an East Roman political whip; for, though he had been gently handled this time, Boris saw himself exposed in perpetuity to the humiliation of being subject to the East Roman government's political control. Only two years after the Romano-Bulgarian agreement of 864, Boris had broken its terms by transferring the ecclesiastical allegiance of Bulgaria from the Ecumenical Patriarchate to the Roman

ORTHODOX MISSION

136 The Byzantine Emperor Michael III and his Empress preside over the baptism of the Bulgarian Khan Boris in AD 865: from a fourteenth-century Slavonic manuscript.

137 Bulgaro-Roman Wars: the expedition of Nikephoros, 811. Above, the
Orthodox Christian Emperor Nikephoros I leads his cavalry into battle;
underneath, after Nikephoros's defeat, the captured Emperor is taunted
before his execution.

See; and, although he voluntarily retransferred his allegiance to the Patriarchate in 870, this first Bulgarian attempt to escape the political implications of allegiance to the Ecumenical Patriarchate was ominous of evils to come.

The prodigal's return to the fold was greeted by a tactfully conciliatory policy on the part of the imperial government. A *modus vivendi* of sorts was reached between Boris and the Emperor Basil, and this persisted until 893, when Boris's son Symeon succeeded to the Bulgarian throne and deliberately forced the political problem into the open again. Educated in Constantinople, Symeon had been captivated in the course of his studies by 'the great idea' of an Hellenic universal state – an idea which had been raised from the dead and enshrined in Constantinople in the imposing political institution of the East Roman *Imperium Redivivum*. With the crown of Bulgaria on his head, Symeon was not long content with the status of an inferior princeling; and, in the circumstances in which he found himself, Symeon could acquire his sovereign independence only by using the throne of Bulgaria as a mounting-block for climbing on to the throne of the East Roman Empire itself. He decided to bid for the imperial crown, and in taking this decision he signed the death-warrants not only of the kingdom which he possessed and of the Empire which he coveted, but also of the society in which these two states had their being.

Symeon's ambition developed in the course of the two wars which he waged with the East Roman Empire in 894–96 and 913–27. Despairing at last of mounting the imperial throne at Constantinople, Symeon resolved to secure his sovereign independence as best he could, by assuming the imperial title within the frontiers of his Bulgarian patrimony and by setting up a local Patriarch of his own. Accordingly he proclaimed himself in 925 'Emperor of the Romans and Bulgars' and, perhaps in the following year, raised the Archbishop of Preslav to the status of Patriarch of the new Empire. The East Roman government naturally enough did not recognize either of these acts; but, in 927, when Symeon died and a peace settlement was negotiated, the East Roman government made the unprecedented concession of recognizing Symeon's successor Peter as an Emperor, with a Patriarch of his own, in exchange for a Bulgarian recognition of the territorial integrity of the East Roman Empire, within the pre-913 frontiers.

The peace which was concluded on these terms lasted for forty-two years; yet, in fact, though not in form, it was no more than a truce. It was a compromise which could not be permanent, for it underlined the incompatibility between ecclesiastical subordination and political independence which Symeon himself had recklessly chosen to emphasize. By 927 it had become impossible to thrust this formidable problem back into the oblivion in which Boris and Basil had sought to bury it fifty years before, and equally impossible to feign blindness to its true solution. It was now conclusively demonstrated that in Orthodox Christendom the jurisdictions of the East Roman Emperor and the Ecumenical Patriarch must be geographically coextensive; and, since Symeon had failed to bring about this necessary and inevitable state of affairs by his expedient of attempting to annex the Empire politically to the Patriarch's foreign

ecclesiastical province of Bulgaria, it followed that sooner or later the indispensable political unification would have to be brought about by the inverse process of annexing Bulgaria to the Empire. Thus the two leading states in the Orthodox Christian World were doomed to continue their struggle until one of them succumbed to a 'knock-out blow'. On a superficial view it might seem as if this evil had been brought on Orthodox Christendom by Symeon's personal wrong-headedness. The fundamental cause of the disaster was, however, the practical subjection of the Church to the state in the East Roman Empire; for it was this that had driven Symeon down the wrong path in the first instance and then made the consequences of his error irretrievable. Within the bosom of a single society there was not room, in perpetuity, for more than one 'totalitarian state'.

The first round of the struggle closed in 972 with the defeat of the Bulgarians and the annexation of Eastern Bulgaria, the original nucleus of Bulgaria, by the East Roman Emperor John Dzimiskes. But within four years the remnant of the Bulgarian state had found leadership in a new dynasty of rulers, and the ensuing half century of war – from 976 to 1018 – wore out the Orthodox Christian Society. The 'knock-out blow', which was the sole practicable means of eliminating one of the two rival Empires, was delivered in 1018 by the East Roman Emperor Basil II; and, at the cost of more than a hundred years of war in all, the whole of Orthodox Christendom now found itself reunited under one imperial rule.[9] Moreover, the victim of this long-drawn-out Romano-Bulgarian contest was not the *ci-devant* Bulgarian state, which was now incorporated in the body of the East Roman Empire; the true victim was the officially victorious East Roman Empire itself, and it duly succumbed to its own nemesis in 1071, when Asia Minor was occupied by the Saljuq Turks after the Emperor Rhomanos Dhioyenes had been taken prisoner.

Moreover, while Bulgaria lived to make abortive attempts to throw off the East Roman yoke in 1040 and 1073, and a successful secession in 1185–87, the East Roman Empire never recovered from the social disorders which it had brought upon itself through its demonic pursuit of military victory. The deep derangement, in this age, of Orthodox Christian social life within the East Roman frontiers revealed itself in the outbreak and progress of two maladies which interacted disastrously with one another. The first malady was an agrarian crisis; the second was a bout of militarism; and both were portents, because they were complaints from which the Orthodox Christian body social had been singularly free in the days of its good health.

When the nascent Orthodox Christian Civilization had emerged from the post-Hellenic interregnum at the turn of the seventh and eighth centuries of the Christian Era, it had started life in possession of one immensely valuable social asset. The legislation of the eighth-century East Roman Emperors Leo Syrus and Constantine V shows that Orthodox Christendom in their day was very much freer than the contemporary West from that concentration of the ownership of land, and consequent polarization of agrarian society into a handful of magnates and a multitude of serfs, which had been one of the mortal diseases of the moribund

Hellenic Civilization in the last days of the Roman Empire. This healthy agrarian foundation was doubtless one of the causes of the rapid growth which the Orthodox Christian Civilization achieved during the next two hundred years; but after the wars between the East Roman Empire and Bulgaria in Khan Symeon's reign (893–927) a sinister change began to show itself. The East Roman legislation of this period contains repeated enactments for protecting the small freeholder against the encroachments of the great proprietor; and, if this may be taken as evidence, we may infer that the evil of *latifundia* was now making its first appearance in Eastern and Central Asia Minor since Justinian had legislated against the great landed proprietors of Cappadocia in the sixth century. It can hardly be an accident that both of these sets of laws dated from times that followed an exhausting foreign war. One of the commonest social effects of war upon a belligerent country is to produce a maldistribution of wealth or to aggravate some existing maldistribution. This was no doubt the connexion between the Bulgarian Wars and the contemporary East Roman agrarian legislation that reached its climax and its unsuccessful termination in the reign of Emperor Basil II 'the Bulgar-Killer'; and such a view would be confirmed by the fact that other and more violent symptoms of social *malaise* appeared as the wars grew longer and more exhausting. One of these symptoms was a series of *pronunciamientos* by magnates in Asia Minor, beginning with Nikephoros Phokas's successful *coup* in 963. The grievances – or ambitions – of these pretenders to the imperial crown got the better of their patriotism. The peasantry in Asia Minor, which had provided the imperial government with tax-payers and with soldiers, was also alienated. When in the eleventh century the heart of Asia Minor was occupied by the Saljuq Turks, the peasantry was glad to see the last of the extortionate imperial taxation officers and the land-grabbing local magnates. The peasants now turned Turk and turned Muslim *en masse*. This wholesale cultural and religious apostasy suggests that before ever their new Turkish masters appeared on the scene the peasants had become spiritually estranged not only from the East Roman political régime, but also from the Orthodox Christian Civilization upon which the East Roman Empire had imposed itself as a crushing incubus. It would have been surprising if the East Roman peasants had not been embittered by their experience, for this had been shockingly ironic. The peasant-soldiers' hard-won victories had freed Asia Minor from the scourge of Muslim raids, only to make the country safe, not for the peasants themselves, but for the tax-collectors and for the land-grabbers.

If the East Roman agrarian crisis had this utterly disastrous dénouement, the extremeness of the disaster is perhaps partly to be accounted for by the fact that the agrarian evil was accentuated by the accompanying malady of militarism. Even before the end of the Bulgarian Wars, which had been forced upon an unwilling East Roman government by Symeon's megalomania, this government had so radically changed its policy that it deliberately embarked on a course of military aggression against its Muslim neighbours on the opposite frontier. From 926, when an East Roman expedition was sent to win territory on the Euphrates, the government persisted for a century and a quarter in pursuing a forward policy which weakened its defences, exposed its heart to attack, and aggravated the internal social strains which the Bulgarian Wars had already produced. The virus of militarism – personified from 963 to 1025 in the officer-emperors Nikephoros Phokas and John Dzimiskes and Basil II 'the Bulgar-Killer' – carried the Empire onwards with an ever-increasing momentum until it precipitated the irretrievable collapse of 1071.

In wantonly opting for this policy of conquest at the expense of stability and security, the East Roman government showed that it had lost that spirit of statesmanlike moderation and restraint which had formerly been the Empire's saving grace; and, when once this spirit was lost, an institution which had always been an incubus upon the life of Orthodox Christendom became intolerable. It was not, however, the irrational play of chance or a malicious stroke of fortune or 'the envy of the gods' that transformed the original ethos of the East Roman Empire into its antithesis, with this fatal consequence. The transformation was due to an inward impulse and not to an external accident; for it was natural that a growing society should expand, and inevitable, in the circumstances of Orthodox Christian social history, that an expansion should bring with it an aggravation of the incubus with which the expanding society was already saddled. Since there was not room for more than one ghost of the Roman Empire to haunt a single house, a life-and-death struggle between the East Roman Empire and its Bulgarian double followed the conversion of Bulgaria inevitably. In this internecine warfare between two idolized ghosts, the Orthodox Christian Civilization went down to destruction.

We have dwelt at some length upon the idolization of the East Roman Empire and its consequences, because this tragic story throws light upon something more than the nemesis that attends the idolization of an ephemeral institution; it shows up the perverse and sinful nature of idolatry itself as a transference of loyalty from the whole to the part and the transference of worship from the Creator to the creature. In Orthodox Christendom from the eighth century onwards the loyalty which should have been reserved for the Orthodox Christian Society as a whole was restricted to a single institution – the East Roman Empire – which was confined to one plane of social life and had been erected there by its worshippers' own hands. From the tenth century onwards, when the expansion of Orthodox Christendom had come to embrace the Bulgars as well as the Greeks within the Orthodox Christian fold, the unworthy object of the idolatrous society's worship was still further narrowed down by being multiplied from the singular into the plural and thereby ceasing to be co-extensive with the society in range, even on its own superficial plane. From 927 onwards the misguided devotion of the Orthodox idolaters to a political fetish was divided between one parochial Empire at Constantinople and another at Preslav. Since both Empires claimed an ecumenical jurisdiction by divine right, a life-and-death struggle between them was inevitable; and, when the idolaters' house was thus divided against itself, it is no wonder that it could not stand.[10]

25 David and Goliath: the idolization of an ephemeral technique

GIANT-KILLERS

138 Above, David and Goliath, fifteenth-century wood-carving.

139 Vietnam guerrilla warfare, contemporary cartoon.

IF WE TURN now to consider the idolization of techniques, we shall find in the history of warfare a classic forum for observing the grave retribution exacted for the commission of this sin. Taking the legendary duel between David and Goliath[1] as our starting-point, we shall see the same drama enacted and reperformed in a continuous series of matches between new-fangled and old-fashioned military techniques.

Before the fatal day on which he challenges the armies of Israel, Goliath has won such triumphant victories with his massive spear and impenetrable armour that he can no longer conceive of any alternative armament, and believes himself invincible. He therefore challenges the enemy of the day to choose a champion to meet him in single combat, on the assumption he too must be a spearman armed *cap-à-pie*, and in the assurance that any Israelite who has the hardihood to fight the Philistine champion with his own weapons will be an easy prey for him. So hard set is Goliath's mind in these two ideas that, when he sees David running forward to meet him with no armour on his body and nothing in his hand that catches the eye except a staff, Goliath takes umbrage, instead of taking alarm, at his adversary's apparent unpreparedness, and exclaims: 'Am I a dog, that thou comest to meet me with staves?' Goliath does not suspect that this youth's impertinence is not a piece of boyish folly but is, on the contrary, a carefully considered manœuvre (David having actually realized, quite as clearly as Goliath himself, that in Goliath's own accoutrements he cannot hope to be Goliath's match, and having therefore rejected the panoply which Saul has pressed upon him); nor does Goliath notice the sling in the hand which does not hold the staff, nor wonder what mischief may be hidden in the shepherd's bag. And so this luckless Philistine triceratops stalks forward pompously to offer his unvizored forehead as a target for the sling-stone which is to slay him at one shot before ever his contemptible adversary comes within range of his hitherto lethal spear.

While this classic tale sums up for all time a philosophic truth that is illustrated by the slowly unfolding history of competition in armaments, it is at the same time a matter of historical fact that the individual hoplite champion did not succumb to a single challenger, but to a phalanx; and the essence of the phalanx did not consist in the equipment of its component men-at-arms, but rather in the discipline which had transformed a barbaric rabble of individual warriors into a military formation whose orderly evolutions could accomplish ten times as much as the unco-ordinated efforts of an equal number of equally well-armed men.

This new military technique, of which we already catch some anticipatory glimpses in the *Iliad*, made its indubitable entry upon the stage of history in the shape of the Spartan phalanx which was forged under the pressure of the Second Messeno-Spartan War (*gerebatur c.* 650–620 BC); but the phalanx's triumph was not definitive, for it succumbed in its turn to new techniques as soon as the Spartans were tempted to 'rest on their oars' after their victory in the

Atheno-Peloponnesian War of 431–404 BC. Within thirty-three years of the Athenian débâcle, this triumphant Spartan phalanx had itself been routed: in 390 by an Athenian swarm of peltasts – light-armed footsoldiers – and then in 371 by a Theban column, a decisive tactical innovation which, with its uneven distribution of depth, weight, and drive, capped the old asset of discipline with the new element of surprise. The Athenian and Theban techniques were, however, as swiftly and surely undone by their own triumphs as the Spartan phalanx itself; for their respective victories were both cancelled at one stroke in 338 BC by a Macedonian formation in which a highly differentiated skirmisher and phalangite had been skilfully integrated with a heavy cavalry into a single fighting force. The list of military Powers defeated by the Macedonian army under Philip II and Alexander is long indeed; yet an even more impressive testimony to its prowess is the avowal of Lucius Aemilius Paullus after his victory at Pydna in 168 BC that 'the Macedonian phalanx was the most formidable and terrifying sight that had ever met his eyes.'[2]

Paullus's eulogy of the defeated Macedonian formation was at the same time a funeral oration pronounced over its dead body by the master of the Roman formation which had dealt the phalanx its death-blow. Through the senile adulation of a hitherto invincible technique, the Macedonian army of the second century BC had become as little able to cope with the Romans as the Athenian or Theban or Achaemenian forces had been able to cope with the Macedonian army of Philip and Alexander five generations earlier. While the Macedonians had 'rested on their oars' after their relatively easy conquest of the Achaemenian Empire, the Romans had been revolutionizing the art of war through an experience gained from their tremendous struggle with Hannibal, and consummated on the fields of Cynoscephalae in 197 BC and Pydna. The Roman legion triumphed over the Macedonian phalanx because it had improved on the Macedonian technique of integration between light infantryman and phalangite, a system which depended upon a meticulously exact co-ordination between two forces utterly distinct in equipment and training and even segregated in separate units. If the co-ordination between these highly specialized units broke down – for example, through such uncontrollable factors as the fog at Cynoscephalae or the broken ground at Pydna – then the formation was dislocated and left at the mercy of a more versatile and efficient adversary. In contrast to this crucial weakness of the Macedonian system, the post-Hannibalic Roman army – forewarned by its fatal reliance on the old-fashioned phalanx at the disaster of Cannae in 216 BC – had developed a superb flexibility, based on a new type of formation and armament which made it possible for any soldier or any unit to play either the light infantryman's or the hoplite's part, and to change over from the one kind of tactic to the other at a moment's notice. It was this versatility, combining the advantages of individualism with those of drill, that was the characteristic feature of the mature Roman military genius; by uniting in each legionary the mobility of the skirmisher with the irresistibility of the hoplite, and refining this technique under the supreme generals who mastered – and misused – it during the last century of the republican régime, the Roman

140   Hoplite champions, detail of relief, c. 400 BC.

141   Greek phalanx, from a vase of the late seventh century BC.

142   Roman and Sarmatian cavalry; detail from Trajan's Column.

army was able to attain the greatest efficiency possible for infantry before the invention of firearms.

At the very moment of reaching this perfection, however, the legionary received the first of a long series of defeats from a pair of mounted men-at-arms – the light horse-archer and the mail-clad lancer or cataphract – who, between them, were eventually to rout the footsoldier. The victorious horse-archers at Carrhae (53 BC), though forestalling by five years the classic infantry combat at Pharsalus, were an omen of the ultimate overthrow of the legionary by the cataphract that took place more than four centuries later at Adrianople (AD 378). In this disastrous engagement the Roman army was defeated by its own over-confidence in its traditional military technique: falling victim to a simple tactical ruse of their Gothic adversaries, Valens's legionaries allowed themselves to be overwhelmed by the enemy's heavy cavalry, which burst upon them 'as a thunderbolt bursts against a mountain-range',[3] and which inflicted unparalleled casualties on the densely packed and helpless Roman formation. The Romans had forgotten the lessons that they had learned at the similar battle of Cannae some six hundred years earlier, when their infantry had been at the mercy of Hannibal's heavy cavalry; they had 'rested on their oars', like the

143 Cataphract – mail-clad lancer – of the second or third century AD.

144 Cavalry versus cavalry: fourteenth-century view of the heavy-armed Mamluk horseman in action.

Macedonian phalangites before them, until they were overtaken and ridden down by an Oriental type of heavy cavalry that was even more formidable than Hannibal's squadrons. Though the Romans had received repeated warnings since Cannae of the legionary's inferiority to Oriental cavalry – in Crassus's disaster of 53 BC, Valerian's of AD 260, and Julian's of AD 363 – they had not been stimulated to make any fresh creative advance in infantry technique. They had left the legion, unreformed, to its fate; and, when disaster duly overtook them at Adrianople, they could think of no more original remedy than to discard the defeated legionary outright and take over the victorious cataphract at second-hand into their reconstituted army.

The cataphract was a degenerate compound of Assyrian heavy-armed infantryman and Nomad horse-archer, yet he had won his ascendancy before the invention of stirrups had made it possible for him to charge home without losing his seat in the saddle. He was to dominate military technique for a millennium, appearing with astonishing uniformity across the length and breadth of Europe and Asia; but already this very range and scale were bad omens for his future. By the end of this chapter the cataphract had lapsed into an armour-plated travesty of himself; in a

repetition of the legendary encounter between David and Goliath, the unwieldy 'Iraqi cataphract at the battle of Nahr Bashir (AD 1258) fell victim in individual combat to the light-armed and mobile Mongol horse-archer – the typical Nomad invader, long known and feared in South-Western Asia.[4] His latest triumph was, however, short-lived, for, just as the heavy-armed phalangite had found success by combining armour with drill, so in the new Cavalry Age the individual Mongol champion was promptly overcome by the disciplined heavy cavalry of the Egyptian Mamluks. These had given warning of the approaching supremacy of their technique at the battle of Mansurah in AD 1250, when the Frankish army of Saint Louis had paid a disastrous penalty for the thoughtless individualism of its knights, each anxious for personal honour at the expense of disciplined formation.[5]

So by the close of the thirteenth century the Mamluks stood in the Levant in a position of unchallenged supremacy, comparable to that enjoyed by the Romans after Pydna; but, like the Romans during the five and a half centuries between Pydna and Adrianople, the Mamluks, too, 'rested on their oars', ignored signs of a vulnerability arising from stagnation, and in AD 1798 were taken unawares in their turn by an old adversary armed with a new

145 Scimitar versus firearm: Egyptian cavalry and French infantry in the battle of the Pyramids, 1798.

146   Prussian ranks on parade, 1871.

technique – in this case Napoleon's French expeditionary force, the unrecognizable heirs of Saint Louis's unruly French knights. Despite the presages of a revival of infantry technique in the victories of the Ottoman Janissaries in 1516–17, and notwithstanding the Mamluks' partial recovery and emancipation from Ottoman domination in Egypt in the eighteenth century, the Mamluks 'had forgotten nothing and learned nothing'[6] as a result of their experience of adversity and eclipse. While they had allowed their military tradition to fossilize and their tactics and equipment to degenerate, the Western World had been rediscovering and reinvigorating the technique of a disciplined infantry force, which this time was equipped with firearms. The motley conscript army raised and drilled in post-revolutionary France was a passable imitation of the Ottoman corps of Janissaries which was now in the last stage of its decline, and by 1798 the French were ready to repeat the exploit of their Ottoman examplars of 1516–17 in conquering Egypt. The humiliating French victory over the blindly self-confident forces of Murad Bey[7] demonstrated conclusively the disastrous effect of four and a half centuries of irremediable stagnation.

We have now traced our chain of destruction from Goliath, the first of the hoplites, to Murad Bey, the last of the cataphracts, and we need not linger long over the latest and more familiar links. The new infantry technique developed in the West in the age of firearms has neither remained static nor been held as a permanent monopoly by a single Western nation. The success of the French *levée en masse* over the small but superbly professional army perfected in eighteenth-century Prussia stimulated the defeated Power to produce a pleiad of military and political geniuses who outdid the French in the new *tour de force* of combining

discipline with numbers; and this with such effect that Prussia's humiliation in the war of 1806–07 was wiped out in the *Befreiungskrieg* of 1813–14. So little did the French learn from the lesson that they brought a yet more calamitous defeat upon themselves in 1871, though in the long run it was the Prussians who suffered more from their victory than the French from their defeat. Dazzled by the brilliance of its own success, the Prussian General Staff allowed its strategic thinking to stagnate, with the result that in the war of 1914–18 the Prussian war-machine brought defeat upon Germany by evoking the unforeseen riposte of a siege on an unprecedented scale. Their blind faith in the successful techniques of trench warfare and economic blockade then concealed from the Western Allies the threat presented by the new technique of mechanized mobility developing in Hitler's armies, which in 1939–40 shattered their adversaries' comfortable prediction of a second *Sitzkrieg* and provoked them to accept a war on these new terms. Since then we have seen the technique of mass mechanization itself challenged on the one hand by the obsolescence of large-scale mobilizations of manpower in the face of the impersonal machinery of atomic warfare, and on the other hand by the impotence of the concentrated resources of a technically sophisticated military Power when faced with bands of guerrilla skirmishers, vastly inferior in equipment but adept at joining battle on their own chosen terrain and their own chosen terms. So in our own times as in previous eras the connexion between breakdown and idolatry has continued to be exemplified; and our final example suggests very forcibly that it is the act of idolization that does the mischief and not any intrinsic quality in the persons or objects or techniques themselves.

26 The Roman See: the intoxication of victory

ONE OF the more general forms in which the tragedy of *koros-hybris-ate* presents itself is the intoxication of victory – whether the struggle in which the fatal prize is won be a war of arms or a conflict of spiritual forces. Perhaps the most notable example of the disastrous consequences of a victory won in the spiritual field is afforded by a chapter in the long, and still continuing, history of the Papacy.

In this chapter, which began in AD 1046 and closed in 1870, the ecclesiastical head of Christendom was compelled twice over to capitulate in his own See to a secular sovereign. In 1046 it was the Emperor Henry III who deposed three rival Popes at the Synod of Sutri and installed his own nominee in their place; in 1870 it was the troops of King Victor Emmanuel who occupied Rome and deprived the Papacy of its last vestiges of territorial sovereignty outside the Vatican; and the eight hundred years which separate these two disasters saw the magnificent creation of the medieval *Respublica Christiana* and the tragic vitiation of this supreme spiritual achievement. Thus the wheel of fortune revolved full circle, bringing the Papacy from an extraordinary defeat to an extraordinary victory, and from victory to defeat again; and the weapon which overcame this greatest of all Western institutions was not wielded by Papal Rome's external foes; it was turned by her own stubborn hands against herself.

When the Tuscan Hildebrand took up his abode in Rome in the second quarter of the eleventh century, he found himself in a derelict outpost of the East Roman Empire which was occupied by a degenerate offshoot of the Byzantine Society, militarily defenceless and morally bankrupt. In this despised and alien city Hildebrand and his successors succeeded in creating the master-institution of Western Christendom. Attempts have been made to compare the Hildebrandine Papacy with other institutions, such as the Theban régime of the chief priest Hrihor, which have combined secular with religious authority, but there is a vein of uniqueness in this Papal *Respublica Christiana* which defies any description of its character by the method of analogy. It is best described in negative terms, as an exact inversion of the East Roman imperial régime which we have looked at in an earlier chapter,[1] and against which it was a social reaction and a spiritual protest; and this description gives perhaps the most fitting measure of Hildebrand's achievement. Papal Rome secured an empire which had a greater hold than the Empire of the Antonines upon human hearts, and which on the mere material plane embraced vast tracts of Western Europe never visited by the legions of Augustus and Marcus Aurelius. Indeed, this Papal dominion was wider than Charlemagne's, who had succeeded – though at ruinous cost – in advancing his frontier from the Rhine to the Elbe and thereby achieving a feat which had been beyond the strength of Augustus; for even Charlemagne never pushed his conquests beyond the Channel or the Baltic, whereas the medieval Papacy had inherited a spiritual dominion over England from the pontificate of Gregory the Great two hundred years before

Charlemagne, and had gone on to make a spiritual conquest of Scandinavia – and of Poland and Hungary too – some two hundred years after Charlemagne's death.

These Papal conquests were partly due to the constitution of the Christian Republic whose frontiers the Popes were enlarging; for it was a constitution which inspired confidence and affection instead of evoking hostility and resistance.[2] The Papal *Respublica Christiana* was based on a combination of ecclesiastical centralism and uniformity with political diversity and devolution; and, since the superiority of the spiritual over the temporal power was a cardinal point of constitutional doctrine, this combination made the note of unity predominant, without depriving the adolescent Western Society of those elements of liberty and elasticity which are indispensable conditions for growth. Indeed, the acceptance of the social unity of Western Christendom, which was implicit in a common recognition of the spiritual authority of the Pope, carried with it a certain guarantee for the political independence of any local community that took upon itself the Papal yoke – a burden which, in the eleventh century, was still apostolically light. It was by entering into direct relations with the Holy See, and thereby becoming acknowledged members of the Western Christian Society in their own right, that the newly converted barbarian kingdoms of Hungary and Poland exorcized the danger of being conquered and annexed by the *Regnum Teutonicum*, as the Saxons, in their day, had been forcibly 'Westernized' by Charlemagne, and as the Irish and the Prussians in a later century were to be subjected, respectively, by the English crown and the Teutonic Order.[3] Thanks to the Holy See, the Hungarians and the Poles were able, like the English, to enjoy the social and cultural benefits of membership in the society of Western Christendom without having to pay the price of forfeiting their political independence. It was also thanks, in large measure, to an alliance or community of interests with the Holy See that the city-states of Lombardy were able to vindicate their political autonomy against the Emperor Frederick I and to maintain it against the Emperor Frederick II.

Nor was the medieval Papacy illiberal in its attitude towards aspirations after local self-government, even in those Central Italian territories over which it claimed secular as well as ecclesiastical authority in virtue of the successive donations of Pepin and Charlemagne and Matilda. It appears to have accepted the situation without protest when the movement which was turning cities into city-states spread from Lombardy, where it had first asserted itself, into Romagna and the Marches and Umbria. In Tuscany in AD 1198 Pope Innocent III gave his recognition to the newly formed league of city-states, and urged Pisa to join it; and this benevolence extended to the *Ducatus Romanus* itself, which was the Papacy's metropolitan province. Papal influence was here exerted to protect the nascent civic liberties of Tivoli and Tusculum and Viterbo against the aggressiveness of the citizens of Rome;

147, 148 Humility and pomp of the Roman Church. A fifth-century Roman mosaic personifies the Church as a modest woman; by the thirteenth century she has become a jewelled empress.

and the Holy See was quick to make peace with the civic movement in Rome itself when it broke out there, in 1143, in a militant and revolutionary form. The Roman revolution of 1143 was followed by the settlement of 1145 between the new republic and Pope Eugenius III; and this settlement was revised and renewed in 1188 during the pontificate of Clement III.

The reason why a majority of the princes and city-states of Western Christendom accepted the Papal supremacy with so little demur was that the Pope was not then under suspicion of attempting to trespass upon the domain of the secular power. So far from claiming a monopoly of territorial sovereignty, like the contemporary Emperors at Constantinople, or a primacy *inter pares*, like the Holy Roman Emperors in the West from Otto the Great onwards in their relations with the independent Kings of France or England or León, the Holy See in this age was not concerned in the competition for territorial rulership. It was exercising on an ecumenical scale an authority of a spiritual character which was on a different plane from any territorial prerogative, and which, so long as it remained on this plane, did not become a danger to local political liberties. This statesmanlike aloofness from territorial ambitions was combined, in the Papal hierocracy at its zenith, with an energetic and enterprising use of the administrative gift which was the Byzantine dowry of Papal Rome. While in Orthodox Christendom this gift had been fatally applied to the *tour de force* of putting substance into the resuscitated ghost of the Roman Empire, and thereby crushing an adolescent Orthodox Christian Society under the incubus of an intolerably heavy institution,[4] the Roman architects of the *Respublica Christiana* turned their administrative resources to better account by building a lighter structure, on a new plan, upon broader foundations. The gossamer filaments of the Papal spider's web, as it was originally woven in the eleventh century, drew medieval Christendom together in an unconstrained unity which was equally beneficial to the parts and to the whole; and it was only later that the silken threads turned into iron bands which threatened to cramp and stunt the Western Society's growth.

In this Papal work of creation it was not, of course, either a capacity for administration or an avoidance of the snare of territorial ambitions that was the vital creative force. The fundamental reason why the Roman See was able in this age to conjure into existence a Christian Republic under a Papal aegis was that the Papacy had consciously taken upon itself the moral leadership of an expanding society in its growth-stage. The Hildebrandine Papacy gave expression and organization to the inarticulate aspirations of the *Plebs Christiana*, transforming them from the day-dreams of isolated individuals or scattered minorities into common causes of supreme value and established authority. The victory of the Christian Republic was won in campaigns for the purification of the clergy from the two moral plagues of illicit concubinage and financial corruption, for the liberation of the life of the Church from the interference of secular Powers, and for the rescue of the Oriental Christians and the Holy Land from the clutches of the Turkish champions of Islam. But this was not the whole nor the best of the Hildebrandine

Papacy's work. A genius for descrying the seeds of noble things and for bringing the crop to harvest was the crowning virtue of the Papacy in the days of its Hildebrandine greatness; and this genius was displayed, not in the 'holy wars' of the crusading Church Militant, but in a fruitful patronage of such promising institutions as the universities and the religious Orders, and in the triumphant enlistment of the best talents of Western Christendom in the service of the Holy See.

The fall of the Hildebrandine Papacy is as extraordinary a spectacle as its rise; for all the virtues that had carried it to its zenith seem to change, as it sinks to its nadir, into their own exact antitheses. The ethereal institution which had been fighting and winning a battle for spiritual freedom against material force was now infected with the very evil which it had set itself to cast out from the body social of Western Christendom. The Holy See which had taken the lead in the struggle against simony now required the clergy throughout the Western World to pay dues at a Roman receipt of custom for those ecclesiastical preferments which Rome herself had forbidden them to purchase from any secular Power. The Roman Curia which had been the head and front of moral and intellectual progress – a tower of strength for the saints who were raising the monastic life to new heights and for the schoolmen who were creating the universities – now turned itself into a fastness of spiritual conservatism. The ecclesiastical sovereign Power in the Christian Republic now suffered itself to be deprived by its local secular underlings – the princes of the rising parochial states of Western Christendom – of the lion's share of the product of financial and administrative instruments which the Papacy itself had skilfully devised in order to make its authority effective. This loss was not made good by the consolation prize of political sovereignty over a minor principality. Has any other institution ever given so great occasion as this to the enemies of the Lord to blaspheme?[5] The downfall of the Hildebrandine Papacy is a more extreme case of *peripeteia* than any that we have yet encountered in our study of the nemesis of creativity. How did it happen, and why?

How it happened is foreshadowed in the first recorded transaction in Hildebrand's public career.

The creative spirits in the Roman Church who set themselves in the eleventh century to rescue the Western World from a feudal anarchy by establishing a Christian Republic found themselves in the same dilemma as their spiritual heirs who are attempting in our day to replace an international anarchy by a political world order. The essence of their aim was to substitute a reign of spiritual authority for the reign of physical force, and in their struggle against violence the spiritual sword was the weapon with which their supreme victories were won. No physical force was exerted in Hildebrand's act of deposing and excommunicating the Emperor Henry IV in AD 1076; yet the moral effect of the Pope's winged words upon the hearts of the Emperor's Transalpine subjects was so intense that within a few months it brought Henry to Canossa. There were, however, other occasions on which it seemed as if the established régime of physical force was in a position to defy the strokes of the spiritual sword with impunity; and it was in such situations that the Roman Church Militant

was challenged to give its answer to the riddle of the Sphinx. Was the soldier of God to deny himself the use of any but his own spiritual arms, at the risk of seeing his advance brought to a standstill? Or was he to fight God's battle against the Devil with his adversary's own weapons, if the only practicable way of ejecting his adversary from his entrenchments was to hoist him with his own petard? Which was the true Christian act of faith?

The question presented itself in an urgent practical form to the would-be reformer Pope Gregory VI when he assumed the burden of Papal office in AD 1045. In order to serve as the instrument of reform, the Holy See must be efficiently organized; to be organized, it must have money; and the necessary supplies of this were not forthcoming; for, while the old Papal revenues from the *Patrimonia Petri* had disappeared with the *Patrimonia* themselves, the new revenues arising from the offerings of pilgrims were being stolen from the very altar of Saint Peter's own church by the brigand-nobles of the *Ducatus Romanus*. No one would dispute that this sacrilegious robbery was as criminal in itself as it was damaging to the interests of the Papacy and the Christian Republic; and there was no prospect of the criminals yielding to any spiritual appeal. Was it then justifiable to meet force with force in this flagrant case? The question was answered when Gregory VI appointed Hildebrand to be his *capellanus*; for the guardianship of Saint Peter's altar, with the gifts which were heaped upon it, was the *capellanus*'s principal duty; and Hildebrand promptly fulfilled it by raising troops and routing the brigands by force of arms.

At the moment when Hildebrand took this first momentous step in his career, the inward moral character of his act was ambiguous and difficult to divine. But in his last hour, forty years later, its true nature had become more apparent. In AD 1085, when he lay dying as a Pope in exile in Salerno, his See had just been looted and burnt by the Normans whom he had called in to assist him in a military struggle which had gradually spread from the steps of Saint Peter's altar until it had engulfed the whole of Western Christendom. The climax of the physical conflict between Hildebrand and Henry IV gave a forecast of the deadlier and more devastating struggle which was to be fought out *à outrance* two centuries later between Innocent IV and Frederick II; and by the time of Innocent IV's pontificate the character of Hildebrand's act had become clear. In choosing the alternative of meeting force with force, Hildebrand had set the Church upon a course which was to end in the victory of his adversaries the World, the Flesh, and the Devil over the City of God which he had sought to bring down to Earth.

If the Papacy became possessed by the demon of physical violence which it was attempting to exorcize, this gives us the explanation of the other changes of Papal virtues into their opposing vices; for the substitution of the material for the spiritual sword is the fatal and fundamental change of which all the rest are corollaries. The establishment and improvement of a system of taxation by a Papacy which had once set out to eradicate simony was manifestly due to the ever-increasing demands upon the Papal Exchequer which were being made by the perpetually recurring warfare between the Papacy and the Empire; and, when the

149 The mounted Pope was a motif of supremacy taken from Roman imperial tradition. A thirteenth-century fresco illustrating the 'Donation of Constantine' shows the Emperor conferring dominion over Rome on Pope Sylvester I, and then leading him into the city.

Papacy succumbed at Avignon to the domination of one of its secular rivals, it was certain that the local secular princes would inherit, sooner or later, the whole of the administrative and financial power which the Papacy had gradually been acquiring for itself throughout Western Christendom. When the Papacy exhausted its strength in its deadly conflict with the Holy Roman Empire, it placed itself at the mercy of the parochial secular states, and was promptly despoiled by them of the panoply with which it had equipped itself for fighting its medieval battle. The sole compensation which the Papacy received from its despoilers was a tiny share in the territorial sovereignty which the local secular princes were forging for themselves out of their Papal spoils. In yielding – or being forced to yield – to this new dispensation of parochial sovereignty, the Papacy was simply allowing itself to drift on a now irresistible tide; and the consciousness that it was now drifting with the tide, and that it had lost control over its own destiny, was no doubt the psychological cause of the conservatism to which the Papacy abandoned itself after the shock of the Reformation. Since it had lost the power of voluntary initiative, the Papacy came to see its safety in stagnation; and it was in this spirit that it set its face not only against the theological and hierarchical innovations of the Protestant Reformation, but also against most of the new discoveries of modern Western physical science and new ideas of modern Western social philosophy.

We have now perhaps found some answer to the question of how the Papacy came to suffer its extraordinary *peripeteia*; but in describing the sequence of events we have not explained the cause. We may be justified in our thesis that the downfall of the Papacy in every sphere can be traced back to its abandonment of the spiritual in favour of the material sword, and that this fatal change can be traced, in its turn, to Hildebrand's first act of his public life. Yet, even if it were demonstrable that Hildebrand's original decision to parry force with force was the ruin of the whole Hilde-

brandine enterprise as a matter of fact, this would not prove that what did happen was bound to happen *a priori*. The single example of the Hildebrandine tragedy proves no more than the truism that the use of material means towards a spiritual end is a dangerous game. To live dangerously, however, is the inevitable condition of being alive at all; and there is no moral law which states that defeat is inherent in the resort to a dangerous manœuvre. It is not enough to show that in Hildebrand's case a disaster did occur; we also have to answer the question why.

Why was it that the medieval Papacy became the slave of its own tools, and allowed itself to be betrayed, by its use of material means, into being diverted from the spiritual ends to which those means had been intended to minister? The explanation of the Papacy's ultimate defeat is to be found, so it would seem, in the untoward effects of an initial victory. The dangerous game of fighting force with force had in this case a fatal result, because, to begin with, it had succeeded only too well. Intoxicated by the success which the hazardous manœuvre obtained for them in the earlier stages of their struggle with the Holy Roman Empire, Pope Gregory VII and his successors persisted in the use of force, and carried it to extremes, until it defeated the users' purpose by becoming an end in itself. While Gregory VII fought the Empire with the object of removing an imperial obstacle to a reform of the Church, Innocent IV fought the Empire two hundred years later with the object of breaking the imperial Power. The downfall of the Hildebrandine Papacy was a supremely tragic performance of the drama of *koros-hybris-ate*.

We can verify the working out of this *Leitmotiv* in two ways: both by contrasting some earlier and later scenes in the play, and by analysing the plot as a whole.

Compare, for example, the outwardly similar but inwardly diverse scenes in which three rival claimants to the Papacy appear before a council of the Church summoned by a Holy Roman Emperor, with the result that two are

150 A fifteenth-century painting repeats the same motif: the Emperor Frederick Barbarossa leads Pope Alexander III into Rome, to symbolize the submission of Frederick to papal authority after the reconciliation of Empire and Pope in 1177.

deposed as illegitimate and a third is compelled to abdicate. In AD 1046 it was Pope Gregory VI who was obliged to abdicate in this way by the Synod of Sutri, which the Emperor Henry III had convened; and in AD 1415 it was Pope John XXIII who suffered the same fate at the hands of the Council of Constance held under the auspices of the Emperor Sigismund. Externally the two scenes might seem almost indistinguishable, but there is a difference in ethos between the two protagonists which gives some measure of the moral débâcle to which the Papacy had succumbed in the course of the four intervening centuries. Pope Gregory VI was an unworldly saint who had rendered himself technically guilty of the offence of simony by purchasing the Papal office in order to rescue it from the hands of his unworthy godson, Pope Benedict IX. The condemnation of Gregory VI was a travesty of justice which aroused indignation all over Western Christendom and inspired Hildebrand to devote his life to fighting for the liberation of the Church from an arbitrary 'Caesaropapism'. Yet the victim of this judicial act of injustice accepted and endorsed his sentence without a murmur. Not so the *condottiere* Baldassare Cossa, 'the most profligate of Mankind',[6] whom the Council of Constance had to deal with as Pope John XXIII. 'He fled, and was brought back a prisoner; the most scandalous charges were suppressed; the Vicar of Christ was only accused of piracy, murder, rape, sodomy, and incest.'[7] The poison of worldliness had worked potently in the course of less than four hundred years to produce the contrast between these two scenes.

There is another pair of scenes in which a Pope invades Southern Italy with an armed force, meets with an ignominious defeat, and dies of chagrin. In the first scene it is Pope Leo IX who is defeated, in AD 1053, by the Normans; and in the second scene it is Pope Innocent IV who is defeated, in AD 1254, by Manfred. Outwardly, Leo was more grossly humiliated at the hands of his conquerors than was Innocent; but, if we compare the two exploits in terms of

151 Dante, in conversation with Pope Nicholas III, rebukes the Papacy for its avarice and prodigality.

152 PAPAL HUMILIATION Pope Gregory VII expelled from Rome. Gregory's presumption of supreme secular and spiritual authority led him into constant conflict with the Emperor Henry IV; despite their reconciliation at Canossa in 1077, Gregory was later deposed by Henry, and ended his days in exile in Southern Italy.

153 Innocent III, self-styled 'Vicar of Christ'; a portrait from Old St Peter's, Rome.

motives and states of mind, we shall see that it was really Innocent who suffered the greater moral defeat. Pope Leo was attempting, in co-operation with the secular arm of the Emperors of both East and West, to carry out a police operation against a band of wholly disreputable brigands; and what broke his heart was not his own defeat but the slaughter of the men who had embraced his cause. Innocent IV, on the other hand, was on the warpath against the son of a dead and defeated enemy against whom he nursed such an implacable hatred that he was prepared to pursue his vendetta into the second and third generation. The chagrin that killed him was his rage at being foiled in an attempt to carry his war into the enemy's country and to chevy out of his ancestral kingdom a prince who had abandoned his father's aggressive ambitions and who was only anxious to be left in peace. Militarily, Innocent's and Leo's expeditions ended in much the same way, but morally there is no comparison between them; and this moral gulf gives the measure of the Papacy's spiritual degeneration during the intervening span of two hundred years.

The operation of *koros-hybris-ate* which we can detect in these comparisons is revealed still more clearly when we take the play as a whole and analyse the plot. The first act opens in AD 1046 with the first steps in the career of Hildebrand, a man who had discerned and accepted the challenge presented to the Papacy by the contemporary reawakening of the Western Christian World from its vegetative lethargy. It was only in a society that was numb with misery – as Western Christendom had been from the twilight of Charlemagne's generation to the dawn of Otto the Great's – that the prerogative of moral leadership could be left, even nominally, in the hands of an institution which was disgracing itself as the Roman See disgraced itself during that profligate passage in its history. From the moment when the Western World as a whole began to shake off its moral torpor and to aspire to a better life, the Roman See was confronted with the alternative of leaping at one bound from the lowest to the highest rung of the moral ladder as it stood in that age, or else being pilloried in its actual state of degradation and seeing its kingdom being numbered and finished and divided and given to the Medes and the Persians.[8] In this hour Hildebrand set himself the tremendous task of substantiating the Church's claim to the moral leadership of the Western World; and in thirty years of titanic labour he succeeded in achieving the impossible. By 1075 the double battle against the sexual and financial corruption of the clergy had been won throughout the Western World, and the victory had been gained by the moral prowess of a Roman See whose profligacy had been the greatest of all the scandals of the Western Church in the preceding century. It was in the moment of his triumph, in the third year of his pontificate, that Hildebrand took a step which, though perhaps inevitable, was almost certain to prove disastrous. In AD 1075 Hildebrand extended his field of battle from the sure ground of concubinage and simony to the debatable ground of investiture.

Logically, perhaps, the conflict over investiture might be justified as an inevitable sequel to the conflicts over concubinage and simony if all three struggles were looked upon as aspects of one single struggle for the liberation of the Church. To Hildebrand at this critical point in his career it might almost seem labour lost to have freed the Church from her servitude to Venus and Mammon, if he were to leave her still fettered by her political subjection to the secular Power. So long as this third shackle lay heavy upon her, would she not still be debarred from doing her divinely appointed work for the regeneration of Mankind? But this argument begs the question whether the possibility of sincere and fruitful co-operation between the Church and the secular Power had in fact wholly vanished by 1075; and on this question the onus of proof lies with the Hildebrandines, for at least two reasons.

In the first place neither Hildebrand nor his partisans ever sought – either before or after the promulgation in 1075 of Hildebrand's decree prohibiting lay investiture – to deny that the secular authorities had a legitimate role to play in the procedure for the election of clerical officers of the Church. In the second place, during the thirty years ending in 1075 the Roman See had found it possible to work hand in hand with the Holy Roman Empire in the older conflict over the issues of concubinage and simony. In these circumstances the need for a deliberate policy of limiting or prohibiting the intervention of the secular authority in investiture must be accounted questionable, for it is conceivable that, if Hildebrand had not chosen to throw down the gauntlet in 1075, a compromise leading to a new and fertile era in co-operation might have been achieved.

The gravity of Hildebrand's action is revealed by the dimensions of the catastrophe which was its sequel. On this issue of investiture Hildebrand staked the whole of the moral prestige which he had won for the Papacy in thirty years; and his hold upon the conscience of the *Plebs Christiana* in the Emperor Henry IV's Transalpine dominions was strong enough, in conjunction with the strength of Saxon arms, to have brought the Emperor to Canossa in AD 1077. Yet, although Canossa may have dealt the imperial dignity a blow from which it perhaps never quite recovered, the sequel to that moral triumph was not an end, but a resumption, of the struggle which Hildebrand had let loose two years before. Despite a series of attempts to settle the dispute in the next fifty years, the conflict remained as an unhealed wound in the Western body social which threatened to break open again under the strain of later crises. The fire which Hildebrand had kindled in 1075 was still burning fiercely a hundred years later.

The second act in the tragedy opens with a respite which coincided in time with the pontificate of Pope Innocent III (*fungebatur* AD 1198–1216). With Germany torn in two by civil war, and with the child-king Frederick of Sicily under Innocent's own guardianship, the young Pope had his hands free to play the part of President of the Christian Republic as Hildebrand had conceived of it; and Innocent III did duly become the Solomon or Suleyman the Magnificent or Harun-al-Rashid of the Hildebrandine Papacy. This was a brilliant role, and it was impressively sustained by a noble figure; yet Innocent's pontificate was not so triumphant in reality as it appeared to be on the surface. As a man of action he was unquestionably noble; but this nobility was tarnished by a touch of *hybris* and baulked by a grain of obtuseness. The fallibility of his judgment is

154 Gregory IX, patron of Saint Francis, as he appears on a mosaic from Old St Peter's.

revealed in his handling of the weapon of the Crusade; in his dealings with the Empire and the House of Hohenstaufen; and in his attitude to the greatest man of his generation, Saint Francis.

Innocent's first act after his accession was to preach a crusade for the rescue of the remnants of the Frankish principalities in Syria from the grasp of the Ayyubid Power; and this enterprise went grievously awry when the Western Christian expeditionary force was diverted from its original objective to take part in an irrelevant and nefarious campaign against the Crusaders' fellow-Christians in the East Roman Empire. In this painful situation Innocent's idealism was convincingly demonstrated in his distress at such a scandalous betrayal of the honour of Western Christendom. But this evidence of a noble spirit only increases our wonder at seeing him, just four years after the lesson of 1204, deliberately launching another assault of Christians upon Christians, and this time not even on the alien soil of Orthodox Christendom, but in Languedoc, at the heart of his own Christian Commonwealth. Did the Pope who had deplored the horrors of the sack of Constantinople by French Crusaders imagine that his French ecclesiastical subjects would behave less brutally if they were let loose upon one of the richest provinces of the Western *Respublica Christiana*, when this time they even had the Pope's official support? And did Innocent suppose that he would succeed any better this time than before in controlling the fearful forces of violence and wickedness that he was letting loose?

This vein of ingenuous ineptitude which comes out in Innocent's handling of his Crusades is also apparent in his dealings with the affairs of the Empire and the Hohenstaufen. He threw himself into the imperial dispute on the anti-Hohenstaufen side, only to be betrayed by his own candidate, the Welf Otto of Brunswick, when the latter eventually attained the imperial crown. Faced with this defection, Innocent could think of no more original plan than to enlist a Hohenstaufen to overthrow the Welf whom he had previously brought into power in order to overthrow a Hohenstaufen. More than this, he actually selected for his new candidate a boy who already wore the Sicilian crown and who would therefore be in a position to execute his father Henry's design of taking the Roman See between two fires if Innocent's assistance enabled him to win the imperial crown as well. Although Innocent, on his deathbed in 1216, exacted from the young Frederick a promise that, as soon as he should have received the imperial crown, he would hand on the Sicilian crown to his son, there was no guarantee that this pledge would be honoured; and thus Innocent left the great institution, which had been placed in his keeping in so prosperous a political condition eighteen years before, at the mercy of a successor of Rome's old imperial enemies, Henry IV and Frederick Barbarossa.

This lack of intuition in divining character, which Innocent showed when he lent his support to two such unsatisfactory protégés, is more flagrantly apparent in his attitude towards Saint Francis; and here it is difficult to draw the line between obtuseness and *hybris*. Innocent's first reaction to this saintly man was negative, and the credit for his subsequent change of mind is due to the

Bishop of Assisi and to the future Pope Gregory IX, who was Francis's solitary champion in Innocent's Curia. Did Innocent's coldness signify an unawareness of Francis's greatness or an indifference to it? Did his aloofness from the deepest spiritual movement of his age reflect the preoccupation of a man of affairs or the superciliousness of an aristocrat? We might give Innocent the benefit of the doubt and acquit him of the charge of *hybris* here, but there is another count on which the charge cannot be rebutted. A Pope whose predecessors had been content to style themselves 'Vicar of Peter' assumed the style 'Vicar of Christ'. This was an ominous departure from the humility of Gregory the Great, who had taken the title *Servus Servorum Dei* when his colleague John the Faster at Constantinople had proclaimed himself 'Ecumenical' Patriarch. Innocent III's failure of judgment can be measured best, like Hildebrand's, by marking its sequel; for the breathing-space which had opened with Innocent's accession did not outlast his death. It was followed by a battle between the Papacy and the Emperor Frederick II which surpassed in fury all the earlier battles between Rome and the Empire, and which produced in Western Europe a devastation and a misery unparalleled since the dawn of the Western Society.

The third act of the Papal tragedy opens on 13 December 1250, which is the date of Frederick II's sudden and premature death. Would the Papacy, now represented in Pope Innocent IV (*fungebatur* AD 1243–54), accept this opportunity of restoring peace to Western Christendom, or would the vendetta against Frederick's house be pursued to the bitter end? Notwithstanding the frightful effects of this latter-day Hannibalic War, Innocent insisted on maintaining the stand which he had taken three years before, when he had declared his determination never to make peace so long as either Frederick or any of his sons remained King or Emperor; and this declaration, which assuredly was no mere error of judgment but was a moral aberration as well, spelled the suicide of the Hildebrandine Papacy.

This stance of implacable hostility was the policy which Innocent IV bequeathed to his successors in the Holy See; and it duly ended in the extinction of Frederick's line through the death of his sons – Manfred in battle in 1265 and Conradin on the scaffold in 1268. The note of *hybris* which Innocent III had struck when he proclaimed himself the 'Vicar of Christ', and Innocent IV when he included Frederick's children in the remorseless vow which he had taken against Frederick himself, was sounded for the third time by Pope Boniface VIII (*fungebatur* AD 1294–1303) when he seized the occasion of the turn of the century to inaugurate the institution of the Papal Jubilee. In the pilgrims who flocked to Rome in the Holy Year 1300 Boniface fancied that he saw the human witness of his own territorial omnipotence; yet at the same time his ears were deaf to the dissenting murmurs of a distant provincial clergy who were still being called upon to pay the Papal war-taxes a generation after the Papal Punic Wars had been brought to their dreadful termination. He did not understand that neither the clergy nor the *Plebs Christiana* would be willing to risk life and fortune to support a Papal against a secular tyranny; he assumed that they would rise at his call as they had risen at Hildebrand's. Under this delusion

155 *Saint Francis weds the Lady Poverty*. For earlier monastic orders, poverty was an incidental part of a régime of self-denial; but Francis chose poverty as an ideal identification with Christ's rule of life.

156 Boniface VIII, inaugurator of the Papal Jubilee: a statue attributed to Arnolfo di Cambio.

157 Martin V, successor to the deposed Pope John XXIII; bronze medal.

he provoked the King of France into drawing his sword, and then ran straight upon the extended sword-point, in the confidence that any secular weapon must crumple under the drum-fire of his own ecclesiastical artillery.

The sequel to this suicidal act was the Pope's arrest at Anagni and the 'Babylonish Captivity' at Avignon and the Great Schism which rent Western Christendom in two; and each of these calamities might have been foreseen and feared and averted by Boniface himself if his vision and judgment and action had not been confounded by the *ate* that was incarnate in him. Precedent could have told him that a *coup de force* against the Pope's own person was the first counter-attack that any Pope had to expect from a secular prince upon whom he had declared war, as Paschal II had been kidnapped in 1111 and Hildebrand himself in 1075. Again, the attraction of the Papacy into the French orbit was a recurrent phenomenon that had a history stretching back to the eleventh century. So long as French power was balanced by imperial power, the pull had not been irresistible. But, when the threat from Germany was removed – as it had been by Boniface's day – who then was left to challenge the ambitions of the King of France? As for the Great Schism, it had already been foreshadowed by the time of Boniface's pontificate in the series of inter-regnums which had been interrupting the Hildebrandine succession for some fifty years past. Enough proof had been given during this period that the electoral machinery which had been installed on Hildebrand's initiative in 1059 was badly out of gear and might quite cease to work if it were subjected to another violent strain or shock. That Boniface should have challenged the King of France when the Papacy was in this parlous state would be inexplicable in a man who was altogether in his right senses.

So we come to the fourth and last act in the Hilde-brandine tragedy, which opens after the turn of the four-teenth and fifteenth centuries with the advent of the Conciliar Movement. The scandal of the Great Schism moved the provincial clergy to come to the rescue of the most venerable institution in Western Christendom, and their attitude, of which the Conciliar Movement was the outcome, combined filial piety with moral reprobation. The reformers were anxious to save the Papacy from suicide, but their anxiety was for the sake of the Christian Republic as well as for the sake of the Papacy itself. They were determined to reconstruct the falling house, but on a new plan which would restore balance to the critically top-heavy Papal edifice. The reconstructed pyramid must be given a lower apex and a broader base. Thus the condition to which the Papacy was asked to assent as the price – and guarantee – of its rehabilitation was the introduction of a parliamentary element into the constitution of the Western body ecclesiastic. Would the Papacy be willing to atone for its past and to assure its future by bowing, in this matter, to the will of Christendom? Once again a Pope had to take a decision which was momentous for the fate of the Western World as well as for that of the Roman See; and, once again, the answer was in the negative. The Papacy rejected the parliamentary principle and opted for an unrestricted sovereignty in a restricted field as the alterna-tive to accepting a limited constitutional authority over a loyal and undivided Christian Commonwealth.

This was the decision which was taken at the Council of Constance in the crucial year 1417 and was confirmed at Basel in 1448. In the thirty years that separated these two occasions, the Papacy did, it is true, attempt to carry out many of the reforms demanded by the Council of Constance. But these Papal efforts at reform were stultified by the fatal weakness of their not being the Papacy's paramount aim or interest. During these critical years the Pope's overriding concern was to assert his own pretension to exercise an autocratic authority; and this Papal impulse to subordinate the reform of the Church to the aggrandizement of the Papacy was perhaps responsible, more than any other factor, for that misunderstanding between the Papacy and the Conciliar Movement which came to an open breach in the quarrel between Pope Eugenius IV and the Council of Basel. In the intoxication of its victory over the Conciliar Movement in this naked trial of strength, the Papacy abandoned itself once more to that lust for power which had been its besetting sin since the days of Hildebrand. With one hand it clung to the despotic ecclesiastical power over the provinces of the Western Church which it had been unexpectedly successful in retaining; with the other hand it continued to build up its secular territorial power in Central Italy; and, in playing their part as fifteenth-century Italian despots, the Popes became steeped in that pride of life which was the dominant note of the medieval Italian culture in its fifteenth-century over-ripeness. Within less than a hundred years after the dissolution of the Council of Basel in 1449 the Papacy was in even worse case than it had been when the Council of Constance had opened in 1414. The Pope had defeated the Conciliar Movement to his own undoing. 'He made a pit and digged it, and is fallen into the ditch which he made.'[9]

The sixteenth century saw the nemesis of the Papacy's fifteenth-century relapse into *hybris*. As a logical consequence of the path that it had chosen to take, the Papacy was treated by the Transalpine Powers as one midget in the covey of Italian secular principalities, and a feeble one at that. It learnt its lesson and withdrew from active participation in the international war-game; but this tardy Papal recognition of the drawbacks of territorial sovereignty did not save Pope Innocent XI from being bullied by Louis XIV or Pope Pius VII from being dragged at the chariot-wheels of Napoleon.

While the Pope suffered a grievous fate as an Italian secular prince, he suffered still worse misfortune as the ecumenical sovereign of the Western Church. The whole of his power was reft away from him in the states that turned Protestant, and four-fifths of it in those that professedly remained Catholic. The sixteenth-century Catholic response to the challenge of Protestantism was not led by the Papacy, but by a band of inspired individual saints; indeed, it was the dead weight of Papal tradition that brought these saints' impetuous advance to a premature halt. They liberated the Papacy from the pride of life, but its lust for power proved too strong for them; and so the sixteenth-century rally failed, after all, to save the day. The Roman Church lapsed into a spiritual torpor, from which it awoke only to stage a counter-revolution against the secular intellectual revival of the eighteenth century. Remaining impervious to the challenge of the new forces of democracy

158 The scholar, diplomatist, and Renaissance patron Aeneas Silvius, later Pope Pius II, travelling to the Council of Basel in 1431.

159 Seal of the Council of Basel, where the Conciliar Movement suffered accumulative defeat as the Papacy struggled to maintain its autocracy.

and nationalism, the Papacy was overtaken on its own ground by the Italian *Risorgimento*, and the extinction of its territorial sovereignty on 20 September 1870 marked the nadir of the material fortunes of the Hildebrandine institution.

This political bankruptcy was, however, far less tragic for the Papacy than its spiritual self-defeat, and the Papacy had inflicted this on itself in a series of acts which began with Saint Francis's patron Pope Gregory IX's excommunication of the Emperor Frederick II in 1227 and culminated in the Papacy's provocation of the sixteenth-century Protestant revolt against the authority of the Roman Church. Since the Reformation, a Church which had once been the institutional expression of Western Christendom's unity has been only one among a number of rival Western Christian sects whose rancorous mutual hostility has torn the Western World in pieces, has brought Christianity itself into discredit there, and has thus opened the way for the supplanting of Christianity by nationalism, a post-Christian resuscitation of the pre-Christian worship of collective human power.

The twentieth century has seen a movement for self-reform in the Roman Church which recalls the fifteenth-century Conciliar Movement and the eleventh-century awakening that found its leader in Hildebrand, Pope Gregory VII; and this time the Roman Catholic clergy and laity has twice been given a Papal lead. Pope Pius XI retrieved the political error of his namesake Pope Pius IX by concluding with the Italian state the Lateran Agreements of 1929, in which the Papacy renounced its claim to temporal power outside the Vatican City, in exchange for Italy's recognition of Papal political sovereignty within this miniature domain. Far more important has been the Church's spiritual *aggiornamento* ('bringing up to date') by Pope John XXIII. In his brief reign (1958–63), this saintly and genial Pope has 'made history'. He has given vent to the most dynamic of any of the movements among the Western Catholic clergy and laity since the eleventh-century spiritual revival. Angelo Giuseppe's assumption of the name 'John' was as intentionally significant as Achille Ratti's assumption of the name 'Pius'. Each of these two Popes was setting out to redeem the reputation of a name that at least one previous Pope Pius and a number of previous Pope Johns had brought into disrepute.

The twentieth-century crisis manifestly resembles the fifteenth-century crisis. It cannot yet be foreseen whether it is going to have a happier outcome, but we can already guess that, if the present movement for reform comes to grief in its turn, the Papacy's claim to autocratic power will have been, once again, the fatal stumbling-block. Will the two sessions of Pope John XXIII's Vatican Council have succeeded in counteracting the effect of the Council of 1869, in which Pope Pius IX compensated the Papacy in advance for its imminent loss of temporal power by obtaining acceptance of the dogma of the Pope's infallibility in his pronouncements *ex cathedra*? And will Pope Paul VI's

160 Pius IX, who made Papal Infallibility a dogma.

efforts to assert his authority enforce submission, or will they provoke revolt?

At all stages of its history the Catholic Church has been a seed-bed of saints. Saint Francis of Assisi is the greatest soul that has appeared in the Western World so far. Yet, time and again, the example given by the saints' self-abnegation has been robbed of its spiritual harvest by a Pope's thirst for power. This tragedy need not repeat itself. The saintly Pope John XXIII's large-hearted policy may prevail, and, if it does, this will benefit the whole of the Western Society by giving a fresh inspiration to the oldest of its Churches. On the other hand, if the present spiritual revival within the Roman Church were to be frustrated once again, the price would be paid, this time, by the Roman Church's own 'Establishment'; for Western Christendom has already paid the price of the Papacy's forfeiture of its former ecumenical leadership. The price has been the replacement of the medieval Western *Respublica Christiana* by a bevy of idolized national states. For the Western Civilization, as well as for the Roman Church, this has been a grievous change for the worse, and the guilt lies with those predecessors of Pope John XXIII who failed, at successive crucial turning-points of history, to rise to the spiritual demands of their high office. They failed spiritually because they had been intoxicated by worldly success. Their failure is a signal illustration of the nemesis of creativity.

PART V

THE DISINTEGRATIONS
OF CIVILIZATIONS

Breakdowns are not inevitable and not irretrievable; but, if the process of disintegration is allowed to continue, I find that it seems to follow a common pattern in most instances. The masses become estranged from their leaders, who then try to cling to their position by using force as a substitute for their lost power of attraction. I trace the fragmentation of society into a dominant minority, an internal proletariat, and an external proletariat consisting of the barbarians on its fringes; and I sketch the social reactions of these diverse groups to the ordeal of disintegration. I also find a corresponding psychological schism in the souls of people who happen to have been born into this unhappy age. Discordant psychic tendencies which are perhaps always latent in human nature now find free play. People lose their bearings, and rush down blind alleys, seeking escape. Greater souls detach themselves from life; still greater souls try to transfigure life into something higher than mere life as we know it on Earth, and sow the seeds of a fresh spiritual advance.

plate 34

A PETRIFIED SOCIETY

A crumbling colossus of King Amenophis III dominates the parched landscape at Thebes, dwarfing the modern village in the background. In the second millennium B C, when this statue was erected, the Egyptiac Society achieved an extraordinary recovery, but the price of her preservation was petrifaction: the society was immobilized by an inflexibly hierarchical structure that impeded new growth. For 2500 years Egypt lingered on in a static and empty life-in-death; the massive monuments left for posterity proclaim the stubborn tenacity of this longest-lived of all known civilizations.

1917 ОКТЯБРЬ 1920

plates 35, 36
SOCIAL MYTHOLOGY,
CHRISTIAN AND MARXIST

A dying society disintegrates in a climax of violence, seen by the victors as a cataclysm in which the forces of evil are destroyed and a new age of peace inaugurated: Christian icon and Marxist poster use the same image of dragon-killing to symbolize this sequence.

plate 37

INTERNAL PROLETARIAT

In a disintegrating society, the 'internal proletariat' – the spiritually dispossessed – are pioneers of regeneration, creating a higher religion drawn from native and alien sources. In the catacomb painting, Christ, who brings God's peace to men, is shown as the Hellenic Orpheus, taming the wild beasts with his lyre.

plate 38

EXTERNAL PROLETARIAT

The 'external proletariat' of transfrontier barbarians 'borrows' and exploits the culture of its civilized neighbours more crudely: here, a Roman coin is transformed into an Anglo-Saxon ornament.

plates 39, 40

SCHISM IN THE SOUL:
ABANDON AND
SELF-CONTROL

The collective crisis of a disintegrating society brings with it a spiritual crisis in the souls of its members. Demoralized by their failures, people resort to parodies of the creative inspiration they seem to have lost. The orgiastic cult of Bacchus, above, appealed to men who saw creativity as the reward of spontaneous self-expression. At the opposite pole to this wild *abandon*, the ascetic tries to recover the power of self-determination by carrying the cult of self-denial to an exaggerated extreme. The Indian fakir, opposite, holding his arms in the air until they waste and die, reveals an astonishing power of self-mastery, yet his discipline, so long as it is pursued as a personal escape from an intolerable world, is as barren as the self-indulgent rites of the ecstatics.

plate 41

BIRTH OUT OF DEATH

The phoenix, symbol of miraculous rebirth, was originally associated with the Egyptiac Sun-God Re; only one bird lived at a time, and each was born from the ashes of a pyre on which its predecessor had immolated itself three days before. The attraction of this powerful image for Christianity is obvious: in the words of the author of a medieval bestiary, 'phoenix signifies Jesus, Son of Mary, that he had the power to die of his own will, and from death he came to life. Phoenix signifies that to save his people he chose to suffer upon the cross' – an image, therefore, of the new life that can be won from the experience of pain.

27 The nature and symptoms of social disintegration

IN PASSING FROM the breakdowns of civilizations to their disintegrations, we should not be too ready to assume that this sequence is automatic and unalterable – that once a civilization has broken down, it must inevitably pass straight through disintegration into dissolution. Although this was the pattern of the Hellenic Civilization, we have already seen[1] that it is not applicable to all civilizations, and we found that we had to turn to an alternative model to take account of the instances which did not conform to our provisional Hellenic norm. On the analogy of the communities which have been arrested at the threshold of growth,[2] a broken-down civilization may itself be 'arrested' at some point before disintegration has had time to run its full course. We have an outstanding example of such an arrest in the Egyptiac Society, which, in spite of having effectively broken down before the end of the third millennium BC, passionately refused to pass away and actually succeeded in surviving for another 2500 years – a span of time that was perhaps nearly three times as long as the combined span of its birth, growth, and first breakdown. Its survival was, however, bought at a price, for the life of the Egyptiac Society during this second aeon of existence was a kind of life-in-death; in fact, it survived by becoming petrified.

This fate of the Egyptiac Society should serve to remind us that disintegration, like growth, is not a single act but a process in time, and, as such, susceptible to changes in tempo. Thus, even when disintegration has unmistakably set in, it does not necessarily run straight out into dissolution, and this fact obliges us to look more closely at the nature of the process.

The conclusions that we reached when we analysed the nature of the growths of civilizations[3] will give us some clues to the nature of their disintegrations. We found that we could identify the essence of growth as an *élan* which carries a challenged party through the equilibrium of an originally effective response into an overbalance which declares itself in the presentation of a fresh challenge; and it is this element of overbalance which converts the single act of challenge-and-response, which we had already detected in the geneses of civilizations, into the repetitive, recurrent rhythm which the concept of growth implies. This repetitiveness or recurrency is likewise implied in the concept of disintegration, which, as we have just suggested, resembles the concept of growth in signifying a process. In each individual performance of the drama of challenge-and-response we must here, of course, write failure for success and change the plus sign into a minus; but the successive defeats through which the process of disintegration works itself out do nevertheless resemble the successive victories which build up the process of growth inasmuch as they, too, constitute a continuous series in which each performance leads on to the next. For example, in the history of the international politics of the Hellenic World, from the time when Solon's economic revolution

PETRIFIED HIERARCHIES

161, 162, 163 A rigid system of stratification had brought the Egyptiac Society to the verge of dissolution by 2000 BC; the ruling élites – administrators and priests, above – arrested the process, but only by tightening their hold. The peasant, below, carried the crushing burden of this strangled society for 2500 years more.

first confronted the Hellenic Society with the task of establishing a political world order, we can see that the failure of the Athenian attempt to solve the problem by means of the Delian League led on to Philip of Macedon's attempt to solve it by means of the Corinthian League, and Philip's failure to Augustus's attempt to solve it by means of a *Pax Romana* upheld by a principate. Similarly, in the history of the Egyptiac Society's struggle with the problem of social incubuses, we can see that the failure to throw off the incubus of a deified kingship led on to a progressive complication of the unsolved problem as the *litteratus* and the priest and the professional soldier successively mounted, behind the king, upon the peasant-pack-horse's back.

In terms of recurrency and rhythm, then, there is an obvious affinity between the nature of growth and that of disintegration; but, on the other hand, our examples will also have revealed a striking point of diversity between the two. It is self-evident that, during the growth process, the same challenge is never presented more than once, for, *ex hypothesi*, so long as growth is being maintained, each successive challenge is being successfully met, or, in other words, disposed of as a living issue and relegated to the history books. By contrast we can see that, in a series in which the outcome of each successive challenge is not victory but defeat, the unanswered challenge can never be disposed of and is therefore bound to present itself again and again until it either receives some overdue and imperfect answer, or else brings about the destruction of a society which has shown itself inveterately incapable of responding to it effectively. Thus, in the disintegrations of civilizations, the perpetual variety and versatility which are the hallmarks of growth give way to a merciless uniformity and uninventiveness; and intensification, instead of diversification, is the form of change which now relieves the monotony of the series of performances. At each performance, now, the challenge is the same as it has been at every performance since the tragic one which witnessed the original breakdown; but, after each successive failure to respond to it, the old unanswered challenge presents itself ever more insistently and in an ever more formidable shape, until at last it quite dominates and obsesses and overwhelms the unhappy souls that are being progressively defeated by it.

Thus the disintegration of a civilization, like its growth, is a cumulative as well as a continuous process; and, at the same time, we might perhaps be less reluctant to apply to this process the metaphor of 'direction' which we hesitated to use in connexion with the growth process.[4] Does not the disintegration of a civilization run to a defeat which culminates either in extinction, or else in a petrifaction which is no true reprieve since it merely condemns the disintegrating society to the temporary limbo of life-in-death before its ultimate and inevitable dissolution? This may in fact be the truth, but we would be wise not to accept this view at face value, before we have applied our usual test of an examination of the evidence. The Solonian *Respice finem*,[5] if it hits the mark at all, is presumably pertinent to all cases; and, until we have actually seen the end of an individual or society, to pronounce an absolute verdict may be premature. 'Whom the Lord loveth he chasteneth' may prove to be as near the ultimate truth as the dictum attributed to Solon by Herodotus, that 'to many people God has given a glimpse of happiness in order to destroy them root and branch'. We cannot say our last word about the nature of the disintegrations of civilizations until we have studied the process from beginning to end, and this in its inward experiences as well as in its outward manifestations.

In our analysis of the breakdowns of civilizations, we found that the ultimate criterion and fundamental cause of breakdown could be described as a loss of harmony which leads to the forfeiture by a society of its power of self-determination;[6] and we then went on to examine at some length the practical ways in which this loss of self-determination is revealed. Let us now pick up this thread of analysis at the point where we left off for our review of the evidence, and bring it a stage further by analysing the loss of harmony itself, as it is disclosed in the process of social disintegration. In essence, the loss of harmony between elements which had formerly coexisted in a society as an integral whole leads inevitably to an outbreak of social discord. The broken-down society is rent in two different dimensions simultaneously by the social schisms in which this discord is expressed. There are 'vertical' schisms between geographically segregated communities, and 'horizontal' schisms between geographically intermingled but socially segregated classes.

In the vertical type of schism, the articulation of society into a number of parochial states gives rise to an internecine warfare on a crescendo note between the unneighbourly members of the same body social. This warfare exhausts the energies of the society, before it brings itself to a violent end through a 'knock-out blow' in which a single surviving state is left staggering among the corpses of its fellow-combatants. We have already seen how frequently the fatal discord takes this vertical form of destructive warfare between states,[7] but at the same time we may observe that the vertical schism is perhaps not the most characteristic manifestation of the discord which propels a broken-down civilization into disintegration. The articulation of a society into parochial communities is, after all, a phenomenon which is common to the whole genus 'human societies' and is not peculiar to the particular species 'civilizations'. The so-called 'civilized' state is simply an imposing, high-powered version of the primitive tribe; and, while the internecine warfare between states in the bosom of a civilization is vastly more destructive in degree than the clashes of tribes within the bosom of a pre-civilizational society, this method of social suicide is merely an abuse of a potential instrument of self-destruction which is within reach of any society. On the other hand, the horizontal schism of a society along lines of class is not only peculiar to civilizations, but is also a phenomenon which first appears at the moment of breakdown, and which is a distinctive mark of the phases of breakdown and disintegration, by contrast with its absence during the phase of growth. This is not, of course, to say that either in a pre-civilizational society or in a civilization in its growth stage horizontal lines of social articulation are unknown. However, at that stage, even where the gulfs between ranks cannot easily be crossed, this hierarchical cleavage is not apt to produce a destructive moral schism, because the

different ranks which are divided in status are apt to be united morally by a common consciousness of having reciprocal functions to perform which are all indispensable for the welfare, and even perhaps for the preservation, of a society which is one and indivisible.[8] In a broken-down society, by contrast, the schism between classes is a product of the disintegration of a coherent social ethos.

We have already come across this horizontal type of schism in an earlier chapter when we were constructing and analysing our Hellenic model of civilization,[9] and we have caught other glimpses of it from time to time in the course of the intervening chapters. So far we have identified the component classes into which a disintegrating civilization breaks – the dominant minority, and the internal and external proletariats. We have also seen something of the nature and origins of these classes: the dominant minority is a perversion of the creative minority whose role of leadership it has inherited, and it embarks on a policy of social repression in order to impose by force the authority which it is no longer accorded in virtue of merit; the internal proletariat comprises that majority within a society which has formerly given its voluntary allegiance to a creative leadership, but which is now increasingly alienated from its own society by the coercive despotism of its corrupted masters; and the external proletariat is formed of the barbarian communities beyond the frontiers of a civilization who have been drawn into its orbit, but who now find themselves similarly alienated. Each of these groups, furthermore, finds an institutional expression of its status: while the dominant minority erects the imposing apparatus of a universal state, the internal proletariat registers its secession from society by adopting a spiritual ethos which is alien in inspiration and which culminates in the creation of a universal church; and the external proletariat shakes off its dependence upon the hitherto dominating civilization and asserts its free existence as a bevy of aggressive barbarian war-bands.

In addition to these preliminary observations on the main features of social breakdown, we have already tried to obtain a clearer view of the nexus of cause and effect between the loss of a leading minority's gift for creation and the loss of its faculty for attracting the allegiance of the majority without having to resort to force.[10] Here we put our finger upon the creative minority's expedient of social drill – a short-cut for bringing the uncreative mass into line – as the weak spot in the relation between minority and majority in the growth stage. On this showing, the estrangement between minority and majority which eventually comes to a head in the secession of the proletariat is a consequence of the breaking of a link which, even in the growth phase, has only been maintained by playing upon a well-drilled faculty of mimesis. The leaders' failure to continue to play upon this faculty in the rank-and-file is a consequence of the same leaders' failure to reply to a particular challenge by making a creative response. It is no longer surprising to find that the link inevitably snaps when the leaders' creativity gives out, considering that, even in the growth stage of the society's history, this link of mimesis has always been precarious by reason of a treacherous duality – the revenge of an unwilling slave – which is part of the nature of any mechanical device.

These are the threads of inquiry into the horizontal schism in a broken-down society that are already in our hands; and perhaps the most promising way of attempting to pursue our inquiry further will be to draw these threads together and then spin out the strands. We will begin by taking a closer look at the pattern of schism, and we will then go on to examine in more detail each of the two fractions – internal and external proletariat – into which the masses in and around a broken-down society split. Our next step will be to turn – as we turned at a certain point in our study of the process of growth[11] – from the macrocosm to the microcosm; for, after we have studied the social expression of discord, we shall want to look at it in its complementary form of an internalized distraction in the soul. Finally, we shall devote our attention to the institutions which arise out of the débris of a disintegrating civilization; and in particular we shall pay close regard to the nature of universal churches, for these, as we have already noted in passing,[12] seem to contain within themselves the seeds of a new evolutionary process which transcends the old limits of the civilizations in which they come to birth.

The social mechanisms which are operative in the transition from growth to breakdown were acutely diagnosed by Saint-Simon, working from his own experience of the shattering social strife which culminated in the French Revolution. Saint-Simon suggested that the histories of societies could be divided into two alternating periods, the 'organic' and the 'critical'. In the socially coherent and harmonious 'organic' periods, the members of a society are united by a common agreement on social organization and social goals; individual and political relationships are stable and accepted, and the disposal of power reflects diverse abilities to contribute to the welfare of society. The 'critical' periods, by contrast, are marked by the collapse of the consensus and by the disintegration of society into dissenting and mutually hostile fragments; status is questioned, relationships become fluid, and in the ensuing struggle for power the relative capabilities of the contending classes and individuals are forgotten.[13] This association of social disintegration and class strife has been made more familiar to modern ears by Marx's more rigorous and substantial analysis of social dynamics in terms of a perpetual class war. Marx's tremendous picture of the proletarian revolution is important to us here, both because it is the classic exposition of the social crisis that accompanies the disintegration of a civilization, and because this formula conforms to the traditional Zoroastrian and Jewish and Christian apocalyptic pattern in unveiling, beyond a violent climax, the vision of a gentle finale. In common with these religions, but perhaps alone of all political dogmas, Marxism offers 'an interpretation of human existence by means of which men may situate themselves in the world and direct their actions to ends that transcend those offered by their immediate situation';[14] and it 'rescue[s] individual lives from the insignificance of finitude . . . by showing the individual that he has or can have some role in a world-historical drama'.[15] In Marxian eschatology, the violent and destructive proletarian revolution, with its temporary sequel of the dictatorship of the proletariat, is to be followed by a New Society in which the disposal of productive forces will be

SOCIAL STABILITY
164–169 'A place and means for every man alive': fifteenth-century engravings of the orders of society, opposite. In a growing civilization – Saint-Simon's 'organic' society – community tells more than class: king, knight, gentleman, merchant, artisan, and servant are held in harmony by mutual interdependence and a common ethos; coherence is the keynote.

SOCIAL IMBALANCE
170 In a period of disintegration – Saint-Simon's 'critical' phase – the ruthless pursuit of incompatible class interests shatters the social pyramid and creates new structures of oppression. The 'lower orders', as in this French Revolution print, must bend under the weight of a privileged élite, until misery spurs them to challenge the minority's monopoly of power.

171 The apocalyptic revelation: Christian. The movement of social disintegration runs through war to peace, from destruction to fresh creation. Biblical tradition prophesies a paroxysm of frenzied violence before the establishment on Earth of Christ's eternal kingdom of peace: Dürer's 'Four Avenging Angels', from his Apocalypse series, *c.* 1497–98.

172 The apocalyptic revelation: Communist. Exposing its origins in Judaeo-Christian tradition, Marxism foretells a pattern of social crisis and rebirth, from an explosion of proletarian destruction to the creation of an ideal commonwealth – the eternal classless society: Soviet revolutionary poster, 1919.

such that class conflict, and the political and social apparatus that this evokes, will be eliminated; the ultimate goal is an age of social cohesion in which men will be finally and permanently free to develop their creative abilities to a hitherto unimaginable degree. This schema does in fact plot out the actual course which the class war, or horizontal schism, in a broken-down society is apt to follow, as a matter of ascertainable historical fact: the phenomenon of disintegration, as it is revealed in history, does exhibit a movement that runs through war to peace; through an apparently wanton and savage destruction of past achievements to fresh works of creation that seem to owe their special quality to the devouring glow of the very flames in which they have been forged.

The schism in itself is the product of two negative movements. First, the dominant minority attempts to hold by force – against all right and reason – the position of inherited privilege which it has ceased to merit; and then the proletariat repays injustice with resentment, fear with hate, and violence with violence when it executes its act of secession. Yet paradoxically this explosive process of disintegration ends in positive achievements – the creation of a universal state, a universal church, and barbarian war-bands. These three achievements are, no doubt, extremely unequal in terms of their respective worth. We have noticed at an earlier point[16] that the universal church, alone of the three, has a prospect in the future as well as a footing in the past, while the universal state and the barbarian war-bands belong to the past exclusively. And it hardly needs to be pointed out that, of the two backward-looking institutions, the barbarian war-bands are poor affairs indeed compared with the universal state. By creating a universal state the dominant minority performs the valuable act of checking, for a time, the process of disintegration which its own past action has precipitated, and of thus enabling the temporarily reprieved society to enjoy a brief Indian summer before its final dissolution. In creating barbarian war-bands the external proletariat has merely prepared itself for a destructive attack upon the dying civilization. Yet there is a gleam of creativity to be discerned, even here, in the contrast that we can see if we compare, in destructiveness and ethos, the war-bands that were led by Theodoric the Ostrogoth to Rome with the hordes of Cimbri and Teutones that had flooded across the Alps at the turn of the second and the last century BC; or the Muslims ruled by Mu'awiyah the Umayyad at Damascus with the pagan hordes of Ituraeans that had silted up, some seven or eight hundred years earlier, out of the North Arabian desert, against the eastern flanks of Hermon and Antilibanus.

Thus the social schism which is the outward criterion of the disintegration of a broken-down society is not just a schism and nothing more. When we grasp the movement as a whole, from beginning to end, we shall find that we must describe it as a movement of 'schism-and-palingenesia'[17] if we wish to give it a title that does it full justice. Moreover, in this double movement, it is the second 'beat' that is its significant feature. The happiness of the palingenesia is not only a reparation for the foregoing bitterness of the schism; it is also the point of the schism, or, in frankly teleological terms, its purpose. And in fact we find that, when once the schism has occurred, nothing but frustration results from a closing of the breach before the necessary palingenesia has been accomplished. A case in point is the *union sacrée* between the dominant minority of the Egyptiac Society and its internal proletariat against the external proletariat as represented by the Hyksos invaders in the eighteenth century BC; for it was this reconciliation at the eleventh hour that prolonged the existence of the Egyptiac Society – in a petrified state of life-in-death – for some two thousand years beyond the date at which the process of disintegration would otherwise have culminated in the expected dissolution.

The outcome of this Egyptiac *union sacrée* suggests that this exceptional sequel to a social schism is one of those exceptions that prove a rule; and we may take the broken rule to be that a new birth, rather than a healing of the breach, is not only the normal ending to a schism, but is also the one possible happy ending. If this is the truth, then it is clear that even during the painful process of disintegration the spirit of creativity – or the ability to respond to challenges – is not utterly overwhelmed; but, in order to carry forward the work of creation in a disintegrating society, some alternative channel must be found. The dominant minority, of course, has condemned itself in advance to have no share in this work, for, by degenerating into a close corporation whose ideas and ideals are fixed and unchanging, it has *de facto* lost that flexible power of response that characterizes a creative minority's action in the growth phase. Even though the personnel of the dominant minority may be radically recast through the admission of *novi homines*, this brings no relief, for they are allowed into its ranks only on condition of accepting the old tradition of the body into which they are being initiated. In this rigid posture, the dominant minority impotently faces a recurring challenge which, as we have seen, is always the same. Its discomfiture, at each successive defeat, is a foregone conclusion. The defensiveness which it substitutes for creativity may be either indolent or recalcitrant; but, whether it is insanely defying the lightning or inertly resting on its oars, in either posture the dominant minority is refusing to hand over to other aspirants the protagonist's role which it has already proved itself incompetent to play.

In making its 'great refusal', however, the dominant minority impoverishes no one but itself. By disqualifying itself from serving as an instrument of creation, it does not thereby bring the work to an end; for, while this civilization is falling and that is rising, the work of creation does still go on. When the growth of a civilization is cut short by breakdown, and the would-be creative minority that has stiffened into a dominant minority begins to repeat an ineffective gesture that never varies at each onset of an unanswered challenge which never ceases to recur, this monotonous celebration of the tragedy of defeat is not the only drama that is played upon the broken-down civilization's social stage. During the disintegration of a civilization two separate plays with different plots are being performed simultaneously side by side. While an unchanging dominant minority is perpetually rehearsing its own defeat, fresh challenges are perpetually evoking fresh creative responses from newly recruited minorities, which proclaim their own creative power by rising, each time, to the occasion. The drama of challenge-and-response continues to be performed, but in new circumstances and with new actors. In this changed constellation of social forces, it is among the mass of erstwhile followers – now deprived of leadership – that creative spirits are born and perform their work. What we are seeing in the secession of the proletariat is thus the familiar process of creative action; but the rise of a creative minority and the process of mimesis are now confined within the limits of a single social class instead of being realized through the society as a whole. The substance of the plot remains the same; but the roles have been reallotted, and the outcome of the drama is unfamiliar – it is a palingenesia. Let us now see how this new act of creation is performed in practice.

173, 174 THE SLAVE, left, archetypal victim of the class war, and his identity token, in case of flight: 'hold me lest I flee, and restore me to my master. . . .'

28 Internal proletariats

WE CANNOT BEGIN our study of internal proletariats better than by quoting a passage from Thucydides in which the historian of the breakdown of the Hellenic Society describes the origins of the social schism that shattered this society after 431 BC.

Such was the savagery of the class war [*stasis*] at Corcyra as it developed, and it made the deeper impression through being the first of its kind – though eventually the upheaval spread through almost the whole of the Hellenic World. In every country there were struggles between the leaders of the proletariat and the reactionaries in their efforts to procure the intervention of the Athenians and the Lacedaemonians respectively. In peacetime they would have had neither the opportunity nor the desire to call in the foreigner; but now there was the war; and it was easy for any revolutionary spirits in either camp to procure an alliance entailing the discomfiture of their opponents and a corresponding reinforcement of their own faction. This access of class war brought one calamity after another upon the countries of Hellas – calamities that occur and will continue to occur so long as human nature remains what it is, though they may be aggravated or mitigated and modified by successive changes of circumstance. Under the favourable conditions of peacetime both countries and individuals display a sweeter reasonableness, because their hands are not forced by the logic of events; but war eats away the margins of ordinary life and, in most characters, adjusts the temperament to the new environment by brutal training. So the countries of Hellas became infected with the class war, and the sensation made by each successive outbreak had a cumulative effect upon the next.[1]

Having thus put his finger on the war-spirit as the demoralizing spiritual force which shattered the Hellenic

Society's moral solidarity, Thucydides goes on to make a brilliant analysis, which is at the same time an overwhelming indictment, of the demonic evil impulses which were thereby let loose in men's souls.

It was a competition of ingenuity in the elaboration of intrigue and in the refinement of reprisals. The customary meaning of words was arbitrarily distorted to cover the conduct of those who employed them. Reckless irresponsibility was treated as courageous loyalty, cautious reserve as cowardice masked under a high-sounding name, restraint as a cloak for poor-spiritedness, and the policy of reason as a policy of *laissez faire*. A frenzied fanaticism was the popular ideal of conduct, while intrigue that took no risks was regarded as a legitimate method of self-defence. Violence of feeling was a warrant of honesty, deprecation of violence a signal for suspicion. Success in intrigue was the test of intelligence and the detection of intrigue a testimonial to superior cleverness, while anyone who so shaped his policy as to dispense with such methods was pilloried as a nihilist towards his own group and a weakling in face of their opponents. In short, approbation was reserved for those who forestalled their enemies in striking a blow or who implanted that suggestion in minds which had not previously conceived of it. The ties of party actually became closer than those of kinship,[2] because partisans were readier than kinsmen to throw themselves into an adventure at a moment's notice, and the associations in question were formed, not to secure the benefits of established institutions, but to gain illegitimate advantages by violating them. Complicity in crime was a more effective sanction for loyalty to engagements than a solemn oath. A fair offer from opponents was received as a signal for practical precautions by the dominant party of the moment, instead of evoking any generous response. The exaction of reprisals was valued more highly than an immunity from wrongs demanding them. The rare covenants of reconciliation were only entered into on either side as a momentary last resort and only observed so long as no alternative resource presented itself. Any one who spied a weak spot in his adversary's armour and had the nerve to seize his opportunity took more satisfaction in obtaining his revenge by treachery than in obtaining it in fair fight, the dominating considerations being the elimination of risk and the added halo of intellectual brilliance investing the triumphs of perfidy. . . .

The cause of this whole phenomenon was the thirst for power arising from the predatory and competitive impulses – impulses which engender conflict, from which passion is engendered in its turn. In all the countries of Hellas the party leaders invented high-sounding catchwords and posed as the champions of political equality for the masses or of moderate conservatism, in order to make spoils out of the public interest which they served with their lips. In their unscrupulous struggle to gain the upper hand over one another they hesitated at nothing and surpassed themselves in the prosecution of their vendettas. So far from attempting to act within the bounds of moral right and national interest, they recognized no limitations on either side except the caprice of the moment. They did not shrink from bringing themselves into power by verdicts immorally obtained against their opponents, if not by naked force, in order to satiate their momentary rancour. In fact, religion had lost its hold upon either party, and they relied upon their powers of misrepresentation to retrieve their good name whenever they had occasion to perpetrate an invidious action. Meanwhile, the moderate elements in every country were preyed upon by the extremists of both camps, partly for their refusal to take sides and partly out of resentment at the prospect of their survival.

Thus the class war plunged the Hellenic Society into every kind of moral evil.[3]

This spiritual débâcle which followed the outbreak of the Atheno-Peloponnesian War in 431 BC continued unchecked during the century of warfare and revolution which was the aftermath of that great catastrophe, and its first social effect was to produce a large and growing floating population of 'stateless' exiles – a phenomenon that had been dreaded but rare during the growth phase of the Hellenic Civilization. By the middle of the fourth century BC the Hellenic World was swarming with these rootless wanderers. This evil was not overcome by Alexander's attempt to induce the reigning faction in each city-state to allow its ejected opponents to return in peace; and the fire made fresh fuel for itself, for the one thing that the exiles found for their hands to do was to enlist as mercenary soldiers; and this glut of military manpower put fresh drive into the wars by which new exiles – and thereby more mercenaries – were being created. This vicious circle of evil cause-and-effect first inflamed the fratricidal warfare in the bosom of Hellas itself, and then discharged the men of war who had been trained in this Hellenic school of arms to wreck the *Pax Achaemenia* through the long-drawn-out wars of Alexander and his Macedonian successors.

The effect of these moral ravages was powerfully reinforced by the operation of disruptive economic forces which the wars let loose. For example, the wars of Alexander and his successors in South-Western Asia gave military employment to one swarm of homeless Greeks at the cost of uprooting another. The mercenaries were paid by putting into circulation the bullion which had been accumulating for two centuries in the Achaemenian treasuries, and this sudden vast increase in the volume of currency in circulation caused a disastrous inflation in those Greek city-states which had so far been spared the flail of political strife. Prices soared without any immediate corresponding rise in wages, and this financial revolution reduced to pauperism the class of peasants and artisans who had hitherto enjoyed a reasonable security. The same effect of pauperization was produced again, a hundred years later, by the economic consequences of the Hannibalic War in Italy, where the peasantry were uprooted from the land, first by the direct devastation that was wrought by Hannibal's troops, and then by the ever-longer terms of military service which the Italian peasantry had to endure, both in the main Italian war-zone and beyond the Apennines and overseas. These distant campaigns in the Po basin, in the Iberian peninsula, in Greece, and in the East did not come to an end when Hannibal evacuated Italy or when Carthage sued for peace, but remorselessly continued to increase in range and scale and to demand ever larger drafts of Italian peasant-soldiers. Under this tribulation the pauperized descendants of the original peasant-conscripts had no choice but to make a profession out of the career which had been imposed upon their ancestors as a *corvée*. During the century of revolution and civil war which began in 133 BC with the tribunate of Tiberius Gracchus and which ended only in 31 BC with the battle of Actium, the 'new poor' derived what little profit they could from their situation by taking mercenary service under the rival war-lords who were now contending for the mastery of the new Roman Empire.

In this cruel process of 'deracination' we cannot doubt that we are watching the genesis of the Hellenic internal proletariat, in the sense – as we have previously defined the term[4] – of a social element which is 'in' but not 'of' its society. The true hallmark of the proletarian is neither poverty nor humble birth, but a consciousness – and the resentment that this consciousness inspires – of being disinherited from his traditional place in the established structure of a society, and of being unwanted in a community which is his rightful home. The Hellenic internal proletariat were actually recruited first of all from the free citizenry, and even from the aristocracy, of the disintegrating Hellenic bodies politic, though of course their spiritual impoverishment was often accompanied, and almost always followed, by a material pauperization; and they were soon reinforced by recruits from other sources who were material as well as spiritual proletarians from the start. The numbers of the Hellenic internal proletariat were vastly swollen by the aggression of Hellenic arms at the expense of both contemporary civilizations and pre-civilizational communities. The conquests of Alexander and his successors swept the whole of the Syriac and Egyptiac and Sumero-Akkadian and Iranic Societies, and a considerable part of the Indic Society, into the Hellenic dominant minority's net, while later conquests swept in half the barbarians of Europe and North-West Africa.

The fate of these aliens was, at first, less wretched than that of the native-born Hellenic proletarians in one respect; though they were morally disinherited and mentally despoiled, they were not, to begin with, physically uprooted. In time the lure of new markets and profits, as well as the need to maintain the level of agricultural production in war-depopulated regions, led to the enserfment of the native inhabitants of conquered lands, and their deportation to the distant plantations of the victorious Power. The use of imported slave-labour – a social evil of which we first catch sight in Greek Sicily in 480 BC – was extended, on a vaster scale, to the devastated areas of Roman Italy after the Hannibalic War. During the last two centuries BC the uprooted Italian peasant-proprietors were progressively supplanted by rootless slave-hoemen and slave-herdsmen. The wastage of this servile economic manpower on the Italian plantations and ranches was perhaps as heavy as the wastage of the nominally free military manpower of the Italian peasantry in its distant theatres of war, but the profits of the wholesale wine, oil, meat, wool, and leather production which was carried on at this human – or inhuman – cost were great enough to bear the capital charge of perpetually having to replace the human raw material. In consequence this age saw all the populations within range of the Mediterranean coast – both Western barbarians and cultivated Orientals – being lawlessly laid under contribution in order to supply the demands of an insatiable Italian slave-labour market.

There were, then, three distinct elements in the internal proletariat of the disintegrating Hellenic Society: disinherited and uprooted members of the Hellenic Society's own native body social; partially disinherited members of alien civilizations or pre-civilizational communities who were conquered and exploited without being torn up by the roots; and doubly disinherited conscripts from these subject populations who were not only uprooted but were also enslaved and deported and worked to death. The sufferings of these three sets of victims were as various as their origins were diverse, but these differences were transcended by their overwhelming common experience of being robbed of their social heritage and being turned into exploited outcasts. Their reactions to a wanton and intolerable oppression were commensurate with the misery of their fate, and a uniform note of desperate passion rings through the pandemonium of bitter proletarian outbreaks in this age.

We catch this note in a series of Egyptian insurrections against the Ptolemaic régime of exploitation – an outbreak which began at the turn of the third and second centuries BC, as soon as the Egyptian fellahin had acquired a stock of arms and *esprit de corps* and self-confidence as a result of the goverment's blunder of conscripting the natives into their army in order to beat off a Seleucid invasion. We hear the same note again in the more celebrated and more momentous series of Jewish insurrections against the Seleucid and Roman policy of Hellenization in Palestine. The outbreak began when Judas Maccabeus took up arms against Antiochus Epiphanes in 166 BC, and it was not quelled by the destruction of Jerusalem in the great Romano-Jewish War of AD 66–70, but burst out again among the Jewish diasporá in Cyrene and Egypt and Cyprus in 115–17, and among the Palestinian Jews in a last forlorn effort under the leadership of Bar Kochba in 132–35. The same reckless fury which inspired the Jews to initiate and maintain their desperate campaign against far more powerful oppressors also moved the semi-Hellenized natives of western Asia Minor to expose themselves to Roman vengeance twice

over: first in 132 BC, when they joined the Attalid Prince Aristonicus upon hearing the appalling news that the last Attalus had bequeathed his kingdom to Rome; and for the second time in 88 BC, when the cities of Asia Minor opened their gates to Rome's rebel client-king Mithridates of Pontus and the citizens took the opportunity to massacre the whole of the Italian business community in their midst.

The rising of Aristonicus is the connecting link between the outbreaks of the subjected Oriental peoples in the conquered provinces and the outbreaks of the imported slaves and pauperized freemen in the homelands of the Hellenic Society. Slaves and 'poor freemen'[5] fought side by side in Aristonicus's rebel band, and his rising was itself perhaps inspired by the news of the slave-revolt which had let loose the first of the two great slave-wars in Sicily (*gerebantur c.* 135–131 BC *et c.* 104–100 BC).[6] These two Sicilian outbreaks were perhaps the largest in scale and the longest-drawn-out of the slave-revolts on the western plantations in the post-Hannibalic Age, but they were neither the first nor the last of their kind, nor perhaps even the most savage. The series began, in the first decade after the temporary restoration of peace between Rome and Carthage in 201 BC, with an abortive conspiracy of the slaves and the Carthaginian hostages at Setia in 198 BC, and a rapidly suppressed rising in Etruria in 196 BC. It was continued in a formidable insurrection in Apulia in 185; and, after a temporary shifting of the scene to Sicily, the climax was reached in the desperate exploit of the runaway Thracian gladiator Spartacus, who ranged up and down the length of the Italian peninsula from 73 to 71 BC. The rancorous resentment against an Hellenic dominant minority was not confined to the revolts of slaves against their masters, but was felt equally by the pauperized free citizens of Rome. The savagery with which the Roman citizen-proletariat turned and rent the Roman plutocracy in the civil wars, and particularly in the paroxysm of 91–82 BC, was quite equal to the savagery of Judas Maccabeus and Spartacus; and the most satanic of all the dark figures that stand out in sinister silhouette against the glare of a world in flames are the Roman revolutionary leaders who had been flung headlong out of the *Ordo Senatorius* itself: Marius and Sertorius and Catiline and Sextus Pompeius.

In these orgies of violence the Hellenic proletariat was repaying the savagery of its oppressors in the Hellenic dominant minority in the same coin, and the ferocity of the outbreaks is hardly surprising when we bear in mind the provocation to which it was a retort. It is, however, both astonishing and admirable to find that this violence was not the only response that was evoked from the Hellenic internal proletariat by the tremendous challenge to which it was subjected. There was also an antiphonal response which was at the opposite extreme of the spiritual gamut, and at this other extremity the internal proletariat not merely attained, but rose far above, the level of achievement which was reached by the lingering residue of the creative spirit in the dominant minority. We find, in fact, that the outbreaks of violence which we have been recording were seldom the only reactions of the victims to their ordeals. While some of the victims were usually moved to answer violence with violence and nothing more, there were usually others who, on each occasion, met force not

175 *Judaea armata*: coin minted during the great Romano-Jewish War of AD 66–70.

176 *Judaea capta*: even the fall of Jerusalem, celebrated here on a Roman coin, failed to crush Jewish militancy.

177 *Judaea resurgens*: coin of the Jews' final forlorn revolt, led by Bar Kochba, in AD 132–35.

by counter-force but by gentleness. Even the frenzied slaves who rebelled against their monstrous master Damophilus had the humanity not to return evil for good, as they showed when they spared Damophilus's tender-hearted daughter while they were dragging to their deaths the tormentor himself and his equally inhuman wife.[7] In the semi-legendary Jewish recollections of Palestinian Jewry's resistance to Antiochus Epiphanes's policy of forcible Hellenization, the passive resistance of the old scribe Eleazar and of the seven brethren and their mother precedes, in the narrative, the militant resistance of the hero Judas Maccabeus.[8] In the story of the passion of Jesus the leader's injunction to his companions – 'he that hath no sword, let him sell his garment and buy one'[9] – is immediately followed by his 'it is enough' when two swords only are forthcoming among all the Twelve;[10] and this perfunctory call to arms is finally stultified by the leader's own deliberate refusal to fight when he is on the point of being arrested.[11] In the next chapter of the story, the famous doctor Gamaliel is profoundly impressed by the striking contrast between the powerful moral resistance to persecution of Jesus's Apostles, and the sterile conventional militancy of the contemporary epigoni of Judas Maccabeus.[12] Here, then, are two responses to an identical challenge which are not only different but are actually contradictory and incompatible. The gentle response is as genuine an expression of the proletariat's will to secede as the violent response is; and in the history of the Oriental proletariat of the Hellenic World from the second century BC onwards we see violence and gentleness striving for the mastery of souls, until violence annihilates itself and leaves gentleness alone in the field.

The issue was raised at the outset, for the gentle way which was taken by the protomartyrs of 167 BC was swiftly abandoned by the impetuous Maccabeus, and his example so dazzled posterity that Jesus's most intimate companions were scandalized by their master's acquiescence in his physical fate.[13] They 'forsook him, and fled'.[14] Yet a few months after the crucifixion Gamaliel was already taking note of the executed leader's miraculously rallied disciples as men who might prove to have God on their side; and a few years later Gamaliel's own disciple Paul was preaching a crucified Christ. This vastly painful but infinitely fruitful conversion of the first generation of Christians from the way of violence to the way of gentleness had to be purchased at the price of a shattering blow to their material hopes; and what was done for Jesus's followers by the crucifixion was done for Orthodox Jewry by the destruction of Jerusalem in AD 70. Before the final catastrophe, one Jewish doctor had spontaneously and unwittingly obeyed Jesus's warning that the Christians in Judaea should flee into the mountains when they saw the 'abomination of desolation'[15] – Hellenic paganism in arms – reappearing on the Palestinian horizon. The rabbi Johanan ben Zakkai independently took the momentous decision to break with the tradition of militancy which Judas Maccabeus had inaugurated; eluding the vigilance of the Jewish Zealots, he slipped out of the embattled city and prevailed upon the Roman High Command to let him through in order that he might quietly continue his teaching out of earshot of the battle. By thus renouncing the path of military resistance he was enabled to re-establish his school and resume his teaching; and he thereby became the founder of a new Jewry whose voluntary abstention from the pursuit of political power has allowed it to survive in all manner of alien and inclement environments, outside its original homeland, down to the present day.

If this change of heart in Orthodox Jewry after the destruction of Jerusalem in A D 70 enabled Jewry to survive as a diasporá, the corresponding change of heart in the companions of Jesus after the crucifixion has opened the way to greater triumphs for the Christian Church. When it faced its first great challenge in the widespread persecutions of the third century, the Christian Church responded in the gentle way of Eleazar and the Seven Brethren, and not in the violent way of Judas the Hammer. In the next ordeal, at the turn of the fourth and fifth centuries, when the converted Roman Empire was breaking up, the Church responded again in this fashion to the invading barbarians (though not to its non-Christian fellow-citizens), and this time its reward was the conversion of the barbarian warbands with whom it found itself face to face in the fallen Empire's derelict western provinces.

Thus in the spiritual history of the Hellenic internal proletariat we see the two incompatible spirits of gentleness and violence perpetually struggling with one another, and gentleness, with the aid of experience, gradually and painfully gaining the upper hand. At the same time, this struggle is not confined exclusively to the proletarian section of society, for there are at any rate hints of it in the spiritual history of the Hellenic dominant minority as well. The contrast between Eleazar the Scribe and Judas the Hammer, or between Jesus and his contemporary Jewish militant Theudas, has its analogue in the contrast between the gentle King Agis and the violent King Cleomenes in the third century B C at Sparta, or between the gentle tribune Tiberius Gracchus and the violent tribune Gaius Gracchus in the second century B C at Rome. Peter's recalcitrance against Jesus's superhuman resignation to the prospect of being wrongfully put to death is anticipated at Athens in Crito's attempt to persuade Socrates to let himself be smuggled out of the prison where he is lying under a death-sentence that he has not deserved. Again, the victory of gentleness over violence in the souls of Peter and Paul and Johanan ben Zakkai has its parallels in the vision of Alexander the Great and in the clemency of Caesar and in the penitence of Augustus.

These famous representatives of the Hellenic dominant minority include, in the Athenian Socrates, the father of all the schools of Hellenic ethical philosophy, and, in the Roman Augustus, the founder of the Hellenic universal state. The two great creative works of the Hellenic dominant minority are at the opposite extreme of the gamut from the deeds of the impenitent conquerors and oppressors. The philosophers and the emperors made it possible for their moribund society to bask for a moment in the pale sunshine of an Indian summer. In the far more lasting spiritual achievement of the internal proletariat, the counterparts to these flashes of a dying power of creation are the higher religion of Christianity and its institutional embodiment in the Christian Church. Each of these achievements will come under our scrutiny at a later stage.[16]

178, 179 THE TRIUMPH OF PEACE 'Like a lion's whelp roaring for his prey': Judas Maccabeus, above, inaugurated the fatal spiral of Jewish militancy. 'They that take the sword shall perish by the sword': below, Christ, in renouncing violent resistance, showed a way out of that spiral.

29 External proletariats

THE EXTERNAL, like the internal, proletariat brings itself into existence by an act of secession from the dominant minority of a civilization that has broken down and gone into disintegration. In this case, the schism in which the secession results is palpable; for, in contrast to the internal proletariat, which continues to live intermingled geographically with the dominant minority from which it has come to be divided by a moral gulf, the external proletariat is not only alienated from the dominant minority in feeling but is also actually divided from it by a frontier which can be traced on the map.

The crystallization of such a frontier is indeed the sure sign that the secession of the external proletariat has taken place. As long as a civilization is still in growth, it has no hard and fast boundaries, except on fronts where it happens to have collided with a member of its own species,[1] for the light with which a creative minority illuminates its own society radiates beyond its frontiers to the pre-civilizational communities round about. There is nothing to limit the beam's range except the inherent limitations of its own carrying-power: the light travels out until it has gradually dimmed to vanishing-point. In a growing civilization, therefore, the creative minority of the day can exercise the same power of attraction upon its pre-civilizational neighbours as it does upon the community in whose midst it has arisen; and it may make its influence felt in places which may be astonishingly remote from the centre of radiation, as witness the adoption of the Syriac alphabet in Manchuria, or the reflexion of Hellenic aesthetic styles in the coins of Celtic Britain and in the statuary of Northern India.

Once a civilization has broken down, however, it ceases to exercise this attraction over adjacent communities, for, if it has lost its own power of self-determination, then, *a fortiori*, it has also lost the power both of exercising any creative influence upon outsiders and of presenting an harmonious whole which can serve as a model for other communities. Moreover, the policy of violence and repression, which a dominant minority in a disintegrating society has to adopt in place of the moral influence exercised by a creative minority, has precisely the same alienating effect upon the external mimics of a society as it has upon the uncreative mass within it. In their own way the pre-civilizational societies round about a disintegrating civilization register their estrangement from it by their own act of secession: they withdraw themselves from the moral orbit of the disintegrating civilization, and thus begin to present a potential menace to it; and, when the dominant minority attempts to secure by military means an allegiance which has hitherto been won by example, the alienated external proletariat reacts by meeting force with force. While the external proletariat performs the negative act of rejecting the once attractive culture of its neighbour, it also performs the positive – albeit destructive – act of continuing to learn from it by borrowing from its superior adversary those military techniques by which it may save itself from the tyranny of the dominant minority. The result

is the onset of prolonged and bitter warfare between the two estranged communities, each of which now threatens the life of the other; and, as the hostilities intensify, so the once fluid frontier between the two crystallizes into an abrupt and impassable barrier. To use the appropriate and expressive Latin terms, which bring out both the kinship and the contrast between the two kinds of contact, the *limen* or threshold, which was a zone, is replaced by the *limes* or military frontier, which is a line that has length without breadth.

The growth phase of Hellenic history offers a classic illustration of the *limen* or buffer-zone with which the home territory of a healthy civilization surrounds itself. Towards continental Europe the quintessence of Hellenism shaded off into a semi-Hellenic Thessaly to the north, and into a semi-Hellenic Aetolia to the west; and Aetolia and Thessaly were themselves insulated by the demi-semi-Hellenism of Epirus and Macedonia from the undiluted barbarism of Illyria and Thrace. Towards Asia Minor, Hellas shaded off, in the hinterland of the coastal city-states, into the semi-Hellenism of Caria and the demi-semi-Hellenism of Lydia, before passing over into the barbarism of the Phrygian interlopers who had settled among the ruins of the Hittite Civilization on the Anatolian plateau. Even in the hinterlands of the Greek colonies in North Africa and Italy, where the cultural gulf between Hellenism and the indigenous communities might have been expected to be far wider, and the political relations between the two worlds proportionately more hostile, there are examples of peaceful contacts and gradual transitions to set against the empire-building of Syracuse and the extermination of the Itali and the Chones. Even more striking than the political reconciliation between Greek and barbarian was the peaceful penetration by Hellenism on the cultural plane. In Sicily in the last century BC, less than five hundred years after the foundation of the latest Greek colony there, it would have been impossible any longer to distinguish the descendants of the native Sicels from those of Greek Siceliots in a population which had long been unified by its common Hellenic culture, its common Greek language, and its common sufferings under Roman misrule. In the continental Italian hinterland of Tarentum, Hellenism spread so rapidly and 'took' so strongly that, as early as the fourth century BC, Apulia was advertising her conversion to Hellenism by becoming the busiest workshop for the production of red-figure vases. Still further afield, the population of Latium took so enthusiastically to the exotic Hellenic institution of the city-state that Greek observers accepted the Latins as Hellenes by adoption, and the earliest extant mention of Rome in Greek literature describes this Latin commonwealth as 'an Hellenic city'.[2]

This picture of voluntary adaptation to the prevailing Hellenic way of life vanishes, however, as soon as the model itself is shattered. The symptom of breakdown in the Hellenic Civilization was the civil war of 431–404 BC; and the first move in a thousand years' war between barbarians

THE RADIATION
OF THE HELLENIC CIVILIZATION

180–183 Portrait busts from Arabia, Central Asia, Asia Minor, and Britain, first to seventh centuries A D. A growing civilization has no rigid frontiers, and its culture radiates out into adjacent barbarian communities; but as it breaks down, its influence on these societies weakens, while the native element becomes stronger.

EMBATTLED EMPIRE

184 By restoring order to a disintegrating world in the last century BC,
Rome committed herself to a ceaseless struggle to preserve it against the
barbarians beyond: border-tribesmen attack a Roman fort.

and Hellenes was made in the third year of this catastrophic conflict, when Macedonia was invaded and laid waste by a Thracian horde. Although this raid was not followed up, it marked the end of the voluntary self-Hellenization of Thrace, and effectively erected a rigid barrier between civilization and barbarism for the first time. While this Thracian front then remained stable for four hundred years, the militant reaction of the external proletariat to the breakdown of the Hellenic Civilization was more violent and more sensational in *Magna Graecia*, where, within a hundred years of the outbreak of the Atheno-Peloponnesian War, the Hellenic colonists had almost been pushed into the sea by the surrounding Oscan tribes. The inflowing barbarians had already crossed the straits of Messina and acquired, in that city itself, a base of operations for the conquest of Sicily before the whole movement was brought to an abrupt end by the intervention of Roman arms. Thereafter, the Romans undertook the massive task of restoring the integrity of the Hellenic World by means of large-scale military campaigns against both the barbarians and the rival Italian contenders for the mantle of the Hellenic Civilization. These successive feats of Roman arms extended the dominion of the Hellenic dominant minority almost as far afield in continental Europe and the Iberian peninsula and North-West Africa as it had already been extended in Asia by the conquests of Alexander of Macedon. But these impressive Macedonian and Roman conquests could not, and did not, relieve a disintegrating Hellenic Society from a social malady that was one of the inescapable penalties of its breakdown. The effect of this morbid military expansion of the Hellenic World was not to eliminate its anti-barbarian fronts but rather to add to their length as it pushed them further afield from the Hellenic dominant minority's base of operations; and this progressive lengthening of the lines of communication, as well as of the front itself, diminished the dominant minority's striking power while increasing its commitments. Indeed, Rome's very success in stepping into the breach and taking over the Etruscans' commitments against the Celts and the Tarentines' commitments against the Oscans and the Macedonians' commitments against the Thracians and Dardanians led her on inexorably, step by step, into assuming the sole responsibility for the maintenance of an anti-barbarian front that ran across the whole length of the European continent from the North Sea to the Black Sea coast. Moreover, this vast extension and aggravation of the anti-barbarian front which the disintegrating Hellenic Civilization had inherited from its own past was only part of the additional burden which the ailing society was wantonly taking upon its shoulders. Simultaneously, the Hellenic dominant minority was taking over anti-barbarian fronts in North Africa and the Iberian peninsula and South-Western Asia from the Syriac Society, which had been forcibly incorporated in the Hellenic World by the Macedonian and Roman wars of conquest.

At the turn of the third and second centuries BC Rome had succeeded in 'knocking out' all the other Great Powers of the contemporary Hellenic World, and thus had acquired a monopoly not only of the assets but also of the liabilities of the Hellenic dominant minority. From the date of the first delineation of the Hellenic universal state's frontiers in the last century BC, down to the transitional period (*c.* AD 375–675) which followed the break-up of the Roman Empire, the Hellenic Society was menaced by barbarian fronts on all sides – in Northern Europe, on the Danube, in Syria, and in North-West Africa. In the course of this prolonged confrontation, bouts of intense military activity alternated with periods of relatively peaceful stagnation on each front: twice the barbarians tried in vain to break through, but at the third attempt they were successful.

At the height of the Hellenic time of troubles during the last two centuries BC we find the Sarmatian barbarians advancing from the east bank of the Don to the Lower and Middle Danube basin, where they hovered menacingly on the north-eastern flank of the Hellenic World from that time onwards. Contemporaneously, at the turn of the second and the last century BC, the Arabs drifted into the derelict domain of the moribund Seleucid Monarchy in Mesopotamia and Syria. On the North-West African front the Numidians took advantage of the overthrow of Carthage in the Hannibalic War and her annihilation in 146 BC in order to encroach upon the derelict Carthaginian province on the African mainland. Lastly, on the North European front, the first extension of Roman rule into Transalpine Europe in the second century BC was answered by the formidable counter-attack of the Cimbri and the Teutones, who bore down on Italy itself along war-paths that were now no longer blocked by the semi-barbarian buffer-Powers which had just been crippled or shattered by Roman arms. On three fronts out of the four the Romans found themselves compelled to intervene in order to bring the barbarian offensives to a standstill; and on the North European front they had to fight for their lives – even in this first of the three historic paroxysms of barbarian aggression. In Europe and in Africa the situation was saved by Marius, who snatched victory out of defeat in the war against the Numidian aggressor Jugurtha (*gerebatur* 112–106 BC) and in the war against the Cimbri (*gerebatur* 105–101 BC). In Asia the last remnant of the Seleucid heritage was salvaged from the depredations of Arab war-bands by Pompey when he organized the Roman province of Syria in 63–62 BC. Thereafter, when a band of Suevi – undeterred by the recent fate of the Cimbri – set their feet upon the same European war-path, Caesar seized the opportunity of improving the Transalpine frontier of the Roman dominions by carrying it (*bellum gerebat* 58–51 BC) up to the line of the Rhine, on which it continued to stand, with a few brief fluctuations, for the next four centuries.

The second abortive attempt, on the barbarian side, at a breakthrough on all four fronts was made in the middle of the third century of the Christian Era. This time it was the Danubian front that was subjected to the heaviest pressure. Here the Goths not only thrust their way overland into the heart of the Balkan peninsula, but also took to the water and harried the coasts of the Black Sea and the Aegean. On the Arabian front the Palmyrene forerunners of the Muslim Arabs momentarily overran not only Syria but Egypt as well. In North-West Africa in the same age the Berbers once more went on the war-path for the first time since Jugurtha's day. On the North European front the Franks and Alemanni now crossed the Rhine and raided Gaul. In this second paroxysm of simultaneous concentric

THE BARBARIAN HYDRA
On all sides, Rome faced a remorseless barbarian reaction to her aggressive
search for imperial security; by A D 200 the tide of war had turned against her.

barbarian attacks the Roman Power succeeded in saving the situation once again. The invaders were cleared out of almost all the provinces they had overrun, and all the broken fronts were again restored. This time, however, the victory had been preceded by heavier reverses and deeper humiliations; it had been purchased at a higher price, and had only superficially restored the *status quo ante*; for, while the old frontiers had been re-established almost everywhere, the relative strength of the Roman and barbarian forces had been permanently changed in the barbarians' favour.

A Rome thus weakened faced the third paroxysm of barbarian aggression which lasted for some three hundred years (*c.* A D 375–675) and ended with the final extinction of the Hellenic universal state. From the fourth to the sixth century the northern front was under continual and intensifying pressure from successive waves of Huns and Avars and Teutons and Slavs, piling up against each other and eventually overrunning the whole of Rome's Empire in the West. In the seventh century the scene of action shifted to Asia Minor and Africa as the Arab Muslims began their organized and purposeful military campaigns. In Asia Minor the Constantinopolitan government succeeded – at

the price of abandoning its commitments and cutting its losses on all other fronts – in pushing the Muslims back from the Straits to the Taurus mountains, and in holding them there, though at the cost of grievously overstraining the nascent body social of Orthodox Christendom. In Africa, however, the Arabs swept on in an impetuous advance from the Nile to the Atlantic, meeting and over-powering the Berbers and the Visigoths and pressing on across the Straits of Gibraltar and through Spain and over the Pyrenees, before their tide was stemmed by the Franks at the line of the Loire and the Rhône in 732. But the out-standing historical event to which the battle near Tours bore witness was not the discomfiture of the Arabs by the Franks; it was the collapse of the resistance of the Roman Power which had been the arch-adversary of the Arabs and the Franks and all the other rival barbarian war-bands alike. By the time when, in the heart of the *Orbis Romanus*, the Frankish war-band encountered and defeated – on derelict Roman ground – the war-bands from beyond the southern frontier, it was manifest that the third attempt by the external proletariat to take the Hellenic universal state by storm had been completely and triumphantly successful.

185 The North: Celtic horsemen and footsoldiers.

186, 187, 188 Below, the Danube frontier: Nomadic horsemen from the steppes.

This cursory review of the impact of the barbarians on the Hellenic Society would suggest that violence was the sole response of the external proletariat to the pressure of the disintegrating civilization, and that it lacked any ability to develop that gentle alternative which, as we have seen, enabled the internal proletariat to achieve an act of positive creation. A ferocious violence was indeed the hallmark of the Hellenic external proletariat, and it is no accident that the Huns should have bequeathed their name to posterity as a synonym for the uttermost in barbarity, or that their most famous leader should have been feared by his contemporaries as 'the Scourge of God'. Yet at the same time we can discern some faint and rudimentary parallels in the behaviour of the external proletariat and of its internal counterpart, and we would be convicting ourselves of historical prejudice if we failed to notice the resemblances and credit them with such value as they deserve. To begin with, there was a distinct difference of degree in the violence of the various war-bands. The Visigothic sack of Rome in AD 410 was without a doubt less savage than the Vandal and Berber sack forty-five years later. Indeed, the impression made upon contemporaries, when they heard the whole story, by the Visigoth Alaric's grant of asylum in the churches of Rome to the inhabitants of the captured city is commemorated in one of the most celebrated passages of Latin literature.

All the devastation, massacre, depredation, arson, and assault of every kind that has been perpetrated in the catastrophe by which Rome has just been overtaken has been done according to the custom of war; but in this catastrophe there has also been a new departure, an unprecedented spectacle. The dreaded atrocity of the barbarians has shown itself so mild in the event that churches providing ample room for asylum were designated by the conqueror, and orders were given that in these sanctuaries nobody should be smitten with the sword and nobody carried away captive. Indeed, many prisoners were brought to these churches by soft-hearted enemies to receive their liberty, while none were dragged out of them by merciless enemies in order to be enslaved.[3]

In another passage[4] Augustine upbraided his pagan Roman contemporaries for their ingratitude towards a God who had shown them an unmerited mercy in allowing the divinely ordained capture of Rome by barbarian hands to be executed in 410 by the relatively enlightened Alaric rather than in 406 by the unmitigatedly cruel Radagaisus. Subsequently, Alaric's successor Atawulf, and the Ostrogoth leader Theodoric, showed that the barbarian yoke could be even lighter than this. The same contrast between an unequivocal and a mitigated barbarism was recognized in Aquitaine, where the inhabitants had resisted the Visigoth invaders in 412, yet found themselves fighting on the same side as their conquerors a century later against a common and more barbarous Frankish enemy. In Spain, on the other hand, the Visigoths were far less preferable as masters than the Muslim Arabs who supplanted them in the eighth century, for the Umayyads treated their Christian and Jewish subjects in both East and West with a toleration that had already made them famous.

These contrasts illustrate the extent to which the external proletariat was susceptible to gentler influences; and we find a similar diversity when we turn to the plane of spiritual creativity. The North European barbarians who had been encamped on a still standing Roman *limes* in the middle of the fourth century of the Christian Era had been converted to the Arianism which at that time was the official form of Christianity in the Roman Empire, and the effect of their conversion was to bring them closer to the spiritual culture of the civilization on whose borders they stood. By the turn of the fourth and fifth centuries, however, when Arianism had been vanquished by Nicene Christianity in the Roman Empire itself, the Arianized barbarians who were now pouring across the breached barriers of the Empire chose to wear their religion as a badge of their social distinction from a conquered population with which they were now determined not to identify themselves; and, the more truculent an Arian war-band was in its treatment of its provincial victims, the more fanatical it was apt to be in its hostility to Catholic Christianity. For instance, the Vandals in North Africa capped economic exploitation and political oppression with religious persecution. But while an Arianism, which its converts had simply taken as they found it, thus eventually became the distinctive mark of particular war-bands in their conquered territories, there were other barbarian groups on other frontiers who showed in their religious life a certain originality, if not true creativity. In the British Isles, for example, the Celts were converted to Catholic Christianity, but, instead of just adopting the alien religion as it stood, they went on to mould it to fit their own native heritage. Beyond the Roman Empire's Arabian frontier the barbarians showed an even greater religious independence. They transmuted into a new higher religion of their own the Judaism and Christianity that had radiated into Arabia. When we turn to the related field of aesthetic creativity, we can see that the barbarians of the external proletariat were not entirely sterile, even if their achievements were not on a par with the creative works which have been an outstanding accompaniment to the higher religions of the internal proletariat. The characteristic mode of cultural expression of the external proletariat has been epic poetry and saga, but the Arabs on the eve of their career of conquest showed the same originality in poetry as in religion. They created a lyric poetry with a personal note that was the forerunner of the rhymed prose of the Qur'an.

We can now summarize our findings so far about the nature of the external proletariat. We have seen that it originates in a reaction to the disintegration of a previously healthy civilization which had once drawn its pre-civilizational neighbours into its orbit, but which has now lost its attractiveness as a model and has ceased to exert any influence upon these outlying barbarian societies. We have also traced the pattern of barbarian assaults on the disintegrating Hellenic Civilization, and we have observed that, although violence is the primary and instinctive response of the external proletariat, traces of an alternative gentler response, comparable with that of the internal proletariat, are also detectable. We have seen that the external proletariat is potentially open to the vision of ultimate spiritual reality embodied in the higher religions, and that it is capable of absorbing or adapting the religious insights of the internal proletariat and thereby displaying a limited but unmistakable power of creation.

30 Schism in the soul

THE SOCIAL SCHISM which we have been examining in the foregoing chapters is an experience which is collective and therefore superficial. Its significance lies in its being the outward sign of a spiritual rift which scars the souls of the individuals who 'belong' to a disintegrating society. Beyond the social expressions of disintegration lie the personal crises of behaviour and feeling and life which are the true essence and origin of the visible manifestations of social collapse. Individual souls which have lost the opportunity (though not of course the personal capacity) for initiating the creative actions by which the growth of a society is sustained are apt to take refuge in a series of alternative reactions to the pressures of disintegration, and these reactions are as it were pathological inversions of some of the growth processes which we tried to identify earlier in this Study.[1] However, if we now attempt a corresponding analysis of these spiritual symptoms of *malaise*, we shall see that, while most of the feelings and actions that they evoke are negative and even destructive endeavours to deny or to arrest the process of disintegration, there are other reactions which may lead on to a genuine attempt to construct an alternative to the disintegrating society; and it is through some of these, in turn, that we shall observe the second part of our movement of 'schism-and-palingenesia' beginning to take shape. In practical life, the distinction between one type of reaction and another may not be hard and fast: the self-mastery of the Stoic may lead on to self-knowledge, and knowledge of self to perception of the divine; an apparently negative act of self-sacrifice may become a positive inspiration to more disciplined souls; the essentially self-indulgent search for a wholly personal salvation may transmute itself into creative social action. Positive and negative are opposite poles of the same magnetized lodestone, and the futile posture may be transfigured into a creative resolve. In other words, we shall find that, once again, we are dealing not with a static situation, but with a dynamic process; and, while we shall see some souls embarking in their despair upon a journey that has no destination in life, we shall also be able to trace the route that leads through torment and tribulation to life's ultimate goal.

We can begin by looking at those forms of behaviour and feeling that seem to betray a loss of the creative faculty, and that involve the actors either in a passive acquiescence in the ruin of their broken-down society, or else in an active but futile endeavour to stem the tide of disintegration by the substitution of an *ad hoc* stratagem for the true creative process. There are two types of personal behaviour which seem to represent alternatives to the exercise of the general faculty of creativeness, in the sense that both of them are attempts at self-expression. The passive attempt consists in an *abandon* in which the soul lets itself go utterly, believing that creativeness comes as the reward of a natural and wholly undisciplined spontaneity – a state of mind in which antinomianism is accepted as a substitute for creativity. The

active counterpart to this attempt to 'live according to Nature' is an effort at stringent self-discipline, based on the inverse belief that Nature is the bane of creativity and not its source, and that a rigorous restraint of the natural passions is the only way to recover the lost faculty. In the Hellenic Society's time of troubles the vulgar hedonists who miscalled themselves followers of Epicurus sought an authoritative sanction for their mood of *abandon* by claiming that it was a life directed by Nature's laws; and, on the other side, the sanction of a 'naturalness' differently interpreted was claimed for the ascetic life of self-denial in the crudely literal practice of the Cynics and, with a greater refinement, by the Stoic practitioners of a kindred philosophy. In all things that were 'indifferent' – and for a Stoic nothing was either good or evil in itself except the wrongness or rightness of his own will – it was the whole duty of the sage to mortify those human desires which were accepted by the hedonist as the promptings of Nature; and to carry this mortification to a degree at which the sage became able to accept as natural, not the impulses of the hedonist's 'natural man', but the trials that were put upon him by the chances and changes of this mortal life. The course of Nature, thus imagined, must be borne by the Stoic sage with cheerfulness if he was capable of rising to this counsel of perfection, and at all events with calmness and tranquillity if he was to be accounted worthy of being numbered at all among the disciples of Zeno.

The melancholy vein of Stoic self-control is reflected in the *Meditations* of the philosopher-emperor Marcus Aurelius, whose philosophy could never quite brace him to bear on his lonely shoulders the Atlantean load of a collapsing world.

The power that rules within, when it is in tune with Nature, has an attitude towards events which enables it to adapt itself easily to anything – within the limits of possibility – that is presented to it. . . .[2]
Be like the headland against which the waves continually break; but the headland stands firm while the tormented waters sink to rest around it. . . .[3]
This infinitesimally short span of time is something to be passed through in tune with Nature and passed out of with a good grace – like an olive that falls when it is ripe with a blessing for Nature who has brought it forth and a gratitude to the tree which has borne it.[4]

The temper to which the careworn Stoic Emperor wistfully aspires in the last of the three sentences above quoted had been duly attained by the lame Stoic slave who had been the most conspicuous wearer of Zeno's mantle in the preceding generation.

What else should we be doing, in public and in private, but singing the praises of the Godhead and speaking good of His name and attempting to express our thanks to Him? Digging or ploughing or eating, should we not ever be singing our hymn to God? . . . And, since most of you have gone blind, was it not meet that there should be somebody occupying this place and

189, 190 THE WINGS OF FORTUNE Fate, fortune, destiny, chance – belief in these uncontrollable forces is attractive to souls adrift in a dying social universe. In Rome the cult of fortune was officially established; its influence permeated life and thought, sapping the creative will.
Above, Fortune shown with the wings of Victory, the wheel of change beside her; opposite, Fortuna–Nemesis, holding the rudder that symbolized her control of destiny, and mounted on a rolling sphere.

191 THE TOUCH OF DEATH Wheel, butterfly, skull and level – symbols of fate, the soul, and inexorable judgment – combined into a melancholy image of overwhelming fatalism: opposite below, mosaic from Pompeii.

singing the hymn to God on behalf of us all? And what else can I, a lame old man, do but sing the praises of God? Were I a nightingale, I would sing like a nightingale; or, were I a swan, I would sing like a swan. But I happen to be a being endowed with reason, and so I must sing the praises of God. This is my work, so I am doing it, and I will never desert this post so long as it continues to be assigned to me. And I call upon the rest of you to sing the same song. . . .[5]

And, when Death overtakes me, I hope to be found by Him practising what I preach, in order that I may be able to say to God: Did I ever transgress Thy commandments? Did I ever use, for any other purposes than Thine, the talents or the senses or the innate ideas [*tais prolepsesin*] that Thou gavest me? Did I ever reproach Thee? Did I ever blame Thy governance? I was sick, when that was Thy will (my fellows were sick likewise, but when *I* was sick, I did not rebel). By Thy will I knew poverty, but I rejoiced in it. I never bore rule, because it was never Thy will that I should; but I never desired it. Didst Thou ever see me turn sullen on that account? Was there ever an occasion on which I presented myself before Thee with other than a cheerful countenance, or without being ready for any command or signal that Thou mightest choose to give? And now it is Thy will that I should leave the festival, so I am taking my leave – with my heart full of gratitude to Thee, because Thou hast deigned to allow me to celebrate the festival with Thee and to behold Thy works and to watch the course of Thy governance. When Death overtakes me, may these thoughts be in my mind and these words on my pen or on the page that my eyes are reading.[6]

Such was the ascetic mastery over Nature that was attained, in the course of the disintegration of the Hellenic Society, by the noblest adepts of the Stoic school of philosophy. And in the final chapter of Hellenic history we can see the ascetic tradition of an expiring dominant minority blending with the less negative asceticism of the proletariat when the Hellenic philosophy, in its Neoplatonic close and climax, rises to a pitch of mystical feeling at which its dying song of praise to God comes almost into unison with the younger and stronger voice of Christianity.

Passing to the Syriac World in a comparable time of troubles, we can see the same unreconciled opposition between *abandon* and self-control in the contrast between the sedately sceptical theory of the Book of Ecclesiastes and the piously ascetic practice of the monastic community of the Essenes. And in another field again, in the philosophic practice of the Sinic time of troubles, we can find Yang Chu suffering Epicurus's fate of being exploited by hedonists and at the same time castigated by moral disciplinarians of the Confucian and Mencian school. In a latter-day time of troubles in Japan which preceded the enforcement of the peace of the Tokugawa Shogunate, a similar antithesis reveals itself in the clash between the abandoned immorality of the Japanese high politics of the age and the almost inhumanly perfect self-dedication of the contemporary samurai to his feudal lord.

Can we see any signs of these conflicting ways of behaviour in the Western Society of our own day? Certainly, the invitation to 'return to Nature' has been clearly audible since it was first uttered by Jean-Jacques Rousseau two centuries ago; and the clamour has reached an unprecedented volume in the claims by initiates of a contemporary 'drug culture' that they have recovered the lost faculty of spontaneous and uninhibited creativity and have found the true model for a society of human perfection. To some extent the progress of the recent science of psychology has also reinforced this modern tendency towards *abandon*, in consequence of its attempt to probe through the layers of acquired social and personal experience which are alleged to mask an inner core of true selfhood and to inhibit its expression. This erosion of the corner-stones of personal discipline may manifest itself in the relatively innocuous form of an individual rejection of the traditional Judaeo-Christian code of sexual morality which, in one shape or another, has been embedded in the Western Society throughout the course of its history. More seriously, it may compose itself into a dangerous reduction *ad absurdum* of the principle of relativity on the social and political plane, undermining the apparently valid concept that an irreducible minimum of fixed poles of orientation is a necessary element in the psychological health of both individuals and societies. On the other hand, the counter-movement of asceticism does not seem to have made much headway in the present-day Western World, though perhaps the first faint stirrings of self-denial, albeit in a somewhat shallow and debased form, can be detected in what is fashionably described as the 'backlash' against 'moral pollution'.

When individual creativity has been replaced by spurious modes of self-expression in this way, we should also expect that the mechanism of mimesis, by which the mass of society is induced to follow its leaders in an age of growth, will be equally unable to operate satisfactorily. The effect of a sudden collapse of social drill is to deprive the individual of his sense of social identity and mutual obligation, and to encourage wholly individualistic reactions to the crisis. In this frame of mind the truant will attempt to escape the consequences of a social breakdown by repudiating his duty to his fellows and deserting the disordered majority in the selfish hope of securing his personal safety at any price. A classic case of truancy, which has come to our notice already,[7] is Athens' desertion of the cause of Hellenic federalism in 228 BC, even though the championship of this cause offered the only hope of saving the independence of both Athens and her sister-states at the heart of the Hellenic World from domination by the giants looming on the periphery of the disintegrating society. The weakness of this reaction is the implicit assumption that individual salvation can be successfully achieved when it is selfishly divorced from its wider social context. However, there is an altruistic form of desertion in which social ends are served precisely by means of an individual act of stepping out of the ranks: the martyr's act of self-sacrifice is equivalent in one sense to a desertion of a disintegrating society; but it differs from truancy in that potentially it has the positive effect of serving as an example to others.[8]

The loss of creative opportunity means also that the Promethean *élan*, which is the active essence of growth, no longer finds vent in action; and in this situation the soul is apt to surrender itself to a hopeless feeling of being adrift in an uncontrollable, if not evil, Universe. In fact, we have already noticed in another context[9] that a common reaction of men who live out their lives in an age of social breakdown is to ascribe their tribulations to the operation of an inexorable law of necessity or fate; and to this we can add the inverse feeling that Man's life and works are rendered equally nugatory by the play of blind and unpredictable

chance. The two notions of necessity and chance are correlative by reason of their very antithesis; for this antithesis does not lie between two alternative and incompatible conceptions of the nature of things, but merely between the human being who feels that he is adrift and the mighty waters that seem to him to be tossing him about as callously as if he were an inanimate piece of flotsam. In a self-regarding mood the castaway views the force that is defeating him in a negative light, as a sheer chaotic disorder, and it is in this mood that he gives the name of chance to his irresistible adversary and mistress. But the notion of disorder, as Bergson has pointed out,[10] is essentially relative, like the notion of order itself. Neither order nor disorder can be imagined except in contrast to its opposite. We make a subjective judgment when we call a thing or a state 'disorder', and what we mean is that we are being disappointed of some form of order which we have chosen, here and now, to impose in thought and act upon the face of the Universe. The intractable state of the facts upon which we are taking a verbal revenge by giving it the bad name of 'disorder' may – and indeed must – at the same time be an exemplification of the principle of order when the situation is viewed from another of the infinitely numerous possible alternative standpoints to that single arbitrary one which happens to be ours at the moment. For instance, the giddy spinning of the potter's wheel, which stands for the acme of disorder in the eyes of an Egyptiac poet[11] whose imagination animates the clay that is whirling helplessly on the wheel's surface, is at the same time an example, on the mathematical plane of existence, of an orderly cyclic motion, while on the teleological plane it is an obedient mechanism for impressing upon the clay the spiritual order that is represented by the potter's will. In a similar way the disorderly motion of a rudderless ship, which stands in Plato's eyes for a Universe abandoned by God,[12] can be recognized, by a mind equipped with the necessary knowledge of dynamics and physics for 'programming' a computer, as a perfect illustration of the orderly behaviour of waves and currents in the media of wind and water. When the human soul adrift apprehends this truth, then the unknown force by which it is controlled loses the subjective aspect of chance and becomes objectified as necessity – but this without any change in the essence of this inhuman power's nature.

The failure to come to terms with the notion of fortune wrought havoc in the Hellenic intellectual world in the age of its decline, for

the ideal of intelligibility thus betrayed took speedy vengeance upon its betrayers as [*tyche*] or *fortuna* assumed the character of a 'principle', to be invoked as the 'explanation' of otherwise unaccountable developments according to the merely subjective whim of the observer. As such, it illustrates in a most sinister form the artistic and philosophic vice of *fantastica fornicatio*.

At Rome the idea of fortune first manifests itself in the *Fors Fortuna* of Servius Tullius. And, though 'she does not appear in the calendar, has no flamen and must have been introduced from outside', her presence in the city at this early stage [in the sixth century BC] marks a recognition by the Romans of a quite illusory belief in luck. But, whatever the significance of the primitive conception, it was overlaid in the later republic by notions which, while perhaps owing their origin to Polybius, assumed ever-increasing prominence until, in the early empire,

they found expression in a regular cult of Fortune. In this connexion we may observe that nothing so clearly exposes the breakdown of classical *scientia* as the deification of chance itself. To make the course of history turn upon such a principle is fatal to intellectual integrity and moral responsibility alike.[13]

The fatalistic passivity which is the common mood of believers in chance and fate alike is also revealed in the Islamic theory of predestination, in the classic form given to it by the theologian Abu'l-Hasan al-Ash'ari (*vivebat c.* AD 873–935). Al-Ash'ari attempts to resolve the apparent contradiction between God's predestination and Man's free will by propounding the doctrine of *Iktisab*, according to which the human will accepts for itself the destiny which God has already assigned to it. On this showing, 'Man is still an automaton although part of his machinery is that he believes himself free.'[14] This tension between human freedom and divine necessity in a God-created Universe has persistently exercised religious minds, and makes its appearance in the higher religions of Christianity and Hinduism, as well as in the vulgarized Taoism of the Sinic World in the second century BC. The Christian doctrine of original sin affirms that the character and conduct of human beings whom we can see alive on Earth today have been causally conditioned by the past action by which Adam fell from grace; though at the same time Christian dogma emphasizes that Adam's sin was of his own willing, and thus by inference Man's free will is not impugned. According to the comparable Indic doctrine of *karma* the spiritual characteristics of all individuals are accumulated as parts of a continuum which appears and reappears in the world of sense through a series of reincarnations, the separateness of these phenomenal existences from one another being merely an hallucination. Thus the word *karma*, which literally means 'action' in Sanskrit, has come to bear the special meaning, in the terminology of philosophy and religion, of moral action flowing from deliberate acts of will, which produces an abiding effect upon the character of the agent, and which mounts up cumulatively, in an ever-open credit-and-debit account, from one incarnation to another.

The personal sense of drift has a social counterpart in the feeling of cultural anomie – a total loss of all sense of particularized form and style which is the inverse of the process of the differentiation of civilizations through growth. The soul surrenders itself to the melting-pot, and a negative sense of cultural promiscuity then comes to pervade every sphere of social activity. In the sphere of social intercourse it results in a blending of incongruous traditions and in a compounding of incompatible values (*pammixia*); in the media of language and literature and visual art it declares itself in the currency of a *lingua franca* or *koine*, and of a similarly standardized composite style of literature and painting and sculpture and architecture; in the realm of philosophy and religion it produces ritual and theological syncretisms. Of the three factions into which a disintegrating society is apt to split, it is the dominant minority that succumbs most readily to the sense of promiscuity. The mentally or physically uprooted expatriates who form the internal proletariat tend not only to keep a firm hold upon the remnants of their native heritage, but even manage to impart some of this to their masters;

and the external proletariat, insulated from the radiation of a dying civilization by the erection of an impassable military frontier, tends on the whole to sustain its vigorous barbarian culture until the moment at which it finally overruns the ruined civilization. This receptivity of dominant minorities is perhaps hardly surprising, since they are the empire-builders, the founders of universal states which are themselves visible manifestations of the need for the securing of secular unity in a disintegrating world.

Common to all these various expressions of spiritual uncertainty is a sense of moral defeat which is liable to divorce the actors from the realities of their social and individual existence, and to encourage them to pursue a utopian chimera as a substitute for an intolerable present. In the twin movements of archaism and futurism we can see two alternative attempts to substitute a mere transfer in the time-dimension for that transfer of the field of action from one spiritual plane to another which is a characteristic movement of growth.[15] In both these utopian movements the effort to live in the microcosm instead of in the macrocosm is abandoned for the pursuit of an ideal world which would be reached – supposing that this were in fact possible – without any challenge to face an arduous change of spiritual clime. This utopian substitute for the true movement of transference declares itself in an attempt either to return to some past 'Golden Age' of the society in question, or else to take a flying leap into the future. The external utopia thus attained is intended to do duty, in place of the inward spiritual cosmos, as an 'other world' of transcendent value; but it is an 'other world' only in the shallow and unsatisfying and ultimately meaningless sense of being a negation of the macrocosm in the momentary present state of the macrocosm's existence here and now. It is a perfunctory fulfilment of the law of life in letter but not in spirit; and, while it may save the soul from spiritual suicide, this attempt to defy the laws of time and motion must ultimately bring disaster upon its practitioners and their society.

The archaistic version may be defined as a reversion from the mimesis of contemporary creative personalities to a mimesis of ancestors, and in this sense it comes near to being a lapse from the dynamic movement of civilization to the virtually static situation of pre-civilizational Mankind. Alternatively, it may be defined as an attempt to arrest a society at a given stage, or forestall a threatening change, by immobilizing the dynamic factors of social growth – and this, as we have seen,[16] is an invariably catastrophic reaction to social challenges. One of the principal impulses towards the archaistic form of utopianism is the virus of nationalism, which we can see at work in the contemporary world. A community which has succumbed to this grave spiritual malady is apt to resent its cultural debt to the civilization of which it is itself merely a fragment, and in this frame of mind it will devote a great part of its energies to creating a parochially national culture, which can be declared free from foreign influence. In its social and political institutions, its aesthetic culture, and its religion, it will try to recapture the ostensible purity of an age of national independence prior to the one in which it finds itself incorporated in the larger society of a supranational civilization.

192 THE CULT OF THE PAST – archaism – offers escape from a deadly present to the myth-memory of an idealized past. In a nationalist variant of this vicious folly, Kaiser William I is shown aping his country's ancestral hero, the Teutonic knight.

The most striking recent example of this backward-looking nationalism in our Western Society has been the National Socialist attempt in Germany to recreate a primitive Teutonic society which would allegedly have corresponded to an ancient 'essence' of Germanism, stripped of all the accretions of the intervening ages. The catastrophic dénouement of this futile and horrific attempt to recover a wholly spurious past illustrates in classic form the nemesis which follows upon the combination of the two spiritual aberrations of archaism and nationalism; and yet it seems that no example, however forceful, carries sufficient conviction to teach later generations the moral, for the same vicious malady is still afflicting communities in the present-day world. The militant nationalism of sectional groups in the modern Western Civilization must be regarded as a clear indication of the spiritual crisis which leads to the idolatrous worship of an allegedly worthy part in place of a no longer accepted whole. As an example of the corrupting effects of such a par-blind pursuit of a utopian past we can cite the black peoples' minority movements within a number of Western nations. In seeking to deny the incontestable and ineradicable links by which recent history has bound an uprooted black community to a white Western Society, and in looking backwards to an African past which is, as a matter of historical fact, lost and buried for these expatriates, the Black Power movements have been guilty of mistaking the part for the whole. They have been in danger of perverting a wholly justifiable search for a dignified identity after centuries of savage white oppression – which has been cultural as well as political – into a violent and ultimately fruitless attempt to detach themselves from their only possible present and future spiritual environment.

Side by side with this type of potentially violent archaism we can set the gentler, but no less corrupting, archaism of those who seek to combine Rousseau's call to 'return to Nature' with their own vision of an older and allegedly more uncomplicated era of Western history. The secessionist tendencies of those who are demoralized by the threatening discrepancy between Mankind's material progress and its spiritual incapacity to cope with the problems that this is creating may perhaps arouse more sympathy at first sight than the naked ferocity of nationalism; yet we ought to recognize quite clearly that this attempt at an archaistic reversion is just as disastrous. Those who fall into either pose are equally guilty of performing a mental manœuvre in the delusion that life may be engineered without first being mastered.

The vain hope that, if reality is denied with sufficient force, then it will cease to be actual, is also at the root of the futurist form of utopianism. The millennarian vision has been one of the commonest manifestations of futurism at periodic times of local crisis in the history of the Western Civilization, but the aberration can also express itself in less spectacularly religious terms. We are most familiar with futurism today in its current guise of political revolution – a concept that, in its very essence and irrespective of its arbitrary ideological label, denies the necessity of undergoing all the pain of experience (*pathei mathos*)[17] by claiming that the intermediate stages between present misery and potential happiness may be leap-frogged with one massive

193   The American black glancing at a socialist tract beneath a romanticizing poster epitomizes the tension between revolutionary futurism and nostalgic archaism in Black Power movements today.

194 BETRAYING THE FUTURE *Demonstration* by Bruno Caruso. The revolutionary cry for immediate release from oppression becomes a meaningless slogan: a cathartic outburst is no substitute for hard-won wisdom.

stride far into the future. The history to date of such revolutionary attempts to recast the structure of local societies has revealed not only the folly of ignoring the limitations imposed on Man by the time-dimension, but also the hazards of abusing a leadership's obligation to carry the mass of society with it;[18] and the combination of these two faults has led in our own time to the erection of tyrannical régimes whose subjects have had to bear the inescapable penalty for their masters' moral and intellectual errors.

We have now perhaps given sufficient attention to the range of spiritual aberrations to which the soul is subject when, under the stress of social collapse, it has abrogated its duty of creativeness. The substitution of stratagem for creation may arguably bring in gains on the short-term account – if this were not possible, no disintegrating society would be safe from immediate and irreversible collapse into anarchy – but on the long-term view we can only make a cumulative entry on the debit side. There is, however, as we have already suggested, a dialectic of disintegration as well as of growth, and the supreme crisis of social collapse, which proves an insuperable challenge to most, has also the power of evoking a supreme response in others. Those who neither acquiesce in the disintegration of their society nor seek to hold back the tide with artificial substitutes for creativity, but who have the vision and the spiritual courage to confront the challenge, have it within their reach to participate in a greater act of creation than is witnessed in even the most vigorous stages of social growth.

THE NEW DEPARTURE   195   The painful crisis of social disintegration challenges the suffering soul
to reject the allurements of easy answers. A fifteenth-century allegory shows
the wisest of the wise turning their backs on Fortune, who stands poised on
wheel and mastless ship, harnessed to the wind's wayward powers. Above
them, Virtue sits flanked by the philosophers Crates and Socrates, the one
casting away his worldly wealth, while the other receives from her the
palm of wisdom.

THE PATH OF GROWTH which is closed by those whose capacity for life and feeling exhausts itself on the mundane level may be reopened by a soul that can see beyond the veil of mundane appearance to the distant view of an 'other world' of a supra-mundane spiritual order. The social catastrophe of disintegration thus reveals itself finally as a crisis of perception in the individual soul. In their very limited way, the modes of life which we have called 'archaism' and 'futurism' are both attempts to escape from a crushing present, which has become manifestly unserviceable as a medium for growth, by pointing to an alternative goal. Yet both these attempts are vitiated by the fundamental error of believing that the soul can be saved from that spiritual sickness which the breakdown of a civilization brings to light without any change of spiritual clime or dimension; and this is as much as to say that the life of Man on Earth is a mere temporal mechanism, a chronological sequence which fulfils itself in the macrocosm of the material world. The bankruptcy of the archaistic and futuristic experiments derives from a stubborn refusal to acknowledge the necessity of that shift from macrocosm to microcosm which we have already recognized[1] as the *sine qua non* of growth in a healthy civilization; yet the illusion that this can be avoided may be shattered at last by the reality of a spiritual defeat which, if it is not accepted as irretrievable, can lead to a new departure in life.

What route must the individual take to arrive at his destination of self-realization in his inner world? He experiences, after all, the same crisis as his fellows in their common ordeal of life in a disintegrating society; yet what is a stumbling-block to them becomes for him a supreme challenge. When the *élan* of growth in a healthy society seems to have given out, the passive individual loses his bearings upon the uncharted seas of the Universe; but the alternative reaction to this sense of a loss of control is, not to look outwards upon a macrocosm engulfed by evil, but to look inwards to the soul's own self and to recognize the moral defeat as a failure of self-mastery. Such a sense of personal sin presents the sharpest contrast imaginable to the passive sense of drift; for, while the sense of drift has the effect of an opiate in instilling into the soul an insidious acquiescence in an evil that is assumed to reside in external circumstances beyond the victim's control, the sense of sin has the effect of a stimulus because it tells the sinner that the evil is not external after all, but is within him, and hence subject to his will.

There is here the whole difference between the Slough of Despond and the faith that moves mountains; at the same time, though, we can see that there may be a margin of common ground between the mountains and the slough in practical life – an intermediate zone of feeling and conduct across which the tormented soul in an age of social disintegration may make, if it will, the arduous passage from resignation to endeavour.

The existence of this no-man's-land in which the two moods overlap is implicit in the Indic concept of *karma*; for although *karma* can be regarded in one aspect as a burden forcibly imposed by the inexorable working of the law of causation, there is an alternative light in which it can be viewed as a burden that is deliberately increased or diminished, assumed or thrown off, by acts which are all within the scope of the agent's own volition. When viewed in this way, *karma* presents itself as the work of the soul that is its subject, and no longer as the work of a destiny that is external to the subject and unamenable to his control; and under this aspect *karma* resolves itself into sin instead of fate. It turns out, that is, to be an evil of which the subject is himself the author, but which, by the same token, he has the power to diminish and perhaps even in the end to extinguish. The same passage to a conquerable sin from an unconquerable fate can be made along a Christian road. In virtue of Christ's death on the cross, the Christian soul is offered a possibility of purifying itself from the taint of original sin, which is its heritage from Adam, by seeking and finding God's grace; and grace comes not as a wholly external transcendent force, but as a divine response to a human effort. The classic case of an awakening to the sense of sin is the spiritual experience of the Prophets of Israel and Judah in the Syriac time of troubles. When these Prophets were discovering their truths and revealing their message, the society out of which they had arisen and to whose members they were addressing themselves had been torn up and half-dismembered by a remorseless Assyrian aggressor. For souls whose society was in such a fearful plight it was an heroic spiritual feat to reject the obvious and specious explanation of their misery as the work of an irresistible external force, and to divine that, in spite of all outward appearances, it was their own sin that was the ultimate cause of their tribulations and that it therefore lay in their own hands to win release.

If thus the passive sense of drift may be turned in the life of an individual soul to an active and potentially creative sense of sin, so also the social feeling of helpless *pammixia* may rise to a positive sense of cultural unity. When it can attain to this perception, a soul will react to the loss of a distinctive cultural style in a disintegrating civilization, not by shrinking from a chaos void of any form at all, but by embracing a cosmos which partakes of what is eternal and universal. The effacement of cultural differentiation brings into view a spiritual edifice whose architecture was previously hidden by Man's local and transitory defences against such an overwhelming vision of eternity and infinity. This awakening to a sense of unity broadens and deepens as the vision expands from the unity of Mankind, through the unity of the cosmos, to the unity of a spiritual presence within and beyond both Man and the whole of the Universe.

The dawn of a sense of unity on the mundane political plane of life is commemorated in the titles by which some universal states have proclaimed their rulers' own conception of their nature and function. For example, the sovereign of the Achaemenian Empire, which served as a

196 Hindu sage in meditation bond; South India.

197 Saint Simeon Stylites; gold plaque from Syria.

universal state for the Syriac World, asserted the ecumenical range of his rule by styling himself 'King of the Lands' or 'King of Kings' – a title which was laconically translated into Greek in the one word *Basileus* without even an introductory definite article. The same claim to exercise an ecumenical authority over a united world is embodied, with complete explicitness, in the phrase *T'ien Hsia* – 'All that is under Heaven' – which was the official title of the Sinic universal state of the Han. The Roman Empire which served the Hellenic World as a universal state came to be equated in the Latin language with the *Orbis Terrarum* and in Greek with the *Oikoumene* in the sense of the whole of the inhabited world. The vision of a unity of the cosmos – foreshadowed in the pedestrian and limited unification of human society in the universal states – has presented itself to men in a series of variations on the theme of a Universe governed by law. The Babylonian astrologer – and the modern Western scientist – has been captivated by a mathematical law; the Buddhist ascetic by a psychological law; the Hellenic philosopher by a social law. Such beliefs have at least the merit of acknowledging the existence of a common principle behind the multiple appearances of the mundane world, but the identification of the unifying principle with law ignores the role of love, and love, as well as law, is an aspect of reality that we encounter in our human experience. We know law as the imposition of unity by the fiat of a sovereign legislator. We know love as the quest for unity by a living being whose divisive self-centredness – another name for life itself – has been overcome by an irresistible impulse to give instead of taking. Our acquaintance with both love and law is in the tiny field of human affairs. The belief that love and law are also aspects of an ultimate spiritual reality is an act of faith. But unverifiable hypotheses are practical necessities of life, and the limitations of human thought make it difficult to think of a hypothetical supra-human reality in non-anthropomorphic terms. In our human vision of a supra-human spiritual reality, the multiplicity of the phenomenal world is reflected in a pantheon of human-like gods, and the awakening to a sense of the unity underlying the multiplicity is reflected in a transition from polytheism to monotheism. In the anthropomorphic religious imagery of all three religions of the Judaic school, the conception of God's ethos and action has changed in an identical direction. God the sovereign legislator has been seen to be God the merciful and compassionate synonym for love.

The soul that has caught the vision of unity, and has seen the unifying spirit as love, is spiritually prepared to perceive, and to respond to, the challenge of an 'other world' that is not just the mundane world translated into an imaginary past or future, but is a world of a different order of reality. Through this revealing vision, the soul may at last discover the truth that the everyday world offers no final answer to the besetting miseries of life in an age of disintegration; and it will be impelled to rise above the mundane level of existence and seek a point of departure in the life of the spirit.

One way of rising above the mundane level is to adopt a stance of detachment from the world and its ills, and this is a philosophy that can be practised in successive degrees from the initiatory act of still-reluctant Stoic resignation to a climax at which the adept deliberately aims at self-annihilation. One may play at detachment in the game of a sophisticated 'return to Nature' that was played by Marie-Antoinette in her Parisian dairy or by Theocritus in his Coan harvest-field. One may carry this game to the length of a pose, as it was carried by Diogenes in his tub and by Thoreau in his tent. One may genuinely stake one's life – as an anchorite in the desert or as a yogi in the jungle – upon the efficacy of this would-be solution to the problem which life presents. But a traveller along the path of detachment who is to reach the goal and win the reward must do more than stake his life upon the quest: he must detach himself from life to the point of being in love with nothing but its negation. To do this, of course, means flying in the face of human nature.

Ethical prowess can and will produce felicity and invulnerability and well-being . . . and there is one way only by which well-being can be reached: the way of detachment from all morally neutral values. You must not allow yourself to have a sense of property in anything; you must surrender everything to God and to Chance . . . and must concentrate upon one thing only – the thing that is truly your own, and in which no outside power can interfere.[2]

Spiritual exercises in the practice of detachment are commended at many other points in this manual of Stoic philosophy; but if we want to follow the path of detachment far enough we shall find ourselves sooner or later turning from an Hellenic to an Indic guide; for, far though the disciples of Zeno go, it is the disciples of the Indic philosopher Siddhártha Gautama that have had the courage to pursue detachment all the way to its logical goal of self-annihilation. The Indic candidate for arhatship knows that the Hellenic expedient of a conducted tour to *nirvana* is a snare and a delusion. If one takes an anaesthetic, one cannot commit *hara-kiri*; and in order to achieve the greater *tour de force* of spiritual self-annihilation one must be alertly aware, from first to last, of what one is about. The key that unlocks the gate of *nirvana* is not an aesthetically agreeable hypnosis but an arduous and painful mental struggle of the kind that is prescribed in the following passage from a work of the Hinayanian Buddhist philosophy:

In one who abides surveying the enjoyment in things that make for grasping craving [*tanha*] increases. Grasping is caused by craving, coming into existence by grasping, birth by coming into existence, and old age and death by birth. . . . Just as if a great mass of fire were burning of ten, twenty, thirty, or forty loads of faggots, and a man from time to time were to throw on it dry grasses, dry cow-dung, and dry faggots; even so a great mass of fire with that feeding and that fuel would burn for a long time. . . .

In one who abides surveying the misery in things that make for grasping, craving ceases. With the ceasing of craving grasping ceases, with the ceasing of grasping coming into existence ceases, with the ceasing of coming into existence, birth ceases, and with the ceasing of birth old age and death cease. Grief, lamentation, pain, dejection, and despair cease. Even so is the cessation of all this mass of pain.[3]

The goal that is the reward of this search is *nirvana*, and *nirvana* is

a condition where there is neither 'earth', nor 'water', nor 'fire', nor 'air', nor the sphere of infinite space, nor the sphere of infinite consciousness, nor the sphere of the void, nor the sphere of neither perception nor non-perception . . . that condition,

SUPERHUMAN INDIFFERENCE By reaching out for perfect detachment from a corrupt world, the ascetic loses hold of the divine passion of pity for Mankind. The yogi, the stylite, and the sage stand coldly aloof from a suffering world, rapt in contemplation of a perfect void.

198 The priest Myo-e meditating: Japan, thirteenth century A D.

Brethren, do I call neither a coming nor a going nor a standing still, nor a falling away nor a rising up; but it is without fixity, without mobility, without basis. It is the end of woe.[4]

This absolute detachment has perhaps never been attained, or at least never as a permanent state, outside the school of Gautama. As an intellectual achievement it is imposing; as a moral achievement it is overwhelming; and yet it has a disconcerting moral corollary, for perfect detachment casts out pity, and therefore also love, as inexorably as it purges away all the evil passions.

> Love cometh from companionship;
> In wake of love upsurges ill;
> Seeing the bane that comes of love
> Fare lonely as rhinoceros.[5]

To the Indic sage's mind this heartlessness is the adamantine core of philosophy; for to give primacy to any of the heart's sensations, however virtuous, is to admit the duality of selfhood into the perfect unity of consciousness. The Buddhist conclusion that all sensation ultimately coincides in reinforcing the fetters of self was reached independently by the Hellenic philosophers as a result of following likewise to the bitter end a parallel line of escape from life (though the Hellenic sage who had struggled out into the sunshine of enlightenment would perhaps feel a greater sense of social obligation to return to the darkness where the vast majority of his former fellow-prisoners were still languishing).

The sage will not feel pity, because he cannot feel it without himself being in a pitiful state of mind.... Pity is a mental illness induced by the spectacle of other people's miseries, or alternatively it may be defined as an infection of low spirits caught from other people's troubles when the patient believes that those troubles are undeserved. The sage does not succumb to suchlike mental diseases. The sage's mind is serene and is immune from being upset by the incidence of any external force.[6]

In pressing its way to a conclusion that is logically inevitable and at the same time morally intolerable, the philosophy of detachment ultimately defeats itself. In the very act of admiring the fortitude of its exponents we are moved to revolt against their denial of man himself. By consulting only Man's reason and not his heart, the philosophy of detachment is arbitrarily putting asunder what God has chosen to join together. This philosophy falls short of the truth by refusing to take account of the soul's duality in unity, and by shutting its ears to the poet's plea 'Where the heart lies, let the brain lie also';[7] and so the philosophy of detachment has to be eclipsed by the mystery of transfiguration. The Hinayana must make way for the Mahayana, Stoicism for Christianity, the arhat for the Bodhisattva, the sage for the saint.

The exponents of detachment seek an illusory form of unity by denying the dualism that Man's own existence implies – the distinction between being and consciousness – and their path of withdrawal from the world of being is for this reason a spiritual blind-alley. The soul must find a route back into the world, if it is not to negate itself in a stultifying philosophy of nihilism; and this route is opened by the religious mystery of transfiguration. At the core of this ideal is the concept of a Kingdom of God which, in so far as it enters into the time-dimension, is not a dream of

the future but a spiritual reality which is at all times present in this world, besides existing – and, indeed, just because it exists – as well in an eternity and infinity that are in a supra-mundane spiritual reality. While the 'other world' of the philosopher is in essence a world that is exclusive of ours on Earth, and an asylum of refuge from it, the divine 'other world' transcends the earthly life of Man without ceasing to embrace it.

And when he was demanded of the Pharisees, when the Kingdom of God should come, he answered them and said: 'The Kingdom of God cometh not with observation; neither shall they say Lo here! or Lo there! for, behold, the Kingdom of God is within you.'[8]

But how can the Kingdom of God be authentically in ourselves in this world and yet also be essentially not of it? This is a question that transcends the limitations of logical solutions; but, if we are willing to acknowledge the hard truth that the nature of transfiguration is a mystery beyond the reach of purely rational thought, we may perhaps be rewarded for a sober recognition of the limits of our intellectual power by finding ourselves able to peer into the mystery through the imagery that conveys the intuition of poets.

> To see a world in a grain of sand
> And heaven in a wild flower,
> Hold Infinity in the palm of your hand
> And Eternity in an hour.[9]

In the words of a poet of the Buddhist Ch'an (Zen) school,

> Infinitely small things are as large as large things can be,
> For here no external conditions obtain;
> Infinitely large things are as small as small things can be,
> For objective limits are here of no consideration. . . .
>
> One in All,
> All in One –
> If only this is realized,
> No more worry about your not being perfect.[10]

The resolution of duality in unity can be achieved in the language of mysticism, but how in practice can God's will be done on Earth as it is in Heaven? In the technical language of theology – whether Mahayanian or Christian – the omnipresence of God involves His immanence in this world and in every living soul in it, as well as His transcendent existence on the supra-mundane plane of being. In the Christian conception of the Godhead His transcendent aspect is displayed in God the Father and His immanent aspect in God the Holy Ghost; but the distinctive and also the crucial feature of the Christian canon is the doctrine that the Godhead is not just a duality but a trinity in unity, and that in His aspect as God the Son the other two aspects are unified in a person who, in virtue of this mystery, is as accessible to the human heart as he is incomprehensible to the human understanding. In the person of Christ the divine society and the mundane society have a common member who in the order of 'this world' is born into the ranks of the proletariat and dies the death of a malefactor, while in the order of the 'other world' he is the King of God's Kingdom. We are bound to ask ourselves how two natures – one human and the other divine – can in any real sense be present both at once in a single person. Answers to this question, cast in the form of creeds, have been worked out by Christian Fathers in terms of the technical vocabulary of the Hellenic philosophers; but this line of approach, which risks reducing the central mystery to a meaningless formula of words, is perhaps not the only one available to us. There is an alternative starting-point in the postulate that the divine nature, in so far as it is accessible to us, must have something in common with our own; and, if we look for one particular spiritual faculty which we are conscious of possessing in our own souls and which we can also attribute with absolute confidence to God – because God would be spiritually inferior to Man (*quod est absurdum*) if this faculty were not in Him but were nevertheless in us – then the faculty which we must think of first as being common to Man and to God will be one which the philosophers wish to mortify, and that is the faculty of love.

Love, rejected by the Buddhist sages of the Hinayana, had to be readmitted to the Indic religion.

> 'This is myself and this is another.'
> Be free of this bond which encompasses you about,
> And your own self is thereby released.
>
> Do not err in this matter of self and other.
> Everything is Buddha without exception.
> Here is that immaculate and final stage,
> Where thought is pure in its true nature.
>
> The fair tree of thought that knows no duality,
> Spreads through the triple world.
> It bears the flower and fruit of compassion,
> And its name is service of others.[11]

Compassion – the love that fulfils itself in service to others – is the motive that inspires the martyrs and that makes their self-sacrifice creative. The example of Socrates' self-sacrifice has been noted already.[12] In the Syriac World in its time of troubles we can see the dissenters offering themselves as martyrs – first the Prophets of Israel and Judah; and then, at a later stage, the opponents of a paganizing faction that was trying, under the Seleucid régime, to escape from the onus of its precious Judaic heritage at the cost of merging its peculiar identity in the standardized form of Hellenism that was being accepted by the Palestinian Jews' non-Jewish fellow-subjects. In the Hellenic World, the two generations which elapsed between the death of the Emperor Alexander Severus in AD 235 and the death of the Emperor Galerius in 311 were signalized by a classic exhibition of martyrdom in the ranks of the Christian Church. The Church was the principal target for the parting strokes of an Hellenic dominant minority which turned savage in its death agony, convinced that it was the victim of a treacherous attack on the part of the proletariat. Under the test of this ordeal the sheep in the Christian fold were divided unequivocally from the goats in being called upon to choose between renouncing their faith and sacrificing their lives. The renegades were legion, but the tiny band of martyrs was spiritually potent out of all proportion to its numerical strength.

Love is, indeed, the core of the New Testament. In the instruction given to Nicodemus, love is revealed as being

199 PASSIONATE PITY Chinese Bodhisattva of the T'ang dynasty. The compassionate saint loves God more by loving His creatures. In reaction against the stern detachment of the early Buddhists, the Mahayana school reconsecrated compassionate love as the crowning ideal of the faith.

both the motive that moves God to redeem Man at the price of incarnation and crucifixion[13] and the means that enable Man to win access to God.[14] The working of love in God's heart – in moving God to suffer death on the cross – is brought out in the Synoptic Gospels in their account of the circumstances in which Jesus announces to his disciples that his destiny is the Passion instead of being to serve as a worldly Messiah for the Jewish futurists. He forbears to reveal this appalling truth until his divinity has been guessed by Peter and has been manifested in the Transfiguration; but, as soon as he has made his epiphany as God, he at once breaks silence about his Passion. The meaning of these revelations in this sequence is surely that a love which loves to the death is the essence of God's nature. And as for the working of love in human hearts as a means of access for Man to God, it is extolled as the sovereign – and sole indispensable – means to this supreme end of Man in the thirteenth chapter of Paul's First Epistle to the Corinthians. The love of Man for God flows on Earth, through all the members of the *Civitas Dei*, along the channel of Man's love for his human brother.

Beloved, if God so loved us, we ought also to love one another. No man hath seen God at any time. If we love one another, God dwelleth in us and His love is perfected in us.[15]

In virtue of this love which is equally human and divine, the Kingdom of God has a peace of its own which is not the philosophic peace of detachment, but the peace of life lived by men in and for God. The member of a disintegrating mundane society who has learned that self-fulfilment is won by self-surrender in God has a surer hope, and therefore a deeper happiness, than the merely 'once-born' member of a society that is still in growth; for he will know that by the suffering of a second birth he may gain entry into the Kingdom of God.

Nothing is more acceptable to God, and nothing more salutary for yourself, than to suffer gladly for Christ's sake. And if it lies in your choice, you should choose rather to suffer hardships for Christ's sake, than to be refreshed by many consolations; for thus you will more closely resemble Christ and all His Saints. For our merit and spiritual progress does not consist in enjoying much sweetness and consolation, but rather in the bearing of great burdens and troubles.

Had there been a better way, more profitable to the salvation of mankind than suffering, then Christ would have revealed it in His word and life. But he clearly urges both His own disciples and all who wish to follow Him to carry the cross, saying, 'If any will come after Me, let him deny himself, and take up his cross and follow Me.' Therefore, when we have read and studied all things, let this be our final resolve: 'that through much tribulation we must enter the Kingdom of God'.[16]

It is not, then, by seeking to escape suffering, but by embracing and responding to it, that the soul born into a disintegrating society can win release and regain, on a higher plane, the path of growth from which his society has strayed; and this movement of return is the second 'beat' of that rhythm of schism-and-palingenesia, in the realm of the soul, which we postulated at the outset of this part of our Study[17] as the characteristic movement of disintegration. Our attempt to analyse the processes by which the power of growth may be recovered from the seemingly fatal catastrophe of social collapse will have shown that the 'recurrence of birth' which we have identified at last is not a mere rebirth of society on any mundane level, but the attainment of a supra-mundane state; and the simile of birth can be applied to it illuminatingly because this other state is a positive state of life – a life shot through with the image of God. That is the palingenesia which Jesus proclaimed as the sovereign aim of his own birth in the flesh.

I am come that they might have life, and that they might have it more abundantly.[18]

PART VI

UNIVERSAL STATES

When a society is in disintegration, each of the three factions into which it splits produces an institution. The dominant minority tries to preserve its threatened power by uniting the warring nations into a universal state. I use this name because these empires, though not literally worldwide, embrace the whole territory of a single civilization. But universal states have sometimes been the work of alien empire-builders, just as the higher religions and the barbarian cultures have been alien in inspiration, and these facts lead me to re-examine my proposition that a civilization is self-contained and is therefore an intelligible field of study. I begin by asking whether universal states are ends in themselves or means to something beyond them. By looking at some of their institutions, I discover that they unintentionally benefit both the higher religions and the barbarians, though it is the religions that profit most. At the same time, although the historic universal states have so far always been local and ephemeral, they seem to be foretastes of a future régime in which the whole of Mankind will live in political unity, and so I conclude by assessing the prospects for this.

plate 42

UNIVERSAL EMPIRE

The creation of a universal state checks the headlong decline of
a disintegrating civilization; such states seem heaven-sent to
those who have been suffering the intolerable miseries of an age
of parochial warfare, and in this frame of mind men are eager to
believe that their empire is destined to be as immortal as the gods
who have ordained it. Their conviction is sustained by the belief
that a universal state embraces literally the whole world, leaving
no external force by which it might be threatened. Although this
is objectively an illusion, in subjective terms it accurately reflects
a situation in which the whole of a civilization has been united
into a single polity. This misplaced but unshakeable confidence
in immortality and universality is exemplified in a detail on
a Roman cameo, showing the Emperor Tiberius, seated beside
Rome, receiving the victor's crown from a personified *Oikoumene*, i.e. 'the inhabited world'. A Roman legend related that
when the Capitol was founded, Terminus – the god of boundaries
– refused to yield his place to Jupiter: 'A favourable inference',
says Gibbon, 'was drawn from his obstinacy, which was
interpreted by the augurs as a sure presage that the boundaries
of the Roman power would never recede.'

plate 43

IMPERIAL PRESTIGE

The prestige of universal states outlives their reality, exciting awe and deference even after power has evaporated. The Europeans visible in the procession of Indian feudatories are representatives of the British East India Company, paying formal homage to the 'Great Mogul'

258

Akbar II; yet since 1803 the Emperor had been the puppet of British masters, whose sole object in still performing this empty ritual was to legitimize their rule by exploiting the Emperor's political prestige.

plate 56

IMPERIAL ARTERIES

For the rulers of universal states a network of communications is an indispensable instrument of military and political control. The most famous road system is probably that of the Roman Empire, the universal state of the Hellenic World. Roman tradition dated its origins to 312 BC, though actually the earliest Roman roads were at least a century older. The system grew with the expansion of the Empire: the road and milestones, opposite, are in Transjordania, which had been converted from a client state into a Roman province in AD 106.

plate 57

CAPITAL CITIES:
REFLEXIONS OF POWER

In a universal state the capital city derives enormous prestige from its status as the seat of government. This fifteenth-century view of Baghdad, right – one of the earliest extant pictures of the city – is a wholly imaginative reconstruction of it as it was believed to have looked in its imperial heyday, before it fell to the Mongol conquerors of the remnant of the 'Abbasid Empire in 1258. Two hundred years after this catastrophe, the memory of imperial Baghdad still haunted the Islamic World.

264

plate 58

CIVIL SERVICES

The degree of efficiency attained by imperial administrations has varied considerably between one universal state and another, and so too has the process by which these civil services have come into existence. In Rome and in British India the commercial middle class was gradually taken into the administration, and was transformed from a corrupt and unprofessional body into a highly proficient service. British administration in India, until the end of the eighteenth century, was in the hands of the East India Company's commercial officers, who would spend their entire working life abroad in its service. Their total isolation from England, before the era of steam transport, plunged them far more deeply into Indian life and culture than their nineteenth-century successors – members of a professional colonial administration who preserved a civil servant's aloofness from 'native' life. This absorption into the local culture – often slightingly referred to as 'going native' – is illustrated in an Indian print of 1800, which shows a British Resident, dressed in Indian clothing and smoking a hookah, entertaining himself at home with a *nautch*, or Indian dancing display.

PRIDE AND PRESTIGE

200, 201 Above, the eagle, a symbol of Roman imperial power also adopted by later empires. Below, the imperial cult: emperor becomes god in a triumphal scene, his defeated foes beneath him.

THE STARTING-POINT of this book was a search for fields of historical study which would be intelligible in themselves within their own limits in space and time, without reference to extraneous historical events; and our first investigations[1] led us to the conclusion that the species of society called civilizations would provide us with a self-contained unit of this nature. Up to the present point we have pursued our inquiries on the assumption that a comparative study of these separate units would give us the perspective that we need for an attempt to chart and to understand the processes of human history. At the same time, however, we have met certain indications of the limitations inherent in our chosen methodology – as, for example, when we noted the intimate link between two civilizations which we described as 'affiliation',[2] or again when we observed that the component classes of society in a disintegrating civilization enter into social and political combinations with alien elements from other contemporary communities.[3] This receptivity of theirs is revealed in the institutions that are their products. Some universal states have been the handiwork of alien empire-builders; some higher religions have been animated by alien inspirations; and some barbarian war-bands have absorbed the rudiments of an alien culture.

Universal states, universal churches, and heroic ages thus link together contemporary as well as non-contemporary civilizations, and this fact raises the question whether it is justifiable to treat these historical phenomena, as we have so far done, as mere by-products of disintegrating civilizations, and to assume that the civilizations themselves are the sole objects of historical study which must be taken into account. If, as seems to be the truth, these three institutions cannot in fact be studied intelligibly within the framework that a single civilization provides, then we ought to inquire whether they themselves form more acceptable units of study; or whether they are each a part of some larger whole which embraces them and the civilizations alike.

We can begin by investigating the claims of universal states to be independently intelligible fields of study. The name that we have attached to them implies that these claims are valid, for universality excludes the notion of anything 'outside' itself. Objectively, no universal state has ever been literally universal in the sense of having covered the entire surface of the globe; but in a significant subjective sense these states have indeed been universal, for they have looked and felt worldwide to the people living under their régime. The Romans and the Chinese, as we have seen,[4] thought of their respective empires as embracing all the peoples in the world that were of any account; and the East Roman Empire, in common with these and others, laid claim to a notional sovereignty over the whole world.[5] This subjective belief in universality has always been an illusion; but we cannot for this reason ignore either its subjective actuality in the eyes of the people who held this belief, or the potency of the substantial effects that even an illusion can evoke. Some empires, as we shall see, have seen through the illusion and have deliberately refrained from claiming an unrealized and unreal universal sovereignty; but such empires seem to have been in the minority. We shall also see that this illusion of universality is not the only chimera to have captivated the imaginations of the inhabitants of universal states. We can test even these subjective beliefs by asking whether universal states, irrespective of their geographical extent, are ends in themselves or whether they are means towards something beyond and more profound than themselves.

Universal states are, let us remind ourselves, essentially negative institutions. In the first place, they arise after, and not before, the breakdowns of the civilizations to which they bring political unity. They are not summers but Indian summers, masking autumn and presaging winter. In the second place, they are the products of dominant minorities: that is, of once-creative minorities that have lost their creative power. There is, however, an element of ambiguity in them, for, while universal states are thus symptoms of social disintegration, they are at the same time attempts to check this disintegration and defy it. The histories of universal states suggest that they are possessed by an almost demonic craving for life, against all odds, and that their citizens are apt not only to desire but to believe very passionately in the immortality of the institution. But to outside observers it seems equally clear that universal states, as a class of polity, are the by-products of a process of social decline, and as such are stamped by their certificate of origin as unmistakably uncreative and ephemeral. From this point of view, the belief in the immortality of a universal state is an astonishing hallucination which mistakes a mundane institution for the Promised Land, the *Civitas Dei* itself; and yet there is no doubt that this illusion can be both widespread and long-lasting.

The deification of the Roman Empire – the Hellenic universal state – by its subjects is notorious, and we can trace this confident belief in Rome's immortality from the date of the establishment of the Empire right through till the eve of its dissolution. Tibullus (*vivebat c.* 54–18 BC) sings of the 'walls of the eternal City',[6] while Virgil (*vivebat* 70–19 BC) makes his Iuppiter, speaking of the future Roman scions of Aeneas' race, proclaim: 'For these I set no bounds in space or time; I have given them empire without end.'[7] The same expectation was expressed in the form, not of a divine communiqué, but of a human hope, by the soldier-historian Velleius (*vivebat c.* 19 BC–AD 31) who, in recording the adoption of Tiberius by Augustus, speaks of 'a hope conceived of the perpetual security and eternity of the Roman Empire'.[8] An historian-propagandist can perhaps afford to be less circumspect, and Livy (*vivebat* 59 BC–AD 17) writes with the assurance of Tibullus: 'the city founded to endure for ever';[9] 'the city . . . founded to endure for ever at the instance of the gods'.[10]

During the century and a quarter that elapsed between the death of Augustus in AD 14 and the accession of Pius in AD 138, the concept of the eternity of Rome and the Roman Empire was cherished by two bad emperors who met their deserts by coming to untimely personal ends. Nero instituted the games 'dedicated to the eternity of the Empire and called "the greatest" [games] by the Emperor's express command'.[11] The *Acta Fratrum Arvalium* record

'votive offering for the eternity of the Empire: a cow'[12] among the proceedings of AD 66, and 'thank-offerings vowed if thou shalt preserve the eternity of the Empire which [the Emperor Domitian] has enlarged in virtue of having undertaken these vows'[13] under the years AD 86, 87, and 90.

In the Age of the Antonines we find a Greek man of letters expressing the Augustan belief in the more delicate form of a prayer, without a suspicion that he was living in an Indian summer and was praying that a fugitive October might be miraculously transformed into a perpetual June.

Let us invoke all the gods and all the children of the gods, and let us pray them to grant this Empire and this city life and prosperity world without end. May they endure until ingots learn to float on the sea and until trees forget to blossom in the spring. And long live the supreme magistrate and his children likewise. Long may they be with us to carry on their work of dispensing happiness to all their subjects.[14]

Thereafter, when a touch of winter begins to make itself felt, its victims defy a change of season which they have not foreseen and cannot face, by insisting more and more emphatically that they have been privileged to enjoy an everlasting midsummer's day. In the Severan Age and its bleaker sequel the contrast between the official eternity of the emperors and the ephemeralness that was their actual lot makes a painfully strong impression. Even after the truth of the Empire's mortality has been proclaimed by Alaric's capture and sack of Rome itself, we can hear above the reverberations of this resounding blow the high voice of a Gallic poet reasserting the immortality of Rome as he travels back from the no longer inviolate imperial city to his own war-ravaged native province.

Rome, raise high the laurels round thy hair and transfigure the hoariness of thy holy head into youthful locks. . . . The flaming stars renew their rises by their settings. You see the moon end, only to begin again. Brennus's victory at Allia did not avert his penalty. The Samnite atoned by subjection for his cruel terms of peace. After suffering many disasters at Pyrrhus's hands, thou didst rout this conqueror of thine. Hannibal lived to bewail his successes. Bodies that cannot be submerged re-emerge with an irresistible *élan*; they spring back from the depths, borne up all the higher. Slant a torch and it will regain its strength; sink, and you will rise aloft all the grander. Promulgate laws to live for Roman aeons; thou, Rome, alone needst have no fear of the Fates' fell distaffs. . . . Thou wilt live out the ages that await thee as thine own mistress – ages that will last as long as the Earth stands and as the firmament bears the stars. Thou wilt be restored by the blows that dissolve other empires. The recipe for rebirth is the capacity to thrive on calamities. So into battle! At last the sacrilegious tribe must fall as thy sacrificial victims. The Goths must tremble and must bow their perfidious necks. Thy dominions, brought back to peace, must yield rich revenues. The spoils of the barbarians must fill the folds of thy majestic robes. To all eternity, Rhine must plough for thee and Nile inundate for thee. The fertile globe must nourish thee, her nurse.[15]

Perhaps the strangest testimony of all to Rome's power of fascination is Saint Jerome's description of the shock that he suffered when the news of the city's fall reached him in his remote retreat in Jerusalem.

While this [theological war] was being waged in Jerusalem, terrible news arrived from the West. We learnt how Rome had been besieged, how her citizens had purchased immunity by paying a ransom, and how then, after they had thus been despoiled, they had been beleaguered again, to forfeit their lives after having already forfeited their property. At the news my speech failed me, and sobs choked the words that I was dictating. She had been captured – the City by whom the whole world had once been taken captive.[16]

The Saint was devoted to the service of a Church that avowedly placed its hopes in the Commonwealth of God, and not in any earthly polity; yet this news, mundane though it might be, affected Jerome so profoundly that for the moment he found himself incapable of proceeding with his literary labours of theological controversy and Scriptural exegesis.

A similar shock was administered to the Arab World by the fall of the 'Abbasid Caliphate in AD 1258. The intense psychological effect that this produced is perhaps even more remarkable than in the Roman case, for, by the time when the Mongol Hulagu sacked Baghdad and gave the 'Abbasid Caliphate its *coup de grâce*, it had long since ceased to exercise more than a nominal sovereignty over the greater part of its original dominions.

It is perhaps comprehensible that a shadow could continue half deliberately to be mistaken for the substance by a dominant minority for whom the moribund universal state represented their own latest achievement and last hope; but it is an extraordinary testimony to the attractive power of the institution that it could also be an object of awe and devotion to the internal and external proletariats who had had little part in its construction. On the strength of this fact, both the legitimate holders and the alien usurpers of the sovereign authority in a universal state may, by stressing a genuine or pretended historic right to that authority, retain a considerable status as the sole dispensers of legitimacy long after they have lost all real power over their nominal empire. Indeed, this monopoly of an imponderable political commodity usually counts for so much that it is rare to find a barbarian conqueror of an imperial province boasting simply that he has seized his prize by force and is holding it by right of conquest alone. There are, to be sure, examples of barbarian conquerors who did permit themselves this indulgence – the Arian Vandals who made themselves masters of Roman Africa, or the Shi'i Kutama Berber conquerors of 'Abbasid Ifriqiyah and Egypt; but both these paid the penalty of being liquidated for their presumption. By contrast, the Amalung leaders of the Arian Ostrogoths and the Buwayhid leaders of the Shi'i Daylamis were wise enough to seek a title for their conquests by ruling them, in official theory, as viceregents of the Emperor at Constantinople and of the Caliph at Baghdad respectively. It was the heretical religion of these Arians and Buwayhids that eventually proved their undoing, for each was later supplanted by a barbarian successor who had taken the extra precaution of matching his claim to political legitimacy with a claim to religious orthodoxy. Even as late as the end of the thirteenth century the 'slave kings' at Delhi felt themselves obliged to legitimize their authority by reaffirming at each succession that it issued from the 'Abbasid Caliphate.

The same exertion of influence unsupported by real power is illustrated in the histories of the Ottoman,

SHADOWS OF POWER

202 The Mongols besiege Baghdad, capital of the 'Abbasid Caliphate. By the time the city fell in 1258, the Baghdad Caliphs had lost most of their real power, but their symbolic prestige for Islam was still enormous. The Islamic World had had a caliph at its head since 632; the death of the last is still lamented in special prayers.

Manchu, and Mughal Empires. The Manchu revival of the Sinic universal state affected to believe that all sovereigns in any part of the world with whom the Celestial Empire might be drawn into diplomatic relations derived their title from the same unique source of legitimacy as did China's own tributary states round about her borders. In the decline of the Ottoman Empire between the disastrous end of the Turco-Russian War of AD 1768–74 and the ignominious outcome of its final trial of strength with Mehmet 'Ali in 1839–40, the ambitious war-lords who were carving out successor-states for themselves in Egypt and Syria and the Balkans were meticulous in claiming to be acting in the Padishah's name while they were actually usurping his power.

The success of both these empires in still retaining, in their decline, a monopoly of the prerogative of serving as the fount of legitimacy was not, however, quite as remarkable as the Mughal Empire's performance of the same diplomatico-psychological · *tour de force*. The Timurid Mughal dynasty continued to assert this prerogative in its dealings with alien Powers who held the shadow of a *ci-devant* Mughal Empire at their mercy after it had sunk to a degree of impotence that neither the Ottoman nor the Manchu Empire ever quite reached. Within half a century of the great Emperor Awrangzib's death in AD 1707, an empire which had once exercised an effective sovereignty over the greater part of the Indian sub-continent had been whittled down to a torso of some few thousand square miles, and within a hundred years of the same date this truncated dominion had been reduced to the circuit of the walls of the Red Fort at Delhi. Yet in 1857 – 150 years after the effective dissolution of the Empire – the puppet Emperor who was still seated on the throne once occupied by Akbar and Awrangzib saw his fantastic pretensions to the legal title of his mighty ancestors' imperial domain vindicated by the mutinous sepoys of the British East India Company's army. The mutineers inaugurated in the Emperor's name the government of a revolutionary counter-raj which they were seeking to substitute by force of arms for the unconsecrated dominion of their British employers; and, in thus exploiting the prestige of a now-impotent Great Mogul, they were only taking account of a persistent state of Indian public opinion with which the British had already been obliged to reckon.

This was the consideration that had led the British East India Company, in 1764 and 1765, to acknowledge the Emperor's suzerainty as the *quid pro quo* for his formal conferment upon them of the right to conduct the administration and collect the revenue in the imperial provinces of Bihar and Bengal. Subsequent British experience confirmed that this imponderable remnant of Mughal imperial power did in fact possess a genuine specific gravity that could not be ignored with impunity. Although, as early as 1773, the British had revoked their recognition of the Mughal Emperor's continuing suzerainty over Bihar and Bengal, they were confronted as late as 1811 with a reassertion of the Emperor's title to a formal sovereignty in these long-since-ceded provinces which they did not find altogether easy to quash; and in the Emperor's last stronghold at Delhi within the walls of the Red Fort the controversy over the question whether he was the suzerain or a pensionary of the

203 Durbar of an Indian maharajah, by an English artist. In Mughal government, the durbar, or public audience, in which subjects performed a formal act of homage to emperor or prince, was a solemn ceremony. Even after the sovereignty of India had passed effectively into British hands, both durbar and homage retained something of their ritual aura.

British East India Company remained unsettled throughout the fifty-five years' interval between the British military occupation of Delhi in 1803 and the suppression of the Indian Mutiny in 1858. The British East India Company's explicit public declaration in 1811 that it was 'unnecessary to derive from the King of Delhi any additional title to the Allegiance of our Indian subjects'[17] was a form of words that, to Indian minds, was less significant than the British Resident's continued performance of a subject's customary visible acts of homage when he attended the Emperor's durbar. The importance still attached in Indian eyes to this symbolic act was given tangible expression by the Mutiny of 1857.

The tenacity of the belief in the immortality of universal states is demonstrated even more forcibly in the paradoxical practice of evoking their ghosts after they have actually proved themselves mortal by expiring. The 'Abbasid Caliphate of Baghdad was thus resuscitated in the shape of the 'Abbasid Caliphate of Cairo, the Roman Empire in the two shapes of the Holy Roman Empire of the West and the East Roman Empire of Orthodox Christendom; the Empire of the Ch'in (Ts'in) and Han dynasties in the shape of the Sui and T'ang Empire of the Sinic Society. Each of these ghosts managed to acquire and retain the status which their originals had once enjoyed, before their passing, as founts of legitimacy.

The Mamluks had been quick to install a refugee 'Abbasid at Cairo in AD 1261 because, being themselves usurpers of their Ayyubid masters' heritage and being faced with the problem of handing it down thereafter from slave to slave, they had the same urgent and recurring need of legitimization as their contemporaries and counterparts the 'slave kings' of Delhi. The Mamluk Sultans and their subjects appear to have treated their 'Abbasid puppets with contempt from first to last, but the more distant Muslim rulers in Hindustan continued to defer to the Cairene 'Abbasid Caliphs as their predecessors had deferred to the last Baghdadi 'Abbasid Caliph Musta'sim. A diploma of investiture was sought and obtained from the Cairene Caliph of the day not only by the parricide and tyrant Muhammad b. Taghlaq (*dominabatur* AD 1324–51) but by his estimable successor Firuz Shah (*dominabatur* AD 1351–88), who did not have his predecessor's incentive for seeking external sanction for his régime. Even Timur Lenk's grandson Pir Muhammad seems to have thought of taking the same step as a manœuvre in the contest for Timur's heritage, and the Ottoman Padishah Bayezid I (*imperabat* AD 1389–1402) seems actually to have applied to the reigning Cairene 'Abbasid in AD 1394 for a grant of the title of Sultan. However, Bayezid's descendant Selim I (*imperabat* AD 1512–20) felt no need of such legitimization, and did not covet a title borne by a puppet of the last Mamluk Sultan whom he had defeated and executed. The new generation of *de facto* rulers of a nascent Islamic World preferred to claim affinity with the Nomad war-lord Chingis Khan rather than with a Meccan Holy Family. In these circumstances the Cairene 'Abbasid Caliphate lost its power of attraction; the title of 'Caliph' forfeited its specific application to ecumenical sovereignty and was debased to the level of a polite honorific for any ruler. The history of the Caliphate might thus have been expected to come to an

end with the death, in obscurity, of the last Cairene 'Abbasid in 1543. Yet this was not, after all, the end of the story. After having thought nothing of the Caliphate for little less than four hundred years, the 'Osmanlis discovered belatedly, in the days of their decline, that this long-despised institution was not quite as worthless as they had thought.

During the hundred years after the negotiation of the Russo-Turkish peace treaty of Küçük Kainarca in 1774 the Ottoman Caliphate became for the first time an active participant in Western international politics; and at the same time it was able to derive great advantage from a misunderstanding among the Western Powers as to the nature of an office which had been obsolete, in all but name, for many centuries. In the West it was widely assumed that the Caliphate was a spiritual office with an authority more or less equivalent to that of the Papacy, while the Sultanate was regarded as being the organ of temporal power; the Ottoman Padishah was thus supposed to be combining in one person two distinct types of authority which might otherwise have been divided between different persons. In truth this assumed analogy between the Papacy and the Caliphate was quite false; and in at least three peace treaties between 1774 and 1913 the Ottoman Power was able to exploit – quite consciously and deliberately – the foreign Powers' error, by retaining in the Caliph's name the temporal authority over territories which it had been compelled to surrender in the Padishah's.

As it turned out, the foreign Powers eventually detected and corrected their error, and thus the deception could not stave off for ever the loss of Ottoman political control over the Empire's former territories. At the same time, however, the refurbishment of the Caliphate as a 'spiritual' office did have an imponderable but appreciable psychological effect upon international politics. It gave pause to the aggressive Western or Westernizing Powers which had taken the measure of the Ottoman Empire's political weakness but still remained in awe of the explosive religious force of Islam. Conversely, it made the Ottoman Empire, shrunken though it was, a moral rallying-point for the Muslim diaspora, not only in the ex-Ottoman territories, but also in distant regions such as India and China which had never been under the rule of any Caliph. These psychological uses of the Ottoman Caliphate, as realized by the Sultan 'Abd-al-Hamid II (*imperabat* AD 1876–1909), were such obviously valuable assets for the Ottoman state that the Sultan's 'New 'Osmanli' liberal opponents sought, not to abolish the Caliphate, but to preserve it for manipulation as an instrument of their own Turkish national policy. The Caliphate thus survived the abolition of the Sultanate in 1922, though only until 1924, by which time the impossibility of drawing any real distinction between the spiritual and the secular title had become clear. The office has now been non-existent for practically half a century, but, in view of the fact that the Caliphate previously managed to retain for more than a thousand years the prestige generated by a power that it had actually possessed for no more than two centuries, it might be wiser even now to regard the office as being merely in abeyance rather than finally extinct.

The Ottoman Padishahs, who treated their heritage of the 'Abbasid Caliphate at first so cavalierly and latterly so astutely, took their heritage of the Roman Empire more seriously. The East Roman Emperors, like the Chinese Emperors, claimed that they had a unique title to a world-wide sovereignty. Rulers of states on the fringes of the world, who were beyond the world-ruler's control *de facto*, were under his suzerainty *de jure* according to this East Roman and this Chinese pretension. The East Roman Emperors based their overweening claim on the fact that their seat of government was 'the New Rome', Constantinople; and this doctrine led the East Roman Empire's neighbours to covet the possession of a city that was held to confer the title to world-dominion on its occupant. In 913, Khan Symeon of Bulgaria came within an ace of installing himself in Constantinople as Emperor of the Romans and the Bulgars,[18] and in the fourteenth century, when the East Roman Empire was already *in extremis*, the prize that had eluded the Bulgar Khan Symeon's grasp might have been seized by the Nemanyid Serb empire-builder Stephen Dushan, but for the accident of his premature death.

A century later, in 1453, Constantinople fell to the Ottoman Padishah, Mehmet II 'the Conqueror'. By that date, East Roman Constantinople was only a tiny unengulfed enclave in the vast Empire, stretching to the Danube and to the Taurus, that Mehmet II's predecessors had conquered; yet Mehmet II has been styled 'the Conqueror' *par excellence* because he and his fellow 'Osmanlis accepted the East Roman doctrine that an emperor who ruled from Constantinople was juridically the sovereign of the whole world, and therefore the acquisition of Constantinople counted for more, in their estimation, than the subjugation of the city's broad European and Asian hinterlands.[19] Thenceforward, non-Ottoman Muslims called the Ottoman Padishah the *Qaysar-i-Rum*, among other titles, and they called the 'Osmanlis 'Rumis'. The survival of the Roman Empire in its East Roman avatar – an Orthodox Christian Greek Roman Empire – has been touched upon in an earlier chapter,[20] and we have also seen[21] how the Phanariot Greek subjects of the Ottoman Empire were betrayed by the 'great idea' of a resuscitated Greek Roman Empire into forfeiting their prospects of becoming partners of the Ottoman Turks in the government of the Turkish Roman Empire. This Turkish Roman Empire survived for a century after the fiasco of the Phanariot Greek Prince Alexander Ypsilandes's invasion of Moldavia in 1821. The last Ottoman Turkish Roman Emperor was deposed in 1922 by the Turks themselves, 116 years after the demise, in the West, of the Roman Empire that had been resuscitated here by Charlemagne.

The East Roman Emperors' claim to worldwide sovereignty had been linked with their fidelity to Christian Orthodoxy, and both of these East Roman pretensions were taken up in Russia – an Orthodox Christian country in which the local church was under the ecclesiastical jurisdiction of the Ecumenical Patriarch of Constantinople till 1589, when an autocephalous Patriarchate of Moscow was created with the blessing of the four older and senior Orthodox Patriarchates. The Grand Duke of Moscow and his subjects repudiated the Greek Metropolitan of Moscow Isidore's signature, at Florence in 1439, of the Act of Union, recognizing the Pope's supremacy (not merely

204 THE CONQUEROR, Sultan Mehmet II. Though his predecessors had already overrun most of the Christian East Roman Empire before Constantinople fell in 1453, it was Mehmet who was remembered by his fellow 'Osmanlis and fellow Muslims as the 'Conqueror' for capturing the Empire's seat of sovereignty, carrying with it the title to world dominion.

primacy) over the whole Church, which had also been signed by the East Roman Emperor John VIII Palaeologus and by the Ecumenical Patriarch, who was the Metropolitan of Moscow's ecclesiastical superior.[22] In 1460 the Metropolitan of Moscow – now a Russian, and no longer a Greek – declared that the fall of Constantinople in 1453 had been God's punishment of the Greeks' betrayal of Orthodoxy at Florence.[23]

The Union of Florence had also been repudiated by the Patriarchs of Alexandria, Antioch, and Jerusalem, and by some eminent clerical subjects of the East Roman Empire itself, including George Scholarius, who, as Gennadius I, became the first of the Ecumenical Patriarchs of Constantinople under the Ottoman régime. However, the Russians' rejection of the Union of Florence was far more important, because from 1439 to 1484, when the Union of Florence was repudiated at an ecumenical council held in Constantinople, at which all four Eastern Patriarchs were represented,[24] the Grand Duchy of Moscow was the only politically independent Orthodox Christian state of any importance[25] that had not compromised itself with Rome, and Muscovy continued to be the only independent Orthodox Christian state until the achievement of independence by the South-East European Orthodox Christian successor-states of the Ottoman Empire in the course of the nineteenth century.

In rejecting the ecclesiastical supremacy of the Papacy and proclaiming the Russian Church's unwavering fidelity to Orthodoxy, the Muscovite government, the Russian ecclesiastical authorities, and the Russian people were unanimous. But the government demurred to the findings of a Russian ecclesiastical synod, convened in 1551, which declared that the Russians were more orthodox than the Greeks,[26] and the government also did not endorse the thesis, propounded by some Orthodox clerics, that Muscovy was the defunct East Roman Empire's heir and that consequently Muscovy had inherited the Empire's title to universal dominion.[27]

In 1492 the Metropolitan of Moscow, Zosimus, called the Grand Duke Ivan III (*imperabat* AD 1462–1505) 'the new Constantine', and Moscow 'the new Constantinople'. This belief was given its classic formulation by an elder of a monastery in Pskov, Philotheus, in an epistle addressed to the Grand Duke Basil III (*imperabat* AD 1505–33).

The Church of old Rome fell [because of] its heresy; the gates of the second Rome, Constantinople, were hewn down by the axes of the infidel Turks; but the Church of Moscow, the Church of the new Rome, shines brighter than the sun in the whole universe. Thou art the one universal sovereign of all Christian folk, thou shouldst hold the reins in awe of God; fear him who hath committed them to thee. Two Romes are fallen, but the third stands fast; a fourth there cannot be. Thy Christian kingdom shall not be given to another.[28]

Two generations later, a paraphrase of this famous passage was written into the installation charter of the first Patriarch of Moscow over the signature of his creator the Ecumenical Patriarch Jeremiah:

Because the old Rome has collapsed on account of the heresy of Apollinarius, and because the second Rome, which is Constantinople, is now in [the] possession of the godless Turks, thy great kingdom, O pious Tsar, is the third Rome. It surpasses in devotion every other, and all Christian kingdoms are now merged in thy realm. Thou art the only Christian sovereign in the World, the master of all faithful Christians.[29]

The Orthodox Christian clerics who made these declarations were trying, officiously, to drape round the shoulders of the political sovereign of the Muscovite state the mantle that, in 1453, had fallen from the shoulders of the last East Roman Emperor; but the Muscovite sovereign shrugged off this piece of finery as if it were a shirt of Nessus; and, indeed, if he had allowed himself to be invested with it, this would have impeded him in the pursuit of his own political objective. It was not the Muscovite government's political ambition to contest the accomplished fact of the 'Osmanlis' conquest of Constantinople; Muscovy's ambition was to reunify Russia politically in a Russian universal state under Muscovite rule.

In the eleventh century the original Russian principality of Kiev had broken up into a number of fragments. In the thirteenth century the westernmost appanage of the Mongol Empire, the Golden Horde, had subjected most of these fragments of Russia to its suzerainty. In the fourteenth and fifteenth centuries, vast tracts of Western Russia, including Kiev itself, had been annexed by Poland and Lithuania. Muscovy's objective was to unite all other surviving Russian states under its own rule, to shake off the suzerainty of the Golden Horde, and to recover the Russian territories that had been annexed by Russia's Western neighbours.

The decisive step in Muscovy's reunification of Russia was its annexation, between 1471 and 1479, of the Republic of Novgorod – a Russian state that had maintained its independence as against both the Golden Horde and Lithuania, and that had expanded its dominions to the shores of the White Sea and to the far side of the Ural mountains. Ivan III, the Grand Duke of Moscow who had succeeded in annexing Novgorod, went on, in 1480, to repudiate the Golden Horde's suzerainty and to proclaim his own independence under the title of autocrat. Ivan III's second successor, Ivan IV the Terrible (*imperabat* AD 1533–84), had himself crowned Emperor in 1547. The recovery of the Russian territories that had been annexed by Poland and Lithuania did not begin till 1667 and was not completed till 1945, twenty-eight years after the Russian Tsardom had been liquidated. In 1945, the Soviet Union reannexed the White Russian and Ukrainian territories that had been held by Poland between the two World Wars, as well as Carpatho-Ruthenia, a strip of ex-Hungarian territory, south-west of the Carpathians, whose inhabitants are Ukrainians.

This Muscovite objective of reunifying 'all the Russias' – Great Russia, White Russia, the Ukraine – was pursued persistently from the fifteenth century onwards. As Obolensky puts it,[30] 'Moscow the Second Kiev', not 'Moscow the Third Rome', was the hallmark of the Muscovite government's foreign policy.

The Muscovite government did seek to establish a Russian universal state that would reunite 'all the Russias' under Muscovite rule, and eventually it attained this objective; but the Muscovite government did not allow the Orthodox Church to saddle it with the defunct East Roman Empire's pretensions to worldwide dominion.

Indeed, the Muscovite government went out of its way to assure its Western neighbours that it did not entertain any such ambition. In 1576, Tsar Ivan IV instructed his ambassadors to the court of the Habsburg Western 'Roman Emperor' to explain that his claim to the title 'Tsar' was based on the fact that he had conquered the 'tsardoms' of Kazan and Astrakhan,[31] which were successor-states of the Golden Horde in the Volga basin. In 1582 Ivan IV declared to the Papal Envoy: 'We do not want the realm of the whole Universe.'[32] This was an explicit repudiation of the role that had been pressed upon the Muscovite government by the Orthodox Church. Ivan IV was declaring that he was not reviving, for his own Empire, the defunct East Roman government's claim to world-dominion on the score of being the Roman Empire's sole legitimate heir – a claim that, in the Middle Ages, had led repeatedly to altercations between the Constantinopolitan Emperors and the predecessors of the Habsburg *Caesarea Majestas*.

Modern Russia did not head towards Constantinople till the reign of Peter the Great, and Peter, when he took Azov and then lost it through his disastrous invasion of Moldavia, was not seeking to replace the Ottoman by a Russian Roman Empire. Peter's objective was not ideological; it was practical. He was seeking to open windows on the sea for his land-locked dominions. At Peter's accession, the Black Sea was an Ottoman lake and the Baltic was a Swedish lake, in consequence of Ivan IV's loss, in the disastrous war of 1558–83, of the narrow sea-board, at the head of the Gulf of Finland, that Muscovy had inherited from the Republic of Novgorod. Peter's motive, like Ivan IV's – and also like Alexander II's, when he annexed the site of Vladivostok in 1858 – was to acquire an ice-free port.

Whether or not we may question the verdict that Eastern Orthodox Christianity is a spent force in modern Russian life, it seems to be indisputable that the Russians were not deceived by the mirage of a Roman world-empire; but it also looks as if this Russian clear-sightedness has been exceptional. The Roman mirage did beguile the Byzantine and Phanariot Greeks, the Bulgar and Serb Slavs, and the Ottoman Turks, and we have seen that the Roman Empire is not the only universal state that has had this posthumous hypnotic effect. On the whole, the evidence that we have mustered would seem to support our original contention that the belief in the immortality of universal states survives for centuries and millennia after it has been decisively confuted by plain hard facts. What are the causes of this strange phenomenon?

One obvious cause is the potency of the personal impression made by the founders of universal states and by their immediate successors – an impression that tends to be exaggerated to legendary proportions with the passage of time. Nowhere is this truth better illustrated than in the official worship of the founder of the *Pax Augusta*, and in the veneration and posthumous deification of his successors. To Augustus were addressed eulogies couched in outright religious language:

[The Most Divine Caesar] has re-established a Universe that had everywhere been in disintegration and had degenerated into a lamentable state. He has put a new face on the whole cosmos – a cosmos that would have been only too happy to pass out of

205 Deified empire-builder: Augustus, the first Emperor of Rome. The feat of bringing peace to a war-torn society confers legendary fame on the founder of a universal state; in retrospect the achievement seems godlike, and the emperor divine.

206 Darius of Persia, appointed 'lord of all men from sunrise to sunset' by the god Ahuramazda, receives his vizier in audience; the incense-burners before him indicate the divine
protection he was believed to enjoy: relief from Persepolis.

existence if, at the critical moment, Caesar had not been born to
be the Universe's universal blessing. . . . The providence that
has organized every detail of human life has exerted and
surpassed itself in order to bring life to perfection in producing
Augustus – whom it has filled with virtue to be the benefactor
of Mankind, sending him to us and to posterity as a saviour
whose mission has been to put an end to war and to set the
Universe in order.[33]

Within a century the logic of divinization had been
accepted.

[Gaius Caligula] was audacious enough to act on assumptions
that were everywhere current about his literal 'God-head'. This
was too much for Roman stomachs at such an early date. But
they were soon to become accustomed to the idea. With Domitian, only forty years later, it had become a convention of polite
speech to hail the emperor as *dominus et deus*, 'my Lord and God'.
In the following century, even constitutionally minded princes
like Trajan had no hesitation in accepting these forms of
address.[34]

Another cause of the persistence of the belief in the
immortality of universal states is the impressiveness of the
institution itself, as distinct from the prestige of the
successive rulers who are its living incarnation. A universal
state captivates hearts and minds because it symbolizes a
recovery from the long-lasting misery of a time of troubles.
It was this aspect of the Roman Empire that eventually won
the respect of originally hostile Greek writers.

There is no salvation in the exercise of a dominion divorced
from power. To find oneself under the dominion of one's
superiors is a 'second best' alternative; but this 'second best'

proved to be the best of all in our present experience of a Roman
Empire. This happy experience has moved the whole world to
cleave to Rome with might and main. The world would no more
think of seceding from Rome than a ship's crew would think of
parting company with the pilot. You must have seen bats in a
cave clinging tight to one another and to the rocks; and this is
an apt image of the whole world's dependence on Rome. In
every heart today the focus of anxiety is the fear of becoming
detached from the cluster. The thought of being abandoned by
Rome is so appalling that it precludes any thought of wantonly
abandoning her.

There is an end of those disputes over sovereignty and
prestige which were the causes of the outbreak of all the wars of
the past; and, while some of the nations, like noiselessly flowing
water, are delightfully quiet – rejoicing in their release from toil
and trouble, and aware at last that all their old struggles were to
no purpose – there are other nations which do not even know
or remember whether they once sat in the seat of power. In
fact we are witnessing a new version of the Pamphylian's myth
(or is it Plato's own?). At a moment when the states of the world
were already laid out on the funeral-pyre as the victims of their
own fratricidal strife and turmoil, they were all at once presented
with the [Roman] dominion and straightway came to life again.
How they arrived at this condition, they are unable to say. They
know nothing about it, and can only marvel at their present
well-being. They are like sleepers awakened who have come to
themselves and now dismiss from their thoughts the dreams that
obsessed them only a moment ago. They no longer find it
credible that there were ever such things as wars; and, when the
word 'war' is mentioned today, it has a mythical sound in most
people's ears. . . .

The entire inhabited world now keeps perpetual holiday. It
has laid aside the steel which it used to wear of old and has

274

turned, care-free, to festivities and enjoyment of all kinds. All other rivalries have died out, and one form of competition alone now preoccupies all the cities – a competition in making the finest show of beauty and amenity. The whole world is now full of gymnasiums, fountains, gateways, temples, workshops, academies; and it is now possible to say with scientific certainty that a world which was in its death-agonies has made a recovery and gained a new lease of life. . . . The whole Earth has been laid out like a pleasure-park. The smoke of burning villages and the watch-fires (lit by friend or foeman) have vanished beyond the horizon, as though some mighty wind had winnowed them away, and their place has been taken by an innumerable multitude and variety of enchanting shows and sports. . . . So that the only people who still need pity for the good things that they are missing are those outside your Empire – if there are any such people left. . . .[35]

If there are any, they are hardly worth speaking of in the estimation of those inside, and this is another reason why the belief in their immortality that universal states inspire is so blindly persistent. Universal states are the supreme expression, on the political plane, of a sense of unity which is one of the psychological products of the process of disintegration.[36] During the time of troubles which disintegrating civilizations undergo, the yearning for unity grows ever stronger as the reality of it vanishes; and when, at the lowest ebb of hope, the long-pursued goal is at last unexpectedly attained, the psychological effect is overwhelming.

Ahuramazda, the creator of Heaven and Earth, has made the King of the Persians 'ruler, far and wide, over this great Earth' – made 'him, the one [lord], to be ruler over many'; made him 'king over many lands and tongues', 'over the mountains and plains this side of the Sea and beyond it' [Babylonian Inscription H]. He can style himself 'the lord of all men from sunrise to sunset' [Aeschines, iii. 132]. All the peoples whose representatives are portrayed on the seat of his throne render him obedience, bring him tribute and serve in his armed forces.[37]

The sense of unity and universality that is here applied to the Achaemenian Empire is also taken up by the Greek Aelius Aristeides in his eulogy of Rome, in which he makes a point of the universality of her rule as well as of the new lease of life which she has brought to a lacerated Hellenic Society.

Of this city of Rome you could not say either that it was left unfortified with a Lacedaemonian bravado or that it was enclosed in fortifications of a Babylonian magnificence. . . . You have not, however, you Romans, neglected to build walls; only you have run them round your Empire and not round your city. You have placed them in the uttermost parts of the Earth; yet they are magnificent walls which are worthy of you and are a sight for the eyes of all who live within their shelter – though it would take an intending sightseer months or even years to reach them if Rome itself were the starting-point of his journey; for you have pushed your way beyond the outermost circuit of the inhabited world and there, in no-man's-land, you have drawn a second circuit with a more convenient *tracé* which is easier to defend – for all the world as if you were simply fortifying a city. . . . This circuit is utterly impregnable and indestructible at every point; it outshines all others; and no system of fortifications that was ever constructed before bears any resemblance to it.[38]

In this passage, a literary contemporary of Marcus Aurelius, in whose anxious reign Rome's magnificent

world-wall was beginning to crack, was re-expounding the theme of a writer of the previous generation, in whose day the world's defences did indeed look impregnably secure. During the last two centuries, says Appian of Alexandria (*vivebat c.* AD 90–160) in the preface to his *Studies in Roman History*,

the [Roman] state has reached its highest point of organization and the public revenue its highest figure, while a long and stable peace has raised the whole world to a level of secure prosperity. A few more subject nations have been added by the emperors to those already under the Roman dominion, and others which have revolted have been reduced to obedience; but, since the Romans already possess the choicest portions of the land and water surface of the globe, they are wise enough to aim at retaining what they hold rather than at extending their Empire to infinity over the poverty-stricken and unremunerative territories of uncivilized nations. I myself have seen representatives of such nations attending at Rome on diplomatic missions and offering to become her subjects, and the Emperor refusing to accept the allegiance of peoples who would be of no value to his government. There are other nations innumerable whose kings the Romans appoint themselves, since they feel no necessity to incorporate them in their Empire. There are also certain subject nations to whom they make grants from their treasury, because they are too proud to repudiate them in spite of their being a financial burden. They have garrisoned the frontiers of their Empire with a ring of powerful armies, and keep guard over this vast extent of land and sea as easily as if it were a modest farm.[39]

In the view of Appian and Aelius Aristeides, the Roman Empire was eternal

just as the sum total of things is eternal, because there is no room, outside it, for its components to fly apart, and there are no extraneous bodies that can collide with it and disintegrate it with a mighty blow.[40]

In these lines of the Roman poet Lucretius, his teacher Democritus's argument looks as impregnable as the Roman *limes* itself.

Nor is there any force that can modify the sum of things. There is no space outside into which any kind of matter can escape out of the totality. Nor is there any space outside from which some new force can arise, break in, transform the whole nature of things, and deflect its motions.[41]

A universal state has indeed as little to fear from outer barbarians as the Universe has from stray star clusters that are *ex hypothesi* non-existent; yet the argument is a fallacy nevertheless, for, as we have seen in an earlier context, 'things rot through evils native to their selves'.[42] In physical Nature there are elements whose atoms disintegrate by spontaneous radioactivity without requiring any bombardment from extraneous particles; and, in human social life, universal states 'are betray'd by what is false within'[43] into revealing, for those who have eyes to see through their specious appearance of impregnability, that, so far from being immortal, these are spontaneously fissile polities.

However long the life of a universal state may be drawn out, it always proves to have been the last phase of a society before its extinction. Its goal is the achievement of immortality, but the attempt to secure immortality in this world is a vain effort, whether blind or deliberate, to thwart the economy of Nature.

207 Britain

208 Argentorate

209 Pannonia

210 Dalmatia

211 Scythia

212 Thebaid

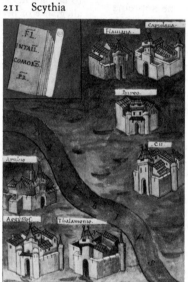

THE WALLS OF EMPIRE

Maps of some of Rome's principal frontier provinces make a composite picture of the vast extent of the Empire. The originals of these fifteenth-century versions came from a lost series of documents, once owned by a fourth- or fifth-century Roman official in Gaul.

There is always innovation to which the old order gives way, and one thing always has to be repaired at other things' cost. There is a perpetual need for raw material to provide for the growth of later ages. These in turn will all follow you when they too have run their course of life. As surely as you, the ages have perished in the past and will continue to perish in the future. This is the law of the Universe. One thing will always be arising out of another. Life is given to none of us in freehold; we all hold it only in usufruct.[44]

How can an institution which is thus dedicated to the pursuit of a mirage be the ultimate goal of human endeavours, even though its citizens persistently mistake the illusion of Gilead for the reality of the Promised Land? On this showing, we must reject the notion that universal states are ends in themselves. On the other hand, we have yet to discover whether they may have some significance as a means for the performance of services in spite of themselves. Certainly the dominant minorities whose handiwork

the universal states are do not enter upon this labour as altruists; on the contrary, their conscious motive is a selfish desire to preserve themselves by conserving the wasting energies of a society with whose fortunes their own are bound up, and their deliberate intention in establishing a universal state is to use it as a means to this self-regarding end. But, although this intention can never be realized, the work devoted to it may yet redound to the benefit of a third party, and thus a universal state may have at least the opportunity of sharing indirectly in a fresh act of creation. The beneficiaries must be one or other of the three groups with which a universal state's establishment comes into contact, namely the internal proletariat or external proletariat of the moribund society itself, or the members of some alien civilization which is its contemporary. Let us now turn to the services which are offered involuntarily by universal states, and look at the uses which may be made of these facilities by each of the potential beneficiaries.

276

33 The boons of conductivity and peace

OUR FIRST PROBLEM is to find out how it is possible for any services at all to be rendered to anyone by an institution that is passive, conservative, archaistic, and in fact negative in every respect.

The world empire of Rome was a negative phenomenon: the result, not of any surplus of power on the one side (the Romans ceased to enjoy that after [their victory at] Zama), but of an absence of resistance on the other side. It would be quite untrue to say that the Romans conquered the world. They merely took possession of something that was lying about for anyone to pick up. The Roman Empire was brought into existence, not by an extreme exertion of Rome's total military and financial energies, as these had once been exerted against Carthage, but through a renunciation, by the contemporary Oriental World, of the externals of self-determination. . . . The petrified remains of imperialism are to be seen in empires like the Egyptian, the Chinese, and the Roman, and in societies like the Indian World and the World of Islam, which remain in existence for hundreds and thousands of years and may pass from one conqueror's hand to another's: dead bodies, shapeless masses of humanity from which the soul has departed, the used-up material of a great historical past. The imperialism that leaves such débris is the typical symptom of social dissolution.[1]

A situation as unpromising as this would hardly seem likely to give rise to any new burst of creative activity. It is easy to see, of course, that if once a seed of creative energy has been planted in a universal state it will have a better chance of coming to fruition than it would have in the choking circumstances of the preceding time of troubles, for a universal state offers a temporary respite from the downward course of a broken-down society towards dissolution. This, however, is a wholly negative service. It does not account for the positive source of that reborn capacity for creativeness which seems to be the supreme benefit that can be conferred by a universal state on its beneficiaries, though it is apparently unable to profit by it for itself. Perhaps one clue is to be found in the tendency shown by dominant minorities in universal states to defeat their own ultra-conservatism by being inveigled into constructive and innovatory work. A universal state is pushed into constructive work primarily, no doubt, by the impulse, which operates in every state, to work for its own self-preservation as an independent polity and to do whatever may be necessary for this purpose. But, strong though this impulse may be, it can hardly be the predominant one; for a universal state is not subject to the pressure of rivals which is so potent a stimulus in the struggle for existence among contending parochial states. The establishment of a universal state brings with it an abrupt transition from internecine warfare to profound peace, since it comes into being through a 'knock-out blow' by which a single parochial state wipes all its competitors off the map and so emerges from battle as the sole survivor. A universal state is *ex hypothesi* unique within its own world, and the pressure of this uniqueness works together with the *vis inertiae* of an exhausted society to keep a universal state in being when once it has been established. Thus, to begin with at least, a

THE FRUITS OF PEACE

213 Rome at rest: scenes of daily life on the estates of a Roman landowner in fourth-century Tunisia. In the upper part, farming; centre, travel; and beneath, produce and accounts are delivered to the lady of the manor.

universal state has little cause to be concerned about its own security, since there is nothing left to threaten it.

On the other hand, there is a strong motive for action in the need to conserve, not a state that is universal in virtue of having no surviving competitors, but the society itself that has been unified politically in the universal state. The need for this form of internal conservation is all the more conducive to some degree of constructive action because the social institutions inherited by the universal state will almost certainly have been badly battered during the anarchy of the preceding time of troubles. It is the menace of this immense and constantly expanding social vacuum that compels the government of the universal state to act against its inclinations by constructing stop-gap institutions to fill the void, as the only means open to it of conserving the society itself – the fundamental task that is such a state's *raison d'être*.

A classic illustration of this necessity of stepping ever further into an ever-widening breach is afforded by the administrative history of the Roman Empire during the two centuries following its establishment after the battle of Actium in 31 BC. The secret of Roman government was the principle of indirect rule. The Hellenic universal state was conceived of by its Roman founders as an association of self-governing city-states with a fringe of autonomous principalities in the regions where the Hellenic culture had not yet struck political root. The burden of administration – which, even at the end of the Hellenic time of troubles, was still publicly regarded as an honourable and covetable load – was to be left resting on the shoulders of these responsible self-governing local authorities; the imperial government was to confine itself to the twofold task of keeping the local communities in harmony with one another and protecting them against attacks from the outer barbarians; and, for these limited imperial activities, a slender military framework and a light political super-structure were all that was required. This fundamental policy was never deliberately revised; yet, if we look again at the Roman Empire as it emerged from a spell of two centuries of Roman Peace, we shall find that its administrative structure had in fact been transformed as a result of innovations that were reluctant and piecemeal, but were far-reaching in their cumulative effect because they were all in the same direction.

By the end of the reign of Marcus Aurelius (*imperabat* AD 161–80), the last of the client principalities had been *gleichgeschaltet* with the provinces, and, more significant still, the provinces themselves had become organs of direct administration instead of remaining mere frameworks for local groups of self-administering city-states. The cause of these far-going moves towards a centralization of world-government was not any desire on the part of the imperial authorities to take over the responsibilities for details; it was a progressive loss of efficiency on the part of the local authorities that forced the imperial government to step in. In the generation of Augustus the government provided by client princes of the stamp of Herod the Great had in general been as effective as it had been ruthless. Among other things, it had been observed that these had been more active than the Roman governors of adjoining provinces in defending their territories against the raids of pirates from

beyond the pale. The city-states, again, whatever their juridical status, had been most successful in still finding sufficient numbers of citizens of sufficient public spirit, integrity, ability, and affluence to administer their affairs without remuneration and to consider themselves richly rewarded by the honour and prestige which local office still carried with it. In the course of the next two centuries, however, the human resources for the conduct of local government gradually ran dry, and the central government, faced with this increasing dearth of the local administrative talent on which it had been accustomed to rely, found itself constrained not only to replace client-princes with imperial governors but to put the administration of the city-states in the hands of 'city managers' who were appointed by the imperial authorities instead of being elected (as the city-state magistrates were) by the local notables, and who were indirectly responsible to the Emperor himself.

In the second century of the Empire's existence, at the very opening of a delusive Indian summer, we can follow the progress of this disquieting administrative development in the famous correspondence between the Emperor Trajan (*imperabat* AD 98–117) and his friend and subordinate Pliny the Younger during the latter's term of service as governor of the province of Bithynia. Before the end of the story, the whole administration of the Roman Empire, from top to bottom, had passed into the hands of a hierarchically organized bureaucracy, while the self-complacent local magistrates and town councillors of the once self-governing city-states had been degraded into becoming the unwilling instruments of the central exchequer for extracting ruinously heavy taxes from the local notables.

The central authorities themselves had been no more eager to impose these changes than the local authorities had been to suffer them. Both alike had been victims of *force majeure*; but, in yielding to such necessity, the government of a universal state is simply defeating its own ends, since the new institutions which it reluctantly constructs with a conservative intention cannot help having an innovatory effect. The consequences are revolutionary because these institutions are highly 'conductive'. The specific effects of a centralization of administration are reinforced by the fact that the empire-builders themselves tend to be unusually receptive of new ideas, notwithstanding the innate conservatism of their intentions; and this undesired and unvalued characteristic of theirs is likely to have been one of the causes of their victory in their life-and-death struggle, during a time of troubles, with their rival competitors for the prize of survival as masters of a universal state. This distinguishing feature of the age endows the new stop-gap institutions thrown up by a universal state with a conductivity comparable to that conferred by physical Nature on the ocean and the steppe.

As the surface of the Earth bears all Mankind, so Rome receives all the peoples of the Earth into her bosom, as the rivers are received by the sea.[2]

The social movements that make their way through the conductive medium of a universal state are both horizontal and vertical. Examples of horizontal motion are the circulation of medicinal herbs in the Roman Empire and the spread of the use of paper from the eastern to the

Thistle

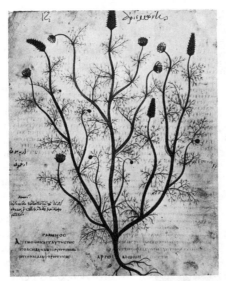

215 Agrimony

216 Poppy

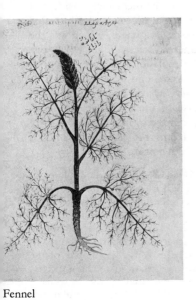

Fennel

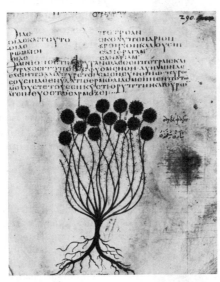

218 Saxifrage

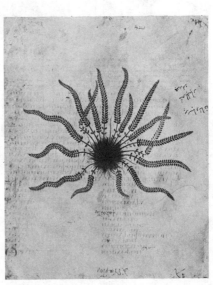

219 Maidenhair

Campion

221 Pumpkin

GEOGRAPHICAL MOBILITY
'Different herbs are brought
to and fro over all the world
for the welfare of the human
race': plants known in the
Roman Empire, from a sixth-
century East Roman
manuscript. The unification of
many nations in one empire
encourages 'horizontal conductivity': peace and the
absence of internal frontiers
permit the free circulation
of ideas and discoveries.

western extremity of the Arab Caliphate. Pliny the Elder reported that

different herbs are brought from different quarters to and fro over all the world for the welfare of the human race. The immense majesty of the Roman Peace reveals to one another not merely human beings, in all their diversity of countries and nationalities, but also the mountains and the ranges that tower up into the clouds, with their flora and fauna. God grant that this divine benefaction may be eternal. The gift bestowed by the Romans on Mankind can be described only as a new form of light.[3]

As for the transit of the Chinese invention of paper across the conductive expanse of the Arab Caliphate, this was impressively rapid. Reaching Samarqand from China in AD 751, the use of paper had spread to Baghdad by 793, to Cairo by 900, to Fez – almost within sight of the Atlantic – by about 1100, and to Jativa in the Iberian peninsula by 1150.

The vertical movements are sometimes more elusive, but often more important in their social effects – as is illustrated by the history of the Tokugawa Shogunate, which was the universal state of the Japanese Society. The Tokugawa régime set itself to insulate Japan from the rest of the world, and was successful for nearly two and a half centuries in maintaining this political *tour de force*; but it found itself powerless to arrest the course of social change within an insulated Japanese Empire, in spite of its efforts to petrify a feudal system, inherited from the preceding time of troubles, into a permanent dispensation.

It was not fear of foreign conquest that led the Tokugawa government to close Japan, but rather a lack of confidence in its own position *vis à vis* dissatisfied elements in the state, notably the *tozama daimyo* [feudal lords of outlying territories] and the *ronin* [masterless warriors]. . . . The Tokugawa Shogunate erected a complicated but very effective structure of control to forestall any possibility of internal revolt. . . . In spite of the Tokugawa determination to preserve a static hierarchical society, very important changes, mostly undesired by the shogunate, were taking place within this society [during the eighteenth century]. Their origin was the spread of money in an economy that was organized from above on the basis of a rice economy. . . . By the early years of the eighteenth century the warriors of Japan, *daimyo* and retainers alike, were in debt to the merchant class. . . . In the course of time some of the more powerful brokers and money-lenders became in effect bankers to the great feudatories. . . . The rise and florescence of this capitalist class was not really compatible with the continued existence of a feudal society.[4]

If we take the year 1590 of the Christian Era, in which Hideyoshi overcame the last resistance to his dictatorship, as the date of the foundation of the Japanese universal state, we find that little more than a century had elapsed before the rising of the lower layers of water from the depths to the surface had transformed a society which Hideyoshi's successor Tokugawa Ieyasu and his heirs had sought to freeze into an almost Platonically utopian immobility. This social upheaval was a result of the operation of internal forces within a closed system, without any impulsion from outside the frontiers of the Japanese universal state. Moreover, for a universal state the Tokugawa Shogunate was culturally homogeneous to an

222 SOCIAL MOBILITY Japanese merchant, from a sixteenth-century print. The government was trying at this time to insulate the Japanese Society from change; but the merchant class, by emphasizing and exploiting its status in Japan's expanding economy, helped to revolutionize this artificially arrested society within a century.

unusually high degree, since, apart from the strictly segregated Dutch trading community at Deshima, the only heterogeneous element in the otherwise uniform society was the socially impotent barbarian Ainu strain in the north. In view of this absence of internal cultural tensions, the effects of the social revolution – achieved against all the efforts of the régime – are doubly impressive.

No other universal state appears to have enjoyed the same degree of cultural homogeneity. The standard pattern seems rather to be a culturally tripartite structure, in which the cultural domain of the civilization from which the universal state has arisen is flanked by culturally alien territories annexed at the expense of both barbarians and neighbouring civilizations. For example, in the Mauryan Empire, which was the original Indic universal state, an Indic cultural core was flanked by an alien province in the Panjab, which had been subjected to both Syriac and barbarian influences; in its other quarters the Empire's Indic core was flanked by ex-barbarian provinces in Southern India and possibly further afield in Ceylon and Khotan as well. The Guptan Empire, in which the Mauryan was eventually reintegrated, possessed an ex-barbarian fringe with an alien Hellenic tincture in Gujerat and the North-West Deccan, and a Hellenized fringe with a Kushan barbarian dilution in the territories under its suzerainty in the Panjab. The Han and Roman Empires also conformed to this pattern.

There are other cases in which this standard cultural pattern has been enriched by some additional element. In the Muscovite Tsardom, a Russian Orthodox Christian core was flanked by a vast ex-barbarian annex extending northwards to the Arctic Ocean and eastwards towards the Pacific, and by a Muslim annex in the Volga basin, the Urals, and Western Siberia. But this pattern was subsequently complicated by Peter the Great's deliberate substitution of a Westernized for a traditional Orthodox Christian cultural framework for the Russian universal state, and by the later annexation of additional alien territories from both the Islamic World in the south and the Western Christian World in the west.

In the Achaemenian Empire, there was an antecedent cultural diversity, within the Syriac core itself, between the Syrian creators of the Syriac Civilization and their Iranian converts, and a geographical gap between Syria and Iran that was still occupied by the dwindling domain of the gradually disappearing Sumero-Akkadian culture. The Achaemenian Empire also embraced the domain of the submerged Hittite culture in Eastern Anatolia, the best part of the domain of the Egyptiac Civilization, fringes torn from the Hellenic and Indic Worlds, and pockets of partially reclaimed barbarian highlanders and Eurasian Nomads. Moreover, after its life had been cut short by Alexander the Great, its work was carried on by his political successors, and especially by the Seleucids, whom it would be more illuminating to describe as alien Hellenic successors of Cyrus and Darius. In the Arab Caliphate, in which the Achaemenian Empire was eventually reintegrated, the Syriac core – in which the earlier diversity between Syrian creators and Iranian converts had been replaced by a cleavage, along approximately the same geographical line, between ex-subjects of the Roman and

ex-subjects of the Sasanian Empire – was united politically, by Arab barbarian empire-builders, with barbarian annexes – in North-West Africa, in the fastnesses of Daylam and Tabaristan, and on the steppe adjoining the Oxus-Jaxartes basin – and with fragments of alien civilizations: a slice of the Indic World in Sind and Multan; the potential domain of an abortive Far Eastern Christian Civilization in the Oxus-Jaxartes basin; a Monophysite Christian majority in Armenia; an Orthodox Christian diasporá among the Monophysite Christian majority in Syria and Egypt; and a fossil of the otherwise extinct Sumero-Akkadian Society at Harran.

A similarly complex picture could be drawn of the Mongol, the Manchu, and the Ottoman Empires, and an only marginally less complex one of the Mughal and the Sumero-Akkadian Empires. It seems, then, that a high degree of diversity is to be expected in the cultural composition of universal states; and, in the light of this fact, it is evident that one effect of the conductivity of universal states is to carry further, by less violent and brutal means, that process of cultural *pammixia* that is started in the aggressive anarchy of the antecedent times of troubles. The refugees, exiles, deportees, transported slaves, and other *déracinés* of that cruel age are followed up, under the milder dispensation of a universal state, by merchants, by professional soldiers, and by philosophic and religious missionaries and pilgrims.

Judgments passed on the effects of this *pammixia* diverge, poles apart, according to the respective social, political, and historical standpoints of the observers who make them. A grandchild of those European Greeks whose heroic resistance had barely saved them from being incorporated, at the height of their own civilization's growth, in the world-empire of the Achaemenidae, could write of 'the appalling present condition of the populations under the Persian yoke, which have been quite disintegrated by being interlarded and kneaded up together.'[5] Another Greek, born more than five hundred years later into the Indian summer of an Hellenic universal state which he could readily appreciate because of the anarchy that had preceded its foundation, could say to Rome, as the highest praise he could give her: 'You have made one single household of the entire inhabited world';[6] and a Gallic poet, writing more than two hundred years later again, at a moment when the Roman Empire in the West had already received its death-blow, could echo this sentiment in the famous epigram: *Urbem fecisti quod prius Orbis erat.*[7] On this controversial question of the value of the result, points of view may differ completely; but there is no disputing the facts themselves, however divergent the attitudes of the writers who present them. Pliny, writing in the first century of the Roman Peace of Roman Italy and of the world empire that she had built up around herself, gave an account that is true, in some degree, of every universal state.

I am not unaware that it may be justly regarded as the lapse of an insensitive and lazy mind to have given so brief and cursory a description of a country that is the nurse of all countries – their nurse and their parent and the chosen vessel of divine grace for the mission of making the skies themselves clearer, gathering the scattered realms into one flock, softening harsh traditional practices, bringing together into mutual converse, through a common medium of linguistic exchange, the discordant and

IMPERIAL MISSION FIELDS
Universal states open up vast new territories for missionary work; their rulers' commitment to peace ensures at first that religious activity is tolerated.

223 Qubilay Khan, Mongol Emperor from 1257 to 1294. Qubilay's Empire stretched from China to the Black Sea, and under his rule these enormous territories enjoyed an unprecedented era of peace and order. Although shamanism was the traditional Mongol religion, Qubilay gave official tolerance to Buddhism, Taoism, Nestorian Christianity, Islam, Confucianism, Manichaeism, and Judaism. His special interest in Buddhism allowed it to win a place in Mongol life that outlasted the expulsion of the Mongols from China in 1368, while during his reign Christians from the West were able to penetrate Central Asia, and Nestorian missions were sent to Baghdad and Europe.

barbarous tongues of innumerable peoples, conferring humanity on Man, and, in a word, becoming the single fatherland of all nations throughout the world.[8]

An indispensable condition for the realization of this degree of supra-national cultural synthesis is, of course, a long-term period of peace. The violent schisms and devastating hostilities which characterize a time of troubles make any kind of fruitful contact well-nigh impossible, as we have already seen; and, of course, a universal state is imposed by its founders, and is accepted by its subjects, as a panacea for precisely this evil of a time of troubles. The immediate and paramount aim of the empire-builders, in making a universal state out of the sole survivor of an age of fratricidal warfare, is to establish concord among themselves and with their fellow-members of the dominant minorities in the former parochial states. Non-violence, however, is a state of mind and principle of behaviour that cannot easily be confined to one compartment of social life; it will tend to apply in some degree to all social relations if it is to apply to any; and therefore the concord which a dominant minority seeks to impose on itself as a class is apt to be extended to the dominant minority's relations with the internal and external proletariats and also with any alien civilization with which the disintegrating civilization may be in contact. Even if no perfect peace can be achieved, there must at least be an armistice and a *modus vivendi*.

This suppression of conflict, which is the prevailing psychological climate under the dispensation of a universal state, profits its various beneficiaries in different degrees. While it enables the dominant minority to recuperate to some extent – and indeed is the condition *sine qua non*, if it is to recuperate at all – it brings a greater relative access of strength to the proletariat. Concord is, after all, a basically negative boon in itself. The life which has already gone out of the dominant minority cannot be revived simply by a belated relief from attrition, whereas the same relief enables the proletariat – which has been stimulated and not crushed by its tribulations in the time of troubles – to 'shoot up and thrive'.[9] Accordingly, during the social armistice inaugurated by the establishment of a universal state, the proletariat will flourish but the dominant minority will wither. Under the common régime of concord the dominant minority's conservation of energy freezes into archaism; but, by contrast, the toleration which this same dominant minority is obliged to practise for the sake of getting rid of fratricidal warfare within its own ranks incidentally gives the internal proletariat the opportunity to demonstrate its creative energy by founding a universal church. At the same time, the atrophy of the martial spirit among the subjects of a universal state, resulting from the monopoly of the military profession by the imperial power and from the political passivity inculcated by it, gives the external proletariat the chance of breaking in and seizing for itself the dominion over the militarily supine state.

The relative incapacity of the dominant minority to profit by conditions which it has itself brought into existence by establishing a universal state is aptly illustrated by its almost invariable failure to propagate a philosophy or 'fancy religion' of its own from above downwards (an apparent exception being the Confucian official religion of

the Sinic universal state). It looks as if the apparatus of
political power which is wielded by the dominant minority
so successfully for the purpose of controlling its subject
populations in the secular side of their life becomes a
positive obstacle to the imposition of an official philosophical or religious doctrine. By contrast, the politically
impotent internal proletariat can exploit most effectively the
opportunity offered by the pacific atmosphere of a universal
state for propagating, from below upwards, a higher
religion and eventually establishing a universal church.

The Neo-Babylonian Empire and its successive avatars,
the Achaemenian Empire and the Seleucid Monarchy, were
used to this effect by Judaism and by its sister-religion
Zoroastrianism. The opportunities offered by the Roman
Peace were seized by a number of competing proletarian
religions – by the worship of Cybele and Isis and by
Mithraism and Christianity, as well as by the Babylonic
religion of astral determination. The corresponding opportunities offered by the *Pax Hanica* in the Sinic World were
competed for by an Indic proletarian religion, the Mahayana, which had originated from a philosophy of the Indic
dominant minority, and by the indigenous Sinic proletarian
religion of Taoism, which likewise created itself out of a
philosophy. The Arab Caliphate provided a comparable
opportunity for Islam, and the Gupta Raj in the Indic
World for Hinduism. The Mongol Empire, which for a
moment extended an effective *Pax Nomadica* across the
length and breadth of Eurasia, fascinated the missionaries
of a host of rival religions by the portentous scale of the
opportunity that this almost literally universal state
appeared to offer; and, considering how brief this passing
moment actually was, it is remarkable how successfully it
was turned to account by the Nestorian and the Western
Catholic Christian Churches and by Islam, as well as by
the Lamaist Tantric sect of Mahayanian Buddhism. The
successive Ming and Manchu avatars of the Mongol
universal state in the Sinic World gave Western Catholic
Christianity a second opportunity for attempting the conquest of a new world, and the same church made a similar
attempt to take advantage of the foundation of a Japanese
universal state in the shape of the Tokugawa Shogunate.
The Ottoman Empire gave an opening for Bedreddinism,
Imami Shi'ism, and Bektashism, and the Mughal Raj in the
Indic World for Kabirism and Sikhism.

The exponents of the higher religions that profited by
the favourable climate of a universal state were in some
cases aware of the special advantages offered by the
situation, which they ascribed to the providence of the God
whose worship they were propagating. In the eyes of the
authors of the books of 'Deutero-Isaiah', Ezra, and
Nehemiah, the Achaemenian Empire was the chosen
instrument of Yahweh for the propagation of Judaism, and
this interpretation of the final cause of a universal state was
shared by one of the Fathers of the Christian Church in
his attitude towards the Roman Empire:

The incarnation of the Word of God united divine nature with
human nature so [completely] that God's nature was able to
stoop to the depths and ours to be raised up to the heights. In
order that the effects of this ineffable act of grace might be spread
throughout the world, God's providence previously brought
into existence the Roman Empire. Its territorial acquisitions

224 The Mughal Emperor Akbar, renowned for his plan to combine the
world's religions into one universal faith, takes part in a debate between
Muslim divines and Jesuit missionaries.

were carried to the lengths required for enabling all nations everywhere to become neighbours in the intimate contact that is established in a universal state. It was thoroughly consonant with the divine plan of action that many kingdoms should thus be confederated in a single empire and that the evangelization of all Mankind should find itself able to make an unimpeded and rapid progress through all the ranks of peoples held together under the rule of a single polity.[10]

An opportunity so marvellous as to seem truly heaven-sent is indeed presented to a higher religion by the establishment of an imperial peace; yet the climate of toleration which gives so favourable a start to missionary work does not always persist to the end of the chapter, but is liable actually to be reversed in reaction to the very success with which the higher religion is exploiting it. In such cases, the peaceful progress of the religion may be interrupted by

official persecutions which either nip it in the bud or else denature it by goading it to adopt a political or a military stance. Western Catholic Christianity, for example, was almost completely extirpated in Japan by the Tokugawa régime in the seventeenth century, and was effectively checked in China in the eighteenth century by the Manchu power. Shi'ism was crushed in the Ottoman Empire in AD 1514 when a Shi'i insurrection was ruthlessly suppressed by Sultan Selim the Grim. Islam was persecuted by the pagan Mongol khaqans, and although this persecution was more than balanced, in the long run, by a temporary political union, under Mongol rule, of China and Dar-al-Islam which led to the permanent introduction of Islam into China, yet Islam missed its possible destiny of becoming the universal church of the main body of the Sinic World. It gained no substantial foothold in China outside

IMPERIAL INTOLERANCE

225, 226 Official indifference gives way to vicious persecution when a religion comes to threaten state authority. Opposite, the first victims of Japan's persecution of Christians. Right, the 'Forty Martyrs', soldiers of a Roman legion who were killed in 320 for defying an anti-Christian imperial decree.

the two far north-western provinces of Kansu and Shensi and the south-western province of Yunnan; and even in these areas the Islamic community never became more than an alien minority which was goaded, by the precariousness of its position, into recurrent outbreaks of militancy. A similar fate awaited Sikhism in India, where this potential embryo of a Hindu universal church was provoked into a sterile political militancy by the sustained and violent persecution which it suffered under the Mughal Raj.

In contrast to these cases, the after-effects of the persecutions of the Christians in the Roman Empire were comparatively slight. During the three centuries ending with the tentative conversion of Constantine in AD 312, while Christianity was benefiting from the facilities unintentionally offered to it by the Roman Peace, the Church was in constant danger of falling foul of Roman policy. Apart from the suspicion of all forms of private associations that haunted the Roman state in the imperial age, there was an older and more deeply graven Roman tradition of special hostility to private associations for the practice and propagation of foreign religions. Although this policy had been twice relaxed – in relation to the worship of Cybele and to Judaism – the suppression of the Bacchanals in the second century BC was an augury of what the Christians were to suffer in the third century of their era. Unlike the Sikh community in the Mughal Raj, however, the Christian Church under the Roman régime resisted the temptation to retort to official persecution by perverting itself from a religious into a politico-military association; and it was duly rewarded for remaining substantially true to its own nature by becoming a universal church and an heir to the future. Yet the Christian Church did not come through this ordeal

227 In fourteenth-century Italy, the Pope and his Curia judge heretics, while a condemned man is burned and others are led into prison. The use of persecution to suppress dissent is a tragic lesson learnt by churches from their own experience of suffering: the Christian Church executed a heretic for the first time in 385.

unscathed. Instead of taking to heart the triumph of Christian gentleness over Roman force, she presented her persecutors with a gratuitous vindication and posthumous moral revenge by herself committing the sin that had consummated their failure. The habit of resorting to persecution as a would-be short cut to overcoming opposition to prevalent practice and beliefs was adopted by the Christian Church before the end of the fourth century, and was maintained by it for thirteen centuries – a spiritual débâcle from which this Church is still suffering.

Such sinister legacies, bequeathed to higher religions by universal states, have not, however, been so significant as the benefits which have been offered to them by the facilities that a universal state provides. It was within, and with the aid of, this political and social framework that Christianity, Islam, Hinduism, and the Mahayana won their way to becoming universal churches.

While the internal proletariat, as the creator of the higher religions, is thus the principal beneficiary on the spiritual plane from the dominant minority's impermanent yet momentous achievement of establishing a universal state, the benefits on the political plane tend to fall into other hands; and this distribution of advantages arises from the very nature of the situation. The enforced peace of a universal state gives the internal proletariat its opportunity for spiritual creativity insofar as it has debarred it from the privilege of exercising political power and has relieved it of the necessity of performing military duties; and even the empire-builders themselves, exhausted by the supreme effort of imposing peace through an overwhelming military master-stroke, are liable to lose the zest that carried their forefathers to their victory in the preceding time of troubles. The military service that was once readily accepted as an honour and as an outlet for ambition now comes to be shunned as an unwelcome burden, and the imperial authorities are obliged to look to the ranks of an untamed external proletariat for their military recruits. The psychology of peace under the auspices of a universal state thus makes the rulers themselves unfit for the task of retaining their own political heritage; and the beneficiaries of this process of psychological disarmament are neither the rulers nor the ruled, but are intruders from beyond the imperial frontiers who may be representatives of the disintegrating society's external proletariat or of some alien civilization. The extinction – as distinct from the breakdown – of a civilization is in fact registered by the occupation of the defunct universal state's domain either by barbarian war-lords from beyond the pale or by conquerors coming from another society with a different culture, or in some cases by both kinds of invader one after the other. Barbarians overran the Empire of Sumer and Akkad, the Guptan Empire, the Empire of Ch'in (Ts'in) and Han, the Roman Empire, the Arab Caliphate, and both the Middle and New Kingdom of Egypt. The Neo-Babylonian Empire, which was the last phase of the Sumero-Akkadian Civilization, was cut short by Iranian barbarians who were in the process of absorbing the Syriac culture and were about to found the original Syriac universal state; and this Achaemenian Empire in its

condemned them as the disreputable adventurers that they were, but for the retrospective glamour of romance and tragedy that their literature has succeeded in casting over their escapades. As for the achievements of the militant representatives of alien civilizations, these too, though seldom so short-lived as the triumphs of the barbarians, are, like them, delusive and disappointing by comparison with the historic achievement of the internal proletariat.

In addition, in at least one case we have seen that a civilization whose universal state has been prematurely cut short by alien conquerors is capable of going to earth and hibernating for centuries, before eventually finding its opportunity to expel the intruders and resume the universal state phase of its history. The Indic Civilization achieved this *tour de force* after nearly six hundred years; the monument of its achievement was the Guptan Empire, in which it resumed the universal state originally embodied in the Mauryan Empire. On the other hand, the Sumero-Akkadian and the Egyptiac Societies were eventually absorbed into a Syro-Hellenic 'culture-compost', though each did manage to maintain a certain degree of independent cultural identity. These examples illustrate the two alternative dénouements to attempts made by one civilization to devour and digest another civilization by force, and the evidence suggests that, in either case, the end result may be long-drawn-out and inconclusive. On this showing, we might be wary of forecasting the ultimate outcome of the Western Civilization's current attempts to swallow its contemporaries, considering how recently these attempts were inaugurated. In the wake of a Western imperialist penetration of the African, Indian, Middle and South American, and Asian Worlds – which has not, however, been the work of a single universal state, but of competing parochial representatives of one civilization – it might have looked for a time as if these areas would be condemned to a forcible Westernization; but the contemporary, and unprecedented, decolonialization of the Western World's overseas empires, taken together with the growing cultural self-awareness of the newly emancipated states and the worldwide diasporás, may have brought with it a decisive break in this process. To take a single but striking example, the Arab countries, which have comparatively recently gained admission to the Western comity of nations as sovereign independent states, were able to achieve this ambition by means of shaking off an Ottoman political ascendancy and an Iranic Muslim cultural veneer with which they had been overlaid for centuries. But is there any reason to suppose that the latent survival power of the Arabic culture, which once enabled the Arabs to resist assimilation to the kindred culture of a sister society, will not assert itself, sooner or later, against the alien influence of the far more alien culture of the West? And if this is conceivable, might it not also be the eventual future of the other societies which are currently exposed to Western influence?

The general effect of this survey of the ultimate consequences of 'cultural conversions' must be to confirm our suggestion that the sole long-term beneficiary from the services offered by a universal state is the internal proletariat. The benefits obtained by the external proletariat are always illusory, while those obtained by an alien civilization are apt to be impermanent.

turn was cut short by Macedonian Greek-speaking barbarians who had already fallen under the influence of Hellenism before Alexander the Great's campaign of conquest. The Mauryan Empire suffered the Achaemenian Empire's fate, 150 years later, at the hands of an Hellenic successor of the Achaemenian Empire in Bactria; and the Empire of the Incas, which was the Andean universal state, was similarly cut short by militant apostles of Western Christendom whose leader emulated the demonic energy, but not the forbearance, of the Macedonian Alexander. At the break-up of the Ottoman Empire, which had provided an alien universal state for the main body of Orthodox Christendom, incipient barbarian invasions were overtaken, and were then either suppressed or transformed, by the mightier march of Westernization: partly in the form of conquests by Western or Westernizing Powers, and partly through the cultural conversion of the subject peoples of the Empire and of the invading barbarians themselves. At the break-up of the Mughal Empire, incipient barbarian invasions were stopped by the restoration of the universal state in the form of the British Raj.

This survey suggests that the benefits secured by barbarian or alien aggressors who take advantage of the psychological climate of a universal state are palpable and, on a short view, imposing. Yet we have observed already[11] that the barbarian invaders of the derelict domain of a crumbling universal state are heroes without a future – a fact that will be confirmed when we come to look more closely at these figures;[12] and posterity would certainly have

34 Communications

WE HAVE SEEN that the general conditions under which a universal state exists are enough in themselves to confer certain benefits on its inhabitants or neighbours. Beyond this, it can also be shown that some of the particular concrete institutions created by universal states to enforce and maintain their rule will tend to offer unintended services to those who know how to take advantage of them. The principal institutions of this kind which we ought now to examine are the geographical and verbal systems of communication, the capital cities, and the civil services founded or adopted by universal states. Communications head the list because they are the master-institution on which a universal state depends for its very existence. They are the instrument not only of military command over its dominions, but also of political control through an overt imperial inspectorate and a secret security police. The maintenance of an efficient system of communications depends partly upon the policing of the principal arteries of travel, and partly also upon the provision of a public means of transportation, since the traveller will find his private resources insufficient or severely taxed if he has to rely exclusively on these for his mobility. In most universal states the public transportation system has usually existed in the form of an imperial postal service; and the imperial postmaster, with his unrivalled opportunity for creating and operating an intelligence network, has usually combined his ostensible function with the headship of the empire's secret security service.

A public postal service seems to have been part of the machinery of government of the Sumero-Akkadian Empire, and in its metropolitan territory of Shinar the embankments of the irrigation canals appear to have served as highways for land-traffic. The 'New Empire' of Egypt, which established its authority over the derelict Syrian and Mesopotamian provinces of the Sumero-Akkadian Empire after an interlude of barbarian Hyksos rule, used the roads which it inherited here from its predecessors for keeping control over the native princelings by a service of diplomatic couriers and travelling inspectors. In the Achaemenian Empire we find the same installations apparently raised to a higher level of organization and efficiency (though this apparent superiority may be an illusion reflecting a mere difference in the amount of our information).

The further the bounds of the Empire were extended, the more powerful became the position of the provincial governors; and this made it the more necessary to create institutions for preserving the Empire's unity and for ensuring a prompt and unhesitating execution of imperial commands. Instruments for holding the Empire together were the great roads converging on Susa and traversing the Empire in all directions in the track of the previously existing trade-routes. . . . These roads were measured in parasangs and were permanently maintained in good condition. The imperial highway was provided, at intervals of about four parasangs on the average, with 'imperial post-stations and excellent inns'. The provincial boundaries and the river crossings were guarded by strongly garrisoned fortresses

(*pylai*) – the desert frontier of Babylonia, among others, was provided with defences of the same kind. At these points the traffic was subjected to searching supervision. All post-stations were manned by mounted couriers whose duty it was to convey imperial commands and official dispatches post-haste, travelling day and night without a break – 'swifter than cranes', as the Greeks put it. There is also said to have been a system of telegraphic communications by beacon-signals. To keep the satraps under control, the Emperor would take every opportunity of sending out into the provinces high officials, like the Emperor's 'eye' or his brother or son, with troops at their back. These would arrive, without warning, to inspect the administration and report abuses. Further safeguards against misconduct on the satraps' part were provided by the presence of the imperial secretary who was attached to the provincial governor, and of the commandants of fortresses and other military officers in his province, who all served as instruments of supervision. These checks were supplemented by a highly developed espionage system. The Emperor had a ready ear for denunciations.[1]

This Achaemenian policy of utilizing the imperial communications system as an instrument for maintaining the central government's control over the provinces reappears in the administration of the Roman Empire, which eventually fell heir to the former Achaemenian dominions west of the Euphrates, and in the Arab Caliphate. The Roman imperial *Cursus Publicus* was instituted by Augustus, and the burden of providing the service, which was originally imposed upon the local public authorities, appears to have been progressively taken over by the imperial treasury in the reigns of Hadrian and Septimius Severus. The Achaemenian inspiration of the Roman system is betrayed in a characteristic use of couriers as spies. The emissaries of the Roman imperial government, who went under the euphemistic name of *frumentarii* ('foragers') and later *agentes in rebus*, were counterparts, in Roman dress, of the Achaemenian emperor's 'eye'. Their administrative duty of superintending the conduct of the imperial postal service was coupled with the political duty of espionage.

A similar dual use of the system was practised in the 'Abbasid Caliphate.

The central government had one department which could obtain information on the activities of the provincial rulers and thus check on them, the *barīd*. The word is of Latin (or perhaps Persian) derivation, and was originally, under the Caliph Mu'āwiya, the term for a mounted messenger carrying governmental correspondence. Under 'Abd-al-Malik, *barīd* came to mean the 'postal service', which ensured written communications between the Caliph and his viceroys or military commanders in the provinces and developed in the reign of the Caliph Mansūr into one of the principal governmental departments (*diwans*). The director (*sāhib-al-barīd*) became a very important and influential office holder in Baghdad. He had under his orders the employees of the numerous 'postal stations' dispersed throughout the vast territory of the Caliphate in cities and on highways laid out as early as Achemenid and Sassanid or Roman and Byzantine times. In each station messengers and their mounts were always on the alert. . . . The duties of the *barīd* employees were not merely to forward official correspondence, but also to collect and convey to Baghdad first-hand and precise information on the state of agriculture and irrigation, the mood of the local population, the activity of the provincial administration and the amount of coined gold and silver money in the local mint (if there was one). The written reports arrived regularly in Baghdad, at the central office of the *sāhib-al-barīd*. The information digested, the *sāhib-al-barīd* reported daily to the *wazīr* on the state of the empire. . . . In fact, the *barīd* was a department of control and detection, making use of numerous spies and informers, male and female, both in the Caliphate and abroad.[2]

Similar institutions were constructed in universal states which had no links with the originators of this South-West Asian pattern. Shih Hwang-ti, the revolutionary founder of the Sinic universal state, was a builder of roads radiating from his capital, which he used for making political inspections and carrying out statistical surveys. His inspectorate was elaborately organized. The inspector-general held office in the capital with his two deputies, and was served by a numerous provincial staff; there were special inspectorates, besides, for 'subject barbarians' and 'subject states'. The Incas, likewise, were builders of roads and fortresses; and, like the Roman conquerors of Italy, they used these instruments to consolidate each gain of ground, in preparation for the next advance in their systematic movement of conquest northward. The completed system consisted of two main roads running parallel, south and north, one along the Andean plateau, and the other along the Pacific coast, with transverse connecting roads at intervals. The roads were carried across rivers and ravines by bridges of stone and wood, by suspension bridges of rope, or by cable and basket; they constituted an engineering feat of such magnitude that it was said that the construction of the bridge of Apurímac was alone enough to overawe and subdue the surrounding hostile Indian tribes.[3] Along these routes store-houses (*tambos*) were strung at intervals, and relays of post-runners stationed at distances of a quarter of a league 'which . . . was how far an Indian could run at speed and in breath, and without being tired'.[4] A message could travel from Cuzco to Quito – a distance of more than a thousand miles as the crow flies and perhaps half as much again by road – in as short a time as ten days. The organization of this service was attributed to the eighth Inca Pachacuti (*imperabat c.* AD 1400–48). The travelling facilities were used by the Inca himself and by itinerant imperial inspectors, intendants, and judges.

The surveillance [of the central government over the provinces] was provided for by inspectors, drawn from the ranks of the *orejones*,[5] who made general tours of the Empire every three years, and by secret agents of the Inca . . . who paid visits, incognito, to all districts. These agents' instructions were to observe, to listen to complaints, and to report, but it was not within their competence to take measures for the suppression of abuses. Under this system, several brothers of the Inca Tupac Yupanqui were successively appointed inspectors. . . . The duties of inspector-in-chief were performed by the Inca himself; he travelled over the Empire in his golden litter, and during the whole period of his visits – which were very long, considering that he sometimes remained absent [from the capital] for as much as three or four years – he would be hearing petitions and dispensing justice.[6]

IMPERIAL ARTERIES

228, 229, 230 The Inca Empire had a magnificent road system running through its dominions, constructed primarily for the use of imperial officials. Above, an official and his wife are carried in a litter; below, an imperial messenger *en route*, and planning a road. Drawings by a sixteenth-century Spanish-Inca observer.

While the means of communication with which the Inca Empire equipped itself were thus assiduously used by the public authorities, including the emperor in person, they were not at the disposal of private travellers. In Central America, by contrast, the road system was pioneered by the merchant guilds which, in their irrepressible eagerness for profits, were continually pushing ahead in advance of the expansion of the Aztec Empire. The Aztec imperial authorities turned these commercial travellers to their own account as sources of military and political intelligence, and took over the tasks of maintaining the roads and bridges and of operating a postal service.

In Japan the Great North-East Road, running up the south-eastern side of the Main Island from the civil capital at Kyoto in the interior to the successive military capitals at Kamakura and Yedo, served first to secure the conquests made by the Japanese Society at the expense of the Ainu barbarians, and afterwards to bring and keep the original metropolitan district, Yamato, under the domination of the Kwanto marchland. Under the Tokugawa régime, which was the Japanese universal state, this trunk road and its branches ministered to the policy of the Shogun's government at Yedo as an instrument not only for keeping an eye on the impotent imperial court at Kyoto, but also for the more formidable task of maintaining control over rebellious feudal lords throughout the Empire. These *daimyos* were required by the Shogun to reside in Yedo for a part of the year, and to leave their wives and families there as hostages when they themselves returned to their fiefs. The twice-yearly migration of these feudal lords between Yedo and their estates was one of the distinctive features of Japanese life in the Tokugawa Age; and the grand trunk road and its ramifications were the media of communication for their perpetual coming and going. While the government had an interest in maintaining these roads for security reasons, it was equally anxious that they should not be kept up well enough to encourage and abet a concerted military march on the capital by disaffected *daimyos*; and thus they deliberately refrained from either constructing bridges or improving the road systems that converged on Yedo.

In China the long-distance transportation of foodstuffs in bulk came to be one of the besetting problems of public administration, owing to a tendency towards political unification under an ecumenical government seated in the north which persisted after the economic centre of gravity had shifted from there to the Yangtse valley.

Commercial growth in China never reached a level which would enable it to overcome the localism and narrow exclusiveness of an agricultural economy. [The] regional groupings were highly self-sustaining and independent of each other, and in the absence of machine industry, modern facilities of transport and communication and an advanced economic organization, state centralization in the modern sense was impossible. In the circumstances, the unity or centralization of state power in China could only mean the control of an economic area where agricultural productivity and facilities of transport would make possible the supply of a grain tribute so predominantly superior to that of other areas that any group which controlled this area had the key to the conquest and unity of all China. It is areas of this kind which must be designated as the Key Economic Areas.[7]

231 Land-borne transport: feudal lord and his retinue travelling on Japan's Great North-East Road. This road was the key to central control of outlying areas, and was used also by feudatories for travel to and from the capital where they were compelled to reside, at ruinous expense, for part of each year.

The Yangtze Valley grew in importance as a productive centre during the Eastern Tsin [AD] (317–420) and the other southern dynasties (420–589), definitely assuming the position of the Key Economic Area from the time of the T'ang dynasty (618–907). Politically, the centre of gravity still lay in the North. . . . This anomalous situation rendered the development and maintenance of a transport system linking the productive south with the political north a vital necessity. The link was provided by the Grand Canal, which engaged the attention of the best minds of China for more than ten centuries, and demanded countless millions of lives and a large portion of the wealth of the country for its improvement and maintenance. . . .[8]

Although traditionally the canal is ascribed to the genius and extravagance of Yang Ti [*imperabat* AD 605–18] of the Sui, it was not built in one period or by one emperor. Like the Great Wall, it was constructed in disconnected sections at different periods. Yang Ti of the Sui completed it by linking the various waterways running in a north and south direction into a connected system and adding long sectors both in the north and south.[9]

The problem of long-distance grain transport automatically fell into abeyance during the bouts of disunion that gripped the Sinic World in the tenth century and in the twelfth of the Christian Era; but, when unity was restored by the Mongol empire-builders in the thirteenth century, this question presented itself again, and this time in far more trying geographical circumstances. The Mongol capital was established at Peking, because the site lay just inside the northernmost limits of China and within convenient proximity to the Nomadic Mongols' native steppes. From this point they had proceeded to conquer the whole of China right down to Canton, and this achievement raised for them the question how they were to administer such a vast and populous domain from a capital located on its extreme northern verge, and how they were to keep this capital supplied from a southern economic centre which was far more remote from Peking than it was from any of the earlier capital cities of the Ch'in, Han, Sui, and T'ang. This problem was inherited from the Mongols by their indigenous Chinese supplanters the Ming, who soon found by experience that the military and political considerations telling in favour of Peking outweighed those considerations of cultural sentiment and economic convenience that had led the founder of the new dynasty to experiment with a transfer of the capital to Nanking. But a reunited China could not be governed from Peking without some effective medium of communication for maintaining the imperial government's political control over the distant Yangtse basin and still more distant southern sea-board, and for bringing northward the rice that was needed in bulk as tax revenue in kind and as food supplies. This problem was solved by a re-alinement of the Grand Canal which made Tientsin instead of Kaifeng its northern terminus. From Tientsin southwards, the Yüan (Mongol) Grand Canal continued to be used, after the expulsion of the Mongols, by their successors the Ming and the Manchus, as the Sui Grand Canal had continued to be used by the T'ang and Sung. The Canal was, in fact, the spinal cord of the Chinese political and economic body until the disintegration of the traditional Chinese state in the nineteenth century.

It will be seen that, in constructing and maintaining their impressive systems of communications, the makers and masters of universal states usually had a clear and precise

232, 233 Water-borne transport: in China, canals have served in place of roads, especially for carrying grain from the agricultural south to the centre of political gravity in the north. Above, section from a map of the Grand Canal, the principal water-route constructed in the seventh century AD and extended by successive imperial dynasties. The canal enters the map in the top left-hand corner, and flows down through a series of locks to the Yellow River, with which it connects by a complicated system of channels. Below, the canal in use: British boats pass through a lock, carrying the ambassador to the Chinese Emperor's court.

idea of the purposes for which they were burdening their subjects with these vast and expensive works. Yet if we look further we shall find that the most deliberately planned and organized system could be exploited by other parties than the imperial government, and for purposes which the government, if it had foreseen them, would have disregarded or have opposed.

A pointed illustration of this unintended effect is provided by the alternative use to which the magnificent communications system of the Roman Empire was put. The splendour of the Roman achievement was admitted by the Greek Stoic philosopher Epictetus, writing in the second century of the Roman Peace.

You see that Caesar appears to provide us with a great peace, because there are no longer any wars or battles or any serious crimes of brigandage or piracy, so that one can travel at any season and can sail from the Levant to the Ponent.[10]

Towards the close of the same century the eulogy was repeated by Aelius Aristeides, a Greek man of letters of a school which had recognized the Roman Empire as the Greek universal state.

The common saying that Earth is the all-mother and the universal home has been demonstrated by you Romans to per-

fection; for today Greek or barbarian, travelling heavy or travelling light, is at liberty to go where he pleases, at his ease; and, wherever he goes, he will never be leaving home behind him. The Cilician Gates and the narrow sandy passage through the Arab country to Egypt have both alike lost their terrors. The mountains are no longer trackless, the rivers no longer impassable, the tribesmen no longer ferocious; it is a sufficient passport to be a Roman citizen or indeed a Roman subject; and Homer's saying that 'the Earth is common to all men' has been translated into fact by you, who have surveyed the whole inhabited world and have thrown all manner of bridges over the rivers and have hewn cuttings through the mountains until you have made the Earth *carrossable* – with your post-houses planted in the wilderness and your system and order spreading civilization far and wide.[11]

If the makers and panegyrists of the Roman imperial system of communications could have foreseen the future they would have found it intolerable no doubt, but not unintelligible in a world in which 'all roads' led 'to Rome', that the thoroughfares which in their time were bringing prisoners, petitioners, and sight-seers to the imperial city should one day convey barbarian war-bands or the armies of rival empires. These imperial highways certainly enabled, and possibly inspired, the barbarian invaders to make straight for the heart of the Hellenic World. The Vandals,

TWO-WAY TRAFFIC   234, 235, 236   The Roman road system was eulogized by contemporaries as the visible sign of the Empire's unity and expansion; a paved road in Syria and, opposite, a milestone a thousand

for instance, entered Spain within three years, and appeared before the walls of Carthage within twenty-four years, of their passage of the Rhine in AD 406. The Arabs arrived in Egypt within six years, at Carthage within sixty-four years, and all but in sight of the Loire within ninety-nine years of their first raid across the Syrian *limes* of the Roman Empire in 633. The Romans' Persian rivals for world dominion reached Calchedon within twelve years, and Alexandria within sixteen years, of crossing the Roman Empire's Mesopotamian frontier in 603. And the inland sea which the Romans had confidently styled *mare nostrum* proved equally serviceable to barbarian raiders – Goths, Franks, Vandals, and Arabs.

Long before the Roman roads had provided this service to Rome's barbarian conquerors, they had already served a far more significant purpose in facilitating the journeys of a single Roman citizen. When Augustus imposed the Roman Peace on Pisidia, a part of Asia Minor that had not been effectively subdued by either the Achaemenids or the Seleucids, he was unconsciously paving the way for Saint Paul, on his first mission-journey from Antioch-on-Orontes, to land in Pamphylia and travel inland, un-molested, to Antioch-in-Pisidia, Iconium, Lystra, and Derbe. And Paul's momentous last voyage from Caesarea

to Puteoli was made possible only because Pompey had swept the seas clear of Cilician pirates. The Roman Peace later proved as propitious a social environment for Paul's successors as it had been for Paul himself. In the latter part of the second century of the Roman Empire's existence, Saint Irenaeus of Lyons – a Christian Father of Asian Greek origin who was an approximate contemporary of Aelius Aristeides – was paying an implicit tribute to the Empire in extolling the unity of the Catholic Church throughout the Hellenic World.

Having received this gospel and this faith . . . the Church, in spite of her dispersal throughout the world, preserves these treasures as meticulously as if she were living under one single roof. She believes in these truths as unanimously as if she had only one soul and a single heart, and she preaches them and expounds them and hands them down as concordantly as if she had only one mouth. While the languages current in the world are diverse, the force of the [Church's] tradition is one and the same everywhere. There is no variety in the faith or in the tradition of the churches that have established themselves in the Germanies or in the Spains or among the Celts or in the East or in Egypt or in North-West Africa, or, again, of the churches that have established themselves at the world's centre. Just as God's creature the Sun is one and the same throughout the world, so likewise the Gospel of the Truth shows its light everywhere.[12]

miles away in Tunisia. At the break-up of the Empire, however, the system acted as a lightning conductor for barbarian invaders, right, carrying them swiftly to the imperial heart-lands.

This successor of Paul's failed to recognize – or at any rate did not acknowledge – how much the Christian Church was indebted for her marvellous unanimity-in-ubiquity to the communications system of the Roman Empire. But the connexion was disagreeably evident two hundred years later, in an age when the Church had become the official partner of the Roman state, to the pagan Ammianus Marcellinus of Antioch.

[The Emperor] Constantius [II] found the Christian religion uninvolved and straightforward and proceeded to muddle it up with old wives' superstitions. As his delight in complicated theological hair-splitting was greater than his sense of responsibility for maintaining harmony, he provoked innumerable dissensions, and he added fuel to the galloping flames by organizing acrimonious debates. One consequence was that crowds of prelates made use of the public post-horses for rushing to and fro on the business of these 'synods', as they call them. The prelates' object was to wrench the whole practice of their religion into conformity with their own caprice; Constantius's achievement was to ham-string the postal service.[13]

Thus the imperial postal service, which was not a facility provided by the government for the convenience of the public but a burden imposed on the public for strictly official purposes, had been taken over by the bishops for the service of the Church.

The Roman system of imperial communications is not the only one that illustrates this particular irony of history. The Sumero-Akkadian Empire was just as hard hit by its own efficiency in this department of imperial administration. Its north-eastern highways eventually conveyed both the flood of the Mitanni Nomad invasion which swept across Mesopotamia, and the sluggish infiltration of Kassite mountain tribes into Shinar. The corresponding north-western highway conveyed Hittite marauders from the Anatolian plateau on the lightning raid in which they sacked Babylon in about 1595 BC. When the Achaemenidae reconditioned the same north-western highway and extended it to the shores of the Aegean and the Hellespont, they, in their turn, were leading a lightning conductor into the heart of their dominions. Their magnificent roads opened the way for the pretender Cyrus the Younger to march his invincible ten thousand Greek mercenaries from Sardis to Cunaxa, and for Alexander of Macedon to follow the trail which they had blazed for an Hellenic conquest of South-West Asia. Yet the political achievements of Alexander and his successors were as negative and ephemeral as they were astonishing. While it took them no longer than five years to break up the Achaemenian Empire, they never succeeded in putting the fragments together again. The long-term beneficiaries of the Achaemenian empire-builders' work were two higher religions, Judaism and Zoroastrianism, and the Macedonian conquerors cleared the field not for a reconstructed empire but for an influx of Hellenic culture.

When, after an interval of nearly a thousand years of Hellenic intrusion, the former domain of the Achaemenian Empire was reunited in the Arab Caliphate, it was the turn of the north-eastern highway – now stretching to the Transoxanian shore of the Eurasian steppe – to act as the suicidally directed lightning conductor for the invasions of Nomadic Turks and Mongols. The Caliphate's other

principal road system in North Africa rendered the same service to other invaders – the barbarian Arab Banu Hilal and Sulaym, the Berber tribes, and the Western Christian Crusaders. Here too, however, the lasting beneficiary from the imperial system of communications was not any of these invaders. The historic service rendered by the wonderful organization described in the *Corpus of Arab Geographers* was to facilitate the propagation of Islam.[14]

In the history of other examples of communications systems which we have already mentioned, we can read the same story. The roads efficiently provided by the Aztecs and the Incas enabled Cortés and Pizarro to overrun two new worlds with the lightning speed of the Macedonian Alexander, and thereby opened the way for Catholic Christianity to make lasting spiritual conquests in these evanescent *conquistadores'* wake. In the Sinic World, the road-building of Shih Hwang-ti was overtaken by the same nemesis.

The construction of roads was a benefit to the empire, but it proved a danger to the Ch'in dynasty. When the great revolt occurred the armies of the rebels found that the new roads served their purposes as well [as], or better than, those of the soldiers of Ch'in. For all the roads centred on the capital. The rebel armies were thus able to move swiftly and easily into the western hill country, hitherto so difficult of access, while the Ch'in generals, endeavouring to cope with rebellion in all parts of China, were hampered by the lack of lateral communications.[15]

Finally, the Grand Trunk Canal, which was the *chef d'œuvre* among the public works of the Sinic universal state, served to convey inland to Peking the Western Catholic missionaries who had lodged themselves in the southern coastal ports, and whose medieval predecessors had already gained a temporary foothold in China via the Mongol-made thoroughfares across the Eurasian steppe.

On the basis of this survey we can hardly escape the conclusion that the long-term historical significance of an imperial communications system in a universal state lies in the contribution that it makes towards the dissemination of cultural, and especially of religious, influences. This conclusion itself raises a momentous question about the future of the contemporary Westernizing world, in which the expansion and sophistication of communications systems are proceeding at a perpetually accelerating pace. It is about a century and a half since the first breakthrough to mechanized forms of transport was achieved; and the intervening years have seen not only an increasingly sophisticated application of technology to transportation, but also the evolution of, first, an entirely unprecedented means of communication which depends, not on the physical conveyance of human bodies, but on the transmission of auditory and visual waves; and, second, a system of information storage and retrieval which offers a potentially infinite expansion of Mankind's capacity for theoretical and practical problem-solving. At the present day the whole habitable surface of the globe is knit together by a system of communications which is literally more than world-wide, since it is based on a string of radio and television satellites that are physically independent of the Earth from which they have been launched.

In the light of the histories of all other known civilizations, the development of this system of communications ought to foreshadow the eventual political unification of the society in which these technological portents have appeared. At the present moment, however, the political prospects of the Western World are still obscure; for, although the choice may seem to lie ineluctably between 'one world or none',[16] only the most faltering steps have yet been taken towards the former goal. It looks as if the familiar method of the 'knock-out blow', by which in the histories of past civilizations one parochial state has imposed its political supremacy on its fellows, will never be employed again, for its price would no longer be paid merely in degrees of devastation but probably in the total annihilation of civilization and the extinction of human life as well. However, it is possible that, if political unification is indispensable and indeed inevitable, this may be achieved by the novel alternative method of voluntary co-operation which has been attempted on a world scale after each of the two world wars of this century, and on a more restricted scale in the current moves towards local but supra-national politico-economic integration in Western Europe. The prospects of these great political experiments are as uncertain as ever, though there is at least a growing recognition among the statesmen and the peoples of the world that a failure would ultimately be catastrophic. At all events, the experience which we have been reviewing in this chapter strongly suggests that the worldwide network of communications which the Western Civilization has already installed for its own purposes is likely to find its historic significance in the familiar ironic role of being turned to account by unintended beneficiaries.

Who would draw the largest benefits in this case? It is quite clear that in the contemporary world the external proletariat of barbarians has shrunk to such miniscule proportions that the remaining pockets of population still untouched by the extant civilizations will scarcely play any independent part in the future. On the other hand, the extant higher religions, whose domains have been linked up with one another by the Western technologist's ever closer-meshed spider's web, have already begun to take advantage of the fresh opportunities thus offered to them. Western Catholic Christianity ventured forth to the East and the West along the routes opened up by the European explorers of the sixteenth and seventeenth centuries, and has been competing since the nineteenth century with an older-established Islam in Africa. In very recent years the new ease of inter-continental travel and contact has facilitated the spread of versions of Hinduism and Buddhism to parts of the world which had been thought to be secure preserves of the Christian faith; and Marxism, which has tried to become an ideological successor to Christianity on its own ground, has achieved an equally impressive penetration.

The issues raised by this stimulation of missionary activities on a worldwide scale are not just those of ecclesiastical geopolitics. The entry of the established higher religions into new missionary fields brings up the question whether the eternal essence of a religion can be distinguished from its ephemeral accidents; the encounters of the religions with one another bring up the question whether they can coexist in fruitful harmony or whether one of them will eventually supersede the rest. Till recently, the higher religions have coexisted, mainly because the past inadequacy of means of communication had set limits to the propagation of even the three principal missionary religions: Buddhism, Christianity, and Islam. By harnessing muscle-power and wind-power, their disseminators had succeeded in capturing entire continents, but not the whole face of the Earth. Present-day means of communication make it possible for each of them, and for other religions too, to win adherents all round the globe; and, for each, this raises the question of coexistence versus competition.

Buddhism has always acquiesced in an amicable coexistence with the previous religions of the countries into which it has spread; and we may hope that this Buddhist tradition will prevail. Our common human nature is differentiated into different spiritual types; these different types find spiritual satisfaction in different presentations of religion; and the recent 'annihilation of distance' has made it possible, now, for the first time, for an individual to choose for himself, when grown-up, the religion that he finds most congenial to him, instead of inheriting a religion automatically through the accident of the time and place of his birth, without regard to his individual temperament.

This freedom of choice would be assured to the individual in a physically unified world if Buddhism were the only missionary religion in the field. Unhappily, Christianity and Islam do not have Buddhism's tradition of tolerance. Hitherto, each of them has demanded from its adherents an exclusive allegiance. Each of them, too, has been unwilling to tolerate the coexistence of any other religion except its own precursors, and these only in an inferior status and on humiliating terms. On these terms, Christianity has tolerated Judaism grudgingly and non-committally – and at periodic intervals has withdrawn even this modified toleration – while Islam, less grudgingly and more bindingly, has tolerated both Judaism and Christianity. Are the Christian and Muslim 'Establishments' capable of extricating themselves from their own traditions? Will they be able to adopt the amicable spirit of Buddhism which answers to the spiritual needs of a physically unified world? If Islam and Christianity prove unable to achieve this revolutionary change of outlook and ethos, will they lose their hold? And, if they do lose it, will their heritage pass to Buddhism, or will Mankind embrace some other religion or religions that have not yet appeared above the horizon? The 'annihilation of distance' has already raised these questions, but it has not yet indicated what the answers to them are likely to be.

The outer surface of a religion reflects the style of the time and place in which the religion originally took shape. The heart of a religion is a response to perennial human spiritual needs. In a time of unusually radical and rapid technological and social change, such as we are experiencing today, religions may present themselves in unfamiliar forms; yet, beneath the surface, their essence may prove to be the same as that of the historic religions which we recognize as being religions, whether or not we adhere to them. Religion is one of the intrinsic faculties of human nature. At any rate, hitherto, every human society, and every individual participant in every society, has had a religion. Neither unawareness nor indifference nor hostility can eliminate religion from human life.[17]

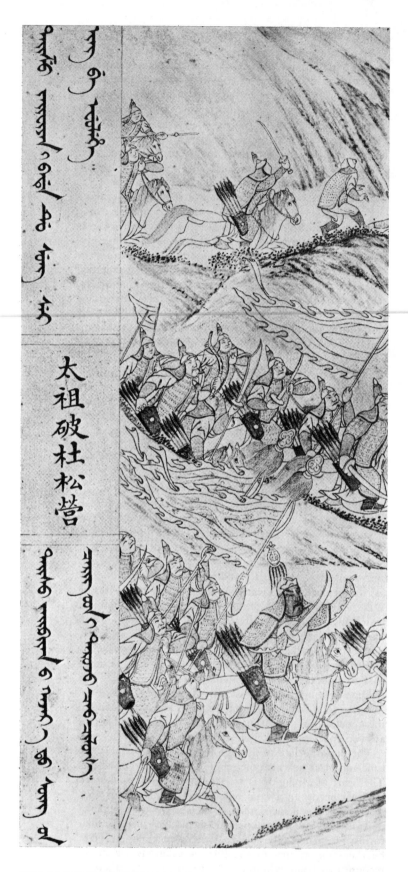

太祖破杜松營

THE ACCENTS OF IMPERIAL RULE

237 Empire-builders usually give official status to several languages in the interests of efficient communication throughout their wide dominions. This scene of the storming of a Chinese garrison comes from a contemporary record of the Manchu conquest of China, and its caption is written in the three current official languages, Manchu, Chinese, and Mongol.

35 Languages and scripts

IT CAN ALMOST be taken for granted that a universal state will have provided itself with official media of mental communication, and that these will include not only one or more languages for spoken intercourse, but also some system of visual records based on a written notation. The language and script chosen by a universal state for these purposes must of course be intelligible both to the imperial Power and to its subject peoples, but this general condition is in practice susceptible of a number of variations. In a few cases – the Japanese Tokugawa Shogunate, for instance, or the Russian Empire – official currency was simply given to the mother tongue of the empire-builders, in virtue of the fact that the universal state comprised no more than a single linguistic domain. This clear-cut situation has not, however, been the rule; for most civilizations have embraced a variety of national languages and scripts, including perhaps wholly alien usages. More often than not, therefore, when it comes to deciding on the official language of a universal state, the empire-builders are faced, not with an accomplished fact to ratify, but with a choice between several competing candidates. In these circumstances, the most usual practice has been for the empire-builders to give official currency to their own mother tongue but without granting it a monopoly. Indeed, in the administration of universal states a plurality of official languages seems to be the rule; and a medium that enjoys the legal primacy may not in practice be the medium most in use. There may be secondary languages that reign supreme in particular regions of the empire, or in particular imperial services, and these may be *lingue franche* that have won this position for themselves *de facto* without having been given recognition *de jure*. A further alternative to either a monopoly or a partnership in language is for the empire-builders to accept the *de facto* primacy of some other language than their own, and to refrain from enforcing their mother tongue. Each of these possible situations can be illustrated in turn from the histories of past universal states.

In the Sinic World the linguistic problem was solved in a characteristically drastic fashion by Shih Hwang-ti (*imperabat* 221–210 BC). This founder of the Sinic universal state gave exclusive currency to the version of the Chinese characters that had been in official use in his own ancestral state of Ch'in (Ts'in), and thereby succeeded in arresting the tendency for each of the Contending States to develop a parochial script only partially intelligible to outsiders. Since the Sinic characters were ideograms conveying meanings, not phonemes representing sounds, the effect of Shih Hwang-ti's act was to endow the Sinic Society with a uniform visual language, which would continue – even if the spoken language were to break up into mutually unintelligible dialects – to serve as a means of ecumenical communication for the literate élite. This standardization of the Sinic characters would not, however, have saved the Sinic Society from the curse of a babel of tongues if there had not been other forces working in the Sinic World in favour of uniformity of speech as well as of script.

To begin with, at the date of the Ch'in (Ts'in) unification in 221 BC, the Sinic World happened still to be unusually homogeneous in language, though by that time it had expanded far and wide from its original nucleus. A great majority of the population even of this vastly extended area spoke some variety of the Chinese branch of the Chinese-Siamese group of the Asian monosyllabic languages, and the heterophone minority largely consisted of speakers of some language of the kindred Tibeto-Burman group. Yet the unifying influence of this original linguistic homogeneity might have been more than counteracted by the combined effect of the geographical expansion and the political disruption of the Sinic Society during its time of troubles if Shih Hwang-ti had not opened a new chapter of Sinic history by imposing political unity, and if his Han successors had not underpinned this edifice of ecumenical government by creating an efficient civil service to administer it. These professional civil servants, recruited from all quarters of the Empire and posted in any province except that of their birth, could not conduct their business in writing alone. The new imperial governing class needed a common means of spoken communication, and it was the resultant standardized official vocalization of a standardized script that saved the Sinic Society from being afflicted with a divisive multiplicity of languages.

A similar monopoly of language was imposed by the Umayyad Caliph 'Abd-al-Malik (*imperabat* AD 685–705) and by the Spanish *conquistadores* of the Central American World. However, the more frequent practice of empire-builders has been to provide their universal state with several official languages, including their own. In the British Raj in India, for instance, the English mother tongue of the rebuilders of the Mughal Raj was, for certain purposes, substituted for Persian, the official language that had been bequeathed by the Mughals to their British and other successors. In AD 1829 the British Indian government made English the medium for its diplomatic correspondence, and in 1835 the medium for higher education in its dominions. But when in 1837 the final step was taken in the deposition of Persian from its official status in British India, the British Indian government did not introduce the use of English for all the other purposes that Persian had previously served. In the conduct of judicial and fiscal proceedings, which were provinces of public administration that personally concerned all Indians of every nationality, caste, and class, the British Indian government replaced Persian, not by English, but by the local vernaculars; and the Sanskritized Hindi vernacular known as 'Hindustani' was actually manufactured by British Protestant missionaries to provide the Hindu population of Northern India with a counterpart of the Persianized Hindi vernacular, known as 'Urdu', which the Indian Muslims had already manufactured for themselves. This humane and sensible decision to forbear from misusing political power by giving exclusive currency to the empire-builders' own alien tongue perhaps partially accounts for the remarkable fact that English has remained in use as an official language in an independent India and Pakistan freed from the shackles of colonial rule.

In the Ottoman Empire the founders' native Turkish was taken as the official language of imperial administration; but, in the heyday of the Ottoman Power in the sixteenth and seventeenth centuries of the Christian Era, the *lingua franca* of the Padishah's Slave-Household was Serbo-Croat, and the language of command in the Ottoman navy Italian. Moreover, on the civil side the Ottoman government, like the British Indian government, followed a policy of allowing its subjects as far as possible to use languages of their own choice in public business that was of personal concern to the individual. The judicial administration was delegated by the central government to autonomous communal authorities which conducted their business in the language traditionally employed by them for public purposes.[1] Since these communal authorities were ecclesiastical, the languages which they used for civil as well as for religious affairs were the sacred languages of their respective religions. The law administered in the communal courts of the Muslim community throughout the Ottoman Empire was written in Arabic, the law of the communal courts of the Orthodox Christian community throughout the Empire in Greek, the law of the Gregorian Monophysite community in Armenian, and so on. It will be seen that the 'Osmanlis in the Orthodox Christian and Arabic Worlds showed the same restraint as the British in India in limiting the scope of the official currency which they gave to their own mother tongue.

The Romans too showed some restraint in the imposition of Latin as an official language in the Greek-speaking provinces of their Empire. They contented themselves with making Latin the exclusive language of military command for units of the imperial army, wherever recruited and stationed, and the principal language of municipal administration for colonies of Italian origin on Greek or Oriental ground. For other purposes they continued to employ the Attic *koine* wherever they found it already in official use; and they made its official status in their own Empire conspicuous by giving it a place, side by side with Latin, in the central administration as well. At Rome under the Principate the imperial chancery was organized in duplicate, with a Greek as well as a Latin side, so that correspondents using either of 'the two languages' (as Latin and Greek were styled *sans phrase*) knew that their business could be transacted in the language of their own choice. This Roman forbearance towards the Greek language was something more than a tribute to the pre-eminence of Greek over Latin as a medium of cultural exchange: it represented a major victory of statesmanship over *hybris* in Roman souls; for, in those vast expanses of the Empire where Greek was not in competition with Latin, the triumph of Latin was so sensational that it might have turned the heads of any but the most sober-minded empire-builders. So far from having to impose the use of Latin upon their subjects and allies in territories outside the Greek language's range, the Romans were in the happy position of being able to enhance its attractiveness by treating the use of it as a privilege that had to be sued for.[2] Even in its contests with those languages and dialects that stood on a cultural and literary par with Greek, Latin was invariably victorious. This triumphal progress of the Latin language elsewhere in the Roman Empire is the setting in which we have to put the Romans'

238, 239 The Achaemenian emperors gave no special status to their own Persian mother tongue. Above, the famous rock inscription at Behistan in Persia records Darius's victories in the Akkadian, Elamite, and Medo-Persian languages. Darius's seal, left, also gives his name in the same three tongues.

deference towards the Greek language in order to appreciate it at its full worth.

An even more remarkable restraint was shown by the Sumerian founders of 'the Empire of the Four Quarters' when they put the upstart Akkadian language on a par with a Sumerian which was not only the empire-builders' own mother tongue but was the historic vehicle of the Sumerian culture. This generous policy was no doubt inspired by the practical consideration that in Ur-Nammu's day (*imperabat c.* 2113–2096 BC) Akkadian was gaining ground while Sumerian was on the ebb; and, in the event, Sumerian had almost become a dead language by the time when the universal state which Sumerian-speaking empire-builders had inaugurated reached the end of its chequered career after the death of Hammurabi (*imperabat c.* 1792–1750 BC). This Amorite restorer of the Sumerian political edifice did not strive against the odds to keep alive the moribund mother tongue of his predecessor Ur-Nammu; but it is significant that he also appears to have made no attempt to fill the Sumerian language's now all but vacant place with his own ancestral Canaanite dialect, but to have allowed Akkadian – which by this time stood at its zenith – to enjoy, unchallenged, the virtual monopoly which by then it had won for itself *de facto*.

The Achaemenidae gave as modest a place in the government of their Empire to their Persian mother tongue as to their Persian mother country. Darius the Great's account of his own acts on the rock of Behistan, overhanging the Great North-East Road, was inscribed in triplicate in three adaptations of the cuneiform script conveying the languages of the three imperial capitals: Elamite for Susa, Medo-Persian for Ecbatana, and Akkadian for Babylon. The same three languages were employed in official inscriptions on imperial buildings in all parts of the Empire. It is to the credit of the Achaemenidae that they should have thus placed two other languages officially on a par with their own mother tongue, but this conscientious even-handedness was too pedantic and too clumsy to meet the practical needs of current imperial administration. The Elamite tongue, for example, though it did happen to be the language of Susa, was not a *lingua franca*, and was already moribund in its own parochial domain; and the version of the cuneiform script that had been specially devised for the notation of the Medo-Persian language failed – in spite of its technical excellence – to win its way into general use, and consequently failed to perpetuate itself. The increasing inaccuracy of its use in the inscriptions of Artaxerxes II (*imperabat* 404–358 BC) and Artaxerxes III (*imperabat* 358–338 BC) betrays the truth that its proper usage was being forgotten within perhaps less than two hundred years of its invention.

This infelicity in the Achaemenids' original choice of official scripts and languages was only partially offset by their liberality in the use of unofficial languages and scripts which had a regional currency – for example, the Greek language and alphabet in the neighbourhood of the Aegean, and, in Egypt, the Egyptian language conveyed either in the hieroglyphic or in the cursive form of the Egyptiac characters. It seems, indeed, to have been their regular practice to provide translations, in the local vernaculars, of official documents addressed to their subjects. But the stroke of statesmanship by which they saved a situation which their own pedantry had created was their act of giving official currency to the Aramaic alphabet and language – side by side with the three hyper-official languages and scripts – in all provinces of the Empire to the west of Babylonia.

The sequel showed that commerce and culture may be more potent instruments than politics for making a language's fortune. In the Achaemenian Empire the speakers of Aramaic were politically of no account, whereas the speakers of Medo-Persian were politically dominant; and, apart from this political 'pull', the Medo-Persian language was by no means at a disadvantage in other respects. The area over which it was spoken as a mother tongue was probably not less extensive, though it was of course much less populous, than the area over which Aramaic was current at the time not merely as a *lingua franca* but as the language of daily life. Moreover, the unknown man of genius who had adapted the cuneiform characters for the conveyance of the Medo-Persian language had endowed it with a script that was almost as convenient as the Aramaic alphabet. Taking his cue, we may suppose, from the alphabet itself, he had achieved with the cuneiform characters what had never been achieved with them by their Sumerian inventors or their Akkadian, Elamite, and Hittite users: he had contrived to convey visually all the sounds of the Medo-Persian language in an all but alphabetic syllabary of not more than thirty-six characters. Yet in the competition between the Medo-Persian and the Aramaic scripts and languages it was the Aramaic that won.

It was not so surprising that the Aramaic language should have beaten the Medo-Persian in a competition for capturing the domain of a faltering Akkadian tongue, for here Aramaic had been the first in the field, and it enjoyed, in addition, the overwhelming advantage of being a sister Semitic language which an Akkadian-speaker might master with far greater ease than he could an utterly alien Indo-European dialect. The really remarkable triumph was achieved by the Aramaic script, which succeeded in replacing the cuneiform as the medium for conveying the Medo-Persian language in its post-Achaemenian phase. This victory must appear the more extraordinary considering that it was accompanied by a lamentably perverse retrogression in the art of writing. Whereas the forgotten inventor of the Achaemenian script for the conveyance of the Medo-Persian language had shown his originality by making an exclusively phonetic use of cuneiform characters that had originated as ideograms, the inventors of the Pehlevi script for the conveyance of the same language in its next phase mishandled a ready-made phonetic alphabet by coining ideograms out of it. Instead of consistently conveying Persian words by spelling them out in Aramaic letters used phonetically, they lapsed into conveying them by writing Aramaic words that were their equivalents in meaning but were, of course, entirely unrelated to them in sound. This ability of the Aramaic alphabet to capture the Persian language even in a usage that stultified the alphabet's own distinctive technical excellence gives some measure of the prestige which it must have acquired by then in Persian minds; and one source of this prestige was undoubtedly the official status that had been given to the Aramaic language and alphabet by Achaemenian emperors whose mother tongue was not Semitic but Indo-European.

In the Mauryan Empire the philosopher-emperor Açoka (*imperabat* 273–232 BC) succeeded in reconciling the demands of impartial justice with those of practical convenience by employing a number of different local living vernaculars conveyed in two different scripts, the Brahmi and the Kharoshthi. This catholicity in Açoka's choice of media for communication with his subjects was prompted by the single-minded purpose of acquainting them with the way of salvation revealed to Mankind by Açoka's master Gautama, as the Spanish successors to the Incas were moved by their eagerness for the propagation of the Roman Catholic form of Christianity to allow the Gospel to be preached in the Andean World in the Quichuan *lingua franca*. This Quichuan had gained the wide currency that it enjoyed at the time of the Spanish conquest because the Spaniards' Inca predecessors had made the learning of Quichuan compulsory, and had imposed this intellectual *corvée* on themselves as well as on their subjects – if it is a fact that the Incas had an esoteric language of their own which they did not choose to vulgarize.

There are other less doubtful examples of imperial peoples' refraining from giving any official status whatsoever to their own mother tongue. The Mongols, for instance, did not take advantage of their immense conquests in order to propagate the Mongol language from the Pacific to the Euphrates and the Carpathians. The Mongol Khaqans employed the Sinic characters and the 'mandarin' dialect for the government of China, and the Mongol Il-Khans the New Persian language and the Perso-Arabic alphabet for the government of Iran and 'Iraq. Even the Khans of Chaghatay's and Batu's appanages, who did not transfer their headquarters from the steppe to the habitat of their sedentary subjects, nevertheless abandoned the use of their Mongol mother tongue in favour of the Turkish that was current among a majority of their Nomad subjects. The succeeding generations of Mongol rulers perpetuated this pattern of extreme linguistic flexibility; and, even at the foundation of the Timurid Mughal Empire in India in the sixteenth century of the Christian Era, by which time the adopted Turki of the empire-builders had developed into an established literary language, the official language selected for the new Raj was not Turki but Persian; moreover, in the unofficial hybrid *lingua franca* that was begotten of the social intercourse between the Mughal court and army and the Hindu subject population, it was Persian again, and not Turki, that was infused into Hindustani.

These, then, are the various ways in which the founders of universal states have met the demand for an official medium of communication in their empires. It is clear, of course, that the essential attribute of an official language – namely, its currency throughout a large domain – will tend to be of service to other parties than the empire-builders alone. In the first place, a language that has been given official currency in an empire is likely to be retained by a restorer of a dilapidated universal state as his own medium of communication with his new subjects, at least temporarily. Akkadian, as we have seen, was taken over from Ur-Nammu's empire by Hammurabi; Greek by the

Umayyad Caliphate from the Roman Empire; and Persian by the British from the Mughal Raj in India; though in the two latter cases the inherited language was eventually superseded by another. The Akkadian language itself actually showed a remarkable resilience, for it continued to be used as a medium of diplomatic exchange, commerce, and culture, not only within the old frontiers of the defunct Sumero-Akkadian Empire, but also in regions never ruled by either Hammurabi or Ur-Nammu, and never even trodden by the great Akkadian war-lords of an earlier age, Sargon and Naramsin. In the fourteenth century BC the Akkadian language and script were being employed in the archives and libraries of Hittite kings at Bogazkale, and, surprisingly, in the correspondence between the imperial government of Egypt and its client princes in Syria, as well as in its transactions with such independent Powers as the Khatti and Mitanni. Latin, too, survived long after the disappearance of the Empire which had conferred an official status on it, and became the accepted medium of international cultural and diplomatic exchange in a European field that was already divided among a number of national vernaculars.

This survival power of a language and its ability to be turned to account by latter-day secular agencies is also illustrated in the fate of Aramaic when, on the overthrow of the Achaemenian Empire by Alexander, it was deposed from its official position and replaced by the Attic *koine*. Deprived of the imperial patronage which it had enjoyed for two centuries, the Aramaic language succeeded, by the first century of the Christian Era, in completing the process that it had already begun of supplanting Akkadian on the east and Canaanite on the west as the living language of the entire Semitic-speaking population of the Fertile Crescent. Likewise, on the strength of its own merits, the Aramaic alphabet achieved, in AD 1599, the greater success of being adopted as the notation for the Manchu language on the eve of the Manchu conquest of China.

This diffusion of the Aramaic alphabet was an intellectual conquest which surpassed in its sweep the military and political conquests of the Mongol and Arab herdsmen-warriors; but the ultimate victors in this field were the higher religions which sped the Aramaic alphabet on its way by taking it into their service. In its 'Square Hebrew' variant it became the vehicle of the Jewish scripture and liturgy; in an Arabic adaptation of its Nabatean variant it became the alphabet of Islam; in its Syriac variant it served impartially the two antithetical heresies of Nestorianism and Monophysitism into which Christianity polarized itself south-east of the Taurus; in an Avestan adaptation of its Pehlevi variant it enshrined the sacred books of the Zoroastrian Church; in a Manichaean adaptation it laboured for a heresiarch execrated by both Christians and Zoroastrians; in a Kharoshthi variant it provided the Emperor Açoka with an instrument for conveying the teachings of the Buddha to his subjects in the former Achaemenian province in the Panjab. This latter-day ecclesiastical use of the Aramaic alphabet has given it an abiding place in history which it would never have won from its ephemeral secular canonization as one of the official scripts of the Achaemenian Empire; and, in this point, it has not been unique.

In like manner the Latin and Attic Greek official languages and alphabets of the Roman Empire won their place in history as the liturgical, theological, and administrative vehicles of the Roman Church in the West and the Greek Church in Orthodox Christendom, while the Neo-Sanskrit official language of the Gupta Empire justified its resurrection by providing a literary medium for both Hinduism and the Mahayana. Even the Emperor Shih Hwang-ti's great work of standardizing the Sinic characters may live to be remembered, not for the service that it did to ethics and politics by providing the Confucian school of philosophy and the imperial civil service with a common instrument of literary expression, but for its service to religion in preserving in translation certain indispensable scriptures of the Mahayana that are no longer extant in the original Sanskrit. The assistance provided for the propagation of Catholic Christianity in the New World was a similarly unintended effect of the Incas' pedagogic imposition of Quichuan on their long-suffering subjects. And it is certain that the Buddha's devoted exponent, the Emperor Açoka, will continue to be revered by Pali-reading Hinayanian Buddhists for his deliberate adoption of the living languages of his subjects as the media for his inscriptions.

240 Assyrian clerks make their records in two languages – one uses a stylus for inscribing Akkadian, while the other writes with a pen in Aramaic: relief from the palace of Sennacherib.

36 Capital cities

THE SEATS of the central governments of universal states show a marked tendency to change their locations in the course of time, and their patterns of movement suggest that the eventual choice of site is strongly influenced by other factors than just the self-interest of the original empire-builders. The founders of universal states usually begin ruling their dominions from a seat of government convenient to themselves alone: either the established capital of their own fatherland, now transformed from a parochial into a universal state; or else on the fringe of the territories which they have subjugated, at a point where these are particularly accessible from the empire-builders' own country. As time goes on, however, the experience of imperial administration or the pressure of events is apt to lead either the original empire-builders or their successors to transfer the capital to a new site which is convenient, not for the empire-building Power alone, but for the empire itself as a whole – a central location, for example, if administrative convenience is the criterion, or a strategic point on a frontier if defence is the most urgent consideration.

The original location and subsequent changes in the location of the capital of a universal state obviously depend to a large extent upon the identity and provenance of the empire-building Power. In universal states founded by representatives of an alien civilization or by barbarians, the imperial capital is apt to start on the edge of the empire and to travel towards its interior. This was the pattern in the case of the 'Osmanli founders of the Ottoman Empire. They started their empire-building operations from a base just beyond the borders of the Orthodox Christian World in the fourteenth century of the Christian Era, and their seat of government travelled *pari passu* with the progressive extension of their dominions in the fourteenth and fifteenth centuries. It moved first from Eskishehr, 'the old city', on the north-western rim of the Anatolian plateau, to Yenishehr, 'the new city', in the lowlands within range of the Sea of Marmara. In AD 1326 it moved on to Bursa, and forty years later leapt the Dardanelles, entered the Balkan peninsula, and found its first site there at Adrianople. Sultan Mehmet the Conqueror (*imperabat* AD 1451–81), who completed the political reunification of the Orthodox Christian World, apart from Russia, under Ottoman rule, subsequently brought the Ottoman seat of government to its final resting-place at Constantinople, the former capital of the East Roman Empire and the cultural metropolis of Orthodox Christendom. Constantinople did not lose the status which Mehmet had conferred upon it until after the dissolution of the Ottoman Empire and the establishment of the Turkish Republic in 1923. Under Article Two of the Turkish Constitution of 1924, Constantinople forfeited juridically to Ankara the role of being the official seat of government of the Ottoman Empire's Turkish successor-state.

The progressive advance of the Ottoman capital towards the heart of the Orthodox Christian World has a parallel in the series of stages by which the capital of the Mongol Khaqans followed the China-ward course of Mongol conquest. The first major successes in Chingis Khan's career were his conquests of the Karayits and Naimans, the two Nestorian Christian Turkish Nomad peoples who occupied the Orkhon basin and dominated the surrounding steppes. When the Mongols acquired both the basin and the concomitant paramountcy over adjacent areas, they signalized their new status as empire-builders by laying out a permanent capital for themselves in the Orkhon basin at Qaraqorum. For this purpose, skilled craftsmen were uprooted from their distant homes in China, Russia, and Western Christendom and were carried away captive to beautify the Khaqan's rising city on the steppe; but before the work was finished it was rendered nugatory by the triumph of Mongol arms on the Chinese front.

Under the Khaqan Qubilay (*imperabat* AD 1260–95), the Mongols overran the whole continental domain of the Sinic Society, including the Yangtse basin and the southern sea-board; and the gravitational pull of this Far Eastern sub-continent immediately made itself felt in the location of the Mongol capital. In AD 1264 Qubilay began to recondition Peking – the site in the north-eastern corner of China where the previous Kin conquerors of North China had placed their seat of government – and in 1267 he removed his own capital to Peking from Qaraqorum. The establishment of the Mongols' capital on this site was to have a more lasting effect than their mere military conquest of the Chinese Empire. When the Manchus followed in the Mongols' footsteps by conquering the whole of China and reconstituting a Sinic universal state in the seventeenth century of the Christian Era, history repeated itself in the location of the imperial capital. Before the Manchus set about the conquest of China within the Wall, they had already made themselves a capital at Mukden, and were more firmly planted there than the Mongols had been in their own first capital of Qaraqorum. The Manchu leaders, at any rate, were already half Sinified before they crossed the Great Wall, and Mukden had become a seat not merely of Manchu government but of Chinese culture. Yet the Manchu conquerors of China took the same decision as the Mongol Qubilay. The guardians of the Manchu boy-king Shun Chih (*imperabat* AD 1644–61), when they made him Emperor, transferred the Manchu seat of government to Peking, and allowed Mukden – which had been 'the education of' the Manchus – to sink to a subordinate status.

In contrast to these examples of movement from the periphery to the interior, the capital cities of universal states founded by some metropolitan Power tend to start in a central position and subsequently to travel towards the frontiers of a politically unified world. The classic example of this tendency is afforded by the history of the Indic universal state, which was both originally founded and then re-established by dynasties whose ancestral domain was the centrally situated state of Magadha. The Mauryas and the Guptas alike retained their seat of government at Pataliputra (the latter-day Patna), which had previously been Magadha's parochial capital. Pataliputra stood at the confluence of the Ganges and the Jumna, and was the natural administrative centre for the Ganges basin; yet, in spite of the practical advantageousness of the site, which worked together with the imponderable forces of tradition and prestige to preserve Pataliputra's prerogative, the seat of government eventually travelled north-westward in both these two parallel chapters of Indic history, and in both cases alike it was drawn in that direction by politico-military pressures from beyond the frontier.

When the derelict domain of the enfeebled Mauryan Empire had been overrun by the Bactrian Greek Prince Demetrius in 200–183 BC, the conqueror transferred the seat of government from Pataliputra to a new site far along the Great North-West Road connecting the former Mauryan capital with Demetrius's own former capital at Bactra (Balkh) on the Central Asian side of the Hindu Kush. Demetrius's New Taxila lay near the old city of the same name, in the neighbourhood of the latter-day Rawalpindi, which, before the foundation of the Mauryan Empire, had been the capital of a parochial Indian state. It commanded the approaches, on the Indian side, to a difficult section of the highway along which a traveller had to negotiate the three successive obstacles of the river Indus, the Khyber pass, and the main chain of the Hindu Kush. This neighbourhood was the natural location for the capital of a Power which was seeking to 'abolish the Hindu Kush' by uniting the Ganges-Jumna basin with the Oxus-Jaxartes basin. The Greek war-lord Demetrius's pioneering and audacious attempt to defy physical geography, however, proved ephemeral. The Bactrian Greek Power had no sooner overrun the Mauryan Empire than it was broken up by fratricidal warfare which opened the way for Nomad invasions of its dominions on the Indian as well as the Central Asian side of the Hindu Kush; but when, after more than two centuries of kaleidoscopic political change, the momentary achievement of the Greek empire-builder Demetrius was repeated in the first or second century of the Christian Era by the Kushan empire-builder Kadphises I and was perpetuated by Kadphises's successors, the seat of government of this reconstituted political union of North-West India with Central Asia came to rest not far from the spot originally selected for it by Demetrius. The capital of the Kushan Empire was planted at Peshawar, on the Great North-West Road between the Indus and the Khyber pass.

After the Mauryan Empire had been re-established by the Guptas, history repeated itself. The Guptas, like their predecessors, ruled the Indic World from Pataliputra; but, when the Guptan Empire collapsed in its turn and was momentarily restored by the Emperor Harsha (*imperabat* AD 606–47), this last of all the Hindu rulers of an Indic universal state placed his seat of government, not at Pataliputra, but at Sthanesvara on the banks of the Upper Jumna, above the site of Delhi, covering the north-western approaches to the Ganges basin from the quarter from which Hun and Gurjara Nomad invaders had swept down on the Guptan Empire from the Eurasian steppe in the preceding chapter of Indic history.

A comparable shift from the centre outwards was made by the capital of the Sumero-Akkadian universal state, 'the Empire of the Four Quarters', which was founded at Ur by the empire-builder Ur-Nammu (*imperabat c.* 2113–2096 BC). The seat of government remained at Ur for more than a century, but – after the break-up of Ur-Nammu's empire and its partial restoration by Hammurabi (*imperabat c.* 1792–1750 BC) – it shifted north-westwards to Babylon in consequence of the expansion of the Sumero-Akkadian World in that direction. Babylon, like Peking, had been founded as a capital for a barbarian parochial state that had encroached on one of the fringes of a faltering civilization's domain. In a different context,[1] it has been noted that the Mongols' indigenous successors in the imperial government of a reunited China, the Ming, were moved by military experiences to transfer their capital from Nanking, in the heart of China, to the Kin's, and the Mongols', geographically eccentric capital of a Chinese Empire under barbarian rule.

Now that we have looked at the common patterns of movement followed by the capital cities of universal states, we can go on to inquire what role these cities can play other than the intended one of serving the empire-builders as their seat of government. The most important accidental characteristic acquired by a capital city does in fact derive directly from its role as a seat of government; for the city that is performing this ecumenical function becomes a microcosm of its own world and the central focus for the life of the state in all its aspects. Its walls enfold, at close quarters, representatives of all nations and classes, speakers of all languages, and adherents of all religious and philosophical persuasions, while its gates lead out on to highways running in all directions to the world's end.

The Incas divided the wards [of the imperial city of Cuzco] according to the four parts of their empire, called Tahuantin-suyu. The division dated back to the first Inca Manco Cápac, who ordered that the savages he had subjugated should be settled according to their places of origin, those from the east to the east, those from the west to the west, and so on. The dwellings of the first subjects were thus disposed in a circle within the limits of the town, and those from newly conquered areas settled according to the situation of their provinces. The *curacas* [lords of vassals] built houses to live in when they came to the capital, each next to one another, but settling on the side nearest his own province. If a chief's province was to the right of his neighbor's, he built his house to the right; if to the left, he built it on the left, and if behind, he built his house behind. The result of this arrangement was that anyone who contemplated the wards and dwellings of the numerous and varied tribes who had settled in them beheld the whole empire at once, as if in a looking glass or a cosmographic plan.[2]

While Cuzco was perhaps unique in being deliberately laid out according to this conscious plan, any capital city is seen by its own inhabitants, by people outside its walls, and by nations beyond the frontiers, as the visible epitome of the world which it governs. For this reason, it is the primary objective of an invading Power, a source of plunder for barbarian hordes, and of legitimacy for alien usurpers. Restorers of dilapidated empires, and revivers of disintegrated empires, are aided in their work of reconstruction by the lingering prestige of the ancient seat of imperial government. When a usurper takes over his victim's former capital as a going concern, the effect is to lighten his task of hoisting himself into the saddle and keeping himself

CHRISTENDOM'S ROMAN EMPERORS

241, 242, 243 Charlemagne's coronation at Rome, below left, recognized the city's prestige and established a precedent for his successors. Many future Holy Roman Emperors sought to make the arduous journey – above, Henry VI *en route* in 1191 – until 1452, when Frederick III, below right, received his crown in Rome in the last performance of this rite.

244 The French Emperor: Napoleon tried to replace the Holy Roman Empire with a new empire centred on France; after dismantling the thousand-year-old institution, he also reversed the tradition of coronation, deporting Pope Pius VII to Paris to crown him there in 1804.

there. Though Peking, for instance, was first promoted to be a seat of imperial government by the intruding barbarian Khitan, and not by any indigenous Chinese dynasty, the subsequent domination of the Chinese people by the Kin in place of the Khitan and by the Mongols in place of the Kin was undoubtedly facilitated by the retention, in both cases, of a capital from which a subject Chinese population had gradually grown accustomed to receiving a barbarian master's word of command. *A fortiori*, in a later passage of Sinic history, the retention of Peking as the seat of imperial government must have facilitated the usurpation of the Manchu barbarians when they took the imperial city over, not from barbarian predecessors, but from the indigenous Chinese dynasty of the Ming.

The prestige of an imperial capital may even survive the decline and fall of the empire at whose head it once stood. In a medieval Western World the 'Roman Emperors' of the German nation could not acquire a perfect title to legitimate investiture with their purple robes without paying at least one visit to the ruins of Rome in order to be crowned in the midst of them by the Pope and be acclaimed by a 'Roman

people' who in their day were, not the *faex* (dregs), but the *faex faecis Romuli*.[3] For German potentates whose strength was derived from hereditary dominions lying north of the Alps, this Italian expedition was always as costly and perilous as it was frequently barren and humiliating. Yet the prestige of a dead Rome's shadow was still so great that, for the sake of it, these moth-kings sacrificed a living Germany's substance; and, though the medieval German Kingdom eventually came to grief through a persistent pursuit of this Roman will-o'-the-wisp, Napoleon's subsequent experience was to indicate retrospectively the difficulties in which the medieval Western Emperors might have involved themselves if they had refused altogether to pay their personal homage to the ex-imperial city's imponderable power. Napoleon's mistake was to summon the Pope from Rome to Paris to assist at his coronation as Emperor of a reconstituted substitute for the Holy Roman Empire; and, by flouting Rome and bullying her sovereign pontiff, he won, not respect for his own political power, but sympathy for the helplessness of his venerable victim.

A capital city of a universal state serves above all as a melting-pot for alien cultures and religions, whose exponents are attracted to it by the unrivalled facilities that it offers – through its cosmopolitan population and its role as the node of a communications system – for the enrichment and diffusion of these cultures and religions. It is through this function that the capital cities of universal states find their lasting links with the future and hence their principal historic significance. The two classic exemplifications of this truth are Rome and Constantinople, each of them the administrative centre of a mighty empire, yet each deriving its immortality not from this function but from its role as a transmitting centre for the higher religion of Christianity. The political power of Rome has been defunct now for more than sixteen centuries, but the city is still exercising a worldwide influence that is a consequence of the work and death in Rome of the two Apostles Peter and Paul almost two millennia ago. As for Constantinople, her religious mission was manifest from the moment of her birth; for this New Rome was founded by Constantine the Great, as St Petersburg was founded by Peter the Great, with a spiritual as well as a geopolitical purpose. When the first Christian Emperor laid out his new capital on ground that had been cleared by his pagan predecessor Septimius Severus's vindictive erasure of Byzantium, he was founding a city that was to be Christian from the start; and it is still clear today that this religious function was of more lasting significance than the superb geographical location that had prompted Constantine to plant his new Christian capital on that particular site. In the course of the following sixteen hundred years, Constantinople has won and lost and twice rewon the political prerogative of serving as an imperial capital – for the Roman Empire, the East Roman Empire, and the Ottoman Empire in turn; yet today such influence as she still exercises in the world beyond the frontiers of Turkey is due to her being the seat of a Patriarch who is still recognized by the ecclesiastical heads of the other Eastern Orthodox Churches as *primus inter pares*.

CAPITALS OF CHRISTENDOM

245, 246 Capital cities are religious centres, a status they retain long after their imperial functions have been forgotten. The memory of secular Rome's Seven Hills was overshadowed by her Seven Churches, left; and in fifteenth-century Constantinople, right, the massive dome of Ayia Sofia outtops all other buildings.

37 Civil services

OUR SURVEY of the institutions of universal states has so far included examples only of those imperial installations which seem to have been features of all such states, for it is hard to imagine any universal state establishing and maintaining itself without some system of language and communications, or without a capital city. By contrast, an imperial civil service is an institution which is found in widely varying degrees of development in different universal states, ranging over the whole gamut from a rudimentary to a highly sophisticated system. The Achaemenian professional civil service, for instance, always remained rudimentary. Its most important representatives were the imperial secretaries who were resident at the headquarters of the imperial governors, but were independent of the satraps and reported directly to the central government. As a further check, the satraps were also kept under observation by itinerant inspectors, expressively nicknamed 'the Emperor's eyes'.[1] The need for a central authority to gather together, hold, and manipulate these widely ramifying threads of administrative control seems to have been met, in the organization of the imperial court, by the evolution of the commander of the imperial bodyguard – the 'Hazarapatis' or 'Chiliarch' – into an imperial chancellor or minister of state, supported by a skilled and numerous administrative and clerical staff. While the Achaemenian civil service never developed beyond this relatively simple stage, the Ottoman government provided for its corresponding administrative needs by creating a civil service that was not just an efficient professional corporation, but was the secular equivalent of a religious order – so rigorously segregated, austerely disciplined, and potently conditioned as to be transfigured into a superhuman, or sub-human, race. The professional civil services of other universal states can be placed at various points between these two extremes, as we shall see if we survey the field.

A barbarian empire-builder who has conquered an already existing universal state by a sudden stroke will probably have no choice but to take over the civil service of that state as he finds it; for instance, the Umayyad possessors of the ex-Roman and ex-Sasanian territories in the Near East left their dominions to be administered by the existing Christian and Zoroastrian civil servants. Arabic was substituted for Greek, Coptic, and Pehlevi as the official language of the public records, but no attempt was made by the Arabs to take over the business of administration itself; and, though under the ensuing 'Abbasid régime the process of conversion to Islam became a landslide which carried into the Islamic fold a majority of the population of the Caliphate of all classes and occupations, the residual unconverted Christian minority continued to play a part in the civil service that was out of all proportion to its eventual numbers. However, although – as in this case – the main lines of action are likely to be dictated by circumstances, there may still be some room for the barbarian usurper to modify the institution that he has received from his predecessors and to preserve some of the more valuable elements from his own native tradition. In the less abrupt course of the establishment of the Manchu Empire over China, the reciprocal relations of the Manchu and the indigenous Chinese administrative institution came to be adjusted more subtly than in the case of the Arabs and their subjects.

Almost half a century before the Manchus embarked on their conquest of Intramural China in AD 1644, their old clan-based feudal administration was replaced by a Chinese-inspired system of administration in the 'banners' or provinces which they were progressively acquiring outside the Great Wall. The Manchus began by employing Chinese scholar-serfs to administer these newly won provinces; but this servile civil service – which resembled the Ottoman Padishah's Slave-Household in embryo – never came to full maturity. The empire-builders were soon made aware of the expediency, and indeed necessity, of taking Chinese civil servants into the Manchu service as free men and of according them the status that had traditionally been theirs under an indigenous Chinese régime. The event that provoked this crucial change of policy was the defection to the Manchu side of the powerful Ming commandant Li Yung-fang; for Li was a potential ally of such importance to the Manchu cause that he was enticed into their service by an offer of admission on terms of equality. This bargain created a precedent for the future, and in 1631 the traditional Chinese bureaucratic system of administration was officially adopted in the Manchu Empire. By the time that the Manchus invaded and conquered Intramural China, the slow maturing of a process of Sinification over two generations had endowed them with an administration that was both familiar to and esteemed by their new subjects. It was, in fact, for this reason that the Manchus were invited into China by the indigenous élite of scholar-gentry, since the cultivated classes reckoned that their prospects would be better under an alien but half-civilized Power than under their subversive rebel compatriots who were at this point unseating the Ming government and threatening to impose a bandit régime. The Manchus' policy of deliberate Sinification had thus not only provided the means of governing their new Empire, but had even helped them to win it in the first place.

The Manchus and the Umayyad Arabs were perhaps exceptional among empire-builders in the scantiness of the indigenous cultural and institutional heritage that they brought with them. Most of the founders of universal states came into the saddle better equipped, and, faced with the unfamiliar and formidable task of governing an empire, they naturally tended to exploit their own pre-imperial heritage as far as practicable. In the cases of the Russian and Roman Empires, for example, an aristocracy descending from a previous age was drawn upon by the empire-builders as material for the creation of an ecumenical administrative structure. The motives prompting these identical policies were, however, quite different. While Peter the Great tried to dragoon the old-fashioned Muscovite nobility into becoming the cultivated, efficient, and industrious administrators in the contemporary Western style whom he needed urgently in large numbers, Augustus took the politically experienced Roman senatorial order into a cautiously regulated partnership with his own new dictatorial régime, not so much because he needed their expertise as because the enmity of this old governing class towards the upstart Caesars had to be appeased and their collaboration secured.

These antithetical problems that confronted Augustus and Peter the Great respectively are the horns of a dilemma that is liable to catch the architect of a universal state who finds himself with an imperial people's pre-imperial aristocracy on his hands. If the aristocracy is capable and experienced, it will probably resent the change in its fortunes that has left it no opening, except the unpalatable service of a dictator, for still exercising those administrative capacities which it has developed during the period of its own political supremacy. Conversely, if the aristocracy is easy-going, the dictator who needs to make use of its services will probably find that the innocuousness of his tool is offset by the bluntness of its edge. After Peter the Great's attempt to turn the Muscovite nobles into Western-style administrators had been tried for two generations, the Petrine imperial government gave it up as a bad job, and granted the hereditary nobility a conditional exemption from public service in AD 1762. On the other hand, Augustus, who was as anxious to dispense with his *viri senatorii* as Peter was to make use of his boyars, had to be content with making them ineligible for the single governorship of Egypt (a province that was a personal conquest of his own, and whose resources were so extensive and so efficiently concentrated in government hands that no Roman emperor could afford to see a Roman senator in control of them). Nearly three centuries had to elapse before Augustus's successor Gallienus (*imperabat* AD 260–68) could venture to set about excluding the senatorial class systematically from key positions of public responsibility and power; and even then the process took nearly half a century more to complete.

A pre-imperial aristocracy is the principal, but not the only, administrative class that empire-builders have brought with them for setting about their ecumenical task. The Spanish Empire in the Americas used the professional skill of middle-class lawyers to turn the unmanageable *conquistadores* into governable subjects; and the British empire-builders in India were only able to reconstruct the derelict Mughal Raj by installing a professional civil service staffed by *novi homines* exported from England. However, in this respect, the most formidably – but, as it turned out, fatally – well equipped of all empire-builders was Shih Hwang-ti.

While the six rival Contending States that succumbed to this last King of Ch'in (Ts'in) and first ruler of a Sinic universal state were still living under the traditional Chou feudal régime, feudalism in the state of Ch'in (Ts'in) had been liquidated by the revolutionary reforms of the Lord of Shang, who had done his work nearly a century before Shih Hwang-ti's accession to the Ch'in throne in 247 BC.

In place of the liquidated aristocracy the Lord of Shang had installed a professional bureaucracy, and the concentration of power in the royal government's hands as a result of this drastic administrative reorganization was the secret of the Ch'in (Ts'in) state's subsequent advance from strength to strength, culminating in Shih Hwang-ti's overthrow of Ch'in's neighbour states and his establishment of a Sinic universal state in 230–221 BC. The cause of this dramatic triumph was, however, likewise the cause of the equally dramatic reversal of the Ch'in (Ts'in) dynasty's fortunes shortly after the first Emperor's death. The revolutionary-minded conqueror committed the unimaginatively fatal blunder of trying to hold his conquests by the use of the same instrument that had won them, notwithstanding the patent unsuitability of this weapon in the circumstances. Not content with subduing and annexing the six rival states, Shih Hwang-ti deposed their feudal aristocracy as well as their royal houses, and put their administration in the hands of alien bureaucrats from his own kingdom of Ch'in (Ts'in). This act imposed on his victims a sharper affliction than they could bear. Even in Ch'in (Ts'in) itself a hundred years earlier, the Lord of Shang's revolutionary policy of bureaucratization might have failed if the Ch'in (Ts'in) state had not been a relatively primitive community in which the aristocracy had less power than elsewhere in China; but the abrupt imposition of bureaucratic rule by a conqueror upon the peoples of these other more highly civilized Chinese states emphasized their loss of independence with an intolerable intensity. Shih Hwang-ti refused to countenance any modification of his radical policy, despite mounting evidence of the opposition that it was provoking; and, in thus recklessly closing every safety-valve, he invited the explosion that took place within a year of his death and that resulted in the extinction of his dynasty by the popular rebel leader Han Liu P'ang.

If Shih Hwang-ti deservedly failed in his attempt abruptly to impose an alien bureaucracy on his subjects, Augustus and Han Liu P'ang well merited the success that attended their careful and statesmanlike policy of creating a new civil service to cope with the problems of the devastated and disorganized world for which each of these men found himself responsible. The administrative systems founded by the Hellenic bourgeois and the Sinic peasant were perhaps two of the finest secular institutions that the world has yet seen, though the critical observer will recognize that their merits were as unequal as their longevity. The Roman imperial administrative system, which went to pieces in the seventh century after its inauguration by Augustus, was not on a par with the Han system which had been founded 150 years earlier and which lasted, with at least a thread of continuity, down to AD 1911.

The defect of the Roman imperial civil service was its reflexion of the discord between the old republican senatorial aristocracy and the new imperial dictatorship which an Augustan compromise had masked but had not healed. In the Roman imperial civil service under the Principate there were two rigidly segregated hierarchies and two mutually exclusive careers in which the senatorial and the equestrian civil servant went their respective ways. This schism in the heart of the service was, as we have just seen, eventually brought to an end in the third century of

PROFESSIONAL ADMINISTRATION

247, 248, 249 The Chinese civil service, recruited by public examination, was the longest-lived and most efficient example of an imperial administration. The Han, Ming, and Manchu officials here span a period of 1700 years; the system itself lasted for two millennia.

the Christian Era, not by the achievement of that *concordia ordinum* which the public interest had always required, but by a high-handed elimination of the senatorial order from all posts of administrative responsibility. Their discomfiture, however, did not leave their equestrian rivals in enjoyment of a monopoly of the imperial civil service; for by this time the decay of local civic self-government[2] had so swollen the volume of the imperial civil service's work that Diocletian found himself compelled to make an inordinate increase in the permanent establishment of the civil service as well as the army; and in the post-Diocletianic Age the entry into the service was open to any Roman citizen possessed of the necessary degree of education, without discrimination between classes. The contrast with the history of the Han imperial civil service is instructive. The opening of careers to talent, which was not achieved in the Roman Empire till more than three hundred years after the establishment of the Augustan Peace, was inaugurated in the Han Empire by Han Liu P'ang himself, within six years of his restoration of order in 202 BC, in an ordinance issued in 196 BC, in which he directed the provincial public authorities to select candidates for the public service on a test of merit, and to send them to the capital for appointment or rejection by the officers of the central government.

This new Sinic civil service received its definitive form when Han Liu P'ang's successor Han Wuti (*imperabat* 140–86 BC) decided that the merit required of candidates should be a proficiency in reproducing the style of the classical literature of the Confucian canon and in interpreting the Confucian philosophy to the satisfaction of the Confucian *litterati* of the day. Under the skilful handling of the Han Emperors the transition from the old feudal order of the Chou Age to the new bureaucratic order of the Han Age was made so smoothly – notwithstanding the violence of the abortively revolutionary Ch'in (Ts'in) interlude – that old names acquired new meanings, and old doctrines new interpretations, by insensible degrees.

The disappearance of feudalism was rendered possible by the policy of the Han Emperors towards a very important and hitherto irreconcilably reactionary class, the *chün tzŭ*. The aristocracy had been virtually destroyed by the revolutionary measures of Shih Huang Ti, but they transmitted their ideals and their political outlook to a new class, the scholars and officials of the centralized empire. From this time onwards the *chün tzŭ* cease to be an hereditary nobility distinguished by membership of a limited number of clans. The revolution had destroyed the territorial and clan basis of the old aristocracy for ever. The *chün tzŭ*, including many of the old aristocratic families, became a class marked off from the mass of the people by education, and only by education. . . . The very meaning of the old terms became obscure. *Chün tzŭ* had meant the son of a lord, member of a noble clan. Under the new régime it gradually came to mean a gentleman in much the same sense as [that in which] that word is used in modern English – one who had received a polite education.

The later Han Emperors adroitly favoured the new educated class. Themselves of peasant origin, with no trace of divine or noble blood to fortify their claim to the throne, it was of vital importance to the new emperors to discover some principle of legitimacy for their power. Noble blood and divine descent they could not claim; force, upon which the Ch'in had relied, had proved to be a double-edged weapon. The master-stroke of the Han Emperors was to enlist in support of the centralized state the very school which had upheld feudalism to the last. . . . Their supreme achievement was to persuade the new scholar class, to whom the feudal age was personally unknown, that the doctrines of Confucius could be applied to the new political régime. . . .

Shih Huang Ti tried to destroy the memory of the past; the Han sovereigns, more subtle than he, succeeded in distorting it. The interpretation of the Confucian doctrine which gained currency during the Han dynasty proved one of the most enduring results of the revolution. The ideal of a centralized state became closely associated with the scholar class and the followers of the Confucian school. Henceforward fissiparous movements are always opposed by the scholars, the very class who had defended ancient feudalism.[3]

The Confucian School of the second century BC which was thus tactfully coaxed into partnership with the Han imperial régime would have astonished Confucius himself by the enormity of its intellectual, as well as its political, departure from the founder's own standpoint. The incorporation of semi-barbarous peoples and their cultures in the Sinic universal state, followed by the violent break in scholarly tradition during the Ch'in interlude, had the effect of making an eclectic version of the philosophy of Confucius into a melting-pot for exotic superstitions. In the latter centuries of the Han régime, the Confucian School did in fact jettison most of these popular accretions, leaving the principal heterodox philosophy of the day, Taoism, to take its place as a widespread religion of the people; but, even in the dehydrated and pedantic form which it eventually acquired, Confucianism was able to inspire a corporate professional ethos within the Han imperial bureaucracy. This bond of a common traditional ethic was lacking among the Han civil servants' Roman counterparts, and this was no doubt one of the reasons for the difference in the fortunes of these two official corporations during the interregnums which followed the break-up of their respective universal states.

While the Han and Roman Empires created their magnificent civil services out of their own social and cultural heritages, Peter the Great and his successors in Russia, when they were creating an administrative apparatus to promote their enterprise of Westernizing their Empire after the hereditary Muscovite nobility had proved useless for the purpose, forced the pace at first by copying Western institutions and even enlisting Western personnel. The cabinet secretary instituted by Peter on a contemporary Western model performed for the autocrat of the Westernizing Muscovite state the service that the Achaemenian emperor received from his Hazarapatis and the Roman emperor from his praetorian prefect. The contemporary organization of Western governments likewise suggested the senate that was established and was endowed with far-reaching powers by Peter in 1711, and the administrative colleges that were set up in 1717–18. Most of these colleges started life with Russian presidents and foreign vice-presidents to teach the Russians the new-fangled Western methods of administration. To provide the staff, Swedish prisoners-of-war were roped in, and Russian apprentices were sent to acquire a Prussian training at Königsberg. In 1722 the office of procurator-general was created for the purpose of keeping a 'king's eye' (to use the Achaemenian term) on both the colleges and the senate.

A Hasaki or an Officer employed by the Grand Signior on messages &c

The habit of an Agiamoglan

Ebrictar Aga or he that brings the bason to the Grand Signior

Selictar Aga or Sword bearer

Tulbentar Aga or he who makes the Grand Signior Turbant

A page of the Hazoda

THE SLAVE-HOUSEHOLD

250–255 Six officials of the Ottoman Empire: all are ex-Christians selected for enslavement in childhood and educated for an administrative career in special schools. Engravings from a seventeenth-century English book.

In cases such as this, where an imperial civil service is fashioned in conscious imitation of an alien model, the need for special arrangements for the training of personnel is, of course, particularly evident. At the same time, this need arises in some degree in all the various situations in which an imperial civil service has to be provided, since it is inherent in the nature of a universal state and is demanded by the usual circumstances in which a universal state comes into being. An ecumenical polity of this type normally takes shape rather suddenly out of a cluster of contending parochial states that have brought a time of troubles to its climax and conclusion by failing to adapt themselves to the necessities of a new age. The problems, experience, institutions, and ethos of these anachronistic predecessors are clearly unlikely to answer fully to the needs of the state that eventually supplants them. A newly-created universal state nearly always has to supply most of its needs itself, and urgently, for its mission is to grapple at once with the troubles of a broken-down society on the verge of dissolution. It cannot afford the time-consuming luxury of learning by experience, but must meet the crisis quickly by improvising the education of a new type of administrator for its new type of government.

In the Inca, Achaemenian, Ottoman, and Roman Empires, the emperor's personal household was both the hub of the wheel of imperial government and the training-school for the administrators required to work the machine. In each of the three former cases, an education system was created within the imperial household, and a cadet corps, drawn from the families of nobles and notables, received instruction in the art of administration. In the Ottoman case the original system was extended by Sultan Mehmet II Fatih (*imperabat* A D 1451–81) to a new administrative cadre of Christian slaves – including renegades and prisoners-of-war, as well as the 'tribute children' levied from the Padishah's Orthodox Christian subjects – who were intended to staff the Ottoman imperial administrative service as a servile class. This élite Slave-Household survived intact for a century; and, even after the Empire's free Muslim subjects had succeeded in forcing an entry into the military branch of the service in the last quarter of the sixteenth century, the educational institutions that had been originally created for 'conditioning' servile recruits retained their monopoly of supplying trained personnel to the civil arm right down to the nineteenth century, when the first official attempt to Westernize the administration was made.

While the Ottoman Padishahs deliberately expanded their personal Slave-Household into an instrument for the government of a rapidly enlarged empire to the exclusion of the free 'Osmanlis who were the Ottoman imperial people, the Roman Emperors, when they found themselves driven to make a similar use of Caesar's Slave-Household in an administrative emergency arising from the bankruptcy of the Roman republican régime, took steps first to limit and then to reduce the role of the imperial freedmen in the task of world government.

We have already noticed that Augustus reserved for members of the senatorial order the posts of highest dignity and heaviest responsibility in the service of the *Princeps*, quite apart from the senatorial monopoly of the administration of those provinces that the founder of the Principate handed back to the senate under his system of 'dyarchy'. No imperial freedman was ever appointed to the governorship of a major imperial province or to the command of a legion; and, when members of the senatorial order were eventually disqualified from holding these high posts, it was the equestrian order that entered into their heritage. The freedmen's stronghold in the administration of the Roman Empire in the early days of the Principate was the central government, in which five administrative offices in Caesar's household – *ab epistulis, a rationibus, a libellis, a cognitionibus*, and *a studiis* – had grown into imperial ministries of state; and even in these posts, which were traditionally the freedmen's preserve, the freedmen became politically impossible as soon as they had impoliticly made themselves conspicuous. The scandal caused by the spectacle of Claudius's and Nero's freedmen-ministers exercising inordinate power led, under the Flavian Emperors and their successors, to the transfer of one of these key posts after another from the hands of imperial freedmen to those of members of the equestrian order, which was the equal of the Emperor's Slave-Household in business ability, and which could be placed in charge of the central administration of the Empire without offence to other free-born Roman citizens.

Thus in the history of the Roman civil service under the Principate the equestrian middle class gained ground at the expense of the slave underworld and the senatorial aristocracy alike. The equestrian order's victory over its rivals on either hand was justified by the efficiency and integrity with which the equestrian civil servants performed their official duties, and this redemption of a class which, during the last two centuries of the republican régime, had risen to wealth and power by a predatory exploitation of army contracts, tax-farming, and usury, was a remarkable moral achievement. The British Indian civil servants, whose record during the last four or five generations of the British Raj, in the service first of the East India Company and afterwards of the Crown, could bear comparison with the record of the Roman equestrian civil servants, were conjured out of much the same unpromising human materials as their Roman counterparts.

The antecedents of the British Indian civil servants, too, were commercial. They had originated as the employees of a private trading organization whose purpose had been pecuniary profit, and one of their original incentives for taking employment far from home in an uncongenial climate had been the possibility of making money for themselves on the side. When the break-up of the Mughal Raj suddenly transformed the East India Company from a mere commercial concern into the virtual sovereign of the Mughals' largest and most lucrative successor-state, the Company's servants yielded to the temptation to make illegitimate and inordinate financial profit out of the political power that they had so opportunely acquired. In this case, as in that of the Roman equestrian class, the start might have seemed to have been so bad as to be beyond hope of retrieving; yet, in both cases, a predatory band of harpies was converted in a surprisingly short time into a body of public servants whose incentive was not personal pecuniary gain, and who had come to make it a point of

PROFESSIONAL BUREAUCRACY

256 Officer of the East India Company, 1775. British rule in India began as a commercial enterprise run by the Company for profit; but under the Crown the Indian administration became a model middle-class profession.

313

honour to wield enormous political power without abusing it. This redemption of the character of the British administration in India was due in part at least to the East India Company's decision to educate their servants for the new political tasks that they had undertaken; and the training system that they created was superior even to that in force for Britain's own civil servants at the time.

Our survey of the methods and sources of recruitment of imperial civil services suggests that neither a pre-imperial hereditary nobility nor an imperial Slave-Household provides the best human material for the purpose. The most promising recruiting-ground is likely to be a middle class which has served an apprenticeship in the responsible management of non-official business, and this is a truth that has become increasingly evident in our own day as governmental administration has grown more intricate. A contemporary bureaucratic system which, because it is supranational, is to some extent comparable to the administrations of the historic universal states is that of the European Economic Community. In this case, a policy of recruiting the Community's administrative personnel from the professional middle classes is being adopted by degrees, in recognition of the particular advantages offered to an international corporation by men who combine business or academic expertise with independence from their national governments.[4] The fact that administrators from this source are gaining ground at the expense of civil servants co-opted from the public services of the Community's member nations is as important an advertisement of the virtues of recruitment from outside the arena of the official administration as was the advancement of a new equestrian class at the expense of the aristocracy and the freedmen in the experience of imperial Rome.

If we now turn to consider who have been the principal beneficiaries from the imperial civil services that universal states have established, we shall see that the most obvious benefits have eventually been obtained by these empires' non-barbarian successor-states: the republican successors of the Spanish Empire of the Indies; the Soviet Union that succeeded the Petrine Russian Empire; the Indian and Pakistani successor-states of the British Indian Raj; and the indigenous successor-states of the Han Empire in the Yangtse basin and along the southern sea-board of the Sinic World. A successor-state that is struggling to establish itself is seldom inhibited by political or cultural animosity from taking over from its imperial predecessor a vital administrative technique or even an existing professional personnel, in order to maintain governmental stability; and, indeed, in this respect the successor-states are conforming to the pattern of utilizing existing institutions that the empire-builders themselves had followed, when these had been faced with the similar task of re-creating order in a devastated world.

While it serves the needs of its imperial creators and their successors, a professional civil service may also be performing the historically more significant function of propagating a culture. The administrators who are sent by an empire-building Power to the furthest corners of its empire are missionaries of the civilization that they represent, and this function has been recognized, and indeed been consciously performed, by the officials of some universal states. The founders of the Inca universal state felt themselves to be charged with a specific civilizing mission when they were extending their dominion over the primitive peoples beyond the pole of the Andean Civilization, and the whole machinery of conquest and rule, over 'backward' and 'advanced' subjects alike, was designed to serve the purpose of assimilation. The British in India were similarly conscious of playing a role in which the political and cultural elements were inseparable; and, as we have seen in an earlier chapter,[5] the language that was the instrument of political dominion became so well absorbed into the public life of India that it survived the departure of the imperial Power and remains a medium of political and cultural intercourse in both India and Pakistan. In the rather different circumstances in which the Western Society – not as a universal state, but as a group of competing parochial nation-states – embarked on the project of creating a set of colonial empires in Africa and elsewhere, the consciousness of being the missionaries of 'civilization' *tout court* ranked at least as high in the minds of politicians and colonial administrators as any mundane political aim; and this aspect of the Western Society's impact on the inhabitants of its overseas empires has, as we now know, outlived the purely political effect.

The most important beneficiaries from imperial civil services have, however, been neither successor-states nor secular civilizations, but churches. The administrative division of an empire into a series of provinces served in a number of instances as the basis for the hierarchical organization of a church. This basis was provided by 'the New Empire' of Egypt for the Pan-Egyptiac Church that was organized by Thothmes III under the Chief Priest of Amon-Re at Thebes; by the Sasanian Empire for the Zoroastrian Church; and by the Roman Empire for the Christian Church. The ecclesiastical pyramid reproduced the features of its secular model from base to apex. At the summit, the Chief Priest of Amon-Re at Thebes was created in the image of a Theban Pharaoh; the Zoroastrian Chief Mobadh in the likeness of the Sasanian Shahinshah; the Pope in the likeness of a post-Diocletianic Roman emperor. The secular administrative corporations performed, however, more intimate services for churches than the mere provision of an organizational framework. They also influenced their outlook and ethos, and in some cases these intellectual and moral influences were conveyed, not merely by example and mimesis, but in the social translation of a personality, in whom they were incarnate, from the secular to the ecclesiastical sphere.

Three historic figures, who each gave a decisive turn to the development of the Catholic Church in the West, were recruits from the secular Roman imperial public service. Ambrosius (*vivebat c.* AD 340–97) was the son of a civil servant who had reached the peak of his profession by attaining the office of praetorian prefect in the Gauls; and the future Saint Ambrose was following in his father's steps as a young and promising governor of the two North Italian provinces of Liguria and Aemilia when, in AD 374, to his astonishment and consternation, he was dragged out of the rut of an assured official career and was hustled by popular pressure into the episcopal See of Milan. Flavius Magnus Aurelius Cassiodorus Senator (*vivebat c.* AD 490–

257 Civil servants and God's servants. Imperial institutions are deliberately imitated by churches seeking an organizational framework. Here the secular and ecclesiastical orders of the medieval West are ranged in parallel hierarchies: Emperor and Pope, king and cardinal, count and archbishop, clerks and clerics.

585) spent his working life on the thankless task of administering Roman Italy in the service of a barbarian war-lord; and it was only after his retirement from secular public life that he found a creative use for the archaistic literary pedantry that he had acquired through his official career. On his rural estate in Southern Italy – the Vivarium, in the district of Squillace – he founded a monastic settlement whose members, inspired by the same love of God that moved Saint Benedict's community at Monte Cassino to labour in the fields, performed the equally laborious mental task of copying the Classics and the Fathers. As for Gregory the Great (*vivebat c.* AD 540–604), he abandoned the secular public service, after serving as a *Praefectus Urbi*, in order to follow Cassiodorus's example by making a monastery out of his ancestral palace in Rome, and was thereby led, against his expectation and desire, into becoming one of the makers of the Papacy. Beside these three great luminaries, we can set, from among the lesser lights, two country gentlemen, Gaius Sollius Modestus Apollinaris Sidonius of Auvergne (*vivebat* AD 430–83) and Synesius of Cyrene (*vivebat* AD 370–415), who were both drawn out of a life of uncreative literary dilettantism when their local countryside was engulfed in the ecumenical catastrophe of their age. Both of them responded to this personal challenge by taking on their shoulders the burdens, anxieties, and perils of local leadership; and each found that he could best perform his arduous duties by acting as bishop of his local community.

Varied as the origins and histories of these five personalities were, they had four things in common. For all of them, except perhaps Cassiodorus, their ecclesiastical career went against the grain. Ambrose was aghast at being made a bishop, while Synesius and Sidonius acquiesced diffidently in a role which obviously struck them as being wholly incongruous. Gregory was as reluctant to be made deacon, apocrisary, and Pope, and even to become abbot of his own monastery, as he had been eager to enrol himself as an ordinary monk. The second common feature in these five ecclesiastical careers was that all these *ci-devant* lay notables were constrained, without regard to their own inclinations, to employ their administrative skill and experience in the service of the Church. In the third place, they found a scope for the use of this faculty in the ecclesiastical field which they had not found in secular life. And, finally, they eclipsed their own performance as ecclesiastical administrators by their genius on the spiritual plane. Thus, when the break-up of the universal state for whose administrative service they had been educated had deprived these Roman gentlemen of the possibility of following secular careers, they responded to this immense challenge by entering the service of the Christian Church and devoting all their powers to assisting in the creation of a new social order.

38 Have universal states a future?

IN THE FOREGOING CHAPTERS of this Part, which have dealt with some of the institutional and other features of universal states in the past, we have drawn illustrations from a number of examples of this species of polity. A few of these empires, of which the Russian is the principal example,[1] have been universal in the sense of having realized a limited ambition to unite under a single régime all the parochial polities of one civilization, i.e. of one cultural 'world'; but we have seen that most empires – the Sinic, the Roman, and the East Roman Empires, for example – which have been universal only in this limited sense have also laid claim to a literally worldwide dominion and have been felt by their subjects to have lived up to this pretension.

However, none of the historic universal states has ever been literally universal, whatever the subjective feeling of their inhabitants may have been. Out of all the specimens of universal states of both types that we have cited, only two – China and Russia – are still in existence today. Of these two, only China has ever laid claim to literal universality; and even China has found herself compelled, by the present political structure of the world, to abate her traditional claim to universality. China has had to accommodate herself to living in a society that has become literally worldwide at the technological level while, at the political level, it has been divided up into an ever larger number of officially sovereign independent fragments of territory. (The number of officially sovereign states on the surface of this planet has doubled since the close of the Second World War.) In strictly political terms, China has now altered her claim to universality to the indirect form of claiming – as the Soviet Union also claims – to be the leading political vehicle of an ideology that, according to the doctrine of the present rulers of both the Chinese and the Russian regional Empires, is the sole true faith for all the world.

This recent Chinese experience might seem, on first thoughts, to suggest that the universal state has no future, however large it may loom in the history of the last five thousand years. One of the greatest reverses that has ever overtaken a polity of this species was the never-retrieved disintegration of the Roman Empire, in the western part of its domain, in the fifth century of the Christian Era. Since then, Western Christendom has never been reunited politically. The Westernization of the world within the last five hundred years has been the work of a number of separate rival local Western states. Their competition with each other has been one of the major driving forces behind the West's expansion, and political divisiveness has been one of the salient features that the process of Westernization has imposed on the political landscape of the globe.

The post-Roman political fragmentation of Western Christendom has now become the political dispensation of the whole world, and in our time the parochial sovereign state is enjoying its heyday. The international anarchy that, on a regional scale, was characteristic of the Sumero-Akkadian World in the early centuries of the third millennium BC, and of the Hellenic World in the last millennium BC, prevails today all round the globe. Have the universal states of past ages any relevance to Mankind's future? Are the two survivors of this species of polity anything more than 'museum pieces'? Can we not write off the universal states as one of the obsolete curiosities of history? This first thought of ours may be judged, on second thoughts, to be premature.

Let us remind ourselves that one of the two surviving specimens of the species is China, a polity which, for most of the time since the year 221 BC, has held together a steadily expanding area and population that, till as recently as the Opium War of AD 1839–42, was the cultural as well as the political focus of half the world. The traditional Chinese *Weltanschauung* has now been tested by more than three millennia of Chinese experience, and one of its key concepts is the dialectic alternation of a dynamic activity, Yang, with a passive state, Yin. When either Yang or Yin is carried to extremes, it automatically restores the balance of Nature by lopping over into its opposite – which eventually reverts to the alternative mode when it, in its turn, has been carried to the furthest length that Nature can tolerate.

Since the break-up of the Roman Empire in the West, the new civilization that has sprung up among the ruins of this outlying part of the Empire's domain has been in a Yang-phase that contrasts sharply with the Yin-condition that is characteristic of universal states; and the West's post-Roman Yang-activity has been accentuated in the course of time. It asserted itself earliest, and most persistently, on the political plane – first in the Roman Empire's barbarian successor-states, then in the medieval Western city-states, and most recently in the modern Western nation-states that have overwhelmed the former city-states in the Western Civilization's original domain, and that have now become the worldwide standard type of polity as a result of the Western Society's global expansion. Even the original ecclesiastical unity of Western Christendom was disrupted in the sixteenth century, and, since the seventeenth century, the sundered fragments of the Western Christian Church have each dwindled in size with the progressive loss of Christianity's hold over Western souls. The worldwide expansion of the Western Civilization in its post-Christian form has spread the West's heritage of disunity and chaos to the ends of the Earth.

This spectacle would lead an observer who had been bred in the Chinese tradition to see in the present worldwide paroxysm of Yang an indication that Yang is going, in the near future, to lop over into a proportionately emphatic reversion to Yin. The traditional-minded Chinese observer would make this forecast *a priori*, but he would also be able to support his prediction by pointing to facts. He could point out that civilizations whose original political structure has been pluralistic have ended as political unities. This has been the course, not only of Chinese history, but of Sumero-Akkadian, Hellenic, and Andean history as well. Our Chinese observer could also point out three contemporary facts that are making stabilization imperative. These three facts are the invention of the nuclear weapon, the population explosion, and the consumption and pollution of the irreplaceable natural resources on which Mankind depends for its survival.

The first steps in the exploration of outer space – modest though these steps are when measured by the apparent scale of the physical cosmos – have taught us already that the resources of our native planet will be all that we shall have at our command for as far as we can see into the future. The harnessing of the forces of inanimate Nature has now given Man the power to use up his limited material patrimony. The reduction of the death-rate thanks to the progress of medicine has removed the former ruthless natural check on the increase in Mankind's numbers. The annihilation of distance by mechanized technology has given Man the power to use the nuclear weapon for committing global genocide. These three facts, in combination, seem to demand the establishment of an effective worldwide government with a mandate for imposing peace, for conserving resources, and for inducing its subjects to limit the number of their children.

A literally worldwide future universal state would be likely to reproduce many of the features of the would-be universal states that have come and gone in the course of the last five thousand years. Like these, it would be a means to ends other than its own perpetuation; but, unlike its predecessors, it would not be foredoomed to be impermanent. There would be no barbarians and no alien civilizations to impinge upon it from outside; and the internal decay that has been the main cause of the disintegrations of previous universal states would be inhibited by the permanence, and the permanent direness, of the need to prevent genocide, to limit population, and to conserve resources. Thus, in the field of human affairs, the rhythm of the Universe may well be arrested. The Yin-state that seems likely to follow the present Yang-phase may not give way to a recrudescence of Yang. A political and human disaster on the scale of the disintegration of the Roman Empire seems unlikely to happen again – though for different reasons than those that seemed convincing to Gibbon.

If there is any truth in these speculations, it should move us to study the characteristics of past universal states with close attention; for, in the histories of the polities of this species, we have a preview of the stable state in which it looks as if Mankind is going to have to live on this planet for so long as the planet remains habitable for human life. The empires that have most significance as pointers to the possible destiny of Mankind are not those established by local states within the body social of some single civilization, such as the recent colonial empires of the modern Western nations, or the similar empires carved out of the carcass of the Achaemenian Empire by the successors of Alexander the Great. They are those that, like the Roman Empire in the Hellenic World, or the Maurya Empire in India, or the Ch'in-Han Empire in China, have given political unity to the whole, or almost the whole, of the domain of an entire civilization at a stage when this civilization has been brought within sight of dissolution by a series of wars and revolutions on a progressively increasing scale of spiritual and material destruction. If we want to avoid finding ourselves living under a perpetual tyranny as the only alternative to the destruction of Mankind, we shall

258 The new society? Athletic display in modern China: Westerners tend to see in China a repulsive modern Leviathan, but behind the ceremonial lies an ideal of mutual solidarity and co-operation from which a fragmented world may learn.

be well advised to study both the positive and the negative sides of the historic universal states.

A future universal state will have to be literally world-wide, but this indicates that it will not necessarily be the creation of one civilization alone, as has been the rule in the past. Westerners should not automatically assume, as they are prone to do, that the values and goals of their own civilization will be permanently dominant. On the contrary, the likelihood is that the world-state of the future will begin by being a voluntary political association in which all the cultural elements of a number of living civilizations will continue to assert themselves. It is true that the West has maintained a cultural assault on the other living civilizations of the world for the past five hundred years, but we still cannot be sure that new civilizations will not emerge in the future or that civilizations which at present seem to be submerged will not be revivified. In any case, a number of civilizations or cultural traditions are likely to have to learn how to live together under a single political dispensation; and thus one of the most instructive lessons that we can learn from the historic universal states is how competing cultures can coexist and can fructify one another.

Most of the universal states that have united a civilization politically have also included portions of the domain of one or more other civilizations, and also portions of their own society's barbarian hinterlands. In the course of time their originally heterogeneous subjects have tended to acquire a sense of solidarity with each other as children of a common human family whose unity has been symbolized for them politically by the world-state in which they have lived. Persecuted minorities and culturally oppressed subject-peoples cannot achieve this feeling of solidarity, and this is a practical consideration that has led the founders of universal states to recognize and tolerate cultural diversity in their domains. One aspect of this characteristic tolerance that has already come to our notice in our review of universal states is the toleration of linguistic variety.[2] Equally, now that a man's religion has become a matter of free personal choice, it would be a profoundly retrograde step if political uniformity were to lead to the imposition of a single religious or ideological orthodoxy, as it has led too often in the past. The Achaemenian Empire's policy of religious toleration is here a promising and inspiring precedent.

One feature of universal states that has come to our notice time and again is the disjunction between their professed aims and their actual effects. If empire-builders have, in general terms, had a purely secular end in view, events have shown that it is not the essentially ephemeral and changing secular world, but Mankind's perennial pursuit of spiritual objectives, that has profited from the empire-builders' labours. We have already[3] considered the religious ends that may be served by the creation of a worldwide system of communications; and it should come as no surprise to us to realize that, while a world-state will probably be instituted initially in response to the mundane challenges which we have identified above, its life thereafter will be likely to minister to a spiritual purpose. This is to be expected, for, although human beings in the mass are seldom moved by other than practical considerations, the very act of creating a political union on an ecumenical scale will confirm the moral truth that life is only practicable in so far as it is grasped as a whole. In this respect, a future world-state seems likely to differ radically from its historical predecessors. So far from being the doomed secular monument to a civilization on the verge of disintegration, it may contain in itself from the start the seeds of a spiritual movement that has already been revealed in the higher religions, and may deliberately and consciously foster their germination and growth.

Here, then, is one possible projection of the future of Mankind's life on Earth. The histories of past universal states allow us to make some general postulates about our own future, and can even offer us some positive lessons; but perhaps the single greatest lesson that we can learn from them is a negative one. Mankind longs today for a world united in peace and freedom, but in the past only the bitter experience of prolonged disunity and war, culminating in intolerable anarchy and distress, has moved men to attempt the salvation of their hard-pressed societies by the forcible unification of rival parochial polities. Even if this has not invariably resulted in the imposition of a tyranny, it has always presaged the eventual downfall of a society. Today we cannot afford the luxury of waiting to learn this lesson by a repetition, at first hand, of our predecessors' experience; for, if we do wait, the choices open to us will be reduced to the alternatives of a world tyranny or the end of life itself. Our knowledge of the past histories of other societies than our own must move us to forestall disaster by taking the future into our hands. If we sit back, we shall find ourselves overtaken by events that have passed beyond our control.

PART VII

UNIVERSAL CHURCHES

The emergence of the higher religions seems to me to mark so important a new departure in human history that these cannot be dealt with adequately in terms of the civilizations whose declines and falls give rise to them. I try to show that they are not parasites on dying civilizations, nor do they simply serve as chrysalises for the births of new civilizations. On the contrary, I believe that the higher religions are themselves societies of a new and distinctive species; their purpose is to enable men to find a direct personal relation with the transcendent reality in and behind and beyond the Universe, though so far they have fallen short of their spiritual aspirations. Most of the religions have achieved the essential step of disengaging themselves from the restrictive matrix of the civilizations in which they came to birth, and have addressed themselves to the whole of Mankind; but some have been betrayed by their institutionalization into becoming rigid in structure and intolerant in outlook. Religions have obviously played an important role in history, but I still have to ask myself what religion is. People have always had something that they call religion, but is the object of their belief real or illusory? I am convinced that it is real, and, although I know that my conviction is partly an unprovable act of faith, I also try to show that only the postulate of a supra-human reality will make some proven human feelings comprehensible to us.

plates 59, 60

HUMAN COMPASSION

Love of God, expressed in the act of worship, is indissolubly linked with compassion for Man, for 'he that loveth not his brother whom he hath seen, how can he love God whom he hath not seen?' This Christian call to charity can be paralleled in Judaism – 'Thou shalt open thine hand wide unto thy brother, to thy poor, and to thy needy'; in Islam – 'For him that give in charity We shall smooth the path of salvation'; and in Buddhism – 'He who clings to the void and neglects compassion does not reach the highest stage.' Such unanimity is impressive, but the Christian faith has distinguished itself by laying special emphasis on Man's duty to love his neighbour. Christian charity, like Christianity itself, is addressed to all Mankind without distinction, and the most hallowed love is that which declares itself in acts of compassion towards strangers and enemies. Christ, in the Gospel according to Saint Matthew, taught that the merciful would inherit the world, and he set out the acts of mercy by which this salvation could be won. A fifteenth-century frieze illustrates the exhortations to feed the hungry and to visit the sick; the other compassionate precepts of Christ were to give drink to the thirsty, to house the homeless, to clothe the naked, and to visit those in prison.

plate 63

DIVINE SELF-SACRIFICE

Self-sacrifice is the supreme expression of the compassionate love that the higher religions have revealed as the ultimate spiritual reality in and behind and beyond the mundane world. For the saint or the sage, self-sacrifice may be part of the supremely painful struggle to win enlightenment by overcoming self-love; in the Christian faith the self-sacrifice of Christ on the Cross translates a fruitful experience of suffering into a unique redemptive act. The combination of suffering and redemption has been symbolized in Christian iconography by the pelican, shown here in a fifteenth-century painting. According to medieval bestiaries, the pelican is a bird that loves its young, but these rebel against their parents and are killed by the father. After three days the mother, inspired by a boundless love for her dead children, revives them by feeding them with her life's blood.

> Then said the Pelican,
> When my birds be slain
> With my blood I them revive.
> Scripture doth record,
> The same died our Lord,
> And rose from death to live. (John Skelton)

Thus the essence of the Christian story of Creation, rebellion, and redemption is contained within this moving legend.

39 Cancers or chrysalises?

WE CAN BEGIN our study of universal churches by examining their relation to the social environment in which they arise. We have already seen[1] that a universal church is apt to come to birth during the time of troubles which follows the breakdown of a civilization, and to unfold itself within the political framework of a universal state. Our study of universal states has brought out two facts about them: first that, in virtue of the fact that a universal state can be no more than a temporary rally in the decline and fall of a civilization, the long-term benefits of this institution are likely to accrue to other parties; and second that, in so far as they become creative in this indirect and vicarious way, through the creative acts of alien beneficiaries, they are creators unintentionally and indeed against their will. Their own primary aim is, not to be creative, but simply to survive; but the experience of losing their lives in order to find them again in the lives of their beneficiaries does not reconcile them to their fate: on the contrary, it provokes them to recalcitrance and indignation. Our survey in the preceding Part of this Study has shown that the principal beneficiaries of universal states are universal churches; and it is therefore not surprising that the champions of a universal state, at a stage in its history when it is clearly entering on its decline, should dislike the spectacle of a universal church within its bosom profiting by the services that the universal state is continuing to render without any longer being able to turn them to its own benefit. The church is therefore likely at first sight to wear the appearance of a social cancer; for in this situation and state of mind the universal state's devotees are apt, not merely to observe and resent the fact that the church is flourishing while the state is decaying, but to assume that the beneficiary must also be a parasite, and that the profit which it is obviously drawing from its host is itself the cause of the host's malady. This diagnosis is as attractive as it is exacerbating, for it is always easier, both intellectually and morally, to debit one's own ills to the account of some outside agency than to ascribe the responsibility to oneself.

In the decline of the Roman Empire an indictment of the Christian Church, which had been mounting up since the first telling shot had been fired by Celsus (*scribebat c*. AD 178), came to a head in the West when the Empire was in its final agonies there. An explosion of this hostile feeling was provoked in AD 416 in the heart of the diehard pagan Gallic devotee of Rome, Rutilius Namatianus, by the sad sight of desert islands colonized – or, as Rutilius would have said, infested – by Christian monks:

As the sea opens out, Capraia rears up. The island is polluted: it swarms with men who have fled from the light. Their own name for themselves is 'monks' – a Greek word signifying their resolve to live solitary lives, out of sight of their fellow-men. . . . Stupid madness of a perverted brain! You are so afraid of life's evil that you cannot bear its good side either.[2]

Rutilius's impersonal hostility towards the monks of Capraia was, however, a less painful feeling than the pang that he suffered shortly afterwards at the sadder sight of another island that had captivated a fellow countryman and acquaintance of the poet's own.

Between the Pisan and the Corsican coast, Gorgon now rises, an islet in mid sea. I shun its reefs: they recall a recent bereavement. Here a citizen has been lost in a living death. Not long ago a youth, once ours – the scion of a well-to-do house, and his ancestors' equal in wealth and wedlock – was hounded by the furies into deserting Mankind and the world. Deluded, self-exiled, he took to this wretched hide-out. The poor fool mistakes dirt for a heavenly banquet. He torments himself; the gods whom he has wronged are not so savage. I ask you, isn't this sect worse than Circe's poisons? In Circe's age, only bodies were transmogrified; now it is minds that suffer this fate.[3]

Through these lines there breathes the spirit of a still pagan aristocracy in the dissolving western provinces of the Roman Empire who saw the cause of Rome's ruin in the abandonment of the traditional worship of the Hellenic pantheon by pagan converts to Christianity and in the suppression of paganism by the Christian Emperor Theodosius.

This controversy between a sinking Roman Empire and a rising Christian Church raised an issue of such deep and general interest that it has stirred the feelings, not only of contemporaries directly involved, but of writers in far-distant generations. In his statement 'I have described the triumph of barbarism and religion',[4] Gibbon not only sums up the seventy-one chapters of his book in nine words, but proclaims himself a partisan of Celsus and Rutilius; and we can see that, in his eyes, the cultural peak, as he saw it, of Hellenic history in the Antonine Age stood out clear across an intervening span of sixteen centuries which, for Gibbon, was a cultural trough. Gibbon's voice echoed sentiments that had been gathering strength since the beginnings of the European humanist 'revival' in the fifteenth century of the Christian Era, and that have since expressed themselves even more explicitly[5] before receding, in our own day, in the face of a more stringent and perceptive scholarship.[6] The weakness of all such interpretations of the effect of Christianity upon the Roman World is that they are based on a mistaken view of the date at which the Hellenic Civilization reached and passed its zenith. The truth is that it had inflicted mortal wounds upon itself long before the appearance, above its horizon, of Christianity or any of the other higher religions with which Christianity eventually competed for the conquest of a moribund Hellenic World. It is indisputable that the Hellenic achievement of parochial self-government and the Hellenic virtue of parochial loyalty had by that time been discredited and extinguished through being misdirected and misused by their own authors and exponents. When, in the fifth century BC, the supreme social need of the Hellenic World had come to be the achievement of political unity, the characteristic features of Hellenic public life had become the bane, instead of the glory, of the Hellenic Civilization; and, even after these parochial patriotisms had brought the Hellenic Society to its breakdown in the outbreak of the Atheno-Peloponnesian War, the Hellenic peoples had continued on their path of self-immolation on the altars of deified parochial states for four more terrible centuries. They were weaned from it, not through a voluntary recognition of their idolatry, but only because life itself had become insupportable.

By the time that Augustus established his universal state, there was nobody in the Hellenic World except the Roman senatorial aristocracy who would still have preferred retaining self-government to getting rid of social disorders, and nobody at all who would still have preferred retaining parochial sovereignty to getting rid of wars. The wounds that the Hellenic Society had inflicted on itself had provoked the social crisis that engulfed its world, and the miseries that it suffered as a consequence produced the revolutionary change of outlook that permitted the imposition of the Augustan Peace. In a post-mortem inquiry into the causes of the death of Hellenism, this reading of Hellenic history, if correct, acquits Christianity and the other higher religions that, in the next chapter of the story, were Christianity's competitors for the spiritual conquest of Hellenic souls. These faiths were filling a spiritual vacuum, not creating one; and the same verdict emerges from an examination of the role of the Mahayana in the history of the Sinic Civilization.

Although it seems clear enough, then, that the higher religions cannot be convicted of having caused the deaths of civilizations in the past, it may nevertheless be true that this is a theoretical possibility – the fact that we can find no historical evidence to support the contention does not absolve us from seeing whether this tragedy might not still come to pass. To get to the bottom of the issue, we must carry our inquiry from the macrocosm of historical facts to the microcosm of individual human experience. Our primary concern is to discover whether the higher religions are essentially and incurably anti-social. When there is a shift in the focus of human interest and energy from the ideals aimed at in a secular civilization to those aimed at in an other-worldly religion, is it true that the social values for which the civilization claims to stand are bound to suffer? In other words, are spiritual and social values antithetical and inimical to one another? Is the fabric of civilization, which is a social achievement, undermined if the salvation of the individual soul is taken as being the supreme aim of life? A recent historian of Rome's decline has affirmed this view:

Pure contentment was reserved for those devoted Christians, particularly the monks, who were putting into practice the precepts which pagan Stoicism had once preached, precepts which constitute the whole burden of Seneca's writing. Such men had turned their backs on the world, happy in the salvation of their own souls. If, instead, with all their fervour, they had gone out into the world, they might have done something to save it.[7]

This argument is, however, based on a false analysis of the relationship between the individual soul and the society in which it finds itself. The supposed antithesis between the two is illusory; for the individual can only express and develop his personality through relations with other personalities, while, conversely, society is no more than the common ground between one individual's network of relations and another's, and it has no existence except in the activities of individuals who, for their part, cannot exist except in society. There is, again, no pre-established antithesis between the individual's relations with his fellow men and his relations with God.

To [Augustine] it is evident that, ultimately, there can be no compromise between the claims of Caesar and those of Christ. Caesar must therefore abandon his pretension to independence and submit to Christian principles, or he must be prepared for the doom which awaits sin and error in its secular conflict with justice and truth. For Christ, as he points out, did not say, *my kingdom is not of* THE *world*, but *my kingdom is not of* THIS *world*. His meaning is best conveyed in the prayer, *Thy kingdom come*. Accordingly, to admit as final any dualism between 'moral man' and 'immoral society' is to perpetrate the most vicious of heresies; it is to deny the Christian promise and to subvert the foundation of the Christian hope.

On the other hand, to accept that promise as valid is to recognize the possibility of a fresh integration of human life in terms of which the manifold forms of secular heresy may at last be overcome. This integration is possible because its basis is a good which, unlike the goods of secularism, is common, comprehensive, inexhaustible, in no wise susceptible of expropriation or monopolization, nothing less indeed than God Himself. Accordingly, in its application to the individual, it does not confine him within the narrow limits of the *polis* (a territorial, racial, and cultural 'unity'), nor does it confront him with the necessity of a choice between alternatives which are equally arbitrary and artificial, viz. the life of 'activity' or that of 'reason', of 'society' or 'contemplation', heresies within a heresy; but, on the contrary, it offers him a 'life' which subsumes them all, the life of 'good will'. And, while thus overcoming the heresies and schisms of individual life, it overcomes those also which vitiate the life of society. For, as it recognizes no element in individual experience which cannot be explained in terms of individual will, so also it denies that there exists any unknown quantity in the 'life' of society which is not to be resolved into terms of association, the deliberate association of individuals in pursuit of such ends as they deem good.[8]

In seeking God, Man is performing a social act.

What [Christianity] prescribes is *adhaerere Deo*, adhesion to God, the source of truth, beauty, and goodness, the supreme reality, as the one fundamental principle for individual regeneration and for social reformation, the point of departure for a fresh experiment in human relationships, on the acceptance of which rests the only real hope of fulfilling the promise of secular life.[9]

If God's Love has gone forth into action in this world in the redemption of Mankind by Christ, then Man's efforts to make himself less unlike a God who has created Man in His own image must include efforts to follow Christ's example in sacrificing himself for the redemption of his fellow men. Seeking and following God in this way that, in a Christian's belief, is God's way, is, in a Christian's eyes, the only true way for a human soul on Earth to seek salvation. The antithesis between trying to save one's own soul by seeking and following God and trying to do one's duty to one's neighbour is therefore false.

Thou shalt love the Lord thy God with all thy heart and with all thy soul and with all thy mind. This is the first and great commandment. And the second is like unto it: Thou shalt love thy neighbour as thyself. On these two commandments hang all the Law and the Prophets.[10]

327

CONTEMPLATIVE LOVE

The anchorite's withdrawal from the world might seem to be the archetypal act of anti-social individualism and selfish indifference, and yet this lone pursuit of spiritual perfection has a profoundly social implication. Men who love God cannot reject His Creation, and the hermit serves God's creatures by offering them an ideal from which they may draw strength and inspiration. Private meditation thus reinforces social effort by revealing the perfection for which all men strive.

259 A Muslim anchorite receives an Indian prince.

The two activities are indissoluble because 'He that loveth not his brother whom he hath seen, how can he love God whom he hath not seen?'[11] The Christian soul that is truly seeking to save itself by loving God in God's way is as fully social a being as the Spartan who saves his personal honour by dying for his community at Thermopylae; only the Christian soul on Earth is enrolled in a different society from the Spartan micro-state or the Roman Leviathan. He is a citizen, not of a secular commonwealth, but of the Kingdom of God, and therefore his paramount and all-embracing aim is, not to identify himself with the genius of an earthly city, but to attain the highest degree of communion with, and likeness to, God Himself; his relations with his fellow-men are consequences of, and corollaries to, his relations with God; his standard for his attitude towards his fellows will be his intuition of God's attitude towards Man; and his way of loving his neighbour as God loves Man will be to try to help his neighbour to win what the Christian is seeking for himself – that is, to come into closer communion with God and to become more godlike.

If this is a soul's recognized aim for itself and for its fellow souls in the Christian Church on Earth, then it is evident that under a Christian dispensation God's will *will* be done on Earth as it is in Heaven to an immeasurably greater degree than in a secular mundane society. It is also evident that, in the Church Militant on Earth, the good social aims of mundane societies will incidentally be achieved very much more successfully than they ever have been or can be achieved in a mundane society which aims at these objects direct, and at nothing higher. In other words, the spiritual progress of individual souls in this life will in fact bring with it much more social progress than could be attained in any other way. It is a paradoxical but profoundly true and important principle of life that the most likely way to reach a goal is to be aiming not at that goal itself but at some more ambitious goal beyond it. This is the meaning of the fable in the Old Testament of Solomon's Choice[12] and of the saying in the New Testament about losing one's life and finding it.[13]

> Ah, but a man's reach should exceed his grasp,
> Or what's a heaven for?[14]

This exposition of the harmony between the conception of Man's duty to God and the conception of his duty to his neighbour has been made here in terms of Christianity, but it might be translated into terms of Mithraism or of the worship of Cybele and Isis, which competed with Christianity for the captivation of the Hellenic World, or into terms of the Mahayana, which did captivate the Sinic World as Christianity captivated the Hellenic. It might also be made in terms of a belief in, and a devotion to, a non-human-like and non-personal ultimate spiritual reality. Within a Christian framework, it is exemplified in the transition during the fourth century of the Christian Era from an anchoritic form of Christian devotion, whose practitioners isolated themselves utterly from their social context, to a 'coenobitic' ('living-in-fellowship') form of monasticism which sought to break down the deceptive dichotomy between the aim of a purely personal salvation and the social implications of Christian love.

The basic problem raised by the enthusiasm of the monks was the separatist and individualist character of the movement. Was the monk pursuing only his own salvation? Or had the movement a social purpose? Insistence on the primacy of the social purpose of the ascetic movement was the central feature of Basil of Caesarea's organization in Asia Minor [in the fourth century], and made his achievement epoch-making. . . . He rejected the hermit-ideal as a private and personal quest, divorced from the Gospel demand of love and service to one's neighbour.[15]

This explicit recognition of the social purpose of Christianity was important at a time when the anchoritic movement was threatening to accentuate its more bizarre and eccentric characteristics at the expense of its central ideal of uncontorted and whole-hearted contemplation; but even the anchorites' personal pursuit of holiness was accorded popular recognition as a valid expression of Christian love, from which contemporaries could draw strength and inspiration: 'The desert fathers in Egypt in the second half of the fourth century were constantly visited by individuals who used to ask according to the regular formula: "Speak to me a word, father, that I may live."'[16] On occasion, moreover, the return of an anchorite to the world to intervene in some secular crisis worked an effect that was commensurate with the degree of prestige that he had acquired during his régime of insulation. Thus in A D 475/76 Saint Daniel the Stylite, at the request of the emissaries of the Orthodox Patriarch of Constantinople, consented to descend from his pillar at Anaplus, up the Bosphorus, in order to save Orthodoxy from the Monophysite proclivities of the usurping Emperor Basiliscus. The mere news of the holy man's arrival in the cathedral church of the Apostles in the imperial city frightened the Emperor into evacuating his own capital and retreating to the imperial palace at the seventh milestone. It was indeed a crushing indictment of the Emperor's conduct of public affairs that the report of his people's affliction should have moved the Saint to re-emerge from a physical isolation in which, by that time, he had been living already for twenty-four years and which was to have lasted unbroken till his death. Working spiritual acts of psychical and physical healing on his way, Saint Daniel led the clergy and people of Constantinople to beard the truant Prince in his suburban asylum; and, when the guards refused the crowd admission to the imperial presence, the Saint directed the people to follow him in the scriptural symbolic act of shaking the dust of the palace precincts off their garments – which they did with such a thunderous reverberation that most of the guards on duty were moved to desert their imperial master and follow in the stylite's train. In vain the Emperor sent messages after the departing Saint to beg him to return to the Hebdomon; in vain he returned to Constantinople himself and besought Daniel to visit him in his palace there. In the end the Emperor was constrained to present himself before the Saint in the cathedral and prostrate himself at his feet; and a public confession of Orthodoxy was the price that he eventually had to pay in order to save his throne by setting Daniel at liberty to resume his station on his pillar-top.

The essential truth that is borne out both by this particular story and by the general advance, in the Christian world, of monastic social charity at the expense of anchoritic individualism is that the contemplative or mystic who can

260 Lancelot, hero of epic romance, visits a hermit to make his confession. The idealized Christian knight combined stringent self-discipline with active works of faith.

261 William Tell consults the anchorite Nicholas of Flue, a Swiss patriot who in 1465 withdrew from politics into a life of contemplation. His wisdom and saintliness brought people flocking to him for advice, and he was the author of the settlement that prevented civil war in Switzerland in 1481.

329

ACTIVE LOVE

262 Charity for Mankind is accorded a central place in most religions as a straightforward means of expressing men's love for God and God's love for the world. Part of the *Seven Works of Charity*, illustrating Christ's teaching on human mercy as recorded in Saint Matthew's Gospel:

extrapolate a social duty from his personal love of God enters into a far more active relation with a far wider circle than the man who pursues his social goals 'in the world' and who spends his life in some secular occupation on the military or political plane. But is this truth peculiar to the Christian faith alone, or is it on the contrary a common possession of all the higher religions which aspire to put themselves in harmony with the ultimate spiritual reality, irrespective of the accidents of local dogma? The Buddhist *sangha* or monastic order, for instance, has long been criticized, by minds schooled in the emphatic Western Christian tradition of 'good works', for its apparent indifference to a social morality of active participation in 'this-worldly' affairs.

It is sometimes argued that such an organization, where men retire from worldly life, earn nothing, beg their food from the common people, and bear no children, is against the welfare of the community. The answer is manifold. What is the purpose of life? If it be to achieve Enlightenment, it is 'a positive social and moral advantage to the community that a certain number of its finest minds, leading a life that may be called sheltered, should remain unattached to social activities and unbound by social

ties'. Such men have from the dawn of history set an example of the ascetic life unfettered by worldly desire, and have proved themselves by their superior self-control and development the counsellors of kings, the teachers of the people, and the exemplars of all.[17]

Certainly this may be as true for Buddhism as it is for Christianity, and the full implications of this truth were recognized in the Bodhisattva doctrine of the Mahayana school of Buddhism.

The Bodhisattva, moreover, is a logical conception. Life is one, say his devotees, and we live for all. It is therefore noble to work for all rather than for oneself. All deeds, whether good or ill, help or harm other human beings, and deliberate acts of goodwill help all living things towards enlightenment. But the really great man grows so self-forgetful that he cares not for the self-reward of his acts of 'merit', and gladly 'turns it over' to the good of all. If, said the would-be Bodhisattva, this doctrine of *Parivarta* or *Parinamana* is contrary to the earlier teaching of Buddhism, so much the worse for the latter. For the doctrine of Karma is cold and hard and difficult; the transference of merit is filled with love and warmth and delight.[18]

This doctrine has remained a stumbling-block to those

330

'For I was an hungred, and ye gave me meat: I was thirsty, and ye gave me drink: I was a stranger, and ye took me in: naked and ye clothed me: I was sick, and ye visited me: I was in prison, and ye came unto me.' The seventh charitable act, added later, was to bury the dead.

Buddhist purists who continue to argue that true enlightenment is the reward of individual effort and merit alone, and that the idea of a vicarious salvation through the merit acquired by others is a dangerous encouragement to the weak-minded and the indolent. We should, indeed, recognize that the purist rejection of the value of 'good works', or action within society, is consistent with Buddhist teaching, in the sense that 'works are all very well for the man who is on the way to liberation, but once this is won they cease to have any relevance'.[19] But the readmission of love and compassion into Buddhism, though it constituted a deliberate denial of the central doctrine of self-extinction, was historically the crucial step towards the necessary recognition that love of God and love of Mankind are not opposites but correlatives.

The conventional criticism of the other-worldly saint finds its legitimate target in the philosophers who cultivate a total detachment in which the process of withdrawal from the secular world does not culminate in an act of returning to it in order to apply in practice the insights won during retirement. The Hinayanian, Stoic, and Epicurean ideal of the sage goes astray through casting Man for a super-human role of godlike self-sufficiency and thereby condemning the adept to seek a way out of an impossible position by restricting himself to a sub-human performance. This philosophy attempts to make of Man, not a saint inspired by God's grace, but a very god in himself; and, since this is too heavy a burden for a human soul to bear, the philosopher cannot even make a pretence of carrying it off unless he lightens his self-imposed task by casting out his God-given feelings of love and pity for the rest of God's creatures. Philosophy's most insidious offence is to refashion Man's ideal of God in the human sage's image; and in place of a primitive God of fear she has nothing better than the idol of intellectualized perfectionism to offer to souls in search of the security of faith.

It is true, of course, that many would-be saints have sinned against their own religious ideal by falling into the unsocial practice of the philosophers. To detach oneself spiritually from the world is an easier option than to take on the travail of sharing God's love for the world and participating in his work of transfiguring it; and in the Hellenic World the higher religions found philosophy already in the field, with an established tradition and prestige, on the wait to captivate souls in whom the flame of divine love was burning low. Many, perhaps a majority, of the aspirants to sainthood fell by the wayside; yet the few who did live up to the Christian ideal in some measure sufficed to secure the survival of the Christian society when Roman hands failed to save the Hellenic Civilization from the final consequences of its own past suicidal acts. It looks as if the higher religions, so far from being a social cancer, have been the bread of social, as well as spiritual, life.

The reverse of the view that universal churches are the sinister destroyers of civilizations is that they are their saviours, or rather that they are the saviours of the species in general though not of individual representatives of it. On this view, universal churches have their *raison d'être* in keeping the species alive by preserving a precious germ of life through the perilous interregnum between the dissolution of one civilization and the genesis of another. In this repetitive process of the reproduction of civilizations, which is assumed to have an absolute value as an end in itself, the churches are useful and perhaps necessary, but secondary and transitory, phenomena. A superficial reading of the historical data might point to this conclusion in some instances: it is clear, for example, that the Christian Church did, as a matter of historical fact, act as a connecting link between the dead Hellenic Society and the Western Society that came to birth on the same ground; and in the Sinic World a similar role was played by the Mahayana during the interregnum that followed the fall of the Han dynasty at the turn of the second and third centuries of the Christian Era. But it does not follow from the mere observation of this fact that the principal purpose of a church is that it should serve as a 'chrysalis' for the emergence of a new civilization. On the contrary, such a hypothetical deduction from the chronological coincidence of events or processes must be rejected as soon as we ask ourselves what the essence of religion or religious faith is. The point is that religious faith comes by grace. Religion cannot be called to heel, like a dog, to suit human convenience.

At certain times and places living religions have been tempted or driven into serving as means to non-religious ends; but to take these episodes of their history as being their *raison d'être* is to misunderstand and misinterpret their mission. So far from this service of secular purposes being a fulfilment of their mission, it is a diversion from it; and, whenever a higher religion has allowed itself to be shunted into this sidetrack, there has usually been a spiritual-minded minority among its adherents who have remained faithful to their religion's true purposes.

When, in the Roman Empire, the Christian Church was not only granted toleration but was made virtually a department of state, the anchorites withdrew into the desert, and the Donatists, Nestorians, and Monophysites successively seceded from a Church which the Monophysites branded as 'Imperialist' (Melchite). When, in the West, a resuscitated imperial government tried to reduce the Roman See, and the rest of the Church within its reach, to the state of subordination to which the 'Melchite' Orthodox Church had already been reduced in the East Roman Empire, this secular challenge to the Church's freedom evoked the mighty resistance movement that was carried to a victorious conclusion, under the Papacy's

auspices, in the eleventh and twelfth centuries. This was the original issue in the conflict between the Empire and the Papacy. When the Papacy had successfully asserted against the West Roman Empire its claim to be the presiding institution in the medieval Western Christian Commonwealth, its assumption of this quasi-political power provoked first the Conciliar Movement and eventually the Protestant Reformation. The Lutheran and Anglican Protestants jumped out of the frying-pan into the fire. They fell straight into the jaws of autocratic parochial princes; and the Calvinists, where they survived, avoided the fate of becoming the slaves of parochial governments only by resorting to Muhammad's expedient of acquiring political control. After the Anglican Protestant Church had been successfully reduced to subordination by the English Crown, the Church's true role was upheld in England by the secession of the Free Churches from the Establishment. Even in Eastern Orthodox Christendom, where the Church has been deprived of its independence more continuously than in any other part of the Christian World, the imposition of an Orthodox ecclesiastical Establishment on Bulgaria evoked an infectious reaction in the form of Bogomilism; and in the modern age there has been at least one great Eastern Orthodox country, Russia, in which the movement of nonconformity has been as vigorous as it has been in the English-speaking countries.

Such assertions of a claim to independence, and refusals to acquiesce in seeing the Church being made to serve non-religious purposes, have not been exceptional incidents in the Christian Church's history; they have been vindications of the rule against exceptional breaches of it. The Hildebrandine movement in Western Christendom in the eleventh century was not the inauguration of a new religion. So far from being a breach with the spirit of the primitive Christian Church, it was a revival of this. And the Nonconformist movement in Protestantism has not been a flash in the pan. Today England and Scotland are the only English-speaking countries in which there are still established churches; in all the rest, including the United States, all Protestant Churches, as well as the Roman Catholic Church, are free from control by the state; and in Russia, since the Communist Revolution of 1917, the boon of hard liberty, that had previously been the dearly bought privilege of the Russian nonconformists, has been thrust upon the Eastern Orthodox Church by a hostile political régime whose intention in disestablishing the Church was doubtless not a benevolent one.

The subordination of higher religions to states or other secular institutions is a relapse into the ancient dispensation under which religion was an integral part of the total culture of some pre-civilizational society or early civilization, limited in spiritual and geographical range. But the higher religions will always be bound to strive to keep themselves disengaged from secular social and cultural trammels, because this is an indispensable condition for the fulfilment of their true mission. This mission is not concerned directly with human beings' social or cultural relations with each other: its concern is the relation between each individual human being and the trans-human spiritual presence, of which the higher religions offer a new vision.

40 Societies of a distinctive species?

In this Study, our first occasion for taking account of universal churches was in connexion with the disintegrations of civilizations.[1] Since the Christian Church was the first example of this species of institutions that we examined, we have used the Christian word 'churches' as a general label for the species. This label is convenient, but it is not altogether apt. The word 'church' implies a unified ecclesiastical government, and this is possessed by perhaps no more than two of the extant higher religions of which the institutions that we have called churches are the social vehicles. The Tantric Mahayana and the Roman Catholic denomination of Christianity are incorporated in 'churches' that are effectively unitary. But the Christian Churches of the Eastern Orthodox and the Western Protestant Episcopalian denomination are respectively in communion with each other without having any common organs of ecclesiastical government, and the ecclesiastical organization of most other extant higher religions – for instance, Islam and the Quaker form of Christianity – is still less closely knit.

In the first six Parts of this Study, we have continued to deal with churches incidentally to our study of civilizations, as phenomena in the histories of societies of the civilizational species. We have found that civilizations are relatively 'intelligible fields of study'[2] by comparison with the political units (i.e. states of various kinds) that have been the more usual fields of historical study in recent times. All institutions are sets of relations between persons, and a set of relations is intelligible if it includes all other relations in itself without being included, itself, in any more comprehensive relation. Intelligibility, thus defined, can be no more than relative, since nothing short of the entire Universe would be wholly intelligible, and our human minds have enough knowledge of the Universe to be aware that our knowledge of it is only partial.

We have undertaken in the present Part of this Study to examine 'churches' for their own sake, and in the opening chapter we reached two negative conclusions about the relations between churches and civilizations. We concluded that churches are not causes of the disintegrations of civilizations, notwithstanding the historical fact that the rise of a church has frequently been contemporaneous with a civilization's temporary or permanent decline. In the second place, we concluded that, while it is true that in some cases a church has served as a chrysalis for the emergence of a new civilization affiliated to one that has declined and fallen, this historical service to the civilizational species of societies is not the churches' *raison d'être*. So far from that, churches, when they allow themselves to be diverted to this alien purpose, are apt to be denatured and to be hindered from performing their own proper function.

The proper function of churches has been suggested, by anticipation, in the final paragraph of the preceding chapter. Churches are the institutional embodiment of higher religions, and the true mission of higher religions, which distinguishes them from religions of earlier kinds, is to enable human beings to enter into a direct personal relation with a trans-human presence in and behind and beyond the Universe, instead of being introduced to this ultimate spiritual reality only indirectly, through the medium of the civilization or of the pre-civilizational society that is the individual's social setting.

This anticipatory account of the mission of a church raises a number of questions that have not been broached in this Study so far. What is the distinctive difference between 'higher religions' and the religions of earlier kinds? Have the higher religions originated, historically, in religions of the earlier kinds, and, if so, how far have they succeeded in disengaging themselves from their historical antecedents? Considering that the higher religions address themselves to human beings as individuals, why have they come to be embodied in churches, and why has the institutional structure of churches been in some cases rigid, in all cases spiritually unsatisfactory, and, in at least a few cases, even scandalous?

These questions lead on to more fundamental questions about the nature of religion itself. Is religion an intrinsic and inalienable faculty of human nature? And, if so, is its field the inner spiritual life of a human being, as contrasted with his social life? Or is religion merely one of a number of expressions of human sociality? And, if so, is this an immature expression which can be and ought to be and, in some cases, already has been discarded *pari passu* with a civilization's advance in secular sophistication and in potency? The final question in this series is the most crucial. Is the object of religion a reality? Or is it an illusion which can be, and ought to be and, in some cases, already has been, exposed and discredited? These questions will now be taken up, in the order in which they have just been presented, in this chapter and in the next.

The distinctive feature of the higher religions, in virtue of which we must regard them as being a new departure from the religions of earlier kinds, is that the higher religions address themselves to human beings direct as individual persons, and not through the medium of the societies in which these persons are participants in their other activities.

Man is peculiar in being a person besides being a social animal. Sociality is a characteristic that Man shares with a number of other species of living creatures – with wolves, for instance, and with termites. Man's personality is the quality that makes him unique among the manifold forms of life on this planet. Our ancestors' acquisition of personality is one way of describing their achievement of human status. But, till a date in human history that is very recent on the time-scale of the age of Mankind so far, sociality continued to be the paramount feature of human life. Human beings lived and felt and thought and acted as a matter of course within the framework of the society in which they had been born and brought up, and their religion was no exception to this rule.

Not only the pre-civilizational societies, but also the earliest of the civilizations – for instance, the Sumero-

Akkadian Civilization and the Egyptiac – are 'intelligible fields of study' in the sense that all sides of their participants' life, their religion included, were comprehended in them. The social structure of these societies was monolithic. Agriculture, animal husbandry, government, and war were religious activities, and consequently there were no religious practices or beliefs that were independent of what, in Christian parlance, would be called 'secular', as distinguished from religious, action and thought. Religion mediated Man's relationships with Man, and Man's relationship with the natural world. Consequently, human history, down to the age of the earliest civilizations inclusive, can be studied adequately in terms of a synoptic view, first of the pre-civilizational societies and then of civilizations, regarded as being so many self-contained 'intelligible fields'. It is not until we arrive at the age of a second set of civilizations, and then not until we reach the stage of disintegration in the history of these later civilizations, that we find ourselves confronted with churches, embodying higher religions, which cannot be treated intelligibly as being nothing but aspects of the culture of the disintegrating civilizations within which these higher religions arose. Their rise was an assertion of the duality of human nature. A human being is not simply a social animal; he is also a personality seeking a direct relation with an ultimate spiritual reality.

From this point onwards – and the point marks the beginning of a new epoch in the history of human affairs – we cannot carry on our study of history in terms of civilizations alone; we have also to reckon with higher religions that liberate human beings from their servitude to their ancestral civilizations, and that are therefore able to win adherents from among the participants in more than one civilization. The tension, latent since our ancestors became human, between Man the social animal and Man the person now becomes manifest; and it is reflected socially in the fission of human history, from this point onwards, into the histories of civilizations and the histories of higher religions. These two strands of recent history cannot be studied in terms of any one single all-inclusive species of society.

The principal higher religions that still survive are Hinduism, Judaism, Zoroastrianism, Buddhism, Christianity, and Islam. They are named here in the historical order of their appearance in the world, but the beginning of the two oldest of them, namely Hinduism and Judaism, cannot be dated precisely, since these two, unlike the later four, were not originated by historically well-attested single founders who claimed, or have been claimed by their followers, to have made a revolutionary break with the past on the religious plane. While all these six higher religions have undergone many changes in the course of their history, the changes in Hinduism and in Judaism have been spread over a longer period of time, and their origins cannot be attributed with certainty to any single founder. In the case of Judaism, Moses may be an historical figure. His name – which looks like an Egyptiac theophoric name with the first part shorn off – may have been the authentic name of a real person, and it is credible that Moses may have inaugurated some form of the monotheistic religion that eventually became Judaism. However, in the history of

SOCIAL RITUAL
263 The Emperor Marcus Aurelius performs a sacrifice. The earliest religions had a social purpose, minimizing men's individual spirituality by socializing their relations with God to confirm the structure and identity of their society. Thus all social functions were religious functions, and worship was a ritual devised to express and reinforce social solidarity.

Judaism, our earliest sure evidence is to be found in the writings of the Prophets of Israel and Judah, which were composed in the course of the eighth, seventh, and sixth centuries B C. In the history of Hinduism, the authors of the Upanishads were the Israelite and Judahite Prophets' approximate contemporaries. On this reckoning, the rise of the higher religions extends over a period of about thirteen centuries running from Amos's and Hosea's generation to Muhammad's.

Common features of all the higher religions are that each of them originated within the framework of some single civilization, that each of them disengaged itself in some degree from this social matrix, and that none of them has disengaged itself completely. They differ from each other considerably, however, in the degree to which their disengagement has been carried.

Hinduism and Buddhism originated within the Indic Civilization, Judaism within the Syriac Civilization, Zoroastrianism within the Iranian Civilization, and Christianity and Islam in a 'culture-compost' in which elements of the disintegrated Syriac and Hellenic Civilizations were mingled.[3]

Hinduism, Judaism, and Zoroastrianism, like the three younger higher religions, conceive of the godhead as being something far above and beyond the communal divinity of the Indic, Israelite, and Iranian Societies. Brahma and Yahweh are omnipotent and omnipresent lords of the whole Universe, and Ahuramazda has the same destiny, though, in the current aeon, his universal sovereignty is being contested by an adversary, Angra Mainyush. Consistently with their universalistic conception of the godhead, the adherents of each of these three higher religions have made some attempt to propagate their respective faiths beyond the bounds of the local society in which these faiths originated. Moreover, in their theology, Judaism and Zoroastrianism have made as radical a break with the past as Buddhism and Christianity and Islam. Judaism has stigmatized all gods, except Yahweh, first as not being legitimate objects of worship, and eventually as being non-existent. Zoroastrianism has transformed most of the gods of the pre-Zoroastrian Aryan pantheon into demons. Yet none of the three oldest higher religions ever took the new road decisively. All three have remained straddled ambiguously astride the line marking the new departure.

In their conception of the role of Almighty God, their adherents became arrested in a state of double thinking which, to Christian and Muslim minds, seems paradoxically inconsistent. After they had come to think of God as being the omnipresent lord of the Universe, they went on thinking of him at the same time as being the peculiar local god of the society or community in which he had originally been worshipped as such. Thus each of these higher religions, in becoming a higher religion, still also continued to be a part of the integrated culture of a particular community or society; and it has never been feasible to be converted to the Hindu, the Jewish, or the Zoroastrian religion without at the same time having to become a member of the Hindu, Jewish, or Iranian Society. Conversion to Judaism or to Zoroastrianism has involved submission to a system of law in which religious observances are inextricably intertwined with what, to Christian minds,

PERSONAL QUEST

264 Alexis, called 'the Man of God', who turned his back on the fifth-century East Roman Society to follow the Christian life as a wandering beggar. The higher religions liberated men from their bondage to a particular civilization with its socially oriented religion, and placed them in a direct relationship with God. Society shrinks in significance when men reach towards a universal spiritual reality that is accessible to all Mankind.

would look like secular regulations. Conversion to Hinduism has involved incorporation in a caste and submission to the restrictions that the Hindu caste-system entails. This explains why conversions to these three religions have been rare, and why their adherents have been no more than half-hearted in their efforts to bring gentiles into their jealously guarded folds.

The failure of the three earliest of the higher religions to disengage themselves from their ancestral social matrix also explains the secessions from them of new higher religions which have broken away in order to impart to all Mankind the universally valid truths and universally applicable precepts that Hinduism, Judaism, and Zoroastrianism had discovered but had reserved for privileged portions of Mankind, namely for the respective heirs of the Indic and Iranian Civilizations, and two of the Syriac communities, Israel and Judah.

The Jain and Buddhist seceders from Hinduism ignored the basic Indic social institution of caste, and the Buddhists were rewarded by their success in converting more than half of the human race, including the whole of the vast Sinic World with its satellite societies in Korea, Japan, and Vietnam – though the price of Buddhism's universalism was its eventual rejection by the Indic Society within which it had come to birth.

The question whether Judaism is bound up inextricably with the culture of a particular community or is a religion that can be embraced by anyone, whatever his ancestral culture or his local nationality may be, was the issue, in the first generation of Christianity, between the original Christian Jewish sect and the gentile Christian Church that was created by the missionary work of Saint Paul; and it is significant that the eventual secession of the gentile Christian Church from Jewry, which followed in spite of Paul's and Peter's concordant desire to avoid the breach, has not been the only case of its kind. Six hundred years later, another new missionary religion inspired by Judaism, namely Islam, parted company with Jewry, as Christianity had done, in order to convert the gentiles to the truths and precepts that the Jews had discovered but had not effectively disseminated.

The history of Zoroastrianism has been the same story. During the age in which Zoroastrianism was the established religion of the Sasanian Empire, Manichaeism seceded from it in the third century of the Christian Era and Mazdakism in the fifth century; and in the following age, when the Sasanian Empire, as well as half the Roman Empire, had been conquered by the Muslim Arabs, the new régime's Zoroastrian subjects in Iran were converted to Islam much more rapidly than its Christian subjects in 'Iraq and Syria and Egypt.

Buddhism, Christianity, and Islam have each been – or become – whole-heartedly universalistic. Each of these three religions has set out to convert the whole of Mankind; and, though the continuing coexistence of all three is proof that none of them has succeeded in achieving their common ambitious aim, each has succeeded in converting whole continents, embracing the regional domains of a number of different civilizations; and each of them has achieved this by means of the rudimentary vehicles of communication that were the only means at their disposal

before the 'annihilation of distance' through the modern advance of technology.[4]

This missionary prowess has been the reward of Buddhism's and Christianity's and Islam's relative success in disengaging themselves from the irrelevant legacy of their historical origins, as contrasted with the strength of the continuing implication of Hinduism, Judaism, and Zoroastrianism in an ancestral civilization's manners and customs. Yet the disengagement of even the three preeminently missionary religions has been only partial.

The Eucharist, which is the supreme rite of Christianity, is a version of the Mediterranean worship of a vegetation god, and the 'elements', bread and wine, are regional products. Their provinciality is borne in on a visitor to Japan, where the rice-spirit, not the corn-spirit, is divine, and where the Mediterranean 'staff of life' is so exotic that the visitor has to use the Portuguese word *pan* if he wishes to ask for bread. In the non-Protestant major part of Christendom, the Great Mother of God has also continued to win worship as the Theotokos; and Protestants agree with other Christians in deifying a human being – a relapse into Egyptiac and Hellenic 'paganism' which is shocking for Jews and which has been renounced by Unitarians at the cost of exclusion from the Christian fold.

Islam, like Unitarianism, stands for a reaction against Christianity's deviation from Jewish monotheism. Islam is as totalitarian in its monotheism as Judaism is. Yet, like Judaism, Islam carries a freight from its pagan past. The pilgrimage to Mecca and the adoration of the black stone embedded in the wall of the Ka'bah are legacies from a pre-Muslim Arabia. The Meccan black stone is a *baetylus* (a Latinization of a Semitic compound word meaning 'the habitation of a god'), and it has older counterparts in the black stones that were brought to Rome from Pessinus or from Pergamon in 204 BC and from Emesa in AD 218. Moreover, Muslim law, like Jewish law and like all primitive law, is monolithic. In Islam, as in Judaism, it is impossible to draw a dividing-line between religious law and secular law.

The transformation of Christianity and Islam into religions for all Mankind was achieved by followers of the founders. It was not the intention of the founders themselves.

In the account of Jesus in the Gospels, there is no indication that Jesus himself was not an orthodox Jew; and, as such, his horizon was bounded by the limits of his own nation. In the Gospel according to Saint Matthew,[5] he is reported to have instructed his emissaries not to visit the gentiles or the Samaritans, but to go rather to 'the lost sheep of the house of Israel'. In the Gospel according to Saint Mark,[6] he is reported to have taken the same line – and this in harsh and wounding language – in his negative first answer to a Canaanite woman's appeal to him.

Muhammad's horizon was likewise bounded by the limits of his own nation. The Arabs' aspiration to become 'People of the Book', like the Jews and the Christians, was nationalistic; and it took a form that is characteristic of barbarians camped on the fringe of a civilization.[7] The Arabs were sufficiently impressed by the culture of the Roman Empire to hanker after a religion of the kind possessed by the Empire's inhabitants; yet at the same time

265, 266 The higher
religions could not dis-
engage themselves totally
from the matrix of earlier
religious traditions. The
legacy of a local pagan past
is discernible in the
Christian adoration of the
Eucharist, a survival from
Mediterranean worship
of vegetation-gods, and in
Islam's veneration of
the 'Black Stone' in the
Ka'bah shrine at Mecca,
right, a cult taken from
pre-Islamic Middle Eastern
religions.

337

THE ISLAMIC HERITAGE

267, 268, 269   Islamic miniatures of Abraham and Isaac, top, and of Samson destroying the temple of the Philistines, centre, demonstrate this faith's Judaic origins. Islam also acknowledged its link with Christianity, an attitude that was not reciprocated: bottom, the flight of Muhammad from Mecca is watched approvingly by Christ.

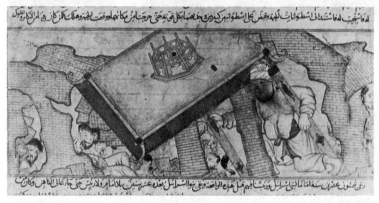

they were sufficiently independent-minded to be unwilling simply to adopt their impressive neighbours' religion as it stood without giving it an Arab national colouring. In the eyes of the Arabs of Muhammad's generation, Christianity was the national religion of the Romans and Judaism the national religion of the Jews; and the picture of God[8] that Muhammad presented to his countrymen was, like the Jewish picture of God, equivocal. Besides being the God of the Universe, he was to be the national god of the Arabs. Islam was to be a revival of the pure religion of Abraham, and this time 'the Chosen People' of Abraham's lineage were to be the Arab offspring of his son Ishmael instead of the Jewish offspring of his son Isaac.

This element of nationalism in Islam was, of course, greatly reinforced when Islam was carried out of Arabia into the former dominions of the Roman and Sasanian Empires as the national religion of Arab conquerors. The conquerors did not much want non-Arab converts. The conquered peoples were more valuable to them as surtax-payers than as less heavily taxed co-religionists. It was the Arabs' Zoroastrian and Christian non-Arab subjects who eventually took the Arabs' kingdom by storm. They forced their way into the fold of Islam, deposed the Arabs from their exclusive ascendancy in the Islamic state, and gave Islam itself an organization and a theology which removed, once for all, the ambiguity that, till then, had kept Islam havering between the two incompatible ideals of nationalism and universality.[9] Thus the non-Arab converts to Muhammad's religion saved for Islam a situation that the founder himself had left unclarified.

This eventual harvesting of Islam's potentialities as a universal religion was an immense cultural, as well as religious, achievement. It is comparable to what had previously been done for Christianity, and it was done by the same people by the same means. The people whose good offices enabled Islam, as well as Christianity, to grow to its full spiritual and cultural stature were the South-West Asian heirs of the combined Syriac and Hellenic cultures. The former participants in these two civilizations had lost their consciousness of their distinctive cultures and had become ecumenical-minded, but they had not lost their cultural fertility. So far from that, the Syriac and Hellenic cultures, in losing their distinctive identities, had blended into a 'culture-compost' which had an unrivalled nutritive power. The feat of nursing not only one but two higher religions into a maturity in which each of them makes a universal appeal is an achievement that it would be hard to match. But for the converts, Christianity might have remained a minor Jewish sect, and Islam might have remained merely an Arab national imitation of Judaeo-Christian monotheism.

Buddhism was never in danger of being merely a Hindu sect. The founder himself had extricated his religion from its ancestral Indic background by ignoring the Indic institution of caste and by dissenting from the prevalent opinion in the Indic World about the nature of the psychic element in the psychosomatic complex of human nature. According to the opinion that was prevalent in the Buddha's day, a human being's psyche is an eternal entity which can be seen, by introspection, to be identical with the ultimate spiritual reality in and beyond and behind the Universe.

Tat tvam asi: 'that is what thou art' – 'thou' being the human soul and 'that' being the ultimate spiritual reality. In sharp opposition to this view, the Buddha held that there was no such thing as a human 'soul' and that the psychic aspect of human nature was merely a flow of discontinuous psychic states.

The breach between the Buddha and his Hindu contemporaries was irremediable. Yet the Buddha's conception of Man's condition, and his prescription for dealing with it, were both founded on an Indic belief which the Buddha shared with his opponents and which he and they alike took for granted. Both parties believed that a human being does not make his appearance in this world once only. They believed that death is followed by rebirth; that the series of recurring births and deaths may be endless; and that this is a far more dreadful fate than death – which would, in fact, be a blessed release if only one could make sure that no rebirth was to follow it. The Buddha's prescription for winning release from rebirth was the extinction of desire; for desire, so he believed, was the force that maintained the flow of psychic states and that, after death, reactivated this flow and thereby caused rebirth. Extinguish desire, and you will be able to make your exit, once for all, into a blessedly irrevocable state of 'extinguishedness' (*nirvana*).[10] This is the essence of Buddhism, at least in its original 'southern' form, as distinct from its later 'northern' form (the Mahayana). So Buddhism is based on a belief that was part of the Buddha's and his Hindu opponents' common Indic ancestral cultural heritage.

Though the higher religions differ from each other in the degree to which they have succeeded in disengaging themselves from the matrices of their ancestral cultures, they are, all alike, attempts to take religion out of the field of social life and to make it a personal affair in which a human being is in direct communion with ultimate spiritual reality, instead of his having to deal with this ultimate reality through the medium of the human society in which he happens to be a participant. In other words, the higher religions are attempts to 'de-institutionalize' religion. Yet we find that, actually, the higher religions are embodied in the institutions that we have called 'churches'. There is an incongruity here which calls for explanation, and we have suggested one explanation already.

Though a human being is a personality, he is also still a social animal, and he cannot escape from his built-in sociality even in his most private personal inner spiritual life. Anchorites involuntarily attract devotees and disciples and produce social effects in the field of mundane affairs, however single-minded they may be in their effort to segregate themselves.[11] Moreover, the anchorite is arrested in his solitary pursuit of ultimate spiritual reality by his social concern to share with his fellow human beings the spiritual discoveries that he has made for himself.

It was open to the Buddha, for instance, to make his exit into *nirvana* as soon as he had attained his own enlightenment, but he voluntarily postponed his own exit in order to show the way to all sentient beings. This, in turn, caused him to found his monastic fraternity, the *sangha*; for the way of salvation cannot be taught by one person to others without some social framework to link the master with his disciples. The inexorableness of the institutionalization of

THE BUDDHIST HERITAGE

270, 271 Doctrinal heterodoxy caused the Buddha to break with his ancestral Hindu religion, yet belief in recurring incarnation was so ingrained in Indic tradition that it was taken over into Buddhism without question; the Buddhist wheel of life, below, shows this perpetual rebirth of souls. Beneath it, the effigy of the Buddha in *nirvana* – the state of extinguishedness that, in Buddhist teaching, offered release from the eternal round.

personal religion can also be illustrated from the history of Christianity. This universal religion was a revulsion from the worship of a universal state, the Roman Empire, symbolized in the goddess Rome and in the god Caesar. In order to hold their own against the mighty power of the Roman imperial government, the Christians built up an ecclesiastical government of their own, organized on the Roman pattern and inspired by the authoritarian Roman spirit.

The adherents of a higher religion are tempted to lapse into authoritarianism not only as a means of collective self-defence but also because they believe themselves to be the depositaries of inestimably valuable truths and prescriptions. They feel themselves to be in duty bound to impart their spiritual treasure to their still unconverted fellow men.

Christianity and Islam have usually regarded the heathen as fair game for forcible conversion. Muslims are com-

manded in the Qur'an to tolerate the Jews and Christians – the 'People of the Book' – in consideration of the fundamental common tenets of the three Judaic religions, but the same consideration has not always led Christians to tolerate the Jews and Muslims; so far from that, the Jewish origins of the Christian faith and the presence of a diasporá that still adheres to Judaism have frequently been causes of grave theological embarrassment for the Christians. In permitting Jews to live and to practise their faith in Christian communities, the Christians have been moved primarily by a practical concern for their own self-interest. Christians have also, like Muslims, been inhibited by a recognition of the unseemliness of persecuting the adherents of a religion that is their own religion's main historical source; but this inhibition has been weaker in the Christian than in the Muslim World, and hence the position of Jews in Christian countries has been very precarious. Christians and Muslims have also imposed the orthodoxy

272, 273 Islam has usually been
generous in its treatment of non-
Muslim 'People of the Book' –
Jews and Christians – sanctified by
the Qur'an as members of sister
religions. Left, an Islamic miniature shows Muhammad conversing
with Christian monks; it was
painted in 1595, when Islam and
Christendom were again at war
after a twenty-four-year truce. By
contrast, Christianity has tried to
support its claim to unique revelation by persecuting the religions
with which it has embarrassing
historical links: Goya's moving
comment on the Inquisition is
simply titled 'For being of Jewish
ancestry'.

of the day on heterodox groups, and have usually tried to
reintern heretics and schismatics in the fold by violent
means. Even when 'unbelievers' have been tolerated, they
have been penalized in Christian and Muslim communities; and Christians and Muslims have waged 'holy wars'
against each other, against the heathen, and against heretics.
'And the lord said unto the servant, Go out into the
highways and hedges and compel them to come in.'[12]

Thus both of these two higher religions have felt that
their overriding duty to convert the 'unbelievers' and preserve orthodoxy outweighs other considerations, including
even some of the moral precepts embodied in their faiths;
and this explains why ecclesiastical authorities have sometimes been as oppressive and atrocious as the most abomin-
able secular governments. Unlike Christianity and Islam,
Buddhism has usually coexisted amicably with other faiths.
It is surely not just a coincidence that Buddhism has been
the most successful of the three missionary religions.

The institutionalization of the higher religions is a perhaps unavoidable tragedy. Its nemesis is a spiritual tension
that is proportionate in its acuteness to the degree to which
the process of institutionalization is carried. In a highly
institutionalized church there is likely to be a conflict between the individual's conscience and the ecclesiastical
'Establishment'. The conscience asserts itself against the
Establishment at its peril; yet society cannot afford to let
the conscience be intimidated and coerced. A human being
has first to master himself spiritually in order to master his
conduct of his social relations with his fellows. Conscience
is a personal, not a collective, faculty. The spiritual level of
a society cannot be higher than the average level of the
participants; the collective level can be raised only on
the initiative of individuals; and, when an individual
does rise above the level of his social environment, this
is the fruit of a previous victory over himself in his own
spiritual life.

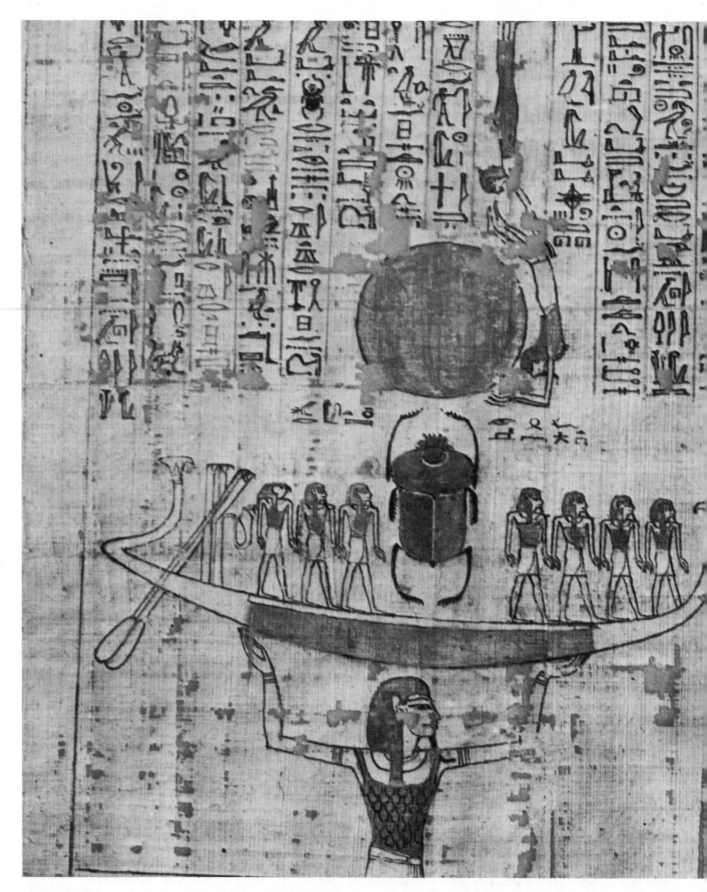

274 Egyptiac religion had a systematic mythology of creation and rebirth. Here, the creation is the principal subject: Nu, image of primordial chaos, supports the boat of the Sun, containing the sacred scarab; reaching towards the Sun's disk are Nut, the sky-goddess, and her son Osiris, god of the dead. On the right, the mummy of Anhai, priestess-donor of the papyrus.

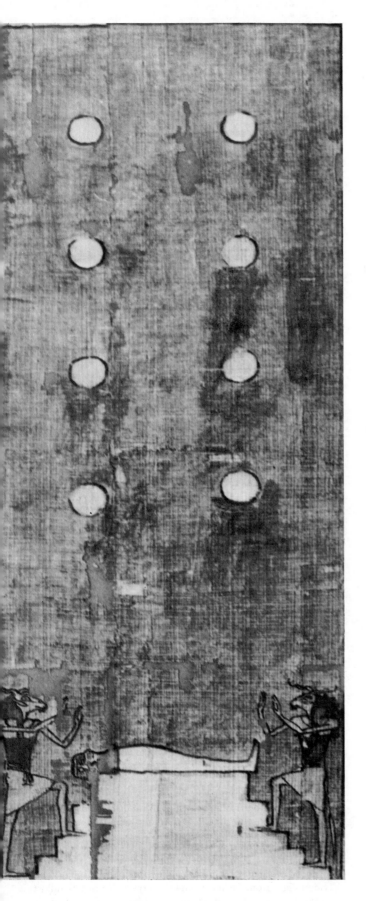

41 Social responses to an illusion or to a reality?

IN THE two preceding chapters of the present Part, we have discussed the relation of churches to civilizations, and we have concluded that churches are a distinctive species of societies that cannot be made intelligible if they are treated, not as being institutions of a new kind, but as being simply the religious facets of the culture of the civilizations within which they have arisen. We have found that this is a practicable way of treating the religious aspect of the histories of the pre-civilizational societies and also of those civilizations that rose and fell without giving rise to a higher religion embodied in a church, but that, after we have reached this point in our inquiry, we can no longer continue to regard civilizations as still being adequately intelligible fields in the sense of being fully comprehensive and self-contained networks of relations. Churches, we have found, break out of the frameworks of civilizations, and this is why churches need to be treated as being societies of a separate and distinctive kind. The distinctiveness of churches is due to the distinctiveness of the character of the religion that is embodied in them. Higher religions are attempts to enable human beings to enter into a direct relation with ultimate spiritual reality; and this is their essential and permanent aim, in spite of their being institutionalized – which is perhaps an unavoidable consequence of Man's being a social animal besides being a person with an inner spiritual life that is not a reflexion of his sociality and is not conditioned by it.

The course of this discussion has raised the question of the relation of religion to the social and to the personal aspect of human nature. This question must now be pursued, but the pursuit of it entails the examination of another question which comes first and goes deeper. What is religion itself?

One manifest feature of religion is that it is a consequence of consciousness. A human being finds himself in a world that he understands and controls only partially. This is an awkward situation for him; yet he has to live in it, and with it, as best he can; and the best that he can do in these strange and disturbing circumstances is to make guesses about what is beyond his ken and to try to come to terms with what is beyond his power.

. . . It is religious experience which lays the foundation of the World. It is ritual orientation, with the structure of sacred space which it reveals, that transforms 'Chaos' into 'Cosmos' and, therefore, renders human existence possible – prevents it, that is, from regression to the level of zoological existence. Every religion, even the most elementary, is an ontology: it reveals the *being* of the sacred things and the divine Figures, it shows forth *that which really is*, and in doing so establishes a World which is no longer evanescent and incomprehensible, as it is in nightmares, and as it again becomes whenever existence is in danger of foundering in the 'Chaos' of total relativity, where no 'Centre' emerges to ensure orientation.[1]

The making of this tentative chart of an enigmatic ultimate reality in order to achieve harmony with it is religion, and, if this definition is correct, it follows that, in religion, there are two elements that are distinct from each other, though they are also interdependent. Religion includes both guesswork about unknown facts, and action in accordance with these guesses. This is true of all religions of every kind; but, within this common framework, there is a wide variation, as between one religion and another, in both the field of the guesswork and the form of the action.

Early Man was acutely conscious of being at the mercy of non-human Nature because of the inadequacy of his understanding of this province of his world. He therefore made guesses about the character of non-human Nature, in the light of his own experience of human relationships, and attempted to identify and propitiate the powers that appeared to him to be at work here. The earliest recorded kind of religion consists of myths about non-human Nature and rites for establishing a harmony with non-human natural powers. Such symbolic confirmations of the patterning of the Universe were the heart of primitive Roman religion; the same principle survives in present-day Japan in Shinto. By now, Man's persistent effort to master non-human Nature – an effort that is coeval with the humanization of our pre-human ancestors – has achieved such success that, in this encounter, Man has turned the tables. So far from being any longer at the mercy of non-human Nature, Man has now subjugated it, and consequently his relation with non-human Nature has dropped out of the field of his religion. Instead of trying to maintain the order of non-human Nature by the performance of symbolic religious rites, Man can exploit and even interfere with the natural order by means of technology; and, instead of guessing about non-human Nature mythically, he explores it scientifically.

Man's subjugation of non-human Nature has gone with a run during the last two centuries, since he has been harnessing, for his service, one after another of the forces of inanimate Nature, which are far more potent physically than the muscle-power of human beings and of domesticated animals. However, Man had already won his decisive victory over non-human Nature towards the close of the fourth millennium BC, when he succeeded in regulating the waters of the Lower Tigris-Euphrates basin and the Lower Nile basin and thereby transforming previously inhospitable jungle-swamps into highly productive irrigated fields.[2] This was the earliest dramatic triumph of organized collective human action, and this exhilarating experience led Man to take his own collective power, in place of non-human Nature's power, as his paramount object of worship. In the Sumerian, and likewise later in the Hellenic, city-states, divinities that had originally stood for forces of non-human Nature were conscripted to stand also for the collective power of the citizens of Ur or Eridu or Sparta or Athens. In the United Kingdom of Pharaonic Egypt, the collective power of the participants in the Egyptiac Civilization was worshipped in a more crudely ingenuous form. The man who wore the Pharaonic double crown was deified *ex officio*.

In making this change in the nature of the object of his worship, Man was succumbing to pride and courting disaster, since pride overwhelms the humility and obscures the insight that are the indispensable safeguards and

CHAOS INTO COSMOS:
CHRISTIAN AND INDIC

275–284 Religion is Man's attempt to order his consciousness of reality and to put himself in harmony with the patterns he discerns. Myths of creation, found in all religions, are fundamental parts of this explanatory process, providing a logical basis for men's guesswork about the world. Above, the primal separation of categories, in the familiar Christian image of God dividing light from darkness. Right, a series of Tantric Buddhist paintings – 'The Evolution and Devolution of the Cosmic Form' – expresses a similar, but more abstract, interpretation of creation as the symbolic establishment of order through the introduction of finite systems into a shapeless cosmos.

हिरण्यगर्भलक्षणम्

वर्तुलंहस्ववदनंच चक्रमध्येतुकोमले ।
श्रीवत्सकोस्तुभाकारंलांछनंचक्रपार्श्वतः ॥
हिरण्यगर्भोभगवान् पद्मनाभिसमन्वितः ।
हिरण्यकर्णमित्रस्तु श्रीप्रदःकुलवर्धनः ॥

हिरण्यगर्भमूर्तिः

शंकर्षणप्रद्युम्नलक्षणम्

लग्रद्धिचक्रोर्काभः पूर्वभागेतुपद्मभृत् ।
शंकर्षणोथ्रप्रद्युम्न सूक्ष्मचक्रस्तुपीतकम् ॥

शंकर्षणमूर्तिः

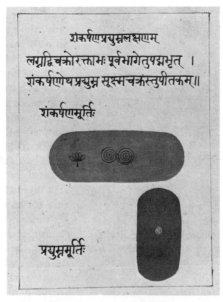

प्रद्युम्नमूर्तिः

स्वयंभूमूर्तिलक्षणम्

स्वर्णैर्वतुलरेखाभिराद्धतोनीलवर्णवान् ।
दीर्घास्यः पृष्ठचक्रस्तु स्वयंभूरितिविश्रुतः ।
केवलंमोक्षफलदो ह्यर्चकस्यनशंसयः ॥

स्वयंभूमूर्तिः ।

श्रीउपेन्द्रलक्षणम्

द्वारस्यवामतश्चक्रं सुक्स्नोदक्षिणेऽपिवा ।
उपेन्द्रमणिवर्णेषे हस्वचक्रातिशोभन ॥

उपेन्द्रमूर्तिः

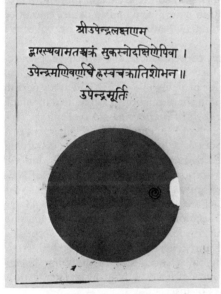

पृष्ठवक्षा नृसिंहोय कपिलोऽय्यात्तिविन्दुकः ।
अथवा पंचविन्दुस्त्पूजनं ब्रह्मचारिएः ॥
कपिलं नारसिंहस्तु प्रथक् चक्रस्ययोत्नते ॥

नृसिंह   मूर्तिः

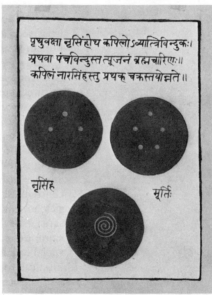

शिवनाभिलक्षणम्

द्विनाभिः पंचरूणाचेड्ड्वेधरिहरात्मिका ।
शिवनाभिरितिस्यातो भुक्ति मुक्ति फलप्रदः ॥

हरिहरात्मिकाशिवनामिः

प्रद्युम्नलक्षणम्

प्रद्युम्नोभगवान् सूक्ष्म चक्रपीतविमिश्रितः ।
मकराभामुखेरेखा वश्यते पृष्ठतोऽपिवा ।
सप्रद्युम्नइतिस्यातास्तूरीयं चावधारयेत् ॥
सर्वसंपत्प्रदंचैव सर्वाकृतिक्षपंभवेत् ॥

प्रद्युम्नमूर्ति

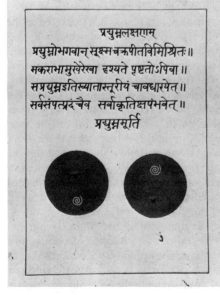

शालग्रामवर्णेफलम्

पीताधनकरीड्येया	रक्ताराज्यकरीस्मृता ॥
अतिरक्तारोगदाच	कृष्णकीर्तिप्रदायिनी ॥
पाण्डुरापापहानित्यं	रूक्षाचेद्रोगदयिनी ॥

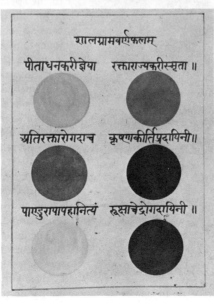

श्रीअनन्तमूर्तिलक्षणम्

नानावर्णेऽनेकमूर्तिर्निर्गभोगीत्वनन्तकः ॥

अनन्तमूर्तिः ।

THE MASTERY OF SELF

Man is by nature self-centred, relating his experience to the infinite 'I' of his conscious personality. The conquest of this innate human egocentricity is indispensable to social harmony, but, as the founders of the higher religions showed, it is attainable only by a painful spiritual struggle in each human soul.

285   The Buddha fasting, an image of extreme physical asceticism.

guides for the conduct of human affairs. Consequently, since the rise of the earliest of the civilizations, Man's worship of his collective power has led him into one disaster after another. This collective form of self-worship is still the paramount religion of a majority of Mankind; indeed, Man's collective power is now greater, and his adulation of it is more extreme, than ever before. It is not surprising that, in our generation, we have brought upon ourselves disasters of unprecedented magnitude and horror.

The truth is that human nature is part of Nature, and is also the field in which our understanding and our control are at their minimum, though it is the field in which a correct understanding and an effective control are more necessary for us than in any other field, since human nature is a far more potent force in our human world than any of the inanimate natural forces that we have harnessed. Human nature, expressing itself in human passions rationalized as human wills, decides how these domesticated inanimate forces shall be used. However far Man may succeed in carrying his conquest of non-human Nature, he will remain at Nature's mercy in so far as he continues to fail to master his own human nature, and human nature cannot be mastered, as non-human Nature has been, by collective human action.

Human emotions, consciousness, and will are not collective; they are faculties of an individual human being; and the inner spiritual life of a person – of each and every person who is a participant in social relations – is the field in which the spiritual battle for self-mastery has to be fought. This is Man's most urgent, and also his most difficult, task. It is difficult because Man is a living being, and every living being is self-centred by nature. Self-centredness is, indeed, another name for life itself, and the overcoming of self-centredness is therefore a *tour de force*. Yet it is only in so far as a human being achieves this *tour de force* that he can have satisfactory social relations with his fellows – and Man cannot contract out of society. He cannot exist except as a social animal, and unregenerate inborn self-centredness is inimical to sociality in a social species of living beings whose sociality is not enforced by built-in instinct, as it is in the social species of insects.

In human life, self-centredness can be prevented from causing social disasters only in so far as it is mastered in the inner spiritual life of each participant in society. 'Suffering is the key to learning',[3] and the spectacle of the self-inflicted sufferings that had wrecked successive attempts at civilization opened the eyes of the founders of the higher religions. They perceived that salvation must be sought, not in the field of social relations, but in the field of a person's inner spiritual life, and that, in this field, salvation can be won only by self-mastery. This is the reason why these seers addressed themselves to their fellow human beings as persons, not as participants in society. It is also the reason why they taught that self-mastery is the indispensable prerequisite for the establishment of a right relation between a human person and the ultimate spiritual reality.

The founder of the youngest of the higher religions, Muhammad, actually called his religion 'submission', meaning self-submission to the unique God, conceived of as being a super-human person who is the ultimate spiritual reality according to Muhammad's belief. 'Submission' is

286   *The Agony in the Garden:* Christ prepares his spirit for submission to physical suffering.

the meaning of the Arabic word *Islam*; and Zarathustra, the Buddha, and Jesus could have called their respective religions, just as aptly, by the corresponding words in their own mother tongues. The unanimity of these four seers in appealing to their fellows individually, and calling for self-conquest and self-surrender, is very striking, because their conceptions of the nature of ultimate reality differed widely. Zarathustra, Jesus, and Muhammad were theists; the Buddha was not – or, at least, if he believed in the existence of his society's ancestral gods, he did not believe in their importance.

These seers' new insight was that the field of religion is a human being's inner spiritual life and not his social life. They took it for granted that religion itself is an intrinsic and inalienable faculty of human nature, and in this they were not innovators. Since our ancestors became human, most human beings have likewise taken this for granted. However, the assumption must be examined, because it has been challenged. In the last century BC, for instance, it was contested by the Roman poet Lucretius in his poem *De Rerum Natura*, in which he expounds the ideas of his master the Greek philosopher Epicurus, whose lifetime straddles the fourth and third centuries BC. Since the later decades of the seventeenth century of the Christian Era, the belief that religion is an intrinsic and inalienable faculty of human nature has been contested again, first by a small band of Western rationalists, but subsequently by an increasing number, not only of Westerners, but also of participants in the surviving non-Western civilizations, as the ideas of the West have spread progressively beyond the West's own borders. The modern Western revival of Lucretius's challenge was provoked by a reaction against the animosity and atrocity of the so-called 'Wars of Religion' between rival sects of Western Christians. Before the close of the seventeenth century, Lucretius's verdict on religion had come to ring true to contemporary Western ears. *Tantum religio potuit suadere malorum*.[4]

Neither Lucretius nor his modern followers have denied that most human beings, so far, have believed that they have religion. Indeed, they have not denied that most people have actually had the religion that people have believed that they have had. What the sceptics have denied is that religion is ineradicable. They have claimed that they have eradicated religion in their own case; that what has been accomplished by them can be accomplished by other people too; and that religion ought to be eradicated. The modern opponents of religion have challenged the thesis of the founders of the higher religions; they have not agreed that religion is a built-in faculty of the human psyche. They have maintained that religion is merely one of a number of expressions of human sociality, and that it is an immature expression. They diagnose it correctly as expressing Man's consciousness of his ignorance and weakness, and therefore they expect, unwarrantably, to see religion discarded progressively, *pari passu* with a civilization's advance in sophistication and in potency. They hold that the recession of religion is an index of this advance. Mankind may have needed religion as a prop while it was in its infancy; it can and should discard this prop now that it is coming of age. These theses are specious, but they are open to challenge in their turn.

The first thesis is that religious beliefs and practices, and likewise ethical codes, are merely part of the manners and customs of a particular time and place, and that, in so far as religion enforces an ethical code, the case for religion – if there is a case for it – is merely utilitarian. On this view, religion is an intellectually untenable but practically effective sanction for the prevalent social pattern of behaviour.

Religion is primarily a social phenomenon. Churches may owe their origin to teachers with strong individual convictions, but these teachers have seldom had much influence upon the Churches that they have founded, whereas Churches have had enormous influence upon the communities in which they flourished.[5]

This view is, however, correct only to the extent to which it identifies religion with religion's mutable social setting and ignores religion's permanent and indispensable role in the personal life of every human being. It is no doubt correct to assert that a structure of belief, a church, an ecclesiastical hierarchy, or a social morality are all sustained by a direct relationship with secular society; and history bears out the materialist thesis that the institutional sides of religion have always expressed and reinforced the social and political structure of the day.

The greatest disaster that has befallen Christendom was, perhaps, the conversion of Constantine and the consequent involvement of Caesar in the affairs of God and of God's Church in the affairs of Caesar. Second to this was the transformation of the Church from the status of a Church persecuted for Christ's sake into a Church persecuting in the name of Christ.[6]

We have already suggested[7] that this disaster of institutionalization and consequent secularization is an unavoidable tragedy, so long as Man fails to master the tension between his individuality and his sociality. The social critique of religion is justified on its own social ground; yet it misses its mark if it tries to apply the same argument to the personal field of spiritual experience and endeavour. The essence of religion is the personal experience of a transcendent spiritual reality and the personal quest for harmony with this experienced reality. Accidents of time and place may clothe this essence of religion with all kinds of externalities, frequently to a degree at which it becomes difficult to distinguish the core of religion from its accoutrements; but the personal belief in transcendence – in an ultimate spiritual reality – cannot be attacked with weapons drawn from the armoury of social criticism.

The second thesis of the opponents of religion is that Mankind's ignorance and weakness are symptoms of a temporary immaturity, and that these symptoms abate as civilization advances in sophistication and in potency. But this advance has been achieved only in Mankind's relations with non-human Nature; and to equate non-human Nature with the whole of Nature is not sophisticated; it is naïvely obtuse. Nature includes human nature, and this is the most intractable and formidable part of Nature that Man has to deal with. This truth was perceived, long ago, by the founders of the higher religions. Man's conquest of non-human Nature by his technology has now made Man a deadlier danger to himself than ever before, by arming him with more lethal weapons and with polluting tools. Since the invention and use of atomic weapons, and the beginning of the employment of 'atoms for peace', it no longer needs a seer to discern this; it is patent to everyone.

Thus history – and, not least, current history – shows that Mankind's ignorance and weakness are not temporary symptoms; they are permanent features of human life. They are inherent in the amphibiousness of human nature. A human being is both an animal and something more; he is both a social animal and a person endowed with a conscience; he has some knowledge and some power, but both his knowledge and his power are limited, and he is aware of this. He is also aware that he is born to die, and death is a formidable prospect for him if he does not believe that he is going to be reborn, whereas, if he does believe this, life is a formidable persistent reality for him. Man's plight is, and is likely to remain, what it always has been. In the Atomic Age it is still what it was seen to be by the Prophets of Israel and Judah and by Zarathustra and by the Buddha. It is misleading to apply the concepts of immaturity and maturity, or of 'infancy' and 'coming of age', to a species of living creatures, such as Mankind is, or to a society, such as a civilization is. The analogy is a false one; for aging and maturing are the experiences of organisms, and neither a species nor a society is an organism. A species is a set of organisms; a society is a network of relations.[8]

We may conclude that neither of these arguments confutes the assertion that religion truly is an intrinsic and inalienable faculty of human nature; and we may surmise that people who deny that they themselves have religion, and deny this in good faith, actually do have religion without recognizing it. Lucretius, for instance, was manifestly a deeply religious man. His missionary ardour to liberate his fellow human beings *from* religion is comparable to the ardour to liberate them *by* religion that has inspired the founders of the higher religions.

But, if it is granted that religion is an abiding reality which is not eradicable from human nature, it does not follow from this that the object of religion is a reality or that the objective of religion is attainable. It is conceivable that beyond our ken there may not be anything that is intelligible or meaningful, and that beyond our power there may be no ultimate spiritual reality with which we can bring ourselves into harmony. To believe in the reality of something beyond our ken can be no more than an unverifiable act of faith. Have we, within our ken, any 'signals of transcendence'[9] – any indications that support the unverifiable hypothesis of the presence of an ultimate spiritual reality behind the phenomena?

One such indication can be put best in negative terms. If it were suggested to us that Man is the highest spiritual presence in the Universe, we should find this suggestion too ridiculous to be entertained. Spiritually imperfect as we are, we have spiritual standards that are far higher than our own highest level of performance. An ideal would surely be inconceivable if there were no reality to which it corresponded. Is this not an indication of the existence of a spiritual reality of a supra-human sublimity? If it is an indication, of course it is not a conclusive one. It is not, and cannot be, a proof.

A positive indication of the presence of a supra-human spiritual reality is the human mind's distinction between right and wrong, and the human conscience's sense of obligation to take sides: to try to do what it believes to be right; to abstain from doing what it believes to be wrong; and to stand for right against wrong in all situations. The distinction and the sense of obligation to take sides seem to be universal. We are able to do what we believe to be wrong, but we are not able to believe that what we believe to be wrong is right. We can say the words 'Evil be thou my Good',[10] but we cannot reverse our ethical values in practice. What is good in our judgment is good, and what is bad in our judgment is bad, irreversibly. Of course there are as many different judgments of what is actually good and bad as there are different persons and different societies. These particular judgments may even sometimes be diametrically opposed to each other; but the people who stand opposed to each other in their judgment of particular cases are in agreement with each other on the two fundamental points of principle: the distinction between right and wrong, and the obligation to take sides.

The concepts of right and wrong, and of good and bad, are relative to each other only logically; imperatively, they are not on a par; for our conscience forbids us to be neutral; it commands us to take action on behalf of what is right and good, against what is wrong and bad. The distinction between right and wrong, and the obligation to take sides, are built into human nature, and this suggests that they are built into the nature of the Universe. If this indication could be verified (and, of course, it cannot be), that would not provide any evidence that what is right is destined to be victorious. It would, however, assure us that every conscious being – human, supra-human, or sub-human – that is capable of making an ethical choice is under a moral obligation to take sides with what is right, and to stake its fortunes on the outcome, whatever the outcome may be.

This suggests that in and beyond and behind the Universe, as well as in a human being's conscience, there is some spiritual power that is making for good. This power may not be omnipotent, and indeed it cannot be omnipotent if it is truly making for good, since the world in which we human beings find ourselves is a mixture of good and evil, and a Creator who was good, besides being omnipotent, would not have made the world like that. This point has been put forcefully by Lucretius.[11]

If we picture the ultimate spiritual reality anthropomorphically, and guess that it is good, we cannot see it in the likeness of Yahweh, the omnipotent and therefore omni-responsible creator of all things, evil as well as good; our God will be Marcion's 'stranger god', who has been moved by love to come to the aid of a world that its creator has mis-made, whether deliberately or because he is incapable of doing better. Moreover, there will be no guarantee that the compassionate divine visitor will succeed in redeeming this world, not of his making, in which he has implicated himself out of love and in obedience to the universal moral imperative to take sides with the good. The compassionate 'stranger god' is likely to have to pay for his intervention by being crucified; and, for him, crucifixion is unlikely to be followed by resurrection. Self-sacrificing love requires no reward other than itself. In being self-sacrificing, love is being self-rewarding.

We have a direct experience of self-sacrificing love in human beings, and also in some non-human living creatures on this planet. This love that is within our ken may be an indication of a love that is beyond our ken; but the love that we know is not uncontested; like right and good, love is a relative term, and love's logical correlative, hate, like right's and good's correlatives wrong and evil, is not an abstraction; it is a reality that frequently prevails in mundane life. If there is a supra-human spiritual reality, and if this ultimate reality is inspired by love, it seems likely that in the Universe, as in our human world, love is perpetually striving to overcome hate, but that, on this larger spiritual battlefield too, love's victory is not assured.

Love is a desire, and desires are emotions that animate living beings. If God is love, this god is not necessarily omnipotent, but he is necessarily alive, and, in being loving, he is human-like. Yet the ultimate spiritual reality need not be conceived of anthropomorphically. Buddhists conceive of it as being a state of 'extinguishedness' (*nirvana*), and what is extinguished here is desire of all kinds, love included. However, Buddhists have shrunk from purchasing spiritual peace at the price of renouncing love. The Buddha is deemed to have postponed his own exit into *nirvana* in order to follow the promptings of his love for his fellow sentient beings, and, according to the Mahayana, the Bodhisattvas have been moved by the same feeling to do as the Buddha did.[12]

Our answer to our final question has inevitably been inconclusive. We cannot be sure that the object of religion is a reality or that the objective of religion is attainable. Why is it, then, that Man has had religion ever since he awoke to consciousness? And why is religion the built-in feature of human nature that it seems to be – a feature that seems destined to continue to be Man's principal concern so long as the human race survives? Is it reasonable for Man to give first place on his permanent agenda to the pursuit of an objective that may be a will-o'-the-wisp? The answer is that ignorance and weakness seem to be permanent banes of human life. 'Man is born unto trouble, as the sparks fly upwards.'[13] In this plight, Man cannot find his way through life without religion, even though his belief in the presence of an ultimate spiritual reality, and his attempt to bring himself into harmony with it, are acts of unverifiable faith.

Moreover, since the rise of the higher religions, Man's never-ceasing spiritual quest has not been fruitless. It has borne out Aeschylus's dictum that 'suffering is the key to learning'. During the age of human history that the rise of the higher religions has inaugurated, recurrent mundane catastrophes have been the occasions for successive spiritual advances.

This inverse variation of Man's secular and religious fortunes is illustrated by the history of Judaism. The age that saw the destruction of the Kingdoms of Israel and Judah was the age of the Prophets. The deportation of the leaders of the Jewish community to Babylonia saw the creation, in exile, of a Judaism, associated with a new institution, the synagogue, which has superseded the earlier form of Jewish religion that was bound up with a ritual that could be performed only in the Temple at Jerusalem. The destruction of the Temple in AD 70 gave occasion for Johanan ben Zakkai to endow Judaism with a form that it still retains today.[14]

The same pattern of relations between the religious and the secular sides of human life is also illustrated by the histories of the three missionary higher religions. Christianity and Islam both sprang from a 'culture-compost' that had been produced by the intermingling of the débris of the disintegrated Syriac and Hellenic Civilizations. The Buddha attained his enlightenment, and imparted his spiritual discovery to his disciples, in an age in which his and their ancestral Indic Civilization was falling into a time of troubles.

The 'sorrowful round' of the recurrent vicissitudes of civilization has carried the higher religions forward in a spiritual movement that has been, not cyclical, but progressive. If we ask ourselves why the descending movement in the revolution of the wheel of civilization has carried the chariot of religion forward and upward, we shall find our answer in the truth that religion is a spiritual activity; for spiritual progress is governed by the law proclaimed by Aeschylus in the words already cited, and by the author of the Epistle to the Hebrews in the verse: 'Whom the Lord loveth he chasteneth, and scourgeth every son whom he receiveth.'[15]

PART VIII

HEROIC AGES

I believe that civilizations have always been brought to grief by their own faults and failures, and not by any external agency; but after a society has dealt itself the fatal blow and is on the point of dissolution, it is usually overrun and finally liquidated by barbarians from beyond its frontiers. The crystallization of a universal state's frontiers seems to be the crucial event, for this cuts the barbarians off from peaceful social contact and pens them up until the moment comes for their destructive descent. I describe how this barbarian pressure builds up, and I show that the barbarians possess an ever-increasing advantage over the embattled civilization, so that their ultimate victory is inevitable. On the desolated homelands of the former civilization, the barbarians enjoy a brief 'heroic age'; but, unlike the higher religions, these ages open no new chapter in the history of civilization. The barbarians are the brooms which sweep the historical stage clear of the débris of a dead civilization; this destructive feat is their historic task, and it has been glorified, to the point of becoming almost unrecognizable, in their myths and poetry.

plate 64

REFLEXION

The equilibrium between a growing civilization and the barbarian communities on its threshold is fragile. It can be shattered abruptly if the civilization breaks down, loses its tenuous appeal, and turns aggressive. Up to this point, the boundary between civilization and barbarism is fluid and permeable, and the barbarians are stimulated by the attraction of the alien society into imitating its culture and its arts; but a broken-down civilization, reconstituted in a universal state, surrounds itself with rigid political frontiers which also serve to inhibit the radiation of civilization into barbarism. The bust of a Gallic warrior illustrates this latent attraction: the sculptor has made a hesitant attempt to reproduce the style of a Roman funerary bust, housed in a niche; it is a crude but genuine effort to copy the standards of an already declining civilization.

plate 65 FRONTIER-BARRAGE   The fluid zone of contact between a growing civilization and adjacent barbarian communities freezes into an impenetrable military frontier as the civilization declines: neighbours become enemies, and cultural

interchange ceases. Hadrian's Wall survives as visible evidence of the Roman Empire's attempt to insulate itself from the barbarian tribes of northern Britain and to protect itself from invasion.

356

plate 66

DISTORTION

The barbarian societies that enjoy their brief 'heroic age' within
the territory of a dead civilization acknowledge an unwilling
fascination for the culture that they have destroyed: its alien
sophistication is both despised and admired. This uneasy coalition between a crude native tradition and a half-absorbed exotic
inspiration is strikingly apparent in barbarian jewellery, a branch
of the plastic arts in which these societies excel, perhaps because
of their penchant for ostentatious display. A Merovingian fibula,
of the sixth or seventh century A D, shows this compound to
perfection: in the centre is a rough cameo, falling far short in
workmanship of the Roman exemplars that evidently inspired it;
but the setting is bold and lustrous, the work of a craftsman
unwilling to make any concessions to classical symmetry or
subtle design.

42 The barbarian past

IN THE two preceding Parts of this Study we have been concerned with universal states established by members of the dominant minority, and with universal churches created by the internal proletariat. Our subject in the present Part is the character of the so-called 'heroic ages' that are episodes in the brief lives of barbarian war-bands. An heroic age is generated in the social and psychological climate produced by the crystallization of a *limes*, which we have already noticed as one of the characteristic manifestations of a civilization in disintegration.[1] If the cultural *limen* of a growing civilization is aptly described as the hospitable threshold of an ever-open door, the military *limes* of a disintegrating civilization can no less aptly be compared to a forbidding barrage astride a no longer open valley. A threshold is an unassuming piece of work; yet the magnificent barrage is as precarious as the humble threshold is secure; for it is a defiance of Nature which cannot be upheld by Man with impunity. The bursting of this military dam by an irresistible flood of barbarian invaders seems to have been the story of every *limes* of every universal state known to history; but is this social catastrophe actually an inevitable tragedy or an avoidable one? To find the answer to this question we must analyse the social and psychological effects of the military barrage-

builder's interference with the natural course of relations between a civilization and its external proletariat.

The first effect of erecting a barrage is, of course, to create a reservoir whose waters pile up against this artificial obstruction to normal drainage; and this effect is inexorable even if we can imagine it to have been unintended and unforeseen. In physiographical terms, the reservoir covers that part of the catchment area which lies immediately above the barrage; but above this there will remain a large unsubmerged hinterland. If we translate this simile back into the social reality, we shall notice a parallel differentiation between the peoples caught immediately above the *limes*-barrage, and those in the region at the back of beyond who are still left high and dry. On the continent of Europe, for instance, the Hyperboraean Slavs continued placidly to lead their primitive life under the shelter of the secluded Pripet marshes throughout the span of two millennia which first saw the Achaean barbarians convulsed by their proximity to the European land-frontier of the Aegean Civilization, and then saw the Teuton barbarians going through the same experience in their turn, some eighteen hundred years later, as a result of their proximity to the Roman Empire's land-frontier. The Achaeans and the Teutons were convulsed because they each happened to be

287 China's Great Wall, consolidated by the Ch'in dynasty in the third century BC, is tangible evidence of an embattled civilization's attempt to establish rigid lines of defence against outer barbarians.

288 Barbarian seen through Chinese eyes: statuette of the T'ang era. T'ang conquests built up a great Empire in the seventh century AD, but eventually it fell victim to successive barbarian invaders.

engulfed in a 'reservoir' created by the erection of a *limes*; the Slavs remained undisturbed because, on both occasions, their physically waterlogged habitat happened to be left culturally high and dry.

Why are the barbarians in the 'reservoir' area so disturbingly affected by the proximity of a military frontier which is at the same time a cultural barrier? And what is the source of the subsequent access of energy which has enabled them invariably to break through the *limes* sooner or later as a matter of historical fact, whether or not this breakthrough is inevitable in theory? The answers to these questions may emerge if we pursue our hydrographical simile further. We have to explain the build-up of water pressure against a dam when we know that the up-stream sources of supply are insufficient to account for the increasing volume of water. We can only assume in this case that the source of supply must lie down-stream, in the ocean into which the basin drains; and we know that, since water cannot flow uphill, it must have risen from the lower to the higher level by the only natural method available to it, namely by evaporating and condensing and falling eventually as rain. Thus the law of gravity can be defied, but the price that the water must pay for its ingeniously contrived passage is the loss of its original composition.

The old traces of sea salt are left behind in the process of evaporation, and a new trace of rock salt is acquired when the streams fed by the falling rain scour out ravines in their descent into the reservoir.

This physical phenomenon is an accurate and illuminating simile of the human phenomenon of the filling of the reservoir of barbarian energy, dammed by a military *limes*, with new dynamic impulses. The activated energy that accumulates in the reservoir and that eventually bursts the barrage is not mainly derived from the transfrontier barbarians' own primitive social heritage; the bulk of it is drawn from the vast stores of the civilization which the barrage has been built to protect. This is the huge source of supply that swells the head of water in the reservoir to a mass that ultimately proves too much for the barrage's powers of resistance; and it is one of the ironies of history that the water which then pours through the breach should have originally been supplied by the very region which the cataclysmic flood now devastates. If in normal circumstances the water flows down-stream in a controlled and fertilizing current, why does it suddenly return as a viciously destructive flood? The answer is to be found partly in the erection of the *limes*-barrage, which is a human act of interference with the ordinary course of

359

Nature, and partly in the transformation of human energy in the course of its passage from the cultivated world within the *limes* to the barbarian reservoir beyond it – a transformation that is Nature's device for surmounting an obstacle which Man has placed in her path.

Some such transformation is no doubt the price of every transfer of culture from one society to another;[2] but the degree and character of the transformation vary according to circumstances. The changes are least when the society that is the transmitting agent is a growing civilization and the receiving reagent is a static pre-civilizational society; and it is at its maximum when both parties are civilizations and both are in disintegration. The case with which we are concerned here must obviously lie somewhere between these two extremes: the transmitting agent is a civilization in disintegration, while the barbarians in 'the reservoir' beyond the *limes* are representatives of pre-civilizational Man, whose resistance to the cultural expansion or radiation of the adjoining civilization is prompted, not by a positive desire to defend an alternative civilization of their own, but only by the negative motive of hostility to an alien culture which in its breakdown has lost its original power of attraction.

This transformation of energy is brought about by a process of decomposition: the invading culture disintegrates into its component parts and is then reconstituted in a new pattern in which these constant components enter into new relations with one another, even if no elements have been either added or removed. A growing civilization may be defined as one in which the components of its culture are in harmony with each other and form an integral whole; on the same principle, a disintegrating civilization can be defined as one in which these same elements have fallen into discord. The diffraction of a culture is thus in itself a symptom of social sickness, and it results, not from the impact of a civilization on an alien society, but from a prior breakdown and disintegration of the civilization itself. The components into which an integral culture splits are an economic element, a political element, and a third which may be called the cultural element *par excellence*; and in the impact between an invading and a receiving culture, the penetrative power of each of the cultural elements, when absorbed in isolation, is exactly inverse to its social value. Thus the economic element is the most readily absorbed, followed by the political element, and lastly by the cultural element; and this is one reason why the diffraction of a culture is a social disaster. War and trade are the principal relations between a disintegrating civilization and its alienated external proletariat; and, of these, it is war that predominates.

It is true that the passage of a barbarian personnel through the *limes* into the civilization's domain, first as prisoners-of-war, then as hostages, next as mercenaries, and finally as conquerors, is reflected on the economic plane in

a counter-flow of money – whether as loot, military pay, or subsidies – out of the world within the *limes* into the barbarian 'reservoir' outside; and this money eventually flows back to its source in payment for goods purchased by its barbarian recipients from merchant representatives of the civilization. Contact of this kind may lead to the barbarians playing a considerable role in the domestic economy of the society on which they have been preying. A classic example is the apparent economic effect of the subsidies paid by the Constantinopolitan imperial government to Attila (*dominabatur* AD 434–53), the war-lord of a confederacy of Hun Nomad war-bands cantoned in the Hungarian Alföld. This remittance of money in specie from the imperial treasury to Attila's camp beyond the *limes* seems to have operated as a roundabout way of transferring purchasing power from the agrarian interests within the Empire, whose taxes provided the means of payment, to the manufacturing and commercial interests, which earned profits by making and marketing goods for purchase by the Huns with the money that these had exacted.[3] This commercial intercourse across a military *limes* is, however, apt to be discouraged and restricted by the imperial authorities. The manifest profitability of the transfrontier trade to the traders on both sides is a plain indication that, in the social situation created by the erection of a *limes*, the marchmen just inside the barrage may acquire a common interest with the barbarians just outside it in the exploitation of the marchmen's fellow-citizens inside the world which the *limes* is intended to protect. Since a common interest might assert itself in a concerted action between marchmen and barbarians which would be a deadly danger to the fenced-in civilization,

an imperial boundary . . . has in fact a double function: it serves not only to keep outsiders from getting in but to prevent the insiders from getting out. . . . It was necessary to restrict Chinese enterprise beyond the Great Wall . . . because Chinese who ventured too far beyond the Great Wall became a liability to the state; the business in which they engaged, whether farming or trade, contributed more to the barbarian community than it did to the Chinese community. They passed out of the Chinese orbit . . . [and] Chinese who left the Chinese orbit and accommodated themselves to an un-Chinese economic and social order inevitably began either to adhere to barbarian rulers or to practise barbarian forms of rule themselves – to the disadvantage of China.[4]

These considerations move an imperial government to restrict the flow of trade across the frontier; and such trade as there is tends to confine itself to the purchase by the barbarians of two classes of imperial products: luxuries for the war-lords and their lieutenants, and weapons both for them and for the rank-and-file of their followers. The trade across the *limes* is in fact sickly as well as precarious, while border warfare flourishes perennially because mutual hostility is the keynote of the confrontation between an alienated external proletariat and a disintegrating civilization.

Under these sinister auspices, such selective mimesis of the dominant minority by the external proletariat as does occur takes place on the barbarians' initiative because the barbarians are politically free.

The needs and motives of the cis-frontier society and state must make concessions to those of the trans-frontier peoples. The very act of drawing a boundary is an acknowledgment that the peoples excluded are not under control and cannot be ruled by command.[5]

The barbarians show their initiative by transmuting those cultural elements that they do accept from the cisfrontier civilization. The lines which this transmutation follows are determined partly by an hostility to the transmitting civilization which makes the barbarians unwilling to allow their borrowings from it to declare their distasteful alien origins; and this negative motive of aversion is reinforced by a positive incentive to turn a loan to practical account by adapting it to suit the different needs of local barbarian life in the reservoir.

Xenophobia and utilitarianism are thus the factors which determine adaptation, and they act in different degrees on different fields of activity, the results varying from the almost indistinguishable takeover to the virtually new act of creation. Yet even the apparently creative achievements of barbarian societies are flawed; for their source may be disguised but cannot be altogether eradicated; and all the cultural products of the transfrontier barbarians are scarred by that schism in the soul which the malady of social disintegration brings with it as its counterpart and concomitant. In the psychological revolution which creates an heroic age out of a primitive way of life, the traditional harmony of the undisturbed static society is disrupted into a tension between the two poles of a more sophisticated individualism and a likewise more sophisticated sense of unity.

The phenomenon which we have called the transfer of energy can now give us the clue for answering our question whether the catastrophic breaching of the *limes*-barrage is, or is not, an inevitable dénouement. In physical engineering a safety-valve against such a flood can be introduced by the construction of sluices which can be opened whenever the pressure of water in the reservoir threatens to exceed the capacity of the dam to resist it. This obviously useful device for safeguarding the dam against catastrophe by providing for a regulated release of the pent-up waters is not overlooked by the political engineers of a military *limes*, as we shall see. In this case, however, the attempted remedy merely precipitates the cataclysm that it is designed to forestall, for the social and psychological materials of which a *limes* is constructed are so frail and friable that, if once this sandstone masonry is breached, the outpouring waters of barbarian energy quickly sweep the whole structure away. In the maintenance of a social barrage, the relief of pressure by a regulated discharge of water is in fact impracticable; and, since the transfer of energy from the civilization below the barrage to the barbarian communities above continues inexorably to add to the pressure on the barrage, the time must come sooner or later when breaking-point will have been reached; and at that juncture a catastrophe will inevitably occur.

The alternative to the hopeless expedient of constructing safety-valves is for the civilization on the defensive to strengthen the structure of the barrage itself, in order to postpone the day of doom. But this cruder counter-measure can at best put off the evil day without being equal to averting it. Time works on the side of the barbarian attackers of a disintegrating civilization, for, as we shall

CULTURAL TRANSMUTATION

292, 293, 294 Barbarian art betrays its makers' unwilling admiration for the civilization they profess to despise: alien cultures are plundered for objects and ideas to be adapted to native use. Opposite, Roman cameos set incongruously in a Frankish cross, and a German fibula of the sixth and seventh centuries. Above, a ninth-century Visigothic relief translates a Roman consular diptych into wholly native terms.

363

also see, each arithmetical increase in the degree of pressure of transformed energy on the *limes* increases the cost of proportionately reinforcing the barrage by a geometric progression.

Thus the erection of a *limes* sets in motion a play of social forces which is bound to end disastrously for the builders; and, for them, the only way of avoiding ultimate disaster would be to preclude this fatal course of events by insulating completely from one another the two incompatible societies whose respective domains the *limes* artificially demarcates. A policy of non-intercourse is, indeed, the counsel of perfection for an imperial government, but in practice the arbitrarily drawn military barrier can never be made permanently or perfectly impermeable, because neither the transfrontier barbarians nor the cisfrontier marchmen can ever be effectively controlled by the imperial Power.

The very fact that the 'barbarians' of the excluded territory are always described as aggressive raiders, attackers, and invaders shows that geographical limits that appear 'natural' and inevitable to one society are not necessarily regarded as geographical obstacles by other societies, which may in fact treat them as merely political obstacles.[6]

And, conversely,

while the general policy of the [universal] state seeks to establish the limit at which its interests can remain centripetal, and to prevent excessive expansion from passing over into centrifugal dispersion, this policy is resisted and evaded by the particular interests of traders, would-be colonizers, ambitious political and military careerists, and so forth, who see opportunities for themselves across the border. Thus there grows up a nexus of border interests which resents and works against the central interest.[7]

A striking illustration of this tendency among the marchmen of a universal state to make common cause with the barbarians beyond the pale is afforded by the history of the relations between the Roman Empire and the Hun Eurasian Nomads who broke out of the heart of the Eurasian steppe towards the end of the third quarter of the fourth century of the Christian Era and established themselves in the Hungarian Alföld. Though the Huns were unusually ferocious barbarians from the back of beyond, and though their ascendancy along the European *limes* of the Roman Empire was ephemeral, a record of three notable cases of fraternization has survived. Attila's secretary of state was a Pannonian subject of the Roman Empire named Orestes, whose son Romulus Augustulus was to make his name by the facile achievement of being the last Roman Emperor in the West. The Greek historian and Roman diplomatist Priscus records meeting in Attila's camp in AD 448 a renegade Greek businessman from Viminacium, who, after having been taken captive by the Huns, had won his way into favour with them.[8] The third member of the trio is 'Eustace, a merchant of Apamea', who, 'about the year AD 484, long after Attila was dead, is found accompanying a band of Hun marauders in the role of their chief adviser on a plundering expedition against Persia'.[9]

The Hun power in Europe came and went far too quickly for this fraternization between the aggressive barbarians and the renegade children of the civilization that was their victim to produce any lasting effect; but it is significant that it should even have gone to the lengths it did, considering that at their first encounter the parties were poles apart in their respective ways of life. Where the barbarian power was built on more durable foundations, this unholy alliance sometimes begot noteworthy political offspring: for instance, the residuary continental European successor-state of the Roman Empire in the West was born of a partnership between Frankish *laeti* (resident aliens) and Gallic bishops and landlords who were the local representatives of the Roman senatorial order. The Manchu Empire, likewise, was born of a similar partnership between Manchu transfrontier barbarians and Chinese marchmen.

Thus the existence of a *limes* in practice always generates social intercourse between the parties whom the barrier is designed to insulate from one another. However, the most common form of contact is not trade but war – a relation which we can justifiably subsume under the heading of contact, for, although it is psychologically estranging, it is at the same time technologically educative. A universal state cannot hold the transfrontier barbarians in check along the line of the *limes* without fighting them; and it cannot fight them without involuntarily training them in its own superior techniques of warfare. The art of war penetrates more rapidly and deeply than any other branch of technique; in the outflow of exports, weapons usually arrive earlier and make their way further afield than non-lethal tools; and the imported weapons of an adjoining civilization are copied by barbarian artificers with a skill that is proportionate to the eagerness of the demand in the local barbarian market. The Eurasian Nomad barbarians 'could not arm themselves at all for purposes of large-scale offensive operations without the assistance of imported weapons. . . . Even the Mongols of the twelfth century – a military nation if ever there was one – had to import their weapons, chiefly from China and Khurasan.'[10]

The effectiveness of these borrowed instruments and techniques can, moreover, be enhanced by the readiness of the barbarians to adapt them to the local terrain. *Ex hypothesi* they already have the advantage of being at home in a theatre of military operations in which their opponents are strangers, since the *limes* is situated in barbarian territory which the civilization has occupied, up to this line, by force of arms in an aggressive previous chapter of its history. When the barbarians combine their hereditary mastery of the local situation with a creative adaptation of borrowed weapons and tactics to suit local conditions of warfare, then they become formidable indeed.

For example, the Cossack barbarians who began as river-pirates to harass the steppe-empire of the Golden Horde added a second and more devastating string to their bow when they also mastered the Tatar art of horsemanship. The Scandinavian barbarians on the fringes of a world which was experiencing the last death-throes of the Roman Empire before the establishment of the new Western Christian Society learnt first the arts of shipbuilding and seamanship from Frisian marchmen, and then the Frankish art of cavalry-fighting. The earlier use of the onager, or wild ass, in warfare, not as a cavalryman's mount but as a charioteer's draught-animal, was borrowed from the

295, 296 Partnership with Chinese marchmen helped the originally barbarian Manchus to complete their conquest of China in 1644; two centuries later the Manchu emperors used barbarian allies against Nomadic tribesmen to extend their Central Asian frontiers. These engravings, from two series commissioned by the Emperor Ch'ien Lung, celebrate battles in the campaigns of 1755 to 1795.

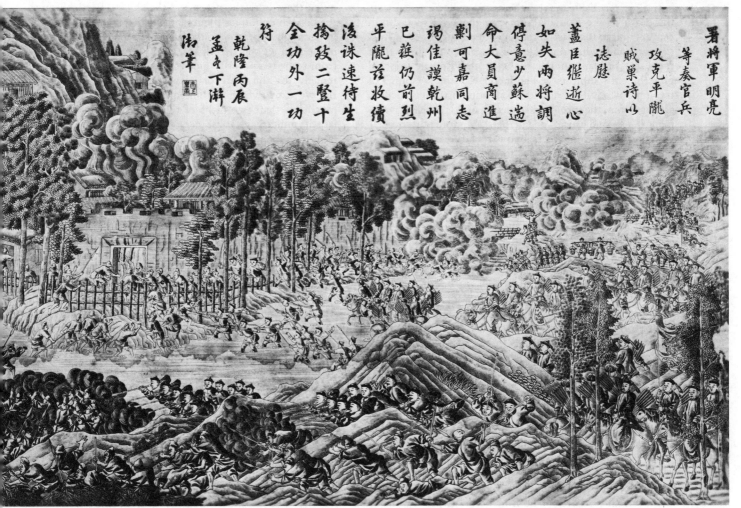

Sumero-Akkadian Society by Aryan Nomad barbarians who eventually used their new-fangled technique against their teachers with deadly effect. In recent times, the experience of the intrusion of the Western Civilization into all the other four continents of the world has shown very clearly that the first lesson learned by technologically primitive societies from their would-be civilizers has been, not just how to employ firearms against them, but also how to exploit this weapon in the local terrain by the use of snipers and sharpshooters and guerrilla tactics.

A further factor that operates against the disintegrating civilization in its encounter with aggressive barbarian communities is the increasingly disruptive effect of prolonged warfare on an economically complex society. Whereas the primitive barbarian communities are occupationally and organizationally devoted primarily to the prosecution of warfare, their civilized opponents' energies are diffused among a number of competing activities; and the need to provide for long-drawn-out hostilities imposes immense strains upon the sophisticated society. Any increase in the numerical strength of a regular standing army entails a corresponding increase in the pressure of taxation upon national income and is liable to set in train a progressive disruption of economic life. The diversion of an intolerably large and still insatiably growing proportion of a dwindling national income to meet the rising costs of public services is the most conspicuous of the social maladies that were the death of the Roman Empire in the West in the fifth century and in the East in the seventh century of the Christian Era; and, while one cause of this cancerous growth of the fiscal burden on the backs of the Roman imperial government's subjects was an increase in the personnel of the imperial civil service to fill an administrative vacuum arising from the progressive decay of local self-government,[11] a second cause – and perhaps the more portentous – was the increase in the manpower of the imperial army which was required in order to meet the increase in the transfrontier barbarians' military efficiency. Septimius Severus (*imperabat* AD 193–211) added three new legions to the thirty that had been maintained since AD 83 for the defence of the static frontiers which Augustus had first marked out; Diocletian (*imperabat* AD 284–305) increased the imperial army's strength in a far higher ratio.

If the chronic warfare between the defenders and assailants of a *limes* is waged in terms of competitive staying power, the defence is bound to collapse sooner or later, since, so far as it is able to hold its own, it can achieve this only by exerting an effort which becomes more and more disproportionate to the effort exacted from its increasingly efficient barbarian adversaries. In this situation there are two obvious courses to which the defence may resort in the hope of arresting this progressive deterioration of its own position. It can mobilize for the defence of the *limes* either its own capacity for organization and technique, in which a civilization is superior to its barbarian neighbours almost *ex hypothesi*, or its barbarian adversaries' capacity for taking advantage of the local terrain through which the *limes* runs. These two policies of elaborating its own organization and armaments and of recruiting barbarian manpower are not of course mutually exclusive, and a harassed Power behind a *limes* usually resorts to both in its desperate search for

some means of reversing the accelerating advance of its barbarian opponents towards victory. In the last struggle of the Hellenic Civilization, which had never been very technical-minded and which had long since lost any faint proclivities in this direction that it might have displayed earlier, it was not technique but organization that was called into play by Diocletian in his attempt to solve the life-and-death problem of the Roman Empire's defence.

Diocletian's solution was to reorganize completely the Roman imperial system of defence, which had been left unchanged in principle during the three centuries that had elapsed since its original institution by Augustus. Augustus's first concern had been to give the Hellenic World the maximum opportunity of recuperating from the exhaustion produced by a hundred years of social revolution and civil war, and one of his measures for attaining this end had been to reduce the numerical strength of the forces that had been mobilized for this fratricidal warfare. For the security of the Empire, the Augustan régime relied, in lieu of the sheer weight of numbers, on the superiority of its professional army over the transfrontier barbarians in military quality and on the deterrent value of the awe inspired by the spectacle of Roman power. By Diocletian's day this hazardously economical security system had long since gone bankrupt. The military efficiency which the barbarians had been acquiring in the school of the *limes* had eventually given them both the nerve and the skill to break through the cordon confining them; and in such an emergency the imperial government's only means of repairing one breach in the frontier was to risk another by the transfer of troops from some temporarily quiet sector. Diocletian's principal remedy for this state of affairs was the institution of a reserve army, which amounted in numbers to perhaps not much less than two-fifths of the total strength of the enlarged military establishment; it was designed to be as mobile as the raiding barbarian war-bands which it was its task to overtake, bring to battle, and destroy.

From the scientific standpoint of a professional soldier, this Diocletianic system of substituting defence in depth for linear defence by organizing a mobile reserve in support of the front line represents a notable advance in the art of war; and it was no doubt partly owing to this military reform that the Empire – which had seemed already to be in the throes of dissolution during the half-century immediately preceding Diocletian's accession – actually held out for a hundred years longer in the West and for three hundred years longer in the East and Centre. Yet the price at which this achievement was bought was immense, and it was paid by the civilian population. Diocletian's professionally admirable military reorganization dealt the civilian population a double blow. On the one hand, the increase in the military establishment had to be paid for by an oppressive system of taxation that depended partly upon an unforeseeable system of price-fixing and that caused alarming social disruption; a contemporary observer remarked that 'the number of men who were supported by the taxes was larger than the number ... who paid them'.[12] On the other hand, the concentration of the élite of the army in the mobile reserve lowered still further the morale, as well as the efficiency, of the cordon-troops stationed on the frontier. The last pretence of the army's being able to hold the barbarians at the *limes* was now virtually abandoned, and it came to be taken for granted that the war-zone was no longer the *glacis* on the barbarians' side of the *limes*, and no longer even the marches of the Empire immediately behind the *limes*, but the territories in the interior that were the Empire's economic and cultural vitals. The scientifically impeccable watchword of 'defence in depth' was in fact a euphemism which disguised the humiliating and disastrous fact that the civilian taxpayer, after having been fleeced once by the imperial treasury to pay for the vast increase in the imperial military establishment, was now exposed to the additional affliction of being fleeced for a second time by barbarian raiders who, after all, could not be prevented from ravaging the Empire's heart-lands.

In addition to the exigencies of sustained warfare having a diverse effect upon the society and economy of a civilization and a barbarian community, the same difference in the degree and type of organization in these respective communities produces a parallel difference in the effects of the warfare itself. To put it in its simplest terms, the dislocation wrought by the descent of a barbarian war-band upon a settled society is far greater than the damage done by the retaliatory raids of an imperial army upon the barbarian communities themselves. It is hard for an imperial army to deal a final blow to its barbarian enemies, for it is hard for it to find an adequate target. This is especially and obviously true in the case of Nomadic communities, which can simply gather themselves up and move on, in the face of an advancing enemy army; but it is to some extent true also of sedentary barbarian societies, since even here the resources of life, though they may be easily destroyed in one raid, are not difficult to restore and reconstruct. In warfare between antagonists that are not on an equality in their level of civilization, the more highly civilized belligerent is apt to win victories that are pyrrhic because they leave the victor exhausted, while his less highly civilized opponent is apt to suffer defeats that are inconclusive because of the recuperative power that is the natural compensation for the handicap of backwardness in organization. The success of guerrilla tactics in some modern theatres of war provides continuing evidence of the practical advantageousness of this theoretical inferiority; for, although the present-day guerrillas are by no means barbarians, they have deliberately and skilfully chosen to adopt and exploit these proven methods of warfare against technologically superior adversaries.

Furthermore, the deterioration of the relations between a civilization and its barbarian neighbours leads the latter to neglect their former peaceful occupations in order to specialize in the art of border warfare. If the barbarian is at first obliged to learn the art of self-defence in order to save himself from subjugation or annihilation at the hands of a civilization that has turned savage, later on – when his growth in military efficiency on his own terrain has gradually reversed the balance of military advantage in his own favour – he is encouraged to practise warfare as an alternative means of making his livelihood. To plough and reap vicariously with sword and spear is more lucrative for the barbarian when once a civilization which has now been thrown on the defensive can be mulcted of its wealth by way of either loot or subsidies; and this is also more con-

genial to him now that the barbarian has become a warrior first and foremost and has remained only secondarily a husbandman. The barbarian adjoining a *limes* thus ceases to be economically self-supporting, and becomes an economic parasite on the civilization on the other side of the military front.

A classical illustration of this characteristic economic regression of the estranged barbarian proselyte of a disintegrating civilization is given by Tacitus's description of the German inhabitants of the barbarian 'reservoir' adjoining the continental European *limes* of the Roman Empire. By Tacitus's time this *limes* had been in existence for about 150 years and had therefore had time to produce its typical social effects. Tacitus affirms that cattle is the Germans' sole form of wealth;[13] but the relative unimportance of agriculture in the German economy of that day, which is implied in this and other passages of the Roman observer's work, cannot have been due to ignorance or even to inexperience; for it is clear from the evidence of modern archaeological research that at one time agriculture was highly developed among the Germanic tribes, and thus its later unimportance points not to an infantile economic backwardness but to a recent economic relapse from a higher state. However, it was only among the immediately transfrontier communities that this agricultural retrogression occurred: beyond the 'reservoir' the Ests (Aestii), as Tacitus observes, 'cultivate cereals and the other fruits of the earth with an assiduity that stands out in contrast to the typical German sloth'.[14] Moreover, the demoralizing effects of proximity to the military *limes* made themselves felt in the political institutions as well as in the agricultural practice of the barbarian communities. Whereas the south-western Germans in the 'reservoir' lapsed into a primitive and unstable form of war-lord-leadership, the communities to the north and east remained loyal to the traditional system of patriarchal kingship.

The militarization of the barbarians in the 'reservoir' is the trump-card in their hand. Thanks to their economic relapse, they have little material wealth to lose; and, having so little to lose by war with the neighbouring civilization, they have little to fear from the continuance of hostilities, or indeed from their intensification. This striking inequality in the material consequences of border warfare for the two belligerents is reflected in a great and growing inequality between them in morale. For the children of a disintegrating civilization that is standing on the defensive the interminable border warfare spells the burden of an ever-increasing financial charge and the anxiety of a never-solved military and political problem. For the barbarian belligerent, on the other hand, the same warfare has the very opposite associations. For him it is not a burden but an opportunity, not an anxiety but an exhilaration. A contest that is always harassing for the civilized party – and utterly devastating for him when he sees that all the resources that he has mobilized are of no avail – is the very breath of life for the militarized barbarian. This great and always increasing inequality in psychological armament makes the discomfiture of the civilized belligerent practically inevitable sooner or later.

In this situation it is not surprising that the party who is both the author and victim of the *limes* should attempt a

297 Pacification of southern Chinese barbarians by a Sung army in the twelfth century A D. Although southern tribes were absorbed into the Sung Empire by a policy of appeasement, the more relentless barbarian pressure in the north could not be checked.

desperate last expedient in order to avert his threatening fate. Since his own resources have proved inefficacious, the temptation to use his barbarian adversary's own disastrously demonstrated prowess becomes irresistible. 'The policy for the Middle Kingdom is to employ the barbarians to knock the barbarians on the head,' wrote a Sinic philosopher in the second century B C;[15] and this policy of setting a thief to catch a thief might seem to have cogent considerations in its favour. The barbarian warrior is the citizen-soldier's superior in the art of border warfare because the barbarian is fighting here on his own familiar ground; and he has also come to be the citizen-soldier's superior in personal prowess because he has acquired a zest for the profession of arms which his adversary has lost. This better military material can be purchased at a very much lower cost to the citizen-taxpayer; and this cheap conversion of an enemy warrior into a friendly mercenary will doubly relieve the pressure on the *limes* by reducing *pari passu* both the power of the 'reservoir' barbarian to take the offensive

and his incentive for going on the warpath. His power will be reduced because his forces will now be divided; and at the same time the temptation to plunder his civilized neighbours will be appreciably diminished, both because the mercenaries' pay will mitigate the need for other sources of income, and because those barbarians who are still tempted to engage in border warfare will now face adversaries who are their equal in military skill.

These considerations have frequently led the rulers of universal states to enlist transfrontier barbarians in their standing armies or to plant them as settlers on the imperial side of the *limes*. The Roman policy is the most notorious example, but the same practice was adopted by the Han Empire and by the 'Osmanlis; yet this expedient for averting a collapse of the *limes* actually precipitates the catastrophe which it is designed to forestall. Part of the explanation of this apparent paradox is to be found in the fact that, in taking the barbarians into its service, the Power behind the *limes* is also taking them into its confidence and is thereby subjecting them to an intensive course of instruction in military and political know-how; and this they can afterwards employ, if they choose, to their own profit at their teachers' expense. Rome faced this problem as early as AD 6, in the revolt of the Pannonian auxiliaries, and from then on her history was punctuated by similar revolts and by campaigns against enemy armies led by commanders, such as Arminius and Tacfarinas, who had gained their experience as one-time members of the Roman army. Besides initiating the barbarians into the Roman art of war, the policy defeated itself – if we are to believe a hostile critic of the Emperor Theodosius I's administration – by appraising the barbarian auxiliaries of the Empire's weakness.

In the Roman forces, discipline was now at an end, and all distinction between Roman and barbarian had broken down. The troops of both categories were all completely intermingled with one another in the ranks; for even the register of the soldiers borne on the strength of the military units was now no longer being kept up to date. The [barbarian] deserters [from the transfrontier war-bands to the Roman imperial army] thus found themselves free, after having been enrolled in Roman formations, to go home again and send off substitutes to take their place until, at their own good time, they might choose to resume their personal service under the Romans. This extreme disorganization that was thus now prevalent in the Roman military formations was no secret to the barbarians, since – with the door thrown wide open, as it had been, for intercourse – the deserters were able to give them full intelligence. The barbarians' conclusion was that the Roman body politic was being so grossly mismanaged as positively to invite attack. [16]

When such well-instructed mercenaries change sides *en masse*, it is no wonder that they are often able to give the *coup de grâce* to a tottering Power behind the *limes*, which has enlisted their services as a last resort. But we still have to explain why they should be moved, as they so often are, to turn against their employers. When once they have been taken into an empire's service, does not their personal interest coincide with their professional duty? They receive regular pay from the imperial treasury that is more secure and more lucrative than the plunder that they used to snatch in occasional raids; and, if they have been settled on land behind the *limes*, does not this too give them a stake in the survival of the empire with whose fortunes their own are now bound up? If their terms of service are so favourable, why should mercenaries turn traitor and virtually invite the transfrontier barbarians to divide with them the benefits that remain their own monopoly so long as they keep the *limes* inviolate?

The answer to these questions is that, in turning against the empire which he has been hired to defend, the barbarian mercenary is indeed acting against his own immediate material interests, but in doing this he is in fact reacting to an impulse that is far stronger than a merely economic consideration. The governing factor in the situation is that the barbarian beyond the pale has long since become estranged from the broken-down neighbouring civilization. This moral breach between two parties cannot be mended by a business deal, however profitable; and, in attempting this expedient, the imperial Power is trying to turn the clock back to a previous age in which a growing civilization and an outer ring of pre-civilizational communities co-existed on a basis of mutual interest, and is refusing to acknowledge the entire sequence of events that has led to the breakdown of the civilization in question and the alienation of its barbarian neighbours. After the breakdown of the civilization and the erection of the *limes*, the enlisted barbarians readily become disloyal because their business contract is not underwritten by any desire on their part to share in the civilization which they have undertaken to defend in return for a material *quid pro quo*. The direction of the current of mimesis has indeed, as we have seen,[17] long since been reversed; the civilization retains little prestige in the barbarians' eyes, while the barbarians themselves are in receipt of the grudging admiration of a forlorn dominant minority. This reversal of the direction of the current of mimesis is fatal for the policy of enlisting barbarism in civilization's defence. In these psychological circumstances a corps of barbarian *foederati* will never turn into a unit of the imperial regular army; it will remain an unassimilated barbarian war-band retaining its own weapons and tactics, taking its orders from its own warlord, feeling its own *esprit de corps*, nursing its own ambitions. In the same circumstances a settlement of barbarian *laeti* will never turn into a civil community of imperial citizens; it will remain an unassimilated *imperium in imperio* which, short of being annihilated, will find its political destiny sooner or later in becoming the nucleus of a dissident successor-state. In short, the policy of hiring barbarians to keep their kinsmen out is foredoomed to failure; and, as this expedient is the last forlorn hope of the tottering Power behind the *limes*, its failure is immediately followed by the *limes*' collapse.

When a barrage bursts, the whole body of water that has been accumulating in the reservoir above the dam runs violently into the sea, and this sudden release of a long-pent-up and ever-mounting force produces a threefold catastrophe. In the first place, the flood destroys the works of Man in the cultivated land below the broken barrage. In the second place, the potentially life-giving water that has made this devastating passage pours uselessly into the sea without ever having served Man for the purposes of irrigation or navigation or the generation of power. In the third place, the emptying of the reservoir leaves its old margins high and dry, deprives of water the vegetation that had once flourished beside this artificial lake, and lets the mountainside relapse into its pristine barrenness.

This natural catastrophe is an apt simile for the human catastrophe that follows on the collapse of a military barrage or *limes*. The resulting social cataclysm is a calamity for all concerned, though the resulting devastation is unequal in its incidence; but the distribution of the damage is the reverse of what might have been expected *a priori*. There is, in fact, a paradoxical reversal of roles.[18] The cost to a disintegrating civilization of saving its tottering *limes* from collapse is, as we have seen, out of all proportion to the degree of the temporary relief that it can give from barbarian pressure. On the other hand, once the doomed civilization is engulfed by the barbarian invasion, the principal sufferers are no longer the ex-subjects of the universal state, but the ostensibly triumphant barbarians themselves. Their long-awaited hour of triumph proves, in

the end, to be the occasion of a discomfiture that neither they nor their defeated adversaries had foreseen.

The explanation of this paradoxical outcome of events is that the triumph of the barbarians releases within them demonically self-destructive forces which have previously been kept in check by the pressure of the *limes* and of the civilization behind it. We have seen that the proximity of a *limes* induces a malaise among the transfrontier barbarian communities because their previously rudimentary economy and institutions are shaken by exposure to the political and cultural influences generated by a broken-down civilization. We have also seen the extent to which the barbarians can adapt to these intrusive influences and even be stimulated by them to acts of creation. This capacity for adaptation and even creation is a symptom that the psychological disturbance to which the barbarians are exposed can be kept within bounds within which it can produce a partially constructive and not wholly demoralizing effect, despite the breakdown of the mechanism of mimesis. This saving curb is provided by the very existence of the *limes*, which, while it stands, acts as a substitute for the indispensable discipline of which a pre-civilizational community is deprived when its traditional cake of custom is broken by the destructive radiation from a disintegrating civilization. This discipline is imposed upon the barbarian community by the demands of perennial border warfare, partly because this trains the barbarian in a stern but instructive military school, and partly too because it imposes upon him an internalized discipline in the sense of giving him tasks to perform and objectives to reach. The *limes* thus acts as a framework in which the barbarian community can continue to exist after the breakdown of the neighbouring civilization.

However, with the sudden collapse of the *limes*, the framework and the safeguard are swept away, and the transfrontier barbarian is suddenly called upon to face a whole new range of problems and to perform new tasks that are altogether too great and too difficult for his immature creative powers; and in this hour of bewilderment the nascent creativity of the barbarian is stifled by impulses of *abandon* and ferocity which lie deep within his native cultural heritage. As soon as the barbarian has left no-man's-land behind him and set foot in a ruined world which is for him an earthly paradise, his malaise rankles into demoralization. This demonic revolution in the barbarian's soul is illustrated by the spiritual catastrophe which overtook the Scandinavians when they overran the Carolingian Empire. When, in the Viking Age, they tore up their life from its traditional roots and launched it into unknown adventure, the price of an excessive liberation was a fatal loss of balance.

When the king's hall was transplanted into a foreign country and his luck plucked out of the fields and grazing grounds surrounding his manor, life necessarily became a round of battles and drinking feasts. [19]

In this exotic environment, the barbarian is apt to surrender himself to the vices of parasitism and sloth that, as we have seen, were already latent in his life along the *limes*. In that previous age, the operation of these demoralizing influences on barbarian souls was mitigated by the necessity of earning the chance to luxuriate in idleness by bouts of mercenary service or by intermittent raids for plunder, so that the sybaritic life was punctuated by periods of intense military activity. But the barbarian master of a successor-state is emancipated from this cycle, and can lapse into utter vegetation – until either he is displaced by a stronger fellow-barbarian, as the Visigoths were by the Franks, or he has quite run through the wasting assets of the *ci-devant* civilization on which he is preying, as the Kassites and the Merovingians did.

The origin of this morally repellent behaviour is to be found in the sudden liberation from the restraint imposed by the *limes*, for which the victim-beneficiary is quite unprepared. Moreover, even though a barbarian military monarchy may once have proved equal to the task of acting as a buffer-state under the auspices of a universal state, the fates of the barbarian successor-states in the interior of an extinct civilization's former domain show that they are quite unequal to the task of bearing burdens and solving problems that are thrown upon them because they have proved too much for the statesmanship of an ecumenical Power that has been heir to the cumulative political experience of an entire civilization. How indeed would a challenge that has defeated the efforts of even a broken-down civilization be expected to receive a victorious response from barbarian interlopers? A barbarian successor-state blindly goes into business on the strength of the dishonoured credits of a universal state that has already gone into bankruptcy; and these boors in office hasten the advent of their doom by a self-betrayal through the outbreak, under stress of a moral ordeal, of something fatally false within.[20] A polity based solely on gang loyalty to a military leader, while it may be adequate for the organization of a raid, or possibly for the administration and defence of a march state, is hopelessly unfit for the government of an ex-civilized community.

The barbarian trespassers *in partibus civilium* have, in fact, condemned themselves to suffer a moral breakdown as an inevitable consequence of their own adventurous act. Yet they do not yield to this self-decreed doom without a spiritual struggle that has left its traces in their literary records of myth and ritual and standards of conduct.

The barbarians' ubiquitous master-myth describes the hero's victorious fight with a monster for the acquisition of a treasure which the unearthly enemy is withholding from Mankind in order to devour it or to hoard it for his own bestial satisfaction. This is the common motif of the tales of Beowulf's fight with Grendel and Grendel's mother; Siegfried's fight with the dragon; Perseus's feat of slaying and decapitating a gorgon, and his subsequent feat of winning Andromeda for his bride by slaying the sea-monster who was about to devour her. The motif reappears in Jason's outmanœuvring of the serpent-guardian of the Golden Fleece and in Herakles' kidnapping of Cerberus. This myth looks like a projection, on to the outer world, of a psychological struggle in the barbarian's own soul for the rescue of Man's rational will or his power of self-determination from the abyss of non-volitional unconscious forces; and this struggle is brought into the open by the shattering experience of the barbarian's passage from the relative security of life beyond the *limes* to the world of uncharted experience behind the breached barrier.

HERO AND MONSTER: WILL AND SELF-WILL

Barbarian mythologies share the striking theme of a fight between hero and monster for a priceless treasure, perhaps symbolic of a psychological struggle within the untamed barbarian soul – the conflict between destructive lust and moral urge that is exposed when the negative values of war-making give way to the positive demands of consolidating a conquest.

298, 299   Opposite, Gilgamesh in battle, and Perseus slaying Medusa.

300, 301   The Gilgamesh motif – man flanked by beasts – found a permanent place in barbarian art, as in the Swedish and Burgundian bronzes, below.

302, 303 Barbarians' enjoyment
of their conquests is short-
lived: they feed passively off
their rich gains, incapable of
building a new society, an
easy prey to demoralization or
conquest. The Vandal landowner, left, followed much the
same life in sixth-century
North Africa as his Roman
predecessor, but never
created a secure society. Right,
the second wave of Europe's
barbarian conquerors: seventh-
century Merovingian horseman.

In the emergence of special standards of conduct
applicable to the peculiar circumstances of an heroic age we
can see an attempt to construct a substitute moral framework. Conspicuous examples are the Homeric warriors'
aidos and *nemesis* (shame and indignation), and the
Umayyad statesmen's *hilm* (a courtly self-restraint). 'Aidôs
is what you feel about an act of your own: Nemesis is
what you feel for the act of another.'[21] In the post-Aegean
heroic age, as depicted in the Homeric Epic, the actions
that evoke feelings of *aidos* and *nemesis* are those implying
cowardice, lying, and perjury, lack of reverence, and
cruelty or treachery towards the helpless.[22] In contast to
these, which enter into all aspects of social life, *hilm* applies
to the political sphere alone. Its virtues were much praised
in Arabic life, but were rarely found.

Hilm is neither patience nor moderation nor clemency nor long-
suffering nor self-possession nor maturity of character. It merely
borrows from each of these qualities certain external traits, to an
extent just sufficient to take in an observer who is not on the
alert. The product of these superficial loans is a virtue that is
specifically Arab.[23]

Hilm is thus something more sophisticated than *aidos* and
nemesis, but also something less attractive. It is emphatically
not an expression of humility; 'its aim is rather to humiliate

an adversary; to confound him by presenting the contrast
of one's own superiority; to surprise him by displaying the
dignity and calm of one's own attitude.'[24] Its practice is not
incompatible with inward feelings of resentment and
vindictiveness, and it presupposes not only the possession
of wealth and power but the possibility of abusing these in
order to injure one's neighbour without having to fear the
consequences of one's action.[25]

These standards of conduct were thus exactly consistent
with the peculiar political, social, and psychological circumstances of the heroic age; their disappearance from social
behaviour was taken by contemporaries as a sign of social
decline and a cause for lamentation. Yet if, as we have
already intimated, an heroic age is no more than a passing
phase, then these virtues do not provide a self-sufficient
moral code, but are only a substitute doing duty for the
values of civilization while these are in eclipse; and the
disappearance of the victorious barbarians' ethical make-
shifts is in fact not a tragedy but a welcome retreat before
the advance of a re-emerging civilization, which makes
them superfluous by bringing back into currency other
more socially constructive virtues.

It is indeed the crucial weakness of the barbarian code of
behaviour that it is a personal and not a social or institutional code. Loyalty to a leader, while it may be based in a

series of individual moral imperatives, is not a long-term substitute for a civilized social system; and it is the utter incapacity of the barbarians for creating stable and enduring political institutions that is their undoing, and that accounts for the extraordinary exhibitions of murderous brutality that have become the characteristic hallmark of heroic ages. A sensationally sudden fall from an apparent omnipotence to an unmistakable impotence is the usual fate of a barbarian Power. Striking historical examples of this play of the motif of *peripeteia* are the eclipse of the Western Huns after the death of Attila, the eclipse of the Vandals after the death of Genseric, the eclipse of the Ostrogoths after the death of Theodoric, and the eclipse of the Serbs after the death of Stephen Dushan. The political potency of the barbarians – displayed in a momentary overlordship over vast tracts of a devastated civilization's domain – hangs on the thread of the single life of some war-lord of genius; and, as soon as this thread snaps, his henchmen relapse into anarchy. The barbarian successor-state of a moribund universal state may be laid low by a last counter-blow from its expiring victim; or it may meet the same violent death at the hands of its fellow-barbarians; or it may languish in exhaustion and impotence, till it is swept off the stage of history to make way either for the re-entry of an old civilization or for the entry of a new one.

In Egyptiac history, the Hyksos barbarians were expelled from the Nile delta by a fresh breed of Theban empire-builders who brought the Egyptiac universal state back to life again. Justinian annihilated the Vandals and the Ostrogoths and restored the Roman Empire from a Levantine base; and the Mongol invaders of China were evicted by the Ming dynasty. The alternative dénouement in which the barbarians reduce their numbers by exterminating one another in fratricidal warfare is exemplified in the progressive elimination of the number of the competing Macedonian barbarian successor-states of the Achaemenian Empire; and, again, in the successive evictions of successive war-bands in the territory of the defunct Roman Empire in the West. This auspicious proclivity of the barbarians for liquidating one another is likewise illustrated in the histories of the break-up of the Arab Caliphate and the break-up of the Khazar Empire in the great western bay of the Eurasian steppe. The third possibility, of lingering on to be snuffed out eventually by the harbingers of a resurgent civilization, was experienced by the Merovingian and Lombard interlopers in Roman Gaul and Italy, who were cleared away by the Carolingians; by the Chaghatay Mongol overlords of Transoxania, who were cleared away by Timur Lenk; and by the Umayyads, who were cleared away by the 'Abbasids.

WHAT ARE WE to make of this unhappy record of viciousness and violence? The mildest judgment will convict it of having been a futile escapade, while sterner judges will denounce it as a criminal outrage. The verdict of futility was once pronounced by a conquered barbarian war-lord whose previous station and subsequent personal experiences entitled him to speak on this point with unchallengeable authority. In AD 534 Gelimir, the ex-King of an ephemeral Vandal barbarian successor-state of the Roman Empire in North-West Africa, could not forget, while he was being paraded through Constantinople in a Roman triumphal procession to celebrate his own overthrow, that his predecessor Genseric had conquered Carthage less than a hundred years back and had sacked Rome herself in AD 455.

The prisoners led in triumph were Gelimir himself, with a purple robe of some sort draped round his shoulders, and the whole of his family, together with the very tallest and physically handsomest of the Vandal rank-and-file. When Gelimir had arrived at the Hippodrome and beheld the Emperor enthroned on a lofty tribune, with the people standing on either side of him, and when, as he took in the scene, he realized the extremity of his own plight, he did not relieve his feelings by weeping or groaning aloud, but repeated over and over again a phrase from the Hebrew scriptures: 'Vanity of vanities; all is vanity.' When he reached the Emperor's tribune they stripped him of his purple and forced him to fall on his face and grovel in adoration of Justinian's imperial majesty.[1]

By contrast, criminality, and not mere futility, is the burden of Hesiod's indictment against a post-Mycenaean heroic age that, in his day, was still haunting the nascent Hellenic Civilization; and, if he had been asked to give his black picture a caption, he could have quoted from the *Odyssey* the goddess Athena's comment on Zeus's tale of Aegisthus: 'All too [fearfully] befitting is the doom that has laid that monster low; thus perish any other wretch who dares such deeds as those.'[2] Hesiod's own judgment on the barbarians is indeed a merciless one:

And Father Zeus made yet a third race of mortal men – a race of Bronze, in no wise like unto the Silver, fashioned from ash-stems, mighty and terrible. Their delight was in the grievous deeds of Ares and in the trespasses of Pride. No bread ever passed their lips, but their hearts in their breasts were strong as adamant, and none might approach them. Great was their strength and unconquerable were the arms which grew from their shoulders upon their stalwart frames. Of bronze were their panoplies, of bronze their houses, and with bronze they tilled the land (dark iron was not yet). These were brought low by their own hands and went their way to the mouldering house of chilly Hades, nameless. For all their mighty valour, death took them in his dark grip, and they left the bright light of the Sun.[3]

In posterity's judgment on the overflowing measure of suffering which the barbarians bring upon themselves by their own criminal follies, this passage in Hesiod's poem might have stood as the last word, had not the poet himself run on as follows:

Now when this race also had been covered by earth, yet a fourth race was made, again, upon the face of the All-Mother, by Zeus son of Cronos – a better race and more righteous, the divine race of men heroic, who are called demigods, a race that was aforetime upon the boundless Earth. These were destroyed by evil war and dread battle – some below Seven-Gate Thebes in the land of Cadmus, as they fought for the flocks of Oedipus, while others were carried for destruction to Troy in ships over the great gulf of the sea, for the sake of Helen of the lovely hair. There verily they met their end and vanished in the embrace of death; yet a few there were that were granted a life and a dwelling-place, apart from Mankind, by Zeus son of Cronos, who made them to abide at the ends of the Earth. So there they abide, with hearts free from care, in the Isles of the Blessèd beside the deep eddies of Ocean Stream – happy heroes, for whom a harvest honey-sweet, thrice ripening every year, is yielded by fruitful fields. [4]

What is the relation of this passage to the one that immediately precedes it, and indeed to the whole catalogue of races in which it is embedded? This episode breaks the sequence of the catalogue in two respects. In the first place the race reviewed here, unlike the preceding races of Gold, Silver, and Bronze, and the succeeding race of Iron, is not identified with any metal; and, in the second place, all the other four races are made to follow one another in a declining order of merit which is symbolized in the descending gradation of the metals from Gold to Iron through Silver and Bronze. Moreover, the destinies of the three preceding races after death are consonant with the tenour of their lives on Earth. The race of Gold 'became good spirits by the will of Zeus – spirits *above* the ground, guardians of mortal men, givers of wealth.'[5] The inferior race of Silver still 'gained among mortals the name of blessèd ones *beneath* the ground – second in glory; and yet, even so, they too are attended with honour.'[6] When we come, however, to the race of Bronze, we find, as we have seen, that their fate after death is passed over in a grimly ominous silence. In a catalogue woven on this pattern, we should expect to find the next race condemned, after death, to suffer, at the lightest, the torments of the damned in the House of Hades; yet, so far from that, we find at least a chosen few of them transported after death, not to Hell, but to Elysium – where they live, above ground, the very life that had been lived by the race of Gold before death.

Clearly, the insertion of a race of Heroes between the race of Bronze and the race of Iron is an afterthought. Both in form and in substance the passages describing the races of these two baser metals ought to stand in immediate juxtaposition to one another. If we do bring them together by allowing the episode of the heroes to drop out, the poem then runs smooth, with no perceptible hiatus at the point

THE AMBIGUOUS IMAGE   304, 305   The civilized victims of barbarian hordes are torn between admiration and contempt for their adversaries: the Roman relief, opposite, shows a Dacian tribesman as a noble hero; but the Chinese emperor, above, receives gifts from a grovelling tributary.

306 The barbarian hero – simple but vigorous images of warriors from a Mycenaean vase of the thirteenth century BC.

where we have excised the incongruous parenthesis. The parenthetic heroes break the poem's sequence, symmetry, and sense; and this discord must have been as painfully obvious to the poet as it is to us. What moved him to make this clumsy insertion at this cost to his work of art? The answer must be that the picture of a race of Heroes was so vividly impressed on the imagination of the poet and his public that some place had to be found for it in any catalogue of the successive ages in their vista of past history; and the irony of the poet's predicament is that this massacre of a work of art for the sake of paying tribute to an historical reminiscence turns out really to have been unnecessary. It was unnecessary because the race of Heroes was already included in the original catalogue under the sign of the third metal of the four. In other words, the race of Heroes is identical with the race of Bronze; and the insertion describing the heroes is thus not an indispensable supplement but a superfluous repetition.

This discovery is surprising, because the impression first made on our minds by the two passages is not one of identity but of contrast. In fact, the difference, as well as the likeness, is real; but the likeness is a likeness of statements about alleged matters of fact, whereas the difference is a difference of aesthetic and emotional atmosphere. The race of Bronze and the race of Heroes are the same people seen through different mental glasses: a lens of faint yet authentic historical reminiscence, and a lens of vivid but hallucinatory poetic imagination.

Hesiod, then, presents the damning truth side by side with an ideal picture; and this dual vision is an authentic reflexion of an ambiguity in the barbarians' own epic poetry. The barbarian poet's concern is not for his heroes' and heroines' moral reputations, but for his poetry's aesthetic merit; and to this end he is ready to fill in his picture, quite unselfconsciously, with light and shade as art demands. His unselfconsciousness is one of the secrets of the epic poet's dazzling artistic success; and this triumph of a barbarian art is the solitary creative achievement amid the welter of catastrophic failures which a barbarian war-band brings upon itself when it crosses the fallen *limes*. In politics, in religion, and in all the other fields in which the barbarians showed rudimentary signs of creativity as long as they were pent up behind the *limes*-barrage, these rudiments are blighted by the demoralization that overtakes the barbarians when they spill out into their Promised Land. In the moral slum of a barbarian successor-state the barbarian's embryonic gift for poetry is the only one of his potentialities that comes to flower; and this bud blossoms so wonderfully that it lends the waste-land the illusory appearance of a paradise. The barbarian poet's magically successful art casts over the barbarian war-lord's commonplace exploits 'in real life' a glamour that captivates and deludes posterity.

A comparison between an historical event and the account of it which appears in barbarian epic poetry will show that, even where the alleged historical event in the epic story turns out to be authentic, there is likely to be no correspondence whatever between the importance that is ascribed to this event in the 'heroic' tradition, and its actual importance as we can estimate it from our knowledge of historical records. For example the Burgundian war-lord Guthhere or Gunther, whose figure looms so large in the

376

Barbarian jewellery is the visual equivalent of their epic poetry – carelessly lavish, crude by comparison with the achievements of the civilizations, but remarkably creative and powerfully attractive.

307 Frankish brooch, *c.* 570.
308 Burgundian fibula, sixth century.
309 Visigothic buckle, seventh century.
310 Anglo-Saxon buckle, seventh century.

311 Visigothic brooch, seventh century.
312 Swedish bracteate, seventh to ninth century.

Nibelungenlied, proves to have played in fact a very minor part in the barbarian infiltration into Gaul in the fifth century of the Christian Era; and, as for the still more famous literary figure of Siegfried, he has been identified with a number of different historical figures, and never at all certainly. It is not the military or political effectiveness, but the literary 'availability' of the barbarian war-lord that makes his literary fortune; and the literary history of a hero of 'heroic' poetry begins to diverge from his authentic history from the moment when his character and actions become the theme for an epic. In fact, the finer the work of art that is the ultimate product of poetic genius, the further the characters and the plot of the epic are likely to have travelled away from the historical persons and events by which they were originally inspired. The *chef d'œuvre* of creative perversion of the historical truth has perhaps been achieved in the 'heroic' poetry of the Serbian external proletariat of Orthodox Christendom, in which an historical hero, Vuk Brankovic, has been transfigured into a 'fictitious' traitor, and an historical traitor, Marko Kraljevic, into a 'fictitious' hero. Besides taking these enormous liberties with the historical persons and events which it does choose to mention, 'heroic' poetry is apt to pass over in silence the persons and events which are actually of the most outstanding historical importance in the age with which the poems are concerned.

It is . . . a curious fact that Clovis and his great achievements seem to be entirely unnoticed in poetry. It appears . . . that though most of the principal Teutonic nations are represented in our stories the relative prominence assigned to them does not at all correspond to what we should expect. Most remarkable is the fact that in stories relating to the Continent nearly all the chief characters (Eormenric, Theodric, Guthhere, Attila, etc.) belong to nations which had passed out of existence before the end of the sixth century. [7]

For the historian it is a paradox that 'the Frankish nation, which ultimately became dominant, is but poorly represented'[8] in the Teutonic Epic; but this is by no means the greatest of the paradoxes with which the Teutonic Epic confronts him. The greatest of all is the fact, at first sight astonishing, that the Teutonic Epic almost entirely ignores the existence of the Roman Empire and *a fortiori* the history of the Hellenic Civilization of which the Roman Empire was the universal state. How is this silence to be explained, when the age with which these Teutonic 'heroic' poems are concerned is precisely the post-Hellenic interregnum which was occupied by the *Völkerwanderung* of the North European and other transfrontier barbarians into the territories of the Roman Empire? Indeed, it is the exhilaration generated by the very experience of the *Völkerwanderung* and the conquest of a derelict Empire that inspires the barbarian poet to perform his feats of romantic imagination. What, then, has moved the authors of the Teutonic Epic to leave unsung the Roman *causa causans* of their own barbarian art and barbarian world?

For the sophisticated historian it is hard to believe that the barbarian poets are not guilty of a conspiracy of silence to which they have been prompted by some inexplicable prejudice or else by sheer caprice. But it is the historian himself who has conjured up this insoluble problem by making the flagrantly unhistorical mistake of ascribing his own interests and outlook to authors who are poets and not historians and whose social milieu is a barbarian war-band and not a civilization. There is, in fact, no warrant for assuming that the authors of 'heroic' poetry are interested in historical truth at all, or in leaving for posterity an accurate account of their age. The silence of the Teutonic Epic in regard to Clovis and to Rome is neither capricious nor deliberate, for what the 'heroic' poet wants is a suitable theme for his art, and, from his point of view, both Rome and Clovis would be 'bad' subjects. It does not occur to him to differentiate between fact and fiction, for the criterion of truth is irrelevant to his art. He simply has an eye for a promising subject and a gift for presenting his theme in a telling way; and in innocently following these lights he has stumbled upon a method which Aristotle has ascribed to him – correctly enough, as regards what the 'heroic' poet actually does, but with a fantastic perversion of the truth in so far as posterity assumes that the barbarian is constructing a deliberate and purposive narrative.

Homer is the great master of the art of telling falsehoods right. . . . From him one learns to prefer what is impossible but plausible to what is possible but incredible. [9]

For the barbarian artist and his audience Beowulf's adventures in Grendel's lair are more credible than the life which a Theodoric begins to lead when, as the guerdon for his victory in the *Rabenschlacht*, he exchanges the Gothic camp for the Roman palace in order to rule the Roman people in Italy as the viceroy of the Emperor at Constantinople. The poet does not seek to follow his lost leader through the folds of the palace-curtains; and as an artist he is right – however culpable his lack of curiosity might have been in the historian that this poet has never set out to be.

Thanks to the barbarian poet's wizardry in approaching his subject on these terms, the squalid realities of the barbarian warrior's slum exhale a phantasy of heroism that long outlives its ephemeral source in the sump of authentic history. This pearl of barbarism is appreciated and appropriated by a posterity that has little use for anything else in the barbarian's otherwise uninviting legacy. The barbarian bard, in the posthumous literary life that is thus conferred on him by the canonization of his works, slily avenges his discreditable comrades the barbarian war-lord and warrior by investing them with an unmerited reputation through an artistic conjuring trick. The fascination exercised by 'heroic' poetry over its latter-day admirers deludes them into mistaking an heroic age which is the changeling child of a poet's imagination for the very different historical reality by which the poet's creative activity has been called into play. The poet's magic touch conjures a 'light that never was, on sea or land'[10] out of the baleful glare of a conflagration kindled by the barbarian incendiaries of a devastated world; and this theatrical lighting makes a slum look like Valhalla. It is a masquerade, but a brilliant one.

PART IX

CONTACTS BETWEEN
CIVILIZATIONS IN SPACE

If it is admitted that single civilizations are not always intelligible fields of study, it seems logical now to look more closely at encounters between civilizations. I want to find out what happens when two civilizations that are contemporaries are brought into close cultural contact, usually at a time when one of them is in the process of disintegration. This type of encounter seems particularly important, because most of the higher religions have arisen in places where several civilizations have intermingled. I first have to establish the facts about encounters, and, with these facts at my command, I examine the effects, which are disturbing and often alarming. I find that 'aggressive' civilizations tend to stigmatize their victims as inferior, in culture, religion, or race; the assaulted party reacts either by trying to force itself into line with the alien culture, or by adopting an exaggeratedly defensive posture. Both reactions seem to me ill-advised. Encounters evoke terrible animosities and create enormous problems of coexistence, but I think that the only positive solution is for both parties consciously to attempt a mutual adjustment. This is how the higher religions have answered the problem, and in our present-day world it is imperative that different cultures should not face each other in hostile competition, but should seek to share their experience as they already share a common humanity.

plate 67

NEW WORLDS

Contacts between separate societies have been a feature of history ever since the birth of the first civilizations five thousand years ago, but the achievement of the late fifteenth-century Western Society in mastering the technique of ocean navigation is a landmark of unique significance in this long-drawn-out process of cultural encounter. The immediate effect of this momentous Western discovery was to bring the Old World into contact with the New, but in the longer term it also made the entire surface of the globe accessible to mariners from the West. Between the date at which ocean-going vessels were first built and the date at which they were superseded by the invention of steam power and other mechanical means of transport, scarcely a corner of the globe escaped the disturbing impact of the expanding Western Society. By the mid-sixteenth century Portuguese pioneers had reached China and Japan, exposing these societies to a 'Western Question' that is still convulsing them today. Here a typical Portuguese *nao de trato*, or trading ship, arrives in Nagasaki, awaited by Western and Japanese merchants on the quayside: detail from a Japanese Nanban ('southern Barbarian', i.e. European) screen of the early seventeenth century.

РАСКОЛЬНИКЪ ГОВОРИТЪ
СЛУШАЙ ЦЫРЮЛЬНИКЪ
Я БОРОДЫ СТРИЧЬ НЕ
ХОЧУ ВОТЬ ГЛЕДИ Я НА
ТЕБЯ СКОРО КАРАУЛЪ ЗАКРИЧ

ЦЫРЮЛНІИКЪ ХО
ДЕТЪ РАСКОЛЬНІКУ
БОРОДУ СТРИЧЬ.

plates 68, 69

RUSSIA'S ENCOUNTER
WITH THE WEST

Early attempts at Westernization were obstructed by Russia's intransigent religious conservatism.
The 'Old Believer', above, is being forcibly shorn in Peter the Great's campaign to Westernize Russian
life and manners. The subconscious tenacity of traditional images is impressive: a Communist poster,
opposite, relies on a frankly biblical figure in its appeal for mass literacy.

ГРАМОТА–
ПУТЬ К
КОММУНИЗМУ

plate 70

JAPAN LOOKS AT THE WEST

In the late sixteenth century a flourishing school of Japanese screen painting was devoted to depicting the arrival of the 'Southern Barbarians' – Western Europeans – and their style of life in Japan. A detail from one such screen shows part of the ceremonial procession of newly-arrived Portuguese merchants in the port of Nagasaki, emphasizing the exotically unfamiliar dress of the foreigners, their height, and their black servants.

plate 71

THE WEST WATCHES
A WESTERNIZED JAPAN

After two centuries of self-imposed isolation, nineteenth-century Japan turned to meet the recurring
Western challenge by a programme of rapid modernization; the success of the new policy was proved
by her wholly unexpected victory over China in the war of 1894–95. The Western journalists here
scrambling after news on the war front were not only reporting a battle: they were witnessing the
arrival on the hitherto Western-dominated world stage of a new Asian Great Power displaying a
Western-style military might.

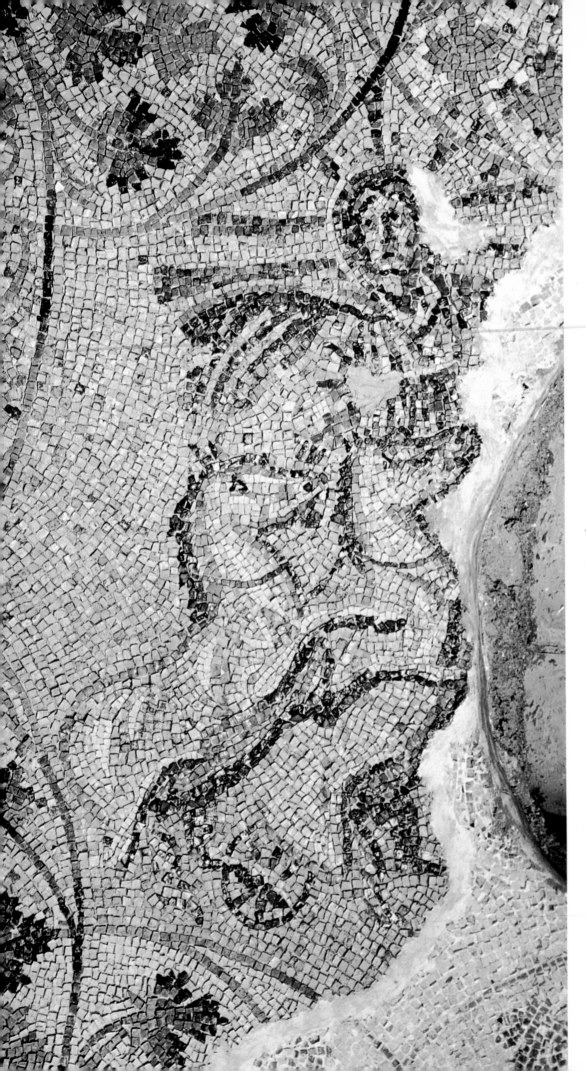

plates 72, 73

CULTURAL ENCOUNTERS:
THE RELIGIOUS SOLUTION

Encounters between contemporary
societies may result not in conflict
but synthesis. With belief in its
own ancestral religions withering
away, the Hellenic Civilization was
hungry for any creed to satisfy its
spiritual want. In the fourth century BC Ptolemy I Soter of Egypt
constructed an artificial religion
out of Hellenic and Egyptiac
elements in order to unite the
motley inhabitants of his Empire.
Its divinities included a Hellenized
version of the Egyptiac Isis,
opposite, and her son Harpocrates
(i.e. Horus).

Among the host of religions
competing for the allegiance of the
Hellenic World at this time,
Christianity triumphed by its ability
to absorb and transform features
from the rest. The depiction of
Christ as the Sun-god Helios, left,
is an unmistakable concession to
Hellenic mythology: by the end of
the third century AD Helios had
become the principal god in the
Roman pantheon, offering Christian
artists a clear image for the supreme
divinity.

plates 74, 75

REJECTION AND ASSIMILATION

In its first expansionist era, the Western Society was still a militantly Christian society and it insisted on trying to impose its own religion on the rest of the world. In this guise the West aroused the suspicion and hostility of the societies it encountered; those that could defend themselves reacted by closing their doors. In Japan, resistance to the Western Christian culture culminated in the rigorous persecution of foreign missionaries and native converts: in the great martyrdom of 1622, opposite, fifty-one Christians, native and alien, were executed at Nagasaki in an attempt to rid the country of their subversive presence.

But Western economic and technological superiority could not be ignored or shut out in the same way: since the late seventeenth century, the world's only choice has been between voluntary and forcible Westernization. The contemporary Nigerian shop-sign, right, is a signal of the West's successful cultural aggression, which has transformed the patriarchal chief of a tribal society into the ubiquitous managerial boss of Western commerce.

FLORA AND FAUNA
OF A NEW WORLD

A civilization that succeeds in dominating a weaker society is liable to dismiss its victims as innately inferior, reducing them to the level of flora and fauna and exploiting or exterminating them as its own interests dictate. In the Flemish painting, left, the conquest of the Americas is represented as an encounter between a pack of naked savages and an advance guard of the civilized, clearing the country for subsequent colonization. The drawing of an American Indian woman and child, below, takes its place in a series of carefully recorded observations of exotic animals and plants that were made by the sixteenth-century English 'discoverers' of the New World.

plate 78

THE CHINESE RESPONSE

China, like Russia, has reacted to the impact of the West by adopting the heretical Western ideology of Marxism as the basis for an equally Western programme of industrialization. Chinese propaganda projects a thoughly Westernized image of Communist industrialism; Mao here plays the familiar part of the Zealotist modernizer, exhorting factory workers to strenuous exertion in the effort to construct a powerful and self-reliant state. Western eyes have had little chance as yet to peer beyond the propaganda, but ignorance of what may lie behind it should not lead to the easy assumption that the whole story is contained in this superficial appearance. China has chosen an imported Western technique to clear away the débris of her stable but suffocating tradition of bureaucratic élitist rule; but Western industrialism, while it can cure some social evils, has created new ones which its originators did not foresee and have no answer for. Yet Western observers should not discount the possibility that China may exercise conscious discrimination in tempering the stability of her own conservative traditional culture with the West's more flexible but more volatile dynamism; the result of such a deliberately controlled attempt at a felicitous synthesis might be a wholly new cultural departure for civilized Man.

44 Encounters between contemporary civilizations

IN THE three preceding Parts of this book we have been following up our general inquiry into the nature and process of the disintegrations of civilizations by making particular studies of each of the three factions into which the body social of a disintegrating civilization splits up. In doing this, we have implicitly found the answer to the question which we asked at the outset of this inquiry, namely, whether civilizations are intelligible fields of study. The conclusion to which our investigations have led us is that a civilization can be studied intelligibly in isolation so long as we are considering its genesis, its growth, or its breakdown.[1] Indeed, the historical evidence that we reviewed in our study of breakdowns seemed to warrant the conclusion that the breakdown of a civilization is usually due to some inward failure of self-determination and is only seldom due to blows delivered by external agencies.[2] After passing, however, to our study of disintegrations, we have found ourselves unable to understand this last phase of a broken-down civilization's history without extending our mental range of vision, beyond the bounds of the disintegrating civilization itself, to take account of the impact of external forces. We have seen that we have to bring into the picture the external proletariat of barbarians from beyond the *limes*, who *ex hypothesi* are not members of the disintegrating civilization, but who have usually given it its *coup de grâce*. Besides, we cannot overlook the alien origin of those elements in an internal proletariat that have been incorporated through conquests at the expense of an alien civilization, and cannot ignore the importance of the part that has been played by creative inspirations from this alien source in the geneses of some of the higher religions that the internal proletariat has brought to birth. We have also seen that universal states have made their mark by unintentionally and unconsciously working, not for themselves, but for alien beneficiaries. Finally, we have seen that the higher religions have proved to be new societies of a different species from the civilizations under the aegis of whose universal states they have made their appearance; and, in so far as universal states have not made their mark by performing services for universal churches, they have made it by performing them for barbarians or for alien civilizations.

These alien civilizations, like the barbarians beyond the pale, have been certified as being alien by the simple and obvious geographical fact that their places of origin have lain outside the frontiers of the universal states on whose domain they have eventually trespassed; and some of the higher religions that have arisen within those frontiers have been no less alien, for their adherents have regarded themselves, and have been regarded by their pagan neighbours, as being 'in but not of' the disintegrating society within which the religion first appeared. This aloofness has indeed been a psychological expression of the historical fact that the source of the religion's creative inspiration has been alien to the tradition of the society within which it has actually presented itself to Mankind. The Roman Empire

provided an Hellenic-made cradle for a mainly Syriac-inspired Christianity, while the Kushan barbarian successor-state of the Bactrian Greek Empire provided a likewise Hellenic-made cradle for a mainly Indic-inspired Mahayana. Although it is true, on the other hand, that Islam and Hinduism each drew its main inspiration from a civilization that provided it with its political cradle as well, it is also true that in the geneses of these two higher religions likewise there had been a previous chapter in which more than one civilization has been concerned. Islam and its political cradle the Caliphate were Syriac reactions on the religious and political plane to the long sustained intrusion of Hellenism on the Syriac World; and a later and shorter intrusion of Hellenism on the Indic World similarly evoked both an Indic-inspired Hinduism and its Indic-made cradle the Guptan Empire. It thus appears that the genesis of four of the higher religions that are still alive in the present-day world becomes intelligible only when we expand our field of study from the ambit of a single civilization to embrace encounters between two civilizations or more.

The importance of the part played in the geneses of higher religions by encounters between different civilizations is indicated by a commonplace of historical geography that is familiar but none the less remarkable. When we mark down the birthplaces of the higher religions on a map, we find them clustering in and around two relatively small patches of the total land-surface of the Old World – in the Oxus-Jaxartes basin, and in Syria (in the broadest sense of this term, covering an area bounded by the North Arabian steppe, the Mediterranean, and the southern escarpments of the Anatolian and Armenian plateaux). The Oxus-Jaxartes basin was the birthplace of the Mahayana in the form in which this religion spread from there over Eastern Asia, and, before that, it had been the birthplace of Zoroastrianism. In Syria, Christianity acquired at Antioch the form in which it spread from there over the Hellenic World as a new religion, after having made its first appearance, as a variety of Pharisaic Judaism, in Galilee. Judaism itself and the sister religion of the Samaritans arose in southern Syria. The Monothelete Christianity of the Maronites and the Hakim-worshipping Shi'ism of the Druses both ensconced themselves in central Syria.

If we extend our horizon to take in the regions adjacent to these two core-areas, this geographical concentration of the birthplaces of the higher religions becomes still more conspicuous. Both the Nestorian and the Monophysite variety of Christianity took shape in and around Urfa-Edessa, in Mesopotamia, while the Hijaz south of Syria saw the birth of Islam at Mecca and Medina. The Shi'i heretical form of Islam was born on the eastern shore of the North Arabian steppe. When we similarly extend the radius of our observation of the Oxus-Jaxartes basin, we locate the birthplace of the Mahayana, in its first appearance as a variation on the philosophy of primitive Buddhism, in the adjacent basin of the Indus; the birthplace of this primitive Buddhism in the Middle Ganges basin, and the birthplace

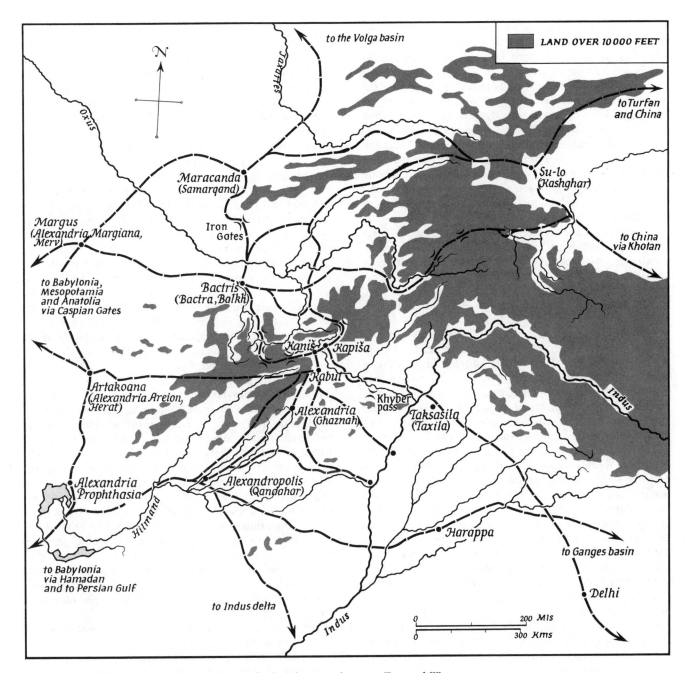

313 The Central Asian 'Roundabout', focus of cultural contact between East and West.

of a post-Buddhaic Hinduism in the same quarter of the Indian sub-continent.

There is in fact a geographical explanation for these remarkable facts. Both Syria and the Oxus-Jaxartes basin are physically constructed to serve as 'roundabouts' where traffic coming in from any point of the compass can be switched to any other point in a great number of alternative combinations and permutations. The physical features actually encourage the convergence of traffic on the cross-roads in these areas, and a glance at the historical past of these two potential traffic-centres shows how they did in fact play the role for which Nature had fitted them.

The Oxus-Jaxartes basin has been the scene of successive encounters between the Iranian, Eurasian Nomad, Syriac, Indic, Hellenic, Sinic, and Russian Civilizations since at least as early as the eighth century BC. The Eurasian Nomad *Völkerwanderung* of the eighth and seventh centuries BC swept over the Oxus-Jaxartes basin on its way to India and to South-West Asia. The region was then incorporated in the Achaemenian Empire and in its Seleucid Asian successor-state. The Seleucid Empire's Bactrian Greek and Kushan successors united the Oxus-Jaxartes basin politically with North-West India. The Arab Empire reunited it with South-West Asia and Egypt. The Mongol Empire incorporated it in a universal state that momentarily united almost the whole of the Eurasian continent except for its Indian, Arabian, and West European peninsulas. Timur Lenk failed in the fourteenth century, but the Russians succeeded in the nineteenth century, in incorporating all the shores of the Eurasian steppe in one of the Mongol Empire's originally subject non-Nomad successor-states. If Timur's empire-building work had proved durable, the Oxus-Jaxartes basin, not the Volga basin, would have been the nucleus of an empire that might have coincided with the present domain of the Soviet Union. Actually, Russia has partitioned the Oxus-Jaxartes basin with Afghanistan – a state between Oxus and Indus which is a replica of the Bactrian Greek and Kushan states that anticipated Afghanistan in straddling the Hindu Kush. These political vicissitudes give the measure of the Oxus-Jaxartes basin's cultural role as a meeting-ground for a number of different civilizations.

Syria's record has been even more extraordinary. To begin with, in and immediately around the Fertile Crescent, civilizations have jostled one another at exceptionally close quarters. Syria is wedged in between the homelands of the two earliest civilizations, the Sumero-Akkadian in 'Iraq and the Egyptiac in the Lower Nile valley. Asia Minor, the homeland of the Sumero-Akkadian Civilization's Hittite satellite, overhangs Syria on the north. Syria is also open to incursions by Nomads from Arabia and by seafarers from the Mediterranean. The Syrians' success in creating a distinctive civilization of their own, which has made a deep mark on Mankind's subsequent history, is a remarkable achievement. The measure of Syria's cultural achievement is given by her political vicissitudes, which surpass even those of the Oxus-Jaxartes basin. In the third millennium BC, empires that arose in the Sumero-Akkadian and in the Egyptiac World occupied northern and southern Syria respectively, from time to time, without colliding. In the second half of the second millennium BC, the Egyptians first occupied the whole of Syria as far north-eastward as the westward elbow of the river Euphrates, and were then forced to partition Syria with the Hittites; but, though the Egyptians made more political impression on Syria than the Akkadians, the cultural impression made by the Akkadian Civilization in the second millennium BC was greater.

During this millennium, a distinctive Syrian civilization was struggling to be born. It was given its opportunity at last by a *Völkerwanderung* that broke upon the Levant from Arabia, Europe, and North-West Africa simultaneously. Egypt and Assyria and Babylonia were all put out of action temporarily, and, in this space/time vacuum, a Syriac Civilization sprang up. It had a rich cultural heritage, drawn from Akkadian, Egyptiac, Aegean, and Hittite sources; and it was as creative culturally, and as disunited politically, as its Hellenic contemporary. Participants in the Syriac Civilization invented the alphabet; they made sea-voyages that outdistanced any that are known to have been made by the Sumerians and Egyptians; and, in the field of religion, they arrived at monotheism, which was both a spiritual and an intellectual feat.[3]

The Syriac Civilization's spell of political independence was brief, and all Syriac communities except the Samaritans and the Jews lost their sense of corporate identity after the destruction of the Achaemenian Empire by the Hellenes; but the 'culture-compost' deposited by the intermingling of the débris of the disintegrated Syriac and Hellenic Civilizations proved to be supremely fertile. This was the soil in which the Orthodox Christian, Western, and Islamic Civilizations germinated, while Syria again paid the political price of being the busiest 'roundabout' on the map of the Old World. From the eighth century BC onwards, Syria was incorporated in, or partitioned between, a series of Empires – the Assyrian Empire and its Neo-Babylonian successor-state; the Achaemenian Empire and its Ptolemaic and Seleucid successor-states; the Roman Empire and the Arab Empire; the Fatimid Caliphate and the East Roman Empire; the Crusader principalities and their Islamic neighbours; the Ottoman Empire and its Arab and Israeli successor-states. Only two out of all these Empires – the Seleucid and the Umayyad – have been governed from a capital on Syrian ground; and there have been only three occasions on which Syria has reverted, on the political plane, to being a cluster of mutually independent local states. This happened in the intervals between the decline of the Seleucids and the onset of the Romans, between the decline of the Fatimids and the rise of the Ayyubids, and after the dissolution of the Ottoman Empire in the First World War. Yet, through all these political vicissitudes, Syria has been playing a leading role in Mankind's affairs since the third millennium BC, and perhaps since the end of the latest bout of the Ice Age.

On the strength of this testimony from the histories of Syria and the Oxus-Jaxartes basin, we may venture the conclusion that, for a study of higher religions, the minimum intelligible field must be larger than the domain of any single civilization, since it must be a field on which two or more civilizations have encountered one another. The encounters in question here must be encounters in the space-dimension between civilizations which, *ex hypothesi*, must be contemporaries. There is of course another form of encounter, a so-called 'renaissance', which takes place in the time-dimension. We might also take note of the possibility of a compound type of encounter which involves both time and space; an example is the renaissance of the Hellenic Civilization in the Western World, whose geographical domain had been marginal in the Hellenic Civilization's domain, and had partly lain right outside it. But we shall leave renaissances to a later Part of this Study,[4] and confine ourselves here to a consideration of encounters in the space-dimension.

Before embarking on a detailed study of some particular examples of encounters between contemporary civilizations, let us take a look at the field as a whole. It is obvious that this field presents a formidably intricate maze of history. The number of civilizations that we originally located on our cultural map was thirty-seven on a maximum count.[5] We can divide these geographically into two groups – one originating in the Old World and one in the New World – which until relatively recently were isolated from each other; and we can further divide our Old-World civilizations chronologically into generations – the maximum number of generations to date being three. This geographical and chronological segregation of civilizations clearly limits the possible number of geographical encounters between contemporaries, but nevertheless the total is still higher than the total number of civilizations. Contemporary civilizations may have had more than one encounter with each other in the course of their histories,

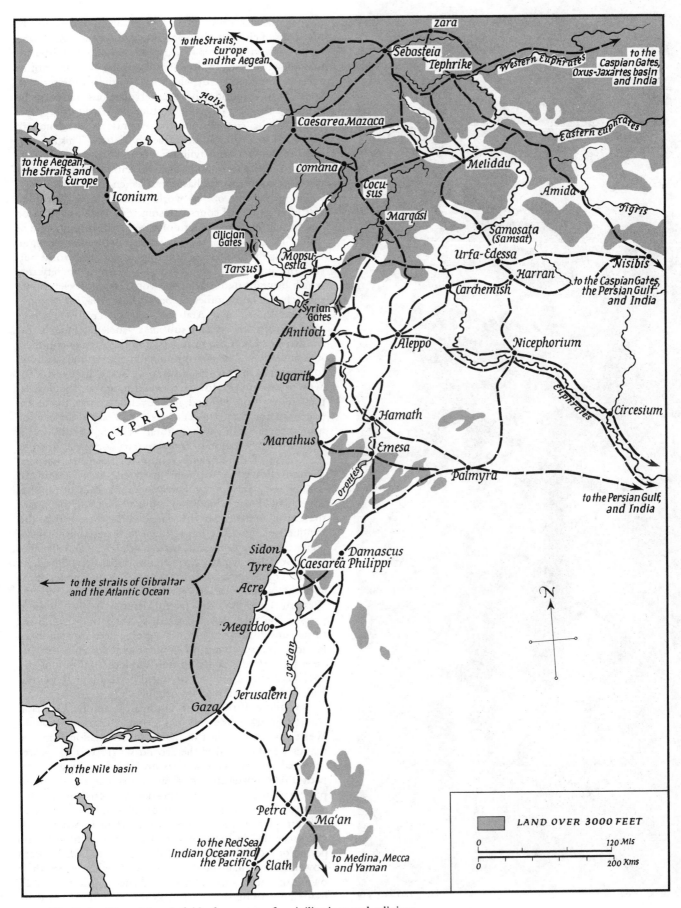

to the Straits,
Europe
and the Aegean

Zara

Sebasteia

Tephrike

Western Euphrates

to the
Caspian Gates,
Oxus-Jaxartes basin
and India

Halys

Eastern euphrates

Caesarea Mazaca

to the Aegean,
the Straits and
Europe

Comana

Meliddu

Cocu-
sus

Amida

Tigris

Iconium

Marqasi

Samosata
(Samsat)

Cilician
Gates

Urfa-Edessa

Nisibis

Mopsu-
estia

Harran

to the Caspian Gates,
the Persian Gulf
and India

Tarsus

Carchemish

Syrian
Gates

Antioch

Aleppo

Nicephorium

Ugarit

CYPRUS

Euphrates

Circesium

Hamath

Marathus

Emesa

Orontes

Palmyra

to the Persian Gulf,
and India

to the straits of Gibraltar
and the Atlantic Ocean

Sidon

Damascus

Tyre

Caesarea Philippi

Acre

Jordan

Megiddo

N

Jerusalem

Gaza

to the Nile basin

LAND OVER 3000 FEET

Petra

Ma'an

0   120 Mls

to the Red Sea
Indian Ocean and
the Pacific

Elath

to Medina, Mecca
and Yaman

0   200 Kms

314   The Syrian 'Roundabout', field of encounter for civilizations and religions.

or there may have been chronological overlaps between the life-spans of civilizations belonging to different generations, or the surviving fossils or diasporás of a dead civilization may have preserved its characteristics within another society. The final factor which has multiplied the series of contacts and collisions between civilizations has been the fusion of the New-World with the Old-World group, as a result of the conquest of the Atlantic by the modern Western Civilization in the fifteenth century. This achievement of the Western Civilization is an historical landmark, and it may help us to find a point of entry into the complex historical maze that we have undertaken to explore.

The expansion of the world from a West European starting-point is, of course, to some extent a visual illusion due to the modern Western observer's distorting angle of vision. It leaves out of account the explorations and emigrations which took place in other quarters of the world outside the purview of the medieval Western Society and which brought numbers of the non-Western societies into contact with one another. In South-East Asia, for example, Chinese, Indian, and Arab explorations created a whole network of contacts and subsidiary societies long before the arrival of Western intruders; and the African continent was similarly the meeting-ground of contemporary cultures for centuries before its geography was 'discovered' by Western explorers. However, even though we should bear these reservations in mind, it is nevertheless true that in the course of the past five centuries the Western Civilization has taken the lead, both culturally and politically, in the aggressive penetration of contemporary societies. When, in the course of the fifteenth century of the Christian Era, Western European mariners mastered the technique of oceanic navigation, they thereby won a means of physical access to all the inhabited and habitable lands on the face of the Earth; and between that date and the present time this conquest of the ocean has resulted in the establishment of contact, on Western terms, between the West and all other living societies, whether pre-civilizational or civilized. In the lives of all these other living societies the impact of the West has come to be the paramount social force and 'the Western Question' the fateful issue. As the Western pressure on them has increased, so their lives have been turned upside down; and it has not only been the frail social fabric of the surviving pre-civilizational societies that has been pulverized; the living non-Western civilizations too have been convulsed and corroded by this literally world-wide revolution of Western origin.

The failure of the second Ottoman assault on Vienna in AD 1683 marked the end of the last offensive by a non-Western society against the Western Civilization; between that date and the end of the Second World War the power acquired by the West was so great that no single competitor nor constellation of rivals was sufficiently strong to present a threat to it. In this age, non-Western Powers – for instance Russia and Japan – were able to play a part in Western power-politics only to the extent to which they had succeeded in Westernizing themselves. Throughout a period of more than two and a half centuries, the Western Powers had virtually no others to reckon with outside their own circle, and, on the material plane, the destiny of all Mankind outside that circle was therefore determined by

CONTACTS AND COLLISIONS

315, 316, 317 Civilizations do not remain isolated, but are constantly interacting, peacefully or otherwise. Among the most outstanding of such collisions was that between the Western Civilization and the New World in the sixteenth century. The Spanish halberdier, opposite, decorates a *conquistador* palace in Mexico. Above, more peaceful encounters. A seventh-century panel, top, showing the 'Silk Princess' bringing silk to Khotan from China, reminds us that Chinese trade created links between widely separated societies long before the intrusion of Western travellers. Beneath, Chinese sages bring history books to the thirteenth-century Mongol ruler of Iran, Ghazan Khan, who commissioned a history of his Nomad forbears' past in Eastern Asia.

این چه حسنت واین چه زیبایی   که در و کا یبات حیران است

شاده ام لبیان و دلبسر وخجلم   که بندم دهن لبیان و دلم

318 China comes to India: a Mughal painting of Chinese ladies, wearing characteristic Chinese dress, at the Indian imperial court in the sixteenth century.

the course of the mutual relations between those Western Powers. Since 1945, however, this Western monopoly of power in the world has come to an end, as a result of the successive entries into the world arena of Japan, the Soviet Union, and China as Powers, in the front rank ideologically or politically, that are modern, no longer just in virtue of having partially Westernized themselves, but on the strength of independent and original achievements of their own. The *Leitmotiv* of power-politics from 1945 to 1972 has no longer been a competition among Western or partially Westernized parochial states for European or world domination, but a competition between the distinctive societies represented by the Soviet Union, the United States, China, and Japan. On a superficial view, it might look as if this development were merely the latest move in the shifting play of international politics. Yet, if we look beyond this consideration of the formal dynamics of power-politics, we shall see that the realinement of political forces after 1945 has been different in kind from any previous alinement since the Ottoman Empire's fall out of the race in 1683. After 1945, and for the first time since 1683, non-Western Powers began once again to play major parts in the arena of power-politics, not in a Western framework, but on their own terms; and this reversion to normality has reintroduced a cultural conflict into a political arena which, for some 250 years past, had been reserved for the domestic political quarrels between Powers that were all alike native or naturalized members of the single modern Western *Kulturkreis*.

Moreover, since this re-emergence of three major non-Western Powers flying their own distinctive cultural colours, there have been significant other developments along the same lines in other parts of the world whose indigenous civilizations had been eclipsed by the Western Society in the heyday of its expansionist era. Parochial representatives of the non-Western societies in South-East Asia, India, and Africa have also begun to assert their claim to an independent political and cultural status. If we add to these the nation-states of the heart-land of the Islamic World, we shall see even more clearly that the post-1945 alinement in international relations has raised an issue of inter-civilizational contact that had been to all intents and purposes in abeyance for 250 years.

These considerations suggest that a scrutiny of the encounters between the modern West and the other living civilizations might be the best way of approaching our subject, besides laying open for discussion one of the principal themes of contemporary history. We can then go on to look at one of the now extinct civilizations which, during its lifetime, made on its neighbours an impact comparable to the West's impact on its contemporaries; and this example will be additionally useful when we come to explore the psychology of cultural encounters. Time is of the essence of the problem, since the psychological reverberations of collisions between contemporary societies do not produce their ultimate social effects until they have completed their slow journey into the individual soul; and therefore we shall be able to follow this process more accurately and fully if we can observe its action from start to finish in the encounters between a long dead society and its contemporaries.

400

45 The Modern West and Russia

WE HAVE DATED the opening of the modern chapter of Western history around the turn of the fifteenth and sixteenth centuries,[1] and the establishment by Muscovy of a Russian universal state towards the end of the fifteenth century.[2] This outstanding event in the political history of Russia thus just anticipated the impact on Russia of the Western Civilization in its modern form; but 'the Western Question' was already familiar to Russians in an older ·shape. In the course of the fourteenth and fifteenth centuries, Western Christian Polish and Lithuanian rule had been established over large stretches of the original patrimony of the Russian Orthodox Christian Society, making of the newly founded capital of the Russian Empire at Moscow a frontier fortress against an encroaching Western Christendom. The political encroachment of the West on Russia's western fringes was consolidated by an ecclesiastical intrusion, in the shape of the imposition, in 1594–96, of union with the Roman Church (subject to the retention of the Eastern rite) on a previously Orthodox Christian population; and the two institutional bonds of politics and religion clamped this detached western fragment of Russia on to the Western World, and provided for the infiltration of other Western cultural influences.

The political sovereignty over these ex-Russian territories in which the Western Civilization was thus gaining cultural converts was one of the stakes in a fluctuating military contest between the Russian universal state and a succession of Western European Powers. Over the centuries Russia succeeded in recovering one after another of the territories which had lain under this Western dominance for varying lengths of time; but the military and political victory which Russia thus gradually obtained over her intrusive Western neighbours was offset on the cultural plane by the consequent propagation of modern Western influences from these semi-Westernized areas into the Muscovite heart-land, which had thus exposed itself to contamination.

Another and possibly more important field in which the encounter between Russia and the modern Western Civilization took place was along the Baltic coast. Here the principals on the Western side were not the relatively backward representatives of the modern Western Civilization who were Russia's immediate continental neighbours in Eastern Europe; they were the maritime peoples on the European shores of the Atlantic who, at the turn of the fifteenth and sixteenth centuries, had taken over from the Italians the leadership of the Western Civilization's expansionist enterprise.

These maritime countries included Russia's neighbours along the Baltic coast from Courland to Finland, which came under Russian sovereignty during the eighteenth century, and which served as one centre for the radiation of Western culture into Russia. But, though the colonial Western German barons and bourgeoisie of the Baltic provinces certainly exercised an influence in Russian life that was out of all proportion to their numbers, the influence of the west-European Western peoples counted for much more, and it was conveyed direct through ports of entry which the Russian imperial government deliberately opened to receive it.

The earliest of these Russian water-gates for the direct reception of the modern Western Civilization from its homelands was the mouth of the Northern Dvina on the coast of the White Sea, which was reached by an English ship in AD 1553. The Muscovite government responded by founding the port-town of Archangel there in 1584, and the Westerners who entered Russia by this route established an inland outpost in 'the Svoboda' on the threshold of Moscow. Direct intercourse between Western Europe and Russia via the White Sea was thus inaugurated on the initiative of Western European mariners in the course of their sixteenth-century conquest of the art of oceanic navigation; but the intensity of Western influence was keyed up to a higher pitch when, in the opening years of the eighteenth century, the circuitous maritime route between Russia and Western Europe via Archangel was short-circuited by the foundation of St Petersburg. Simultaneously, the field within which this alien influence was allowed to exert itself was expanded from the narrow limits of the Svoboda to embrace the entire domain of the Russian Empire, which, in Peter the Great's day, already stretched all the way from the Baltic to the Pacific.

In the prolonged drama of the impact of the West on Russia, which has now been active for more than 250 years at this high pitch, and in a lower key for some two hundred years before that, the plot was dictated by a perpetual interplay between the intense technological prowess of the modern Western World and Russia's no less intense determination to preserve her own independence against all comers and to extend her Empire into Central and Eastern Asia. The challenge of the West evoked two antithetical reactions.

A small and politically insignificant 'Zealot'[3] minority resisted the Western intrusion on a unique Holy Russian state which, in their belief, was 'the Third Rome' and the last surviving guardian of true Christian orthodoxy.[4] These were the fanatical 'Old Believers' who had broken with the official Muscovite Church and state in the seventeenth century over the question whether the traditional Muscovite version of Orthodox Christian ritual and practice should or should not be brought into line with seventeenth-century Greek practice. They had obstinately refused to change one jot or tittle of their own parochial Muscovite custom; and the intransigence thus displayed in a family quarrel within the bosom of the Orthodox Christian Church declared itself, a fortiori, against a policy of adopting anything at all from a schismatic Western World. They rejected point-blank a Western technology which was tainted by association, and they carried their refusal to the point that they were unwilling to applaud the use of Western weaponry even for safeguarding Holy Russia's independence against the lethal assaults of a superior enemy.

319 In Russia, a tenacious loyalty to traditional observance was the hallmark of the Orthodox Christian Church. This sixteenth-century icon commemorates the foundation of the Solovetski monastery in the White Sea, a citadel of religious conservatism that the government reduced by siege in 1668–70.

The totalitarian Zealot response to the pressure of the modern West was both logical and sincere. The Zealots trusted wholly in God and were willing to stake the existence of Orthodox Christian Russia on their belief that God would preserve His people as long as they observed His law. This belief was never put to the test, owing to the numerical insignificance of the Old Believers; yet, though their reaction was repressed, it was not without some effect as a subterranean influence. For example, the Slavophil movement, which was one of the nineteenth-century cultural phenomena of the 'Herodian'[5] Petrine régime, had a dual aspect. It could be explained in Herodian terms as a Russian variation on the contemporary Romantic movement in the West; but from another standpoint it might be viewed as a muted expression of the native Russian Zealot hostility to the Western culture – an hostility which, in an age when Westernization was the dominant tendency in Russia, found itself compelled to masquerade in some Western garb or other and thus fastened upon an archaizing Western movement which itself was a native criticism of Western industrialization.

The thorough-going Herodianism which was at the opposite extreme of the psychological gamut from the totalitarian Zealotism of the Old Believers was first translated from aspiration into act by the genius of the Zealots' bugbear Peter the Great (*imperabat* AD 1689–1725). The Petrine policy was to convert the Russian Empire from a Russian Orthodox Christian universal state into one of the parochial states of the modern Western World, in which the Russian people would take its place as one among a number of Western or Westernized nations. This policy sought to save Russia's political independence and cultural autonomy, in a world in which the modern Western way of life was becoming the rule, by gaining admission for Russia to membership of a Westerners' club bound by certain rules of international conduct; it was the first example of voluntary self-Westernization by a non-Western Power.

The West was calling the tune to which the Russians had to dance; and the Herodian policy of Peter the Great and his successors was an improvised response to a Western pressure which took the tangible form of a series of military assaults. The effect of these encounters was at first to demonstrate Russia's relative inferiority and hence to lead her to adopt Western techniques with success; but the final outcome revealed how superficial this policy of Westernization had been.

The first of these encounters took place during the sixteenth and seventeenth centuries, when a newly established Muscovy, in attempting to expand and consolidate her territories westwards, came into collision with Sweden and with Poland-Lithuania. Although the emergent Russian state did make some territorial gains in the course of these wars, the true measure of the relative strengths of Russia and her Western neighbours was not given by any fluctuations in frontiers, but by the constant ability of Western armies in this age to defeat contemporary Russian armies in the field; and this was patently accounted for by the West's technological superiority over its adversary. The alarming experience of the inadequacy of native Russian military technique in warfare with Russia's modern Western neighbours was a challenge which found its

320, 321 HERODIANISM Peter the Great dragged Russia from the Middle Ages into Western modernity. Symbolic of the new era was his foundation of the Baltic port of St Petersburg, below, as a 'window on the West'.

403

response in the Petrine Herodian revolution. Peter faced the task of bringing Russia's civil and military organization up to the contemporary Western standard;[6] and the success of his policy was foreshadowed in his own victory over a rash Swedish invader of the Ukraine in 1709, and was consummated just over a century later in the expulsion of Napoleon's armies.

The post-Napoleonic era saw a superficially Westernized Russia standing on a pinnacle of apparent ascendancy; yet this appearance was already an illusion, for the Revolutionary and Napoleonic Wars of 1792–1815 were the last Western wars on the grand scale that were fought with a pre-industrial Western technique. In the Crimean War (*gerebatur* AD 1853–56) Russia was still able to fight her Western adversaries on more or less equal terms, but only thanks to the conservatism of contemporary French and British military minds. The American Civil War and the three Prussian wars of aggression (*gerebantur* AD 1861–71) saw the new industrial technique duly applied to warfare by Western Powers; and the inefficacy of Russia's half-hearted attempts to catch up with the latest Western

advances in industrial and military technology was revealed in her humiliating defeat at the hands of a Westernized Japan in 1904–05, and in her total collapse when she challenged the German military machine in the First World War. These were shattering proofs of the inadequacy of the Petrine dispensation for enabling Russia to hold her own in a rapidly industrializing world; and the Russian Communist Revolution was the response. The abortive revolution of 1905 was a reaction to the Petrine Russian Empire's defeat by Japan. The utter disaster of 1914–18, and its remorseless revelation of the extreme industrial and social backwardness which had made it inevitable, brought the Bolsheviks into power and eventually determined their programme.

The effect of Russia's Herodianism thus proved to have been relatively shallow, even though it had been her policy for more than two centuries ending in the collapse of Peter the Great's Russia. One explanation of this was that Westernization had been rigidly confined to a few fields of life only, and had never made any deep impression upon the life and culture of Russia.

A backward country assimilates the material and intellectual

Русткой ратникъ
Иванъ Гвоздила

У басурмана ношки тоненки
душа коротенка

Што мусье промахну
лся анъ вотъ тебе разъ
другой бабушка дастъ

Русткой Милицiйской
мужикъ Долбила

Вить очнется Басурманъ
Не вдавайся Братъ въ обманъ

Што мусье кувырнулся
расъ два три ась не прива
битли мусье

322 Naval technology was Peter the Great's consuming interest; he made secret visits to Western shipyards to learn modern techniques, though the ships of his fleet, left, are less advanced in design than contemporary Western vessels.

323 In spite of Peter's Westernizing programme, a deep-seated belief in Russia's rugged superiority persisted. This popular nineteenth-century print, appealing to traditional patriotic sentiment, glorifies the victory of the Russian peasant soldier over his better-equipped French adversary.

conquests of the advanced countries. But this does not mean that it follows them slavishly, reproduces all the stages of their past. . . . The possibility of skipping over intermediate steps is of course by no means absolute. Its degree is determined in the long run by the economic and cultural capacities of the country. The backward nation, moreover, not infrequently debases the achievements borrowed from outside in the process of adapting them to its own more primitive culture. In this the very process of assimilation acquires a self-contradictory character. Thus the introduction of certain elements of Western technique and training, above all military and industrial, under Peter I [the Great], led to a strengthening of serfdom as the fundamental form of labour organization. European armament and European loans – both indubitable products of a higher culture – led to a strengthening of czarism, which delayed in its turn the development of the country.[7]

Thus the Westernization of certain aspects of Russian life actually helped to inhibit progress across the whole gamut. Strong traditional cultural forces resisted a fully effective Westernization of the Tsarist autocracy; in practice, the Petrine policy of Herodianism became half-hearted, for the Tsarist régime could not tolerate the liberalization of

Russian political and social life, even though the adoption of the Western capitalist technique might demand this as the price for maintaining Russian independence and military parity with the West.

At the climax of a backward Russia's confrontation with the society which she had so inadequately attempted to imitate, it was an alternative political model of no less Western origin that captured the Russian revolutionary movement. Marxism was a Western futurist criticism of a latter-day industrial form of modern Western life which the Western Romantic movement had attacked from an archaistic angle. The Russian Revolution of October 1917 combined a subjective uprising against the Tsarist autocracy with – in Marxist terms – an objectively necessary proletarian anti-capitalist revolt: in other words, the West's own style of radical opposition to the established form of Western Civilization had seeped sufficiently deeply into Russian life to ensure that the Russian movement of political liberation would be carried out in a Western guise. The Revolution was, indeed, anti-Western only in so far as 'the West' stood for capitalism; but, in any other sense, hostility to the Western or to any other particular civilization was irrelevant. Marxist doctrine recognized none of the vertical lines of demarcation between nation and nation, or between one society and another, but only the horizontal lines of class that cut across the accepted international and cultural frontiers. Like the historic higher religions, it promised a release that was to be universal.[8]

Communist Russia was perhaps the first non-Western country to recognize the possibility that the Western technique of industrial production could in practice be divorced from its Western cultural matrix, so long as it were supported by an effective substitute social ideology. Petrine Russia had tried to graft a slip of Western industrialism on to the unreceptive stock of the traditional Russian Orthodox Christian Society, and had failed because it had pursued a reform programme of modernization only as far as the half-way mark. It was left to Russia under a Marxist dispensation to explore the full implications of an industrialized, but non-capitalist and non-Western, social system; and it remains to be seen whether Communism may perhaps offer a practical and humane solution to the problems of industrialism which capitalism has so far been unable to solve.

Whether this solution will be found by Communist Russia is, however, a separate question; for, on the morrow of her proletarian revolution, she lapsed into a curiously revived Zealotism. It is easy to see that there were cogent practical reasons for the isolationism that was adopted by – indeed, forced upon – Communist Russia after the end of the revolutionary war; yet the internationalist ideology of Marxism was peculiarly ill-suited to serve as the vehicle for a belated Russian Zealotist movement. Communism was, for Marxists, 'the wave of the future' in all capitalist societies at a certain stage of their development; yet Russia under Stalin arrogated to herself a unique status in the history of the proletariat's road to power; in effect she tried to appropriate the Marxist ideology for herself alone. In a secular imitation of the Old Believers, the Russian Communist régime considered itself to be the sole repository of Marxist orthodoxy, implying that Marxism as a doctrine and in practice was valid only in terms of the Russian experience. Mere priority in the revolutionary field thus gave Russia the opportunity to reassert a claim to a unique destiny that was latent in the Russian cultural tradition and had been taken over by the Slavophils from the Russian Orthodox Church, though it had never before received any official secular sanction. (The Communist 'Establishment' was, of course, not solely secular; it was also the embodiment of an ideology that was an atheistic form of religion.) The substance behind this Russian Communist pretension is the primacy that Russia assumed in the Communist bloc in Eastern Europe, after having drawn these nations out of their mainly Western setting into her own orbit. The seriousness of Russia's assumption of this role can be gauged by the bitterness with which Russia has resented 'defections' from the Russian Communist camp, whether the defectors have been individuals or whole nations.

Russia since the Revolution thus presents the paradoxical picture of a society that has received an alien ideology in Herodian style, in order to exploit it as the vehicle for a Zealotist policy of cultural self-sufficiency.

324 ZEALOTISM REVIVED A Russian Revolution poster exhorts workers to celebrate the First of May by giving extra effort to the work of reconstruction. Modern Russia has opted decisively for the Western industrial system: even the Marxist formula is a Western importation, though it is pursued with all the fanaticism of the Old Believers.

46 The modern West and Eastern Asia

THE RUSSIAN CIVILIZATION had already had some experience of the Western Society before it had begun to be affected by the impact of the Western culture in its modern phase; but, by contrast, the existence of the West was all but unknown to the civilizations in China and Japan down to the moment when the West's pioneer navigators impinged on both these societies. Their ignorance of the West perhaps helps to explain the paradoxical fact that these remoter civilizations showed, at the first encounter, a greater readiness to open their arms to the modern West than was shown by any of the West's better-informed next-door neighbours. The West's nearest neighbours – the Jews, Orthodox Christians, and Muslims – had felt the full force of Western religious fanaticism in the era of Western expansion before the secularization of the Western Society; and the reception of the modern Western culture by these societies did not begin until the alien Western way of life was able to offer itself to them in a secularized version – with technology enthroned in religion's former place at the apex of the Western pyramid of values. Less prudence in dealing with the importunate Western stranger at the gate was shown by the Sinic and Japanese Societies, and by the indigenous societies of the New World. So far from waiting for the abatement of a Western religious fanaticism of which they had not been forewarned by any past experience of it, they laid themselves open to the full impact of the West in its early modern phase, when its traditional religious aggressiveness was still in the ascendant.

Despite the fact that the Sinic and the Japanese Societies were in generally bad case by the first half of the sixteenth century, when the ocean-faring Westerners first appeared above their horizon, both succeeded in holding their own against the West in its early modern phase. They managed with impunity to weigh the Western Civilization in the balance, find it wanting, make up their minds to cast it out, and muster the necessary force for putting into effect a deliberate policy of virtual non-intercourse. This, at least, was how the first chapter of the encounter unfolded itself; but it was followed by a sequel in which the story was quite different.

In breaking off relations with the West in the form in which the West had presented itself to them in its early modern phase, the Chinese and the Japanese had not disposed of 'the Western Question' once for all; for the West did not remain fixed in the form that it had attained at the moment when Eastern Asia had dismissed it. The secularization of Western culture opened a new chapter in Western history at the turn of the seventeenth and eighteenth centuries; and the substitution of technology for religion as the highest Western cultural value reopened 'the Western Question' for China and Japan. In abandoning its traditional insistence that aliens must become converts to some Western form of religion as a condition *sine qua non* for admittance to the Western Society, the West was jettisoning the bigotry that had previously made it appear repellent and menacing in Chinese and Japanese eyes. Conversely, in

325 WESTERN APPROACHES East meets West in a strikingly exotic encounter. The Chinese painter of this scene showing the first aircraft in China, in 1910, clearly had little concept of powered flight: he has constructed his plane like a Chinese paper kite, making no attempt to illustrate the means of propulsion that has launched the machine on to his horizon. The result is graceful, naïve, and wholly misleading.

dedicating its energies to technology the West was launching itself on a course of material progress that was rapidly to eclipse its own or any other society's previous achievements in this line. This Western technological superiority had, at the earlier encounter, already seemed formidably attractive to China and Japan; and, now that it was being raised to ever higher degrees of potency, the Eastern Asian peoples, like their counterparts in the Indic, Islamic, and Orthodox Christian Worlds, found themselves confronted with a choice between mastering this superlative skill or succumbing to it.

The reactions of the Chinese and the Japanese to their successive encounters with the West resemble each other in some respects and not in others. A point of likeness is that in the second encounter the reception of the secularized modern Western culture was initiated from below upwards, as a result of the failure of both the Manchu and the Tokugawa régime to take the necessary lead. On the other hand, the nineteenth-century Japanese Westernizing movement quickly parted company with the contemporary movement in China by acquiring government sponsorship and becoming an official and coercive policy. In the original sixteenth-century Westernizing movements, too, the two societies had taken different courses from the outset: the initiative had come from above downwards in the Sinic Society, and from below upwards in the Japanese Society.

If we plot out the courses of the two societies' reactions to the West from the first half of the sixteenth century down to the present day, we shall see that the Chinese curve comes out relatively smooth and the Japanese curve relatively jagged. By comparison with the Chinese reactions, the two successive periods of Westernization in Japan and the intervening periods of anti-Western reaction all went to extremes, and the two successive reversals of policy – from reception to rejection in the seventeenth century and from rejection to reception in the nineteenth – were relatively abrupt. The Chinese never went so far as the Japanese in surrendering themselves to the modern Western culture on either occasion or in insulating themselves from contact with the West in the intervening stage of anti-Western xenophobia; and the reversals of policy that were decreed in Japan by the fiat of a dictator or by the verdict of a revolution were allowed in China to work themselves out more gradually and more spontaneously.

In both societies the early modern Western Christian missionaries made converts who eventually proved their sincerity by sacrificing their lives rather than obey their government's command to renounce their exotic adopted faith; but the dominant motives in both societies for tentatively embracing the early modern Western Christian culture were not religious but secular, and the unconvincing and bigoted religious propaganda of the missionaries was grudgingly tolerated only for the sake of the material benefits which might be gained through them, either directly or indirectly. In this chapter of the story, the Chinese imperial court's cultivation of the Jesuits was less utilitarian or more frivolous – in whichever of the two lights we may prefer to regard it – than the contemporary cultivation of them in Japan. In Chinese minds the dominant incentive was curiosity; and, though, in their curiosity about sixteenth-

EASTERN RESPONSES

326, 327, 328 Jesuit missionaries from Western Europe, bringing Western technology as well as the Christian religion, reached Japan in 1549 and China in 1552. Japan seized on the new technology, but the alien religion and its missionaries were effectively proscribed in 1614. The print of Christ, opposite, is a rare example of Japanese Christian art, made before the ban. Above, a priest celebrates mass in the Jesuit residence at Nagasaki, the port to which all Westerners were confined. China was more tolerant in religion but was ambivalent towards Western science. The Jesuit Adam Schall, right, was official astronomer at the Chinese court in the 1640s; his knowledge fascinated the Chinese but alarmed them too, since it invalidated their own faulty calendrical calculations.

329 Westerners as pariahs: view of the Dutch factory in Nagasaki, c. 1690. After 1639 Japan tolerated the profitable presence of Western traders, but signified its hostility to the aliens and their religion by confining them to a ghetto and forcing them each year to perform an humiliating act of homage and a sacrilegious ritual involving the desecration of the cross.

century Western firearms, the Chinese as well as the Japanese had practical considerations in mind, the Ming régime's desire to fortify its tottering authority by equipping itself with these new-fangled weapons was far less intense than the eagerness of contemporary Japanese warlords to master a new military technique which might play a decisive part in their struggles for the prize of ruling a reunified Japanese Empire.[1]

Nor did the Ming or Manchu imperial government see in the development of trade through Western middlemen those dazzling prospects of commercial profits that excited Japanese cupidity. Towards the close of the sixteenth century it looked as if the adoption by the Japanese of the contemporary Western art of war and their engagement in commerce with Western traders might draw Japan at this stage out of the ambit of the Sinic Society into the ambit of a Western Society which had made itself ubiquitous by conquering the ocean. Before the advent of the Western ocean-farers in Eastern Asia, the Japanese had already taken to the sea in a counter-stroke to the abortive attempts of the Mongols to invade Japan in AD 1274 and 1281. The Japanese had been making piratical descents on the coasts of China since 1369, and, when, after the suppression of Japanese piracy by Hideyoshi at the end of the sixteenth century, Japanese seamen followed the example of the Western newcomers by taking to trade, they rapidly extended the range of their maritime activities over the Pacific as far afield as the straits of Malacca in one direction[2] and the Spanish Viceroyalty of Mexico in the other.[3]

The other side of the picture was that, by the turn of the sixteenth and seventeenth centuries, a Japan whose political unification by indigenous military force was then still incomplete and insecure had come to be perilously exposed to the danger of having political unity imposed on her from abroad at the eleventh hour. The Spanish conquest of the Philippines in 1565–71, the union of the Portuguese with the Spanish Crown in 1581, and the Dutch conquest of Formosa in 1624 were object-lessons of the fate which might befall this other group of West Pacific islands with which the Portuguese had been in contact since the mid-sixteenth century. By contrast, the vast sub-continent of China had nothing more to fear from the advent of Western pirates in the sixteenth and seventeenth centuries than she had found to fear from the activities of Japanese pirates in the fourteenth and fifteenth centuries. For China, the still unmechanized early modern Western sea-raiders were not potential conquerors, however annoying they might be; the dangers that gave serious cause for anxiety to the Chinese imperial government in this age were the possibilities of domestic revolt and of overland invasion from the Eurasian steppe beyond the Great Wall or from the Manchurian forests. After the enfeebled indigenous Ming dynasty had been supplanted by the vigorous semi-barbarian Manchu dynasty in the course of the seventeenth century,[4] a recurrence of the conjuncture of invasion and revolt which had brought the Manchus into the saddle did not present itself on the Chinese political horizon for the next two hundred years.

This difference in the geographico-political situation of China and Japan in the early modern age of Western oceanic expansion goes far towards explaining why it was that in China the repression of Roman Catholic Christianity was postponed till the turn of the seventeenth and eighteenth centuries and was the outcome, not of any apprehensive calculations in the field of power-politics, but of an academic theological controversy; while, by contrast, Christianity was promptly and ruthlessly suppressed in Japan, and all threads but a solitary Dutch one in the nexus between Japan and the Western World were cut. The succession of blows delivered by the newly established Japanese central government began in 1587 with the first ordinance decreeing the banishment from Japan of Western Christian missionaries, and culminated in the ordinances of 1636 and 1639, forbidding Japanese subjects to continue to travel abroad and Portuguese subjects to continue to reside in Japan.

In Japan, as in China, the eventual abandonment of a self-imposed insulation from contact with the West was initiated from below upwards; and it was inspired by a purely intellectual interest in modern Western scientific knowledge that preceded any desire to exploit this knowledge for the same practical ends which had allowed the West to acquire its unprecedented economic and military power. Like the early seventeenth-century Japanese converts to Roman Catholic Christianity, the early nineteenth-century Japanese devotees of modern Western secular science demonstrated their sincerity by exposing themselves to a similar risk of martyrdom.

The Tokugawa régime signalized the last years of its existence by banning all Dutch studies outside the field of medicine: and, from the government's standpoint, the only thing wrong about this repressive policy was its impracticability. Yet this welling up of a disinterested intellectual curiosity concerning the achievements of modern Western science was an indirect outcome of the government's own cultural policy. In their anxiety to conserve their arduously attained achievement of freezing Japanese life into immobility on the once feverishly agitated military and political planes, the Tokugawa had wisely looked for alternative vents for unabated Japanese energies, and they had encouraged the pursuit of learning as one innocuous outlet. The mental discipline that they had favoured had been the cultivation of Neoconfucianism, which was the legacy of the Sung and Ming Ages in China; but it proved impossible for a reactionary régime in Japan at the turn of the eighteenth and nineteenth centuries to permit its subjects to supplement their authorized cultivation of a conservative vein of indigenous thought by making a strictly utilitarian study of modern Western medicine without thereby opening a passage for the mighty flood of modern Western knowledge in its entirety.

While the inspiration of the nineteenth-century Japanese Westernizing movement from below upwards thus came from modern Western secular scientific thought, the inspiration of the corresponding and contemporary movement in China came from modern Western Protestant Christianity, whose missionaries accompanied the British and American salesmen of the industrialized West's exports, as in the sixteenth century Roman Catholic missionaries had accompanied the Portuguese pioneers of early

330 Westerners as paragons: Japan's re-entry into the Western ambit was as dramatic as her exit. The first railway, connecting Tokyo with Yokohama, was opened in 1872, less than twenty years after the first intrusion of the modern West in the person of Commodore Perry. Industrialization began in earnest in the last decade of the century, laying at great speed the foundations of the heavy industries that were to secure Japan's commercial and military success in competition with the older-established Western Powers.

331 Westerners as barbarians: the Emperor Ch'ien Lung receives Lord Macartney's embassy in 1793. The mission – as impressive a demonstration of Western power as Perry's – was one of several unsuccessful attempts to persuade China to establish diplomatic relations with Britain and open her cities to British trade.

modern Western commercial enterprise. The T'aip'ing politico-religious insurrectionary movement, which came near to overthrowing the Manchu régime in the 1850s and 1860s, was not merely a 'Zealot' indigenous revolt against the incipient Western influences in the Manchu 'ascendancy'; it was also in its own way a translation of Protestant Christianity into indigenous Sinic terms. In the last decades of the nineteenth century, the Chinese initiators of a movement for secular political reform were likewise influenced by Western Protestant Christian missionaries. Sun Yat-sen, the founder of the Kuomintang, was the son of a Protestant Christian father; and another Protestant Christian ,Chinese family played a paramount part in the Kuomintang's subsequent history in the persons of Sun Yat-sen's wife, her sister, who was the wife of Chiang Kai-shek, and their brother, T. V. Soong.

Thus, from the outset, the nineteenth-century Chinese Westernizing movement differed from its Japanese counter-part in having a Protestant Christian instead of a secular scientific Western inspiration; and the two movements also rapidly diverged on the political plane. Both movements were confronted with the formidable task of having to liquidate and replace a well-established indigenous ecumenical régime which had demonstrated its unfitness to survive by revealing its insensitivity to the imperative need

for coping with the impact of the powerful modern Western Civilization. In this political emergency, however, the Japanese Westernizers were more alert, more prompt, and more efficient than the Chinese. Within fifteen years of the first appearance of Commodore Perry's squadron in Japanese territorial waters in 1853, the Japanese Western-izers had not only overthrown the Tokugawa régime when it failed to rise to the urgent occasion; they had achieved the far more difficult feat of installing in its place a new régime capable of putting into operation a comprehensive Westernizing movement from above downwards. The Chinese took 118 years to accomplish even the negative political result that the Japanese achieved in fifteen. The arrival of Lord Macartney's embassy at Peking in 1793 was a no less illuminating demonstration of the growing strength of the Western Civilization than the arrival of Perry's squadron in Yedo Bay sixty years later; yet in China the overthrow of the *ancien régime* did not follow till 1911, and the discarded universal state was then replaced, not by any effective new Westernizing political order, but by a familiar anarchy which the Kuomintang was unable to overcome.

The nineteenth-century shock that jolted both Eastern Asian peoples out of their ruts was the impact of new high-powered Western armaments carried by British warships in

JAPAN'S ROAD

332–339 Advance to power: stages in the modernization of the Japanese army from 1867 to 1894. With the collapse of the isolationist Shogunate and the Meiji Restoration in 1867–68, Japan entered on a period of rapid self-Westernization. Military conscription was introduced, breaking the *samurai*'s traditional monopoly of martial service and prestige, and the army was brought to a new standard of efficiency in training and armament. The success of the policy was first demonstrated in 1877, when the new army suppressed a conservative rebellion.

413

JAPAN'S ROAD

Achievement of power: Japan needed less than half a century after the Meiji Restoration to bring her policy of Westernization to a triumphant conclusion. Her dramatic achievement of Great Power status was foreshadowed in the attempt to create a sphere of influence on the Chinese mainland in 1895, and was confirmed by her unexpected victory over Russia in 1905.

340 Japanese troops in action in Korea during the Sino-Japanese War.

341 Japanese warship in the Russo-Japanese War. Japan's astonishing naval victory at Tsushima marked her arrival among the Great Powers.

the war of 1839–42 and by American warships in the visitations of 1853–54; and thus Japan's flying start over China in the race towards the goal of economic and political Westernization can be measured in terms of Japan's military superiority over China during the fifty years running from the outbreak of the Sino-Japanese War of 1894–95. During that half century, China was militarily at Japan's mercy. Although an effective conquest of the whole of China eventually proved to be beyond Japan's resources, it is clear that, if the Japanese war-machine had not been shattered in the Second World War by the United States, the Chinese would never have been able, unaided, to recapture from the Japanese invaders the ports, industrial areas, and railroads that were the keys to the Westernization of China.

Moreover, Japan's facile, albeit inconclusive, victories over China were the cheapest of the trophies which adorned the triumphal progress of Japanese militarism to its ironical finale of unprecedented military and political disaster, within a span of fifty years. Between 1894 and 1945 Japan extracted military dividends from a process of technological Westernization with a virtuosity that eclipsed the achievements of Petrine Russia between her victory in the Great Northern War of 1701–21 and her defeat in the Russo-Japanese War of 1904–05. In this trial of strength between the two Westernizing nations, a victorious Japan won recognition as a Great Power in the Western comity of states, as Russia had won recognition after her victory over Sweden some two hundred years previously. Thereafter, Japan achieved the *tour de force* of making herself one of the three leading naval Powers in a twentieth-century world in which naval strength was a function of industrial potency in terms of Western industrial technique. Her final fling was to smite the United States navy in Pearl Harbor and overrun all the colonial possessions of the Western Powers in South-East Asia in the course of a suicidal leap into the jaws of disaster.

The prostration of China and Japan after the Second World War marked in both societies, though in different ways, the end of the first chapter in their second period of Westernization. Japan had adopted the Western way of life to the extent of assuming a role in the competition of Western power-politics; while China's belated and incomplete attempt at self-Westernization had served to expose the inappropriateness of the traditional Western political model for China's own internal organization. Since 1945, each of these two societies has made new approaches to the impact of the West.

Japan's disastrous experience of involvement in a Western war, which was underlined in a unique fashion by her role as the testing-ground for the West's latest achievement in the field of military technology, has led her to renounce her own military heritage, at least officially, and to concentrate on the achievement not of military but of economic supremacy in Eastern Asia. The extreme tensions evoked in the internal life of the Japanese Society by a forced march towards this goal are evident in the bout of severe political disturbances that began in 1960, and in the strains imposed both on the physical environment and on human nature by the unrestrained advance of industrial production. One may perhaps hazard the guess that

342 China's Great Leap Forward: striving to make up for lost time. John Bull is outpaced by a Chinese rider, symbolizing China's current determination to beat the Western Society at its own industrial game.

Western bafflement at the 'enigma' of Japan is no more than the confusion felt by a society that has seen its own movement of cultural aggression outflanked by its victim; for, in the act of appearing to have been captivated by the West, Japan may actually have disarmed her assailant. Whether the present cultural *mélange* in Japan will develop into a distinctive amalgam of Western and indigenous traditions is a question that can hardly be answered at the present time, for Japan's own impact on the rest of the world has doubtless only just begun and will certainly become a major issue in the near future.

China, on the other hand, has been facing a more complex challenge than Japan, for her 'Western Question' has, since 1949, been presented in a dual form. Communist China has a Russian Marxist 'Western Question' as well as a Western 'Western Question'. The path which China may adopt will be discussed in a later chapter of this Part;[5] meanwhile, we may observe that China and Japan now stand for the two principal cultural exports of the Western World – capitalism and Communism – while the underlying current of technological prowess that unites these two Western movements is flowing through both societies at a different rate. Experience suggests that this Western technological export is likely to lose its exotic significance as an alien culture-element, and become a taken-for-granted component of all or most societies. If this is a correct forecast, the next chapter of the cultural encounter between the Western and non-Western societies will be expressed in terms of how these societies learn to cope with the contents of a Pandora's box that the West has opened with disconcerting consequences for the whole world. The mere degree of a society's industrialization or mechanization will be less significant than the measure of its success in providing solutions to the problems of pollution, of resource exhaustion, and of social tension that are at present the unexorcized concomitants of the industrial system. The future may reveal a non-Western answer to a problem that was originally presented to the world by the West.

47 Encounters with the post-Alexandrine Hellenic Society

IN A POST-ALEXANDRINE Hellenic view of Hellenic history the generation of Alexander the Great (*imperabat* 336–323 BC) marked a break with the past and the beginning of a new era as sharply as, in a modern Western view of Western history, the transition from a medieval to a modern age was marked by the conjuncture of discoveries and inventions at the turn of the fifteenth and sixteenth centuries of the Christian Era.

In both these new chapters of history the most obvious ground for a hybristic depreciation of the achievements of the past by comparison with present experiences and expectations was the consciousness of a sudden immense increase in power, both over other human beings by military conquests and over physical Nature by geographical exploration and scientific discovery. The Macedonian *conquistadores*' feat of overthrowing the Achaemenidae was as exhilarating as the Spanish *conquistadores*' feat of overthrowing the Incas. If a handful of military adventurers could thus shatter, at one blow, a universal state that, for its subjects, had come to seem part of the permanent order of Nature, the society which had given birth to these adventurers might seem to be the potential future mistress of all Mankind. But this enhanced sense of military and political power was not the whole, and indeed not the essence, of a new experience which expressed itself in the feeling that a new era had begun. If either a Hellene of the third century BC or a Westerner of the sixteenth century of the Christian Era had been asked to describe the sensations by which his consciousness of a new era was sustained, he would probably have given less weight to his society's increment of material power than to his sense of an expansion of its mental horizon. In the sensation produced by the discovery 'in real life' of a hitherto fabulous India, to which the Macedonians made their way by opening up a continent and the Portuguese by mastering the ocean, the successful performance of a mighty feat of exploration was accompanied and qualified, on both occasions, by a sense of wonder at the revelation of a marvellously alien world endowed, apparently, with inimitable skill and wisdom. In the sensation produced in the Hellenic World by the scientific discoveries of Aristotle and Theophrastus, and in the Western World by Copernicus and Galileo, the sense of power arising from a notable addition to knowledge was likewise accompanied and qualified by a sense of impotence in the face of the reminder of Man's relative ignorance which every addition to Man's understanding of the Universe is apt to bring with it.

A comparison between the post-Alexandrine Hellenic World and the modern West is legitimate in these generalized terms, but we must qualify it by pointing out two important differences. The encounter between the modern Western Civilization and its contemporaries began at a date when the West still held to a Christian *Weltanschauung*, and the culture radiated by the West included the religious element that was its original essence. By the end of the seventeenth century, however, the Western Society was in the process of secularizing itself, and thus the culture which the West was propagating from then on was only a secular extract from the old integral culture. There was no corresponding division of chapters in the post-Alexandrine history of the radiation of Hellenism, for the Hellenic Civilization had already relieved itself of its religious element at a precociously early age. The enlightenment of the Hellenic World took place towards the end of the fifth century BC; by Alexander's day this enlightenment was thus a hundred years old already, and there was no chapter of post-Alexandrine Hellenic history in which Hellenism was propagated in its original integrity. One of the possible reasons for the Hellenic Civilization's comparative precocity in bursting out of the intellectual strait-jacket of traditional religion may have been the apparent poverty of the Hellenic Society's religious heritage from the antecedent Aegean Society, by comparison with the richness of the Christian heritage bequeathed to the Western Society by a Hellenism which had been converted to Christianity on its death-bed. In Hellenic history the comparative insignificance of a religious legacy, which, in Western history, was to act as both a powerful stimulus and a heavy incubus, can be seen to have had a twofold effect. On the one hand it allowed rationalism to raise its head more easily, and, therefore, earlier, in the Hellenic Civilization than in the Western; but on the other hand the intellectually enlightened Hellenic World never showed itself so prone as the secularized Western World to intellectual *hybris*.

In the Western World the rationalists were first embittered by the length and arduousness of their struggle with a formidably entrenched institutionalized Church, and then intoxicated by the apparent completeness of their eventual victory; and these successive experiences bred in them a spirit of arrogance – though, ironically, this arrogance of the modern Western enlightenment was itself partly a legacy of the Judaic religion against whose dominion it had revolted. This heritage of course also governed the attitude of the Christian Church to other religions. In the second phase of its age of expansion, the Western World was inclined to dismiss the teachings of the non-Christian religions as the Western rationalists had dismissed Christianity. The rationalists looked upon religion in all its guises as being, at best, illusory and superfluous, and, at worst, deliberately fraudulent. Modern Western Christians felt the Western rationalists' contempt for all religions except the Western Christians' own. In spiritual matters, then, the Western rationalists and the Western Christians shared a common outlook of disdain. The rationalists studied non-Western religions out of intellectual curiosity; the Christians studied them for polemical purposes. But neither rationalist nor Christian Westerners took any of these religions seriously as spiritual discoveries or revelations that might conceivably have some value for Western souls.

343, 344 The Western Society rejected as inane superstitions the alien religions that it encountered through
contact with other civilizations. Right, the devilish 'God
of the Tatars', from a fifteenth-century manuscript of
Marco Polo's travels. Below, European settlers in
America are shown a column, erected by an earlier
explorer, which the Indians are ignorantly worshipping
as a god.

417

The Hellenic experience was quite different. A revulsion against the immaturity of the traditional Hellenic religions had already begun to torment Hellenic souls before the fifth-century enlightenment deprived them even of these unsatisfying substitutes for a mature expression of religious faith. When the triumphal progress of their military and intellectual conquests brought the post-Alexandrine Hellenes into contact with full-blooded non-Hellenic religions, whose spiritual value and efficacy seemed to be guaranteed by the large-scale voluntary allegiance that they commanded, the Hellenic reaction was rather to envy their adherents as privileged possessors of a spiritual pearl of great price than to pity them as the dupes of an unscrupulously fraudulent priestcraft. Even the syncretistic religious cults devised by coldly calculating post-Alexandrine Hellenic statesmen – such as Ptolemy Soter's attempt to bring his Egyptiac and Hellenic subjects together on common religious ground through his manufacture of the hybrid divinity Sarapis, or the Romans' institution of Caesar-worship as the religious symbol for their Hellenic universal state – were tributes to their Hellenic subjects' horror of a religious vacuum, besides being designs for taking advantage of their non-Hellenic subjects' religiosity. This receptive attitude of the post-Alexandrine Hellenic conquerors towards the religions of the societies which Hellenism had taken captive on the intellectual as well as on the military plane was one cause of the momentous religious consequences of the aggressive Hellenic Civilization's impact on its contemporaries.

The second difference between the expansion of Hellenism and the expansion of the Western Society is also the more crucial. The most fateful single event in all Hellenic history was the ideological and religious collision, in Coele Syria in the second century BC, between Hellenism and a Syriac religion, Judaism, which, by that date, had adopted some elements of an Iranian religion, Zoroastrianism (e.g. the beliefs in God's Holy Spirit and in a future Last Judgment). Eventually the Hellenic World was converted to a religion of Jewish origin that was, and remained, essentially Judaic in its inspiration and its principles, notwithstanding its compromises with Hellenism in the fields of theology and visual art, and its adoption, into its pantheon, of the Great Mother of God – a deity that had been evicted from Judaism but had survived as Cybele in Asia Minor and as Isis in Egypt. This conversion of the Hellenic World to Christianity was the end of the Hellenic Civilization. As a result of the conversion, Hellenism lost its identity.

Thus, unlike the West as far as we know to date, the Hellenic Civilization was ultimately dissolved as a result of the most momentous of its encounters with its contemporaries. The Syriac Civilization in fact took its conqueror captive by a subtle process of cultural decomposition and amalgamation. The reciprocal influence and counterinfluence of the Syriac and the Hellenic Civilizations on each other was exerted over a long period of time, and, as time went on, ever more intensively. The eventual effect was to disintegrate each of the two, and to compound their tissues into a new fabric which, though composite, was so closely compacted that it became difficult to analyse it into its original components. At least as early as the eighth

CULTURAL COALESCENCE

345–350 The Hellenic and Syriac Societies exercised a reciprocal influence on each other over many centuries, ultimately disintegrating together into a single 'culture-compost'. The main Syriac contribution was its religion. Mystery and salvation cults answered a spiritual need left unsatisfied by Hellenic religion. A fresco from Dura Europos, above, shows the worship of Palmyrene gods, whose cult had reached Rome by the first century AD. The Phoenician Baal, opposite, was their forerunner and prototype, while Phoenician sculpture in a syncretistic Egypto-Babylonian style had a strong influence on the 'orientalizing' Hellenic art of the seventh century BC. In the opposite direction, infiltration of Hellenism into Syriac culture is illustrated by fifth-century BC Greek and Achaemenian coins; the Athenian coin shows the usual figures of Athena and owl with the inscription *Ath(enaion)*: on the Achaemenian copy beneath, the inscription becomes *Bas(ileos)* (king) while a satrap's head replaces that of the goddess.

century BC, four hundred years before Alexander's campaigns, the Syriac Civilization produced a permanent effect upon the Hellenic by giving it the Phoenician alphabet. In the seventh century it gave it a Phoenician style of art which was itself an amalgam of the Egyptiac and Akkadian styles. In the fourth century it gave it a Phoenician code of ethics and system of cosmology – the Stoic philosophy, whose founder, Zeno, was a citizen of the Cypriot Phoenician city-state Citium. The cultural intercourse between the Syriac and Hellenic Worlds was reciprocal, and Hellenism was radiating into Syria long before the time of Alexander the Great.[1] By the fifth century BC Syria was importing Hellenic pottery and other Hellenic wares and works of art, and was also adopting the Attic standard of coinage. 'By the middle of the fourth century Greek coins were being imitated by the Persian satraps and local rulers of Cilicia, Syria, and Palestine'[2] (including the priest-presidents of the autonomous Jewish state in Judaea). Even at the opposite extremity of the Syriac World from its Phoenician façade facing the Hellenic World, 'the South Arabians then fashioned crude imitations of Attic coins'.[3] The potency of this previous radiation of Hellenic culture into the Syriac World goes far towards explaining the rapidity with which the Syriac World succumbed to Hellenism after Alexander's military conquest of the Achaemenian dominions in South-West Asia and Egypt. The eventual result, however, was the decomposition of Hellenism as well.

The Syriac Civilization did not achieve this posthumous revenge by making a frontal attack on Hellenism. It was, indeed, no longer in a position to mount a counter-offensive, since by this time it was no longer in being. Moreover, a frontal attack on Hellenism by an alien culture would have courted a repulse at any time from the fifth century BC onwards. In the post-Alexandrine Age the alien cultural agencies that eventually brought Hellenism down found that they could not stalk their quarry with any hope of success unless they approached it obliquely, disguised in the reassuring dress of Hellenic thought and art. Stoicism, for example, presented in terms of Hellenic philosophy a *Weltanschauung* that was akin to that of the Prophets of Israel and Judah. But this self-transformation was no mere sly and superficial masquerade; it was a genuine metamorphosis; and the decomposition of Hellenism was achieved by an instrumentality that was, itself, already semi-Hellenic. When the Hellenic Civilization that had decomposed the Syriac Civilization was hoist with its own petard, there was an Hellenic as well as a Syriac ingredient in the lethal charge of gunpowder. The final dissolution of Hellenism was the work of Christianity; and it is significant that, of all the non-Hellenic religions that competed for the conversion of Hellenic souls in the age of the Hellenic universal state, Christianity went the furthest in Hellenizing itself. Besides presenting itself visually in the established forms of Hellenic art, Christianity, like its forerunner Stoicism, expressed itself intellectually in terms of Hellenic philosophy. More than that, its crucial departure from its parent religion, Judaism – namely, the belief that Jesus was the Son of God and was, in fact, one of the three persons in a triune godhead – was, from the standpoint of Jewish monotheism, a shocking concession to two Hellenic religious aberrations: man-worship and polytheism.

351, 352 THE CHRISTIAN SYNTHESIS The higher religion of Christianity grew in the fertile soil created by the 'compost' of Hellenic and Syriac culture, and the influence of each is clearly discernible in Christian thought and art. The Hellenic contribution can be judged by comparing details from two sarcophagi: above, third-century AD sarcophagus of a Greek philosopher, perhaps the Neoplatonist Plotinus. Underneath it, a fifth-century Christian sarcophagus makes explicit reference to the artistic style of the Greek original and the philosophy behind it: Christ teaches his followers in precise imitation of the pose of philosopher and pupils.

It is also significant that Islam, which was a conscious and deliberate reaction against Christianity's Hellenizing departure from Jewish monotheism, did not revert to Judaism's strictly un-Hellenic tradition. When Islam was confronted with the need to equip itself with a systematic theology, the Islamic theologians found, as their Christian predecessors had found, that they needed to draw upon Hellenic philosophy for their theological purpose and that they could not do this effectively without going back to the Hellenic fountain-head. From the ninth century of the Christian Era onwards, the works of the Hellenic philosophers and scientists became part of the recognized, and even obligatory, apparatus of Islamic culture, as they had become part of the apparatus of Christian culture; indeed, it was often through Islamic versions that the works of Hellenic philosophers first came to the notice of the medieval Western Society. Thus it is true to say that Islam and Christianity both have roots in a composite Helleno-Judaic soil.

The compositeness of the soil in which Islam and Christianity both germinated is one key to the explanation of the fission of Judaic religion into three separate and rival sects. Part, at least, of the explanation of this unhappy course of Judaic religious history is to be found in a residual incompatibility between the Syriac and the Hellenic element in the Syro-Hellenic 'culture-compost' that had been compounded in the course of the five centuries ending with the fourth century of the Christian Era. The coalescence of the two elements had been nearly complete but not quite; and the resulting cultural amalgam had been acceptable to nearly but not quite all the peoples in the section of the *Oikoumene* between India and the Atlantic. Thus the psychological harmony produced by this all but completely successful feat of cultural fusion had been subject to strains, and these strains partly account for the subsequent religious schisms.

The Jews and the Iranians (except for the Iranians in the Oxus-Jaxartes basin) could not stomach the Hellenic ingredient in the compost; and they reverted uncompromisingly to their pre-Hellenic ancestral traditions. The population of the South-West Asian Fertile Crescent and Egypt, which had been subjugated politically by the Greeks, and had then been kept subject by the Greeks' Roman heirs in the region to the west of 'Iraq, behaved like the Jews and the Parsees in expressing their anti-Hellenic reaction in religious terms. First the Nestorian Christians and then the Monophysite Christians broke away from the 'Melchite' ('Imperialist') Christian Church of the Graeco-Roman 'Establishment'. The Muslims and their ex-Nestorian and ex-Monophysite converts then broke away from Christianity altogether; but, as has been noted already, even Islam – and *a fortiori* the two anti-Melchite Christian sects – found that they could not dispense with an Hellenic philosophical formulation for their theology; and their inability completely to discard Hellenism debarred Nestorianism, Monophysitism, and Islam from carrying their anti-Hellenic reaction to the length of adopting Judaism, which offered an uncompromisingly anti-Hellenic form of Syriac religion. The ironic result has been that the Jews themselves have been left as a scattered dissenting minority in the vast area – half the Old World and the whole of the Americas – in

THE ISLAMIC SYNTHESIS

353 Islam sprang from the same Syro-Hellenic 'culture-compost' as Christianity, and however forcefully it might try to renounce its Hellenic past, the links remained. Many Greek texts, lost in the West, survived in Islam. This page is from an Arabic translation of Galen, the second-century Greek philosopher and physician.

which the majority of the population has been converted to one or other of the two non-Jewish Judaic religions, Christianity and Islam.

The Syriac and the Hellenic elements are both ineradicable, not only in Christianity and Islam themselves, but also in the Christian and Islamic Civilizations for which they have respectively served as chrysalises. Both these religions have both Syriac and Hellenic antecedents, and in both religions both these elements are of capital importance. Islam, Christianity, and the several civilizations that these two religions have mothered, are all products of an identical compost consisting of both Syriac and Hellenic elements.

The eventual outcome of the post-Alexandrine Hellenic Society's impact on other civilizations has a topical interest for Westerners today; for, in this comparable case of contact between contemporary civilizations, we know the whole story, whereas in our own modern Western case the impact has not yet worked itself out to its conclusion. In the Hellenic case, the encounter began with a military conquest and ended in the religious conversion of the conquerors that brought with it the disintegration of the conquerors' ancestral civilization. The significant point, in this case, is that the original offensive and the counter-offensive that was eventually victorious were launched on different planes. The offensive had been military; the ultimate counter-offensive was religious.

It has also to be noted that a counter-offensive on the religious plane against the Hellenic military conquerors was not the conquered societies' first resort. Their first reaction was to reply to military force in kind. Within less than two centuries after Alexander's destruction of the Achaemenian Empire, Greek rule had been liquidated in Iran and 'Iraq; but the effect of this military counter-offensive was incomplete, and this in two respects. It did not put an end to Hellenic rule either in the Levant to the west of the river Euphrates or in the Oxus-Jaxartes basin. Both the Oxus-Jaxartes 'roundabout' and the Syrian 'roundabout' remained under Greek rule; and the political successors of the Greek heirs of the Achaemenidae paid for ousting the Greeks politically by succumbing to the Hellenic culture. This is notorious in the case of the Romans, who maintained the Hellenic régime to the west of the Euphrates until the seventh century of the Christian Era. The Eurasian Nomad Parni, who created a 'Parthian' Empire in Iran and 'Iraq at the Seleucid Greek monarchy's expense, were likewise Hellenized to some extent.

As for the Oxus-Jaxartes basin, this remained under Greek rule after the establishment of the Parthian state had insulated the Bactrian Greeks from the main body of the Hellenic World; and, early in the second century BC, Bactrian Greek conquerors crossed the Hindu Kush and imposed Greek rule on a larger part of India, for a longer time, than Alexander himself had managed to do in his brief foray into the Indus basin. Under the rule of the Bactrian Greeks and their ex-Eurasian Nomad Kushan successors, the nothern branch of Buddhism, the Mahayana, sprouted from an Indo-Greek 'culture-compost', and then Hellenic art travelled north-eastwards, in the service of the Mahayana, to Eastern Asia, while south-eastwards it became one of the stimuli of Indian art of the Gupta Age.

Thus, under Kushan, Arsacid Parnian, and Roman rule, Hellenism pervaded the *Oikoumene* from India to the Atlantic coasts of Africa and Europe in the second century of the Christian Era; and manifestly the modern Western Civilization is in a comparable political and cultural situation today. The non-Western majority of Mankind has now passed out of its brief but revolutionary spell of subjection to Western colonial rule; but the Western Civilization is continuing to gain ground beyond the Western Society's own bounds. Is the story of the world's encounter with the West going to follow, in the future, a parallel course to the world's encounter with post-Alexandrine Hellenism? Will a new 'culture-compost' breed new religions, to be followed by the rise of new civilizations? Today we can only put these questions. The answers still lie hidden below our horizon, but already we can see that, on the technological plane, the two situations differ; and this difference may lead to a different dénouement in the contemporary case. At all events, we have seen[4] that Mankind's choice is effectively limited to 'one world or none';[5] and we can guess that, in a world united in the future by voluntary agreement, the Western Society must abate the energy of its cultural aggression, both because of the destructive tendencies of some Western attitudes and objectives, and because of the rival claims of other cultural value systems.

354 AN HELLENO-INDIC SYNTHESIS Gandhara, in Central Asia, was for a brief period the meeting-place of the Hellenic and Indic Societies; its sculpture rings with echoes of this Hellenic encounter, exemplified in this head of a Brahman ascetic, from the third or fourth century AD.

48 The social consequences of encounters between contemporary civilizations

As WE HAVE SEEN very clearly in the previous chapter, the social price that a successfully aggressive civilization has to pay is a seepage of its alien victims' exotic culture into the lifestream of its own internal proletariat, and a proportionate widening of the moral gulf that already yawns between this alienated proletariat and a would-be dominant minority.

The effects of a successful assault on the body social of the assaulted party are more complex, without being less pernicious, than the corresponding effects on the aggressor society. The two principal effects are succinctly expressed in the proverbs 'One man's meat is another man's poison', and 'One thing leads to another.' In other words, elements of a culture which have been harmless or beneficial in their native environment are apt to turn dangerous and destructive when absorbed as isolated intruders into an alien social context; and, on the other hand, these pioneer elements of a culture tend, once they have succeeded in establishing themselves in their new environment, to draw in after them the other elements of the original home culture.

The operation of the first of these processes is familiar to us by analogy in the field of the physical and natural sciences. The fate of Hiroshima and Nagasaki has demonstrated that a hitherto innocuous substance may become lethally explosive if an atom's Sun-like nucleus is stripped of the electrons that are its planet-like satellites; and the explanation of this is obvious. The latent physical energy, of a deadly potency, that is released through the splitting of an atom, was kept in store in the intact structure of an integral atom through being neutralized there by an equilibrium of forces that expressed, in terms of dynamics, the atom's structural pattern. It will be seen that, in the atom, the destructive potentialities of the constituents were kept in check by an inanimate equivalent of the sociality which is the working constitution of physical as well as social life. This relation of interdependence and consequent reciprocal obligation between cells composing a living body and the organism constituted by these components is indeed the elixir of life – as is demonstrated by the deadliness of the cancer by which a living organism is afflicted whenever any of its cells seek to live just for and by themselves without regard to the social reciprocity which is the necessary condition of survival for body and cells alike.

It is evident that the disruptive effects produced by unimpeded activity on the part of one particle or cell torn from its natural context is due to the inability of the whole organism to accommodate itself to a new dynamic force. The pertinence of these physical analogies to the sphere of social life becomes clear when we think of our earlier investigations into the nature of harmony and disharmony in the careers of civilizations.[1] The challenge presented by the introduction of a new force into the domestic life of a society cannot be ignored with impunity. In the new situation that the new event has produced, social health can be preserved only through the adjustment of the old pattern to accommodate the new element; and this adjustment is tantamount to a replacement of the old pattern by a new one, or, in other words, to a thorough-going reconstruction of this particular social universe. The penalty for ignoring the necessity of making this new adjustment, or for seeking to evade it, is either a revolution, in which the new-born dynamic force shatters a traditional culture-pattern that has proved too rigid to adapt to it, or else an enormity engendered by the introduction of the new force's driving-power into the structure of an obstinate culture-pattern whose fabric has proved tough enough to withstand the new force's unprecedentedly powerful pressure. The encounter between a new culture-element and an old culture-pattern is always governed by the same set of circumstances, whether the new element happens to emerge from within or to impinge from outside. In both these variations on a situation which is ultimately the same in both cases, the introduction of the new element condemns the old pattern, *ipso facto*, to undergo a change in either its structure or its working. Unless this inexorable summons of new life is effectively met by an evolutionary adjustment of the culture-pattern's structure, the visitant, which in another context is either harmless or even creative, will actually deal deadly destruction.

In the present place we are concerned with the situation in which the new dynamic force is an alien intruder, uprooted from its native soil, divorced from its former associates, and driven into exile in a strange and hostile land. The isolated vagrant culture-element plays havoc in the foreign body where it lodges because the diffraction that has sundered it from its native setting has, at one stroke, deprived it of its previous *raison d'être* and released it from the discipline of its previous counterweights and antidotes.

We can illustrate this by looking at the effect on the African World of the introduction of a Western cultural institution, democratic government, which has had an honourable history in its native cultural context. Traditionally, the key institution of African government has been monarchy, a system which imposes a sharp distinction between ruler and ruled. Among African communities where no such hierarchical political system exists, authority is liable to be diffused throughout society as a whole, without being located in identifiable specialist agencies. In the modern Western Civilization, by contrast, democracy has become the standard stable institution of government: in theory it blurs the distinction between ruler and ruled, and this is confirmed on a few rigidly defined occasions; but at the same time the exercise of practical authority is confined to a few groups of specialists – legislators, judges, policemen, and the like. Western democracy and African kingship are thus two political systems with very little in common; and, when we add to this the fact that modern African states, being defined by frontiers drawn without reference to traditional tribal or national units, lack the cohesive sense of corporate identity which is a practical precondition for the reasonable functioning of democracy, we can see that the likelihood of this exotic transplant striking firm root in its alien environment would be quite small.

In the eyes of Western democrats, there is clearly a crisis of political articulation in liberated Africa today, and one tendency is to ascribe this to a failure of one kind or another on the part of the colonial Powers which were supposed to have introduced 'civilized' government to Africa.

Between the wars the argument most often heard was that the political systems existing before colonial rule were 'natural growths', to be fostered rather than destroyed for the sake of something deemed to be more appropriate to the contemporary world. Now we are told that the recognition of traditional authority was a mistake from the first, that it supported the influences which are most opposed to necessary changes, and that it entrenched the sentiments of 'tribal' separatism which are proving so disruptive in some of the new African states.[2]

It is debatable whether the argument can be pitched in terms of what the colonial Powers thought best for their possessions, since they were perhaps not primarily interested in fitting them for independence; but in any case,

the truth is that there is no one course which would have been the correct one all through the history of colonial rule in Africa. The ideal would have been a flexibility such as is hardly possible for any large-scale organization. The explanation is really rather a simple one, though it does not provide a simple guide to action. When Africa was independent, traditional rulers commanded the respect of all their people, and to have set them aside would have created bitter resentment in the grandfathers of those who today condemn the policy of recognizing them. But under the new influences that colonial government brought with it, some Africans began to make the same criticisms of the traditional way of life that their European rulers made, and to temper their respect for the traditional rulers with criticism. If colonial governments had had superhuman wisdom, they would at exactly the right moment have given their backing to these forward-looking members of the populations under their authority. But could any ordinary human being have judged that moment aright?[3]

In other words, there might have been a point at which the disruptive effects of the introduction of an alien novelty could have been minimized by a careful control of the circumstances. But this did not occur. The transfer of power from colonial to independent régimes was performed in a somewhat peremptory fashion, and a form of government extracted wholly from a Western experience was left to function as well or as badly as it might.

Thus we can identify three key elements in the political configuration of contemporary Africa: a decayed indigenous tradition; a colonial interregnum which created problems of identity for artificially constructed political units; and an exotic importation of Western culture. The difficulty of incorporating this foreign importation into the indigenous culture is illustrated, for example, by the issue of corruption in public life – the procurement by those in power of status and posts for fellow-kinsmen, which is (in theory at least) anathema to the Western democrat, but normal and even laudable in an African context.[4] Again, the unfamiliarity of a political structure which includes the alien idea of a 'loyal opposition' has led to the dismantling of multi-party systems in most states soon after independence.[5] In these

circumstances, the construction of a functional system for legitimizing the transfer of political power is clearly a grave problem.

These examples will serve to show the sort of difficulties that can be expected to arise when an isolated culture-element is lodged in an alien environment; and the alternative results of revolution or enormity are only too apparent in the African World. There is a pointless and potentially damaging gap between a superficial ideal of democratic government and an actuality which is often far from democratic. It is pointless, because this Western culture-element becomes meaningless when it is dissociated from its native cultural context, and therefore value-judgments are inappropriate outside this context; and it is damaging, because such judgments are made, with the effect of evoking uncertainty and uncontrollable conflict internally, and condemnation or ridicule externally.

The second stage in the process of an encounter between two contemporary civilizations is the tendency of an integral culture-pattern that has established itself in the assailant society to reassert itself in the receptor society through the reassemblage and reintegration of the constituent culture-elements that have become divorced from one another in the process of transmission. This nisus towards reintegration has to contend with the opposing tendency of an assaulted society to resist the penetration of alien culture-elements and to admit them, if it must, only in the smallest possible quantities and at the slowest possible rate. Accordingly, when some single intrusive alien element has succeeded in opening a way for its old associates, the tension betweeen the pioneer trespasser's constant pull and the invaded body social's no less constant resistance constrains the associated culture-elements to make their entry one by one, in isolation from their pristine cultural context. The assaulted body social's resistance to the painful and disruptive intrusion of an alien culture can be taken as a matter of course; but its ultimate defeat is almost equally inevitable. The stimulus towards the recombination of the diffracted elements is irresistible, because integration, and not disaggregation, is the natural and normal state for a set of culture-elements. This impulse to return to normality is the explanation of the successful entry of all the other elements of a culture after the first pioneer, and for their subsequent reintegration once they are inside the receptor society. The assaulted society succumbs to *force majeure*; the most it can hope to achieve is to delay this process of entry and reintegration; and in fact even this delaying tactic usually serves only to draw out the agony of the encounter, without being able to put an end to it.

The future course of events is thus foreshadowed in the first intrusion; and assaulted societies are not always blind to the consequences that are likely to follow from allowing even the most trivial and innocuous of alien culture-elements to make an entry. We have already taken note of the Zealotist reaction to an external cultural invasion in a Russian context;[6] it is an uncompromising policy of deliberate self-insulation that has often been attempted but seldom with success. While a Zealot's characteristic ethos is, as we shall see,[7] emotional and intuitive, there have also been Zealots whose isolationist stance derives from their empirical discovery of the truth that cultural intercourse is governed by the social law that 'one thing leads to another'. A classic case of this rationalist variety of Zealotism is the severance of relations between Japan and the Western World that was gradually carried through, after careful investigation and deliberation, by Hideyoshi and his Tokugawan successors in the course of the fifty-one years ending in AD 1638. An equally deliberate adoption of the Zealotist policy in modern China culminated in the Great Cultural Revolution which began in AD 1966.

In the name of Marxism and Leninism the [Red] Guards have denounced Balzac and Hugo, and Shakespeare and Beethoven, as the products of a rotting bourgeois culture; they have defaced Pushkin's monument in Shanghai, and have vented their contempt for the works of Chernyshevsky and Herzen, the progenitors of the Russian revolutionary movement of the nineteenth century. . . . We have been presented with long lists of streets and boulevards, the names of which have been changed from 'Eternal Peace' to 'The East is Red', from 'Well of the Prince's Palace' to 'Prevent Revisionism', from 'Glorious Square' to 'Support Vietnam', from 'Eastern Peace Market' to 'East Wind Market', and so on. We are asked to rejoice . . . that certain culinary establishments are no longer called 'Collection of All Virtues', but 'Peking Roast Duck Restaurants'. Hosts of hairdressers and dressmakers have pledged themselves to produce no more outlandish haircuts, such as 'duck tail' and 'spiralling' hairdoes, or cowboy jeans and tight fitting shirts and blouses and various kinds of Hongkong-style skirts. 'We should not regard these matters lightly', the Chinese Agency says gravely, 'because it is here that the gates to capitalist restoration are wide open.' . . .

Like Russia in the last years of the Stalin era, so China has now plunged headlong into a self-centred isolationism and nationalism and has shut herself off more hermetically than ever from the outside world and from all its political and cultural influences.[8]

Here a nationalist rejection of non-Chinese styles and attitudes is intermingled with a political commitment to a Communist as against a bourgeois culture. Communism itself is a Western import, and, for the Chinese makers of the Great Cultural Revolution, this is an unexpurgated incongruity; but the recognition that 'one thing leads to another' is none the less the guiding light of the policy.

The truth is that an intrusive alien culture-element cannot easily be purged of its dangerous capacity for attracting to itself the other elements with which it was associated in its original cultural pattern. Once one of these elements has been allowed to gain a foothold within a society, it can only be demagnetized if the recipient can metabolize and assimilate it so that it can be absorbed into his native culture as an enrichment and not a dissolvent of the prevailing harmony. If the assaulted party proves unable to neutralize the unwelcome visitant in this way, then his only hope of social survival lies in making a psychological *volte-face*. He may still be able to save himself by abandoning the Zealot attitude of tooth-and-nail opposition to an irresistible invader's inexorable advance and adopting instead the Herodian's opposite tactic of fighting a superior adversary with his own weapons as a prelude to winning his goodwill by welcoming him with open arms.[9] The practical value of this policy is illustrated in two successive stages of the encounter between the 'Osmanlis and the modern West. Sultan 'Abd-al-Hamid's grudging policy of Westernization at a minimum was never practical politics when once the

355 PLANNED WESTERNIZATION Mustafa Kemal Atatürk, seen here teaching the Roman alphabet that he substituted for the Turkish language's traditional Arabic script, gave Turkey a promising start in her attempt to come to terms with the West. Instead of trying to solve 'the Western Question' for the entire Islamic World in the tradition of the Ottoman Caliphate, Atatürk deliberately restricted himself to the limited but practicable aim of creating a modern Turkish state, fully prepared for the task of holding its own in a Westernizing world.

356 Mehmet 'Ali discusses the route of a planned desert road with English and French engineers in 1839.

invading Western culture had forced its way through the Porte and entrenched itself in the Ottoman imperial government's war department, whereas Mustafa Kemal Atatürk's whole-hearted policy of Westernization to a maximum offered the 'Osmanlis a just practicable way of salvation even when adopted as a last resort at the eleventh hour.

'Abd-al-Hamid's policy of modernizing his military machine was based on the delusion that he could confine the Western education of military and naval officers to a professionally indispensable minimum of technical instruction, and prevent their imbibing any other Western ideas. The Ottoman state was indeed in a dilemma from which it could not escape. If it was to insure itself against a danger of being conquered by militarily efficient neighbours, it must win military efficiency for itself by providing itself with fighting forces on the modern Western pattern; but it could not do this without exposing itself to the alternative danger of being destroyed, not by foreign conquest, but by domestic revolution, through the reception of subversive Western political ideas by the professionally Western-trained military officers on whose technical proficiency the military quality of the autocracy's fighting forces depended.

The Sultan's delusion was overtaken and confuted in AD 1908 when the political revolution which cost him his throne was led by junior officers who had acquired their 'dangerous thoughts' at this unenlightened Ottoman despot's sterilized military academy. 'Abd-al-Hamid's dilemma accounted for the emergence of a characteristic figure – the liberal revolutionary military officer – who was a natural phenomenon in the social no-man's-land between two conflicting cultures, though in Western eyes the conjuncture of 'liberal' and 'military' appeared paradoxical. The same figure existed in pre-revolutionary Russia; and his descendants are to be seen in the present-day military leaders of revolutionary *coups* in, for example, Africa or the Middle East, where an underlying current of conflict between the realities of a local culture and ideals imported from the West has frequently been brought to a head by Western-trained officers. By contrast with 'Abd-al-Hamid, Kemal's campaign of Westernization in Turkey extended to all departments of social life; and, shattering though the experience of the secularization of a traditional Islamic society was, Kemal's policy reached its limited and practicable aim of creating and maintaining an independent Turkish national state after the First World War.

426

The contagious effects of allowing an alien virus to invade one department of social life are illustrated in an earlier chapter of the encounter between the West and the Ottoman Empire. Early in the nineteenth century in Egypt Mehmet 'Ali set himself the limited objective of Westernizing his fighting forces in order to be able to hold his own in a Westernizing world; yet the sequel to this demonstrated that a new departure in the military field could not be completed successfully unless it were supported by a series of further innovations in the other departments of social life.

At an early period of his military career, Mahomet Ali saw enough to convince him of the superiority of European tactics over those of the East; for he was himself engaged against the French Army in Egypt, and conceived a high opinion of the value of martial science. But the introduction of Western organisation into the armies of the Levant brought with it other important results; for the appliances of mechanical art, of education, of medical knowledge, and a general system of dependence and subordination, were the needful companions of the new state of things. The transfer of the military power from unruly and undisciplined hordes to a body of troops regularly trained through the various grades of obedience and discipline was in itself the establishment of a principle of order which spread over the whole surface of Society.[10]

Thus in Mehmet 'Ali's Egypt, as in Peter the Great's Russia, the pursuit of an originally limited objective led to a far-reaching and ambitious Herodian educational programme. In order to secure an intake of military and naval cadets equipped with a general cultivation in the Western style as a background for their technical training in the Western art of war, Mehmet 'Ali realized that he must create a reservoir of boys endowed with a preparatory education on these non-technical Western lines. At the same time he also realized that, however effective an education he might manage to provide in his cadet schools and in the civilian preparatory schools leading up to them, these new institutions by themselves would not succeed in producing and maintaining that fighting force of a Western pattern and standard that was the practical objective of his educational endeavours. Such a fighting force required auxiliary services which in turn required a special technically trained personnel; this expensively elaborate establishment could not be kept up without an expansion of the public revenue; the revenue could not be expanded without a rise in the taxable income of the community; production could not be increased without technical improvements in agriculture and industry; none of these requirements could be met without providing a further personnel of Western-educated civil servants and economic experts; and the requisite intake of civilian cadets could only be secured by providing a general preparatory education on the same model as that utilized for the education of military cadets.

The Westernization of education, then, followed naturally from the originally limited policy of military reform. The infantry, cavalry, and artillery schools under Western commandants were supplemented by engineering and naval schools, and were reinforced by the establishment of a mathematical and drawing school and a cannon-foundry. This technical training of personnel for the fighting forces and their auxiliary services was underpinned by the introduction of a system of general education on a French model in Egypt, and was additionally improved by

PIECEMEAL WESTERNIZATION

The nineteenth-century Egyptian ruler Mehmet 'Ali's primary aim was Westernization in the military sphere and the creation of a modern fighting force, but he found this limited objective unattainable without a simultaneous modernization in numerous related fields, from education to medicine. His successors were unable to keep control over this haphazard process.

357 Cairo street in Mehmet 'Ali's day: the medieval background to his policy of modernization.

358 Traditional school in Cairo in the mid-nineteenth century. One of Mehmet 'Ali's major contributions to the development of modern Egypt was the replacement of this type of schooling with an education system on the Western model, required initially for training personnel for his army's ancillary services.

arrangements for enabling an élite of the students to pursue courses of Western study in Europe itself.

The first school was established in Cairo as early as AD 1812, and four years later Mehmet 'Ali himself opened a school of engineering in his own palace with eighty Egyptian students and with Western instructors and instruments. In 1833 a polytechnic was founded, as a preparatory school for the military cadet colleges, with two French, two Armenian, and two Muslim instructors; primary schools were established in Cairo and Alexandria to feed the polytechnic, and several local schools were also established in each provincial department. The year 1836 saw the inauguration of a French-inspired Council of Education administering fifty elementary and secondary schools distributed over the country. The pupils of these schools were recruited by conscription and the secondary schools were organized on military lines, with the schoolboy-conscripts drawing pay and rations from the government. According to a return made in 1839, a total of 1215 students was receiving instruction in the non-military special schools – in languages, medicine, agriculture, bookkeeping, and the like. This systematic network of special and general educational establishments on Western lines

was eventually completed in 1867; side by side with the development of the educational system within Egypt itself, Mehmet 'Ali and his successors maintained from 1826 until about 1870 an Egyptian Scientific Mission in Paris, to which an annual contingent of students was sent to complete their studies. The extent and the limits of this progressive broadening of a Westernizing educational system that had been introduced originally for the particular technical purpose of creating a modern army go far to explain both the subsequent rise of a nationalist movement among the Egyptian intelligentsia, and the failure of this movement at its first outbreak; for, in the very act of acquiring its Western notions and culture, the intelligentsia had become culturally alienated from the illiterate masses of the peasantry, and was thus unable to enlist their support.[11]

Another illustration from the same field shows very forcefully the strength and speed with which a traditional social pattern may be disintegrated, once its outer defences have been breached. In 1825 a French medical officer, Dr A. B. Clot, arrived in Egypt to organize a medical service for the Egyptian Army, and managed eventually to secure the adoption by it of the French Army's health regulations and other improvements in the military medical system.

The great achievement of his career, however, was his success in extending his medical attentions beyond the barracks and into the vast field of Egyptian civil life. Against a violent opposition – inspired by a general spirit of Islamic conservatism and a particular Islamic prejudice against the practical study of anatomy by dissection – Clot succeeded in persuading Mehmet 'Ali to found a medical school in 1827, together with a midwifery school, a maternity hospital, a pharmaceutical school, a preparatory school, and a school for learning French (the language of medical instruction). Eventually Clot was also able to convert the former exclusively military hospital into a civilian hospital, and to expand vastly the number of beds available for both military and civilian cases. The establishment of this hospital system, including a maternity hospital, helped to break down within less than fifty years one of the strongest of all traditional Islamic tabus. The medical examination and treatment of Muslim women had previously been forbidden except under conditions which would not offend against an inexorable sense of propriety, with the result that any effective medical attention had been impossible. Clot's success in destroying this tabu was thus nothing short of revolutionary.

The current progress of Westernization in the 'Third World' nations seems at first sight to be the latest confirmation of our proposition that 'one thing leads to another' in cultural encounters. Initially, Westernization in underdeveloped countries has meant industrialization – the adoption of Western technology for economic development – and it has been pointed out that an underdeveloped nation cannot 'simply import the industrial revolution from abroad, uncrate it like a piece of machinery, and set it in motion'.[12] On the contrary, 'it must be emphasised that the process of industrialisation is a total process. . . . To make the break into the process of industrialisation . . . requires some special transformation in the total situation.'[13] In adopting the Western industrial system, the nations of South America, Africa, and Asia have found themselves constrained to acquiesce in a degree of Westernization in almost every department of their social and indeed their individual lives. Western standards of public health, of education, and of urban organization, for instance, are imported and implanted in these widely diverse societies in order to supply the system with a healthy, trained, and available working force. The structures as well as the standards of political administration and public life come to be measured against Western models; and each nation has to find and hold a place in the worldwide nexus of economic and political relationships.

To a great extent, then, the underdeveloped nations of the non-Western world are being carried along on a wave of Westernization following their adoption of Western standards in the sphere of economic production. Yet their relation with the Western World is, in some cases at least, by no means as clear cut as this might suggest.

In the colonial era the Western Civilization was a relatively concrete and composite whole, and the aggression by which it certified its cultural superiority was carried out successfully by means of the West's technological precocity. Western culture might be welcomed as enlightenment by the Western-educated élite of the invaded societies; or it might be anathematized by the Zealotist intransigents who hoped for a resurgence of native culture; but in either case the Western Civilization could be seen as a stable and definable entity. In the present-day world, however, the Western Civilization no longer presents this integral image. The values and the objectives of the West's technological culture are no longer secure; even the originally Western salvationist doctrine of Marxism has now been filtered and mediated through non-Western societies; and thus there are signs of an alternative, non-Western starting-point for dealing with problems of social and moral equity which the West itself has conjured up but cannot answer.

The present encounter between the Western Civilization and the non-Western societies represented in the Third World is thus taking place in a radically different context from that in which the earlier encounters between the West and Russia or Japan or China ran their course. The experience of imperialism has left the ex-colonies with equivocal attitudes towards the society from whose political control they have escaped but whose cultural values still seem to dominate the world. But the technology which was once the key to this Western dominance now seems to have turned against itself, and to be exacting penalties where once it gave rewards. Social injustice, spiritual suffering, and the wastage of Man's natural patrimony have been the unexpected harvest of a century of unbridled industrial expansion in the Western World; and it seems that a growing number of erstwhile converts to the Western industrial creed have begun to doubt the advisability of paying a similarly grievous price for a belated and also probably exiguous share in the West's material wealth. In Tanzania, for instance, the struggle for capital accumulation and industrialization has been demoted to second place, to make way for concentration on policies of agricultural reorganization based on peasant co-operatives. The implications of this movement are very significant, for it suggests that a goal of economic development which was originally adopted by analogy with the West may now be sought by means different from those used in the West itself.

Of course, it is still largely true that the modernization of any aspect of the life of these societies will entail corresponding changes in the total structure. The modernization of agricultural production is, after all, unthinkable without at least some use of machinery and artificial fertilizers; these must be manufactured or purchased from abroad, and thus the problems of industrialism cannot be entirely avoided. Similarly, the considerations which lead an industrializing nation to embark on educational and health programmes will still be operative. Yet the difference of emphasis does mark a genuine difference of spirit, for it represents an actual as well as a symbolic relegation of technology to second place, which is where it ought to belong in the scale of cultural values. If this interpretation is correct, then the way may lie open for a selective adoption of some elements of Western culture, and the rejection of others, by non-Western societies. A deliberate discrimination of this kind between the positive and the destructive or alien values of the Western Civilization would mark a turning-point in the history of Man's efforts to control his collective destiny.

359 CLASSIFICATION: aggressive civilizations label the alien societies they encounter as inferior; but in the area of religion at least this inferiority can be overcome by conversion. To the Western *conquistadores*, the culture of the New World was acceptable if it could be Christianized. An eighteenth-century painting from Peru shows the Virgin Mary as an Inca princess, the curl on her forehead being a traditional Inca fertility symbol.

WHEN TWO or more civilizations encounter each other, they are likely, at the start, to differ in the respective degrees of their potency. Human nature is tempted to exploit an advantage, and therefore a civilization that is more potent than its neighbours is likely to make an aggressive use of its ascendancy, so long as this ascendancy lasts.

The representatives of an aggressive civilization that has successfully penetrated an alien body social are prone to succumb to the *hybris* of the Pharisee who thanks God that he is not as other men are.[1] The nemesis attending this particular vein of *hybris* is ironical. The truth that the self-designated 'top-dog' unconsciously reaffirms in treating his fellow humans as 'under-dogs' is that all souls are equal in virtue of being equally human, and it is impossible for a human being to commit the sin of denying the humanity of others without incurring in the act the penalty of de-humanizing himself. There are, however, different degrees in this inhumanity.

The least inhuman form of inhumanity tends to be shown by representatives of an aggressive civilization in whose culture religion is, and is felt and recognized to be, the governing and orienting element. In a society which has not secularized its life, the denial of the under-dog's humanity will take the form of an assertion of his religious nullity. A dominant Christendom will stigmatize him as an unbaptized heathen; a dominant Islamic Society, as an uncircumcized unbeliever. This is certainly a form of *hybris*; yet, in recognizing that the under-dog too has a religion of a kind, albeit one that is erroneous and perverse, the top-dog is implicitly admitting that the under-dog is, after all, a human soul; and this means that the gulf fixed is not a permanently impassable one when the distinction between sheep and goats has been drawn in terms of religious practice and belief. The ugly line dividing the human family into a superior and an inferior fraction could be obliterated eventually through the progressive conversion of everyone who has been living in so-called 'error' to the dominant religion in question; and, according to the tenets of most of the higher religions, this is not just a theoretical possibility but a practical goal which the true believer must do his utmost to help his church to attain.

We have already remarked[2] that this potential universality of the Christian Church was symbolized, in the visual art of medieval Western Christendom, by the convention of portraying one of the Magi as a black. When the Western Society, in the next chapter of its history, came to force its presence on most other living societies by its conquest of the ocean, the same sense of the Catholic Church's universality showed its sincerity in action. The Spanish and Portuguese *conquistadores* proved ready to go to all lengths of social intercourse, including intermarriage, with bona fide converts to Roman Catholicism, without any longer taking account either of a transcended difference of religion or of an abiding difference of language and race. The Muslims likewise had from the outset intermarried with their converts, without regard to differences of race; and Islam had also inherited, from a precept enshrined and consecrated in the text of the Qur'an by the Prophet Muhammad himself, a recognition that there were certain non-Islamic religions which, in spite of their inadequacy by comparison with Islam, were authentic partial revelations of divine truth and goodness. The affinity with Islam that was to be recognized in Judaism and Christianity as two morning stars preceding and heralding an Islamic sunrise was acknowledged in the Islamic ecclesiastical vocabulary by the bestowal on their adherents of the name 'People of the Book' (*Ahl-al-Kitab*). This spiritual recognition carried with it a practical political corollary. The Islamic *Shari'ah* declared that, once any non-Muslims who were 'People of the Book' had submitted to Muslim rule and had agreed to pay the taxes that were a token of their submission, carrying with it a guarantee of their security, they acquired a right to be protected by the Muslim 'ascendancy' without being obliged to renounce their non-Muslim faith. This privilege was probably confined originally to the Jews and Christians and Sabians, but it was tacitly extended, in the event, not only to the Zoroastrians[3] but also even to the polytheistic and idolatrous Hindus; so that in practice the Muslims came to recognize that the adherents of all other higher religions had a moral claim to be tolerated by the followers of Islam on the implicit ground that they too, in their degree, had been recipients of revelation from the One True God.

The positive attitude, manifested in this Islamic concept of 'People of the Book', towards another religion that can be recognized as being spiritually akin to one's own, has its antithesis in a negative attitude manifested in the Christian concepts of 'schismatics' and 'heretics'. From this anti-thetical negative standpoint a heterodox faith's spiritual affinity with orthodoxy is not a merit carrying a title to toleration; the heresy's secession in spite of its affinity is felt to be a perversity calling for extirpation by physical force if moral persuasion fails. Islam as well as Christianity adopted this attitude towards aberrant sects; and death was also the inexorable penalty for apostasy in Islamic communities. Moreover, there was also a reverse side to the Western Christian disregard of all but the religious distinction between peoples. Acceptance of the Christian faith was a passport to social acceptance, but, by the same token, a refusal to embrace Christianity put the recalcitrant beyond the pale. For the heathen in the New World, as on many unpredictable occasions for the Jew in the Old World, the choice was baptism or annihilation – and annihilation not indeed as a punishment for refractoriness, but as, in Christian eyes, the only alternative means of salvation. In medieval Western Christendom, any Jew could save his life in times of murderous anti-Semitic militancy by agreeing to baptism,[4] though thousands chose to pay the final penalty rather than apostatize from their faith. The choice was certainly an inhuman one, since it offered only the alternatives of profound spiritual suffering or profound physical suffering. Yet if we look at the other forms of inhumanity practised by the top-dogs, the religious form will come to seem relatively humane by comparison.

360 While Christians rejected all other religions as false and idolatrous, Muslims gave a certain toleration to Judaism and Christianity in recognition of these faiths' historical affinity with their own. The sixteenth-century Mughal Emperor Jahangir refused conversion but respected the Christian religion: these marginal illustrations from the 'Jahangir album' are copies of Christian figures from paintings presented to him by Jesuit missionaries.

361–364 Submission: non-Christians have usually been regarded by the Church as enemies of God to be overcome by force, but if they submit to baptism these inferior idolaters will be accepted as equal members of the community of true believers. Conversion may involve spiritual suffering, but it is an escape from physical penalization. Above, the Church Militant triumphs over the vessels of the faithless, among them heretics, Jews, and magicians (Faustus). Opposite, the Church Evangelical baptizes the heathen: left, the refugee Inca ruler Saire Tupac, who was baptized and made a marquess by his Spanish conquerors; right, Michael Alphonsus Shen Fu-tsung, a seventeenth-century Chinese convert; below, the Maori chief Te Puni undergoing baptism in 1853.

The next worse form of the top-dog's denial of the under-dog's humanity is the assertion of the under-dog's cultural nullity in a society that has secularized its culture. In the history of the cultural aggression of secularized civilizations, this was the connotation of the distinction drawn by members of the Hellenic Society between 'Hellenes' and 'Barbarians', and by members of the Sinic Society between their own cultivated selves and 'the rest'. In the modern world the various national perpetrators of the Western Society's cultural aggression made a similar distinction between 'Civilization' with a capital 'C', and the 'barbarians' or 'savages' whom they encountered in their expansion over the surface of the globe. This attitude led to a political and cultural paternalism in the West's overseas colonial empires, and a denial of the rights of citizenship to the subject peoples, and thus to the erection of a cultural barrier that could not be passed by means of the simple formula which permitted the magical translation of heathen into believer. Nevertheless, the possibility of 'civilizing the savage' was not utterly denied; in the West's colonial empires, the circumstances of the encounter determined that the test of 'civilization' would be a candidate savage's ability to rise to certain standards of literacy and polite behaviour, as defined by his Western masters. The candidate who passed muster on these terms might take his place among the ranks of the civilized, irrespective of the political relationship between his native land and the imperial Power.

This purely cultural distinction has, however, rarely been the sole criterion by which an aggressive modern Western Society has certified its superiority to non-Western Mankind. The savage who wishes to become *salonfähig* in a Westernizing world must in any case conform to a quite arbitrary and external standard of civilization which is in itself a denigration of his own ancestral culture; and, even if he is prepared to undergo this degree of dehumanization in order to enjoy the questionable benefits of honorary membership of an alien society, he will probably find himself defrauded of his prize by the other dehumanizing presumptions of the top-dogs.

Another tendency of imperialist conquerors of foreign lands is to class the indigenous inhabitants as 'natives' – a word now almost devoid of any but the most pejorative associations, though originally its moral content was nil. In stigmatizing the members of an alien society as 'natives' of their homes, the top-dog is denying their humanity by asserting their political and economic nullity. While admitting the indisputable fact that he has found them already in possession at the time of his own appearance on the scene, he is making this admission without conceding that these 'natives'' mere priority of occupation gives them any title, either legal or moral, as against himself (though the same claim to prior occupation will become his own outraged defence if any rival intruder tries to wrest the prize from his grasp). By designating the inhabitants as 'natives' *sans phrase*, he is implicitly assimilating them to the non-human fauna and flora of a virgin 'New World' that has been waiting for its predatory and acquisitive latest human discoverers to enter in and take possession on the basis of a right of 'eminent domain' over a 'Promised Land' deemed to be in the gift of some war goddess of private enterprise.

365 EXPLOITATION: by calling the members of an invaded society 'natives' an aggressive civilization asserts its right to treat them as commercial objects. The African slave trade was the ultimate expression of this pretension. Here, slaves on an ivory tusk from the Congo kingdom of Loango; Portuguese explorers baptized the Congo king in 1491, but their commercial interest in the profits of slavery took precedence over mere religious sentiment, and his people were ruthlessly exploited.

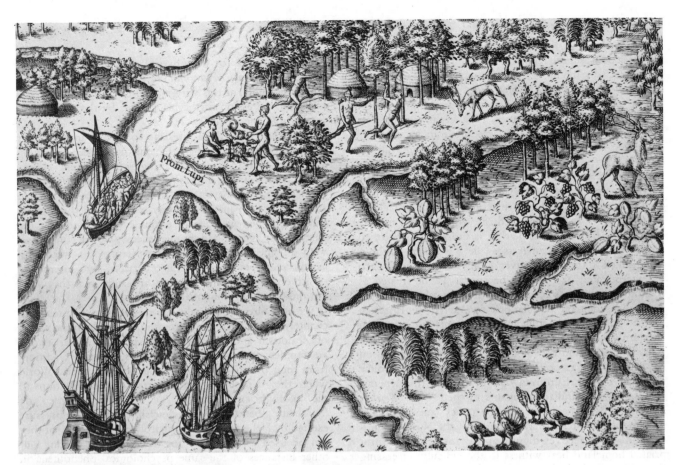

366, 367 EXTERMINATION: 'natives' are easily seen as flora and fauna awaiting efficient domestication for the profit of their discoverers. Above, natives of Florida figure in a sixteenth-century print as equivalents of the fabulous trees. Left, unprofitable or dangerous natives must be exterminated like vermin: a nineteenth-century French colonialist does his bit for civilization.

On these premises the fauna and flora of the wilderness may be regarded by the human pioneer in one or other of two alternative lights. Either he may treat them as vermin and weeds to be extirpated in order to clear the ground for profitable agricultural activities, or alternatively he may treat them as valuable natural resources to be carefully conserved and efficiently exploited. The pioneer's choice of economic policy will be determined partly by his estimate of the value of the natural environment and partly by his own temperament; but, whatever the policy that he may elect to adopt, and whatever the considerations or feelings by which he may be prompted, he will be acting in any event on the assumption that he is morally at liberty to pursue his own best interests as he sees them, without being called to treat the 'natives' as anything but wolves to be exterminated or sheep to be shorn. To be treated as economic chattels has been the fate of many subject peoples, from the sedentary populations conquered by Eurasian Nomad hordes to the indigenous inhabitants of the modern Western Society's several colonial empires in Africa and Asia. The adoption of a policy of physical extermination has been perhaps rarer, though this was certainly the policy practised by the European colonists of North America against the Red Indian occupants of their 'New World'; and, though in the latter case the policy was eventually renounced, the present-day struggles of the North American Indians to recover dignity and status in their expropriated homeland bear witness to the difficulty of erasing the stigma with which the 'native' is stamped.

From the attitude which makes 'natives' out of alien human souls, it is but a short step to asserting the utter and incontrovertible inferiority of the 'natives' by branding them as the spawn of inferior races; and this is the last and the worst form of the stigmata with which the under-dog has been branded by the top-dog. In the first place, it is an assertion of the under-dog's nullity as a human being without any qualification whatsoever. In the second place, this racial dichotomy of Mankind differs from all the religious, cultural, and politico-economic dichotomies alike in fixing a gulf that is wholly and permanently impassable. In the third place, the racial stigma is unique in singling out for its criterion of distinction between one hypothetical kind of human being and another the most superficial, trivial, and insignificant aspect of human nature that could be selected for this inauspicious purpose.

In practice, in the modern world, the cultural, politico-economic, and racial criteria of inferiority have become intertwined, the racial hypothesis having been deduced from the illusion of cultural superiority which the Western Society – and especially its English-speaking representatives – entertained in its encounters with the non-Western civilizations. Racial and cultural arguments reinforce each other with insidious power, for the racialist will be confirmed in his prejudice whether he deduces racial inferiority from the primitiveness of a culture, or whether he sees this primitiveness as an example of an inferiority deriving from the 'plain facts' of racial differentiation. In either case it is clear that a racialist stigma is readily combined with any of the other stigmata of inferiority. The vicious effects of this most heinous of moral crimes scarcely need, unhappily, to be pointed out today: within living memory racialism has been responsible for the physical extermination of many million racial *Untermenschen* in the Western Society, and it is still responsible, at this very moment, for the physical and spiritual oppression of the black races by the white races throughout the world.

The reaction of the aggressive society in an encounter between contemporaries to the spiritual ordeal of finding alien souls at its mercy is thus a single-track *descensus Averni*; the only perceptible diversification of an essentially uniform response's character is produced by the passage to some lower step in the one-way traffic down this sinister stairway. When we turn to examine the response of the party at bay against an inhuman enemy, we are confronted with an apparent contrast. The victim of a successful assault seems to have a choice between two alternative possible reactions which look at first sight as if they were not only different but antithetical.

We have already noticed these reactions in the preceding chapters of this Part, and we have given to them the names of 'Zealotism' and 'Herodianism' respectively. These names are familiar to anyone educated in a Christian tradition, from their original historical context in the Syriac World where they denoted the two contrary Jewish reactions to the onslaught of Hellenism. The example is particularly illuminating because the two Jewish reactions to a pressure exerted by Hellenism were so sharply pronounced that they can be used as indicators for detecting and sorting out other instances of the same psychological phenomena in other passages of the histories of encounters between contemporaries.

In that age, Hellenism was pressing hard upon Jewry on every plane of social activity – not only in economics and politics, but also in art, ethics, and philosophy. No Jew could escape or ignore the problem of the impact of Hellenism, and the question of his response was something by which every Jew was inevitably obsessed. There appeared to be only two alternative ways of meeting this insistent challenge; and this was the issue over which the Zealots and the Herodians parted company to strike out separate paths for themselves in apparently opposite directions.

The Zealot faction was recruited from people whose impulse, in face of attacks delivered by a stronger and more energetic alien civilization, was to take the clearly negative line of trying to fend off the formidable aggressor. The harder Hellenism pressed them, the harder they strove, on their side, to keep themselves clear of Hellenism and all its works; and their method of avoiding contamination was to retreat into the spiritual fastness of their own Jewish heritage, lock themselves up within this mental donjon, close their ranks, maintain an unbroken and unbending front, and find their inspiration, their ideal, and their acid test in the loyalty and sincerity of their observance of all the minutiae of traditional Jewish law. The faith by which the Zealots were animated was a conviction that, if they were so meticulous in abiding by their ancestral tradition and in preserving it utterly intact and unchanged, they would be rewarded by being accorded a divine grace and strength to resist the alien aggression, no matter how overwhelming the aggressors' material superiority over the Zealots might appear to be. The Zealots' posture was that of a tortoise who has withdrawn into his shell, or of a hedgehog who has rolled into a spiny defensive ball – though an Herodian might perhaps be more inclined to describe his rival's attitude as that of an ostrich who has buried his head in the sand.

The anti-Zealot Herodian faction was recruited from the servants, supporters, and admirers of the Idumaean King Herod the Great. His prescription for Jewry's problem of coping with Hellenism was, first, to take the objective measure of this alien social force's irresistibly superior power with a sober eye, and then to learn and borrow from Hellenism every Hellenic accomplishment that might prove useful to the Jews for equipping themselves to live in an inescapably Hellenizing world.

In a Zealot's eyes this Herodianism was a compromise that was dangerous, impious, and cowardly; but the Herodians could argue plausibly on behalf of their policy that it was preferable to the Zealots' impulse in every respect. It was positive instead of being negative, and was therefore free to be active instead of condemning itself to be passive, whereas the Zealot line was hopelessly passive in spirit, however violently active its occasional outbreaks might seem. Moreover, the Herodians could claim that, in following their line, they were showing greater moral courage than the Zealots, since the attitude which the Zealots denounced as Herodian opportunism was in fact the realism of minds strong enough to look the indisputable facts in the face, and to frame a straightforward policy on this basis.

Hellenism, the Herodians would argue, was a hard fact which had successfully intruded itself into Jewry's social universe, and from which there was no possibility of escape. The Zealots' attitude of uncompromising non-recognition of the presence and power of this triumphant alien force was an attitude of moral cowardice entailing an impolicy that courted certain defeat. The one effective way for Jewry to cope with Hellenism was for the Jews to accept the manifest limitations of their own power; to recognize that their social universe could never be the same again since the emergence of Hellenism above the Syriac World's horizon; and to grasp, and act upon, the truth that Hellenism could be fought successfully only by the adoption and exploitation of Hellenic weapons. According to the Herodian exposition of the case, the real choice lay between a voluntary Hellenization of Jewish life to whatever extent might prove in practice to be necessary, and on the other side an irresponsible Zealot impulse to ride for a fall in which Judaism would succumb to Hellenism altogether, with nothing to show for such a purposeless sacrifice.

We cannot listen to the Herodian and Zealot claims without being prompted to ask two questions. How do these melodramatically contradictory attitudes stand to one another in fact? And does either of them prove to be an effective retort to the successful aggression of an alien civilization? We shall be able to answer these questions if we examine the evidence offered by the historic encounters between civilizations, using what we already know from the examples that we have considered in the preceding chapters of this Part.

In the history of the Jews' encounter with Hellenism the phenomenon of Herodianism is discernible more than two hundred years before Herod's seizure of power in 40 BC. According to tradition, the Jewish scriptures were translated from Hebrew and Aramaic into the Greek by the Septuagint at the command of Ptolemy Philadelphus (*regnabat* 283–245 BC), and, even if this tradition is somewhat clouded by legend, the beginnings of the voluntary self-Hellenization of the immigrant Jewish community in Alexandria certainly date back to the infancy of this melting-pot city. In the hill-country of Judaea the High Priest Joshua-Jason was busy as early as the third decade of the second century BC on his work of Hellenizing the dress and manner of life of his younger colleagues in the Jewish ecclesiastical hierarchy. The damning account of this episode in the Second Book of Maccabees[5] is a revealing exhibition of the animus that Herodian policies aroused in Zealot hearts, just as was the Zealotist denunciation of the Septuagint's Greek testament as a sin equal to the worship of the golden calf.

A similar contrast between Zealotism and Herodianism can be observed in a later chapter of the history of the Jewish diasporá, when the modern Western Society embarked upon a policy of emancipation which eventually was to break down all the civil distinctions between Jew and non-Jew. The latter-day Jewish Herodians seized the opportunity that Western liberalism offered, by carrying forward the policy of assimilation into the national communities of the day, which had hitherto been open only to those Jews who were prepared to apostatize from their faith and to undergo the ritual of baptism which certified that they had become members of the Christian Commonwealth (though baptism still remained attractive as the final seal of respectability, and Jews or ex-Jews still had to contend with the unofficial anti-Semitism of their non-Jewish fellow-citizens). The ending of their civil penalization in Western Europe during the eighteenth and nineteenth centuries made it possible for Jews to enter, as Jews, the public and social life of their national communities on an equal footing with Gentiles. The experience of long centuries of bitter discrimination as outcasts acted on Jews as a strong stimulus to attempt the alternative of assimilation, once this became both possible and practicable; and, by the end of the nineteenth century, many assimilationist Jews were able to identify themselves with their Gentile neighbours to the extent that they resented the dangerous intrusion on their new-found solidarity that was represented, in their eyes, by the arrival in emancipated Western Europe of traditionalist immigrant Jews from the unemancipated Jewish communities in Eastern Europe.

By contrast, the Zionist movement's deliberate and enthusiastic recultivation of a distinctively separate Jewish political consciousness stamped them with the authentic hallmark of Zealotism. Yet these Zionist neo-Zealots were anathema to diasporan devotees of the ritualistic Zealot tradition that was still alive in the European ghettoes. In the eyes of the traditionalists, the Zionists were guilty of flagrant impiety in presuming to bring about on their own initiative a physical return of the Jewish people to Palestine which it was God's prerogative to accomplish at His own good time. On the other hand, in the assimilationist Jews' estimation the political ambition of the Zionists to found a Jewish national state in the modern Western style did not atone for a Zealot vein in Zionism which, for the

368 Assimilation: Jewish emancipation in nineteenth-century Western Europe gave Jews their first opportunity to attempt an Herodian policy of assimilation into local culture. Benjamin Disraeli's attitudes epitomized this new departure: for him Christianity was 'completed Judaism', and, though proud of his Jewish origins, he saw baptism and assimilation as the logical course for Jews in a Christian society.

assimilationists, was deplorably retrograde. The assimilationists could not bear the Zionists' relapse into their common ancestors' irrational belief that the Jews were 'a peculiar people'. Thus at the present time the Jewish community in the world is divided among a majority which remains outside Israel (though not in every case by choice), and two factions among the minority within Eretz Israel. The persistent tension in the state of Israel between the diehard meticulous observers of ancestral tradition and the increasingly secular-minded legatees of Zionism testifies to the ambivalence of the Zionist reaction to Jewry's situation. A secularized Zionism may indeed achieve the Herodian objective of assimilation, by means of a corporate transformation of the Jewish community in Israel into the likeness of 'all the nations';[6] though at the root of this there must still lie the special claim of a chosen people to implement its divinely ordained title to the Land of Israel. At all events, the attempted Israeli-Jewish responses to the problem of 'peculiarity' will all of them fail unless the policy of national and religious exclusivity is renounced forthwith.

If we turn back to the cultural context in which the Zealot and Herodian responses originally arose, we can find other examples of the pair in the reactions to Hellenism of other Oriental societies that had shared the Syriac World's experience of military conquest. The outburst of Jewish Zealotism in Judaea in the first half of the second century BC had been anticipated in the last part of the previous century by a Zealot *émeute* in Egypt,[7] while the swift failure of Joshua-Jason's audacious Herodian attempt to Hellenize the Jewish priesthood at Jerusalem was offset in the Egyptiac World by the eventual success of a gradual movement towards converting the metropoleis of the Egyptian nomes into simulacra of Hellenic municipalities. In post-Alexandrine Babylonia a dwindling band of astronomer-priests, who were fighting a losing battle to preserve a more and more esoteric Sumero-Akkadian cultural heritage against the invading Syriac culture's progressive encroachments, were so zealously bent on eluding the contaminating touch of the Syriac aggressor that they leaned over backwards into an Herodian Philhellenism, welcoming their Hellenic conquerors with open arms. In the Indic World, which had been forced into intimate contact with Hellenism by the Bactrian Greek warlord Demetrius's invasion of the Mauryan Empire in about 200–183 BC, we can likewise observe symptoms of the two reactions in the Herodian Philhellenism of Mahayanian Buddhist religious art and in the Zealot attitude of some forms of Hinduism.

This survey of the psychological reactions to encounters with post-Alexandrine Hellenism would be incomplete if it failed to notice one figure in whom both Herodianism and Zealotism were incarnated. Mithridates VI Eupator, the Iranian-descended King of a successor-state of the Achaemenian Empire on the Hittite soil of Pontic Cappadocia, presented an attractively Herodian countenance to the eyes of European as well as Asiatic Hellenes who welcomed him in 88 BC as their deliverer from a barbarous Roman yoke; yet the same war-lord wore the opposite appearance of an anti-Hellenic Zealot to the Cyzicenes who closed their city's gates against him in 74 BC and greeted the Roman general

Lucullus as their saviour from the doom of falling under the alien yoke of an Oriental despot. A similar cultural ambivalence is presented by the figure of Ducetius in the pre-Alexandrine chapter of the same Hellenic story. After having made his name as the unsuccessfully gallant Zealot leader of his Sicel fellow-barbarians in the last round of their losing battle against Hellenic imperialism, Ducetius lived to return to Sicily, from his exile in the heart of the Hellenic World, on the Herodian errand of founding in his homeland a new commonwealth in which Greek colonists and Sicel natives were to fraternize in virtue of the natives' voluntary adoption of the intruders' alien culture.

Our pair of antithetical psychological reactions can also be detected in the histories of the respective encounters of Ottoman Orthodox Christendom and of the Indic World with the aggressive Islamic Civilization. In the main body of Orthodox Christendom under the *Pax Ottomanica*, a majority of the *ra'iyeh* belonging to the *Millet-i-Rum* still clung to an ancestral religion whose ecclesiastical independence they had chosen to preserve at the price of submitting to an alien political régime. However, this Zealotism was partially offset, even on the religious plane, by the Herodianism of a minority who were lured into apostasy from Christianity to Islam by tempting social advantages and dazzling political prizes that were the rich rewards for conversion to the religion of the Ottoman 'ascendancy'. Such political ambition became a far stronger incentive to Herodianism when, in the course of the seventeenth century, new exigencies created by the rising pressure of the Western Christian Powers upon the Ottoman Empire moved the Porte to create new-fangled high offices of state to be held by the Orthodox Christian *ra'iyeh* without their being called upon either to renounce their ancestral faith or to forfeit their personal freedom.[8] Meanwhile, the rank-and-file of the *Millet-i-Rum*, who, short of becoming free Muslims or Ottoman public slaves, did not enter the Ottoman public service even as unconverted freemen, had long since succumbed to Herodianism in much larger numbers in the more trivial, yet still significant, ways of learning to talk their Ottoman masters' language and aping their dress.

The story of the Hindus' psychological reaction to the rule of an Islamic 'ascendancy' in the Indic World runs on much the same lines. While a vast majority of the Hindu *ra'iyeh* of the Timurid Mughal Muslim emperors of India and their Afghan and Turkish Muslim forerunners emulated the Orthodox Christian *ra'iyeh* of the 'Osmanlis in zealously resisting the temptation presented by potent social and political inducements to apostatize, there were local mass-conversions to Islam – particularly among the socially depressed *ci-devant* pagan converts to Hinduism in Eastern Bengal – that would appear to have been on a greater scale than the corresponding mass-conversions to Islam among the Christian subjects of the Ottoman Porte. Moreover, the Brahmans showed the same alacrity as the Phanariots in entering the Muslim Power's public service as unconverted freemen, and the same facility in adopting their Muslim masters' language and dress.

When we come to the encounters with the modern Western Civilization, which have overtaken all the contemporaries of this potently expansive society, we see the

369 Exclusion: Jews in nineteenth-century Samarqand. Eastern Europe and Western Asia offered little chance of assimilation to their Jewish inhabitants; crushed by discrimination and persecution, they developed a defensively Zealotist culture that emphasized their religious and racial singularity.

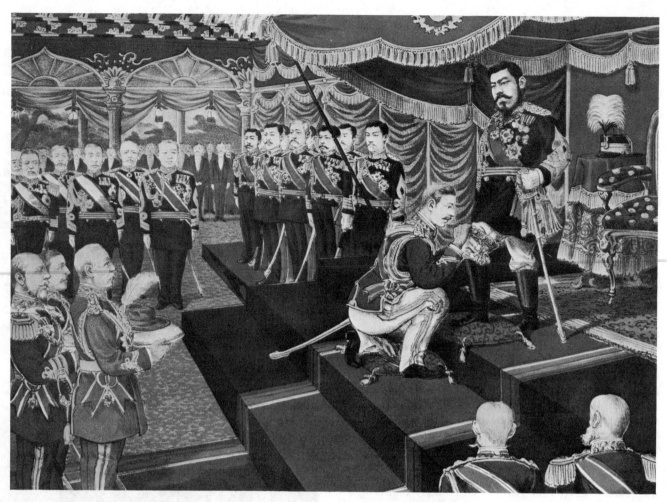

370 The Japanese Meiji Emperor is received into the Order of the Garter after the conclusion of the Anglo-Japanese Alliance in 1906. Japan's entry into the world club of Great Powers had an ambivalent significance: though apparently the climax of a new policy of Herodian relaxation, it still looked back to Japan's Zealotist past, for modernization was a device for preserving an independent destiny for Japan in an inescapably Westernizing world.

offshoot of the Sinic Society in Japan reacting to the impact of the West with vigour along both the two alternative lines. The strength of the Herodian current in Japan was demonstrated impressively by its persistence in adversity. The adoption of the Western weapons, dress, and religion imported by the Portuguese traders and missionaries towards the end of the sixteenth century was little more than the facile expression of a simple curiosity. This was, however, vindicated after the Tokugawa régime had ordered its subjects on pain of death to break off relations with the West and to renounce the imported Western religion; for a remnant of Japanese crypto-Christians remained secretly loyal to their proscribed alien faith for more than two hundred years – as became apparent when the Meiji Restoration of 1868 made it possible for them at last, in the ninth or tenth generation, to come out into the open again.

This second outburst of Herodianism in Japan in the middle decades of the nineteenth century was also, as we have seen, partly the work of other heroes who had risked and lost their lives in a non-religious Herodian cause by secretly studying modern Western science in a Dutch medium, without waiting for the fall of the intolerantly Zealot-minded Tokugawa Shogunate. In this light, the Meiji Restoration in its day looked like the deferred but definitive triumph of an Herodianism which had been the predominant vein in the original Japanese response to the challenge of the West. Yet, in this second bout as in the first, the experience of half a century was to put a Zealot face on the reality behind Herodian first appearances – with the implication that the Tokugawa period, in which Zealotism had been in the ascendant, had after all been something more than an irrelevant interlude in a basically Herodian drama.

The strength of the Zealot current in Japan had been indicated from the outset by the assiduity with which the Japanese had equipped themselves for holding their own against the formidable Western strangers by the ostensibly Herodian feat of learning how to make, as well as use, new-fangled Western firearms. It was moreover significant that, when the Tokugawa government set itself to sever relations between Japan and the West, it cannily refrained from following up its veto on Western commodities and Western religion by renouncing the employment of Western weapons. This statesmanlike disregard for logic was justified by the sequel. The Tokugawa eventually forfeited a political ascendancy founded on military force as a result of their military impotence to prevent Commodore Perry's squadron from entering Yedo Bay in 1853; and this demonstration of Japan's nineteenth-century military inferiority made it clear that, in the course of 215 years of deliberate isolation, the régime had allowed its stationary seventeenth-century Western armaments to be left so far behind by the progress of Western military technique that it was no longer competent to fulfil its self-appointed task of keeping the West at bay. Between 1853 and 1868 a growing public zeal for an effective fulfilment of the Tokugawa's neglected Zealot mission expressed itself not only in insubordination towards the authority of this now discredited régime but in rising xenophobia against the Western intruders who had at last begun to force an entry into Japan.

While the Japanese revolution which liquidated the Tokugawa can be presented as a triumph for Herodianism in the sense that its economic and political programmes were inspired by a Western example and were directed towards Westernization, the same revolution can equally well be presented as a triumph for Zealotism in the sense that the ultimate intent of Japan's self-Westernization was to allow her to hold her own in an irreversibly Westernizing world. The latent Zealotism of the strategy behind the Herodianism of Japan's tactics during the seventy-seven years ending in 1945 was indeed divulged as early as 1882 in the official organization of the State Shinto. In this artificial movement a resuscitated pre-Buddhaic paganism was utilized as a vehicle for the deification of the living Japanese people, community, and state through the symbolism of an archaistic cult of the imperial dynasty, which was reputed to be the divine offspring of the Sun goddess and which offered its hereditary collective divinity for worship here and now in the epiphany of a god perpetually incarnate in the person of the reigning emperor.

It will be seen that, during the last four hundred years, the Japanese psychological reaction to the ordeal of encountering the West has been ambivalent through and through. We have perhaps reviewed enough cases by now to realize that this Japanese example of ambiguity between Zealotism and Herodianism is not unique; and in fact the impression left on our minds by our review of the evidence is confused and bewildering. As often as not, we have seen that these ostensibly antithetical attitudes tend to turn back in on themselves and meet on a middle ground. This Janus-faced ambivalence may, however, give us the clue for interpreting and explaining this at first sight surprising conclusion. Let us see whether we can understand the phenomena of Zealotism and Herodianism more accurately by starting from this common feature, rather than by examining the two currents separately as we have done hitherto.

If we remind ourselves of the nature of the emergency that brings both Zealots and Herodians into action, we shall see that their ambivalent appearance, far from being surprising, is actually quite understandable. Both parties alike are engaged in the same enterprise of counter-attacking an alien enemy in their midst. The common objective of both the Zealot and the Herodian defenders of their common home is to retrieve this perilous situation; and, in

JAPANESE JANUS

371 The historic sun symbol of Japan is given a graphic form derived from Western art on a poster advertising the World Fair of 1970, held in Osaka.

441

so far as they may be taking different lines, these are merely different tactical approaches to an identical strategic objective. Moreover, it is clear that neither warrior can hope to achieve a common practical purpose if he insists on pushing his own tactical theory to the extremity of its logical conclusions. The Herodian who succeeded in making himself utterly like his attacker would achieve only a suicidal self-stultification. Even those Herodian potentates who went furthest in imposing an aggressive civilization's alien culture on their subjects on the technological, economic, social, and intellectual planes usually went to these unwelcome lengths with the object of thereby preserving intact at least the continuity and independence of the commonwealth for whose government they were responsible. Non-violent Herodians whose policy was not dictated to them by any political responsibilities were usually aiming at the preservation of some other element in their own assaulted cultural heritage – for instance, an ancestral religion, or, at a minimum, the bare memory of the submerged society's former existence through the registration of an entry in the records of the victorious aggressor society. Equally, every practical-minded Zealot must make concessions to Herodianism if he is to avoid a similar fate of suicidal self-sacrifice. On this showing, the Zealot and Herodian standpoints look, not so much like two isolated peaks sundered by an unbridgeable gulf, as like the upper and lower ranges of a gamut between which lies an infinite series of gradations. If we are right in concluding that the ostensible contrast between Zealotism and Herodianism masks a family likeness, and that these two psychological reactions to the intrusion of an alien culture are actually two variations on an identical theme, we should expect to find this affinity being reflected in a similarity of effect. In fact, we do find this unmasked resemblance between Zealotism and Herodianism betraying itself in their common failure.

The ineffectiveness of this Zealot-Herodian response to the challenge of a cultural assault is manifest in the historic case that we have taken as our prototype. In Jewry's encounter with post-Alexandrine Hellenism, neither variant of the assaulted society's defensive reaction was able to achieve the common purpose of finding a solution for Jewry's Hellenic problem that would be practicable and at the same time tolerable. Herod the Great and his school of Herodians were unable to persuade or compel their Zealotist compatriots to acquiesce in a political autonomy under Roman hegemony which would have given the Palestinian Jewish community a chance of coming to terms with Hellenism without losing its own communal identity in its ancestral home; and the Zealots succeeded in sabotaging this Herodian policy, only to bring the Palestinian Jewish community to the destruction which the Herodians had foreseen and foretold as being inevitable if the Zealots should once succeed in taking the bit between their teeth. The catastrophes of AD 70 and AD 135 proclaimed the bankruptcy of Herodianism in closing the door on the possibility of a cultural compromise between Judaism and Hellenism, and at the same time exposed the folly of Zealotism by turning the holy city of Jerusalem into the pagan abomination of Aelia Capitolina. After this disaster the Jews had to choose between the two extremes of either abandoning Judaism for gentile Christianity, or else embracing an inward-looking and isolated diasporan Pharisaism.

This inbuilt tendency to fail in both Zealotism and Herodianism can be explained if we take a closer look at the nature of the two attitudes and the context in which they are brought into action. Both are in practice desperately defensive attempts to ignore or forestall a new situation produced by the introduction of a novel dynamic element into the life of a society. In this connexion the impact of newly encountered forces impinging on a society from outside is analogous to the emergence of newly created forces welling up from within; and we have seen[9] that a failure to control the resulting tensions produces either an enormity or a revolution. Zealotism and Herodianism are condemned in advance to irrelevance, since they mistake the superficial features of invasion for the underlying essence of cultural collision. The Zealot freezes – like the archaist[10] – while the Herodian dismantles or disguises the invader's cultural target; yet these camouflaged postures only facilitate the passage of the invader. The responses are thus self-defeating.

This conclusion would present a gloomy prospect for the assaulted party in an encounter if the respective roles of the parties were destined to remain unchanged. However, the dominance of a dominant party saps this party's strength, and thus dominance has a built-in weakness which condemns it to be ephemeral. Conversely, an assaulted party that is apparently retreating is all the time unobtrusively infiltrating into territory behind the assailant's advancing lines. In Hegelian terms, the clash between thesis and antithesis tends to produce a synthesis that is composed of elements derived from each of its two parental opposites, but which, just because of this fruitful diversity of its origins, is a new departure with distinctive features of its own that were not to be found in either of its sources.

In the history of the encounter between the Hellenic and Syriac Civilizations, the synthesis that issued from the clash between Hellenism and Judaism expressed itself mainly in terms of religious doctrines, practices, and institutions. A Syro-Hellenic 'culture-compost' was the seed-bed of Christianity and Islam. The current clash between the West and all the surviving non-Western societies may produce a more varied and perhaps still more fruitful 'culture-compost' after the West's no doubt ephemeral dominance has subsided in its turn. In this present case, it looks as if the synthesis is likely to present itself in an economic and cultural form – though the fundamental form of any human drama usually proves to be spiritual when we analyse the parties' actions in depth.

Today the entire habitable surface of the globe is enmeshed in the net of Western technology – military and civil – and this superficial Western unification of Mankind has implicated a number of different societies with dramatically diverse ways of life. The Western and Westernized, or partially Westernized, communities still amount, all told, to no more than about a quarter of Mankind. Three-quarters of Mankind still consist of Neolithic-Age peasantries with the top-dressing of a largely parasitical 'establishment' by which one of these peasantries after another has been overlaid within the last five thousand years. The polar contrasts are presented by the ultra-industrialized Western countries on the one side and by China on the other.

Both the ultra-Western and the Chinese ways of life are potentially self-destructive. The Western way is explosive; the Chinese way – that is to say, the traditional Chinese way – is petrifying. At the same time, each of these two ways offers something that is indispensable for human welfare. The explosive Western way is dynamic; the petrifying Chinese way is stable. If the present dominance of the West is followed, as seems likely in the light of comparable past sequences of events, by a unifying and blending of cultures, it is conceivable that Western dynamism might mate with Chinese stability in proportions that would produce a new way of life for all Mankind – a way that would not only permit Mankind's survival but would secure its welfare.

Within the last five hundred years, the West has proved its capacity to shake the rest of the world out of its traditional torpor. The West has at last aroused even China, which was the most static of all surviving non-Western civilizations till it was hit by the West's impact. The Sinic Society has surpassed the extinct Egyptiac Society in longevity, and, for 2060 years, ending in the outbreak of the Opium War in AD 1839, the Sinic Society was also as stable as the Egyptiac Society was during the third and second millennia BC. If the Egyptiac Society had lived on to be hit by the West, it too would, we may guess, have been galvanized by the impact, as the Sinic Society has been.

The West can galvanize and disrupt, but it cannot stabilize or unite. The West's history has been as unstable as Chinese and Egyptiac history has been static. The break of continuity between Western history and the antecedent Hellenic Society's history was extreme, as compared with the parallel case of the Orthodox Christian Society. There had also previously been an extreme break of continuity between Hellenic history and the antecedent Aegean Society's, as compared with the parallel case of the Syriac Society's relation to its Aegean, Hittite, Egyptiac, and Akkadian predecessors. By contrast, the Egyptiac Society took shape earlier than the Aegean Society and lasted as long as the Hellenic; and the Sinic Society, which took shape earlier than the Hellenic Society, is still in existence at the present day, notwithstanding the mounting pressure of the West on China during the last four centuries.

When we turn our attention to the Western Society's internal history, we find – as has been noticed already[11] – that it has been politically fractured ever since the fall of the Roman Empire in the West – that is to say, for fifteen centuries, reckoning back from the present day. No other civilization has remained in this politically fractured plight for that length of time, so far as we know. Moreover, the West's political disunity has been aggravated by religious disunity and, since the Industrial Revolution, by a class conflict that has been more violent than the conflict between the peasantry and the 'establishment' in the pre-industrial societies.

We may conclude that the political and spiritual unification of the world is not going to be achieved for Mankind by any Western agency. At the same time, it is clear that, in the long run, and more probably in the short run, the world must be unified politically by some agency or another, since this is, for Mankind, the only alternative to self-destruction now that Western technological virtuosity has produced nuclear weapons, the consumption of irreplaceable natural resources, the pollution of Mankind's non-human natural environment, and the population explosion.

In the enigma of Mankind's future, two points are manifest. Western dynamism has made it impossible for the non-Western majority's traditional pre-industrial way of life to continue unmodified, while Western explosiveness has made the continuation of the modern Western way of life impossible likewise, without some drastic curbing and abatement.

Since the fifteenth-century Portuguese and Spanish conquest of the ocean, and in a still greater degree since the eighteenth-century British Industrial Revolution, the essence of the modern Western way of life has been a constant economic growth and territorial expansion. A few non-Western countries have succeeded in adopting this Western way. Russia, for instance, has both industrialized her metropolitan area and has populated relatively empty outlying areas; Japan has been more successful than Russia in industrialization, but less successful in territorial expansion. However, it is impossible for all the rest of Mankind to follow Russia and Japan in their Westernizing course. The natural resources accessible to Mankind will not suffice for this.

Even if industrialization were to be limited to the Western countries, together with Russia and Japan, economic growth and territorial expansion on an increasing scale and at an accelerating rate – a programme that the so-called 'advanced' countries still take for granted – could be maintained only at the expense of the 'backward' majority of Mankind and of the irreplaceable natural resources that are Mankind's sole material patrimony. However, the Western and Westernized countries are so demonically bent on this disastrous course that it is improbable that any of them will have the vision and the strength of mind to save themselves and the rest of Mankind from this course's inevitably fatal ending. It might be guessed that the West will become increasingly harassed and preoccupied by the domestic, social, and economic problems that it has created for itself. Eventually, on this forecast, the conveyor-belts would cease to revolve because it would become impossible, at any price, to continue to find recruits for manning the assembly lines. If Mankind's life, which the West has unsettled, is to be re-stabilized, and if Western dynamism is to be tempered to a degree at which it will be a vivifying and no longer a destructive force in human affairs, we must seek outside the West for the initiators of this next movement. It is not inconceivable that these will make their appearance in China.

China already contains perhaps as much as one quarter of the total human population of the planet, and her quota is likely to increase. The immense territory that sustains this huge population has been held together politically under a single government since 221 BC, with 'intermediate periods' of disunity and disorder that have been as transient as those that occasionally punctuated the equally long course of the history of the United Kingdom of Pharaonic Egypt. Like the Pharaohs and the Emperors of Sumer and Akkad and the Achaemenidae and the Roman and East Roman Emperors, the Chinese Emperors regarded themselves, and were regarded by their subjects, as being the sole legitimate rulers of a 'Middle Kingdom' that was, itself, the legitimate suzerain of 'All that is under Heaven' (*T'ien Hsia*). This conception of China's destiny, and the practical vindication of this conception in the maintenance of the Chinese Empire's political unity, made a deep imprint in the Chinese people's consciousness through an experience that persisted for the 2060 years from 221 BC to AD 1839. The Chinese people survived the ensuing century of humiliation at Western and Japanese hands, and, in the world of the late twentieth century, the Chinese are still the imperial people *par excellence*. Their historic *Weltanschauung*, which is a reflexion of their historic achievements, designates them for playing the unifying and stabilizing role that will now have to be played by some portion of Mankind if Mankind is to survive into the twenty-first century.

Since the establishment, in 1949, of the Communist régime in the whole of China except Taiwan, the Peking government and the administration at Washington, which have been at loggerheads with each other on all other points, have both been working to prevent the non-Chinese three-quarters of Mankind from knowing what the Chinese quarter was doing. For non-Chinese, the intention and result of Chairman Mao's Great Cultural Revolution are still obscure. To these baffled foreign observers – or, rather, conjecturers – of the Chinese scene, it looks as if the Communist régime has had two negative objectives. On the one hand, the régime seems to be determined not to let China relapse into its traditional political and social configuration. It does not mean to allow the Chinese peasantry to be oppressed, as they have been since the dawn of Chinese history, by a top-heavy 'establishment'. The Communist régime has realized that the peasantry's lot will not be alleviated if Marxism-Leninism is substituted for Confucianism as a justificatory philosophy for a new generation of mandarins. Mao and his colleagues are aware that the mandarinate itself must be abolished, once for all, never to be re-established. Yet, if it is true that the leaders of the Communist régime in China are determined to break irrevocably with the traditional social structure of a pre-industrial peasant civilized society, it seems also to be true that they are determined not to follow the Russians and the Japanese in carrying an industrialization and urbanization of their way of life to Western extremes.

The Chinese appear to be searching for a middle way which would combine the merits, and avoid the defects, of both the traditional pre-industrial way of life and the industrial way by which this has been supplanted recently in the Western and Westernized countries. The traditional way sets a relatively low ceiling on a society's productivity and burdens an indigent peasantry with the incubus of a partly unproductive cultural and political élite. The industrial way does not eliminate the invidious traditional schism of society into a privileged and an exploited class, while it subjects both human nature and Man's non-human natural environment to an increasing strain which, if not relieved, seems bound, sooner or later, to reach breaking-point. If Communist China can succeed in its pioneering enterprise of social and economic selection, it may prove able to give to the whole world the gift that both China and the rest of the world need; and this gift would be a felicitous mixture of modern Western dynamism with traditional Chinese stability. The fate of China's long-delayed essay in adventurous social experimentation still lies on the knees of non-Western gods. It cannot yet be foreseen whether the Chinese, or any other section of Mankind, will succeed in producing the synthesis between a traditional thesis and a modern Western antithesis that is called for in order to enable Mankind to save itself from self-destruction.

Let us assume that the saving synthesis is going to be achieved. This is a highly optimistic assumption, and it must also be accompanied by a word of warning. There have been successful syntheses in the past. The alternative syntheses between Hellenism and Judaism that are represented by Christianity and Islam are notable cases in point. But these two cases are reminders that even the most successful syntheses cannot meet everyone's needs. Neither the Christian nor the Islamic synthesis was acceptable to the Jews. They were not tempted by either of these options to renounce their distinctive separate communal identity. The non-militant Pharisaic dispensation instituted by Rabbi Johanan ben Zakkai[12] made it possible for them to survive as a separate community in diasporá – always penalized and often murderously persecuted; and this was the way of life to which the Jews clung. At the opposite extreme of the Syro-Hellenic cultural gamut, the Hellenist die-hards would have liked to take the same uncompromising course,[13] but they failed for lack of the resoluteness and cohesiveness and staying-power that have enabled the Jewish diasporá to maintain its identity since AD 70.

The Jewish example – and the Parsee example too – suggests that, even if the Chinese or some other non-Western people were to succeed in working out a synthesis between modern Western dynamism and traditional stability, there would be likely to be some intransigents on either wing who would insist on holding aloof and opting out. But the historical precedents also suggest that these dissenting minorities would probably be neither so numerous nor so powerful that their abstention would prevent the synthesis from being adopted by a decisive majority. History also warns us that it would be a heinous crime in the future, as it has been in the past, to penalize and persecute dissenting minorities. Mankind needs unity, but, within a prevailing unity, it can afford a modicum of variety and its culture will be the richer for this.

PART X

CONTACTS BETWEEN CIVILIZATIONS IN TIME

Encounters between contemporary civilizations are not the only way in which one civilization comes into contact with another. A living civilization has an encounter with an extinct one when it brings this back to life in a renaissance. I do not think that this term should be confined to 'the' renaissance of Hellenism in Italy: renaissances have been quite common in many other societies, and have also occurred in other aspects of life than those resuscitated in late medieval and early modern Italy. Many people appear to look upon this Italian renaissance as a marvellous cultural rebirth, but I think that a ghost is intrinsically less valuable than a living being. I try to make this point clear by reviewing some examples of these artificial revivals of institutions, ideas, and arts, and I find that the native genius of a civilization is liable to be stifled if the society comes to accept the revival of the old as a sufficient substitute for fresh creative departures.

plate 79

IDEAL COMMONWEALTH

The revival of Hellenism in medieval Italy was not confined to
the artistic plane, but had a political incarnation which predated
the artistic renaissance by some three hundred years. From the
eleventh century, Italian cities were winning self-government
from imperial and ecclesiastical authority, and these 'communes'
modelled their republican constitutions on the resuscitated ideal
of the Hellenic city-state. Without doubt it was the creation of
such small-scale polities, with their local patriotism and fierce
civic pride, that encouraged the florescence of art and literature
in later centuries: in this fruitful conjunction of politics and
culture they accurately reproduced the distinctive character of
their Hellenic models. The Palazzo Pubblico at Siena is decorated
with frescoes illustrating and celebrating every aspect of civic
life; a detail from the *Allegory of Good Government* (1338–39)
shows an assembly of citizens below the figures of three presiding
virtues, Peace, Fortitude, and Prudence.

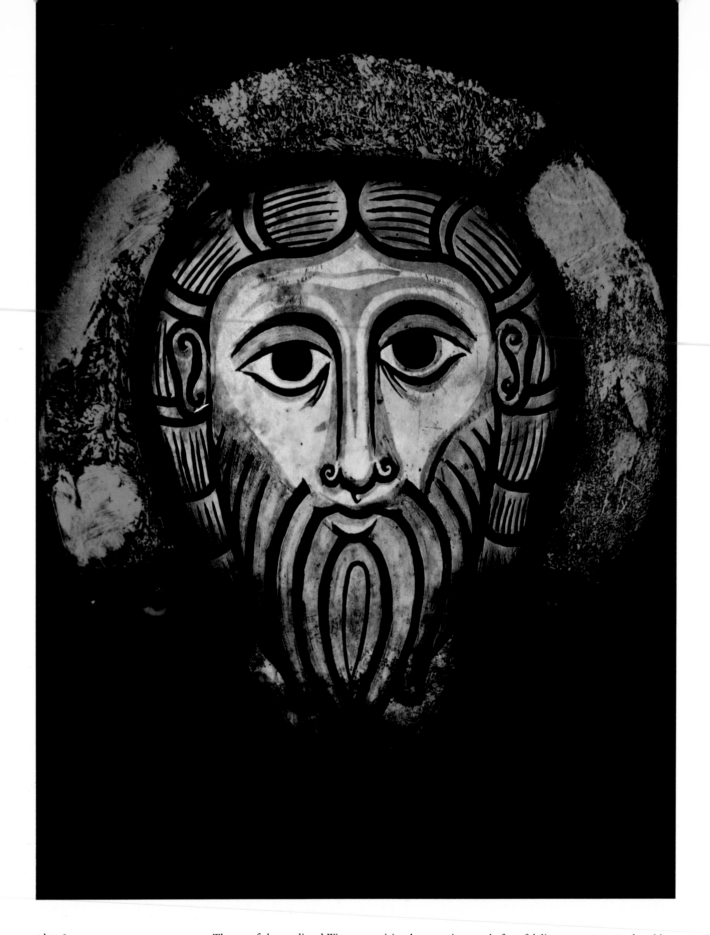

plate 80

The art of the medieval West put spiritual expressiveness before fidelity to appearance, breaking with the idealized naturalism of late Hellenic art: eleventh-century stained glass window from the Abbey Church of Wissembourg.

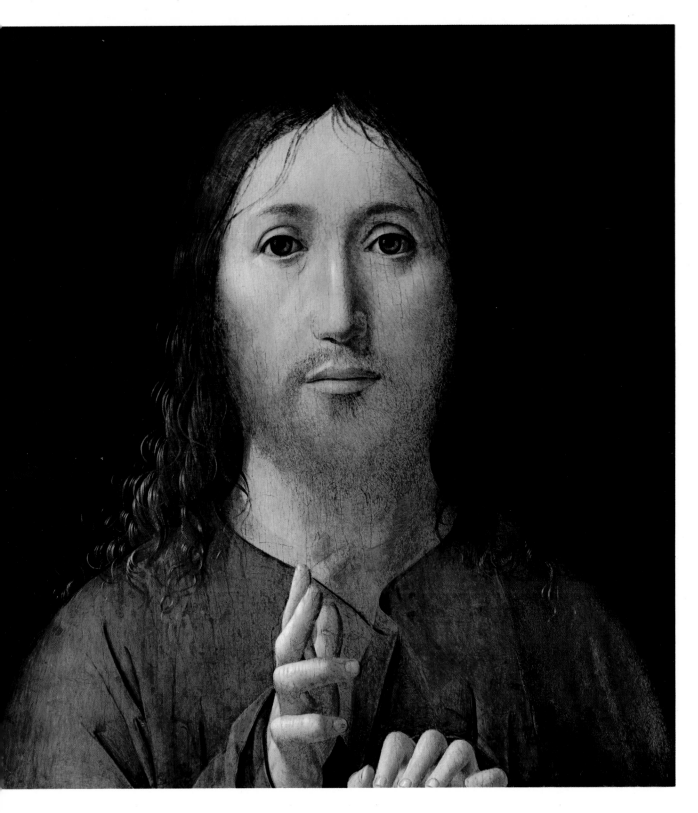

plate 81

HELLENISM RETURNS

The renaissance of Hellenism in late medieval Italy led to a new preoccupation with reproducing reality as it appeared to the eye – hence the invention of oil painting, with its potential for technical subtlety: Antonello da Messina (*c.* 1430–79), *Salvator Mundi*.

plate 82

BEYOND HELLENISM

By the mid-nineteenth century, Western artists had achieved proficiency in photographically perfect representation: Ingres (1780–1867), *Madame Moitessier*. But this proficiency was then unexpectedly made otiose by the invention of photography itself.

plate 83

HELLENISM REJECTED

The camera's conquest of the visual world left twentieth-century artists free
to explore the hidden worlds of the mind and its modes of perception; art
finally exorcized its Hellenic ghost: Picasso, *Woman with a Fan,* 1908.

plates 84, 85

CHRISTIANITY'S
JUDAIC
CONSCIENCE

The Catholic church, above, is centred on an altar adorned with images and dominated by the Son of God – clear evidence of the early Church's Hellenic independence from the Judaic tradition that abhorred image-worship and the Trinity. In the Reformation, Christianity's suppressed Judaic origins again rose to the surface; the Protestant church, right, is empty of images, and the focus of attention is not the altar but the pulpit.

plate 86

CHRISTIANITY'S JUDAIC ROOTS

'And there shall come forth a rod out of the stem of Jesse, and a branch shall grow out of his roots' – Isaiah's prophecy of the coming of the Messiah was given a literal form in Christian art, showing the generations from Jesse to the Christian Messiah growing out of the recumbent body of Jesse. The link between the Old and the New Testament that the Tree of Jesse illustrates so vividly is not merely symbolic: although the Church has frequently tried to ignore or minimize the debt it owes to Judaism, the Christian faith is rooted in its Jewish past, and elements from this antecedent tradition have been intermittently revived in Christian ritual and doctrine. In particular, a reassertion of the profound Jewish commitment to monotheism and aniconism, which were both weakened by the infiltration of Hellenic ideas into Christianity, has been apparent in the prolonged and bitter debates over attempts to define the dogma of the Trinity, in periodic outbursts of iconoclasm, and in the Protestant rejection of the cult of the Virgin and the Saints.

50 Renaissances of institutions, laws, and philosophies

THE METAPHORICAL APPLICATION of the French word *renaissance* to denote the 'rebirth' of an extinct culture or of an obsolete phase of a surviving culture is a specifically modern Western usage; and, in this technical sense, the term has come to be used in the singular, not in the plural, and as a proper name, not as the label of a species. In ordinary modern Western parlance, the singular expression 'the Renaissance' has been used to denote something that happened in one local province of one civilization in one age of history on two principal planes of its activity. The particular civilization in question was Western Christendom, the particular province was Northern and Central Italy, the particular age was the late medieval period of Western history (*c.* AD 1275–1475), the particular activities were the literary and visual arts. The occurrence that was identified by this *ad hoc* label was the evocation of the 'ghost' of a 'dead' civilization; and the *revenant* thus called up by this feat of necromancy was the shade of the Hellenic culture to which Western culture was affiliated.

From time to time in the course of this Study we have put ourselves on our guard against the distortions to which the egocentric illusion exposes us; and with this in mind we would be well advised to reconsider this customary Western conception of 'the Renaissance' in a critical spirit. In fact, we shall find that the popular usage of the term to describe the late medieval Italian literary and artistic movement is at variance with the historical facts in at least three respects. In the first place the popular usage has tended to be applied only to the strictly cultural features of the late medieval Italian renaissance, to the exclusion of the political facet. In the second place the use of the word *renaissance* as a proper name for the evocation of Hellenism in late medieval Italy ignores the fact that there have been other renaissances of Hellenism in other provinces of Western Christendom at other times of Western history (later, as well as earlier, than the late Middle Ages), and that these other Western renaissances of Hellenism have extended to other facets of the Hellenic culture besides the literary, artistic, and political. In the third place the customary usage ignores the still more significant fact that there have been other renaissances of Hellenism in the history of at least one other Hellenistic Civilization besides Western Christendom, and other renaissances of other 'dead' cultures besides Hellenism as well as renaissances of obsolete phases of surviving cultures in the histories of other, non-Western, civilizations.

As soon as these facts are marshalled, it becomes clear that the use of the word *renaissance* as a proper name is inappropriate, for it quite erroneously labels as a unique occurrence an event which in reality was no more than one particular instance of a recurrent historical phenomenon. The evocation of a dead culture or of an obsolete phase of a surviving culture by the living representatives of a civilization that is still a going concern proves to be a species of historical event for which the correct label is, not 'the Renaissance', but 'renaissances'. Renaissances are, as we have already noted,[1] a form of encounter. Here the difference of location between the colliding parties is a distance measured not in the space-dimension of the geographer but in the time-dimension of the chronologist. The encounter takes place between a living civilization and the ghost of a dead civilization or of an obsolete phase of the living civilization's own past.

The evocation of such a ghost is a risky venture. At best, it may introduce a disturbing and stimulating element into an alien social context; but it may have the alternative effect of stifling the native genius of the society which has summoned it into its life. Besides widening our field beyond the single example of the late medieval Italian renaissance of Hellenism, we can push our search for renaissances into other facets of cultural life besides those recaptured by this Italian renaissance. It will be convenient to group these into renaissances in the fields of politics, law, and philosophy; of languages, literatures and the visual arts; and of religions.

The political manifestations of the late medieval Italian renaissance have attracted relatively little attention, but they preceded the cultural manifestations for which this renaissance is remembered. On the aesthetic plane the Italian renaissance of Hellenism did not begin earlier than the generations of Dante (*vivebat* AD 1265–1321) and Giotto (*vivebat c.* AD 1266–1337) and Petrarch (*vivebat* AD 1307–74), but the political renaissance began to take effect as early as the eleventh century, when the government of the cities of Lombardy passed out of the control of their bishops into the hands of lay magistrates who were appointed by and responsible to the citizens. The resuscitated Hellenic political ideal which made this impact on eleventh-century Western Christian urban communities in Northern Italy made a corresponding impact on the peoples of the feudal monarchies in Transalpine Europe after the spread of the late medieval Italian sub-culture into the other provinces of Western Christendom. In both its earlier and narrower and its later and wider field the influence of this Hellenic *revenant* on Western politics was the same. The superficial effect was to propagate a cult of constitutional self-government which eventually conferred upon itself the flattering Attic title of 'democracy', after having proved its potency by stimulating the English, French, and American Revolutions. By the end of the nineteenth century democracy seemed to have won a conclusive victory over absolute monarchy in Western Europe; but the ideal of internationalist brotherhood that this political ethic implied was overwhelmed by the actuality that democracy had become 'nationalized' and dehumanized in the modern post-Christian West. In this sense it was an accurate reproduction of that idolatrous worship of collective humanity embodied in a parochial state which had overtaken the pre-Christian Hellenic World. This ghost was evoked in medieval Italy some three or four hundred years earlier than the ghosts of an Hellenic literary and artistic culture that, in its authentic original appearance in

372 A dying ideal: Democracy crowns the people of Athens, on a stele of 336 BC inscribed with a decree against tyranny. The conjunction of date and decree is significant: Athens had recently been forced to join a Greek league organized by Philip of Macedon, and the true era of the democratic Hellenic city-state had thus drawn to a close.

the fifth and fourth centuries BC, had been raised to its highest level of achievement by the Attic worshippers of parochialism.

The Italian renaissance of Hellenic political parochialism was not, however, either the sole or the earliest political renaissance of Hellenism in Western history. In the course of Hellenic history itself a religion of state-worship had been taken over and universalized in the adulation of *Dea Roma* and *Divus Augustus*; and a post-Diocletianic autocratic version of this secularized worship of ecumenical power was formally revived in Western Christendom, 250 years before the revival of city-state worship in Lombardy, when Charlemagne was crowned as a Roman Emperor by Pope Leo III on Christmas Day AD 800.

This first abortive attempt to create a 'Holy Roman Empire' was followed by a regular series of subsequent attempts to impose an ecumenical political authority upon the fragmented polities of Western Christendom. Saxon, Hohenstaufen, and Habsburg princes successively tried to appropriate this imperial prerogative; and its attraction survived into the present century, when the regalia of the Holy Roman Empire were presented to Hitler after the *Anschluss* of Austria to the short-lived German Reich. But this ideal of ecumenical unity in the form of an imperial régime, which has hitherto invariably proved abortive on Western soil, was only one aspect of the ghost of the senile Hellenic universal state that was raised by Leo and Charlemagne. The absolutism of the Diocletianic Roman Empire's demands upon its subjects was as characteristic a feature of this late Hellenic political institution as its claim to world-wide dominion; and the intensive, as well as the extensive, potency of the original was reproduced in the wraith that haunted Western Christendom.

The Carolingian Empire . . . was conceived as the society of the whole Christian people under the control of a theocratic monarchy, and [it] attempted to regulate every detail of life and thought, down to the method of ecclesiastical chant and the rules of the monastic order by legislative decrees and governmental inspection. . . . The fusion of temporal and spiritual powers was far more complete in the Carolingian state than it had been in the Christian barbarian kingdoms, or even in the Byzantine Empire.[2]

Charlemagne and his successors condemned this resuscitated absolutism to miscarry by attempting to bring, not only every plane of activity, but also every geographical province of Western Christendom under the sway of this 'unitary Church State';[3] but the different circumstances under which Frederick II Hohenstaufen reattempted the Carolingian *tour de force* made it possible for Frederick's political ecumenicalism to fail without involving his absolutism in the disaster as well.

When Charlemagne had ventured on his enterprise of reinaugurating a Roman absolutism through his widespread and still expanding dominions, he was hampered by having to try to reconstruct entirely, from the foundations, a sophisticated social structure that had long since been destroyed in all the former provinces of the Roman Empire that lay within his frontiers. By contrast, the Emperor Frederick II inherited in the Kingdom of Sicily a base of operations in which absolutism was already a going concern, thanks to the effective local revival there of the late

373, 374 THE GHOST OF CAESAR The ideal of the Roman Empire has haunted the Western Society since the last Emperor abdicated in 476. Charlemagne attempted to resuscitate it in AD 800. He aimed at creating a society worthy to inherit Rome's imperial glory and her Christian mission, and he pursued a deliberate policy of reviving Hellenic culture. Alcuin called Charlemagne's capital at Aachen 'the second Rome', and conferred names such as Horace and Homer on Carolingian notables. The coin, above, shows Charlemagne as a Roman *Imperator Augustus*. A second highly conscious revival of Roman absolutism came in thirteenth-century Sicily, where Emperor Frederick II, shown with his wife on the relief opposite, was able to build on a surviving Byzantine tradition. Frederick's Sicily resembled the East Roman Empire in having a professional civil service, unique in the Western Society of that age; government was so secure that Frederick's court, unlike those of other contemporary states, did not have to be ambulatory. Byzantine autocracy was also recalled in the practice of prostration before the Emperor, and in the doctrine that to dispute a royal decision was to commit an act of sacrilege.

458

Roman system by earlier Byzantine and Muslim rulers. The failure of Frederick's attempt to unite Central and Northern Italy with Southern Italy under a centralized ecumenical autocratic rule did not prevent him from making, as King of Sicily, the mark on Western history that he could not make as Holy Roman Emperor. This limited but successful revival of Roman absolutism on Sicilian soil did serve as an example and a stimulus for a host of would-be autocrats in other Western parochial states.

The earliest of these successful experiments in establishing counterparts of the Byzantine Kingdom of Sicily in other provinces of Western Christendom were the work of despots who, in the 250 years after Frederick's death in AD 1250, swept up the seventy or eighty self-governing city-states of Central and Northern Italy into ten miniature empires, all of which proved true to the Sicilian prototype by being so many local graves of Italian civic liberties. This was the region from which the Italian revival of Roman absolutism spread into Transalpine Europe; and the medieval parliamentary liberties of the non-Italian parts of Western Christendom came within an ace of suffering the same fate. Only in the ex-feudal Kingdom of England was the challenge of Italianate autocracy successfully met by a marriage between parliamentary liberties and autocratic efficiency which bore fruit in the creation of a modern parliamentary constitutional government. This was, however, merely a local exception to the general course of political development in Western Christendom in the early modern age. In this period of Western history, the spectre of Roman absolutism won a sweeping victory; it took two hundred years for the tyranny of King Philip II (*regnabat* AD 1555–98) to refine itself into the enlightened absolutism of the Emperor Joseph II (*imperabat* AD 1765–90), and three centuries for the 'divine right' of kings, who had converted their limited hereditary feudal rights into an unlimited prerogative of power, to water itself down to the prosaic 'legitimacy' pleaded by the restored post-Napoleonic monarchies. Even after the progressive democratization of the Western régimes in the second half of the nineteenth century, a vestige of autocracy still survived in the Western World in the Habsburg government of Austria-Hungary and in the Hohenzollern government of Prussia-Germany; and, though both these anachronistic autocracies were eventually overthrown after their defeat in the First World War, the transplanted system of responsible parliamentary government failed to take root there. The anti-parliamentarian dénouement in Europe between 1919 and 1939 may have come as something of a shock to the liberal devotees of parliamentary democracy; yet it was, in fact, one more reanimation of the absolutist ghost that had bedevilled the Western Society since it had first been resuscitated from its Hellenic death-bed some eleven centuries previously. At the present day, the signs are that the ghost has been laid at last; the vision of unity has lost none of its lustre, but the decision to attempt unification by means of voluntary co-operation in the form of the EEC represents a break with the *karma* of the past.

In the non-Western World, corresponding renaissances on the political plane can be observed. The ghost of a Roman Empire that had served as the Hellenic Society's universal state was raised by the Orthodox Christian as well

as by the Western Christian Hellenistic Society; and we have seen[4] that in Orthodox Christendom this necromantic *tour de force* was performed with such virtuosity that it broke the Society's back. We have also watched the ghosts of other empires playing the same malignant role in the histories of other civilizations. The ghost of a Sinic universal state that had been embodied in the Ch'in-Han Empire returned to haunt the society in the shape of the Sui and T'ang Empire; and, when the Sinic Society propagated an offshoot on to Japanese soil, this Sinic political incubus was exported to Yamato in AD 645 as an integral part of the Chinese culture-package.

Turning from politics to law, we can again begin our survey of renaissances in this field by looking into the history of the Western Society. We have seen that, after the post-Hellenic interregnum had declared itself on the political plane in the break-up of the unitary Roman Empire into a mosaic of successor-states, the emergence of two new Hellenistic Christian civilizations found its political expression in attempts to raise this Roman Empire from the dead. On the legal plane, the Roman Law, which in the course of the ten centuries ending in Justinian's generation had been slowly and laboriously elaborated to meet the complicated requirements of the sophisticated ecumenical Hellenic Society, was swiftly left stranded by the rapid obsolescence of the whole way of life to which it had come to be so closely geared.

Eventually the symptoms of decay and death were followed by manifestations of fresh life on the legal, as on the political, plane; but, in both the nascent Orthodox and Western Christian Worlds alike, the impulse to provide a live law for a living society did not find its first vent in any move to reanimate the rarefied system of Roman Law. In the legal sphere, the first move in both these new worlds was, not to raise a ghost, but to perform an act of creation. Each of these two Christian societies demonstrated the sincerity of its religious beliefs by attempting to create a Christian law for would-be Christian people. In both Christendoms, however, this new departure in a would-be Christian direction was followed by a renaissance, first of the Israelitish Law that was latent in Christianity's scriptural heritage from Jewry, and then of the Justinianean Law which began to become less inappropriate as the new civilizations began to mature.

In Orthodox Christendom the Christian new departure was announced, in the joint reign of the two Syrian founders of the East Roman Empire, Leo Syrus III and his son Constantine V, in the promulgation in AD 740 of 'a Christian law book' which was 'a deliberate attempt to change the legal system of the Empire by an application of Christian principles'.[5] This revolutionary work was published under the conservative title of *A Selection [Ecloga], in Abridgment, of the Institutes, Digest, Code, and Novels of the Great Justinian*[6]; but its two imperial promulgators showed their hand and gave notice of their aspirations by adding that the work was 'also a Rectification in the Direction of Greater Humanity'; and, in the first paragraph of the preface, the source of law was declared to be, not legislation enacted by the Roman people, but revelation vouchsafed by God, and the sanction of law to be, not human enforcement, but divine retribution.

Our God who is lord and maker of all things, the creator of Man who has endowed Man with the privilege of free will, has (in the language of prophecy) given Man, to help him, a law in which God has made known to Man everything that Man ought to do and to shun. The conduct prescribed by the law is to be adopted because it is a passport to salvation; the conduct prohibited by the law is to be eschewed because it brings punishment on the transgressor. No one who keeps these commandments or who – save the mark – disregards them will fail to receive the appropriate recompense for his deeds of whatever character. For it is God who has proclaimed both the positive and the negative commandments in advance [of the human legislator]; and the power of God's words – a power that knows no variation and that rewards every man's works according to their deserts – shall (in gospel language) not pass away.

To a modern student, the main humanizing reform to the Justinianean Law would appear to be here the liberalization of the severe Roman family law by which a parent enjoyed an unlimited power over his children; and Christian influence would be most strongly seen in the redefinition of marriage law, by which, in conformity with Christian teaching, marriage ceased to be a private and dissoluble contract and became a public sacrament. An Orthodox Christian in any generation from the eighth century down to the present day might, however, single out as the most humane and Christian part of this *Ecloga* the chapter on penalties for crimes. Mutilation was substituted for capital punishment in many cases, the law thereby recognizing that the criminal was also a sinner who must be given an opportunity to repent.

These radical new departures were inspired by Christian theology; but, since the Christian Church counted the books of the Old Testament as being the divinely revealed word of God, as well as the New Testament, it was almost inevitable that the birth of a new Christian Law should be followed sooner or later by a renaissance of the latent Law of Israel to which the Christian Church was thus affiliated. When we add up the references or allusions to the Bible in the preface to the *Ecloga*, we find that the Old Testament is cited half as many times again as the New Testament. It is true that all the six citations from the Old Testament are taken from 'the Prophets' and not from 'the Law'; yet, in this Orthodox Christian evocation of the Old Testament in the field of Law, it was inevitable that in the long run 'the Law' and not 'the Prophets' should prevail. Sure enough, an *Ecloga Legis Mosaïcae* did eventually make its appearance in a later version of the original *Ecloga*. It seems likely, in view of this, that the *Ecloga*'s revolutionary partiality for punishments in the form of mutilations derived from a literal application of the Old Testament Mosaic 'Covenant Code', and not from an incorrect interpretation of a passage of poetic symbolism in the New Testament.[7]

In contrast to the gradualness and unselfconsciousness of this renaissance of the Mosaic Law out of the Orthodox Christian Law's Israelite scriptural heritage, the renaissance of the Roman Law out of Orthodox Christendom's own Hellenic predecessor was both self-conscious and abrupt. In the preface to 'the Handbook' promulgated between the years AD 870 and 879 by the founder of the Macedonian dynasty of East Roman Emperors, Basil I, in conjunction with his sons and colleagues Constantine and Leo (VI), the new legislators gave notice that the *Ecloga* was to be abrogated, not indeed entirely, but 'to the requisite extent'; while, in the preface to a subsequent draft for a second edition of 'the Handbook' published between AD 879 and 886, notice was given that 'Our Imperial Majesty . . . has totally rejected and scrapped the imbecilities promulgated by the Isaurians[8] in defiance of . . . the Divine Dogma and to the undoing of the salutary laws.'

The *odium theologicum* which is here advertised as the motive for superseding the existing legislation was probably a less powerful stimulus to action than the practical need to adapt the law to the increasingly complicated demands which the growing civilization was making on it. The relatively simple system that had satisfied the legal requirements of the nascent Orthodox Christian Society in the eighth century was inadequate now that a century and a half of social progress had intervened. A more subtle legal apparatus had become one of the crying needs of the ninth-century Orthodox Christian Society; and this, rather than the theological discrepancy between the Syrian and Macedonian dynasties over iconoclasm, was the origin of the resuscitation of the Justinianean Law. 'The Handbook' and 'the Second Edition' were followed up promptly by the promulgation, in about 888–90, of 'the Imperial Decisions' (*Vasilika*) in no less than sixty books, and tardily by the foundation of an imperial school of law at Constantinople in 1045.

The ninth-century Vasilican ghost of the sixth-century *Corpus Iustinianeum* resembles its original in presenting an imposing appearance which it is incapable of sustaining under closer examination. It was a compound of material drawn from numerous earlier sources, most of them commentaries and revisions rather than originals. The only touch of originality was the substitution of a single unitary system of classification for Justinian's dispersion among four works of materials concerning the same subjects.

To quarrel with a renaissance for being unoriginal is a criticism that might perhaps be discounted as captious; but the ineffectiveness that is another characteristic of the Macedonian dynasty's attempt to reinstate the Roman Law is a more serious weakness; for a ghost, after all, is only distinguishable from a nonentity in so far as it succeeds in making an impression on the living beings whom it is haunting. The ninth-century renaissance of Roman Law in Orthodox Christendom showed itself conspicuously impotent to supersede in reality the iconoclast Emperors' new Christian Law which it was abrogating verbally, and even impotent to exorcize the rival ghost of the Mosaic Law which was re-emerging out of the Christian Law's Old Testament foundations.

It is significant that both 'the Handbook' and 'the Second Edition' reproduced the provisions of the *Ecloga*, in spite of the fact that the *Ecloga*'s authors were attacked in the prologue. The strength of the *Ecloga*, in this encounter with a revived Roman Law, lay in the fact that the *Ecloga* was a faithful reflexion of the Orthodox Christian ethos, whereas the Hellenic spirit expressed in the late Roman Law was an alien presence in an Orthodox Christian environment. In the spheres of both family law and marriage law, the intention of returning to the Justinianean practice was compromised, for in practice a modified form of the now entrenched Christian system could not be

dispensed with. In criminal law too the *Ecloga*'s system of punishments was retained and was even developed further. The vigour with which the recently established Christian tradition continued to assert itself against the attempted revival of the Roman tradition is betrayed in the preface to 'the Second Edition', leading up to the passage quoted above in which the Macedonian legislators denounce their Syrian predecessors and all their legal works.

The experience by which Our Majesty has been aroused and stimulated to bestir itself to retrieve and proclaim the good world-saving law with the utmost zeal and utmost care is what we can only describe as our initiation in the secret chambers of the heart by the divine intervention of the Trinity in Unity.

Thus, though the Macedonian Emperors were bent on reinstating a Roman Law that had been disestablished – wrongfully, as they believed – by the preceding Syrian Emperors' innovations, it never occurred to them to look for the sanction of law in autonomous acts of human volition. In historical fact, the Roman Law, whose champions the Macedonian Emperors professed to be, had been the unequivocally man-made act of the Roman people. Yet, in defiance of Roman legal history, the Macedonians showed themselves true Orthodox Christians in assuming without question that no law could be validated by any other sanction than the ordinance of God. In other words, the Macedonians, no less than their Syrian iconoclast bugbears, believed in 'the divine dogma' as the foundation of law; and the apparent conflict of ideologies dwindles in this light down to a family quarrel between the opposing advocates of two scarcely distinguishable variants of the same Orthodox Christian creed.

A second great school of law that underwent a similar history of eclipse and renaissance is the Islamic Law. The Arabic *Shari'ah* of the Caliphate was partially replaced by barbarian codes in those parts of the Islamic World that fell under Mongol and Ottoman rule, though it was maintained in full force in Egypt in the Mamluk Empire. However, when the Ottoman Empire began to expand into populous territories in which the Arabic language and the *Shari'ah* had never lost their hold, the *Shari'ah* was revived and re-established for use throughout the enlarged Ottoman dominions. The comprehensive codification that was undertaken in the sixteenth century on Sultan Suleyman I's orders then remained the basis of Ottoman Law until the modern reforms of the nineteenth century.

Our final task in this chapter is to examine the renaissances of philosophies. In another context we have watched the Confucian *litterati* surviving the dissolution of the Han embodiment of the Sinic universal state and eventually regaining their monopoly of the imperial civil service after the Han Empire had been revived by the Sui dynasty and maintained by their successors the T'ang. In achieving this remarkable recovery of lost ground on the plane of public administration, the Confucians were also winning a victory over Taoist and Mahayanian Buddhist rivals. The re-establishment in AD 622 of an official examination in the Confucian classics as the method of selecting recruits for the imperial civil service signified that the Taoists and Buddhists had let slip an opportunity for supplanting the Confucians which had seemed to be well within their grasp. The contrast between this political failure of the Mahayana

461

THE GHOST OF CONFUCIUS

375   Chinese civil service examination in the seventeenth century, supervised by the Emperor. Proficiency in the Confucian classics had become the test for entry into the Chinese civil service in the last century BC, but the system fell into disuse in the fourth century AD. Its revival in AD 622 not only signified a return to older tradition, but also represented a victory for Confucianism over its new rival Buddhism.

in the interregnum between the fall and rise of successive Sinic universal states and the success with which the Christian Church exploited its chances in Western Europe in the post-Hellenic Age brings out the fact that – by comparison with Christianity at any rate – the Mahayana was a politically incompetent religion. Even the patronage of the parochial princes of Northern China during the period from the break-up of the Ch'in (Ts'in) Empire in AD 316 and the re-establishment of the Empire by the Sui in 589 had failed to give the followers of the Mahayana a firm seat in the political saddle. However, as soon as the encounter between the Mahayana and Confucianism was transferred from this alien political plane to the spiritual, their respective fortunes were dramatically reversed.

The Confucians exposed themselves to the risk of this *peripeteia* when they followed up their political triumph in the civil service by an attempt to reanimate the thought latent in their literary canon. This process of reconstituting a philosophy out of an examination subject was started by the Neoconfucian thinkers Han Yü (*vivebat* AD 768–824) and Li Ao (*mortuus c.* AD 844). In the eleventh century this Neoconfucianism branched into two schools led by the brothers Ch'eng Yi (*vivebat* AD 1033–1108) and Ch'eng Hao (*vivebat* AD 1032–85); the former's 'School of Principles' was carried to its culmination by Chu Hsi (*vivebat* AD 1130–1200), while the elder brother's 'School of Mind' culminated in the thought of Wang Shou-jen (*vivebat* AD 1473–1529). Neoconfucianism began and ended with declarations of dissent from both Taoism and the Mahayana, yet in fact it had adopted some of the most fundamental tenets of both of its rival schools of religious thought. The Yin-Yang cosmology of the Taoists was absorbed into Neoconfucianism, and the Ch'an (Zen) School of the Mahayana exercised a particularly potent influence on post-Buddhaic Confucianism. Neoconfucianism thus took over from the Mahayana the metaphysical element which Confucianism itself had always lacked; and, though in some respects it did try to recapture the authentic spirit of Confucianism which it had set out to resuscitate, such attempts were feeble and fitful by comparison with the assiduity with which Mahayanian Buddhism continued to insinuate itself into a philosophy that had originally been intended to revivify a pre-Buddhist ideology. This captivation of the Neoconfucian philosophical renaissance itself by the spirit of the Mahayana made nonsense of the reinstated Confucian imperial civil servants' efforts to destroy the hold of the exotic Mahayana Church on the now politically reunited and socially advancing Sinic World.

The Confucian campaign against Buddhism had begun even before the reunification of the former domain of the Han Empire and the reinauguration of the public examinations in the Confucian classics; but as soon as they had acquired a hold upon the government of a resuscitated ecumenical empire the Confucians began to abuse this power systematically for the purpose of suppressing their hated Buddhist rivals. From AD 626 onwards, the Buddhist monasteries in the T'ang imperial crown's dominions were placed under an increasingly severe Confucian official control. A series of anti-Buddhist memorials addressed to the T'ang imperial throne between 624 and 819 at length produced their cumulative effect in 842–45 in a systematic

official persecution which, though mild compared with the persecutions of which the Christian Church was either victim or perpetrator, was an exceptionally violent and bloody incident in the less unhappy history of the relations between church and state in the Sinic World.

As it turned out, this Confucian attempt to repress and if possible eradicate the Mahayana in China was abortive: the Mahayana has remained a living force in the Sinic World. However, even if the Mahayana had been successfully extirpated in China eleven centuries ago, this discreditable political triumph of the Confucians would have been stultified by the Neoconfucian philosophical school's surrender to the Mahayana on the metaphysical plane. As we have seen, the pioneers of Neoconfucianism had already set their course on these Mahayanian lines before the launching of the great persecution in 842; and elements of a thinly disguised Ch'an Buddhism continued after this date to be incorporated in the officially recognized canon of Neoconfucian thought.

Clearly, the Neoconfucian philosophers' *odium philosophicum* towards the Indic Mahayana was as self-frustrating as the Macedonian legislators' *odium theologicum* towards the would-be Christian legislation of their Syrian iconoclast predecessors on the East Roman imperial throne. There is a common moral to be drawn from this common failure of two similar attempts to substitute ghosts raised from the dead for living ideas or institutions. It is all very well for the necromancer to evoke a wraith, but he courts failure if he then goes on to try to merge his own identity in the spectre that he has succeeded in conjuring up. A phantom is, after all, nothing if not transparent, and a creature of flesh and blood that seeks to take cover behind such a *revenant* will remain conspicuously visible through his would-be disguise. The shape of the Mahayana shows through the shimmer of Neoconfucianism as plainly as the solid substance of the Syrian Emperors' would-be Christian legislation can be discerned beneath the patches of the Justinianean veneer with which it was partially covered by the Syrians' Macedonian successors.

On the other hand, if we look at the renaissance of Hellenic Aristotelian philosophy in Western Christian history, the plot takes a rather different turn. Neoconfucianism succumbed to a religion that, in the official view of the Confucian imperial régime, was an alien and unjustified interloper; Neo-Aristotelianism imposed itself on a theology in whose view Aristotle,—even though Aquinas habitually referred to him as 'the Philosopher' *sans phrase* – was a pagan to be treated with suspicion and circumspection. In fact, the Hellenic philosopher's ghost captivated a Christian Church that had readmitted this pagan *revenant* on sufferance into the Western part of the Hellenic Civilization's former domain after the Church had gained possession of the title-deeds; conversely, the Sinic philosopher's ghost was captivated by the Mahayana, which the Confucians had attempted to evict from the homeland of the Sinic Civilization to which the Confucians had persistently maintained their claim. Thus the common feature of these two variations on a ghost-story is that the party which actually has the law on its side is worsted in the event by an opponent who has no case at law, and hence has relied on his merits.

51 Renaissances of languages, literatures, and visual arts

RENAISSANCES in the literary and visual arts are very different from those at which we have already looked in the fields of law and politics; for, unlike Man's social activities, or indeed his scientific and technological pursuits, the fine arts are not tied directly to function. A style of art is not constrained to the same extent as is a system of government or a legal system to reflect the practical exigencies of a particular time and place. Doubtless the social milieu is of primary importance in determining both the form and the content of works of art, and the artist is to this extent the prisoner of his age and his class; yet our subjective experience tells us that an element of the arbitrary and the unpredictable in the fine arts must always escape precise definition and classification, however painstaking our analysis, for art expresses a relation with reality which is quite different from the relations that are established in the other fields of human activity. Art mediates Man's perceptions and reflexions in such a way that the validity of the insights embodied in it is not limited by the temporary local circumstances of historical time and place in which it was created, however instrumental these may have been in the act of creation. Although a work of art can be instantly assigned to its correct historical context by observation of style and subject – and, indeed, can be used as an almost infallible token for establishing the identity of a social milieu – nevertheless the most essential element of what we call art is precisely that part which remains comprehensible, or revealing, or mysteriously 'true', far beyond the age of its birth.

The fine arts thus combine and reconcile the logically incompatible categories of necessity and freedom, and this ambivalence is the secret of the influence that a literature or a visual art is able to exercise over the life of the society in which it has originally been created. Moreover, this magic power is felt with a heightened potency in the life of an affiliated society in which the ghost of an obsolete art has been conjured up. An aesthetic style that has been arbitrary in one sense even in its original social milieu becomes doubly arbitrary when it is revived within an alien milieu which has already created a native style of its own. Yet the exponents of this native aesthetic style have little ground on which they can defend themselves against an alien intruder. No style of art can plead, like a system of government or law, that it is the only practicable solution of local contemporary social problems; it cannot plead either, like the natural sciences or technology, that it is the only rational integration of the sum of knowledge within its field that has been accumulated to date. In default of these natural defences which may be deployed by law or by science, the issue on which the battle between native and alien will be decided is the question which of the two presents the identical substance of an unvarying reality in an alternative form that better satisfies the abiding and ubiquitous spiritual needs of men and women, irrespective of the local temporary social milieu in which they happen to live. The respective merits of the combatants are weighed in balances that render their accounts in terms of eternal and universal values, without being much subject to the distorting pulls of date or locality. Under these conditions, the odds are even. The invader from the past has just as good a chance of success as the living defender of an open city. It is for these reasons that *revenantes* literatures and visual arts present such markedly ambivalent appearances and arouse such bitterly violent and stubborn controversies, as we shall see if we now go on to survey the field.

A living language has a life of its own apart from any literature that may employ it as a medium; *ex hypothesi* it will predate the appearance of a literature, and it may subsequently go its own way as an aural means of communication independent of its written literary career. This original relation between a language and a literature is inverted when the same literature and the same language are raised from the dead, for the ghost of a language can haunt the living world only as a parasite on the ghost of a literature. In surveying the renaissances of languages and literatures, we cannot separate the two. The hard labour of recapturing a 'dead' language has seldom been undertaken except for the sake of regaining access to monuments of literature in which this language was enshrined; and the usual course of a literary renaissance has been to recover not the interpreter's power of speaking a dead language as it was originally spoken, but the scribe's power of writing it as it was originally written.

The first step in this arduous and unpromising enterprise is to retrieve the dead literature's remains; the second step is to remaster their meaning; the third step is to reproduce them in counterfeits which might be mistaken for parodies, were it not patently obvious that they are solemnly clumsy tributes inspired by a superstitious reverence for the originals. We can follow the chronological sequence of these successive stages in our survey, though in the course of it we shall find that the stages may overlap, and that each stage is distinguished from the others by more than just the chronological difference.

In a dawning literary renaissance, the execution of the preliminary and preparatory tasks of scholarship has usually been a collective and not an individual enterprise. The typical monument of a literary renaissance in its first or second stage is an anthology, thesaurus, corpus, lexicon, or encyclopaedia compiled by a team of scholars at the instance of a prince; and the princely patron of such works of co-operative scholarship as these has frequently been the ruler of a resuscitated universal state which itself has been the product of a renaissance on the political plane. The five outstandingly eminent representatives of the type who are known to history – namely, Asshurbanipal, Constantine Porphyrogenitus, Yung Lo, K'ang Hsi, and Ch'ien Lung – were all emperors of *imperia rediviva*.

In their dedication to the pioneer work of collecting, editing, annotating, and publishing the surviving works of a 'dead' classical literature, the emperors of successive resuscitations of the Sinic universal state have probably never been rivalled. Enormous collections of the Sinic classics were made under the auspices of the Emperors Yung Lo (*imperabat* AD 1403–25), K'ang Hsi (*imperabat* AD 1662–1722), and Ch'ien Lung (*imperabat* AD 1736–96), some of them running to so many thousand volumes that

cum religiofo tripudio plaudendo & iubilando, Quale erano le Nymphe Amadryade, & agli redolenti fiori le Hymenide, riuirente, faliendo iocunde dinanti & da qualúq; lato del floreo Vertunno ftricto nella fronte de purpurante & meline rofe, cum el gremio pieno de odoriferi & fpectatiffimi fiori, amanti la ftagione del lanofo Ariete, Sedendo ouante fopra una ueterrima Veha, da quatro cornigeri Fauni tirata, In uinculati de ftrophie de nouelle fronde, Cum la fua amata & belliffima moglie Pomona coronata de fructi cum ornato defluo degli biódiff:mi capigli, parea ello fedéte, & a gli pedi dellaquale una coctilia Clepfydria iaceua, nel le mane tenente una ftipata copia de fiori & maturati fructi cum imixta fogliatura. Præcedéte la Veha agli trahenti Fauni propinq; due formofe Nymphe añfignane, Vna cú uno haftile Trophæo gerula, de Ligoni· Bidenti· farculi· & falcionetti, cú una ppendéte tabella abaca cú tale titulo.

INTEGERRIMAM CORPOR. VALITVDINEM, ET STABILER OBVR, CASTASQVE MEMSAR. DELI TIAS, ET BEATAM ANIMI SECVRITA TEM CVLTORIB. M. OFFERO.

376, 377, 378 ORIGINAL AND COUNTERFEITS: Hellenism resuscitated in Western typographical design. The original model, opposite above, is a leaf from a fifth-century AD Latin manuscript of Virgil's *Georgics*. Beneath it, a partly successful attempt to reproduce the lost Hellenic style in a Carolingian sacramentary: the script is Carolingian miniscule, even, and legible, but the design of the page is unhellenically clumsy and confusing. Above, a printed page from the *Hypnerotomachia Poliphilii* published by Aldus Manutius in 1499, typical of the fine work produced by his press and revealing a deliberately Hellenizing style in typography and design. Aldus's model was the script of the humanists, who had in turn copied that of Carolingian scholars.

it was beyond the resources of the state to print them. By comparison with these huge enterprises, the corresponding works of the East Roman Emperor Constantine Porphyrogenitus (*imperabat* AD 912–59) were puny, even though by any other standard his collection and classification of the extensive remains of Hellenic classical literature would be regarded as a considerable feat of scholarship.

In the complementary task of interpreting the meaning of an anthologized literature, Sinic scholarship again puts all competitors into the shade. At least three notable encyclopaedias of Sinic knowledge were compiled during the T'ang régime and four during the Sung. In the Ming Age and the Manchu Age, these were used as the basis for even more comprehensive works of lexicography. There are corresponding works to the credit of Byzantine scholars, but none which can compare in scope or in scholarship with the Chinese achievement.

The next stage in the development of a literary renaissance is the counterfeiting of a classical literature, and here the palm must be awarded to the band of Byzantine historians who, from the eleventh century onwards, found their medium of literary expression in the renaissance of an obsolete Attic Greek *koine*. This linguistic and literary make-believe was carried to its preposterous extreme by the Orthodox Christian historians, Nicholas ('Laonikos') Khalkokondhylis and Kritopoulos ('Kritovoulos'), who were among the last cultivators of the genre in the fifteenth century. They aspired to imitate Thucydides and Herodotus, the most illustrious and elusive of all Hellenic originals. The measure of their failure is to be found in the countless glaring solecisms of syntax, vocabulary, and morphology that stud their writings – faults of style that are incongruous with the genuineness of the writers' historical vision.

If we now extend our synoptic view of the Sinic, Orthodox Christian, and Western renaissances of a classical language and literature to embrace the whole course of each of these three movements from beginning to end, we shall notice that the Sinic and Orthodox Christian renaissances resemble each other, but differ from the Western renaissance, in two respects. In the first place, each of the two non-Western movements succeeded, once it had got under way, in going forward without any serious set-backs; whereas the Western literary renaissance that got under way in Italy in the fourteenth and fifteenth centuries had an eighth-century precursor of Northumbrian origin that had been abortive. In the second place, the counter-movement by which each of the two non-Western literary renaissances was eventually overcome was not a revival of the domestic culture. In both the Sinic World and Orthodox Christendom, the haunted society never even attempted to exorcize the ghost; in each case, the alien intruder was expelled by another alien in the shape of the Western Civilization, which captivated Orthodox Christendom in the course of the seventeenth century and China at the turn of the nineteenth and twentieth centuries. By contrast, the modern Western renaissance of Hellenic literature was eventually brought to an end by a reinvigoration of the native Western culture which resulted, before the close of the seventeenth century, in a decisive victory for an anti-Hellenic 'counter-revolution'.

The abortive first attempt at a literary renaissance of Hellenism in Western Christendom was coeval with the birth of the Western Christian Civilization itself. The insular prophet of this movement in Northumbria was the Venerable Bede of Jarrow (*vivebat* AD 675–735); its continental apostle in Carolingia was Alcuin of York (*vivebat* AD 735–804); and, before it was prematurely extinguished by a blast of barbarism from Scandinavia, it had already begun to revive Hellenism in its original Greek as well as in its Latin dress. Alcuin had dared to dream that, in partnership with Charlemagne, he would be able to conjure up a ghost of Athens on Frankish soil; but the vision vanished almost as soon as it had appeared, and, when it was recaptured at last after seven centuries by the band of Italian humanists, it proved as evanescent and insubstantial as any shade must be.

The illusory semblance of solidity which this phantom displayed at its long-delayed second appearance was so well simulated in its first flush that the pioneers of humanism might be forgiven in their day for believing that they had made Alcuin's dream come true. However, this conviction could only have been justified by the event if the humanists had been right in their underlying assumption that the genii of the Western Civilization and Hellenism were two persons of one substance; and this was indeed the crucial article of faith for these modern Western humanists.

In making this assumption the humanists were simply applying to their own venture in the art of necromancy one of the necessary tenets of the necromancer's ideology. The motive for raising a ghost is to produce some change in the outlook and conduct of the living people whom the ghost is intended to haunt. If the haunted party were to show no signs of being affected by the apparition, its evocation would be so much labour lost. The measure of the necromancer's success is the degree to which the ghost's intrusion effectually deflects the haunted party from his previous course, but in doing this the necromancer must avoid exposing himself to the charge that his familiar spirit is not a guide but a misleading will-o'-the-wisp. For this reason, every successful necromancer has to justify what he has done by contending that, at the moment when he took it upon himself to raise a ghost from the past, the living individual or society for whose benefit he claims to be acting was wandering off the beaten track into the wilderness, and that therefore he was doing a beneficent service by guiding the wayfarer back on to the highroad. This was the view of their work which the authors of the modern Western literary renaissance of Hellenism endeavoured to impose on their contemporaries, and it is a view that has found its champions up to the present time. In the event, the Western World did exorcize the ghost of Hellenism by the close of the seventeenth century, some two or three hundred years after it had first been conjured up; but, before this ghost was finally exorcized, its hold upon the society had become so strong that a further two or three hundred years had to pass before it could be said that the ghost had been well and truly laid to rest.

In this cultural civil war, the counter-attack against Hellenism was launched by Bodin in the sixteenth century and was carried on more boldly by Bacon and Descartes before being pressed home to a decisive victory by

A

Full and True Account

OF THE

BATTEL

Fought laſt *FRIDAY*,

Between the

Antient and the *Modern*

BOOKS

IN

St. *JAMES*'s

LIBRARY.

LONDON:

Printed in the Year, MDCCX.

Before the Title of the Battle.

379 Frontispiece and title-page to the 1710 edition of Swift's satire on the controversy between ancient and modern learning (i.e. Hellenism and the scientific method), first published in 1697. Swift gave the advantage to the ancients, though historically the dispute was eventually decided in favour of the moderns.

Fontenelle in France and William Wotton in England. The two telling shots to which 'the Ancients' finally succumbed were Fontenelle's *Une Digression sur les Anciens et les Modernes* and Wotton's *Reflections upon Ancient and Modern Learning*, both of which were published towards the close of the seventeenth century. One of the signs of the passage of the Western Civilization into the modern chapter of its history was the publication at Rotterdam in 1695–97 of Pierre Bayle's *Dictionnaire Historique et Critique*. Bayle was one of the prophets of a rationalism which was a revulsion from the wars of religion, and one of the founding fathers of a 'Republic of Letters' which was a secular substitute for the lost medieval Western *Respublica Christiana*. His dictionary was the parent of Diderot's and d'Alembert's *Encyclopédie*, and thus the grandparent of all subsequent works of co-operative intellectual engineering, whose promoters acknowledged their debt to the mother

of modern Western encyclopaedias by converting its title into a generic name for a line of literary activity.

Dictionaries and encyclopaedias were not, of course, products of this age alone. They had been invented in the disintegrating Hellenic World in its post-Diocletianic Age and in the disintegrating Sinic World in the Age of the Posterior Han as strong-boxes for preserving an accumulated cultural wealth that was under threat of being lost through oblivion; and they had been revived, as we have seen, in Orthodox Christendom and in the later Sinic World as a first step towards recovering command of the buried treasures of an antecedent culture with the intention of eventually bringing them back into circulation. In sheer physical bulk, the monuments of Sinic encyclopaedism dwarf the most imposing structures of the kind that the technological resources of the modern West have been able to produce until very recently. But the novelty of the late

Charles Panckoucke aux Auteurs de l'Encyclopédie

380 THE VICTORY OF THE MODERNS Diderot, d'Alembert, and other contributors to the *Encyclopédie*, a project conceived by Diderot and published in thirty-five volumes between 1751 and 1776. Unlike the earlier Sinic encyclopaedias, it was not a compendium of classical literature but a work of original scholarship, propounding the new learning of the Enlightenment. As a work of propaganda for rationalist philosophy, it earned bitter condemnation from orthodox and clerical thinkers, and was twice banned from publication.

modern Western encyclopaedias lay, not in their structure or in their scale, but in their purpose and their spirit. In stealing this weapon from the armoury of post-Diocletianic Hellenism, the Western champions of the Moderns against the Ancients in the seventeenth-century *Kulturkampf* were employing it neither for the preservation nor for the resuscitation of a dead culture, but for the assertion of a living culture's pretension to be worth more than its predecessor's ghost.

The successive encyclopaedias that were published and republished, on an ever larger scale and at ever shorter intervals, in the West from 1695 onwards were so many manifestos giving notice of the Westerners' claim to have outstripped the wisdom of the Hellenes; and they were also so many *comptes rendus* of the progress achieved by Western intellectual pioneers in virgin fields of knowledge. In the fields of mathematics, natural science, and technology, the self-confident Western belief in the originality of its contributions might retrospectively prove to have been justified. In aesthetic, moral, and religious fields in which the concept of progress is inapplicable and the search for wisdom a perennially fresh one, it is impossible to predict whether a Western Faust has become an any more acceptable candidate for divine grace than an Hellenic Prometheus. But meanwhile one thing is certain, and this is that, before the close of the seventeenth century, a living and lively Western World gave the ghost of a dead Hellenism unequivocally clear notice to quit.

Can we put our finger on any distinctive feature in this renaissance which might account for the Westerners' eventual success in shaking off, by their own unaided efforts, the incubus of the past, when this feat proved to be beyond the strength of both the Orthodox Christians and the Chinese? One clue at least can be found in the contrast, which we have noticed already, between the spasmodic course of the linguistic and literary renaissance of Hellenism in the West and the uninterrupted progress of the corresponding renaissances in Orthodox Christendom and in China. The interruptions of the Hellenic ghost's importunate activities in the West were so many opportunities for an original literature in the living vernacular languages of the Western peoples to strike root too deeply to be overthrown when the spectre returned after its temporary absence. The new native Western poetry in the vernacular had discarded the Hellenic mode of versification, based on the quantitative value of syllables, in favour of a mode based on the accentuation of words, which was the natural mode for poetry in the living Romance and Teutonic languages of the Western Christian peoples. This native Western Christian accentual verse had been enriched by the adoption of a contemporary Arabic poetry's device of rhyme, which was alien to the literary tradition of the Hellenic World and Western Christendom alike. The triumph of this revolutionary Western new departure was portended in the success of the rhymed accentual Provençal poetry of the troubadours, and was assured when Dante chose the same medium for his *Divina Commedia* in preference to Latin hexameters. In taking this historic decision, Dante was able to express the spirit of his world and age by combining the cultivation of a vernacular poetry with a cult for a resuscitated Hellenic cultural past. He contrived – but without strain – to be the exponent of a renaissance and of a new life simultaneously. His ability to achieve this magically creative harmony was at least partly due to the fortunate fact that, in Italy at the turn of the thirteenth and fourteenth centuries, the influence of the resuscitated Hellenic culture was not overwhelmingly strong.

The impotence of this ghost to stifle the growth of a new and original culture that was springing up under its shadow is revealed in the success with which the living creature turned the tables on the *revenant* from a dead world; for in this case the spectre was dexterously captivated by its intended victim. When we examine the poetry composed in Latin in Western Christendom from the turn of the eleventh and twelfth centuries onwards, we hear the accents of Jacob's voice while we are feeling the hands of Esau. The medieval Latin poetry written between the twelfth and the fifteenth centuries could be described not inaptly as vernacular poetry masquerading in a Latin dress. Though the words are Latin, the rhythm, rhyme, sentiment, and spirit of this ostensibly Latin poetry have all been breathed into it by the creative spirit of a contemporary Western literature in the vulgar tongue. When fifteenth-century Italian humanists, in their injudiciously pedantic enthusiasm for the genuinely Hellenic article, proved clever enough to write classical Latin quantitative verse that might occasionally pass for the work of Lucan or even Ovid, they merely succeeded in killing the vernacular poetry in Latin dress without ever coming within sight of their ulterior objective of installing a resuscitated Hellenic literature in place of a long since securely established vernacular poetry in the vulgar tongue. The humanists' revival of the art of writing classical verse was followed, not by an eclipse of the native Western literature, but by a fresh outburst of it in a blaze which effectively took the shine out of the humanists' frigid academic exercises.

The spontaneously generated native vernacular literature which came to this fine flower in the Western World had its counterpart in Orthodox Christendom and in the Sinic World; but here the seed fell among the thorns of the resuscitated language and literature of the past, and was choked by them. The Modern Greek language resembled the Western vernaculars in being accentual and not quantitative, and it found a congenial form of accentual versification – the so-called 'Metropolitan Metre' – which was quite alien from Ancient Greek quantitative verse. Modern Greek accentual verse provided the vehicle for the eleventh-century epic poem of Basil Dhiyenes Akritas which was the Byzantine counterpart of the *Chanson de Roland*. Yet, whereas the eleventh-century *Chanson* was able to become the parent of a vernacular literature, in all the living Western languages, which is still bearing fruit some nine hundred years later, the contemporary Byzantine Greek epic was cheated out of its own manifest destiny through being sterilized by the triumph of an Orthodox Christian renaissance of Ancient Greek language and literature; and even the stimulating example offered to the Greeks by French and Venetian vernacular literature failed to produce a comparably vigorous Greek vernacular literature with a distinctive character of its own.

In the nineteenth century, when the Greek Orthodox Christians' feeling towards the West had changed from contempt and hostility to admiration and receptivity, it might have been expected that one of the first fruits of this cultural conversion would be the liberation of the Modern Greek language from the dead hand of a Hellenism that had been resuscitated in Greek Orthodox Christendom before the beginning of this Christian civilization's long encounter with its sister society in the West. Unfortunately for the Greeks, however, they imbibed the toxin of nationalism from the same Western spring; and this had the effect of heightening the nineteenth-century Greeks' consciousness that their language was lineally descended from the Ancient Greek, and that their ancestral Orthodox Christian Civilization was affiliated to the Hellenic. These irrelevant historical facts led them to take refuge in the cultivation of linguistic archaism, and to denature their mother tongue by forcing into it as gross an infusion of Attic Greek vocabulary, inflexion, and syntax as they could compel this living language to swallow. Thus, on the linguistic and literary plane, the Greeks' 'reception' of modern Western culture, whose distinctive gift it was to use living vernaculars as its literary vehicles, had the paradoxical result of fettering the living Greek language instead of liberating it.

In the Sinic World too, a popular literature in the living vernacular tongue had succeeded in springing up under the shadow of a moribund classical language and literature, thanks to the culturally shattering effect of the Mongol domination. However, the authority of the Chinese classical language and style was sustained by the fact that these were the hidebound official media of education and administration; and consequently the flourishing new vernacular literature was deprecated, even by its own authors, as being vulgar and contemptible. It was not until after the abolition of the civil service examinations in Chinese classical literature in AD 1905 that the Chinese vernacular literature was enfranchised. The living 'mandarin' *lingua franca* which was the vernacular literature's linguistic vehicle was then able to claim the status of legitimacy which had at last been forfeited by the dead language in which the Confucian classics were embalmed.

If we now turn our attention to the visual arts, the first point that will strike us is that renaissances in this field are a relatively common phenomenon. Among the more familiar instances of it we can pick out the renaissance of the 'Old Kingdom' style of sculpture and painting, after a two-thousand-years-long lapse, in the Egyptiac World of the Saïte Age in the seventh and sixth centuries BC; the renaissance of an Akkadian style of carving in bas-relief in the Sumero-Akkadian World of the ninth, eighth, and seventh centuries BC, when this resuscitated Akkadian art was practised with the greatest virtuosity in Assyria; and the renaissance, in miniature, of an Hellenic style of carving in bas-relief – of which the most exquisite exemplars were Attic masterpieces of the fifth and fourth centuries BC – on Byzantine diptychs, carved not in stone but in ivory, in the tenth, eleventh, and twelfth centuries of the Christian Era. These three visual renaissances, however, were all left far behind, both in the range of the ground covered and in the ruthlessness of the eviction of the previous occupants, by the renaissance of the Hellenic visual arts in Western Christendom. This evocation of the ghosts of Hellenic visual arts occurred in the three fields of architecture,

469

sculpture, and painting; and, in all these fields, the *revenant* established itself so securely that, after the West had been released from its thrall, Western artists no longer knew how to exploit their newly recovered liberty.

This paralysis of the native genius affected all three provinces of the visual arts; but the most extraordinary episode was the triumph of the Hellenic renaissance in the province of sculpture. In this field, the thirteenth-century French exponents of an original Western style had produced masterpieces that could stand in comparison with those of the Hellenic, Egyptiac, and Mahayanian Buddhist schools at their zeniths. In the field of painting, by contrast, Western artists had not yet shaken off the tutelage of the more precocious art of the Orthodox Christian Society; and in the field of architecture the Romanesque style – which, as its name indicates, was an inheritance from the last phase of the Hellenic Civilization – had already been overwhelmed by an intrusive 'Gothic' style that, despite its misleading label, had actually originated in the Syriac World.

The struggle between a doubly defeated Western visual art and its Syriac and Hellenic assailants can still be seen in the architecture and sculpture of the chapel that was built in Westminster Abbey between 1503 and 1519 under the auspices of King Henry VII (*regnabat* AD 1485–1509). In the vaulting of the roof the 'Gothic' style has achieved a final *tour de force* in defiance of the Hellenic invasion. The stone figures on high represent the swan-song of a Transalpine school of native Western Christian sculpture. The centre of the stage is triumphantly occupied by the Hellenizing masterpieces of the Italian sculptor Torrigiani (*vivebat* AD 1472–1522), confident in their mastery of the future.

The 'Gothic' architecture which thus continued to hold its own until the first quarter of the sixteenth century in Northern Europe had long since been driven off the field in Northern and Central Italy; for here, in any case, it had never succeeded so decisively as in Transalpine Europe in supplanting the Romanesque style. Italy was the bridgehead in which an alien presence, conjured up from a dead Hellenic World, first entrenched itself on Western soil. The successive stages in the triumphant progress of a Hellenizing style of architecture, which was eventually to replace both the Romanesque and the 'Gothic' throughout the Western World, can be traced in the history of the building of the Cathedral of Santa Maria del Fiore at Florence between 1296 and 1461. The Florentines' decision, taken in 1294, to scrap their medieval cathedral dedicated to Saint Reparata in order to erect a modern building on the site may be taken as a symbolic act signifying a resuscitated Hellenism's declaration of aggressive war upon the prevailing medieval style. The climax of this long-drawn-out architectural drama was the victory of Filippo Brunelleschi (*vivebat* AD 1377–1446) in a public competition, opened in 1418, for designs for a cupola to crown the cathedral.

Brunelleschi's cupola made so deep an impression on the imagination of the astonished Western World that the homely Italian word *duomo*, signifying 'the house [of God]', thereafter acquired the secondary meaning of a specific architectural structure which Western builders had lacked the skill to erect before Brunelleschi rediscovered the secret through his study of late Hellenic architecture. Yet Brunelleschi's cautiously high-pitched dome, which created this sensation in the West, would have looked clumsy to the eye of the contemporary Ottoman architect of the Green Mosque at Bursa, which was built for Sultan Mehmet I (*imperabat* AD 1413–21). Four hundred years after Brunelleschi's day, when his successors had run through all the resources of the resuscitated Hellenic technique, and had gone on to apply them to the revolutionizing of domestic as well as public architecture, the ultimate effect of their technical ingenuity was to make an aesthetic desert. The native Romanesque and the exotic 'Gothic' vein had been quenched long before the imported Hellenic cornucopia had been emptied by these successive generations of architects.

The sterility with which the Western genius had been afflicted by a renaissance of Hellenism in the domain of architecture was proclaimed by the West's difficulty in reaping a due harvest from the Industrial Revolution. Industry gave the Western World an incomparably versatile new building material in the iron girder, but nineteenth-century Western architects were for the most part content merely to incorporate the use of iron into otherwise uninventive buildings in the prevailing classical and 'Gothic' revival styles. Only a few buildings – Cyrus Hamlin's Hamlin Hall built on the shores of the Bosphorus in 1869–71, or the Halle des Machines built in Paris in 1889 – attempted an unashamed and full exploitation of the new technique. It was left to a much later generation of architects to explore all the potential of iron- and steel-framed construction in styles which owed nothing to either classical or 'Gothic' models.

This sterilization of the West's artistic genius, which for so long was the nemesis of the Hellenizing renaissance in the realm of architecture, was no less conspicuous in the realms of painting and sculpture. For more than half a millennium since the generation of Giotto (*vivebat c.* AD 1266–1337) the modern Western school of painting unquestioningly accepted the naturalistic ideals of Hellenic visual art in its post-archaic phase. It worked out, one after another, many different ways of conveying the visual impressions of light and shade, until this long-sustained effort to produce the effects of photography through prodigies of artistic technique were suddenly stultified by the invention of photography itself. After the ground had thus been cut away from under their feet by the shears of modern Western science, some Western painters made a Pre-Raphaelite movement in the direction of their long since repudiated Byzantine provenance. Others, however, made a genuinely new departure by turning to explore the new world of psychology which had been opened up by the advance of science, and used their paint to convey the spiritual experience of Psyche instead of the visual impressions of Argus. The same movement of psychological exploration eventually captured the field of sculpture too; and in both fields it has broadened out into a more intensive investigation of the structure of the physical world which science has been laying bare.

Thus, at the time of writing, it looks as if, in all three visual arts, the sterilization of the native Western genius by an exotic Hellenizing renaissance may at last be overcome; but the slowness and the difficulty of the cure show how serious the damage has been.

381, 382, 383 ARTISTIC CROSSROADS King Henry VII's Chapel in Westminster Abbey, built between 1503 and 1519, stands as a permanent monument to the contemporary struggle between local tradition and resuscitated Hellenism. The fan vaulting of the roof, opposite, is one of the last masterpieces of 'Gothic' masonry, and the stone figure from the wall belongs similarly to the final phase of a Northern European school of sculpture. Outshining both these examples of a native art is Torrigiani's triumphantly classical tomb for Henry and his wife, the first harbinger in England of Italy's Hellenistic renaissance.

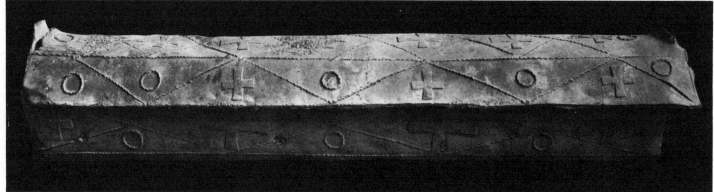

IMAGE-WORSHIP: HELLENIC ORIGINS

384, 385, 386 Three sarcophagi illustrate the alternation of Hellenic iconolatry and Judaic aniconism in Jewish and early Christian religious art. The first is Jewish, from the third or fourth century A D: an Hellenic infection is clear in the use of floral motifs and even human figures. An austere Christian sarcophagus of the same date, centre, shows a striking revival of Judaic aniconism, but a fifth-century Christian sarcophagus rejects this in favour of lavish decoration in the Hellenic style.

52 Renaissances of religions

IN THE REALM of religion, the classical example of a renaissance has been Judaism's perennial feat of redisclosing its accusatory yet ineradicable presence within the bosom of Christianity. The relation of Christianity to Judaism was as damningly clear to Jewish eyes as it was embarrassingly ambiguous for Christian consciences. In Jewish eyes the Christian Church was a renegade Jewish sect which had taken up the misleading teachings of a misguided though idealistic Galileean Pharisee. Christianity's captivation of the Hellenic World was not a divine miracle, but a pagan exploit; for this facile conquest had been achieved by means of a betrayal of Judaism's two cardinal principles, monotheism and aniconism, which were Yahweh's supreme revelations.[1] If Jewry had been willing to betray the Lord's trust by compromising with Hellenic polytheism and Hellenic idolatry, Jewry too could have cajoled the Hellenes into a nominal acceptance of Judaism at the price of Judaism's capitulating to Hellenism on these two crucial points of substance.

After Christianity had made this transparent compromise with Hellenism, the watchword for Jewry was to persevere in bearing her witness to the Lord's everlasting revelations and commandments. In the words of a renegade disciple of Gamaliel's:

Take unto you the whole armour of God, that ye may be able to withstand in the evil day, and, having done all, to stand. Stand therefore, having your loins girt about with truth.[2]

Jewry's disdain for the sensationally triumphant Christian Church might have been discounted by the victorious Church as the pique of a discomfited competitor if Christianity itself had not combined a sincere theoretical loyalty to its Jewish legacy of monotheism and aniconism with those practical concessions to Hellenic polytheism and idolatry for which it was being attacked by its Jewish critics. The Christian Church's reconsecration of the Jewish Scriptures as the Old Testament of the Christian faith was the weak spot in the Church's armour through which the shafts of Jewish criticism went home to Christianity's heart. 'Thou shalt have no other gods before Me' and 'Thou shalt not make unto thee any graven image, or any likeness of anything that is in Heaven above or that is in the Earth beneath or that is in the water under the Earth, thou shalt not bow down thyself to them nor serve them',[3] were commandments which the Christian believed, just as unquestionably as the Jew, to be words of God which Man was required to obey without any reservations.

The Ten Commandments were of the essence of an Old Testament which the New Testament was perpetually invoking as its authority and hallowing as the scripture that Christ had come to fulfil. The Old Testament was consequently one of the foundation-stones on which the edifice of Christianity rested; but so, too, was the doctrine of the Trinity, so again was the cult of the saints, and so likewise was the visual representation of the saints and of all three

387, 388 'THERE IS ONE GOD': Judaism's uncompromising monotheism is inscribed in Greek on a capital from a Palestinian synagogue of the sixth century A D. The New Testament Trinity was abhorrent to Jews – and to Muslims – as being a concession to Hellenic polytheism: a medieval miniature, *The Coronation of the Virgin*, represents the three Persons of the Trinity anthropomorphically, showing how close Christianity comes to being guilty of this charge.

IMAGE-WORSHIP: ORTHODOX REACTION

389 The cult of images in the early Christian Church, with its disturbing implications of idolatry, led Jewish critics to accuse Christianity of paganism. Conscious of its vulnerability on this score, the Church began to revive its inheritance of Judaic aniconism as early as the fourth century. In the eighth-century East Roman Empire, iconoclasm temporarily triumphed. The Emperor Leo Syrus removed the figure of Christ from the gate of his palace and representations of Christ in churches were whitewashed – an action equivalent in the eyes of iconophiles of the next century (when the manuscript above was produced) to recrucifying Him.

Persons of the Trinity in three-dimensional as well as two-dimensional works of art. None of these foundation-stones could be pulled out from under the building without danger of bringing it down. Yet how could the Christian apologists answer the Jewish taunt that the Church's Hellenic practice was irreconcilable with its Judaic theory? Some reply was required that would convince Christian minds that there was no substance in Jewish arguments; for the tellingness of the Jewish exposure of the hypocrisy of the Christian Church lay in the responsive conviction of sin which this Jewish indictment evoked in Christian souls. Judaism was thus able to take its revenge on Christianity by forcing the Church to fight on two fronts simultaneously; and the foreign war waged against an obstinately unconverted Jewry was less formidable for the Christian ecclesiastical authorities than the domestic struggle, waged deep within each Christian soul, between an Hellenically easy-going Christian paganism and a Judaically tender Christian conscience.

The duality of the conflict is reflected in Christian polemical literature in the distinction between the genre of apologias for Christianity against Jewish attacks on it, and the genre of controversies within the bosom of the Church between Christian iconodules and Christian iconoclasts, though the arguments bandied about in both genres, and taken over by successive generations of controversial writers, are of course identical to a large extent. After the nominal conversion *en masse* of the Hellenic Gentile World in the course of the fourth century, the domestic controversy within the pale of a now pan-Hellenic Church tended to overshadow the polemics between Christians and Jews. However, the theological warfare on this older front seems to have flared up again in the sixth and seventh centuries, as a result of a puritanical house-cleaning in Jewry which had begun towards the end of the fifth century in the Palestinian Jewish community. This domestic campaign within Jewry's bosom against a Christian-like laxity that had latterly been tolerating the visual representation of animals, and even of human beings, in the mural decorations of synagogues, had its repercussions on the Jewish-Christian battle front in a resumption of offensive-defensive Christian operations against the Jewish denunciation of Christian idolatry. When we turn to the parallel controversy between Christian iconophiles and Christian iconophobes, we shall be struck by its persistence and ubiquity. From the morrow, and indeed from the eve, of the Christian Church's victory over the pagan Diocletianic imperial régime, we find this conflict bursting out in almost every province of Christendom in almost every succeeding century of the Christian Era.

In a still unfissured Catholic Church a ferment of iconophobia can be seen spreading in and after the fourth century. The exhibition of pictures in churches was forbidden by the thirty-sixth canon of the Council of Elvira (*sedebat c.* AD 300–11). Eusebius of Caesarea (*vivebat c.* AD 264–340) refused to oblige Constantine the Great's sister Constantia by granting a request of hers to him to send her a holy image. Epiphanius, Bishop of Constantia (alias Salamis) and Metropolitan of Cyprus (*vivebat c.* AD 315–402), tore up a curtain with a picture embroidered on it which he found hanging in a church. In the Syriac Orient an attack against image-worship was launched, in about AD 488, by Xenaïas the Monophysite Bishop of Mabbug; and in the sixth century there were iconoclast riots at Edessa and at Antioch. In the same century in the Greek heart of the Christian *Oikoumene* the strength of iconoclastic feeling is indicated by the recorded fact that Julian, Bishop of Adramyttium, prohibited the exhibition in churches of his diocese of any visual representations in the round, and of any two-dimensional representations in stone and wood, and permitted sculpture-work on the doors only. In the same century in the Latin West a bishop of Narbonne found it advisable to drape a picture of Christ on the Cross, and Bishop Serenus of Marseilles broke or removed all images found by him in churches in his diocese. Iconophobe activity is recorded in the sixth and seventh centuries in Constantinople, Cyprus, Armenia, and Transcaucasia.

The evidence attests the vitality of the iconoclast cause in both the heart and the extremities of Christendom over a period of four hundred years up to the date at which the East Roman Emperor Leo Syrus made this cause his own; and it explains how it was that, in Orthodox Christendom, the ghost of a Judaic iconophobia was able to assert itself so brusquely. In AD 726, when the campaign for the destruction of images began, it was not a question of calling up a ghost from the dead, for by that date it had already been hovering for centuries, on the wait for any opportunity to fasten upon its victim's conscience.

In Orthodox Christendom the renaissance of Judaic iconophobia has a history not unlike that of the literary renaissance of Hellenism in the West. It broke out in two distinct eruptions, in 726–87 and 815–43, separated by an interval of quiescence; and the augury of eventual failure that could be discerned in the intervening set-back was fulfilled when the compromise between the two positions, which was agreed in 843, proved in the event to be a lasting peace in this five-centuries-old theatre of conflict.

This apparently permanent settlement of the controversy over images in Orthodox Christendom was not, however, the last that was to be heard of this vexed question in Christendom at large. The temporary re-establishment of the cult of images in Orthodox Christendom by the decisions of a council held at Nicaea in 787 evoked expressions of dissent and disapproval in Charlemagne's dominions; and, though this protest was quashed by Pope Hadrian I (*fungebatur* AD 722–95) when he rejected Charlemagne's suggestion that they should co-operate in a joint condemnation of the Second Nicene Council's acts, the eruption elsewhere in Transalpine Europe which these anticipatory rumblings portended did burst out at long last. The explosive sixteenth-century renaissance of a Jewish iconophobia in Germany was no less violent than the eighth-century explosion had been in Anatolia; and by now its effects have proved more persistent.

In this Protestant Reformation in Western Christendom the aniconism that was one of the two fundamental tenets of Judaism was not the only Judaic ghost that succeeded in reasserting itself. Judaic Sabbatarianism also captivated the sixteenth-century secessionists from the Roman Catholic Church; and the renaissance of this other element of Judaism in Protestant Western Christendom is less easy to explain. The meticulous observance of the Sabbath and of

IMAGE-WORSHIP: PROTESTANT REACTION

390 Dutch Protestant soldiers systematically destroy every representation of God or Man in a church: paintings, statues, windows, tombs, and altar are all desecrated in a furious attempt to purify the house of God from the intrusive idols. Western Christendom felt the iconoclast controversy less deeply than the East; the use of images, implanted by Hellenism in pre-Christian Italy, had been firmly established in the more naïve Western Church, and Papal Rome's break with imperial Constantinople over East Roman iconoclasm was one of a series of incidents that led ultimately to the schism between the Eastern Orthodox group of churches and the Roman See. A Western revival of Judaic iconoclasm was postponed until the sixteenth-century Reformation, when a vigorous reaction against images and against cults of saints became a central feature of the Protestant revolt – an issue that still divides the Western Church today.

other rituals had been the Jewish diasporá's effective response to the challenge of having to preserve its identity and its corporate existence under extremely adverse conditions; but the triumph of Jewish Sabbatarianism in the Western Christian World could not be ascribed to these unusual circumstances in which the Jewish dispersion had found itself.

The Protestants' paramount objective was to return to the pristine practice of the primitive Church; yet here we see them obliterating a difference of practice between primitive Christianity and Judaism which the primitive Church had introduced expressly to serve as a distinguishing mark. The primitive Church had advertised its secession from Jewry by transferring its weekly holy day from the Sabbath to the first day of the week; and the Protestants were now doing their best to cancel the intended effect of this primitive Christian new departure by applying to the 'Lord's day' both the Judaic name of the Sabbath and the Judaic tabu associated with it. Could these 'Bible Christians' be unaware of the logion 'the Sabbath was made for Man, and not Man for the Sabbath'?[4] Could they have read, without understanding, the numerous passages in the Gospels,[5] illustrating this thesis, in which Jesus is reported to have gone out of his way to break the Sabbatarian tabu? Could it have escaped the Protestants' notice that Paul, whom they honoured above all the other Apostles, had made himself notorious by repudiating and denouncing the Mosaic Law, root and branch? The answer to these questions is that, in appealing from the authority of the Papacy to that of the Bible, the Protestants had reanimated not only the New Testament, but the Old Testament as well, and that, in a contest between the two resuscitated spirits for the dominion over Protestant souls, the spirit of Judaism had prevailed. The consequent renaissance of a Judaic Sabbatarianism was an impressive testimony to the lasting power of a ghost by which Gentile Christianity had been haunted and harassed ever since its birth.

Although these renaissances of Judaic elements in Christianity are impressive, they are not the only examples of the phenomenon in the field of religion. The commonest form that it takes is the revival of selected features of an ancestral religion, often with the object of stimulating a resurgence of religious conviction and fervour. The Western Christian World experienced successive movements of this kind, sometimes amounting to no more than a slight emphasis on one particular aspect of orthodoxy, but occasionally rising to an explosive surge of reform and purification, and culminating, as we have seen, in the Protestant Reformation of the sixteenth century. Japan, after her disastrous defeat in the Second World War, spawned numerous new religious sects. The majority of these were based on some element taken from traditional Shinto or Buddhist belief, refurbished for the use of a people who – demoralized by the demotion of their Emperor from divine status and by the consequent emasculation of the official State Shinto religion – was seeking to fortify itself with an artificially resurrected faith.[6]

When a gulf opens between traditional religious orthodoxy and actual material experience, it is apt eventually to be closed by some form of religious revival. The obsoleteness of a religious doctrine may for a time appear to confirm the view that religion itself is unnecessary and illusory;[7] but there is a strong tendency for Man's spiritual aspirations to reassert themselves, frequently by means of a revival of the spiritual beliefs of a past more remote than the age from which the discarded religion sprang. It might not be too fanciful to see in the current reaction against Man's pollution of his natural environment a rediscovery of the ancient belief in the sacrosanctity of Nature. Our ancestors understood by intuition that Man could not violate Nature with impunity; and the experience of modern times has reaffirmed the truth that the natural world is not a public utility that is at Man's disposal for endless exploitation, but is an ecological system in which Man himself is inextricably involved and which Man therefore cannot abuse without harming himself.

PART XI

WHY STUDY HISTORY?

My study of history would be incomplete if, after having surveyed the process of history, I failed to ask myself what history is and how an account of it comes to be written. I do not think that history, in the objective sense of the word, is a succession of facts, nor history-writing the narration of these facts. Historians, like all human observers, have to make reality comprehensible, and this involves them in continuous judgments about what is true and what is significant. This requires classification, and the study of the facts has to be synoptic and comparative, since the succession of facts flows in a number of simultaneous streams. Historians who accept the full implications of their task are in danger of erecting deterministic explanations, but I do not think that this need be so. I believe that human beings are free to make choices within the limitations of their human capacity. I also believe that history shows us how men may learn to make choices that are not only free but effective by learning to achieve harmony with a supra-human reality that makes itself felt although it is impalpable. A curiosity to explain and understand the world is the stimulus that has excited men to study their past, so I conclude by looking at some of the impulses that have moved individual historians to embark on their work of discovery and explanation.

plate 87

THE SHAPE OF HISTORY

Man has to dissect reality into innumerable isolated fragments in order to be able to understand it. This process of articulation and classification undoubtedly misrepresents reality, but it is an inescapable consequence of conscious thought – the alternative is the mystic's wholly passive intuition of divine unity. This 'Tree of History' is one such attempt to make history intelligible by classifying its data and then presenting them as a reintegrated whole. It illustrates the philosophy of the twelfth-century Christian thinker Joachim of Fiore, whose scheme has a basically theological structure. The Tree is divided into three ages, presided over by the Father (the age of law and fear), the Son (grace and faith), and the Holy Ghost (love and freedom). Among the significant persons and events represented by the branches are the Twelve Tribes of Israel, the mission of John the Baptist, the first coming of Christ, the foundation of the Churches, the sequence of Popes thought to herald the dawning of the last age, and the second coming of Christ. The Tree culminates in the consummation of the third and final age: Joachim prophesied that it would be foreshadowed in the middle of the thirteenth century, and that after its establishment it would endure as a Kingdom of Saints until the Last Judgment. His interpretation of history is clearly that of a medieval Western Christian, yet similar millennarian ideas continued to be popular in later centuries and can even be discerned in Marx.

plates 88, 89

CURIOSITY AND
CATASTROPHE

The Western archaeologist, left,
is fascinated by the relics of a
vanished civilization which are
meaningless for the shepherd
guarding his flock and for the
Muslim intent on his prayers:
such curiosity, born of 'emotion
recollected in tranquillity', inspired the work of Gibbon and
of Ibn Khaldun. More rarely,
the historian's curiosity may be
kindled by his own experience
of catastrophe: the sudden
shattering of a stable world,
portrayed by the painter of
War, opposite, jolted the author
of this Study into action in
August 1914, as a similar shock
had jolted Thucydides in 431 BC.

plate 90

LIFE'S CONSUMMATION

A detail from Fra Angelico's *Christ Glorified in the Court of Heaven*
presents his vision of the communion of Saints. It is a visual
declaration of a Christian's belief that all things work together
for good to them that love God. The artist is addressing fellow-
Christians in the style of his own time and place, yet simultaneously he is conveying a universal message. The beauty and
the holiness of his work transcend the difference between
historic religious and cultural traditions. His joy and hope
communicate themselves to anyone who gazes at his picture and
meditates on its meaning. The host of beatified souls converges
on the figure of Christ who has been their inspiration and their
goal. They are adoring their saviour and are celebrating a
triumph which, because it is his, is also the consummation of
their own pilgrimage. This imagery interprets the ultimate
spiritual reality in terms of one particular monotheistic religion;
yet Fra Angelico's depiction of an ineffable mystery also lends
itself to other interpretations. The Christ on whom the pilgrims'
paths converge is Teilhard de Chardin's 'Omega Point'; the
choir's unison is an intuition of a Hindu monist's experience of
unity; the scene's serenity anticipates a Buddhist arhat's exit
into *nirvana*.

391 Clio, the muse of history, from a Roman sarcophagus. The name comes from the Greek, *kleos*, meaning fame won by glorious deeds; in Hellenic mythology Clio celebrated the deeds of heroes. Herodotus, the first servant of Clio, wrote his *Histories* 'lest the great and wonderful deeds performed by Greeks and barbarians should become lost to fame'.

WE HAVE now brought to a close the plan of operations that we set ourselves in the first Part of this Study. We have surveyed the lives of civilizations, the relations between them, and the emergence of the higher religions as societies of a distinctive species. The object of these intellectual labours has been to make our human history comprehensible as a whole, by examining the evidence that is available to us as twentieth-century men. We have so far assumed that this object must be attainable, but we have not yet asked ourselves whether this assumption is legitimate, nor have we made any critical appraisal of the mental tools that we have employed in this self-imposed task of explanation. All study, whether of human affairs or of non-human Nature, is subject to the limitations of human thought; and the first and greatest of these is that thought cannot help doing violence to reality in the act of trying to apprehend it.

For all we know, reality is the undifferentiated unity of the mystical experience. We cannot know whether it is or not, because we cannot be conscious without our mental image of reality – or reality's image of itself, mirrored in a human mind[1] – being diffracted or articulated into subject and object. This is the first link in a chain of articulations that we forge as fast as we go on thinking.

Our human consciousness, after its self-generating – or reality's generating – articulative act, goes on to dissect reality further into the conscious and the subconscious, soul and body, mind and matter, life and environment, freedom and necessity, creator and creatures, god and devil, good and bad, right and wrong, love and power, old and new, cause and effect. Such binary structures are indispensable categories of thought; they are our means of apprehending reality, as far as this is within our power. At the same time they are so many boundary-marks indicating the limits of human understanding, since they misrepresent reality by breaking up its unity in our apprehension of it. They are as baffling as they are enlightening. We cannot do without them, yet cannot do with them either. We cannot afford either to discount them completely or to take them at their full face value.

We cannot think about the Universe without assuming that it is articulated; and, at the same time, we cannot defend the articulations that we find, or make, in it against the charge that these are artificial and arbitrary. It can always be shown that they break up something that is indivisible and let slip something that is essential. Yet, without mentally articulating the Universe, we cannot ourselves be articulate – cannot, that is, either think or will. And we cannot go on thinking or willing if we regain the unity of the mystical experience. So we have to dissect – and, in dissecting, misrepresent – reality in order to apprehend reality sufficiently to be able to act and live in the light of the truth as far as we can discern it. Our inability to apprehend reality completely is, of course, not surprising. It is a paradox that one part of a whole should be able to distinguish itself from the rest and should then be able to achieve even a partial apprehension of the whole,

including itself. This feat is miraculous, however imperfect. How far it does fall short of attaining a true mental image of reality it is impossible for a human mind to tell.

Thought has no sooner set itself going by mentally breaking reality up than it gets to work to put reality together again. After having analysed, thought operates by classifying: that is, by identifying a number of different objects as being specimens of one and the same kind.[2] These objects between which the mind finds sufficient resemblance to allow it to bring them together mentally under some single head are no more than particular facets of phenomena. The facets of any phenomenon are innumerable, as is demonstrated by our ability to classify one and the same phenomenon in innumerable different ways, each corresponding to some different facet that it displays. So any one classification apprehends no more than a fraction of each of the phenomena that it brings together; and, when we have classified the same phenomenon under as many different heads as it displays facets whose like we can detect in other phenomena, we are still left with an unidentifiable residue that has eluded all classification. This is what we mean when we say that in every phenomenon there is something 'unique'. This word 'unique' is a negative term signifying what is mentally inapprehensible. The absolutely unique is, by definition, indescribable.

A high valuation of this element of uniqueness within the realm of human nature is evidently what has made its status a burning question in the study of human affairs, while it is not one in the natural sciences. This also perhaps explains why it is that among the various schools of students of human affairs – philosophers, theologians, logicians, psychologists, anthropologists, sociologists, historians – it is the historians who have made it their business to be not only the exponents of the element of uniqueness, but also its champions. The most obvious definition of history is that it is the study of human phenomena as we see them on the move through time and space; but a different definition has been proposed by A. L. Kroeber. The essence of the historian's approach, he suggests, is not the vision of human affairs as temporal events; it is 'the endeavour to achieve a conceptual integration of phenomena while preserving the integrity of the phenomena'.[3] This is the antithesis to the analytical and classificatory procedure, but these two alternative definitions of history do not conflict with each other. History must aim at preserving the complexity of individual events 'while also constructing them into a design which possesses a certain coherence of meaning'.[4] The truth is that 'no description of any individual object or event can dispense with predicates or abstract repeatable traits',[5] and that therefore 'no statement about the past can avoid some element of generality'.

If . . . there is genuine novelty in the Universe, and if events occur that have never occurred before, history must be an incomplete explanation of the present. In order to learn from the past there must be recurrences and similarities both throughout the past and between it and the present. There are enough recurrences and similarities to enable history to give us some account of the past and some explanation of the present. Thus our choices are at least partially illuminated and enlightened.[6]

Change, novelty, and creation in human affairs are manifestations of the element of uniqueness in them, and one of the most cherished aims of historians is to catch change, novelty, and creation in their mental grasp; but they have to employ an instrument of thought which can analyse and classify points of likeness, but cannot cope with elements in phenomena that display no relations with any others. In seeking to apprehend what is unique, historians are, in fact, trying to swim against the current of the operational movement of the intellect.

The starting-point of historical interpretation, as of any intellectual enterprise, is the assumption that reality has some meaning for us which is accessible to us by the mental process of explanation. We assume that reality makes sense, even if perhaps not completely. That is to say, we assume that there is at least a certain amount of order and regularity in the relations between the myriad phenomena into which our image of reality is dissected in our human consciousness. 'All induction *assumes* the existence of *connexions* in nature, and . . . its only object is to determine between what elements these connexions hold.'[7] Two expressions of this assumption are the beliefs in the uniformity of Nature and in causation. Since this is true of all thought, it is true of thought about human affairs. 'The historian employs concepts and hypotheses because of the general assumption that underlies all social science: *History is not exclusively chaos or chance: a degree of observable order and pattern, of partially predictable regularity, exists in human behavior.*'[8] If we ask what justification we have for making these assumptions, all we can say is that to deny the uniformity of Nature and the category of causality is to resolve the Universe into items that have no intelligible connexion with each other.

In this sense determinism is the epistemological basis of the human search for knowledge. Man cannot even conceive the image of an undetermined universe. In such a world there could not be any awareness of material things and their changes. It would appear a senseless chaos. Nothing could be identified and distinguished from anything else. Nothing could be expected and predicted. In the midst of such an environment man would be as helpless as if spoken to in an unknown language. No action could be designed, still less put into execution. Man is what he is because he lives in a world of regularity and has the mental power to conceive the relation of cause and effect.[9]

The truth of this proposition has not, however, prevented the defence of the unique from becoming and remaining the primary concern of the historian; but 'history is concerned with the relation between the unique and the general. As a historian, you can no more separate them, or give precedence to one over the other, than you can separate fact and interpretation.'[10] The juxtaposition of these two pairs of concepts is by no means arbitrary, for they are clearly related to each other in a way that reaches beyond the confines of epistemology.

The historian's common assumption that 'the facts are there to be used'[11] is surely mistaken. Facts are not really like boulders that have been detached and shaped and deposited exclusively by the play of the forces of non-human Nature, waiting – ready-made though not man-made – to be picked up and used by the historian; nor does the historian find facts strewn along his way as he strolls through the past. They are like flaked and chopped flints, hewn stones, or bricks. Human action has had a hand in making them what they are, and they would not be what they are if this action had not been taken. The facts of history are not 'brute things or events outside the mind, for they have been filtered through minds before I have word of them'[12] – and, one might add, before my own mind apprehends them. Facts are, in truth, exactly what is meant by the Latin word *facta* from which the English word is derived. They are 'things that have been made' – that is to say 'fictitious' things rather than 'factual' things – and this truth about them cannot be evaded by calling them 'data' ('gifts') instead. Gifts imply the existence of a giver, as inescapably as manufactures imply the existence of a maker. Whether we call the phenomena 'data' or call them 'facts', we are admitting that they have been given or have been made by somebody. We may attribute the maximum amount of credit for them to non-human Nature or to God, but we shall not be able to clear ourselves of the charge that we, too, have had a hand in the transaction, and that our contribution, however small we may reckon it to have been, has nevertheless been an indispensable one.

This is true both of the facts themselves and of our reception of them. 'Facts do not "speak for themselves". Concepts do not "emerge" from the evidence.'[13] 'The facts speak only when the historian calls on them: it is he who decides to which facts to give the floor, and in what order or context. . . . The belief in a hard core of historical facts existing objectively and independently of the interpretation of the historian is a preposterous fallacy.'[14] For this reason, it is quite inappropriate to regard history as being a sequence of facts, and the historian's job as being merely to accumulate as great a number of facts as he can muster. Not only do facts not 'speak for themselves', but 'those who tried to create theory out of facts never understood that it was only theory that could constitute them as facts in the first place'.[15] That is to say, 'there is no abstract thing called "History" which bestows significance upon events in time'.[16] History is the framing of questions by a particular human being in a particular space-time context; he asks questions, and he adduces evidence to support his answers, and in both these acts he makes use of hypothesis before ever he 'finds' a fact. This is true even of the barest narrative form of history, which makes no other claim than 'to show how things really were'.[17] The simplicity of this pretension is nothing but an illusion: it merely leaves unspoken the historian's working hypotheses – the criteria by which he has articulated his questions and his answers. Otherwise, the historian would be convicting himself of an absurd belief that 'all facts are equal, but some are more equal than others'.

Facts cannot, then, come into existence without the good offices of an hypothesis. If it is true that every fact is – as the etymology of the word implies – something that has been constructed, and, if it is also true that part, at least, of the indispensable work of construction has been done by the apprehending human mind, it seems hazardous to try to classify some so-called 'facts' as genuine on the illusory ground that they are objective, while rejecting other so-called 'facts' as spurious on the solid ground that they are constructions of a human mind. If it is true that all facts are partly constructions of human minds, the presence or absence of this man-made element in them cannot be an effective criterion for distinguishing the spurious from the genuine.

Does this conclusion commit us to an inescapable relativism? There cannot be observation without inter-action between the observer and the object under his observation, and in interacting they are bound to affect each other reciprocally. If historical study is one instance of such interaction – in this case, between the historian and his facts – what prevents us from seeing in the histories written by historians merely so many alternative acts of imagination, each competing on equal terms for our allegiance? In every case the historian's view of the past will be conditioned by the ever-changing position of his own present observation-point; and in this sense relativity is a limitation that is imposed upon human studies in all fields by the very nature of the situation in which the conscious human mind has to operate. But it follows from this that

objectivity in history . . . cannot be an objectivity of fact, but only of relation, of the relation between fact and interpretation, between past, present and future. . . . The historian . . . in his task of interpretation needs his standard of significance, which is also his standard of objectivity, in order to distinguish between the significant and the accidental; and he . . . can find it only in relevance to the end in view. But this is necessarily an evolving end, since the evolving interpretation of the past is a necessary function of history. The traditional assumption that change has always to be explained in terms of something fixed and un-changeable is contrary to the experience of the historian.[18]

What are the objectives which historians have had in view in their studies of history? To begin with, we can take it as axiomatic that the study of human affairs has some meaning, and that the historian undertakes to explain this meaning or to 'make sense of' history. As soon as he posits a causal connexion between two events, he is beginning to make sense of the past; that is, to marshal it in some sort of orderly system and so make it accessible to human understanding. All historians are committed to this purpose; but for many this is not the end of the story. They have felt impelled to strike out further along the road towards a systematic formulation and interpretation of history as a whole, and not just of parts of it. Perhaps we can distinguish between these two approaches by calling them respectively 'history' and 'metahistory'. 'Metahistory is concerned with the nature of history, the meaning of history and the cause and significance of historical change.'[19] It arises out of the study of history, and is akin to metaphysics and theology. The metahistorian seeks to integrate his study of reality in some higher dimension than that of human affairs as these present themselves to him phenomenally.

A classic work of metahistory, in this sense, is Saint Augustine's *De Civitate Dei*, as contrasted, for example, with the histories written by Thucydides or by Livy. Thucydides and Livy each set out to describe and explain a particular series of events that seemed important to them (and that seem important still to a modern student of history). Thucydides's subject was the origin and course of the great war that convulsed the Hellenic Society in 431–404 BC; Livy's was the majestic rise and culmination of the Empire in which he lived and which he felt to be in decay in his own time. But Saint Augustine 'give[s] us a synthesis of universal history in the light of Christian principles'.[20]

Ideally, perhaps, every historian needs to be a meta-historian in some degree, since 'history properly so-called can be written only by those who find and accept a sense of direction in history itself'.[21] In practice, though, there has usually been a disagreement about the nature of the historian's craft between historians who have committed themselves to the metahistorical viewpoint, and those who have seen their own chief merit in their resolute refusal, on principle, to indulge in large-scale synthetical writing. The attempt to discover some central principle of order or regularity in the historical process – by analogy with the world of physical Nature – is, in truth, an enterprise that bristles with difficulties for the human intelligence; yet this in itself is no reason to condemn the attempt as futile. The historian who seeks to understand the broad connexions of past, present, and future has embarked on at least the first stages of a search for the ultimate cause, but he does not expect to reach his goal any more than the natural scientist believes he will discover the ultimate nature of matter.

The principal pitfall for the metahistorian is perhaps the temptation to emphasize the deterministic aspect of causation and thereby to deny at least implicitly the possibility of free will. We have already seen in this chapter that a belief in determinism is an epistemological precondition for human knowledge and action, but it does not follow from this that Man's action are unfree in the sense of being pre-ordained by some non-human or suprahuman force, for 'the notion of contingency . . . refers to a limitation of the human search for knowledge, not to a condition of the universe or of some of its parts'.[22] None the less, the belief has proved irresistibly attractive to many human minds; in an earlier chapter,[23] we saw how its attractions tend to be greatest in times of profound social upheaval, when men's actions seem impotent to arrest the process of social decay. In that context, we concluded that determinism and fatalism are the refuge of minds that are too defeatist or too vain to face the humiliating but liberating truth that 'we are betray'd by what is false within'.[24]

Determinism derives its force from the observation of 'laws of Nature' which manifestly affect human lives – for instance, the unalterable succession of the seasons, or of day and night, or, in the realm of animate Nature, the succession of generations of creatures that are predestined to die. The same observation must also have suggested the cyclical interpretation of human history, a doctrine that, as we have seen,[25] dominated Indic minds and was enter-tained by Hellenic minds too. The application of the 'theory of eternal recurrence' to human affairs is a counsel of despair for humanity, since this doctrine denies that Man has any power ever to effect a permanent change in his condition, and teaches him that he is condemned to suffer the meaningless revolutions of the wheel of existence.

It is true that, when we survey the surviving records of Mankind's past acts and experiences, both personal and corporate, we do observe recurrences that have been not only numerous but also, in some cases, momentous. The evidence for this is manifest and massive. It cannot be explained away, and this makes it probable that, in some departments of human life, there will continue to be recurrences in the future. But it is a fallacy to interpret these observations as being proofs that the theory of inevitable, and therefore eternal, recurrence holds good for human history. The fact that such and such an event has recurred, perhaps many times over, does not prove that it was ever bound to recur; and, *a fortiori*, this does not prove that it is bound to recur again in the future. In the inner lives and in the social relations of human beings, the patterns that we discern in the record do not have any built-in capacity or impulse to reproduce themselves. To credit acts and experiences and relations with this capacity is to misunderstand their nature. A patterned set of acts or experiences or relations is something quite different from an organism. The recurrences of historical events and situations are consequences, not of physical heredity, but of moral *karma* (in the Buddhist usage of the word).

Although a commitment to determinism is implicit in the cyclical view of human history, the alternative 'linear' or one-way view of it is also not immune from this fallacy. The belief in a progressive historical process inevitably begs the question whether the process has or does not have a goal, and the assumption that it does have a goal leads in turn to the question whether human beings are impelled or compelled to head for this goal either deliberately or involuntarily. A tension between the belief in the predetermination of the goal and a belief in the genuineness of some degree of freedom in moving towards this inevitable goal is evident in Christian historical philosophy: Saint Augustine released the late Hellenic World from the belief in Man's enslavement to a wholly arbitrary fate or fortune, but he accomplished this at the apparent price of re-subjecting Man to the tyranny of an unknowable Divine Will. The same paradoxical relapse into determinism is implicit in Islam, the religion whose name means 'submission' to God. In the secularized modern Western World determinism was given new force by the revolutionary progress of scientific discovery in the sphere of physical Nature, and it reappeared in the materialist dialectic of Marxism.

However, neither Western Christian philosophy nor the post-Christian Western philosophy of Marxism involves a belief that Man is helplessly at the mercy of necessity. Man's freedom from this servitude is vindicated when the nature of the dialectical process is properly understood. Man is not condemned to be the plaything of fortune or the tool of an enigmatic and perhaps arbitrary Deity. Under the law of God or the laws of Nature, Man is free to make choices and to pursue objectives in so far as he knows the laws and takes care to act in accordance with them. Engels described the dialectical process as 'an ascent from the kingdom of necessity to the kingdom of freedom';[26] a Christian might describe it as the process by which Man freely embraces God's law of love. What does this mean in practice? In Engels's words:

Freedom is the appreciation of necessity. 'Necessity is *blind* only *in so far as it is not understood*.' Freedom does not consist in the dream of independence of natural laws, but in the knowledge of these laws, and in the possibility this gives of systematically making them work towards definite ends. . . . Freedom of the will therefore means nothing but the capacity to make decisions with real knowledge of the subject. . . . Freedom therefore consists in the control over ourselves and over external nature which is founded on knowledge of natural necessity; it is therefore necessarily a product of historical development.[27]

In Christian terms, the 'glorious freedom of the sons of God', which they enjoy under the law of love, is the perfect freedom possessed by God Himself, which an all-loving Creator has exercised at the sacrificial price of emptying himself[28] of almighty power for the sake of coming to the rescue of his creature, Man. Under a law of love which is the law of God's own Being, God's self-sacrifice challenges Man by setting before him an ideal of spiritual perfection; and Man has perfect freedom to accept or reject this. The law of love leaves Man as free to be a sinner as to be a saint; it leaves him free to choose whether his personal and his social life shall be a progress towards the Kingdom of God or towards the kingdom of night.

In neither of these formulations is there any externally applied coercion; yet, when Man does voluntarily comply with – in Christian terms – God's law, or – in Marxist terms – the laws of Nature, he becomes progressively more self-aware and thus more self-determining, in the sense of being more free to make choices that, besides being free, are effective.

392 'The peace of immortal man with immortal God is an orderly obedience unto His eternal law. . . . The devil transgressed the peaceful law of order, yet could not avoid the powerful hand of the Orderer': miniature from a fourteenth-century edition of Augustine's *De Civitate Dei*.

54 Historians in action

In the preceding chapter we have examined the nature of historical thought and have surveyed the principal schools of interpretation of the phenomena of history. This investigation has been made possible by the work of the historians: by their thoughts, their feelings, and their communication of these thoughts and feelings to their fellow human beings.

Writing has been the historians' principal means of communication in societies in which, within the last five thousand years, there has been a literate public. But literate, as well as pre-literate, societies have also erected architectural monuments to commemorate notable persons or events, and the purpose of these monuments has not been explained by accompanying inscriptions in all cases. In some pre-literate societies, genealogies, extending in some cases backwards over many generations, have been memorized, and, in all states of society in all ages since our ancestors became human, there have also been unwitting historians: for instance, people who have piously buried precious equipment with the dead, or who have casually thrown away blunted tools or broken pots. This piety and this slovenliness, between them, have provided our archaeologists with mute records that reveal far less than the written word but extend our knowledge of what they do reveal over a far wider range of time and space.

Unlike the archaeologists' insouciant informants, the memorizers of genealogies, the builders of monuments, and the writers of narratives have taken deliberate action for recording events; and the impulse that has prompted this action has been curiosity. This impulse may be defined as being an intellectual and emotional concern for things that are not of any obvious practical use for the person who feels this concern or for other members of his family or of his community. (The discoveries that have resulted from curiosity have, of course, repeatedly proved to be unexpectedly useful eventually.)

Curiosity is a distinctively human impulse. It is a consequence of consciousness; for consciousness confronts a human mind with phenomena that are evidently no more than a fragment of reality and are certainly superficial, and possibly delusive, even as far as they go. Curiosity is an impulse to probe through the phenomena in search of the reality that the phenomena mask. Curiosity remains unsatisfied unless and until it has attained its objective; and therefore, though it may begin as a pastime, it will end, if pursued perseveringly, in a religious experience. An encounter with the reality behind the phenomena is not just a mental feat; it is an imperative commitment for the human self to put itself in harmony with ultimate reality by bringing its own human will into conformity with it.

The phenomena, presented by consciousness, that may arouse curiosity may be found in one or more of several different fields. One field is non-human Nature, another is social human affairs, yet another is a human being's inner spiritual life, and this third field is the one in which ultimate reality may be encountered by a human being who presses his quest of reality to its conclusion. The lengths to which people carry this quest differ greatly from person to person, and these differences in degree of perseverance are due, not only to innate differences of personal character, but also to differences in people's cultural environment. For instance, the Indic cultural environment stimulates curiosity about the inner spiritual life, whereas the modern Western cultural environment tends to direct curiosity towards non-human Nature.

Curiosity about social human affairs is stimulated by different cultures to different extents. The stimulus is at its minimum in arrested societies or communities, and we may guess that it was also minimal throughout the Lower Palaeolithic Age. In the Islamic World the Western traveller C. F. Volney found curiosity at a low ebb in AD 1783–85. He observed that his Muslim contemporaries were incurious about the stupendous monuments of the past among which they were squatting.[1] Since then, the Islamic peoples' curiosity has been reawakened by the impact of the West which hit Egypt in 1798 and has been sustained since then with ever-greater vigour. Today, explorations are carried out in Middle Eastern countries by national as well as by foreign archaeologists.

Moreover, before the thirteenth century of the Christian Era, when the Islamic World fell into adversity, Muslims had shown more curiosity about non-human Nature than contemporary Westerners; and, even in the subsequent Islamic dark age, the Islamic Society demonstrated its abiding interest in social human affairs by producing a series of historians, including Volney's and Napoleon's eminent Egyptian contemporary 'Abd-ar-Rahman al-Jabarti and his Tunisian predecessor Ibn Khaldun (*vivebat* AD 1332–1406), the most illuminating interpreter of the morphology of history that has appeared anywhere in the world so far.[2] The Muslims' concern for history is not surprising, since Islam, unlike Hinduism, but like Islam's two sister Judaic religions, Christianity and Judaism itself, is embedded in the history of human affairs.

Without the impulse of curiosity, there cannot be intellectual action in any field. There can, however, be curiosity that does not generate action. The acquisitive curiosity of the collector and the apprehensive curiosity of the examinee are cases in point. In these cases, the information that is accumulated by curiosity is used only passively, not actively. The subject of the present chapter is curiosity that has led to action in which the explorer has taken the initiative. The original field of the action surveyed in this chapter has been the study of mundane human affairs; but some of the historians who have started their operations in this field have pressed on beyond it to explore Man's relations with the reality behind the phenomena. The two Tunisian historians, Ibn Khaldun and Augustine, have carried their inquiries to the point at which history is transfigured into theology – a folly in the opinion of many modern Westerners, but no stumbling-block for medieval Western minds.

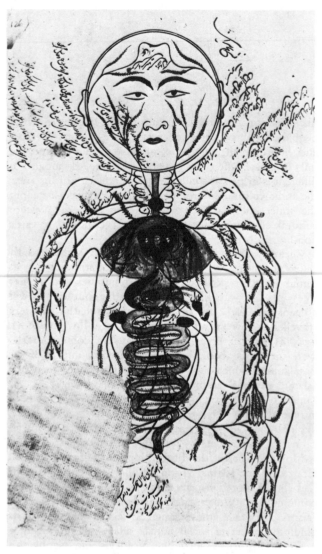

393 Until its decline in the thirteenth century, the Islamic Society maintained a standard of proficiency in scientific and historical study that was unequalled in the medieval West. This illustration of the digestive system comes from a seventeenth-century manuscript of the *Canon of Medicine* by the eleventh-century Arab physician and philosopher Avicenna (ibn Sina), which remained the standard medical textbook in the Western World until the seventeenth century.

394, 395 History-writing waits upon curiosity. The stupendous monuments of Egypt, opposite above, had been visible for six or seven thousand years to those who lived there, but had awoken no desire to investigate them. It was left to visitors from outside to begin probing their meaning. Beneath, *savants* accompanying Napoleon's expeditionary force in 1798 start work on the reinvestigation of Egypt's past.

Action is the crux. To fail to take action, or to miss the right moment for taking it, is as disastrous for intellectual work as it is for practical work; and in the intellectual field the danger of miscarriage through inaction is more insidious, because the nemesis is usually not so quickly manifest. Since curiosity is the generator of intellectual action, an imperative and pertinacious curiosity is the intellectual worker's prime need. If his curiosity is strong enough, it can move mountains.

Heinrich Schliemann (*vivebat* A D 1822–90), the discoverer and excavator of the site of Troy, had his curiosity aroused by an engraving, in a book given to him by his father when he was not yet eight years old, of Aeneas carrying his father Anchises out of the burning city of Ilion. The child's father explained to him that the massive city-walls depicted in this engraving were imaginary. The child declared his belief that Ilion must have had real walls, and he announced his intention to unearth them. The father was a drunkard; the son started life penniless. From his fifteenth to his forty-second year (1836–63), Heinrich earned a fortune, and educated himself simultaneously. He spent his forty-seventh to his sixty-ninth year (1868–90) on disinterring, first the seven or eight strata of Troy, and then the Mycenaean sites on Ithaca and at Mycenae, Orchomenos, and Tiryns.

George Grote (*vivebat* A D 1794–1871), the author of *A History of Greece* (a magisterial work), was the son, not of an impoverished drunken pastor, but of a well-to-do selfish banker, who put his son to work in the family business in his sixteenth year, without allowing him any margin of either time or money, in order to enable the historian's father himself to live at leisure and in affluence. George Grote's lifework was in double jeopardy; for he was inclined to dissipate ineffectually, on diverse worthy non-commercial pursuits, the meagre residue of his working time that his commercial duties did not occupy. The situation was saved for Grote by his father's death and by his own marriage. His wife prevailed upon him to concentrate, from 1843 onwards, on carrying out the *magnum opus* that he appears to have planned as early as 1822, and he passed the proofs of the twelfth (the concluding) volume of *A History of Greece* on 23 December 1855.[3] Though Grote seems to have been disinclined temperamentally to concentrate his intellectual energies, the severe discipline of commercial business had schooled him, as it had schooled Schliemann (who was endowed already by nature with an heroic self-control and pertinacity), when at last he devoted his time to the particular intellectual work that was his true vocation.

Schliemann's and Grote's curiosity enabled them to surmount difficulties imposed on them by their personal lot in life. Ibn Khaldun, the outstanding genius in the field of the study of the morphology of history, and Giambattista Vico (*vivebat* A D 1668–1744), the pioneer in this line of historical study in the Western World, were moved by their curiosity to surmount a difficulty of a different kind. They had to contend with the dearth of the information at their command for carrying out their enterprise.

The method of studying morphology is necessarily comparative. The morphologist has to take a synoptic view of the largest number of specimens of his subject that he can assemble. For studying the morphology of history, an assemblage of civilizations and higher religions is needed. Since 1798, the year in which Napoleon landed in Egypt with a working party of *savants* attached to his expeditionary force, Western archaeologists and orientalists have been expanding the Western World's historical horizon by making large additions to the number of known societies of these two species. They have been acquainting modern Westerners with all the living non-Western civilizations and non-Western-Christian forms of higher religion, and they have been disinterring the material relics of extinct civilizations that had fallen into oblivion or that had become intellectually inaccessible even when, as in the case of the Egyptiac Civilization, posterity had continued to be reminded of a civilization's former existence by the survival, above ground, of conspicuous monuments.

By the year 1927, when I began to make the notes for the original version of the present work, I was able to survey twenty-one civilizations, thanks to the work of the archaeologists and orientalists during the preceding 130 years. In the year 1961, I was able to survey thirty-one; and I have now been able to add the African Civilizations. By contrast, Vico, working at Naples in the early eighteenth century, had only two civilizations within his historical horizon, namely his own Western Civilization and its Hellenic predecessor, while Ibn Khaldun, working in North-West Africa and Egypt in the fourteenth century of the Christian Era, had only a single civilization – his own Islamic Civilization – at his command, since his knowledge of non-Islamic civilizations, contemporary or antecedent, was dim. Yet Vico, by comparing just two specimens with each other, was able to discern that the histories of these two had followed parallel courses which corresponded with each other, phase by phase. He demonstrated that the Hellenic and the Western Civilizations were comparable to each other morphologically, though chronologically their respective time-spans hardly overlapped. As for Ibn Khaldun, he was able, by noting the difference in the effects of two Arab invasions of North-West Africa, to arrive at illuminating general conclusions about the relation between politics and religion.

The Arab invasion of North-West Africa in the seventh century of the Christian Era had not only left this region's economic life intact; it has been followed by an increase in North-West Africa's economic prosperity. By contrast, the effect of the invasion of the same region, in and after AD 1051, by two Arab tribes, the Banu Hilal and the Banu Sulaym, had been devastating economically and disruptive politically. Ibn Khaldun was familiar with the history of a number of states, beginning with the Caliphate, which, in the course of Islamic history, had been founded by intrusive pastoral Nomads in the territories inhabited by sedentary populations. He had perceived that the intruders had been able to establish states because they were animated by an *esprit de corps* ('asabiyah), a 'group feeling', making for social solidarity, which their sedentary subjects lacked. Both sets of Arab invaders of North-West Africa must have been endowed with *esprit de corps*, since both sets were pastoral Nomads. Why was it, then, that the eleventh-century invasion had worked havoc where the seventh-century invasion had been innocuous, or perhaps even beneficial?

Ibn Khaldun's answer was that *esprit de corps*, though indispensable for empire-building,[4] was not sufficient by itself. 'Arabs can obtain royal authority only by making use of some religious colouring, such as prophecy, or saint-hood, or some great religious event in general.'[5] 'Dynasties of wide power and large royal authority have their origin in religion based either on prophecy or on truthful propaganda.'[6] 'Religious propaganda gives a dynasty at its beginning another power in addition to that of the group feeling it possessed as the result of the number of its supporters.'[7] Ibn Khaldun's perception of the inadequacy of a secular-sociological explanation of the history of North-West Africa in the Islamic Age thus led him to include God among the dramatis personae of history and, in so doing, to give history itself a new dimension.

The brilliance of Ibn Khaldun's and Vico's insights illustrates the triumph of curiosity over the obstacle presented by a dearth of information. The modern archaeologists' decipherment of scripts to which the key had been lost, and their interpretation of the long-since 'dead' languages that these scripts conveyed, have been triumphs of curiosity in solving intellectual puzzles.

The starting-point of the decipherment of the Egyptiac script was the discovery, in 1799, of the 'Rosetta Stone', on which the text of a decree, promulgated in 196 BC by King Ptolemy V, was engraved in the Greek alphabet and language and also in both the hieroglyphic and the cursive form of the Egyptiac script and in the Pharaonic Egyptian language. In this case the cipher was broken by the observation that, in the hieroglyphic text, an identical group of characters recurred at points corresponding to those at which the name 'Ptolemaios' recurred in the Greek text. The interpretation of the Pharaonic Egyptian language was aided by the survival, in liturgical use, of Coptic, which is descended from it (though Coptic was of no help for the decipherment of the hieroglyphs, since Coptic is written, not in these, but in a version of the Greek alphabet).

The interpretation of the Sumerian language, conveyed in the cuneiform script, has been an even more amazing intellectual *tour de force*, considering that Sumerian has no affinity with any other known language, and that the deciphering of cuneiform had to start with the identification of proper names (previously known only in garbled Greek and Hebrew versions of them) in the Medo-Persian text of the Achaemenian Emperor Darius I's inscription on the cliff-face at Behistan, in which thirty-six out of the vast repertory of cuneiform characters are used alphabetically for conveying an Indo-European language. The full range of the cuneiform script, and the distinction between its ideograms, its phonemes, and its determinatives, had then to be explored in another part of Darius I's trilingual inscription, and in older Assyrian documents, in which the cuneiform script had been used for conveying the Akkadian language. The interpretation of Akkadian, like the interpretation of Pharaonic Egyptian, was aided by this language's kinship with, in this case, not only one still surviving language but with a whole family. Akkadian is a Semitic language, like Hebrew (i.e. Canaanite), Aramaic (and its descendant Syriac), Arabic, Himyaritic, and Ethiopic. The final move from the interpretation of Akkadian to the interpretation of Sumerian, with which

Akkadian has no linguistic affinity, was made possible by the discovery of bilingual Akkadian and Sumerian vocabularies, glosses, and texts compiled in Assyria in the seventh century BC in the penultimate phase of the Sumero-Akkadian Civilization's long history.

These triumphs of curiosity over formidable obstacles of diverse kinds testify to the power of this psychic impulse. When the objective of curiosity is the study of social human affairs, the explorer has to break out of his own segregated and self-centred personality and to enter into the feelings and thoughts and lives of other people – and these not only his fellow-participants in his own civilization or religion, and not only his own contemporaries, whose civilizations and religions are different from his, but also other fellow human beings of his who have lived in long-past ages in distant parts of Mankind's habitat.

> Whate'er I feel I cannot feel alone.
> When I am happiest or most forlorn,
> Uncounted friends, whom I have never known
> Rejoicing stand or grieving at my side,
> These nameless, faceless friends of mine who died
> A thousand years or more e'er I was born.[8]

This empathy through ecstasy – a word which means literally an escape from imprisonment in the self – is something more than an emotional and intellectual experience; it is a spiritual feat. To achieve it, the spiritual athlete has to be aware of the great cloud of witnesses with which he is compassed about,[9] and he has to lose himself in the communion of sinners and penitents and saints with whom Dante consorted in the three successive stages of his vision of the *Divina Commedia*.

Some sensitive souls have achieved empathy through an inner spiritual illumination, without any stimulus from external phenomena; but often, and perhaps usually, curiosity is aroused by an encounter with some external object or event. We have already taken note of the engraving of an imaginary scene that excited Schliemann's curiosity before he was eight years old, and that thus led him to disinter Troy forty-nine years later. Narratives and landscapes can produce the same evocative effect. For me, a passage in Geoffroi de Villehardouin's *Conquête de Constantinople*[10] has brought to life Constantinople as it was on the eve of its sack by Venetian and French 'Crusaders' in AD 1204, and a passage of Bernal Diaz's *The Discovery and Conquest of Mexico*[11] has brought to life Tlaltelolco as it was in AD 1519, on the eve of its destruction by the Spaniards. In these two cases 'winged words' have had the effect of transporting me, in spirit, to those two cities and those two dates, to participate there in calamities that were repetitions of Troy's. A similar effect has been produced on me by views of landscapes. I have had the experience of being transported, in spirit, across a time-gulf on the battlefields of Gettysburg and Chattanooga and Port Arthur, and in surveying, from one of the twin summits of the citadel of Pharsalus, the battlefields of Pharsalus and Cynoscephalae; and on 11 February 1921, standing on the topmost tier of the auditorium of the theatre of Ephesus, I lived through the tumultuous drama, performed there nearly nineteen centuries earlier, which is described so vividly by the author of The Acts of the Apostles.[12]

Curiosity that has borne fruit in the writing of history has sometimes been awakened by contemporary events, either public or personal to the historian or, in some cases, events of both kinds. The contemporary stimulus may be the fall of a great and famous city or the outbreak of a great and destructive war or the building of an empire whose architects have aspired to establish a literally worldwide world-state and have come within an ace of achieving their ambition. These dramatic experiences may inspire an historian to write the history of his own time and place; they may also lead him on to ground that lies far afield, in both dimensions, from his initial act of recording events within close range.

We have already taken note of Villehardouin's response, as an historian, to the sack of Constantinople in AD 1204 and of Diaz's response to the destruction of Tlaltelolco in AD 1521. The sack of Baghdad by the Mongols in AD 1258, and the destruction of Jerusalem by the Romans in AD 70, moved Ibn al-Tiqtaqa and Josephus to write the history of their own times, but it also moved each of them to enlarge the scope of his historical work by including in it the whole history of the society – the historian's own society in each case – that had culminated in a dire catastrophe in the historian's own age.

Ibn al-Tiqtaqa was born at Hillah in south-eastern 'Iraq after the sack of Baghdad in AD 1258. Josephus was a combatant in the Romano-Jewish War of AD 66–70, and he had a unique opportunity of observing this war from both sides, since he allowed himself to be taken prisoner and then to be employed by his Roman captors as a political adviser.[13] Both these historians were concerned, not only to satisfy their own curiosity, but to imbue their society's conquerors with some curiosity about the civilization that these conquerors had victimized.

Josephus had originally written his history of the war of AD 66–70 in his Aramaic mother tongue for the Aramaic-reading public in the Fertile Crescent. He then translated this work of his into Greek for a Greek-reading public[14] whose domain extended, in Josephus's day, from Seleucia-on-Tigris all the way to Marseilles. He followed this up by writing, for the instruction of this same Greek-reading public, *The Ancient History of the Jews*.

Ibn al-Tiqtaqa's *Al-Fakhri*[15] is a history of Islam from its radiant dawn to the catastrophe in AD 1258 which had turned out, by the time when Ibn al-Tiqtaqa was writing, to have been, after all, only a temporary eclipse. The abiding potency of Islam was demonstrated by the definitive conversion, in AD 1295, of the Mongol war-lord Ghazan Khan and his Mongol *comitatus*, only thirty-seven years after Ghazan's ancestor Hulagu had sacked Baghdad, had extinguished the 'Abbasid Caliphate, and had turned 'Iraq and Iran into an appanage of the far-flung Mongol universal state. Ibn al-Tiqtaqa wrote in his native Arabic, but, in dedicating his work to Ghazan Khan's governor of Mosul, Fakhr-ad-Din 'Isa, the author must have been hoping to interest his Mongol masters in the history of their subjects' religion, to which the descendants of the conquerors had now adhered.

Saint Augustine was led still further afield than either Ibn al-Tiqtaqa or Josephus had been led from contemporary mundane events by his response to the challenge

396 Pompey enters the Holy of Holies in the Temple after capturing Jerusalem in 63 BC: illustration from a medieval manuscript of Josephus's *Antiquities of the Jews*. Josephus's historical studies were inspired by his desire to explain the events leading to the great conflict between Rome and the Jews – 'I saw that others perverted the truth of these actions in their writings.' His first book, the *Wars of the Jews*, aimed at presenting an unbiased account of the military struggle, but he returned in the *Antiquities* to his original plan of recording in Greek the full story of Jewish history since the Creation. The scale of the undertaking had deterred Josephus from pursuing this plan, but he was persuaded to complete it by his conviction that Jewish history ought to be made accessible to the Greek-speaking world.

397 Map of the world, from a contemporary manuscript of Ibn Khaldun's *Muqaddimah*, the Prolegomena to his *Universal History*; the map is oriented towards the south, with Africa at the top and Europe below. Ibn Khaldun's brilliant study was inspired by his curiosity to explain the different effects of the two Arab invasions of North Africa in the seventh and eleventh centuries A D: the first had been followed by political and social progress, while the second had led to chaos and ruin. From his observations he developed a penetrating analysis of social morphology, embracing, in a panoramic vision, the rises and falls of empires and civilizations.

presented, to Christian and non-Christian alike, by the Visigoth warlord Alaric's sack of Rome in A D 410. Augustine was moved to write his *De Civitate Dei* by a zeal to refute the anti-Christian Romans' thesis that the catastrophe of A D 410 had been a retribution for the Christian Roman imperial government's forcible suppression of its non-Christian subjects' ancestral religions.[16] The first five of the twenty-two books of Augustine's *magnum opus* are a polemical tract on this controversial issue, but his answer to this original question led him to ask and answer two more questions. In a second batch of five books he argued that the non-Christian religions have no more utility for a life after death than they have for life on Earth. His final and fundamental question, with which the last twelve of the twenty-two books of *De Civitate Dei* are concerned, is: 'What is this other commonwealth that remains standing now that the mundane commonwealth, embodied in the Roman Empire, has fallen?' Augustine, like his latter-day fellow Tunisian Ibn Khaldun, was led, by his concern with an event in mundane history, to carry his exploration to the point at which history acquires a supra-mundane dimension.

The impulse to write history may also be aroused by the experience of the outbreak of a great war.

Thucydides of Athens has written the history of the war between the Peloponnesians and the Athenians. He began to write as soon as war broke out, in the belief that this war would eclipse all its predecessors in importance.[17]

He began to write, but the first call on his time was for the performance of his public duty as an Athenian citizen, and he might not have had the leisure for carrying out his private literary project if he had not been cashiered and exiled in the eighth year of this twenty-eight-years-long war as the penalty for a reverse that he had suffered as a naval officer.

In Thucydides's case, an unhappy personal experience conspired with a tragic public experience to bring a masterpiece of historical literature to birth; and Thucydides is only one star in a Pleiad of eminent historians who have been frustrated men of action. Another of these, the prisoner-of-war Josephus, has been noticed already. The list includes the deportee Polybius, the exiles Xenophon and Clarendon, and the rusticated civil servant Machiavelli. The personal histories of these six historians were the inverse of Schliemann's and Grote's. Schliemann and Grote deliberately withdrew from their involvement in practical affairs in order to give themselves the leisure for carrying out long-since-planned researches. By contrast, the six had their fruitful leisure thrust upon them. They had started as men of action, and their careers in this original field had been unkindly cut short. Their eviction from the field of action had, however, been a blessing in disguise. It had constrained them to find and follow their true vocation, which was to write histories that have become 'permanent possessions'[18] for Mankind.

Polybius is one of the historians whose curiosity has been stimulated by the rise, in his time, of a great empire.

What mind, however commonplace or indifferent, could feel no curiosity to learn the process by which almost the whole world fell under the undisputed ascendancy of Rome within a period of less than fifty-three years?[19]

The still more rapid rise of the Achaemenian Persian Empire stimulated Herodotus, and the meteoric rise of the Mongol Empire stimulated two great Persian historians, 'Ala-ad-Din Juvayni (*vivebat* A D 1226–83) and Rashid-ad-Din al-Hamadani (*vivebat c.* A D 1247–1318).[20] The unification of Mankind was achieved on a vast scale in the Achaemenian, Roman, and Mongol Empires. This fascinating spectacle led the historians whose curiosity had been excited by it to extend their field of observation still further, to embrace as much of Mankind's habitat as lay within their horizon.

A particularly potent stimulus to historical curiosity is the confrontation, in an historian's mind, of a contemporary experience, either public or personal, with a knowledge of some situation in the past to which the contemporary situation presents a striking contrast. A confrontation of this kind raises the question: 'How has this come out of that?' This question goes to the root of historical inquiry, since history is concerned with human affairs as these are observed on the move in the time-dimension.

We have already noted the stimulation of Ibn Khaldun's and Volney's curiosity by their recognition of the contrast between the forlorn condition of the Islamic World in their respective lifetimes and this region's former prosperity and grandeur. A similar experience inspired Gibbon to write *The History of the Decline and Fall of the Roman Empire.*

It was on the fifteenth of October, in the gloom of evening, as I sat musing on the Capitol, while the barefooted fryars were chanting their litanies in the temple of Jupiter, that I conceived the first thought of my history.[21]

Nearly twenty-three years elapsed between 15 October 1764, the day on which Gibbon received his inspiration, and 27 June 1787, the day on which he wrote the last words of the last chapter of the mighty work that his experience on the Capitol had moved him to produce.[22] Like Saint Augustine and Ibn Khaldun, Gibbon was carried by his curiosity far further than he had foreseen. The last chapter of *The Decline and Fall* comprises the whole of the work as this had originally been planned,[23] but, in the work as eventually executed, this is chapter seventy-one. In the course of execution, the work had grown from a history of the decay of the public buildings of imperial Rome into a history of the decline and fall of the Roman Empire.[24]

In a minor way, I too have been stimulated by confrontations between an experience of my own and my knowledge of something in the past that was relevant to it. For instance, on 23 May 1912, I was sitting on the summit of the citadel of Mistra and was gazing eastward, across the vale of Sparta, at the Menelaïon, visible on a bluff overhanging the east bank of the river Eurotas. This spectacle demonstrated to me that the medieval French lords of Mistra and the Mycenaean Greek lords of the site of the Menelaïon were counterparts of each other, though, in chronological terms, they were sundered from each other by the twenty-four centuries that had elapsed between the sacking of the Mycenaean palaces in the twelfth century B C and the founding of Mistra in A D 1249. Then, in August 1914, I became aware that I had been overtaken by the experience that Thucydides had had in May 431 B C. In terms of experience,

these two dates manifestly marked comparable turning-points in Hellenic and in Western history, though, in terms of chronology, they were just over 2345 years apart. These two confrontations between events in Greek history and events in Western history convinced me of the correctness of Vico's intuition that the histories of these two civilizations are parallel and comparable[25] in spite of their being non-contemporaneous. This conviction led me on from Vico's comparison in two terms only to a comparative study embracing all the civilizations that had risen above a Western inquirer's mental horizon since Vico's day, thanks to the work of orientalists and archaeologists in the course of the 170 years between A D 1744 and 1914.

The pursuit of historical curiosity is not just an intellectual exercise; it is also an emotional experience; and one of the emotions induced by it is awe. Gibbon did not readily succumb to awe. Both his personal temperament and the *Zeitgeist* of the eighteenth-century 'Enlightenment' were inimical to it. Yet, in writing the last lines of *The History of the Decline and Fall,* Gibbon was moved to describe his subject as 'the greatest, perhaps, and most awful scene in the history of mankind'. As for Villehardouin and Diaz, they admitted to having been awestricken by their first sight of the great and splendid cities that they were going to sack. We may guess that Alaric had the same feelings when he sighted Rome in A D 410, and Hulagu, too, when he sighted Baghdad in A D 1258, notwithstanding the Nomad's contempt for the works of his sedentary victims. Scipio Aemilianus, when in 146 B C he was consummating the annihilation of Carthage, was seen by his friend and companion Polybius to burst into tears and was heard by him to quote a passage of the *Iliad*[26] that foretold the destruction of Troy. Scipio then confessed to Polybius that he was filled with foreboding for Rome by his vision of the destinies of Man.[27]

In a minor way I had a similar experience on 19 March 1912, *en route* from Khandra to Palaikastro at the eastern end of the island of Crete. Rounding the shoulder of a mountain, I found myself confronted by the shell of a Baroque villa, which must have been evacuated by its Venetian occupants at an early stage in the Turco-Venetian war of 1645–69. If this derelict Jacobean country-house had stood in England, it would assuredly have been as full of life in 1912 as it had been before 1645. It would never have ceased to be inhabited. Actually, in 1912, this modern Western building in Crete was a lifeless relic of 'Ancient History', on a par with the ruins of the Minoan palaces, built in the second millennium B C, that I had been visiting a few days earlier. In 1912 the Venetian Empire was as dead as the legendary 'thalassocracy' of King Minos. Lines from Browning's 'A Toccata of Galuppi's' were now running through my head, and, in a flash, it occurred to me that the British Empire might perhaps be heading, in its turn, for the Venetian Empire's fate.

At the time, this thought glanced off my mind; for in 1912 the British Empire appeared still to be at its zenith. I had a lively memory of the celebration of Queen Victoria's Diamond Jubilee in 1897, when I had been an impressionable eight-year-old, and I had not taken to heart Kipling's prescient forebodings in his 'Recessional'. Yet, through the personal accident of longevity, I have lived to see the

ENDLESS DEATH OR ETERNAL LIFE?

398, 399 Details of Brueghel's *Triumph of Death* and Fra Angelico's *Christ Glorified in the Court of Heaven* symbolize the opposite poles of Man's interpretation of his Universe. Is life condemned to end in nothing beyond the meaningless inanity of the grave, or is death the

British Empire liquidated within the three-quarters of a century between the years 1897 and 1972; and on 15 June 1960, at Razmak in Waziristan, I saw a relic of a vanished empire which, on this occasion, actually was the British Empire itself. The cantonment at Razmak had been built, on the grand scale, to house two divisions; it was a replica of Aldershot and Catterick; yet in 1960, thirteen years after the British had evacuated the Indo-Pakistani sub-continent, the doors of the deserted houses at Razmak were parting from their hinges and shrubs were sprouting in the empty streets. The forts at Howsteads and Chesters, on Hadrian's Wall, must have looked like that in the fourteenth year after the Roman evacuation of Britain. Soon Razmak will look as Howsteads and Chesters look today.

Scipio Aemilianus's inward agony in his hour of outward triumph was characteristically Hellenic – and would have been characteristically Jewish too; for the Hellenic and the Jewish *Weltanschauungen*, which on many points are worlds apart, are in accord with each other in their common conviction that the nemesis of triumph is disaster and that pride goes before a fall.

A feeling of awe at sensational reversals of fortune is the keynote of Herodotus's work. In the first six of his nine books, Herodotus builds up for his readers the mighty Achaemenian Empire, only to cast it down for them in the last three books, in which he records this hitherto invincible super-power's astonishing and humiliating defeat, in the years 480–479 BC, by an ephemeral coalition of a minority of the petty states in one third of the Hellenic World. This ironical discomfiture of a puissant empire by the envy of the gods is a play that has been reperformed at more recent dates in other theatres. The world-conquering Mongols were defeated sensationally by the Egyptian Mamluks in AD 1260, and the sub-continent-conquering British by the Afghans in 1842. While the present lines are being written, the Americans are being defeated by the Vietnamese.

The Mongols' disaster at 'Ayn Jalut was as portentous an event in human history as the defeat of the Persians at Salamis and Plataea and Mykale. The decisive battle in AD 1260 snatched Islam, as the decisive battles in 480–479 BC had snatched Hellenism, out of the jaws of destruction.

496

prelude to a glorious consummation for souls that have striven to lead a holy life on Earth? The answer to this question is unknown, yet, though the intellect is unable to apprehend the reality behind and beyond the phenomena, the spirit has intuitions of the ineffable Truth.

These two dramatic reversals are illustrations of Herodotus's observation that 'God loves to cut short everything that overtops its kind',[28] and the equality in catastrophe that the envious gods demand is imposed for them by Death the Leveller.

> Sceptre and Crown
> Must tumble down,
> And in the dust be equal made
> With the poor crooked scythe and spade.[29]

Death is the universal, inescapable, and conclusive retort to the audacious declaration of independence that is made by every living being. The creature sets itself up as the centre of a counter-universe. Death demolishes this pretension. Thus the awe induced by the pursuit of historical curiosity is an indication that the inquisitive explorer has caught a glimpse of the reality behind the phenomena. His awe is his reaction to what he has seen. It is Arjuna's reaction to Krishna's terrifying disclosure of his naked self at Arjuna's importunate request.[30] But awe is not the only emotion that is aroused in the explorer by his quest. The spectacle of the enigmatic phenomena also evokes two other emotions – compassion and exultation – and these, like awe, are responses to glimpses of the reality that the phenomena veil.

The Buddha's and the Bodhisattvas' compassion opens the way for an exit out of the phenomenal world into a state of 'extinguishedness' (*nirvana*) – a mortification of desire which brings with it a cessation of pain. Translated into Christian theistic terms, the reality that is reflected in compassion is the Johannine God who 'so loved the world that he gave his only begotten son',[31] and it is Marcion's 'stranger god' who is voluntarily exposing himself to tribulation in order to redeem a Universe for whose ills he bears no responsibility. The exultation that is another reaction to the spectacle of the same phenomena has been given utterance by a Jewish psalmist and by a Christian saint. 'The heavens declare the glory of God, and the firmament sheweth His handiwork.'[32] 'Laudatu si', Mi Signore, cum tucte le Tue creature.'[33] The vision of reality that these jubilant voices announce is depicted on the altarpiece, now in the National Gallery in London, which was painted by Fra Angelico for the Church of Saint Domenico at Fiesole.

How is it possible for the ultimate reality behind the phenomena to reveal itself in such different guises? What is there in common between an annihilation through death, an exit into *nirvana* through self-extinction, and an entry into a communion of saints? On first thoughts, these three visions of ultimate reality look as if they were irreconcilable with each other, but on second thoughts we can see that they each present a picture of an identical goal. They each testify that the cause of sin and suffering and sorrow is the separation of sentient beings, in their brief passage through the phenomenal world, from the timeless reality behind the phenomena, and that a reunion with this reality is the sole but sovereign cure for our ailing world's ills. Communion, extinguishedness, and annihilation are alternative images of reintegration. They are symbols of a consummation that is ineffable because it is the antithesis of Man's experience in his ephemeral life on Earth. They are variations on a single theme: the return from discord to harmony, or, in Sinic terms, from Yang to Yin. 'To Him return ye, one and all.'[34] 'Das Unbeschreibliche, Hier ist's getan.'[35]

MAPS

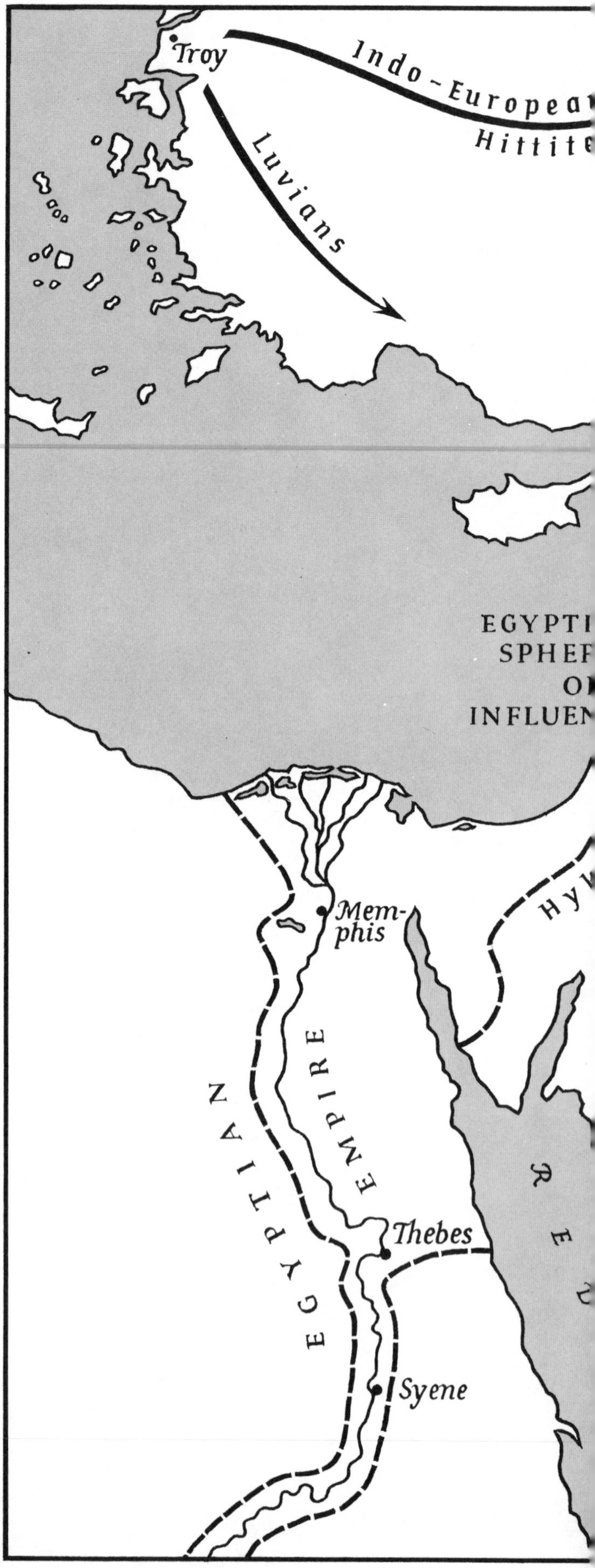

Troy

Indo-Europea

Hittite

Luvians

EGYPTI
SPHEF
OI
INFLUEN

Mem-
phis

Hy

Thebes

Syene

R
E
D

E G Y P T I A N   E M P I R E

400 SOUTH-WEST ASIA AND EGYPT IN THE
EIGHTEENTH CENTURY BC This century
saw the destruction of the Egyptian Middle
Kingdom by Hyksos invaders, the foundation
of Hammurabi's Babylonian Empire, and the
Völkerwanderung of Eurasian Nomads into South-
Western Asia.

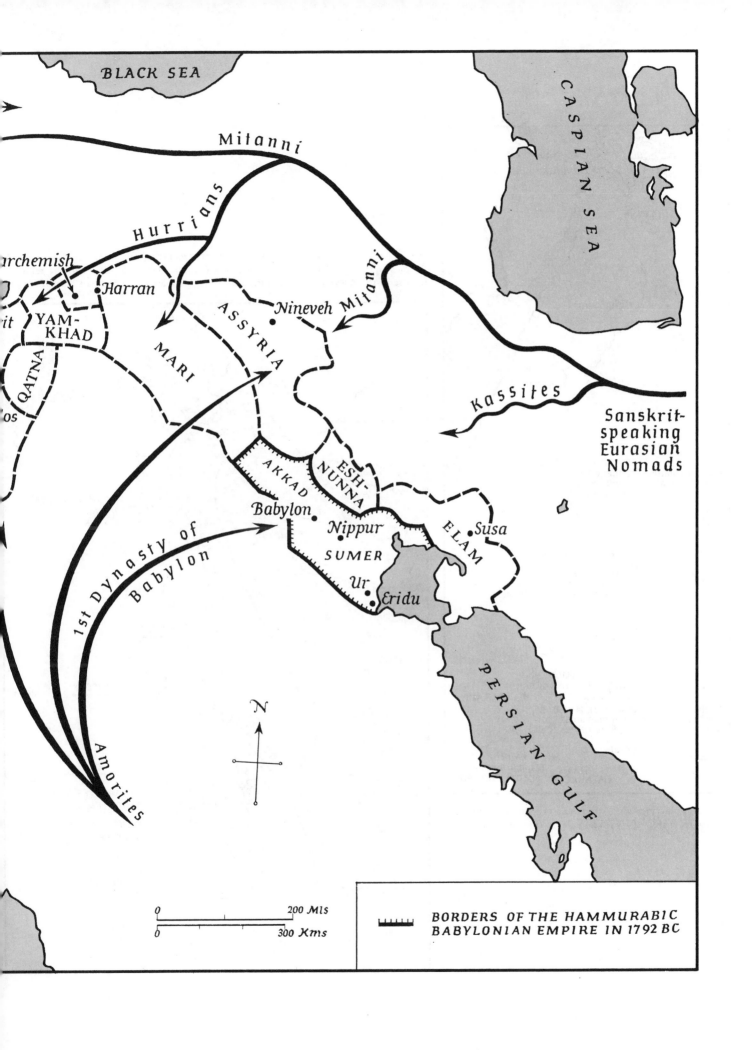

BLACK SEA

CASPIAN SEA

Mitanni

Hurrians

Carchemish

Harran

YAM-KHAD

ASSYRIA

Nineveh

Mitanni

MARI

QATNA

os

Kassites

Sanskrit-
speaking
Eurasian
Nomads

AKKAD

ESH-
NUNNA

Babylon

Nippur

ELAM

Susa

SUMER

1st Dynasty of Babylon

Ur

Eridu

Amorites

N

PERSIAN GULF

| 0 | | | 200 Mls |
| 0 | | | 300 Kms |

BORDERS OF THE HAMMURABIC
BABYLONIAN EMPIRE IN 1792 BC

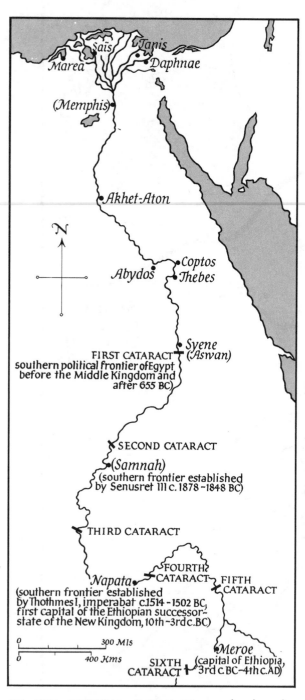

401 THE EGYPTIAC CIVILIZATION, showing the gradual extension of Egyptian rule up the Nile valley.

402 THE CRADLE OF THE SYRIAC CIVILIZATION, from the repulse of the S Peoples by Egypt at the battle of the Nile (1191 or 1171 BC), down to the tempora repulse of the Assyrians by a coalition of Syrian peoples at the battle of Karkar (853 BC

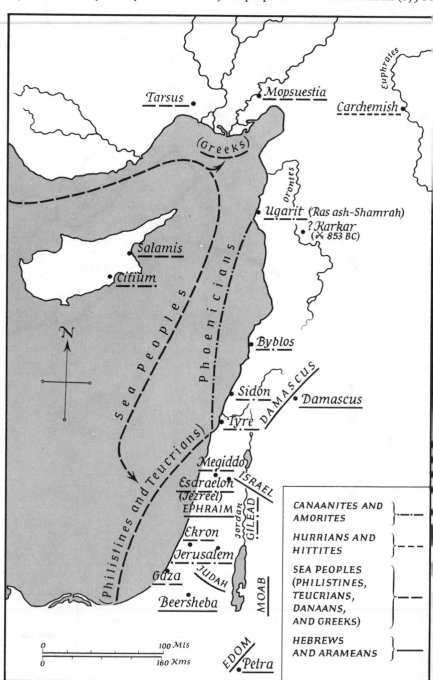

| CANAANITES AND AMORITES |
| HURRIANS AND HITTITES |
| SEA PEOPLES (PHILISTINES, TEUCRIANS, DANAANS, AND GREEKS) |
| HEBREWS AND ARAMEANS |

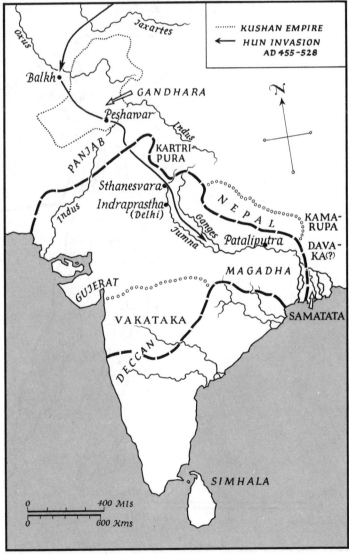

403 THE MAURYAN EMPIRE in the time of Açoka (273–232 BC) Inscriptions left by Açoka throughout his Empire allow its extent to be mapped. After his death, the Empire began to break up, succumbing eventually to Bactrian Greek invaders, led by Demetrius (? I or II), at the beginning of the second century BC.

404 THE GUPTAN EMPIRE, c. AD 450 The Gupta dynasty, founded by Chandra Gupta, re-established the imperial unity that had been lost with the disintegration of Mauryan India; the capital, as in Mauryan times, was Pataliputra, chief city of the state of Magadha in which both dynasties had originated. The Guptan Empire declined under the impact of Hun and Gurjara invasions between 455 and 528.

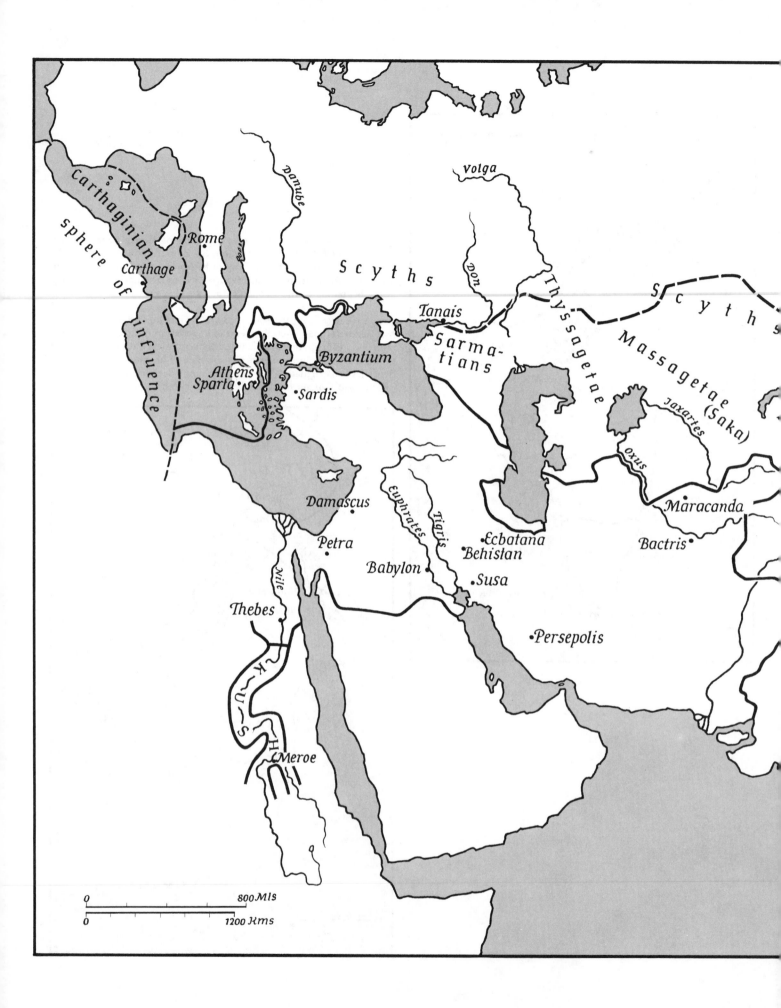

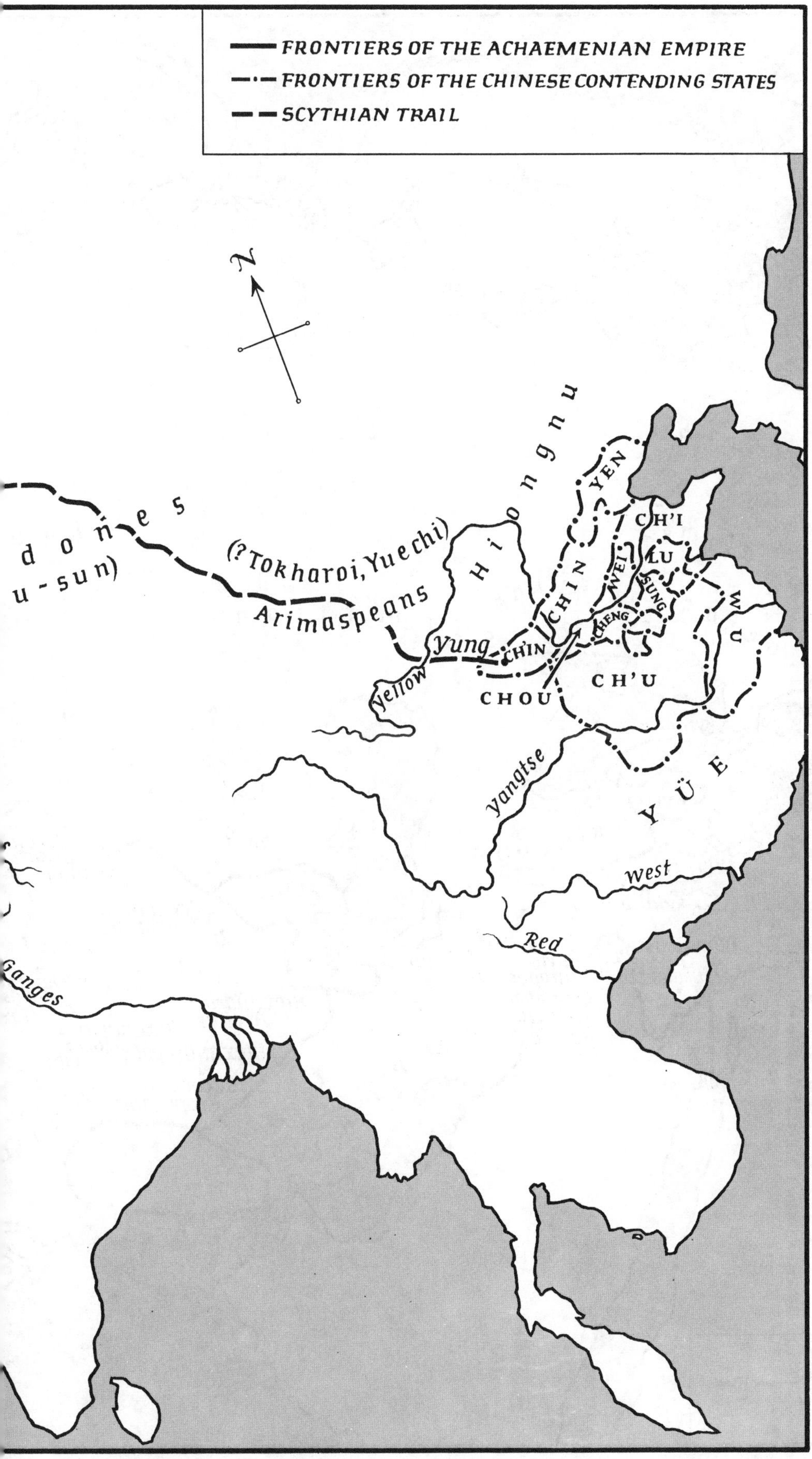

FRONTIERS OF THE ACHAEMENIAN EMPIRE

FRONTIERS OF THE CHINESE CONTENDING STATES

SCYTHIAN TRAIL

N

do n e s

u - sun)

(?Tokharoi,Yuechi)

Arimaspeans

H i o n g n u

YEN

CH'I

CHIN

LU

WEI

Yung CHIN

CHENG SUNG

W U

CHOU

CH'U

Yellow

Yangtse

YÜE

West

Red

Ganges

405 THE ACHAEMENIAN EMPIRE AND THE CONTENDING STATES OF CHINA, *c.* 480 BC While the civilizations at the extreme east and west of the Old World were in a phase of political disunity, the Achaemenian Empire united the Syriac and Iranian Worlds in one universal state. East and west were linked by a precarious trade route – the 'Scythian Trail' – across steppes occupied by pastoral Nomad barbarians.

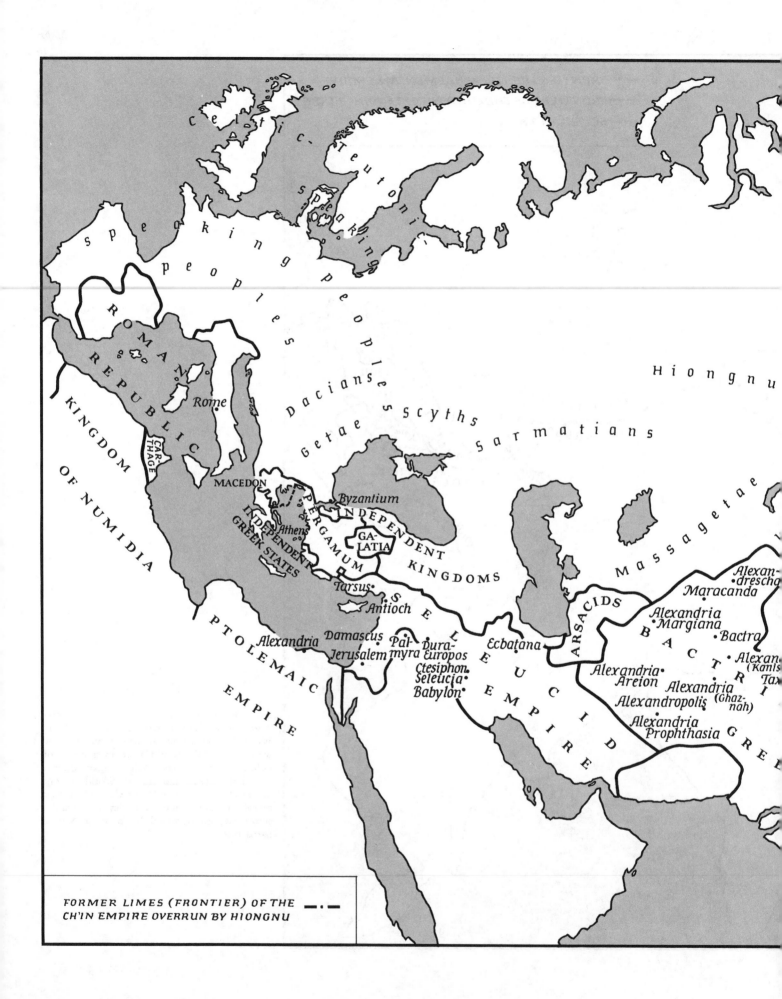

FORMER LIMES (FRONTIER) OF THE
CH'IN EMPIRE OVERRUN BY HIONGNU   — · —

Hiong nu

Yuechi (Tochari, Doghras)
174 BC

Loyang

Ch'ang Ngan

HAN

YÜEH

EMPIRE

Pataliputra

PIRE

0   1000 Mls
0   1600 Kms

406 THE HELLENIC AND SINIC WORLDS,
171 BC In the east, the Ch'in-Han Empire
had brought unity to the fragmented Chinese
states; but the dissolution of the Achaemenian
Empire had left a number of local states contending for the mastery of an Hellenic World
that had been brought to the gates of India by
the conquests of Alexander the Great. The
migration of the Yuechi from their Asian
homelands contributed to the accumulating
barbarian pressure against the borders of the
Hellenic World.

407 THE HELLENIC WORLD, *c.* 200 BC to
AD 235 A detail from the preceding map,
showing the location of the principal cities and
regions discussed in this Study.

• Panticapaeum

• Sinope
• Trapezus

• Heraclea

THRACE
• Adrianople
• Byzantium
• Calchedon
BITHYNIA
Philippi
(✕ 42 BC)
• Maronea
• Aenus
GALATIA
CAPPADOCIA
• Abdera
• Dicaea
• Nicaea

• Pessinus

• Caesarea Mazaca
• Comana

• Pergamon
PHRYGIA
• Antioch
Edessa •
• Carrhae
(✕ 53 BC)
• Magnesia-
on-Hermus
• Iconium
Smyrna •
LYDIA
• Lystra
Tarsus
• Ephesus
• Magnesia-
on-Maeander
PISIDIA
• Derbe
Seleucia •
• Antioch
Miletus •
CARIA
PAMPHYLIA
• Apamea
DELOS
LYCIA
CILICIA
Dura Europos •
NAXOS
• Emesa
RHODES
CYPRUS
Palmyra

• Damascus

CRETE • Itanus

• Jerusalem

N

• Raphia

• Alexandria

• Memphis

0   300 Mls
0   500 Kms

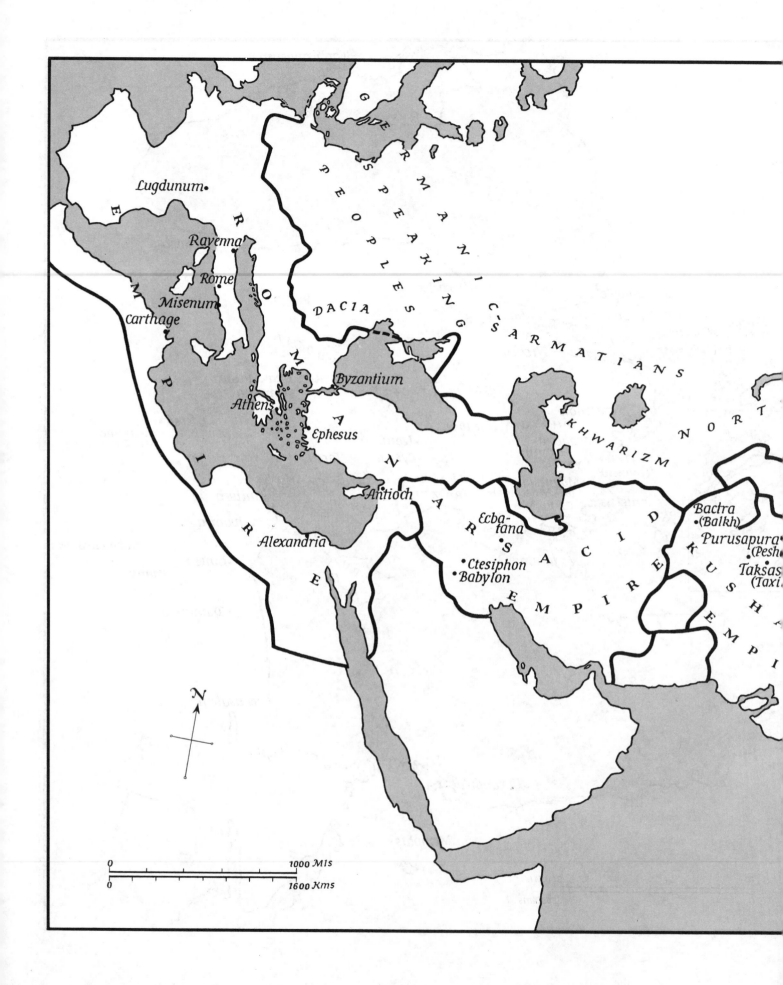

Lugdunum

Ravenna

Rome

Misenum

Carthage

R O M A N   E M P I R E

GERMANIC-SPEAKING PEOPLES

DACIA

SARMATIANS

Byzantium

Athens

Ephesus

Antioch

Alexandria

KHWARIZM

NORT

Ecbatana

Ctesiphon

Babylon

A R S A C I D   E M P I R E

Bactra
(Balkh)

Purusapura
(Pesh

Taksas
(Taxi

KUSH

EMPI

N

0 ——————————— 1000 Mls
0 ——————————— 1600 Kms

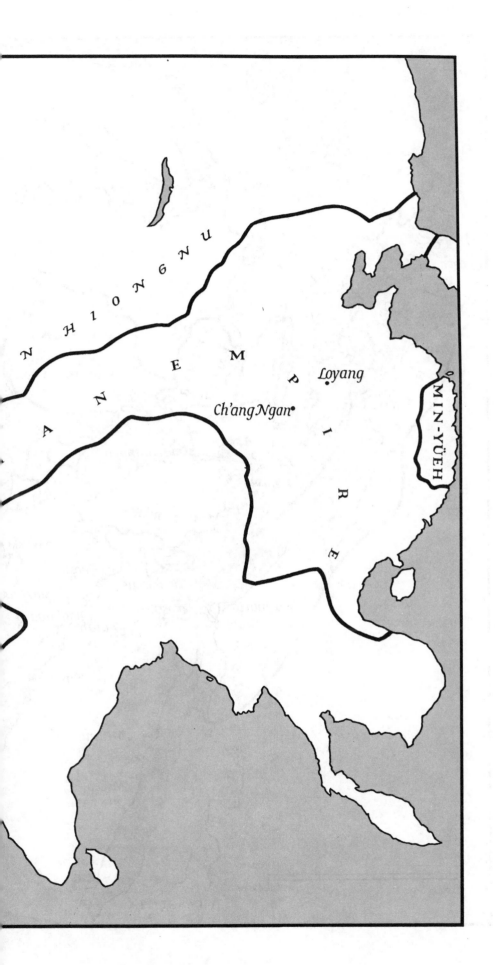

HIONGNU

N

HAN EMPIRE

Loyang

Ch'ang Ngan

MIN-YÜEH

408 THE HAN, KUSHAN, ARSACID, AND ROMAN EMPIRES, *c.* AD 100, including their respective satellites. The two great universal states of the Old World, the Roman and Han Empires, were kept from direct contact by the Parthian Arsacid and Kushan states both founded by originally barbarian Nomad dynasties. There were hostile relations between the Roman and the Arsacid Empire, and between the Han and the Kushan Empire. Consequently, Roman-Kushan and Han-Arsacid relations were friendly. A cordon of barbarian peoples was pressing upon the northern frontiers of all the Empires.

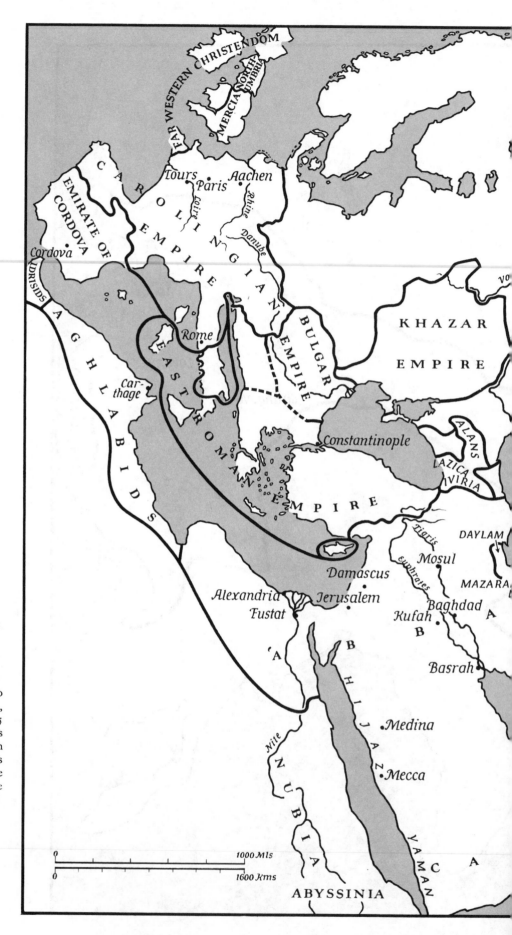

409 THE T'ANG EMPIRE, THE 'ABBASID
CALIPHATE, THE EAST ROMAN EMPIRE,
AND THE CAROLINGIAN EMPIRE, *c.* AD 815
The T'ang and 'Abbasid Empires were revivals
of the disintegrated Han and Achaemenian
universal states, but the Roman Empire was
now divided into two states that were to become
the bases of two Christian civilizations – the
Western, and the Eastern Orthodox.

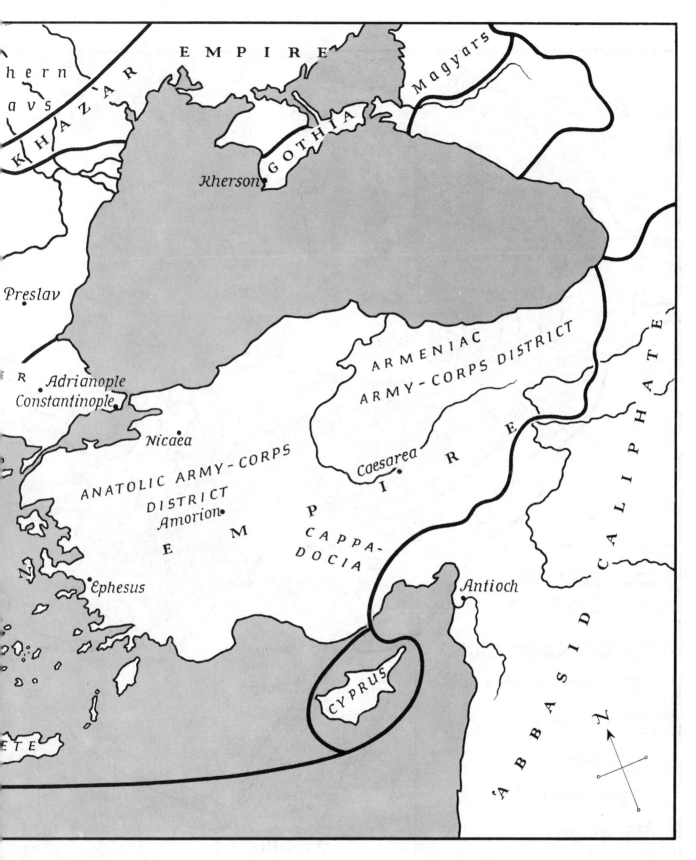

hern

avs

K H A Z A R

GOTHIA

Magyars

Kherson

Preslav

ARMENIAC

ARMY-CORPS DISTRICT

R

Adrianople

Constantinople

Nicaea

ANATOLIC ARMY-CORPS

DISTRICT

Amorion

E   M

P

CAPPA-

DOCIA

I   R   E

Caesarea

Ephesus

N

Ephesus

A B B A S I D   C A L I P H A T E

Antioch

CYPRUS

ETE

N

410 THE EAST ROMAN EMPIRE, *c.* AD 815
A detail from the preceding map, showing the
extent of the Empire on the eve of Bulgaria's
south-westward expansion into the Balkans.

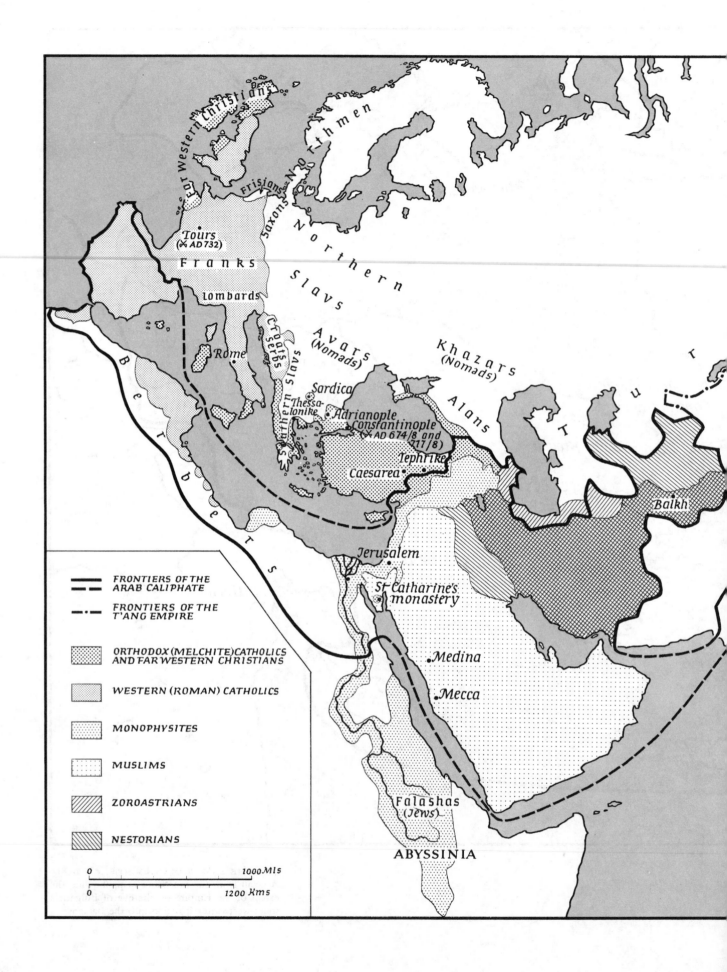

FRONTIERS OF THE
ARAB CALIPHATE

FRONTIERS OF THE
T'ANG EMPIRE

ORTHODOX (MELCHITE) CATHOLICS
AND FAR WESTERN CHRISTIANS

WESTERN (ROMAN) CATHOLICS

MONOPHYSITES

MUSLIMS

ZOROASTRIANS

NESTORIANS

0   1000 Mls

0   1200 Kms

Far Western Christians

Frisians

Saxons

N o r t h m e n

Tours
(× AD 732)

F r a n k s

Lombards

N o r t h e r n

S l a v s

Croats

Serbs

A v a r s
(Nomads)

K h a z a r s
(Nomads)

Rome

S o u t h e r n   S l a v s

A l a n s

Sardica

Thessa-
lonike

Adrianople

Constantinople
(× AD 674/8 and
717/8)

Tephrike

Caesarea

Balkh

B e r b e r s

Jerusalem

St Catharine's
monastery

Medina

Mecca

Falashas
(Jews)

ABYSSINIA

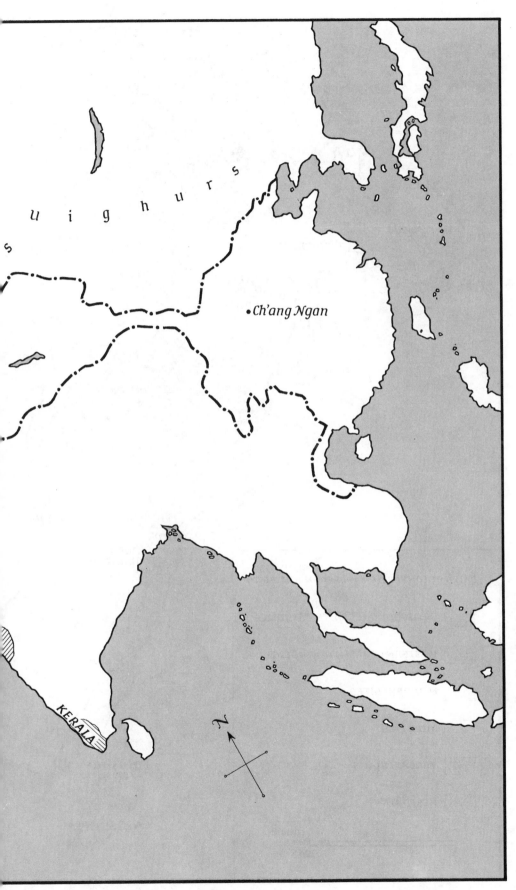

uighurs

s

•*Ch'ang Ngan*

KERALA

N

411 THE DISTRIBUTION OF THE JUDAIC
RELIGIONS, *c.* AD 732, before the mass
conversions to Christianity and Islam. Christianity was still confined largely within the
borders of the old Roman Empire; the Celtic
fringes of north-western Europe had an independent Celtic Church, the basis of the abortive
Far Western Christian Civilization. Zoroastrianism still dominated Iran, sharing its
territory with the Nestorian Christianity brought
there by refugees from the Roman Empire.
Islam had spread throughout the Arabian
peninsula, but had not yet made much progress
in any of the vast areas, outside Arabia, that the
Arabs had conquered.

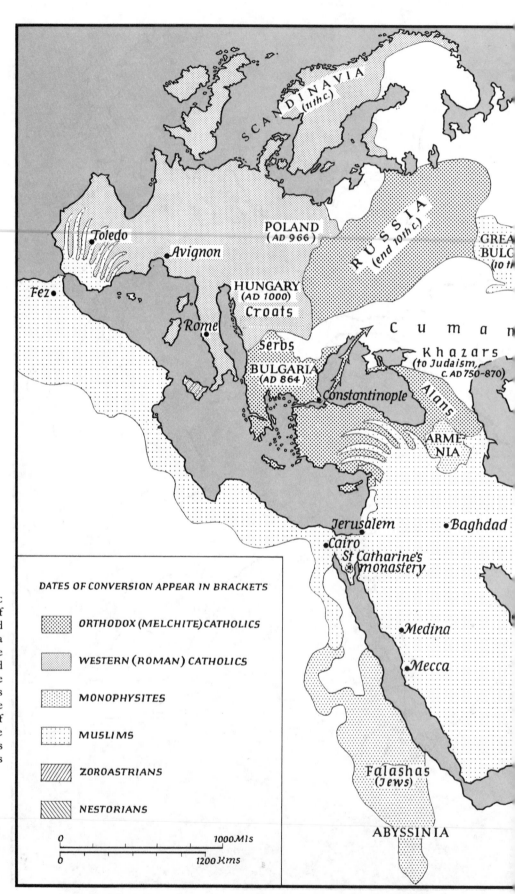

412 THE DISTRIBUTION OF THE JUDAIC RELIGIONS, *c.* AD 1200 By now the whole of Western and Central Europe had been converted to Roman Catholic Christianity, while Russia had received Orthodox Christianity from the East Roman Empire. Nestorian missions had converted some of the Nomad tribes to the north of China. As a result of several centuries of Arab rule, Islam had not only survived the Turks' and the Western Crusaders' invasions of the Caliphate's domain: it had reduced the Christian and Zoroastrian population of this region to a minority, through mass conversions to Islam beyond the limits of Arabia itself.

Within the map:

SCANDINAVIA (11th c.)

POLAND (AD 966)

RUSSIA (end 10th c.)

GREA BULG (10 t

Toledo

Avignon

HUNGARY (AD 1000)

Croats

Fez

Rome

Serbs

BULGARIA (AD 864)

C u m a n

Khazars (to Judaism, c. AD 750–870)

Constantinople

Alans

ARME-NIA

Jerusalem

Baghdad

Cairo

St Catharine's monastery

Medina

Mecca

Falashas (Jews)

ABYSSINIA

DATES OF CONVERSION APPEAR IN BRACKETS

ORTHODOX (MELCHITE) CATHOLICS

WESTERN (ROMAN) CATHOLICS

MONOPHYSITES

MUSLIMS

ZOROASTRIANS

NESTORIANS

0   1000 Mls
0   1200 Kms

Mongols

Tatars

Khitan

Naimans
(post AD 1009)

Karayits
(AD 1009)

Q I T A Y

Beshbalyq

Q. *Qarakhocho*

U i g h u r s
(to Manichaeism, AD 763)

S U N G

Nestorian stele (AD 781)
Ch'ang Ngan

K I N E M P I R E

(p c h a q)

Q A R ( )

Balasaghun

Kashghar (to Islam, AD 960)
Khotan

Balkh

Ghaznah

Meliapore

KERALA

N

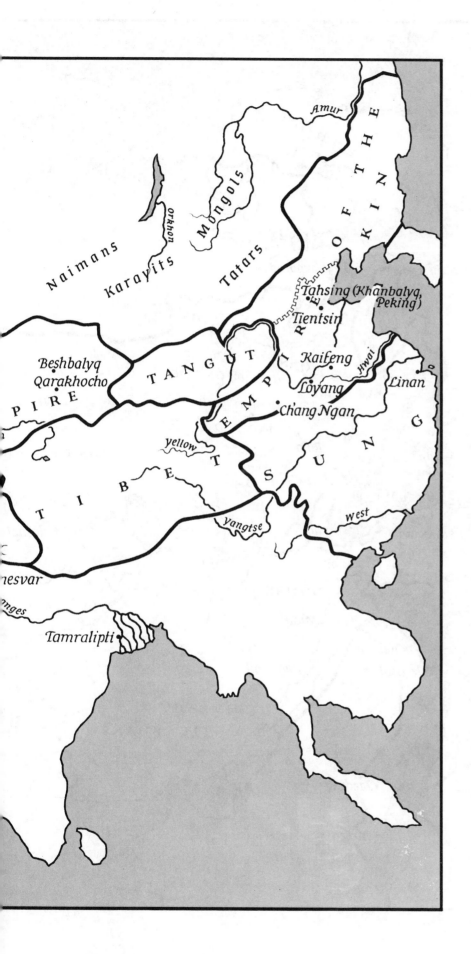

413 SUCCESSOR-STATES OF THE T'ANG
AND 'ABBASID EMPIRES, AD 1175 The
break-up of the Arab and Chinese universal
states left a mosaic of smaller states in their
former territories. In the West, the Carolingian
Empire had long since disintegrated, and
Western Christendom was divided among a
number of parochial states. The Holy Roman
Empire was merely the largest of these: the rest
did not recognize its suzerainty, though all
Western Christians, including those in the
Celtic fringe, now recognized the ecclesiastical
supremacy of the Roman See.

CHRISTENDOM

NOVGOROD

Paris • •Hamburg •Lübeck
Wisby
•Danzig •Novgorod

Toledo •
Seville •Cordova Avignon •Marseilles
•Granada Genoa •
Venice •
Rome •

WESTERN

LITHU-
ANIA

TRIBUTARY RUSSIAN PRINCIPALITIES
Kiev

(G O L D E N

H O U S E   O F   J U

H O R D E,   Q I P C H A

BLUE HORDE

EAST
ROMAN EMPIRE
Caffa
Constantinople
'OSMANLIS
Trebizond

Tana

WHITE HOR

Volga

KHWARIZM

Jaxartes

Balasagh

HOUSE O

Samarqand
Oxus •Balkh

Kabul•

SIND

MAMLUKS

HOUSE

Mosul •

OF

Damascus
Cairo • Jerusalem

Euphrates
Tigris

• Baghdad

HULAGU
(IL - KHANS)

DOMINIONS

Nile

• Medina

• Mecca

0   1000 Mls
0   1600 Kms

Qaraqorum

Tatu (Khanbalyq, Peking)
Tientsin

Grand Canal

Kaifeng
Hwai
Linan

Beshbalyq
Qarakhocho

wei

GHATAY

otan

yangtse

Canton

west

D · O · M

Red

Ganges

MIEN

ALJI

IRE

K · H · A · Q · A · N' · S

M · A · I · N · S

414 THE MONGOL EMPIRE, *c.* AD 1310 The sweeping conquests of the Mongols united almost the entire Eurasian land-mass in one universal state. Only two Muslim states, one in India and the other in Syria and Egypt, retained their independence. In European Christendom, the Mongols imposed their suzerainty on the greater part of Russia, but not on the Balkan peninsula or on any part of the ecclesiastical domain of the Papal See.

FRONTIERS OF GRAND DUCHY OF MOSCOW IN 1300

FRONTIERS OF GRAND DUCHY OF MOSCOW IN 1462

FRONTIERS OF RUSSIAN EMPIRE IN 1598

FRONTIERS OF RUSSIAN EMPIRE IN 1725

FRONTIERS OF RUSSIAN EMPIRE IN 1861

FRONTIERS OF RUSSIAN EMPIRE IN 1972 (INCLUDING 'SATELLITES')

AREA OF USSR IN 1972

Berlin
Prague
Vienna
Budapest
Sofia
Bucharest
Constanti-
nople
Danube
Dniester
POLAND
Warsaw
LITHUANIA
COURLAND
LIVLAND
ESTLAND
Dnieper
Kiev
UKRAINE
Odessa
Azov
Don
Pskov
Novgorod
Moscow
Kazan
volga
Astrakhan
St Petersburg
(Leningrad)
Archangel
Dvina
White
Sea
FINLAND
Murmansk
Ural mountains
Oxus
Jaxartes
Altai mts
Gob
des
PEOPLE'S REPUBLI

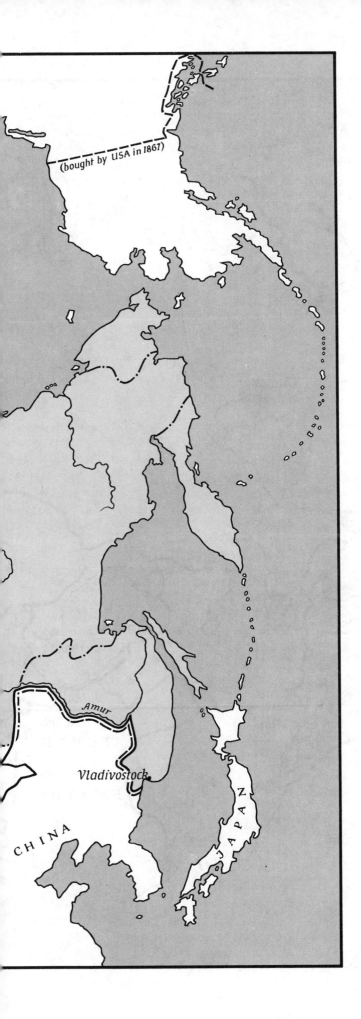

(bought by USA in 1867)

Amur

Vladivostock

CHINA

JAPAN

415 THE EXPANSION OF RUSSIA FROM AD 1300, showing the gradual growth of the multinational Russian universal state beyond its Russian Orthodox Christian nucleus.

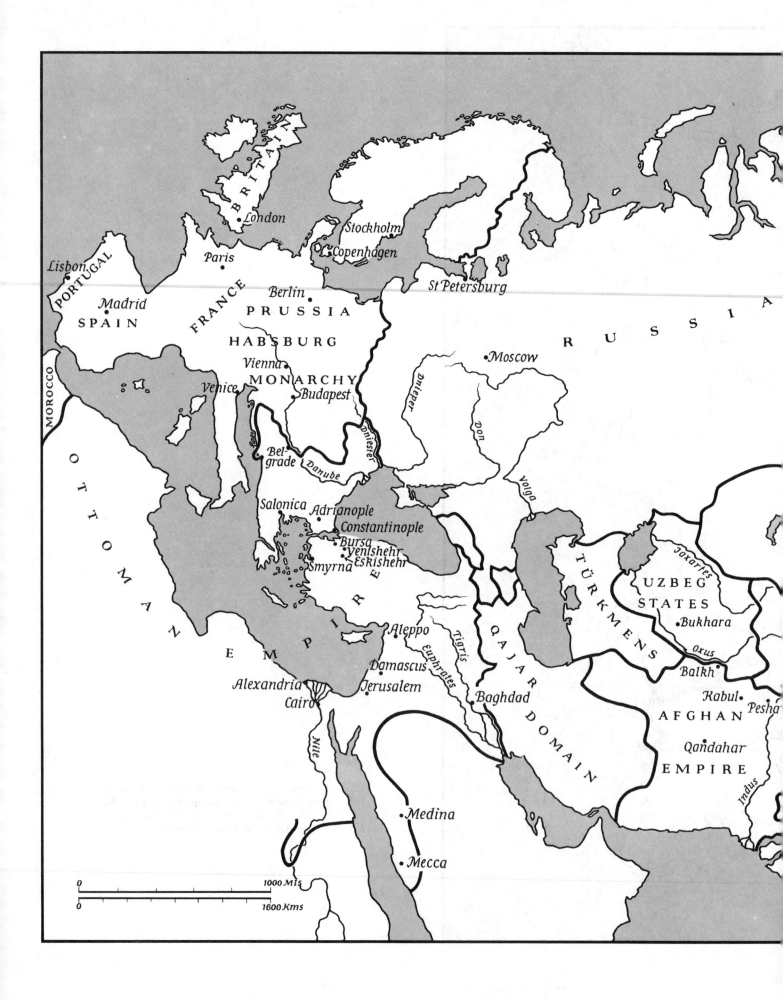

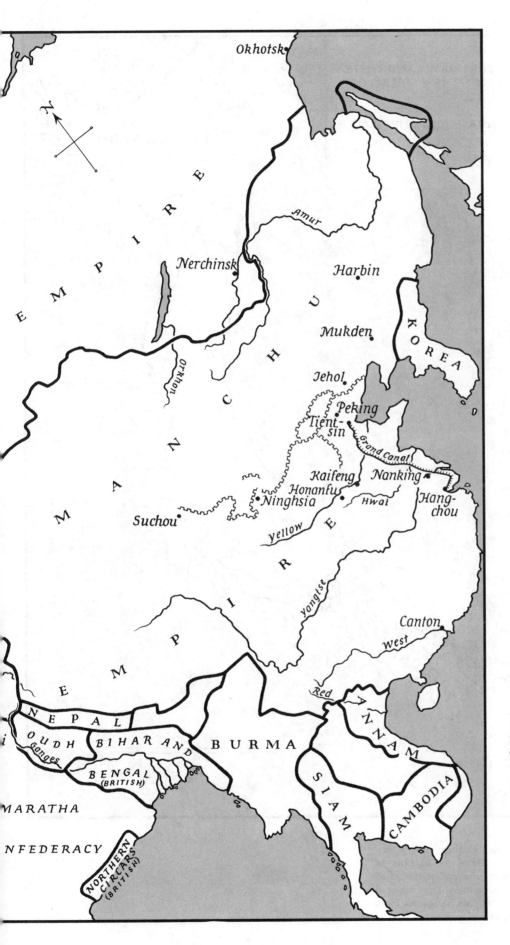

Okhotsk

N

EMPIRE

Amur

Nerchinsk

Harbin

MANCHU

Mukden

KOREA

Orkhon

Jehol

Peking

Tient-sin

Grand Canal

Kaifeng

Nanking

Honanfu

Ninghsia

Hwai

Hang-chou

Suchou

yellow

EMPIRE

Canton

West

yangtse

Red

NEPAL

ANNAM

OUDH

BIHAR AND

BURMA

Ganges

BENGAL
(BRITISH)

SIAM

CAMBODIA

MARATHA

NFEDERACY

NORTHERN
CIRCARS
(BRITISH)

416 THE OTTOMAN, RUSSIAN, AND
MANCHU EMPIRES, AD 1795 The three vast
empires based on Turkey, Russia, and China
dominate the map geographically, but the
political destiny of the world was in the hands
of the territorially insignificant Great Powers
on the Western fringes of Europe.

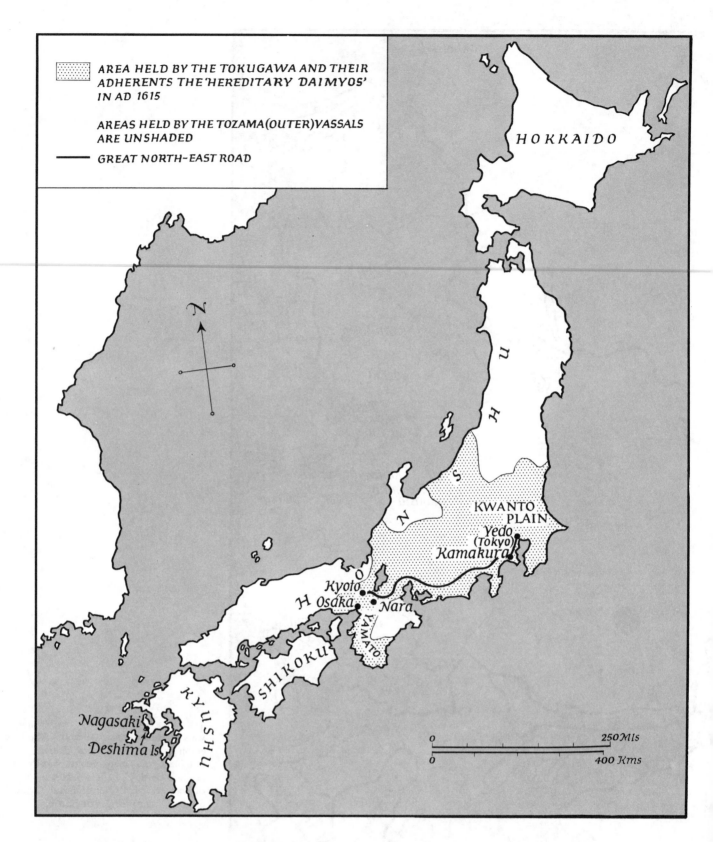

THE JAPANESE CIVILIZATION During Japan's isolationist period, foreign trade was confined to the port of
Nagasaki, and a ghetto of Dutch merchants was permitted to
reside on the island of Deshima. Kyoto remained the imperial
residence, but Yedo, the seat of the Tokugawa Shogunate from
1603 to 1868, became the *de facto* capital.

CHRONOLOGIES

The Sumero-Akkadian Civilization
The Egyptiac Civilization
The Syrian 'Roundabout'
The Central Asian 'Roundabout'
The Indo-Pakistani Sub-continent
The Sinic Civilization
The Japanese Civilization
The Hellenic Civilization
The Orthodox Christian Civilization
The Islamic Civilization

The Sumero-Akkadian Civilization

c. 4300–3100 BC	Gradual reclamation of the jungle-swamp in the Lower Tigris-Euphrates Valley; beginnings of a distinctive Sumeric Civilization
c. 3100–2400 BC	A mosaic of Sumerian sovereign city-states, more and more violently at war with each other
c. 2396–2371 BC	Sumerian city-states united politically by conquest into an empire extending from the head of the Persian Gulf to the Mediterranean coast of northern Syria
c. 2371–2316 BC	Sargon of Agade, an Akkadian-speaking community somewhere near the future site of Babylon, conquers the Empire
c. 2371–2230 BC	Agade Empire of Sumer and Akkad (universal state)
c. 2230–2120 BC	First Intermediate Period of political disunity and weakness; *Völkerwanderung* of Amorite founders of Babylon from west, and of Gutaeans from east
c. 2113–2096 BC	Ur-Nammu, founder of Third Dynasty of Ur, re-establishes Empire of Sumer and Akkad
c. 2113–2006 BC	Third Dynasty of Ur (revived universal state)
c. 2006–1755 BC	Second Intermediate Period
1894–1595 BC	First Dynasty of Babylon
1792–1750 BC	Hammurabi of Babylon (revived universal state)
c. 1732–744 BC	Third Intermediate Period
18th to 17th centuries BC	*Völkerwanderung* of Mitanni, Kassites, Hurrians, Hyksos; Assyria falls under Mitanni's suzerainty
c. 1732–1136 BC	Kassite Dynasty in Babylonia
1595 BC	Babylon sacked by Hittites
14th century BC	Assyria recovers independence and becomes militaristic instead of commercial
13th to 12th centuries BC	*Völkerwanderung* of Aramaeans, Chaldaeans, Hebrews, Sea Peoples, Phrygians
1244–1208 BC	Assyria conquers Babylon
12th to 10th centuries BC	Assyria repels Phrygians and Aramaeans
932–859 BC	Assyria conquers Aramaean states east of Euphrates
853 BC	Battle of Karkar: Assyrians repulsed by coalition of Syrian states
744–727 BC	Tiglath-Pileser III of Assyria
744–609 BC	Assyrian Empire: most of Syria, Babylonia, Egypt, and Elam annexed; Aramaic language and alphabet spread throughout Fertile Crescent (revived universal state)
625–539 BC	Chaldaean successor-state of Assyrian Empire, i.e. Neo-Babylonian Empire (revived universal state)
612 BC	Nineveh sacked by Medes and Chaldaeans
539 BC–AD 1258	Babylonia incorporated successively in Achaemenian, Seleucid, Arsacid, Sasanian, and Arab Empires, and serves each empire in turn as its economic base

The Egyptiac Civilization

4th millennium BC	Gradual reclamation of the jungle-swamp in the Nile Valley below the First Cataract and in parts of the Nile Delta; development of a distinctive Egyptiac Civilization
c. 3100 BC	Sudden unification of the Egyptiac World through conquest of Northern Kingdom by Southern Kingdom
c. 3100–2160 BC	Old Kingdom
c. 2686–2613 BC	Third Dynasty
c. 2613–2494 BC	Fourth Dynasty (pyramid-builders)
c. 2494–2345 BC	Fifth Dynasty (king becomes 'son' of Sun-god Re)
c. 2345–2181 BC	Sixth Dynasty
c. 2160–2052 BC	First Intermediate Period of political disunity and weakness; ? invasion by Asians
c. 2052–1786 BC	Middle Kingdom
c. 2052–1991 BC	Eleventh Dynasty
c. 2052–2010 BC	Mentuhotpe II reunites Egypt, starting from Thebes
1991–1786 BC	Twelfth Dynasty; administration gradually recentralized; suzerainty imposed on northern Nubia and on southern Syria
1786–1567 BC	Second Intermediate Period
c. 1730 BC onwards	*Völkerwanderung* of Hyksos and subjugation of northern Egypt by them
1567 BC	Ahmose, starting from Thebes, expels Hyksos from northern Egypt
1567–c. 1320 BC	Eighteenth Dynasty
1567–1085 BC	New Kingdom; expansion up Nile to Napata, just below the Fourth Cataract
1468 BC	Battle of Megiddo: Egyptian victory in Syria
1457 BC	Egypt invades Mitanni

1379–1362 BC	Iknaton (abortive religious and artistic, but permanent linguistic, revolution; weakening of hold on Syria)
13th to 12th centuries BC	*Völkerwanderung* of Libyans and Sea Peoples
c. 1320–1200 BC	Nineteenth Dynasty
c. 1286–1270 BC	Egyptian-Hittite War
c. 1200–1085 BC	Twentieth Dynasty
1191 or 1171 BC	Battle of the Nile: Egyptians repel Sea Peoples
1085–656 BC	Third Intermediate Period; political disunity; infiltration of Libyans
c. 935–730 BC	Libyan Dynasty
c. 730–664 BC	Contest for possession of Egypt between Ethiopians (Kushites) based on Napata, and Assyrians
664–525 BC	Twenty-sixth Dynasty
525 BC–AD 639	Egypt incorporated successively in Achaemenian, Ptolemaic, and Roman Empires
c. 464–455 BC 404/395–342 BC	Independent native Egyptian régimes
3rd to 4th centuries AD	Conversion to Christianity
c. 3rd to 4th centuries AD	Art of reading and writing the three Egyptiac scripts is lost

The Syrian 'Roundabout'

(*see map on page 397*)

3rd millennium to 18th century BC	Sumero-Akkadian sphere of influence and exploitation in north, and Egyptian sphere in south; no overlapping
18th to 17th centuries BC	*Völkerwanderung* of Hurrians, Mitanni, Hyksos
15th to 13th centuries BC	Egyptian Empire in Syria (but *lingua franca* is Akkadian)
12th century BC	*Völkerwanderung* of 'Hieroglyphic Luvians', Hebrews, Aramaeans, Philistines
? 11th to 10th centuries BC	Earliest inscriptions in Phoenician alphabet
c. 10th century BC	Aramaic alphabet derived from Phoenician
858–856 BC	Assyria conquers Bit Adini, the Aramaean state astride westward elbow of River Euphrates
853 BC	Battle of Karkar: Assyrians repulsed by coalition of Syrian states
c. 800 BC	Phoenicians begin to plant colonies in western Mediterranean Basin

8th to 6th or 5th centuries BC	Extant writings of Prophets of Israel and Judah
732 BC	Assyria liquidates Kingdom of Damascus
722 BC	Assyria liquidates Kingdom of Israel
586 BC	Neo-Babylonian Empire liquidates Kingdom of Judah
539–333 BC	Syria incorporated in Achaemenian Empire
333–332 BC	Alexander conquers Syria; Greek replaces Aramaic as official language and as *lingua franca* in former Achaemenian dominions
301 BC	Syria partitioned between Seleucus I and Ptolemy I
after 301 BC	Foundation of Antioch and other Greek settlements in northern Syria; Hellenization of Transjordania
201–198 BC	Antiochus III conquers southern Syria for Seleucid Empire from Ptolemaic Empire
c. 175 BC	Hellenizing movement in temple-state of Jerusalem
168 BC	Antiochus IV persecutes Judaean Jewish opponents of Hellenization
166–129 BC	Hasmonaean Dynasty wins independence from Seleucid Empire for Palestinian Jewry
2nd to 1st centuries BC	Arabs infiltrate Syria
64 BC	Pompey creates Roman province of Syria
63 BC	Pompey extinguishes independence of Hasmonaean state
37–4 BC	Herod the Great King of Palestinian Jewish state under Roman hegemony
? before 4 BC to AD 27	Jesus
c. AD 40–64	Paul's missionary journeys, based at first on Antioch
66–70	First Romano-Jewish War
70	Destruction of Jerusalem
130	Hadrian orders foundation of Aelia Capitolina on site of Jerusalem
132–35	Second Romano-Jewish War
262–72	Palmyrene régime in Roman Empire's eastern provinces
272–602	Syria reincorporated in Roman Empire; but secession of Monophysite Christianity from the 'Melchite' (Imperialist) Church
633–41	Muslim Conquest of Syria
641–969	Syria incorporated in Arab Empire
661–750	Arab imperial capital at Damascus

531

969	Syria partitioned between East Roman Empire and Fatimid Shi'i counter-caliphate
1098–1291	Western Christian Crusaders in Syria
1169–1516	Syria held by Ayyubids and their Mamluk successors
1516	'Osmanlis conquer Syria
1831–50	Syria held by Mehmet 'Ali, Pasha of Egypt
1840–1918	Restored Ottoman régime in Syria
1918–20	Syria partitioned between French and British mandated territories
1948	Syria partitioned between states of Syria, Lebanon, Jordan, Israel, and Egypt

The Central Asian 'Roundabout'

(see map on page 395)

? 17th century BC	Aryas traverse Oxus-Jaxartes Basin *en route* from the Eurasian steppe, advancing south-west to Mesopotamia (Mitanni), and south-east to India
? 14th century BC	Iranians occupy Oxus-Jaxartes Basin
8th to 7th centuries BC	Cimmerians and Scyths traverse Oxus-Jaxartes Basin *en route* from the Eurasian steppe, advancing south-west to South-West Asia, and south-east to the Indus Basin
6th century BC to 331 BC	Oxus-Jaxartes Basin and Kabul River Basin incorporated in Achaemenian Empire
329–328 BC	Alexander conquers Oxus-Jaxartes Basin
after 311 BC	Oxus-Jaxartes Basin incorporated in Seleucid Empire
c. 250 BC	Bactrian Greek successor-state of Seleucid Empire in Oxus-Jaxartes Basin makes itself independent
c. 200–140 BC	Bactrian Greek state straddles the Hindu Kush and splits up into rival principalities
c. 135–125 BC	Bactrian Greek rule north of Hindu Kush extinguished by Yuechi Eurasian Nomads
c. AD 48–after AD 224	Kushan Yuechi Empire straddles Hindu Kush (remnant survives till Hun *Völkerwanderung*)
1st century AD onwards	Mahayana Buddhism traverses Oxus-Jaxartes Basin *en route* from India to Eastern Asia
? before 359	Ephthalite Huns occupy Oxus-Jaxartes Basin
5th to 7th centuries	Nestorian Christianity traverses Oxus-Jaxartes Basin *en route* from Roman Empire to China
c. 455	Huns and Gurjaras invade India across Hindu Kush

c. 563–68	Sasanian Persian Empire and Western Turks partition Ephthalite dominions along line of River Oxus
c. 661–71	Persian share of Ephthalite dominions (Tokharistan) incorporated in Arab Empire
739–41	Transoxania definitively incorporated in Arab Empire
874–999	Samanid successor-state of 'Abbasid Caliphate in Oxus-Jaxartes Basin
962–1161	Ghaznevids straddle Hindu Kush
999	Ilak Khans from Tarim Basin conquer Transoxania
1141	Refugee Khitans (Qaraqitay) from northern China conquer Transoxania
1161–1215	Ghuris straddle Hindu Kush
1215–20	Khwarizm Shahs straddle Hindu Kush
1220	Mongols conquer Qaraqitays' and Khwarizm Shahs' dominions
1227	Mongols' Central Asian dominions partitioned between Golden Horde and Chaghatay's appanage
1369–1494	Timurid Empire based on Oxus-Jaxartes Basin
1500	Uzbeks conquer Oxus-Jaxartes Basin
1747–	Kingdom of Afghanistan bestrides Hindu Kush with northern frontier along line of River Oxus
1865–95	Russia conquers what is now Soviet Central Asia, i.e. the Uzbek territories (except Afghan Uzbekistan between Hindu Kush and Oxus), together with Türkmenistan

The Indo-Pakistani Sub-continent

c. 2500–1500 BC	*Floruit* of the Indus Civilization
c. 1500 BC	Entry of the Aryas into the sub-continent
last millennium BC	Rise of the Indic Civilization and its spread throughout the sub-continent
7th century BC	*Völkerwanderung* of Eurasian Nomads into Indus Basin
7th to 4th centuries BC	Period of contending local states in northern India
c. 567–487 BC	The Buddha
after 539 BC	Cyrus II annexes Kabul River Basin to Achaemenian Empire
after 522 BC	Darius I annexes Indus Basin to Achaemenian Empire
327–325 BC	Alexander in the Indus Basin

323–185 BC	Maurya Empire (first universal state)
273–232 BC	Emperor Açoka; adopts Buddhism in 261
2nd century BC to 2nd century AD	Simultaneous gradual rise of Mahayana Buddhism and theistic Hinduism
c. 200–183 BC	Bactrian Greek King, Demetrius (?I or II), invades India
c. 200 BC–AD 48	Greek principalities in North-West India
1st century BC	Sakas supersede Greeks progressively in Indus Basin
c. AD 48–after 224	Kushan Empire astride Hindu Kush range between Oxus and Jumna rivers; Graeco-Indian Buddhist art in Gandhara
1st century AD onwards	Peaceful maritime expansion of Indic Civilization into South-East Asia and Indonesia
after 224	Kushan Empire annexed by Sasanian Empire (a remnant of the Kushan Empire survives until the Hun *Völkerwanderung*)
320–590	Gupta Empire in northern India (revived universal state)
c. 455–528	Huns and Gurjaras invade India; they are defeated but not dislodged and are converted to Hinduism
606–47	Emperor Harsha (revived universal state)
711	Arabs conquer Sind
c. 788–838	Sankara preaches Monistic philosophy
962–1161	Turkish Muslim Ghaznevid Empire astride the Hindu Kush (survives in Panjab till 1186)
11th to 12th centuries	Ramanuja preaches modified Monism
1175–c. 1202	Muhammad Ghori conquers northern India
1206–1398	Turkish 'slave-kings' at Delhi
1302–11	North Indian Muslims conquer Deccan
c. 1336–1565	Hindu Vijayanagar Empire in South (remnant survives till 1646)
1398	Timur Lenk sacks Delhi
1419–1539	Nanak, founder of Sikh religion
1526–40 and 1555–1707	Mughal Empire (remnant at Delhi 1707–1857) (revived universal state)
1556–1605	Emperor Akbar
1659–1707	Emperor Awrangzib
1757–65	British East India Company takes possession of Bengal and Bihar
1818	British rule or suzerainty established throughout India to the south-east of the Indus Basin
1834–86	Ramakrishna
1843–49	British conquer Indus Basin
1849–1947	British Indian Empire (revived universal state)
1857–58	Mutiny of British East India Company's Indian troops
1858	East India Company's régime in India replaced by British government rule
1869–1948	Gandhi
1947	British Indian Empire replaced by three successor-states: the Indian Union, Pakistan, and Burma
1972	Bangladesh secedes from Pakistan

The Sinic Civilization

c. 1500–1027 BC	Beginning of the Sinic Civilization: Shang Kingdom in North China plain
1027–256 BC	Chou Kingdom in Wei River Basin and Lower Yellow River Basin
771 BC	Chou government driven from Wei River Basin to Loyang by northern barbarians
771–221 BC	First Intermediate Period (Period of Contending States): political disunity and increasingly violent warfare among local states, but progressive expansion of Sinic Civilization's area and growing technological, economic, and intellectual vigour
c. 551–479 BC	Confucius
5th century BC	Beginnings of water control
c. 479–438 BC	Moti rejects Confucius's grading of ethical obligation
c. 4th century BC	Taoist classics
4th to 3rd centuries BC	Legist school of Philosophers
c. 4th century BC	Ox-drawn plough and iron tools and weapons
247–210 BC	King Cheng of Ch'in (Ts'in)
221 BC	Cheng becomes first Emperor (Shih Hwang-ti) of Sinic universal state
221–207 BC	Ch'in imperial dynasty
207–202 BC	Second Intermediate Period
202–195 BC	Emperor Liu P'ang, founder of first Han dynasty
202 BC–AD 9	First Han Dynasty (universal state)
140–87 BC	Emperor Wuti; Confucianism established as official philosophy; beginning of partial recruitment of civil servants by examination

AD 25–220	Second Han Dynasty; Buddhism (carrying Graeco-Roman art) makes entry into China
184–589	Third Intermediate Period
4th to 6th centuries AD	China divided politically between barbarian successor-states of the Empire in the north and refugee régimes in the south; Sinification of the south; apogee of Buddhism throughout China
311	Hiongnu (Hun) Eurasian Nomads take Loyang
589–618	Sui Dynasty; Grand Canal completed from Hangchou to Loyang
618–909	T'ang Dynasty
622	Recruitment of civil servants by examination revived and systematized
8th to 9th centuries	Block printing of books begins
842–45	Persecution of Buddhism and other foreign religions
875–979	Fourth Intermediate Period
960–1279	Sung Dynasty
1114–1234	Kin Dynasty in northern China
1126	Sung Dynasty evicted from northern China by Kin (Jurchen Manchus)
1131–1200	Neoconfucian philosopher Chu Hsi
1234	Mongols complete their conquest of Kin Empire
1260–1368	Yüan (Mongol) Dynasty; northern section of Grand Canal realined to reach Tientsin (for Peking) instead of Loyang (for Ch'ang Ngan)
1260–94	Qubilay, suzerain of whole Mongol Empire, sovereign of China
1267	Qubilay moves his capital to Peking from Qaraqorum
1279	Mongols complete their conquest of Sung Empire and thus reunify China politically
1315	Recruitment of civil servants by examination revived
1368–1644	Ming Dynasty
1473–1529	Neoconfucian philosopher Wang Shou-jen (alias Wang Yang-ming)
16th century	New food-plants start population explosion
1514	The first Portuguese reaches China
1644–1912	Ch'ing (Manchu) Dynasty
1662–1722	Emperor K'ang Hsi
1689	Sino-Russian Treaty of Nerchinsk
1726–96	Emperor Ch'ien Lung

1839–1949	Fifth Intermediate Period
1839–42	Opium War: Britain annexes Hong Kong and forces China to open several ports for foreign trade and settlement
1850–64	T'aip'ing Rebellion
1854–60	Russia annexes left bank of Amur and a seaboard further south
1894–95	First Sino-Japanese War, followed by incipient partition of China among foreign Powers
1905	Ending of civil service examinations
1911–12	Ch'ing Dynasty deposed; imperial régime abolished
1931–45	Second Sino-Japanese War
1949	Kuomintang régime replaced by Communist régime in continental China
1965/6–68	Cultural Revolution in continental China

The Japanese Civilization

c. AD 550–75	Buddhism introduced via Korea
646	T'ang system of imperial administration introduced from China; beginnings of distinctive Japanese Civilization
710–94	Imperial capital at Nara
794–1868	Imperial capital at Kyoto
858–1185	Emperors dominated by regents at Kyoto
12th and 13th centuries	Zen Buddhism acclimatized in Japan
1185–1590	Intermediate Period of political disunity and civil war
1205–1333	Shoguns dominated by regents at Kamakura
1222–82	Nichiren, founder of Hokke school of Buddhism
1274 and 1281	Unsuccessful Mongol invasions of Japan
1335–1597	Ashikaga shoguns at Kyoto
1542	Portuguese reach Japan
1587–1640	Christianity banned; Japan attempts complete self-insulation
1590–98	Hideyoshi dictator at Osaka (foundation of universal state)
1592–98	Unsuccessful Japanese invasion of Korea
1598–1616	Tokugawa Ieyasu in power
1603–1868	Tokugawa shoguns at Yedo

1853–54	Commodore Perry with US naval squadron enters Yedo Bay
1868	Meiji Restoration
1894–95	First Sino-Japanese War
1904–05	Russo-Japanese War
1931–45	Second Sino-Japanese War
1941–45	Japan intervenes in Second World War
1945	Atomic bombs dropped on Hiroshima and Nagasaki
1950	Japanese economic boom starts

The Hellenic Civilization

12th to 9th centuries BC	Dark Age in the Aegean Basin
12th to 10th centuries BC	Greek settlements along west coast of Asia Minor
12th to 11th centuries BC	*Völkerwanderung* of north-west-Greek-speaking war-bands into the Aegean Civilization's domain
by 8th century BC	Hellenic World articulated politically into a mosaic of sovereign local city-states
8th century BC	The Greeks adopt the Phoenician alphabet: the Homeric epics take definitive form
8th century BC	Greek population explosion starts; Greek colonial city-states planted in southern Italy and Sicily
7th century BC	Greek colonial city-states planted along north coast of Aegean, round coasts of Sea of Marmara and Black Sea, in Cyrenaïca, and along French riviera
7th century BC	In some Hellenic city-states, subsistence farming replaced by cash-crop farming and by manufacturing industry for export
7th century BC	Etruscans and some native Italian peoples adopt Hellenic culture, including the alphabet; Egypt opened for Greek traders
7th century BC	Intensification of warfare between Hellenic city-states
7th to 6th centuries BC	Hereditary monarchies and aristocracies replaced by dictatorships in economically advanced states
6th century BC	In Greece, dictatorships replaced by oligarchies of property-owners; in Sicily, dictatorships begin, uniting clusters of city-states
6th century BC	Beginnings of Hellenic science and philosophy
c. 620–550 BC	Thales of Miletus
c. 570–490 BC	Pythagoras of Samos and Croton
6th century BC	Further plantations of Greek colonial city-states prevented by rise of Carthaginian Empire in West, and of Lydian, succeeded by Achaemenian Persian, Empire in East
480–479 BC	Achaemenian Emperor Xerxes' attempt to conquer European Greece defeated by coalition of minority of European Greek states led by Sparta and Athens
479 BC	Victorious Greek coalition liberates Greek communities under Achaemenian rule along north and east shores of Aegean and round Sea of Marmara
478 BC	Liberated Greek communities transfer leadership from Sparta to Athens; Atheno-Persian War continues
469–399 BC	Socrates (Athenian)
466 or 464 BC	*Entente* between Sparta and Athens breaks down
461 BC	Radical democratization of Athens
459–449 BC	Athens at war simultaneously with Achaemenian Empire and with Sparta's allies in European Greece
454 BC	Athens completes transformation of league of liberated Greek states into an Athenian Empire
449 BC	Atheno-Persian peace settlement at continental Greek states' expense
445 BC	Atheno-Spartan peace settlement confirms liberation of central European Greece from Athenian rule
431–338 BC	Chronic indecisive warfare between Greek states, accompanied by intense artistic and intellectual activity and continuing progress of Hellenization of northern Greece and peninsular Italy
429–347 BC	Plato (Athenian)
405–404 BC	Overthrow of Athenian Empire by Sparta
4th and 3rd centuries BC	Gallic and Celtic *Völkerwanderung*
386 BC	The Great King's Peace re-establishes Achaemenian Empire's sovereignty over the Greek states of Asia Minor and confirms Sparta's supremacy in European Greece
384–322 BC	Aristotle (Stageirite)
371 BC	Sparta overthrown by Thebes
359–336 BC	Philip of Macedon
341–270 BC	Epicurus of Samos
340 or 339–266 BC	Rome unites peninsular Italy politically; Hellenization of Italy progresses

338 BC	All Greek states between Dardanelles and Straits of Otranto, except Sparta, confederated under *Pax Macedonica*
336–323 BC	Alexander the Great King of Macedon, and, from 331 BC, also Emperor of former Achaemenian Empire
333 (?)–261 BC	Zeno of Citium, the Phoenician Cypriot founder of the Stoic philosophy
331 BC	Overthrow of Achaemenian Empire by Alexander opens up its former dominions for colonization by Greeks and for Hellenization
323 BC	At Alexander's death, *Pax Macedonica* collapses
323–146 BC	Resumption of chronic warfare in expanded Hellenic World
218–146 BC	Rome breaks power of Carthage, Macedon, and the Seleucid Monarchy and dominates Mediterranean Basin
2nd century BC	Palestinian Jews reject Hellenization
133–31 BC	Political and social revolution in Roman Commonwealth and its dependencies
31 BC–AD 14	Octavian (Augustus) Emperor
31 BC–AD 235	*Pax Augusta*: Hellenic World at peace under Roman rule (universal state)
c. AD 40 onwards	Spread of Christianity through Hellenic World
204–270	Plotinus of Alexandria
235–84	Breakdown of *Pax Augusta*; barbarian breakthrough retrieved
250	First systematic attempt to extirpate Christianity
284–305	Diocletian Emperor; military and administrative reform: universal state restored; survives in West till 5th century and in Levant till 602
303–311	Last and most determined attempt to extirpate Christianity
311	Imperial edict conceding toleration to Christianity
313–95	Completion of conversion of Hellenic World to Christianity – by force in final stage
313–602	Symbiosis of disintegrating Hellenic Civilization and nascent Orthodox Christian Civilization
378–476	Barbarian breakthrough retrieved in the Levant but not in the West
533–68	Partial and temporary re-establishment of the Roman imperial régime in the West, at cost of exhaustion in the Levant
602	Collapse of Roman Empire in the Levant

The Orthodox Christian Civilization

AD 306–37	Emperor Constantine I the Great (master of the whole Roman Empire 324–37)
311	Imperial edict conceding toleration to Christianity
313–95	Completion of conversion of Hellenic World to Christianity – by force in the final stage
313–602	Symbiosis of disintegrating Hellenic Civilization and nascent Orthodox Christian Civilization
	The Cappadocian fathers – theologians and ecclesiastical organizers:
c. 329–92	St Gregory of Nazianzos
c. 330–79	St Basil the Great, founder of the Eastern Orthodox monastic order
c. 335–95	St Gregory of Nyssa
6th to 7th centuries	Slav *Völkerwanderung* to the south of River Danube
527–65	Emperor Justinian I
7th century	Administrative, economic, and social revolutions in East Roman Empire: militarization of provincial government; rise of freeholding peasantry, providing a provincial militia
602	Murder of Emperor Maurice; collapse of Constantinopolitan imperial government
610–41	Emperor Heraclius
626	Constantinople withstands siege by Avars and Persians
674–78	Constantinople withstands siege by Arabs
680	Bulgar Nomads win foothold to south of Lower Danube
717–41	Emperor Leo III ('Isaurian', i.e. Syrian)
717–18	Constantinople withstands second Arab siege
726	*Ecloga* lawbook promulgated
726–843	Conflict between supporters and opponents of cult of icons
741–74	Emperor Constantine V
809–904	Bulgarian Khanate expands south-westwards over the interior of the Balkan Peninsula
843	Conflict over icons ended by compromise favourable to iconophils
863	Mission of SS. Constantine-Cyril and Methodhios to Moravia
863	Turn of the tide in the East Roman Empire's favour in its perennial warfare with the Arabs

864	Bulgaria converted to Orthodox Christianity
by 867	Orthodox bishop installed at Kiev
867–86	Emperor Basil I (Adrianopolitan)
870	Bulgaria's allegiance to Orthodox Christianity confirmed, in preference to subordination to Roman See
c. 870–79	'The Handbook' of laws promulgated
c. 874	Orthodox archbishop installed at Kiev
c. 879–86	Second edition of 'the Handbook' promulgated
c. 889–90	*Vasilika* lawbooks promulgated
893–927	Khan Symeon of Bulgaria, 'the semi-Greek'
10th century onwards	Renaissance of Hellenic style in Byzantine visual art
10th century	Bogomil religion starts in Bulgaria and subsequently spreads into East Roman Empire and into Western Christendom
913–27	Symeon fails to incorporate East Roman Empire in Bulgaria by force
926–1046	East Roman Empire expands into Islamic and Armenian territories
928/9 (?)–1003/4	Unsuccessful East Roman legislation for preserving peasant freeholds
c. 961	The first important monastery (the Great Lavra) founded on Mount Athos
976–1025	Emperor Basil II, 'the Bulgar-killer'
976–1018	Great Bulgaro-Roman War
989	Definitive conversion of Russia to Orthodox Christianity
1018	Bulgaria incorporated in East Roman Empire
1042–51	Debasement of East Roman gold coin – financial crisis
1071	Saljuq Turks defeat and capture Emperor Rhomanos Dhioyenes and subsequently occupy interior of Asia Minor; Normans take Bari
1204	Venetian and French Crusaders take Constantinople; East Roman Empire partitioned among Latin and Greek successor-states
1261–1453	Greek East Roman Empire re-established at Constantinople, but supplanted in western Asia Minor by Turkish successor-states
1353	'Osmanlis take Gallipoli (their first foothold in Europe)
c. 1361	'Osmanlis take Adrianople
1371–93	'Osmanlis conquer Serbia and Bulgaria
1439	Abortive union of Eastern Orthodox Churches with Roman Church
1453	'Osmanlis take Constantinople
1638	Russians advance the frontier of Orthodox Christendom to the coast of the Pacific Ocean at Okhotsk
17th century	Beginning of reception of secular Western Civilization by Eastern Orthodox Christian peoples (Russians, Serbs, Greeks)

The Islamic Civilization

8th century BC	Arabs erupt out of Arabia; repulsed by Assyria
2nd century BC	Arabs erupt out of Arabia; not repulsed by the Seleucid monarchy; permanent lodgments of Arab communities left in Syria and Mesopotamia
c. AD 70–570	Religions of the Fertile Crescent seep into the Arabian Peninsula
AD 570–632	Muhammad, founder of Islam
622	Muhammad's flight (*hijrah*) from Mecca to Medina and foundation of Islamic state at Medina
630	Mecca capitulates to Muhammad
632–61	First four Caliphs (Khalifahs, i.e. political successors of Muhammad)
633–37	Conquest of 'Iraq
633–41	Conquest of Syria, including Palestine
639–41	Conquest of Mesopotamia and Egypt
642–51	Conquest of Iran
647–98	Conquest of North-West Africa
653	Capitulation of Armenians and Georgians
661–750	Umayyad Caliphate with capital at Damascus
661–71	Conquest of eastern Khurasan
674–78 and 717–18	Failure to take Constantinople
710–12	Conquest of most of Iberian Peninsula
711	Conquest of Sind
732	Failure to conquer Gaul
739–41	Definitive conquest of Transoxania
750–1258	'Abbasid Caliphate with 'Iraq as metropolitan province
750	'Abbasids unable to establish their rule in Islamic dominions in the Iberian Peninsula
756–1031	Refugee Umayyad state in Iberian Peninsula

788–1258	Progressive break-up of the 'Abbasid Caliphate in Africa and Asia	1502–1895	Russia subjugates Muslims in Volga Basin, Siberia, Crimea, and western Turkistan
1016–90	Political disunity in former Iberian Umayyad domain	1529 and 1682–83	'Osmanlis fail to take Vienna
1090–1235	First the Murabits, then the Muwahhids from Africa reunite the Islamic dominions in the Iberian Peninsula	after 1707	Mughal Empire disintegrates
		1722	Safawi Empire collapses
1169–1250	Ayyubid state in Egypt	after 1774	Beginning of reception of secular Western Civilization by Muslim peoples
1250–1517	Mamluk successor-state of Ayyubids — Crusaders expelled; Mongols repulsed and converted	1911–18	Liquidation of Ottoman Empire
13th century	Refugee Ottoman state founded on the Islamic World's border in north-west Asia Minor	1919–23	Creation of Turkish Republic
		1924	Abolition of Ottoman Caliphate
1453	'Osmanlis take Constantinople (Istanbul)	after 1945	West European Powers, but not the Soviet Union, China, and Israel, relinquish their rule over Muslim peoples
16th and 17th centuries	Most of the Islamic World comprised in three empires: the Ottoman, Safawi, and Mughal	1947	Creation of Pakistan

NOTES
ON THE TEXT

LIST OF
ILLUSTRATIONS

INDEX

Notes on the text

PART I
THE SHAPE OF HISTORY

1 The relativity of historical thought

1 Greek text as in E. Diehl, *Anthologia Lyrica*, Leipzig, Teubner, 1922, I, 58–9.

2 For the Western World as a whole the close of this preceding age may be equated approximately with the end of the third quarter of the nineteenth century of our era. The idea that the 'sixties and 'seventies of the nineteenth century were a time of transition from one age of our common civilization to another is familiar to continental Europeans and to Americans (both in the United States and in Canada). It is less familiar to people brought up in Great Britain, who usually think of these decades not as the close but as the zenith of an age – the Victorian Age – which began earlier and ended later than this. From the standpoint of Great Britain, that is perhaps the natural view; but it will be suggested below (in ch. 2) that the position of Great Britain in the Western World at that time was exceptional. In the invention of industrialism and 'democracy' the people of Great Britain had been pioneers; and the process by which the supremacy of these two institutions was established was already past history in Great Britain at the time when it was attaining or approaching completion in other parts of the Western World. Hence the people of Great Britain were conscious of relative continuity at a time when the peoples of most other countries in the Western World were conscious of a transition from one age to another. The sense of the majority must be taken as the standard when we are considering the Western World as a whole.

3 On this point, see W. Dilthey, *Gesammelte Schriften*, Leipzig and Berlin, Teubner, 1927, VII. The *Geisteswissenschaften* tend to borrow the methods of the *Naturwissenschaften*, owing to the seniority of these latter disciplines, notwithstanding the fact that their respective *Verfahrungsweisen* differ *ab initio* (p. 130). 'Die realen Kategorien sind . . . in den Geisteswissenschaften nirgends dieselben als in den Naturwissenschaften' (p. 197). The usefulness of a 'scientific methodology' is one of the principal problems of modern sociology; see for example Peter Berger, *Invitation to Sociology: A Humanistic Perspective*, New York, Doubleday, 1963, pp. 11–62.

4 It is noteworthy that, while many historians still acquiesce in this régime, the leading minds in the field of contemporary physical science have already passed the stage of study in which the industrial system seems to be a fruitful and adequate method of research. Refuting the view that 'scientists are becoming ever narrower and more specialized', P. B. Medawar suggests that 'the opposite is the case. One of the distinguishing marks of modern science is the disappearance of sectarian loyalties. . . . Isolationism is over; we all depend upon and sustain each other' ('Two Conceptions of Science', reprinted in *The Art of the Soluble*, London, Methuen, 1967, pp. 111–28.)

5 'Established', that is, in the subjective meaning of the French verb *constater*.

6 See Eduard Meyer, 'Der Gang der alten Geschichte' in *Kleine Schriften*, Halle, Niemeyer, 1910; and *Blüte und Niedergang des Hellenismus in Asien*, Berlin, Curtius, 1925. In another place, Meyer points out that the historian's access to historical evidence is always and everywhere at the mercy of chance, so that there is no rational correspondence between the intrinsic importance and interest of any given historical event and the quantity and credibility of the historical evidence that is at our disposal for the study of it (*Geschichte des Altertums*, 4th edition, Stuttgart and Berlin, Cotta, 1921, I (i), 211–12).

7 The pioneers of today in the field of physical science would probably admit this description as being true of the *laboratorium* of their 'classical' predecessors, but would indignantly – and perhaps justly – deny that their own work was being conducted on 'classical' principles or under the shadow of 'classical' traditions.

8 See Bergson's inquiry into the 'Fonction Primordiale de l'Intelligence' in *L'Évolution Créatrice*, 24th edition, Paris, Alcan, 1921, pp. 164–79. In this suggestion, Bergson has been anticipated by Turgot. See the 'Plan de Deux Discours sur l'Histoire Universelle' in *Œuvres de Turgot*, nouvelle édition, 2 vols., Paris, Guillaumin, 1844, II, 626–8.

9 Bergson (see n. 8), especially ch. 3.

10 Camille Jullian, *De la Gaule à la France: Nos Origines Historiques*, Paris, Hachette, 1922.

11 Jullian (see n. 10), ch. 2, p. 62, 'L'Époque des Agricolteurs (Temps Néolithiques)'.

12 H. W. V. Temperley's masterly *History of Serbia*, London, Bell, 1917, illustrates the difficulties with which a historian

has to contend in attempting to write a history of a nation of this calibre. In order to make Serbian history intelligible and consecutive, he has to present it within the successive frameworks of Byzantine and Ottoman history and finally in relation to the 'Eastern Question': that is to say, as a function of the modern European balance of power. There are few chapters in which he succeeds in disengaging Serbian history from its context and treating it in isolation.

2 The field of historical study

1 See Part XI, ch. 53, pp. 486–7, below.
2 Virgil, *Eclogues*, I, 66: 'And the Britons totally cut off from all the rest of the world.'
3 i.e. 'a second world'; see E. A. Freeman, *Historical Essays*, fourth series, London, Macmillan, 1891, ix, 'Alter Orbis'.
4 Marc Bloch, *Feudal Society*, London, Routledge and Kegan Paul, 1961, pp. 181–9.
5 In a lecture on Henry IV and Richelieu, printed in *Lectures on Modern History*, London, Macmillan, 1906.
6 Eric Hobsbawm, *Industry and Empire*, London, Weidenfeld and Nicolson, 1968, p. 21.
7 The only Spartan overseas colony was Tarentum, and the foundation of Tarentum appears to have been an exceptional measure.
8 See M. P. Nilsson, 'Die Grundlagen des spartanischen Lebens' in *Klio*, xii, 1912.
9 Thucydides II, 41.
10 See Part IV, ch. 23, p. 173, below.

3 Some definitions of terms

1 F. A. Hayek, *The Counter-Revolution of Science*, London, Allen and Unwin, 1952, p. 34.
2 Presumably derived from the simile in the New Testament in which the adherents of the Christian Church are spoken of as members of the body of Christ (e.g. 1 Cor. vi. 15; Eph. v. 30).
3 P. Bagby, *Culture and History*, London, Longmans, 1958, pp. 84 and 95.
4 Bagby (see n. 3), p. 124.
5 A. L. Kroeber, *The Nature of Culture*, Chicago, University Press, 1952, p. 104.
6 Bagby (see n. 3), pp. 162–3.
7 See H. Frankfort's criticism of Childe's phrase in *The Birth of Civilization in the Near East*, London, Williams and Norgate, 1951, pp. 57–8 and p. 57, n. 2.
8 R. Redfield, in *The Primitive World and its Transformations*, Ithaca N.Y., Cornell University Press, 1953, equates civilization with the rise of cities (p. ix) on the ground that it was in the cities that 'the administrative élite', 'the literate priest', and 'the specialized artisan' made their first appearance (p. 30).
9 Frankfort (see n. 7), pp. 7–8.
10 A. N. Whitehead, *Adventures of Ideas*, Cambridge, University Press, 1933, pp. 13–14.
11 Christopher Dawson, *The Dynamics of World History*, London, Sheed and Ward, 1957, p. 41.
12 The Western statue must be pre-Renaissance if it is to be characteristic and distinctive. It must antedate the Western reception, at 'the' Renaissance, of the Hellenic style of visual art.
13 A. L. Kroeber, *Style and Civilizations*, Ithaca N.Y., Cornell University Press, 1957, pp. 2–3 and 155–6.
14 Kroeber (see n. 5), p. 402.
15 Kroeber (see n. 5), p. 403.
16 Kroeber (see n. 13), p. 150.
17 Bagby (see n. 3), p. 108.
18 Bagby (see n. 3), pp. 108–9.
19 Frankfort (see n. 7), p. 16.
20 Bagby (see n. 3), p. 109.

4 The need for a comprehensive study of human affairs

1 M. R. Cohen, *The Meaning of Human History*, La Salle, Open Court Publishing Company, 1947, p. 210.
2 J. Needham, *Science and Civilization in China*, Cambridge, University Press, 1954, II, 336; and C. Lévi-Strauss, *The Savage Mind*, London, Weidenfeld and Nicolson, 1966.
3 Among many other contemporary observers, Jan Romein testifies that, in our day, 'one world or none' is the truth about our situation (M. F. A. Montagu (editor), *Toynbee and History*, Boston, Porter Sargent, 1956, p. 350).
4 This point has been made by Polybius in his *Ecumenical History* I, 4: 'The coincidence by which all the transactions of the world have been oriented in a single direction and guided towards a single goal is the extraordinary characteristic of the present age, to which the special feature of the present work is a corollary. The unity of events imposes on the historian a similar unity of composition in depicting for his readers the operation of the laws of Fortune on the grand scale, and this has been my own principal inducement and stimulus in the work which I have undertaken.'
5 R. Coulborn in *Phylon*, 1940, offprint, p. 62.
6 'Die Erkenntnis der Geschichte der Menschheit soll ein Gemeingut der Menschheit sein': a fragment written by Ranke in the 1860s, printed on pp. xiii–xvi of A. Dove's preface to the Ninth Part, Second Section, of Ranke's *Weltgeschichte*, 9 parts, Leipzig, Duncker and Humblot, 1881–8. The passage here quoted is on pp. xv–xvi.
7 In a critique of my work, J. Romein judges that I am right in thinking that the unity of the world is now in the making. As Romein puts it, world unity has been created by the technicians; we have now to raise this technological unity to the level of creativity (*Toynbee and History* (see n. 3), p. 350).

5 The transitional societies

1 See Part IV, ch. 20, p. 155, below.
2 Jacquetta Hawkes and Sir Leonard Woolley, *History of Mankind*, published for the International Commission for a History of the Scientific and Cultural Development of Mankind, London, Allen and Unwin, 1963, I, 363–4.
3 Hawkes and Woolley (see n. 2), p. 414.
4 Hawkes and Woolley (see n. 2), p. 466.
5 V. G. Childe, *What Happened in History*, Harmondsworth, Penguin, 1942, p. 70.
6 Hawkes and Woolley (see n. 2), p. 597.
7 Hawkes and Woolley (see n. 2), p. 419.
8 R. J. Braidwood, *The Near East and the Foundations of Civilization*, Eugene, Oregon State System of Higher Education, 1952, p. 16.
9 Braidwood (see n. 8), p. 5.
10 F. Borkenau in *Merkur*, July 1949, p. 629.
11 Braidwood (see n. 8), p. 42.
12 Braidwood (see n. 8), pp. 5–6 and 42.
13 Borkenau (see n. 10), p. 631. It is noteworthy that, in Peru as well, technological progress was characteristic of the Formative Age (W. C. Bennett, 'A Reappraisal of Peruvian Archaeology', p. 6, in *Memoirs of the Society for American Archaeology*, Menasha Wisc., 1948, pp. 121–2).
14 Borkenau (see n. 10), p. 630.
15 V. G. Childe, *Man Makes Himself*, London, Watts, 1936, p. 122.
16 In the Andean World as well, the transition from the Formative Age to the Classic Age, in which the valley bottoms in coastal Peru were mastered and irrigated, was accompanied by a shift in interest from technology to the social and political enterprise of manipulating manpower (W. C. Bennett and J. B. Bird, *Andean Culture History*, American Museum of Natural History Handbook Series no. 15, New York, 1949, pp. 181–2; W. C Bennett in 'A Reappraisal of Peruvian Archaeology' (see n. 13), p. 6).
17 Childe (see n. 15), p. 120–2.
18 In Egypt the whole land was owned by a single god incarnate, Pharaoh. In Sumer it was parcelled out among the territories of a number of independent city-states, and each of these city-state territories contained the estates of several gods. These Sumerian gods were not incarnate.
19 Braidwood (see n. 8), p. 37. Compare page 39 and also page 35: 'Fig. 25: Physiographical and rainfall map of Nuclear Western Asia, with major sites of occurrence of Ubaid phase antiquities or of materials judged to be contemporary with the Ubaid phase.' This was the phase in which the alluvium of the Lower Tigris-Euphrates basin was occupied by Man (p. 36).
20 Childe (see n. 5), pp. 79–80.
21 R. Redfield, *The Primitive World and its Transformations*, Ithaca N.Y., Cornell University Press, 1953, p. 6.
22 Childe (see n. 5), p. 80.

6 The comparative study of civilizations

1 This obvious but fundamental point is made by H.E.Barnes in *An Introduction to the History of Sociology*, Chicago, University Press, 1948, p. 732.

2 G.Buchdahl, in *The Australasian Journal of Philosophy*, December 1956, p. 168, quotes a dictum of Newton's about Newton's own method of work: 'In this philosophy, propositions are deduced from phenomena and afterwards made general by induction.' Buchdahl labels Newton's first step 'the inductive process' and the second step 'the inductive inference'.

3 I hold, as Bagby holds, that 'we shall only be able to judge our scheme when we have applied it to the actual facts of history and seen what results it gives us' (*Culture and History*, London, Longmans, 1958, p. 202).

7 Hellenic and Chinese models

1 M.R.Cohen, *The Meaning of Human History*, La Salle, Open Court Publishing Company, 1947, p. 114.

2 This view has certainly been widely held among Egyptologists in the past. However, E.J.Baumgartel, in *The Cultures of Prehistoric Egypt*, revised edition, London, Oxford University Press, 1955, p. 12, maintains that 'it is not generally recognized that the nomes are survivals of pre-Menite states.'

3 T.A.Sumberg questions 'whether churches are universally the link between the death and birth of related civilizations' (*Social Research*, September 1947, pp. 267–84).

4 Sinic history, by itself, offers all the necessary data for constructing the improved model. If Chinese scholars had not done violence to early Chinese history in their excessive zeal for symmetry and self-consistency, it would not have been necessary to resort to an Hellenic model, as we have had to do in order to correct the traditional Chinese misrepresentation of the configuration of early Chinese history.

5 H.Frankfort points out that, if we view Egyptiac history through Hellenic and Western spectacles, we shall fail to see it as it really was (*The Birth of Civilization in the Near East*, London, Williams and Norgate, 1951, pp. 27–31). As Frankfort sees it, 'the ideal of a marvellously integrated society had been formed long before the Pyramids were built; it was as nearly realized, when they were built, as any ideal social form can be translated into actuality; and it remained continuously before the eyes of rulers and people alike during subsequent centuries. It was an ideal which ought to thrill a Western historian by its novelty, for it falls entirely outside the experience of Greek or Roman or modern Man,

although it survives, in an attenuated form, in Africa. It represents a harmony between Man and the divine which is beyond our boldest dreams, since it was maintained by divine power which had taken charge of the affairs of Man in the person of Pharaoh. Society moved in unison with Nature. Justice, which was the social aspect of the cosmic order, pervaded the commonwealth' (pp. 27–31). Frankfort's thesis that the Egyptians' 'polity was not imposed but evolved from immemorial predilections' (p. 99) is convincing. On the other hand, when Frankfort goes on to say that this polity 'was adhered to, without protest, for almost three thousand years', his contention here is contradicted by the evidence of the surviving Egyptiac literature of the age of the Middle Kingdom. This testifies that the ideology of the Old Kingdom régime, and the measures (e.g. pyramid-building) through which this ideology was put into practice, did eventually provoke a moral reaction that went to the length of political revolution in the last days of the Sixth Dynasty.

6 This exceptional case is underlined by K.W.Erdmann in *Archiv für Kulturgeschichte*, 1951, pp. 174–250, on pp. 224–5.

7 This economic revolution was made possible by an advance, not in the realm of technology, but in the realm of politics (see ch. 5, pp. 48–52, above).

8 E.A.Thompson (editor and translator), *A Roman Reformer and Inventor: De Rebus Bellicis*, Oxford, Clarendon Press, 1952.

8 A Jewish model

1 During this period, there were states – e.g. the Kingdom of Adiabene and the Khazar Empire – in which the royal family and some of their grandees were converts to Judaism. There were also oases in the Hijaz and fastnesses in Abyssinia, the Caucasus, and the Crimea in which converts to Judaism held their own, perhaps with some admixture of Jewish refugees. But only a minority of the Jews in the world ever lived, or ever could have lived, in these holes and corners.

2 The stimulus of penalizations is discussed in Part II, ch. 16, below.

3 In the case of the Lebanese, this has been true *de jure* as well as *de facto* since the establishment, in 1861, of an autonomous vilayet of the Lebanon which became the Lebanese Republic in 1920.

4 The present worldwide Lebanese diasporá mostly dates from times subsequent to 1861, i.e. from the period in which the Lebanese people have had a state of their own. Since 1861, the one great ordeal to which they have been subjected has been the Turkish blockade during the First World War.

5 This has been one of the spurs by which the Irish, too, have been driven abroad. But, unlike the Scots and the

Lebanese, the Irish have been driven by political oppression as well.

6 R.Redfield, *The Primitive World and its Transformations*, Ithaca N.Y., Cornell University Press, 1953, p. 49.

9 A survey of civilizations

1 The rival claims of unity and diversity in African history are controversial. In the chart on page 72 a practical chronological distinction has been made between East and West Africa; but the question is still open. For a discussion of it, see Basil Davidson, *The Africans*, London, Longmans, 1969, pp. 36–41, and references.

2 See P.L.Shinnie (editor), *The African Iron Age*, Oxford, Clarendon Press, 1971.

3 See P.L.Shinnie, *Meroe*, London, Thames and Hudson, 1967, pp. 165–9.

4 See J.S.Trimingham, *The Influence of Islam upon Africa*, London, Longmans, 1968.

5 See J.S.Trimingham, *Islam in West Africa*, Oxford, Clarendon Press, 1959; *A History of Islam in West Africa*, Oxford, University of Glasgow Press, 1962; *Islam in East Africa*, Oxford, Clarendon Press, 1964.

6 See J.Desmond Clark, *The Prehistory of Africa*, London, Thames and Hudson, 1970, pp. 219–22.

7 See Lucy Mair, *Primitive Government*, Harmondsworth, Penguin, 1962, p. 9.

8 See Part I, ch. 3, pp. 43–4, above.

9 See Brian Fagan, *Southern Africa during the Iron Age*, London, Thames and Hudson, 1965.

10 See Davidson (n. 1), pp. 35–6.

11 See ch. 3, p. 44, above.

12 See C. Daryll Forde (editor), *African Worlds: Studies in the Cosmological Ideas and Social Values of African Peoples*, London, Oxford University Press, 1954.

13 See Davidson (n. 1), pp. 54–67, and pp. 137–42.

14 For the notion of 'challenge-and-response', see Part II, ch. 13, p. 97, below.

15 See Part III, ch. 18, below.

16 See Davidson (n. 1), pp. 235–43.

17 In each case the pre-universal-state phase of the civilization, if there was such a phase (and in most cases there was), has been distinguished from the universal-state phase, if the civilization in question ever entered into that phase. For this purpose the universal-state phase has been taken as including all successive avatars of the original universal state, in cases in which this was reconstituted either once, or more than once, after a temporary lapse, or repeated temporary lapses, into political disunity. In cases (e.g. those of the Aegean Civilization and the Indus Civilization) in which we do not know whether the society did or did not ever enter into the universal-state phase, this civilization's total time-span has been marked uniformly in a different shading again.

In cases of affiliation the interregnum between the submergence of the antecedent civilization and the emergence of the affiliated civilization has been included in the time-spans of both civilizations, instead of being excluded from both. This has been done in order to make it clear that the time-spans of the two civilizations overlapped below the surface.

The time-span of the five Christian and Islamic civilizations has been reckoned as starting from the date at which Islam and each of the four main Christian sects began to make mass-conversions. The starting-dates of the Christian and Islamic civilizations have, of course, to be distinguished clearly from the starting-dates of the two religions, Christianity and Islam, themselves. During the first three or four centuries of these two religions' existence, which were their formative centuries, their adherents amounted numerically to no more than a diasporá scattered among a majority that professed other religions; and the religion of a minority can inspire a community to maintain its identity without the prop of a national territory of its own, but it cannot provide the framework or basis for a new civilization. The eventual mass-conversions made the emergence of Christian and Islamic civilizations possible for the first time. The Islamic diasporá became a ruling minority within twenty years of the *hijrah*, whereas the Christian diasporá remained a subject minority until not much less than three hundred years after the crucifixion. But the political difference is not to the point. The religion of a ruling minority is no more capable than the religion of a subject minority is of serving as the matrix of a new civilization. In the age in which the Umayyad and 'Abbasid Caliphate was at its zenith, there was an Islamic political Power but not yet an Islamic society constituting a civilization.

18 By far the greater part of our information about the Middle American and Andean Civilizations is archaeological. The archaeological evidence enables us to distinguish local cultures within each of these two civilizations, and different stages in the history of each of them. On the other hand, the archaeologists have not yet reached firm conclusions about the datings. As recently as 1958, the beginning of the 'classic' phase in Middle America and in Peru – i.e. the beginning of the phase which, in the history of the Old World, we call 'civilization' – was dated, at the earliest, later than the beginning of the Christian Era. In 1971, the zenith of the Middle American Olmec culture was dated 1150–900 BC by Professor Michael D. Coe, in the light of excavations conducted by him in 1966–68 at San Lorenzo, on the isthmus of Tehuantepec – a site that seems to have been the Olmec culture's earliest centre. In the chart on page 72 of the present work, the beginning of civilization (i.e. of the 'classic' phase of culture) in both the Middle American and the Andean region is still placed at the beginning of the Christian Era, with question-marks to allow for the possibil-

ity that its true date may prove to have been earlier than 1000 BC.

19 The Babylonic last phase of the distinctive civilization of the Lower Tigris-Euphrates basin was still Sumeric in its inspiration. Asshurbanipal's library was stocked with texts in the Sumerian language and with glossaries of it. But it would, nevertheless, be misleading to apply the label 'Sumeric' to the civilization current in Assyria and Babylonia in the seventh century BC, considering that, by that date, the Sumerian language had been a 'dead' language for more than a thousand years. Since the age of Hammurabi the Semitic Akkadian language had replaced the Sumerian language as the living vehicle of the Sumeric Civilization. Therefore, Sumero-Akkadian is a more illuminating label than 'Sumeric' for the whole span of a civilization that did not lose its identity till the first century of the Christian Era.

20 This covers not only the 'Minoan' society, but also the contemporary 'Helladic' variant of the Aegean Civilization in continental European Greece, as well as the 'Mycenaean' last phase of both 'Minoan' and 'Helladic'.

21 The African Civilizations are not the only ones that have been drawn into such an intimate relationship with the Western Civilization since the closing decades of the seventeenth century. It may be thought more accurate to describe them all as 'satellites' rather than 'affiliates' of the West. Today it might be hard to find any living non-Western society, either of the civilizational or of the pre-civilizational kind, that has not been drawn into the orbit of the Western Civilization to some degree, either voluntarily or involuntarily. This relation between them and the West may, however, turn out to have been only a phase, judging by what happened after the Syriac Civilization had been drawn into the field of the Hellenic. In the light of this historical precedent it seems possible that the civilizations of the West and its satellites may blend into a new ecumenical civilization drawing contributions from all of them.

22 i.e. a Pre-Columbian civilization in what is now the south-west of the United States.

23 In what are now Ecuador and Columbia.

24 In what are now northern Chile and north-western Argentina.

25 Elam is the basin of the Karkheh and Karun rivers in present-day Iran, adjoining the lower basin of the Tigris and Euphrates rivers in present-day 'Iraq. Is the Elamite culture to be classified, not simply as a local cultural province of the Sumero-Akkadian Civilization, but as a distinct civilization affiliated to the Sumero-Akkadian? The grounds for classifying it as a separate civilization are its language, which is not related either to Sumerian or to Akkadian Semitic, and its native script. But the invention of this script may have been inspired by an

acquaintance with the Sumerian script, and during some important periods of Elamite history a version of the Sumero-Akkadian script was used for conveying the Elamite language.

26 The civilization labelled 'Hittite' in this book would have been described more adequately by a geographical name like the Aegean, Andean, and Middle American Civilizations. This Civilization's domain was Asia Minor (in present-day Turkey), but to call it 'Asian' or 'Asiatic' would have been confusing, since the word 'Asia' has come to stand for a whole continent, and no longer just for Asia Minor. The Hittites, including the Indo-European-speaking Hittites' local predecessors, occupied only one of this Anatolian civilization's provinces, and the civilization had reached, and perhaps passed, its zenith before the Indo-European Hittites and Luvians (the Hittites' western neighbours) had arrived in Asia Minor.

27 Urartu (the name of this country survives in the name of Mount Ararat) coincides in area approximately with the eastern end of present-day Turkey together with the present-day Soviet Republic of Erivan. The heart of the Kingdom of Urartu (ninth to seventh centuries BC) was the basin of Lake Van, but Urartu also included the upper basins of the river Aras and the river Euphrates, i.e. both arms of the Upper Euphrates.

28 The area of the Meroitic Civilization extended from the First Cataract of the Nile upstream to at least as far as the Sixth Cataract, and perhaps included the Jezirah ('Island') between the White and Blue Niles as well as the country between the Blue Nile and the Atbara. This area coincides approximately with the present-day Egyptian piece of Nubia, together with the northern part of the present-day Sudan. The area as a whole was called Ethiopia by the Greeks and Romans. The present-day Ethiopia (alias Abyssinia) lay outside it. The Pharaonic Egyptian Empire had extended as far up the Nile as the Fourth Cataract in the period of the Eighteenth Dynasty. The Kingdom of Ethiopia was never united with Egypt politically after 654 BC. The Meroitic Civilization gradually developed distinctive features of its own, and it also expanded its domain southwards.

29 This would be a civilization common to the Etruscan immigrants into Italy in the last millennium BC and the peoples previously established in Italy. The common elements in their civilization (e.g. literacy in the Cumaean alphabet) were of Hellenic origin. The indebtedness of the civilization of Italy in the Hellenic Age to the Hellenic Civilization was so great that it seems more instructive to regard Italy as having been, in this age, a province of the Hellenic World rather than a satellite of it.

30 Including the Mongol and Calmuck converts to the Tibetan form of Mahayana Buddhism.

31 See Part II, ch. 17, below.

PART II

THE GENESES OF
CIVILIZATIONS

10 The nature of the geneses of civilizations

1 In this study, the Greek word *mimesis*, from *mimeisthai*, is used in order to avoid the connotations of 'unintelligent imitation' which attach to the derivative English word 'mimicry'. Mimesis, as used here, denotes social imitation 'without prejudice'.

2 The historical importance of mimesis was discerned by David Hume, as witness the following passage in his essay *Of National Characters*: 'The human mind is of a very imitative nature; nor is it possible for any set of men to converse often together, without acquiring a similitude of manners, and communicating to each other their vices as well as virtues. The propensity to company and society is strong in all rational creatures; and the same disposition which gives us this propensity, makes us enter deeply into each other's sentiments, and causes like passions and inclinations to run, as it were, by contagion through the whole club or knot of companions.'

3 Walter Bagehot, *Physics and Politics*, 10th edition, London, Kegan Paul, 1894, pp. 27 and 35.

4 On this point see Bagehot (n. 3), p. 42.

5 Tacitus, *Agricola*, 45.

6 Ps. cvii. 10.

7 J. C. Smuts, *The League of Nations: A Practical Suggestion*, London, Hodder and Stoughton, 1918, p. 71.

8 Herbert Spencer, *First Principles*, 4th edition.

9 G. W. F. Hegel, *Phänomenologie des Geistes*.

10 *Œuvres de Saint-Simon et d'Enfantin*, Paris, Leroux, 1877, XLI, 86–7, 170–2, 177, 179, 205.

11 William Blake, 'The Marriage of Heaven and Hell'.

12 They are always mentioned in this order – Yin, the static condition, first, and Yang, the dynamic activity, second – and never the other way round.

13 Johann Wolfgang von Goethe, *Faust*, ll. 12104–11: 'All that is transitory is only an image; the imperfect here becomes achievement; the ineffable is performed; the eternal spirit of womanhood draws us onward.'

14 Goethe, *Faust*, ll. 501–9: 'In floods of life, in the storm of action, I surge up and down, I weave to and fro! Birth and grave an eternal sea, a shuttling weaving, a glowing life – thus I work at the roaring loom of time, and make a living vesture for the Godhead.'

11 The cause of genesis: race?

1 See Part IX, ch. 49, pp. 434–6, below.

2 This is not to say that the condition of non-white populations under white rule in Spanish and Portuguese Africa and in Latin America is happier than the condition of non-white populations that were formerly under British or American rule. On the contrary, the condition of the non-white populations in the Hispanic countries and their present or former colonies, in the Old World and the New, is probably almost everywhere the less happy of the two. This, however, is because the Spanish- and Portuguese-speaking peoples of the Western World are at present on the whole in a less happy condition themselves than the English-speaking peoples. As far as the non-white populations in the Hispanic countries suffer, they suffer equally with their white fellow countrymen of the same social classes; that is to say, they suffer from the prevailing political disorders and economic injustices – but not from any racial discrimination.

12 Environment?

1 *Influences of Atmosphere, Water, and Situation*, ch. 13.

2 Herodotus II, 33.

3 1 Cor. xiii. 2.

4 O. H. K. Spate in *The Geographical Journal*, December 1952, p. 419.

5 *The Social Sciences in Historical Study*, New York, Social Science Research Council, 1954, p. 119.

13 Challenge-and-response

1 See Part I, ch. 1, p. 34, above.

2 In Easter week, 1931, when I wrote the first version of the present chapter, I fancied that the phrase 'challenge-and-response' was a new coinage of my own; but, about a dozen years after I had first put it on paper, I came upon it in the fourth stanza of Robert Browning's 'Master Hugues of Saxe-Gotha'.

> O you may challenge them, not a response.
> Get the church-saints on their rounds!

The collocation of the two words must have lain submerged on some subconscious level of my mind for a quarter of a century since the Christmas holidays of 1905–06, when I had first read the poem with my mother. When I fancied that I was inventing this phrase, I was really hauling it up from the hold of my memory.

3 A. C. B. Lovell, *The Individual and the Universe: B.B.C. Reith Lectures 1958*, London, Oxford University Press, 1959, pp. 23–4.

4 e.g. the catalogue in the *Odyssey* XI, 225–332, a passage which is probably a fair sample of the lost Hesiodic *Ehoiai*.

5 *Mephistopheles*: 'Von Zeit zu Zeit seh' ich den Alten gern' (*Faust*, l. 350).

6 *Faust*, ll. 249–50: 'God's works, sublime beyond all understanding, are glorious, as they were in the beginning.'

7 Job i. 1–5.

8 Matt. xiii. 24–30.

9 Pierre Teilhard de Chardin, *The Phenomenon of Man*, London, Collins, 1959, p. 164.

10 *Faust*, ll. 340–3: 'Man's activity can all too easily slumber, he is eager for unlimited repose; so I gladly give him a companion who stirs up and works up and perforce, in a devil's way, creates.' In the oddly different language of rationalism, precisely the same idea is expressed by Turgot in his 'Plan de Deux Discours sur l'Histoire Universelle': 'La Raison et la Justice, mieux écoutées, auraient tout fixé, comme cela est à peu près arrivé à la Chine. . . . Le genre humain serait resté à jamais dans la médiocrité. . . . Mais ce qui n'est jamais parfait ne doit jamais être entièrement fixé. Les passions tumultueuses dangereuses, sont devenues un principe d'action, et par consequent de progrès' (*Œuvres de Turgot*, nouvelle édition, 2 vols., Paris, Guillaumin, 1844, II, 632). Turgot has had a presentiment of the French Revolution nearly half a century before the date of its outbreak.

11 *Faust*, ll. 1338–44: 'I am the spirit who always rejects! I am in the right; for everything that comes up deserves to go under: so, if nothing came up, that would be better. It follows that everything that you call sin, destruction, or, in one word, evil, is my native element.'

12 *Faust*, ll. 11575–6: 'He alone earns freedom and life itself who has to win them daily.'

13 *Faust*, ll. 249–50, quoted above, p. 100, and n. 6 thereto.

14 2 Cor. iii. 18.

15 2 Cor. iii. 17.

16 *Faust*, ll. 1566–9: 'The god who dwells in my breast can arouse my innermost being to its depths; he reigns over all the forces within me; yet he is powerless to move anything outside.'

17 Matt. xiii. 27–30.

18 Euripides, *Hippolytus*, ll. 1327–30, Gilbert Murray's translation, London, Allen and Unwin, 1902.

19 Murray (see n. 18), ll. 1420–2.

20 V. Grönbech, *The Culture of the Teutons*, London, Oxford University Press, 1931, Part II, p. 302.

21 *Faust*, ll. 312–17.

22 *Faust*, ll. 1692–1706: Faust. If ever I lay me down contentedly on a sluggard's bed, let me be done for, straight away! If you can ever cajole and delude me into feeling satisfied with myself, if you can inveigle me with enjoyment, let that be my last day! It is a bet. Will you take it? *Mephistopheles*. Done! *Faust*. And stroke on stroke! If I say to the fleeting moment: 'Do tarry! You are so beautiful!', then

you may clap fetters on me, then I will gladly go under! Then the death knell may peal, then you are free from your service, the clock may stop, its hand may fall, time may, for me, be ended!

23 See ch. 10, p. 86, above.

24 The hint of a future reversal of fortune which is darkly conveyed in 'it shall bruise thy head and thou shalt bruise his heel' is hardly more comforting than Artemis' assurance to Hippolytus that he shall become the object of a cult and the hero of a song (*Hippolytus*, ll. 1423–30).

25 Luke xxii. 53.

26 John xix. 11.

27 R.H.J.Steuart, *The Inward Vision*, London, Longmans, 1930, pp. 62–3. An expression of the same truth, in remarkably similar language, from the standpoint of a contemporary psychologist, will be found in C.G. Jung, *Modern Man in Search of a Soul*, London, Kegan Paul, 1933, pp. 274–5.

28 *Faust*, l. 336: 'I grant you, here too, only a *show* of freedom.'

29 *Faust*, l. 343, quoted above, p. 100, and n. 10 thereto.

30 *Faust*, ll. 1335–6: 'A portion of that force which always wills evil and always works good.'

31 *Faust*, ll. 337–9: 'I have never hated such as you are. Of all the spirits that reject, the knave is the least irksome to Me.'

32 *Faust*, ll. 11167–843.

33 *Faust*, ll. 11581–2 and 11585–6: 'I *should like* to say to the fleeting moment: "Do tarry! You are so beautiful!" In anticipation of such sublime bliss, I enjoy the supreme moment *now*.'

34 Grönbech (see n. 20), Part II, pp. 331 and 332.

35 This is the motif of the Syriac myth (preserved in Gen. xxxii. 24–32) of the mysterious being – man or angel or demon or God Himself – who assails Jacob before dawn and, in doing so, goes out of his way to bring about his own discomfiture. The assailant, in virtue of his nature, must be gone before dawn; and when he fails to overcome Jacob's resistance and break free – even after using his supernatural power in the hope of putting Jacob out of action – he is driven to confess that Jacob has prevailed and to comply with Jacob's terms: 'I will not let thee go except thou bless me.'

36 It would seem to follow that, if the Devil had known his business, he would have played just the opposite game. Instead of naïvely vaunting his own ability to ruin one of God's creatures – a Faust or a Job – he would have hypocritically chimed in with the Archangels in hymning the omnipotence of God and the perfection of His works. His song would have been not a candid satire on God's chief creation, Man,

Der kleine Gott der Welt bleibt stets von gleichem Schlag,
Und ist so wunderlich als wie am ersten Tag

(This world's godling stays always true to form; he is as amazing as he was on the first day), but a disingenuous

God's in His Heaven,
All's right with the World.

37 Ps. cii. 25–7.

38 *Faust*, ll. 510–17; compare lines 1744–7: *Faust*. Thou who dost encircle the wide world, thou active spirit, how near I feel myself to thee. *Spirit*. You are like the spirit whom you understand; you are not like me (*vanishes*). *Faust* (*collapsing*). Not like thee! Like whom, then? I have been made in God's image, and I am not even like thee!

39 Isa. liii. 3.

40 Plato, *Respublica*, II, 361E–362A.

41 *Faust*, ll. 354–417.

42 *Faust*, ll. 418–517.

43 Job iii.

44 *Faust*, l. 4596.

45 *Faust*, ll. 2607–8.

46 *Faust*, ll. 3376–413:

My peace is past,
My heart is sore;
I shall find my peace never,
Nevermore.

47 Dream of a woman undergoing an operation under insufficient ether, cited by William James in *The Varieties of Religious Experience*, 33rd impression, London, Longmans, 1922, pp. 392–3.

48 Matt. iii. 13–14 and iv. 11; Mark i. 9–13; Luke iii. 2–22 and iv. 1–13.

49 The non-violence of Jesus and his followers, and its contrast with the militancy of the abortive messianic movements of a Theudas or a Judas of Galilee, did not escape the observation of Gamaliel (Acts v. 34–40).

50 Job iii.

51 *Faust*, ll. 418–521.

52 *Faust*, ll. 602–807.

53 *Faust*, ll. 1224–37.

54 *Faust*, ll. 1583–1606.

55 *Faust*, ll. 1607–26: 'Woe! Woe! Thou hast destroyed it – destroyed this beautiful world – destroyed it with mighty fist; it crashes, it falls to pieces! A demigod has shattered it! We bear its ruins away into the void, and we lament over the beauty that has been lost. Mighty one among the sons of Earth, build the world again, grander than before; build it up within thine own breast! Start a new course of life with radiant sentience, and let new songs ring out in answer.'

56 *Faust*, ll. 1627–8.

57 Grönbech (see n. 20), Part II, p. 302. There is a curious congruity between the language of the anonymous author of the *Voluspà* and Virgil's language in the *Georgics* I, 505–11:

A world where right spells wrong, and wrong spells right!
So many wars! So many shapes of crime!
The plough despised! The ploughmen reft away!
The widowed fields unkempt! The sickle's curve

Melted to mould a sword-blade's stiff straight edge . . .
Neighbours break bonds of friendship, take up arms;
The wicked war-god rages everywhere.

58 *Ho epi Kronou bios.* (See, for example, Plato, *Leges*, 713C–D, where the myth is adapted to illustrate the philosopher's social theory.)

59 The story of Cain and his descendants, which is given as an epilogue (Gen. iv. 16–24) to the story of Cain and Abel (Gen. iv. 1–15), represents Cain as the father of civilization in general and all its works. In this epilogue, Cain himself builds a city and his descendant, Lamech, has two sons, Jubal and Tubal-Cain, who are respectively 'the father of all such as handle the harp and organ' and 'an instructor of every artificer in brass and iron'. Here we have the picture of a civilization with an agricultural basis evolving an urban life and industry. At the same time, Jubal and Tubal-Cain are given a brother, Jabal, who is 'the father of such as dwell in tents and such as have cattle', so that Cain's descendant, Lamech, is made progenitor of the Nomadic stock-breeding civilization and the sedentary agricultural and industrial civilizations alike.

60 Hesiod, *Works and Days*, 289.

61 Virgil, *Georgics* I, 121–4.

62 Origen, *Contra Celsum*, iv. 76, xix, cited by A.D.Nock in his edition of Sallustius, *Concerning the Gods and the Universe*, Cambridge, University Press, 1926, p. xlv.

63 Matt. xxv. 24.

64 Hesiod, *Works and Days*, 174–5.

65 Matt. xvi. 13–23; Mark viii. 27–33; Luke ix. 18–22.

66 Matt. xvii. 10–12; Mark xi. 11–14.

67 Matt. xxvi. 36–46; Mark xiv. 32–42; Luke xxii. 39–46. Compare John xii. 23–8.

68 Matt. xxvi. 42.

69 Matt. xxvii. 46; Mark xv. 34.

70 Luke xxviii. 46.

71 John xix. 30.

72 Rom. vii. 24–5. The whole of chapters vii and viii is a lyrical meditation upon this theme.

73 Job xl. 3–5 and xlii. 2–6.

74 *Faust*, ll. 4405–612.

75 *Faust*, ll. 11384–510.

76 *Faust*, ll. 4601–12: *Margaret*. What is this that is rising up from the ground? He! He! Send him off! What does he want in this holy place? He wants me! *Faust*. You must be saved alive! *Margaret*. God's judgment-seat! I have delivered myself into thy hands! *Mephistopheles* (*to Faust*). Quick! Quick! Or I will leave you in the lurch with her. *Margaret*. Our Father, I am thine! Save me! Ye angels! Ye heavenly hosts! Encamp around me, to preserve me! Henry, I shudder at you. *Mephistopheles*. She is condemned! *Voice* (*from above*). Redeemed! *Mephistopheles* (*to Faust*). Away to me (*vanishes with Faust*). *Voice* (*from within, dying away*). Henry! Henry!

This is, psychologically, the end of the play; for Mephistopheles' defeat is irrevocable; and although the light which has broken upon Gretchen's soul in this dawn does not enlighten Faust till many more years have passed over his head, yet his ultimate salvation is ensured by hers, and the labyrinthine second part of the play is therefore psychologically as well as artistically superfluous. By comparison with the last scene of Part I, the corresponding scene in Part II, in which Faust confronts and defies the four grey women – Want and Guilt and Care and Need – is an anti-climax. The last ten lines of Part I already convey the mystery – 'Das ewig Weibliche/Zieht uns hinan' – which is uttered, in the last two lines of Part II, by the Mystic Choir. The poet had no need to point his meaning by an epilogue which almost quadruples the length of his work.

77 Grönbech (see n. 20), Part II, pp. 302–3. Compare Virgil, *Eclogues*, IV.
78 Job xlii. 12–17, compared with i. 2–3.
79 Contrast the fable of Solomon's choice (1 Kgs. iii. 5–15), in which the hero merely forbears to ask for long life or riches for himself, or for the life of his enemies, in order to ask for an understanding heart to judge the people, yet is rewarded by being given, not only a wise and understanding heart, but riches and honour into the bargain.
80 *Faust*, ll. 243–70.
81 *Faust*, ll. 1583–1606.
82 *Faust*, ll. 11866–89.
83 *Faust*, ll. 12106–9, quoted in Part I, ch. 10, p. 89, above.
84 Pater Profundus, in *Faust*, ll. 11872–3: 'Thus it is the almighty love that fashions and cherishes all that is.'
85 Heb. xii. 6 and Aeschylus, *Agamemnon*, 186–7.
86 Matt. vii. 14.
87 In the Hellenic story of Prometheus, the two services are incompatible, and the hero suffers because he has served Man in God's despite. For an interpretation of Aeschylus's version of the Promethean myth, see Part III, ch. 19, below.
88 Job xlii. 7–10.
89 *Faust*, ll. 12069–111.
90 Matt. xvi. 24–8; Mark viii. 34–8; Luke ix. 23–7.
91 John xii. 32.
92 Robert Turgot, 'Plan de Deux Discours sur l'Histoire Universelle', in *Œuvres de Turgot*, nouvelle édition, 2 vols., Paris, Guillaumin, 1844, II, 647. Compare E. Meyer, *Geschichte des Altertums*, 4th edition, Stuttgart and Berlin, Cotta, 1921, I (i), 83 and 174.
93 1 Cor. xv. 57.

14 The arduousness of excellence

1 P.E.Newberry, 'Egypt as a Field for Anthropological Research', in *Report of the ninety-first meeting of the British Association*, London, Murray, 1924, p. 176.

2 Newberry (see n. 1), p. 176.
3 A distinguished geographer, O.H.K. Spate, has in fact made this pertinent objection.
4 S.A.Pakeman, *Ceylon*, London, Benn, 1964, pp. 33–5, quoted by permission of the publisher.

15 The stimulus of hard countries

1 Herodotus VII, 102.
2 Plato, *Critias*, 111 A–C.
3 Herodotus IV, 144.
4 See Polybius IV, 45.
5 Num. xxxii.
6 i.e. 'the land of the Philistines'. *Palaistine* is the Greek and *Filastin* the Arabic form of the modern 'Palestine'.

16 The stimulus of penalizations

1 The phrase was coined by J.O'Sullivan in *U.S. Magazine and Democratic Review*, 1845, p. 5.
2 2 Kgs. xviii. 21.
3 *Ra'iyeh* means literally 'the flock' of which the Ottoman padishah was the shepherd. The term was not applied exclusively to his non-Muslim subjects. The Muslim peasantry of Anatolia were called *ra'iyeh* as well as the Christian merchants and ecclesiastics of Constantinople.
4 See Part I, ch. 8, above.
5 This abortive Far Eastern Christian Civilization is discussed further in ch. 17, below.

17 Abortive civilizations

1 See Part IX, ch. 47, below.
2 See Part IX, ch. 47, pp. 418 ff., below.

PART III

THE GROWTHS OF CIVILIZATIONS

18 Examples of the arrest of growth

1 See Part I, ch. 10, p. 86, above.
2 See Part V, ch. 27, pp. 222–3, below.
3 For the origins of Nomadism, see E.D.Phillips, *The Royal Hordes*, London, Thames and Hudson, 1965.
4 For this view see R.Pumpelly, *Explorations in Turkestan: Expedition of 1904: Prehistoric Civilizations of Anau*, 2 vols., Washington D.C., Carnegie Institution, 1908.

5 See P.J.Ucko and G.W.Dimbleby (editors), *The Domestication of Plants and Animals*, London, Duckworth, 1967, especially pp. 73–100.

19 The criterion of growth

1 For an analysis of this myth, see Part II, ch. 13, above.
2 Gilbert Murray, *Prometheus Bound translated into English Rhyming Verse*, London, Allen and Unwin, 1931, pp. 8–9.
3 Murray (see n. 2), ll. 230–8.
4 Murray (see n. 2), ll. 443–4.
5 Murray (see n. 2), ll. 241–3.
6 Henri Bergson, *Les Deux Sources de la Morale et de la Réligion*, Paris, Alcan, 1932, p. 55.
7 See Part II, ch. 17, and Part III, ch. 18, above.
8 Goethe, *Faust*, ll. 3249–50:

From appetite I flounder to enjoyment
And, in enjoyment, crave for appetite.

9 *Mater Gloriosa* (Mary) to *Una Poenitentium* (Gretchen), speaking of *Doctor Marianus* (Faust), in *Faust*, ll. 12094–5:

Come, raise thyself to higher spheres!
Lead! He will follow heeding thee.

10 Bergson (see n. 6), pp. 188–9.
11 See Part II, ch. 18, above.
12 See p. 140, below.
13 See Part I, ch. 3, p. 43, above.
14 Bergson (see n. 6), pp. 333 and 73.
15 Bergson (see n. 6), p. 251.

PART IV

THE BREAKDOWNS OF CIVILIZATIONS

20 Is determinism convincing?

1 Lucretius, *De Rerum Natura* II, 1148–52 and 1157–74.
2 Cyprianus, *Ad Demetrianum*, 3. Compare Saint Augustine, *Sermo* lxxxi, 8 (apropos Ps. ciii. 5).
3 i.e. the so-called 'heat death of the Universe'; see Sir James Jeans, *Eos, or the wider Aspects of Cosmogony*, London, Kegan Paul, 1928, pp. 52 ff.
4 Compare Pierre Teilhard de Chardin, *The Phenomenon of Man*, London, Collins, 1959, pp. 285–90 and 308–10.
5 P. Moore, *Suns, Myths and Men*, revised edition, London, Muller, 1968, p. 224.
6 O.Spengler, *Der Untergang des Abendlandes*, Vienna and Leipzig, Wilhelm Braunmüller, 1918, I, 152–3.
7 Part I, ch. 3, p. 43, above.
8 Spengler (see n. 6), I, 160–1.
9 'The species boundary between *H.*

erectus and *H. sapiens* is generally and arbitrarily drawn at between 500,000 and 300,000 years ago' (David Pilbeam, *The Evolution of Man*, London, Thames and Hudson, 1970, p. 15). Both species are members of the same genus, but for our present purpose we can take the date of the appearance of the species *H. sapiens* as marking the advent of 'a recognizably human form' of the genus *Homo*.

10 Plato, *Respublica*, 546A–B.
11 Book of Common Prayer, Ps. cvii. 10.
12 For a survey of theories of recurrence see M. Éliade, *Le Mythe de l'Éternel Retour*, Paris, Gallimard, 1949.
13 See G. Cairns, *Philosophies of History*, London, Peter Owen, 1963, pp. 26–31.
14 Éliade (see n. 12), pp. 131–2.
15 Plato, *Leges*, 677A; compare *Critias*, 109D.
16 Plato, *Timaeus*, 21E–23C.
17 Plato, *Politicus*, 269C–273E.
18 Virgil, *Eclogues* IV, 4–7 and 34–6.
19 Marcus Aurelius, *Meditationes* IX, 28; compare V, 13, and VII, 1.
20 R. Thapar, *A History of India*, Harmondsworth, Penguin, 1966, p. 161.
21 Matt. vi. 7.
22 F. Nietzsche, *Also sprach Zarathustra*, III 13 2; English translation by R. J. Hollingdale, *Thus Spoke Zarathustra*, Harmondsworth, Penguin, 1961.
23 Aristotle, *Meteorologica* I, 3.
24 Aristotle, *Problemata*, xvii. 3.
25 Virgil, *Georgics* I, 501–2, 505–8, 510–14.
26 Alphonse Karr, *Les Guêpes*, January 1849.
27 See Part II, ch. 13, above.
28 See Part III, ch. 19, p. 136, above.
29 M. Griaule and G. Dieterlen, 'The Dogon' in C. Daryll Forde (editor), *African Worlds*, London, Oxford University Press, 1954, p. 84.
30 Horace, *Carmina* I, 35, 17.
31 Judg. v. 20.

21 The mechanicalness of mimesis

1 See Part III, ch. 19, p. 140, above.
2 George Meredith, *Modern Love*, stanza 43.
3 C. F. Volney, 'Les Ruines' in *Œuvres Complètes*, Paris, Didot, 1860, pp. 12–13.
4 Menander, fragment 540.
5 Ambrose, *Hexameron* I, vii, 31, quoted in P. Brown, *Augustine of Hippo*, London, Faber and Faber, 1967, p. 85.
6 Basil Davidson, *The Africans*, London, Longmans, 1969, p. 147; and see also chs. 12–15.
7 For an examination of this doctrine see Part IV, ch. 20, pp. 154–5, above. For Volney's analysis, see his 'Leçons d'Histoire' in *Œuvres Complètes* (n. 3).
8 The two analyses are analogous inasmuch as they both fly in the face of the prevailing philosophy of the day. Volney's intuition, as we have observed, gives the lie to the fundamental doctrine of eighteenth-century Western philosophy,

while the passage here quoted from Cyprian contradicts another passage from Cyprian's own pen which occurs in the same tract *Ad Demetrianum*. In this other passage (which has been quoted above in ch. 20, p. 154) Cyprian advocates the view that the Hellenic Society of the age is suffering from an automatic process of senile decay. A judicious admirer of Cyprian will not attempt to explain this manifest contradiction away. He will be content to observe that in chapter 3 of the tract the author is simply reproducing one of the commonplaces of Hellenic philosophy, while in chapter 10 he is expounding a Christian doctrine which has become a living part of Cyprian's own thought.

9 Cyprianus, *Ad Demetrianum*, 10.
10 See Part III, ch. 19, above.
11 Matt. vii. 14.
12 Heb. xii. 1.
13 Matthew Arnold, *Culture and Anarchy*, London, Murray, 1869, pp. 13–14.
14 Henri Bergson, *Les Deux Sources de la Morale et de la Réligion*, Paris, Alcan, 1932, p. 251 (quoted in Part III, ch. 19, p. 140, above).
15 Plato's letters, no. 7, 341D.
16 See Part I, ch. 10, p. 85 and n. 1 thereto, above.
17 See Bergson (n. 14), pp. 98–9: 'How is one to get purchase upon the will [of another person]? There are two ways open to the educator. The one way is by drill (*dressage*) . . . the other is by mysticism. . . . The first method inculcates a morality consisting of impersonal habits; the second induces the imitation of another personality, and even a spiritual union, a more or less complete identification with it.' The second method is of course that counselled by Plato.
18 Matt. vii. 13.
19 William Wordsworth, *The Excursion* IX, 188–90.
20 Bergson gives two pertinent examples of the practice of mechanization: the actor who in a public performance re-experiences only formally the emotions which he had made himself experience genuinely when he was learning his part; and the stereotyped 'laws' of magic in a primitive society, which no longer reproduce the natural *élan* which generated the magic; see Bergson (n. 14), pp. 177–8.
21 See Part I, ch. 10, p. 85, above.
22 See Part I, ch. 10, p. 89, above.
23 See Part III, ch. 19, pp. 135–6, above.
24 Matt. xv. 14.
25 See Part III, ch. 18, above.
26 See Part I, ch. 7, p. 56, above.
27 John xxi. 18.

22 The reversal of roles

1 See Aristotle, *Poetica* VI, 18, *et alibi*.
2 Luke iii. 12–13 and vii. 29–30; Matt. xxi. 31–2.
3 Isa. ix. 1; Matt. iv. 15.
4 See Matt. xxi. 31.
5 See Luke iv. 16–32.

6 Luke xviii. 9–14.
7 Luke x. 25–37.
8 Matt. xxi. 42 (quoting Ps. cxviii. 22). Compare Mark xii. 10; Luke xx. 17; Acts lv. 11; Eph. ii. 20; 1 Peter ii. 7.
9 Mark ix. 35 = Matt. xxiii. 11. Compare Mark x. 43–4 = Matt. xx. 26–7.
10 Luke ix. 48.
11 Matt. xviii. 3–5 = Mark ix. 37 = Luke xviii. 16.
12 Matt. xxi. 16, quoting Ps. viii. 2.
13 1 Cor. i. 27–9. The theme is enlarged upon in 1 Cor. ii; and in 1 Cor. iii. 18–21 the *peripeteia* between 'wisdom' and 'foolishness', which is the first of the four antitheses in i. 27–8, is taken up again and carried further. Compare Col. ii. 8.
14 Herodotus VII, 10.
15 Compare the latter-day British boast of possessing an empire 'on which the sun never sets'.
16 Herodotus I, *passim*; III, *passim*.
17 Horace, *Carmina* I, 3, 37–40.
18 Lucretius, *De Rerum Natura* V, 1222–5.
19 The *Tao-te Ching*, ch. 9; translated by Arthur Waley, *The Way and its Power*, London, Allen and Unwin, 1934.
20 Isa. ii. 12–17. Compare Obad. 3–4 (echoing Jer. xlix. 16).
21 Ecc. ix. 11–12.
22 The *Magnificat*, in Luke i. 51–2.
23 Gilbert Murray, *Prometheus Bound translated into English Rhyming Verse*, London, Allen and Unwin, 1931.
24 Eph. iv. 18.
25 See Part III, ch. 18, above.
26 For the role of the Serpent see Part II, ch. 13, above.
27 1 Cor. x. 12.
28 Prov. xvi. 18.
29 Plato, *Leges*, 691C.
30 See the list in Part I, ch. 9, p. 72, above.
31 John iii. 4.
32 Matt. xviii. 3.

23 Athens and Venice: the idolization of an ephemeral institution

1 See Part I, ch. 1, pp. 34–7, above, for the nature of idolatry as exemplified in the modern Western political aberration of nationalism.
2 Goethe, *Faust*, l. 249, quoted in Part II, ch. 13, p. 100, above.
3 Mark xiii. 14 = Matt. xxiv. 15. Compare Luke xxi. 20. These passages in the New Testament are reminiscences of Dan. ix. 27 and xii. 11.
4 In Part III, ch. 19, pp. 138–9, above.
5 The phrase, as we have it, occurs in the rendering of Pericles's funeral oration by Thucydides in II, 41.
6 Job xlii. 6.
7 See Plato, *Leges* IV, 704D–705B. This passage reads like a deliberate rejoinder to part of Pericles's funeral oration, recorded by Thucydides in II, 38 (2); similarly *Leges* IV, 707 A–C is Plato's reply to Thucydides II, 39 (3) and 40 (2).

8 Plutarch, *Life of Sulla*, XIV, 5.
9 For the differences in ethos, and consequent divergence in action, between the Achaeans and Arcadians on one side, and the rest of the Ten Thousand on the other, see Xenophon, *Cyri Anabasis, passim*, especially VI, 1–3.
10 Polybius XVIII, 14.
11 See the account in Acts xvii. 16–34.
12 The superiority of Italian over Transalpine culture, which was so striking towards the end of the fifteenth century, is sometimes placed to the credit of the foregoing renaissance in Italy of Latin and Greek letters (the authentic renaissance of a defunct Hellenic culture in Italy must be distinguished from the Transalpine mimesis of this wholly Italian achievement). But the Italian renaissance was not the cause, but rather partly the instrument or medium, and partly an incidental consequence, of the special local advance in civilization which Italy made in the fourteenth and fifteenth centuries. The true cause of the advance was not an Italian mimesis of Hellenic culture, but a series of creative Italian responses to contemporary challenges. For the phenomenon of renaissances in general, and the Italian example in particular, see Part X, below.

24 The East Roman Empire: the idolization of an ephemeral institution

1 i.e. the Nestorian and Monophysite reaction in Mesopotamia, Syria, and Egypt against the official Catholic Christianity of the Empire.
2 See ch. 26, p. 199, below.
3 The assertion is attributed to Leo in these terms by Pope Gregory II in a letter (Ep. xiii) replying to a no longer extant letter of Leo's. See A. A. Vasiliev, *Histoire de l'Empire Byzantin*, 2 vols., Paris, Picard, 1932, I, 341.
4 The Western universities largely owed their stimulus and their liberty to the fact that they were under the aegis and auspices of the Papacy, instead of being under the thumb of the local temporal lord or the local bishop. For the attitude of the Papacy to the emergent Italian city-states in the twelfth century, see ch. 26, p. 201, below.
5 The essence of the 'Adoptionist' as opposed to the 'Conceptionist' faith is a belief that Jesus was not born divine, but that in virtue of his human spiritual achievements and merits he was designated by God as the son of God when, at the moment of his baptism, he was taken possession of by the Holy Spirit as a human vehicle for its divine activity. In the Paulician sect's Armenian homeland the Paulicians' original 'Adoptionist' doctrine survived till the nineteenth century. On the other hand, on East Roman soil Paulicianism appears to have been transformed, in the early ninth century, from

an 'Adoptionist' form of Christianity into a 'dualistic' religion in which the power of evil was credited with at least a partial independence of the power of good. See N. Garsoïan, *The Paulician Heresy*, Paris and The Hague, Mouton, 1947.
6 See ch. 26, p. 206, below.
7 On p. 180, above.
8 See Part III, ch. 19, p. 137, above.
9 Russia, which had been converted to Orthodox Christianity in 985, had tacitly acquiesced in its implicit subjection to the imperial government's nominal sovereignty.
10 Matt. xii. 25 = Mark iii. 24 = Luke xi. 17.

25 David and Goliath: the idolization of an ephemeral technique

1 See the story as it is told in 1 Sam. xvii.
2 Polybius XXIX, 17.
3 See the description of the battle in Ammianus Marcellinus, *Res Gestae* XXXI, 11–13.
4 See the eyewitness account by Falak-ad-Din Muhammad b. Aydimir, quoted by Ibn-al-Tiqtaqa in *Kitab-al-Fakhri*; English translation by E. G. Browne, *A Literary History of Persia*, London, Fisher, Unwin, 1906, II, 462.
5 See the contemporary account in Jean, Sire de Joinville, *La Vie du Saint Roi Louis mise en nouveau langage par Henri Lognon*, Paris, A l'enseigne de la Cité des Livres, pp. 87–8. English translation by M. R. B. Shaw, Harmondsworth, Penguin, 1963.
6 'Personne n'a su ni rien oublier, ni rien apprendre.' Chevalier de Panat in a letter dated London, January 1796, in *Mémoires et Correspondance de Mallet du Pan*, 2 vols., Paris, Amyot et Cherbuliez, II, ch. 9, p. 197.
7 See the eyewitness account in Shaykh 'Abd-ar-Rahman al-Jabarti, *Aja'ib-al-Athar fi't-Tarajim wa'l-Akhbar*, 4 vols., Cairo, A.H., 1322, III, *ad init.*; French translation in *Merveilles Biographiques et Historiques*, 9 vols., Cairo, Imprimerie Nationale, 1888–96; Paris, Leroux, 1888–96, VI *ad init.*

26 The Roman See: the intoxication of victory

1 See ch. 24, above.
2 On this point see ch. 24, pp. 189–90, above.
3 The subjugation of Ireland by the English Crown was sanctioned in advance by an incumbent of the Papal office who was perhaps unable to forget that, before he became Pope Hadrian IV, he had been the Englishman Nicholas Breakspear; but this case seems to have been exceptional. Indeed, it is the only notable

instance in which the medieval Papacy lent its authority to promote the conquest of a small and weak community within the bosom of Western Christendom by a large and strong one. The part played by the Papacy in helping Hungary and Poland to escape the heavy yoke of the Holy Roman Empire, and the city-states of Lombardy to throw it off, is more characteristic of the Papal policy towards the political system of medieval Western Christendom.
4 See ch. 24, pp. 183–5, above.
5 2 Sam. xii. 14.
6 Edward Gibbon, *The History of the Decline and Fall of the Roman Empire*, ch. lx.
7 Gibbon (see n. 6), ch. lx.
8 Dan. v. 25–28.
9 Ps. vii. 15.

PART V
THE DISINTEGRATIONS OF CIVILIZATIONS

27 The nature and symptoms of social disintegration

1 See Part I, ch. 7, p. 59, above.
2 See Part III, ch. 18, above.
3 See Part III, ch. 19, p. 136, above.
4 See Part III, ch. 19, pp. 136–7, above.
5 Herodotus I, 32.
6 See Part IV, ch. 21, p. 166, above.
7 In Part I, ch. 7, above.
8 An example of this unity in diversity is the social relation between knights and villeins which was the ideal – though not always the practice – of the medieval Western feudal system.
9 See Part I, ch. 7, p. 56, above.
10 See Part IV, ch. 21, p. 166, above.
11 See Part III, ch. 19, pp. 137–8, above.
12 See Part I, ch. 7, pp. 56–7, above.
13 See A. Bazard, 'Exposition de la Doctrine Saint-Simonienne' in *Œuvres de Saint-Simon et d'Enfantin*, Paris, Leroux, 1877, XLI, 171–4.
14 A. MacIntyre, *Marxism and Christianity*, London, Duckworth, 1969, p. 2.
15 MacIntyre (see n. 14), p. 112.
16 See Part I, ch. 7, pp. 56–7, above.
17 The literal meaning of 'palingenesia' is 'a recurrence of birth', which has an ambiguous connotation: while it may mean a repetitive rebirth of something that has been born before, it is used here in its other meaning of an unprecedented new birth of something that is now being born for the first time.

28 Internal proletariats

1 Thucydides III, 82.
2 Compare Matt. x. 21, and 34–7 = Luke xii. 51–3, xiv. 25–7, and xxi. 16–17 (quoting Mic. vii. 6); Matt. xii. 46–50 =

Mark iii. 31–5 = Luke viii. 19–21 –
A.J.T.
3 Thucydides III, 82–3.
4 In Part I, ch. 7, p. 56, above.
5 The phrase may be coined on the pertinent analogy of the 'poor whites' of the Southern States of the USA or of South Africa today.
6 'As the news [of the outbreak of the first Sicilian slave-war] spread, slave-revolts flared up everywhere. At Rome a hundred and fifty persons entered into a conspiracy, in Attica over a thousand, and others in Delos and elsewhere' (Diodorus of Agyrium, *A Library of Universal History* XXXIV–XXXV, 2, §19 (fragments)). Delos, which was the principal slave-market of the Hellenic World in the second century BC, was on the threshold of the Attalid kingdom in western Asia Minor, which was the theatre of Aristonicus's tragic adventure.
7 Diodorus of Agyrium (see n. 6), 2, §§39 and 13. Diodorus says of the slaves' treatment of Damophilus's daughter: 'This was a demonstration that the treatment meted out to the others was not the expression of any innate barbarity in the slaves, but was simply retribution for the wrongs which had previously been inflicted upon them.'
8 2 Macc. vi–viii., in contrast with the remainder of the book.
9 Luke xxii. 36.
10 Luke xxii. 38.
11 Luke xxii. 49–51.
12 Acts v. 35–9.
13 Matt. xvi. 21–6.
14 Matt. xxvi. 56.
15 Matt. xxiv. 15–28 = Mark xiii. 14–23 = Luke xxi. 20–4.
16 In Parts VI and VII, below.

29 External proletariats

1 This phenomenon will be examined in Part IX, below.
2 Rome is so described in a surviving fragment of a lost work by Plato's pupil Heracleides Ponticus; see Plutarch, *Camillus*, 22.
3 Saint Augustine, *De Civitate Dei* I, 7.
4 Saint Augustine (see n. 3) V, 23.

30 Schism in the soul

1 See Part III, ch. 19, and Part IV, ch. 21, above.
2 Marcus Aurelius, *Meditationes* IV, 1.
3 Marcus Aurelius (see n. 2) IV, 49.
4 Marcus Aurelius (see n. 2) IV, 48.
5 Epictetus, *Dissertationes* I, 16, §§15–16 and 19–21.
6 Epictetus (see n. 5) III, 5, §§7–11.
7 See Part IV, ch. 23, p. 171, above.
8 See ch. 31, p. 253, below.
9 See Part V, ch. 20, above.
10 See Henri Bergson, *L'Évolution Créatrice*, 24th edition, Paris, Alcan, 1921, pp. 239–58.

11 'The Admonitions of a Prophet' in A. Erman, *The Literature of the Ancient Egyptians*, English translation by Aylward M. Blackman, London, Methuen, 1927, p. 95.
12 Plato, *Politicus*, 272D6–273E4.
13 C. N. Cochrane, *Christianity and Classical Culture*, Oxford, University Press, 1940, pp. 478–9.
14 *The Encyclopaedia of Islam*, London, Luzac, 1927, II, s.v. Kadar.
15 See Part III, ch. 19, pp. 137–8, above.
16 See Part III, ch. 18, above.
17 Aeschylus, *Agamemnon*, 186–7; first quoted in Part II, ch. 13, p. 109, above.
18 See Part IV, ch. 21, pp. 160–1, above.

31 The challenge of disintegration

1 In Part III, ch. 19, pp. 137–8, above.
2 Epictetus, *Dissertationes* I, 4, §3, and IV, 4, §39.
3 *Upadana-sutta* II, 84, quoted in E. J. Thomas, *The History of Buddhist Thought*, London, Kegan Paul, 1933, p. 62.
4 *Udana*, ch. VIII, quoted in T. C. Humphreys, *Buddhism*, Harmondsworth, Penguin, 1952, p. 127.
5 *Sutta Nipata*, quoted in E. Conze, *Buddhist Scriptures*, Harmondsworth, Penguin, 1959, p. 79.
6 Seneca, *De Clementia* II, 6 and 5.
7 Robert Browning, 'One Word More', xiv.
8 Luke xvii. 20–1.
9 William Blake, 'Auguries of Innocence'.
10 Seng-ts'an, *Sin sin ming*, quoted in Conze (see n. 5), pp. 174–5.
11 Saraha, *Dohakosha*, quoted in Conze (see n. 5), p. 179.
12 In Part IV, ch. 23, p. 171, above.
13 John iii. 16–17.
14 John iii. 3–8.
15 1 John iv. 11–12.
16 Thomas à Kempis, *The Imitation of Christ* II, 12; English translation by Leo Sherley-Price, Harmondsworth, Penguin, 1952, pp. 87–8.
17 See Part V, ch. 27, p. 228, above.
18 John x. 10.

PART VI
UNIVERSAL STATES

32 Universal states:
ends or means?

1 See Part I, chs. 2 and 5, above.
2 See Part I, ch. 2, p. 42, above.
3 See Part V, ch. 27, p. 224, above.
4 In Part V, ch. 31, p. 250, above.
5 See below, pp. 271–2.
6 Tibullus, *Carmina* II, 5, 23–4.
7 Virgil, *Aeneid* I, 278–9.

8 Velleius Paterculus II, 103.
9 Livy IV, 4, §4.
10 Livy XXVIII, 28, §11.
11 Suetonius, *Nero*, 11, §2.
12 G. Henzen (editor), *Acta Fratrum Arvalium Quae Supersunt*, Berlin, Reimer, 1874, p. lxxxi.
13 Henzen (see n. 12), pp. cxv, cxix, cxxvi.
14 P. Aelius Aristeides, *In Romam* XXVI, §109.
15 C. Rutilius Namatianus, *De Reditu Suo* I, 115–16, 123–34, 137–46.
16 Saint Jerome, *Epistola* XXVII, 12, written in AD 412, in J.-P. Migne, *Patrologia Latina*, Paris, 1844–64, XXII, col. 1094.
17 Dispatch from the Court of Directors, quoted in T. G. P. Spear, *Twilight of the Mughuls*, Cambridge, University Press, 1951, p. 44.
18 See Part IV, ch. 24, p. 192, above.
19 For Mehmet II's acceptance of this doctrine, see H. Inalcik, 'The Policy of Mehmed II towards the Greek Population of Istanbul and the Byzantine Buildings of the City' in *Dumbarton Oaks Papers*, nos. 23 and 24, 1969–70, pp. 229–49, on p. 233.
20 In Part IV, ch. 24, above.
21 In Part II, ch. 16, pp. 119–20, above.
22 See Steven Runciman, *The Great Church in Captivity*, Cambridge, University Press, 1966, pp. 110 and 321.
23 See D. Obolensky, *The Byzantine Commonwealth and Eastern Europe 500–1493*, London, Weidenfeld and Nicolson, 1971, p. 363.
24 Runciman (see n. 22), p. 228.
25 The Georgian Church had been represented at Florence in 1439, and it may have compromised itself on this occasion. In any case, the Georgian principalities came under Ottoman and Safavi suzerainty in the sixteenth century, leaving Muscovy as the sole surviving independent Orthodox Christian state.
26 Runciman (see n. 22), pp. 329–30.
27 Runciman (see n. 22), p. 323; Obolensky (see n. 23), p. 363.
28 Philotheus of Pskov, as cited by N. Zernov, *The Russians and their Church*, London, Society for the Promotion of Christian Knowledge, 1945, p. 50. See also the citation in Obolensky (n. 23), p. 363.
29 Text as cited in Zernov (see n. 28), p. 71.
30 Obolensky (see n. 23), p. 366.
31 Obolensky (see n. 23), p. 366.
32 Obolensky (see n. 23), p. 365.
33 Inscription, probable date 9 BC; text as in W. Dittenberger, *Orientis Graeci Inscriptiones Selectae*, Leipzig, Hirzel, 1905, II, 48–60.
34 C. N. Cochrane, *Christianity and Classical Culture*, Oxford, University Press, 1940, p. 130.
35 Aelius Aristeides (see n. 14) XXVI, §§68–70.
36 See Part V, ch. 31, pp. 249–50, above.
37 E. Meyer, *Geschichte des Altertums*, Stuttgart, Cotta, 1901, III, 24–5.
38 Aelius Aristeides (see n. 14) XXVI, §§79–84.

39 Appian of Alexandria, *Studies in Roman History*, Preface.
40 Lucretius, *De Rerum Natura* V, 361–3.
41 Lucretius (see n. 40) II, 303–7.
42 Menander, fragment 540; quoted in Part IV, ch. 21, p. 160, above.
43 George Meredith, *Modern Love*, stanza 43; quoted in Part IV, ch. 21, p. 161, above.
44 Lucretius (see n. 40) III, 964–5 and 967–71.

33 The boons of conductivity and peace

1 O. Spengler, *Der Untergang des Abendlandes*, Vienna and Leipzig, Wilhelm Braunmüller, 1918, I, 51. The pith of the point that Spengler is making is concentrated in Francis Bacon's dictum that 'it was not the *Romans* that spread upon the *World*; But it was the *World* that spread upon the *Romans*' (in *The Essays, or Counsels Civil and Moral* XXIX, 'Of the True Greatness of Kingdoms and Estates').
2 P. Aelius Aristeides, *In Romam*, §62.
3 C. Plinius Secundus, *Historia Naturalis* XXVII, i, §63.
4 R. Storry, *A History of Modern Japan*, Harmondsworth, Penguin, 1960, pp. 66–7, 73–5.
5 Plato, *Leges*, 693A.
6 Aelius Aristeides (see n. 2), §102.
7 C. Rutilius Namatianus, *De Reditu Suo* I, §66.
8 Plinius Secundus (see n. 3) III, v, §39.
9 The phrase used by Herodotus (I, 66) to describe the progress of Sparta under the impetus that she received from the institution of the Lycurgean agoge.
10 Pope Leo the Great, *Sermo* LXXXII, ch. 2, in J.-P. Migne, *Patrologia Latina*, Paris, 1844–64, LIV, col. 423.
11 In Part V, ch. 27, p. 228, above.
12 In Part VIII, ch. 43, below.

34 Communications

1 E. Meyer, *Geschichte des Altertums*, Stuttgart, Cotta, 1901, III, 66–8.
2 E. A. Belyaev, *Arabs, Islam and the Arab Caliphate*, London, Pall Mall, 1969, pp. 224–5.
3 Garcilaso de la Vega, *Royal Commentaries of the Incas and General History of Peru*, translated by H. J. Livermore, Austin and London, University of Texas Press, 1966, Part I, pp. 48–52.
4 Garcilaso de la Vega (see n. 3), p. 328.
5 The nickname given to the ruling minority in the Inca Empire by their Spanish conquerors – A. J. T.
6 L. Baudin, *L'Empire Socialiste des Inca*, Paris, Institut d'Ethnologie, 1928, pp. 120–1.
7 Ch'ao-ting Chi, *Key Economic Areas in Chinese History as Revealed in the Development of Public Works for Water-Control*, London, Allen and Unwin, 1936, pp. 4–5.
8 Ch'ao-ting Chi (see n. 7), p. 113.
9 Ch'ao-ting Chi (see n. 7), pp. 113–14.
10 Epictetus, *Dissertationes* III, 13, §9.
11 P. Aelius Aristeides, *In Romam* §§100–101.
12 Irenaeus, *Contra Haereses* II, x, 2, in J.-P. Migne, *Patrologia Graeca*, Paris, 1857–66, VII, cols. 552–3.
13 Ammianus Marcellinus, *Res Gestae* XXI, xvi, §18.
14 M. J. de Goeje (editor), *Bibliotheca Geographorum Arabicorum*, Leiden, 1870 seqq.
15 C. P. Fitzgerald, *China, A Short Cultural History*, London, Cresset Press, 1935, p. 138.
16 J. Romein in M. F. A. Montagu (editor), *Toynbee and History*, Boston, Porter Sargent, 1956, p. 350, quoted in Part I, ch. 4, n. 3, p. 541, above.
17 On these points see further Part VII, chs. 40 and 41, below.

35 Languages and scripts

1 The non-Muslim autonomous communities were known by the name of *millet* – a word of Arabic origin with a meaning betwixt and between the connotations of the Western words 'nation' and 'church'. Though the dominant Muslim community was not called a *millet*, its constitution and status were in essence the same as those of the Jewish *millet* and of the several Christian *millets* of different denominations.
2 For example, in 180 BC the municipality of Cumae, whose citizens had possessed the passive rights of Roman citizenship (the Roman *civitas sine suffragio*) since 338 BC, was allowed, in response to a petition from the municipal authorities themselves, to substitute Latin for the community's native Oscan as its official language. (See Livy XL, 43.)

36 Capital cities

1 See ch. 34, p. 291, above.
2 Garcilaso de la Vega, *Royal Commentaries of the Incas and General History of Peru*, translated by H. J. Livermore, Austin and London, University of Texas Press, 1966, Part I, pp. 421–2.
3 See Cicero, *Ad Atticum* II, i, §8.

37 Civil services

1 See ch. 34, p. 288, above.
2 See ch. 33, p. 278, above.
3 C. P. Fitzgerald, *China, A Short Cultural History*, London, Cresset Press, 1935, pp. 153–5.

4 See D. Coombes, *Towards a European Civil Service*, London, Chatham House and Political and Economic Planning, 1968, p. 39.
5 See ch. 35, p. 297, above.

38 Have universal states a future?

1 See ch. 32, pp. 271–3, above.
2 See ch. 36, above.
3 In ch. 34, pp. 294–5, above.

PART VII

UNIVERSAL CHURCHES

39 Cancers or chrysalises?

1 In Part V, ch. 27, p. 228, and Part VI, *passim*, above.
2 C. Rutilius Namatianus, *De Reditu Suo* I, 439–42, 445–6.
3 Rutilius Namatianus (see n. 2) I, 515–26.
4 Edward Gibbon, *The History of the Decline and Fall of the Roman Empire*, ch. lxxi.
5 For example: 'The Graeco-Roman world has descended into the great hollow which is roughly called the Middle Ages, extending from the fifth to the fifteenth century, a hollow in which many great, beautiful, and heroic things were done and created, but in which knowledge, as we understand it, had no place. The revival of learning and the Renaissance are memorable as the first sturdy breasting of Humanity of the hither slope of the great hollow which lies between us and the Ancient World. The modern man, reformed and regenerated by knowledge, looks across it and recognizes on the opposite ridge, in the far-shining cities and stately porticoes, in the art, politics and science of Antiquity, many more ties of kinship and sympathy than in the mighty concave between, wherein dwell his Christian ancestry, in the dim light of scholasticism and theology.' J. C. Morison, *The Service of Man: an Essay towards the Religion of the Future*, London, Kegan Paul, Trench, 1887, pp. 177–8.
6 See for example, S. Mazzarino, *The End of the Ancient World*, London, Faber and Faber, 1966, for a discussion of historical approaches to the fall of the Roman Empire.
7 J. P. V. D. Baldson, *Rome: The Story of an Empire*, London, Weidenfeld and Nicolson, 1970, p. 246.
8 C. N. Cochrane, *Christianity and Classical Culture*, Oxford, University Press, 1940, pp. 510–11.
9 Cochrane (see n. 8), p. 501.
10 Matt. xxii. 37–40.
11 1 John iv. 20.
12 1 Kgs. iii. 5–15.
13 Matt. x. 39 and xvi. 25; Mark viii. 35;

Luke ix. 24 and xvii. 33; John xii. 25.
14 Robert Browning, 'Andrea del Sarto', ll. 97–8.
15 H.Chadwick, *The Early Church*, Harmondsworth, Penguin, 1967, p. 178.
16 Chadwick (see n. 15), p. 178.
17 T.C.Humphreys, *Buddhism*, Harmondsworth, Penguin, 1951, pp. 132–3, quoting A.K.Coomaraswamy, *Buddha and the Gospel of Buddhism*, London, Harrap, 1916, p. 120.
18 Humphreys (see n. 17), p. 160.
19 R.C.Zaehner, *Concordant Discord: The Interdependence of Faiths*, Oxford, Clarendon Press, 1970, p. 134.

40 Societies of a distinctive species?

1 See Part V, ch. 27, above.
2 See Part I, ch. 6, p. 52, above.
3 See Part IX, ch. 47, below.
4 See Part VI, ch. 34, pp. 294–5, above.
5 Matt. x. 5–6; xv. 21–8.
6 Mark vii. 24–30.
7 See Part VIII, ch. 42, below.
8 'Allah' means '*the* god', i.e. the unique god of Judaism and Christianity, in the Syriac language as well as in Arabic. In Syriac translations of the Greek texts of the Bible and the Christian Fathers, the Christian Greek term 'Ho Theos' is translated as 'Allah'.
9 For the transformation of the Arab successor-state of the Roman and Sasanian Empires into an Islamic universal state in which all Muslims had the status of first-class citizens regardless of their nationality, see M.A.Shaban, *The 'Abbasid Revolution*, Cambridge, University Press, 1970, and *Islamic History AD 600–750: A New Interpretation*, Cambridge, University Press, 1971.
10 See Part V, ch. 31, pp. 251–2, above.
11 See ch. 39, pp. 327–30, above.
12 Luke xiv. 23.

41 Social responses to an illusion or to a reality?

1 M.Éliade, *Myths, Dreams and Mysteries*, London, Harvill Press, 1960, pp. 17–18.
2 See Part I, ch. 5, pp. 48–52, above.
3 Aeschylus, *Agamemnon*, 186–7, quoted in Part II, ch. 13, p. 109, above.
4 Lucretius, *De Rerum Natura* I, 101: 'So vast is the sum of the iniquities that religion has induced [people to perpetrate].'
5 Bertrand Russell, 'Has Religion made Useful Contributions to Civilization?' in *Why I am not a Christian*, London, Allen and Unwin, 1957, p. 18.
6 R.C.Zaehner, *Concordant Discord*, Oxford, Clarendon Press, 1970, p. 22.
7 In ch. 40, p. 341, above.
8 See Part IV, ch. 20, p. 155, above.
9 The phrase is Peter Berger's; see

A Rumour of Angels, London, Allen Lane, 1970.
10 John Milton, *Paradise Lost* IV, l. 110.
11 In *De Rerum Natura* V, 195–227.
12 See Part V, ch. 31, pp. 251–3, above.
13 Job v. 7.
14 See Part V, ch. 28, pp. 232–3, above.
15 Heb. xii. 6.

PART VIII
HEROIC AGES

42 The barbarian past

1 See Part V, ch. 29, p. 234, above.
2 See Part IX, chs. 48 and 49, below.
3 An illuminating and entertaining analysis of this three-cornered economic relationship can be found in E.A.Thompson, *A History of Attila and the Huns*, Oxford, Clarendon Press, 1948, pp. 184–97.
4 Owen Lattimore, *Inner Asian Frontiers of China*, London and New York, Oxford University Press, 1940, pp. 240 and 242.
5 Lattimore (see n. 4), p. 243.
6 Lattimore (see n. 4), p. 239.
7 Lattimore (see n. 4), pp. 243–4.
8 Priscus of Panium, *History of His Own Times*, in L.Dindorf (editor), *Historici Graeci Minores*, Berlin and Leipzig, Teubner, 1870, I, 305–9.
9 Thompson (see n. 3), p. 175, quoting Zachariah of Mytilene.
10 Thompson (see n. 3), pp. 173 and 172.
11 See Part VI, ch. 33, p. 278, above.
12 J.P.V.D.Balsdon, *Rome: The Story of an Empire*, London, Weidenfeld and Nicolson, 1970, p. 225; the observation was made by Caecilius Firmianus Lactantius.
13 Tacitus, *Germania*, 5.
14 Tacitus (see n. 13), 45.
15 The maxim is in an essay by Kia Yi, the general tenor of which is reproduced by O.Franke in *Geschichte des Chinesischen Reiches*, Berlin, de Gruyter, 1930, I, 132–3.
16 Zosimus, *Historiae* IV, xxxi, §§ 1–3.
17 On p. 364, above.
18 The play of this motif in human affairs – for which Aristotle coined the term *peripeteia* – has been discussed in Part IV, ch. 22, above.
19 V.Grönbech, *The Culture of the Teutons*, London, Oxford University Press, 1931, Part II, p. 305.
20 George Meredith, *Modern Love*, first quoted in Part IV, ch. 21, p. 161, above.
21 Gilbert Murray, *The Rise of the Greek Epic*, 3rd edition, Oxford, Clarendon Press, 1924, p. 84.
22 Murray (see n. 21), pp. 85–7.
23 Père H.Lammens, S.J., 'Études sur le règne du Calife Omaiyade Mo'âwia Ier' in *Mélanges de la Faculté Orientale* II, Paris, London and Leipzig, 1908, p. 67.
24 Lammens (see n. 23), p. 68.
25 Lammens (see n. 23), pp. 72 and 79.

43 The image and the reality

1 Procopius, *A History of the Wars of Justinian* IV, 9.
2 Homer, *Odyssey* I, 46–7.
3 Hesiod, *Works and Days*, 143–55.
4 Hesiod (see n. 3), 156–73.
5 Hesiod (see n. 3), 122–6.
6 Hesiod (see n. 3), 141–2.
7 H.M.Chadwick, *The Heroic Age*, Cambridge, University Press, 1912, pp. 31–2.
8 Chadwick (see n. 7), p. 39.
9 Aristotle, *Poetica* XXIV, 18.
10 William Wordsworth, 'Elegiac Stanzas suggested by a Picture of Peele Castle in a Storm'.

PART IX
CONTACTS BETWEEN CIVILIZATIONS IN SPACE

44 Encounters between contemporary civilizations

1 See Part VI, ch. 32, p. 266, and Part VII, ch. 40, p. 336, above.
2 See Part IV, above.
3 See Part III, ch. 15, p. 118, above.
4 See Part X, below.
5 See list in Part I, ch. 9, p. 72, above.

45 The modern West and Russia

1 See ch. 44, p. 398, above.
2 See Part VI, ch. 32, p. 272, above.
3 For an explanation of this term, see ch. 49, pp. 436–7, below.
4 See Part VI, ch. 32, p. 272, above.
5 For an explanation of this term, see ch. 49, pp. 436–7, below.
6 See Part VI, ch. 37, p. 311, above.
7 L.Trotsky, *The History of the Russian Revolution*, London, Gollancz, 1965, p. 24.
8 See Part V, ch. 27, p. 225, and Part VII, ch. 41, above.

46 The modern West and Eastern Asia

1 The distinction between the Japanese and the Chinese interest is explored in C.M.Cipolla, *European Culture and Overseas Expansion*, Harmondsworth, Penguin, 1970, pp. 95–6 and 167–70.
2 A Japanese colony established itself at Manila between 1593 and 1614 (see C.R.Boxer, *The Christian Century in Japan, 1549–1650*, London, Cambridge University Press, 1951, p. 302), and during the first quarter of the seventeenth century similar colonies of Japanese traders and mercenaries made their appearance at various points in South-East Asia (see Boxer, pp. 296–7).

3 There were Japanese traders in Mexico in 1597 (see J.Murdoch, *History of Japan*, Kobe, Kobe Chronicle, 1903, II, 292). Japanese traders were doing business all over the Pacific by the time at which they were suddenly prohibited from engaging in foreign trade by the non-intercourse ordinance of 1636 (see Murdoch, p. 692).
4 See Part VI, ch. 37, p. 308, above.
5 See ch. 49, pp. 443–4, below.

47 Encounters with the post-Alexandrine Hellenic Society

1 See W.F.Albright, *From the Stone Age to Christianity*, 2nd edition, Baltimore, Johns Hopkins University Press, 1957, pp. 337–8.
2 Albright (see n. 1), p. 338.
3 Albright (see n. 1), p. 338.
4 In Part VI, ch. 38, above.
5 The phrase is J.Romein's, first quoted in Part I, ch. 4, n. 3, p. 541, above.

48 The social consequences of encounters between contemporary civilizations

1 See Part IV, ch. 21, p. 166, above.
2 Lucy Mair, *Primitive Government*, Harmondsworth, Penguin, 1962, pp. 254–5.
3 Mair (see n. 2), p. 255.
4 J.Maquet, *Power and Society in Africa*, London, Weidenfeld and Nicolson, 1971, pp. 122–3.
5 Maquet (see n. 4), p. 118.
6 See ch. 45, pp. 401–3, above.
7 See ch. 49, pp. 436–42, below.
8 Isaac Deutscher, *Russia, China, and the West*, edited by F.Halliday, Oxford, University Press, 1970, pp. 333 and 334.
9 See ch. 49, pp. 437–42, below.
10 John Bowring, *Report on Egypt and Candia* dated 27 March 1839, and addressed to the Right Hon. Lord Viscount Palmerston, London, Clowes and Clowes, 1849, p. 49.
11 For these developments see P.J.Vatikiotis, *The Modern History of Egypt*, London, Weidenfeld and Nicolson, 1969, especially pp. 49–125.
12 Quoted in E.S.Mason, 'The Planning of Development' in *Scientific American*, September 1963, p. 235.
13 M.Barratt Brown, *After Imperialism*, London, Heinemann, 1963, p. 407.

49 The psychological consequences of encounters between contemporary civilizations

1 Luke xviii. 11.
2 In Part II, ch. 11, p. 91, above.
3 See the Qur'an, Surah xxii. 17.
4 See Norman Cohn, *The Pursuit of the Millennium*, revised and expanded edition, London, Temple Smith, 1970, p. 80.
5 2 Macc. iv. 7–17.
6 1 Sam. viii. 5 and 20.
7 See Part V, ch. 28, p. 231, above.
8 See Part II, ch. 16, pp. 119–20, above.
9 See Part IV, ch. 21, p. 166, and Part IX, ch. 48, pp. 423–4, above.
10 See Part V, ch. 30, pp. 245–6, above.
11 In Part VI, ch. 38, above.
12 See Part V, ch. 28, p. 232–3, above.
13 See Part IV, ch. 23, p. 171, above.

PART X

CONTACTS BETWEEN CIVILIZATIONS IN TIME

50 Renaissances of institutions, laws and philosophies

1 In Part IX, ch. 44, p. 396, above.
2 Christopher Dawson, *Religion and the Rise of Western Culture*, London, Sheed and Ward, 1950, pp. 15 and 89.
3 Dawson (see n. 2), p. 89.
4 In Part IV, ch. 24, above.
5 J.B.Bury, in his edition of Edward Gibbon, *The History of the Decline and Fall of the Roman Empire*, London, Methuen, 1898, V, Appendix 11, p. 525.
6 See C.E.Zachariä von Lingenthal, *Collectio Librorum Juris Graeco-Romani Ineditorum: Ecloga Leonis et Constantini; Epanagoge Basilii, Leonis, et Alexandri*, Leipzig, Barth, 1852.
7 Matt. v. 29–30; Matt. xviii. 8–9; Mark ix. 43–7.
8 i.e. by the Emperors of the Syrian dynasty – A.J.T.

52 Renaissances of religion

1 See Part IX, ch. 47, p. 419, above.
2 Eph. vi. 13–14.
3 Exod. xx. 3–5.
4 Mark ii. 27.
5 e.g. Matt. xii. 1–13; Mark ii. 23–8 and iii. 1–6; Luke xiii. 11–17; John v. 1–18.
6 See Part IX, ch. 49, p. 441, above.
7 See Part VII, ch. 41, above.

PART XI

WHY STUDY HISTORY?

53 The nature of historical thought

1 'The consciousness of each of us is evolution looking at itself and reflecting': Pierre Teilhard de Chardin, *The Phenomenon of Man*, London, Collins, 1959, p. 221.
2 Compare Part I, ch. 4, pp. 46–7, above.
3 A.L.Kroeber, *The Nature of Culture*, Chicago, University Press, 1952, p. 70.
4 Kroeber (see n. 3), p. 79.
5 M.R.Cohen, *The Meaning of Human History*, La Salle, Open Court Publishing Company, 1947, p. 42.
6 Cohen (see n. 5), pp. 289–90.
7 H.W.B.Joseph, *An Introduction to Logic*, 2nd revised edition, Oxford, Clarendon Press, 1916, p. 401.
8 *The Social Sciences in Historical Study*, New York, Social Science Research Council, 1954, p. 95.
9 L.von Mises, *Theory and History*, London, Cape, 1958, p. 74.
10 E.H.Carr, *What is History?*, London, Macmillan, 1961, p. 59.
11 Pieter Geyl, *Debates with Historians*, London, Batsford, 1955, p. 140.
12 M.C.D'Arcy, *The Sense of History*, London, Faber and Faber, 1959, p. 48.
13 *The Social Sciences in Historical Study* (see n. 8), p. 131.
14 Carr (see n. 10), pp. 5–6.
15 G.Stedman Jones, 'English Historians' in *New Left Review*, November–December 1967, p. 42.
16 Stedman Jones (see n. 15), p. 42.
17 Leopold von Ranke, *Geschichte der germanischen und romanischen Völker 1494–1535* I, Anhang: 'Zur Kritik neuerer Geschichtsschreiber'.
18 Carr (see n. 10), pp. 114–15.
19 Christopher Dawson, *The Dynamics of World History*, London, Sheed and Ward, 1957, p. 287.
20 Dawson (see n. 19), p. 295.
21 Carr (see n. 10), p. 126.
22 von Mises (see n. 9), p. 93.
23 See Part IV, ch. 20, above.
24 George Meredith, *Modern Love*, first quoted in Part IV, ch. 21, p. 161, above.
25 In Part IV, ch. 20, p. 154, and Part V, ch. 30, pp. 243–4, above.
26 Friedrich Engels, *Socialism Utopian and Scientific*, London, Swan Sonnenschein, 1892, p. 82; quoted in R.C.Zaehner, *Dialectical Christianity and Christian Materialism*, London, Oxford University Press, 1971, p. 45.
27 Friedrich Engels, *Anti-Dühring*, London, Lawrence and Wishart, 1934, pp. 128–9; quoted in Zaehner (see n. 26), pp. 59–60.
28 Phil. ii. 7, as translated in the Revised Version.

54 Historians in action

1 See C.F.Volney, 'Les Ruines', in *Œuvres Complètes*, Paris, Didot, 1860, pp. 12–13.
2 Ibn Khaldun, *Muqaddimah, An Introduction to History*; English translation by F.Rosenthal, 3 vols., London, Routledge and Kegan Paul, 1958.
3 See H.Grote, *The Personal Life of George Grote*, London, John Murray, 1873, p. 224.

4 Ibn Khaldun (see n. 2), I, ch. 3, §1, p. 313: 'Royal authority and large dynastic power are attained only through a group and group feeling'; I, ch. 3, §6, pp. 322–7: 'Religious propaganda cannot materialise without group feeling'.

5 Ibn Khaldun (see n. 2), I, ch. 2, §26, pp. 305–6.

6 Ibn Khaldun (see n. 2), I, ch. 3, §4, pp. 319–20.

7 Ibn Khaldun (see n. 2), I, ch. 3, §5, pp. 320–2.

8 Rosalind Murray.

9 Heb. xii. 1.

10 Geoffroi de Villehardouin, *Conquête de Constantinople*, text and translation by N. de Wailly, 3rd edition, Paris, Didot, 1882, p. 72.

11 Bernal Diaz de Castillo, *The Discovery and Conquest of Mexico, 1517–21*; English translation by A.P.Maudslay, London, Routledge, 1928, pp. 297–310.

12 Acts xix. 29–41.

13 See Josephus's preface to his *Contra Apionem* I, 47–50.

14 See Josephus's preface to *De Bello Judaico* I, 1–16.

15 Ibn-al-Tiqtaqa, *Al-Fakhri*; Arabic text edited by H.Derenbourg, Paris, Bouillon, 1895; French translation of this

edition by Émile Amar, in *Archives Marocaines*, xvi, Paris, Ernest Leroux, 1910.

16 Saint Augustine, *Retractiones* (*Reconsiderations*) II, ch. 43.

17 Thucydides I, 1.

18 Thucydides I, 22.

19 Polybius I, 1.

20 'Ala ad-Din 'Ata Malik Juvayni, *The History of the World-Conqueror*; English translation by J.A.Boyle, 2 vols., Manchester, University Press, 1958, of Muhammad Qazvini's edition of the Persian text of the *Ta'rikh-i-Jahan Gusha*, 3 vols., London, Luzac, 1912, 1916, 1937. There is an incomplete edition, by E.M. Quatremère, of the Persian text of Rashid-ad-Din, *Jami'-al-Tawarikh* (*A Comprehensive Collection of Histories*), Paris, Imprimerie Royale, 1836.

21 John Murray (editor), *The Autobiographies of Edward Gibbon*, London, Murray, 1896, pp. 405–6 (Memoir D). Compare p. 302 (Memoir E) and the slightly variant account of the same experience on p. 270 (Memoir C).

22 Read the moving account of Gibbon's feelings on this second eventful occasion in Murray (see n. 21), pp. 333–4 (Memoir E).

23 Murray (see n. 21), pp. 270–1 (Memoir C), and p. 406 (Memoir D).

24 Murray (see n. 21), p. 284 (Memoir C), and p. 411 (Memoir D).

25 The recognition that the history of the Western Civilization is parallel and comparable to the history of the antecedent Hellenic Civilization is, of course, no more than an observation that Western history has actually followed the same course so far. It does not commit the observer to the dogma that this repetition was inevitable. On this point see ch. 53, p. 488, above.

26 Homer, *Iliad* IV, 164–5.

27 Polybius XXXVIII, 22, reconstructed from Appian's paraphrase in *Roman Studies*, 'The Book of Africa', ch. 132.

28 Herodotus VII, 10; quoted in Part IV, ch. 22, p. 167, above.

29 James Shirley, *The Contention of Ajax and Ulysses* I, iii.

30 *Bhagavadgita* XI.

31 John iii. 16.

32 Ps. xix. 1.

33 Saint Francis of Assisi, *Laudes Creaturarum*, 1, 5.

34 Qur'an x. 4.

35 Goethe, *Faust*, ll. 12108–9: 'The ineffable – why, here, this is accomplished'; quoted in Part II, ch. 13, p. 109, above.

List of illustrations

Colour plates

1 *Mappa mundi*; manuscript illumination from Beatus's *Commentary on the Apocalypse*, early 13th c. Bibliothèque Nationale, Paris

2 The Deposition from the Cross; full-page illustration from an Ethiopic manuscript of the *Miracles of the Virgin Mary*, mid 17th c. British Museum, London

3 The Deposition from the Cross; gouache on paper, copied from a Flemish engraving by a Mughal artist, *c.* 1598. Victoria and Albert Museum, London

4 The Five Regions of the World; illustration from the so-called 'Mayer-Fejérváry Codex', Mixtec, before AD 1350. Public Museums, Liverpool

5 Mandala Vasudhara (goddess of Abundance); Nepal, AD 1504. British Museum, London

6 Icon of Saint Alypios the Stylite; painting by Constantin Cantorinis, Corfu, 1716. By courtesy of Dr Siegfried Amberg-Herzog, Switzerland

7 Chinese philosophers studying the Yin-Yang symbol; Chinese embroidery, 19th c., probably after an earlier design. British Museum, London. (A similar scene is found on a large porcelain vase of the 17th c. in the Victoria and Albert Museum, London)

8 Passover ceremony; illumination from a Hebrew liturgical manuscript, Italy, 1466. British Museum, London

9 The Passover meal; illumination from a Haggudah illustrated by Moses Leib ben Wolf of Trebitsch, Moravia, 1716–17. Hebrew Union College, Cincinnati

10 Tutankhamun and his Queen; detail from the back of Tutankhamun's throne; relief on wood in gold and silver with inlay of coloured glass-paste and glazed ceramic, *c.* 1361–1352 BC. Egyptian Museum, Cairo. Photo Werner Forman

11 Slaves carrying earth for the building of Sennacherib's palace; detail of a relief from the palace, Assyrian, 8th c. BC. British Museum, London. Photo Werner Forman

12 The Earth seen from space; photographed from artificial satellite, November 1967. Photo NASA/USIS

13 Primary divisions within the fertilized world-egg; gouache on paper from Rajasthan, India, 18th c. By courtesy of Ajit Mookerjee Esq., New Delhi

14 The baptism of Moriscos; detail of polychrome wood reredos by Felipe Bigarny in the Chapel Royal of Granada Cathedral, 1520–22. Photo Mas

15 Detail of the central panel of the triptych *The Garden of Delights*, by Hieronymus Bosch, *c.* 1500. Prado, Madrid. Photo Mas

16 The Tree of Death and Life; full-page illumination by Berthold Furtmeyer from a missal made for the Archbishop of Salzburg, 1481. Bayerische Staatsbibliothek, Munich. For an Italian example of a similar image, linking the Tree of the Fall and that of Redemption, see p. 100. For further references see J.B. Trapp, 'The Iconography of the Fall of Man' in C.A. Patrides (editor), *Approaches to Paradise Lost*, London, Edward Arnold, 1968, pp. 223 et seq.

17 William Blake, *The Fall of Man*; watercolour, 1807. Victoria and Albert Museum, London. For a description of this probably unique representation of the 'Fortunate Fall' see David Bindman, 'The Artistic Ideas of William Blake', PhD thesis, University of London, 1971, pp. 149–50

18 The Wilderness of Judaea. Photo Middle East Archive

19 Group of Japanese and Portuguese Christians; two-leaf Nanban screen, painted on leather, late 16th c. By courtesy of Christie and Co.

20 Worshipper from the Nestorian temple at Qarakhocho (Turfan), Sinkiang, late 9th c. Museum für Indische Kunst, Berlin

21 Two Mongol Nomads in conversation; Mongol drawing, 14th c. Topkapı Saray Museum, Istanbul

Monochrome illustrations

Special photography commissioned for this book was undertaken by A.C.Cooper, Werner Forman, J.R.Freeman, Eileen Tweedy, and John Webb.

Index

Numbers followed by the letter m refer to maps, by the letter t to chronological tables; those in italics refer to illustrations. Dates of Popes, Emperors, and monarchs indicate reigns.

as alleged cause of 154; loss of harmony resulting in 166; racial degeneration rejected as cause of 155; responsibility of leaders for 166; self-determination, failure of, as cause of 161, 166, 394

Civilizations, disintegration of 222–9: achievements of 229; and dominant minority 224, 228; and schisms in society 223, 224; as cumulative process 223; definition of 360; institutions arising out of 225; reaction to 240; role of creative minorities in 228

Civilizations, encounters between 394–400: at Central Asian 'Roundabout' 394, 395, 396, 422; at Syrian 'Roundabout' 394–6, *397*, 422; impact of alien cultures in 423–4; psychological consequences of 430–44; social consequences of 423–9

Civilizations, geneses of 51, 85–9: causes of 91–6, 111; effect of excessive challenges on 123; multiple causes of 97, 109; race and environment as causes of *80*, 91–6; stimulus of penalization on *81*, 119–22

Civilizations, growth of: criteria for 135; definition of 360; problems of 132, 135; role of creative minorities in 161, 234; shift from microcosm to macrocosm necessary to 248

Clarendon, Earl of 494

Claudius, Emperor (AD 41–54) 313

Clement III, Pope (AD 1187–91) 200

Cleomenes III, King of Sparta (236–222 BC) 233

Clio, muse of history *484*

Clot, Dr A.B. 428–9

Cohen, M.R. 55

Coleridge, S.T., *Ancient Mariner* as illustration of challenge-and-response 105, 106

Communications: contemporary system of 294; in universal states 288–95

Communism: apocalyptic revelation of 225; Judaeo-Christian origins of 58; *see also* China; Marxism; Russia

Confucianism 58, 59, 63, 533t: as ethic in Chinese bureaucracy 210–11; as religion of Sinic universal state 282–3; campaign against Buddhism 463; Neo-confucianism 463; renaissance of 461, 463

Confucius (*c.* 551–479 BC) 59, 60, 533t

Conradin, King of Sicily (AD 266–68) 206

Constance, Council of (AD 1414–18) 203, 209

Constantine I, the Great, Emperor (AD 306–37) 60, 184–5, 536t

Constantine V, Emperor (AD 741–75) 184, 192, 460

Constantine VII Porphyrogenitus, Emperor (AD 912–59) 465, 466

Constantinople 187, 329, 536t, 537t: as capital city 302, 307; penalization of Christians in 119; sack of (AD 1204) 60, *176*; seat of Roman government at 60, 183, 271; *see also* Istanbul

Constantius II, Emperor (AD 350–61) 294

Copan 112

Copernicus, Nicolaus (AD 1473–1543) 416

Corinth 41, 42, 508–9m: Canal 115

Corinthian League 223

Crassus, Marcus Licinius 197

Crates (*fl. c.* 325 BC) *248*

Creative minorities *see* Minorities

Crimean War (AD 1853–56) 404

Crito 233

Croesus (560–546 BC) 168

Cromwell, Oliver 109

Cronos 135

Crusaders 132, *176*, 206, 532t, 537t

Ctesiphon 173, 506–7m, 510–11m

Culture: definition of 43; development of, compared with technological development 48; of other civilizations 47; *see also* Renaissance and under individual civilizations

Culture-compost *see* Syro-Hellenic culture-compost

Cuzco 303

Cybele, worship of 283, 285, 328

Cynoscephalae 508–9m: battle of (197 BC) 195

Cyprian Saint (*c.* AD 200–58) 154, 161

Cyrene *116*, 508–9m

Cyrus, the Younger (d. 401 BC) 171, 294

Cyzicenes 438

Czechoslovakia 37

D'Alembert, Jean le Rond 467, *468*

Damaratus, King of Sparta 114

Damascus 117

Damophilus of Enna 232

Danes, invasion of England by 39

Daniel the Stylite, Saint (AD 409–93) 329

Dante Alighieri (AD 1265–1321) 202, 456, 492

Darius I, the Great, Emperor (521–480 BC) 274, *298*, 299, 492

David and Goliath, legend of *150*, 194

Dawson, Christopher 44

Daylam 512–13m, 520–1m

Daylamis 268

Delian League 116, 223

Demetrius, Bactrian Greek prince (*c.* 190–167 BC) 303, 438, 503m

Democracy, as dominant institution of Western Civilization 30, 456

Demography 41, 133

Demosthenes (384–322 BC) 172

Descartes, René 466

Determinism: as cause of breakdown of civilization *143*, 154–9; attractiveness of 487; dangers of belief in 487; *see also* Christianity

De Villehardouin, Geoffroi 492, 493, 495

Dhiyenes Akritas, Basil 469

Diasporás 65, 120–1: economic basis of 65; effects of technology on 67; future of 67, 69; Lebanese 66; preservation of identity by 65; Scottish 66; *see also* Jews

Diaz, Bernal 492, 493, 495

Dicaearchus of Messene 161

Diderot, Denis 467, *468*

Diocletian, Roman Emperor (AD 284–305) 60, 310, 536t: military reforms of 366

Diogenes (*c.* 400–325 BC) 251

Disraeli, Benjamin *438*

Dominant minorities *see* Minorities

Domitian, Emperor (AD 81–96) 267

Donatists 332

Dorians, in Crete 135

Drift, sense of 244: in contrast to sense of personal sin 249; results of 244

Druses 394

Ducetius (d. 440 BC) 439

Dukhobors, in Canada 65

Dzimiskes, Emperor John (AD 969–76) 192, 193

Earth, exhaustion of natural resources of 154

East Roman Empire 65, 71, 85, 512–13m, 514–15m, 520–1m, 522–3m, 532t, 536–7t: agrarian situation in 193; alienation of peasants in 193; as ghost of Roman Empire 180, 181, 183, 184, 193, 270; as incubus upon Orthodox Christendom 181, 193; belief in universality of 266, 271, 316; Bulgaria, relations with 188–93; civil service of 184; collapse of 182; deportation policy of 188; fidelity to Christian Orthodoxy of 271; foundation of 184; Hellenic Civilization, in relation to 186–7; incorporation of Syria in 396; militarism of 192, 193; Muslim invaders in 193; opportunity for restoration of 183; Orthodox Church, relations with 180–4, 185, 189; reaction of Hildebrandine Papacy to 199; Saljuq Turks, relations with 192, 193; suppression of Paulician heresy by 187–8; *see also* Orthodox Christian Church; Orthodox Christian Civilization

Ecbatana 299, 504–5m

Ecclesiastes, Book of 169, 242

'Échelles du Levant' 120

Ecloga Legis Mosaicae (AD 726) 460, 461, 536t

Egypt: basis for church in New Kingdom of 314; change in physical condition of 111; collapse of Old Kingdom of 63; continuity of history of 71; Coptic Monophysites in 65, 121; creation of Upper 52; education in 427–8; invasions of 132, 286; irrigation in, *50*, 344; Islamic law in 461; Mamluks in 198, 496; medical reforms in modern 429; physical environment of 96; Ptolemaic régime in 32–3, 531t; religion in 51, 117, *342*, *343*; Seleucid Monarchy, relations with 231; spread of metallurgy from 71; unification of 57–8; union of Upper and Lower Nile in *51*; Western influence on modern 427–8

Index compiled by Marie Forsyth